Guile Reference Manual 1/2

A catalogue record for this book is available from the Hong Kong Public Libraries.

Published in Hong Kong by Samurai Media Limited.

Email: info@samuraimedia.org

ISBN 978-988-8381-89-0

Table of Contents

6   API Reference   99

Appendix A   GNU Free Documentation License

Preface

This manual describes how to use Guile, GNU's Ubiquitous Intelligent Language for Extensions. It relates particularly to Guile version 2.0.11.

Contributors to this Manual

Like Guile itself, the Guile reference manual is a living entity, cared for by many people over a long period of time. As such, it is hard to identify individuals of whom to say "yes, this person, she wrote the manual."

Still, among the many contributions, some caretakers stand out. First among them is Neil Jerram, who has been working on this document for ten years now. Neil's attention both to detail and to the big picture have made a real difference in the understanding of a generation of Guile hackers.

Next we should note Marius Vollmer's effect on this document. Marius maintained Guile during a period in which Guile's API was clarified—put to the fire, so to speak—and he had the good sense to effect the same change on the manual.

Martin Grabmueller made substantial contributions throughout the manual in preparation for the Guile 1.6 release, including filling out a lot of the documentation of Scheme data types, control mechanisms and procedures. In addition, he wrote the documentation for Guile's SRFI modules and modules associated with the Guile REPL.

Ludovic Courtès and Andy Wingo, the Guile maintainers at the time of this writing (late 2010), have also made their dent in the manual, writing documentation for new modules and subsystems in Guile 2.0. They are also responsible for ensuring that the existing text retains its relevance as Guile evolves. See Section 2.6 [Reporting Bugs], page 12, for more information on reporting problems in this manual.

The content for the first versions of this manual incorporated and was inspired by documents from Aubrey Jaffer, author of the SCM system on which Guile was based, and from Tom Lord, Guile's first maintainer. Although most of this text has been rewritten, all of it was important, and some of the structure remains.

The manual for the first versions of Guile were largely written, edited, and compiled by Mark Galassi and Jim Blandy. In particular, Jim wrote the original tutorial on Guile's data representation and the C API for accessing Guile objects.

Significant portions were also contributed by Thien-Thi Nguyen, Kevin Ryde, Mikael Djurfeldt, Christian Lynbech, Julian Graham, Gary Houston, Tim Pierce, and a few dozen more. You, reader, are most welcome to join their esteemed ranks. Visit Guile's web site at http://www.gnu.org/software/guile/ to find out how to get involved.

The Guile License

Guile is Free Software. Guile is copyrighted, not public domain, and there are restrictions on its distribution or redistribution, but these restrictions are designed to permit everything a cooperating person would want to do.

- The Guile library (libguile) and supporting files are published under the terms of the GNU Lesser General Public License version 3 or later. See the files COPYING.LESSER and COPYING.

- The Guile readline module is published under the terms of the GNU General Public License version 3 or later. See the file COPYING.
- The manual you're now reading is published under the terms of the GNU Free Documentation License (see Appendix A [GNU Free Documentation License], page 807).

C code linking to the Guile library is subject to terms of that library. Basically such code may be published on any terms, provided users can re-link against a new or modified version of Guile.

C code linking to the Guile readline module is subject to the terms of that module. Basically such code must be published on Free terms.

Scheme level code written to be run by Guile (but not derived from Guile itself) is not restricted in any way, and may be published on any terms. We encourage authors to publish on Free terms.

You must be aware there is no warranty whatsoever for Guile. This is described in full in the licenses.

1 Introduction

Guile is an implementation of the Scheme programming language. Scheme (`http://schemers.org/`) is an elegant and conceptually simple dialect of Lisp, originated by Guy Steele and Gerald Sussman, and since evolved by the series of reports known as RnRS (the Revised^n Reports on Scheme).

Unlike, for example, Python or Perl, Scheme has no benevolent dictator. There are many Scheme implementations, with different characteristics and with communities and academic activities around them, and the language develops as a result of the interplay between these. Guile's particular characteristics are that

- it is easy to combine with other code written in C
- it has a historical and continuing connection with the GNU Project
- it emphasizes interactive and incremental programming
- it actually supports several languages, not just Scheme.

The next few sections explain what we mean by these points. The sections after that cover how you can obtain and install Guile, and the typographical conventions that we use in this manual.

1.1 Guile and Scheme

Guile implements Scheme as described in the Revised^5 Report on the Algorithmic Language Scheme (usually known as R5RS), providing clean and general data and control structures. Guile goes beyond the rather austere language presented in R5RS, extending it with a module system, full access to POSIX system calls, networking support, multiple threads, dynamic linking, a foreign function call interface, powerful string processing, and many other features needed for programming in the real world.

The Scheme community has recently agreed and published R6RS, the latest installment in the RnRS series. R6RS significantly expands the core Scheme language, and standardises many non-core functions that implementations—including Guile—have previously done in different ways. Guile has been updated to incorporate some of the features of R6RS, and to adjust some existing features to conform to the R6RS specification, but it is by no means a complete R6RS implementation. See Section 7.6 [R6RS Support], page 622.

Between R5RS and R6RS, the SRFI process (`http://srfi.schemers.org/`) standardised interfaces for many practical needs, such as multithreaded programming and multidimensional arrays. Guile supports many SRFIs, as documented in detail in Section 7.5 [SRFI Support], page 550.

In summary, so far as relationship to the Scheme standards is concerned, Guile is an R5RS implementation with many extensions, some of which conform to SRFIs or to the relevant parts of R6RS.

1.2 Combining with C Code

Like a shell, Guile can run interactively—reading expressions from the user, evaluating them, and displaying the results—or as a script interpreter, reading and executing Scheme code from a file. Guile also provides an object library, *libguile*, that allows other applications to easily incorporate a complete Scheme interpreter. An application can then use Guile as an extension language, a clean and powerful configuration language, or as multi-purpose "glue", connecting primitives provided by the application. It is easy to call Scheme code from C code and vice versa, giving the application designer full control of how and when to invoke the interpreter. Applications can add new functions, data types, control structures, and even syntax to Guile, creating a domain-specific language tailored to the task at hand, but based on a robust language design.

This kind of combination is helped by four aspects of Guile's design and history. First is that Guile has always been targeted as an extension language. Hence its C API has always been of great importance, and has been developed accordingly. Second and third are rather technical points—that Guile uses conservative garbage collection, and that it implements the Scheme concept of continuations by copying and reinstating the C stack—but whose practical consequence is that most existing C code can be glued into Guile as is, without needing modifications to cope with strange Scheme execution flows. Last is the module system, which helps extensions to coexist without stepping on each others' toes.

Guile's module system allows one to break up a large program into manageable sections with well-defined interfaces between them. Modules may contain a mixture of interpreted and compiled code; Guile can use either static or dynamic linking to incorporate compiled code. Modules also encourage developers to package up useful collections of routines for general distribution; as of this writing, one can find Emacs interfaces, database access routines, compilers, GUI toolkit interfaces, and HTTP client functions, among others.

1.3 Guile and the GNU Project

Guile was conceived by the GNU Project following the fantastic success of Emacs Lisp as an extension language within Emacs. Just as Emacs Lisp allowed complete and unanticipated applications to be written within the Emacs environment, the idea was that Guile should do the same for other GNU Project applications. This remains true today.

The idea of extensibility is closely related to the GNU project's primary goal, that of promoting software freedom. Software freedom means that people receiving a software package can modify or enhance it to their own desires, including in ways that may not have occurred at all to the software's original developers. For programs written in a compiled language like C, this freedom covers modifying and rebuilding the C code; but if the program also provides an extension language, that is usually a much friendlier and lower-barrier-of-entry way for the user to start making their own changes.

Guile is now used by GNU project applications such as AutoGen, Lilypond, Denemo, Mailutils, TeXmacs and Gnucash, and we hope that there will be many more in future.

1.4 Interactive Programming

Non-free software has no interest in its users being able to see how it works. They are supposed to just accept it, or to report problems and hope that the source code owners will choose to work on them.

Free software aims to work reliably just as much as non-free software does, but it should also empower its users by making its workings available. This is useful for many reasons, including education, auditing and enhancements, as well as for debugging problems.

The ideal free software system achieves this by making it easy for interested users to see the source code for a feature that they are using, and to follow through that source code step-by-step, as it runs. In Emacs, good examples of this are the source code hyperlinks in the help system, and edebug. Then, for bonus points and maximising the ability for the user to experiment quickly with code changes, the system should allow parts of the source code to be modified and reloaded into the running program, to take immediate effect.

Guile is designed for this kind of interactive programming, and this distinguishes it from many Scheme implementations that instead prioritise running a fixed Scheme program as fast as possible—because there are tradeoffs between performance and the ability to modify parts of an already running program. There are faster Schemes than Guile, but Guile is a GNU project and so prioritises the GNU vision of programming freedom and experimentation.

1.5 Supporting Multiple Languages

Since the 2.0 release, Guile's architecture supports compiling any language to its core virtual machine bytecode, and Scheme is just one of the supported languages. Other supported languages are Emacs Lisp, ECMAScript (commonly known as Javascript) and Brainfuck, and work is under discussion for Lua, Ruby and Python.

This means that users can program applications which use Guile in the language of their choice, rather than having the tastes of the application's author imposed on them.

1.6 Obtaining and Installing Guile

Guile can be obtained from the main GNU archive site ftp://ftp.gnu.org or any of its mirrors. The file will be named guile-*version*.tar.gz. The current version is 2.0.11, so the file you should grab is:

```
ftp://ftp.gnu.org/gnu/guile/guile-2.0.11.tar.gz
```

To unbundle Guile use the instruction

```
zcat guile-2.0.11.tar.gz | tar xvf -
```

which will create a directory called guile-2.0.11 with all the sources. You can look at the file INSTALL for detailed instructions on how to build and install Guile, but you should be able to just do

```
cd guile-2.0.11
./configure
make
make install
```

This will install the Guile executable guile, the Guile library libguile and various associated header files and support libraries. It will also install the Guile reference manual.

Since this manual frequently refers to the Scheme "standard", also known as R5RS, or the "Revised[5] Report on the Algorithmic Language Scheme", we have included the report in the Guile distribution; see Section "Introduction" in *Revised(5) Report on the Algorithmic Language Scheme*. This will also be installed in your info directory.

1.7 Organisation of this Manual

The rest of this manual is organised into the following chapters.

Chapter 2: Hello Guile!

A whirlwind tour shows how Guile can be used interactively and as a script interpreter, how to link Guile into your own applications, and how to write modules of interpreted and compiled code for use with Guile. Everything introduced here is documented again and in full by the later parts of the manual.

Chapter 3: Hello Scheme!

For readers new to Scheme, this chapter provides an introduction to the basic ideas of the Scheme language. This material would apply to any Scheme implementation and so does not make reference to anything Guile-specific.

Chapter 4: Programming in Scheme

Provides an overview of programming in Scheme with Guile. It covers how to invoke the `guile` program from the command-line and how to write scripts in Scheme. It also introduces the extensions that Guile offers beyond standard Scheme.

Chapter 5: Programming in C

Provides an overview of how to use Guile in a C program. It discusses the fundamental concepts that you need to understand to access the features of Guile, such as dynamic types and the garbage collector. It explains in a tutorial like manner how to define new data types and functions for the use by Scheme programs.

Chapter 6: Guile API Reference

This part of the manual documents the Guile API in functionality-based groups with the Scheme and C interfaces presented side by side.

Chapter 7: Guile Modules

Describes some important modules, distributed as part of the Guile distribution, that extend the functionality provided by the Guile Scheme core.

Chapter 8: GOOPS

Describes GOOPS, an object oriented extension to Guile that provides classes, multiple inheritance and generic functions.

1.8 Typographical Conventions

In examples and procedure descriptions and all other places where the evaluation of Scheme expression is shown, we use some notation for denoting the output and evaluation results of expressions.

The symbol '⇒' is used to tell which value is returned by an evaluation:

```
(+ 1 2)
⇒ 3
```

Some procedures produce some output besides returning a value. This is denoted by the symbol '⊣'.

```
(begin (display 1) (newline) 'hooray)
⊣ 1
⇒ hooray
```

As you can see, this code prints '1' (denoted by ' ⊣ '), and returns hooray (denoted by '⇒').

2 Hello Guile!

This chapter presents a quick tour of all the ways that Guile can be used. There are additional examples in the `examples/` directory in the Guile source distribution. It also explains how best to report any problems that you find.

The following examples assume that Guile has been installed in `/usr/local/`.

2.1 Running Guile Interactively

In its simplest form, Guile acts as an interactive interpreter for the Scheme programming language, reading and evaluating Scheme expressions the user enters from the terminal. Here is a sample interaction between Guile and a user; the user's input appears after the `$` and `scheme@(guile-user)>` prompts:

```
$ guile
scheme@(guile-user)> (+ 1 2 3)                    ; add some numbers
$1 = 6
scheme@(guile-user)> (define (factorial n)    ; define a function
                       (if (zero? n) 1 (* n (factorial (- n 1)))))
scheme@(guile-user)> (factorial 20)
$2 = 2432902008176640000
scheme@(guile-user)> (getpwnam "root")         ; look in /etc/passwd
$3 = #("root" "x" 0 0 "root" "/root" "/bin/bash")
scheme@(guile-user)> C-d
$
```

2.2 Running Guile Scripts

Like AWK, Perl, or any shell, Guile can interpret script files. A Guile script is simply a file of Scheme code with some extra information at the beginning which tells the operating system how to invoke Guile, and then tells Guile how to handle the Scheme code.

Here is a trivial Guile script. See Section 4.3 [Guile Scripting], page 41, for more details.

```
#!/usr/local/bin/guile -s
!#
(display "Hello, world!")
(newline)
```

2.3 Linking Guile into Programs

The Guile interpreter is available as an object library, to be linked into applications using Scheme as a configuration or extension language.

Here is `simple-guile.c`, source code for a program that will produce a complete Guile interpreter. In addition to all usual functions provided by Guile, it will also offer the function `my-hostname`.

```
#include <stdlib.h>
#include <libguile.h>

static SCM
```

```
my_hostname (void)
{
  char *s = getenv ("HOSTNAME");
  if (s == NULL)
    return SCM_BOOL_F;
  else
    return scm_from_locale_string (s);
}

static void
inner_main (void *data, int argc, char **argv)
{
  scm_c_define_gsubr ("my-hostname", 0, 0, 0, my_hostname);
  scm_shell (argc, argv);
}

int
main (int argc, char **argv)
{
  scm_boot_guile (argc, argv, inner_main, 0);
  return 0; /* never reached */
}
```

When Guile is correctly installed on your system, the above program can be compiled and linked like this:

```
$ gcc -o simple-guile simple-guile.c \
    `pkg-config --cflags --libs guile-2.0`
```

When it is run, it behaves just like the `guile` program except that you can also call the new **my-hostname** function.

```
$ ./simple-guile
scheme@(guile-user)> (+ 1 2 3)
$1 = 6
scheme@(guile-user)> (my-hostname)
"burns"
```

2.4 Writing Guile Extensions

You can link Guile into your program and make Scheme available to the users of your program. You can also link your library into Guile and make its functionality available to all users of Guile.

A library that is linked into Guile is called an *extension*, but it really just is an ordinary object library.

The following example shows how to write a simple extension for Guile that makes the j0 function available to Scheme code.

```
#include <math.h>
#include <libguile.h>
```

```
SCM
j0_wrapper (SCM x)
{
  return scm_from_double (j0 (scm_to_double (x)));
}

void
init_bessel ()
{
  scm_c_define_gsubr ("j0", 1, 0, 0, j0_wrapper);
}
```

This C source file needs to be compiled into a shared library. Here is how to do it on GNU/Linux:

```
gcc 'pkg-config --cflags guile-2.0' \
  -shared -o libguile-bessel.so -fPIC bessel.c
```

For creating shared libraries portably, we recommend the use of GNU Libtool (see Section "Introduction" in *GNU Libtool*).

A shared library can be loaded into a running Guile process with the function `load-extension`. The `j0` is then immediately available:

```
$ guile
scheme@(guile-user)> (load-extension "./libguile-bessel" "init_bessel")
scheme@(guile-user)> (j0 2)
$1 = 0.223890779141236
```

For more on how to install your extension, see Section 4.7 [Installing Site Packages], page 55.

2.5 Using the Guile Module System

Guile has support for dividing a program into *modules*. By using modules, you can group related code together and manage the composition of complete programs from largely independent parts.

For more details on the module system beyond this introductory material, See Section 6.19 [Modules], page 381.

2.5.1 Using Modules

Guile comes with a lot of useful modules, for example for string processing or command line parsing. Additionally, there exist many Guile modules written by other Guile hackers, but which have to be installed manually.

Here is a sample interactive session that shows how to use the (ice-9 popen) module which provides the means for communicating with other processes over pipes together with the (ice-9 rdelim) module that provides the function `read-line`.

```
$ guile
scheme@(guile-user)> (use-modules (ice-9 popen))
scheme@(guile-user)> (use-modules (ice-9 rdelim))
scheme@(guile-user)> (define p (open-input-pipe "ls -l"))
scheme@(guile-user)> (read-line p)
$1 = "total 30"
scheme@(guile-user)> (read-line p)
$2 = "drwxr-sr-x    2 mgrabmue mgrabmue     1024 Mar 29 19:57 CVS"
```

2.5.2 Writing new Modules

You can create new modules using the syntactic form `define-module`. All definitions following this form until the next `define-module` are placed into the new module.

One module is usually placed into one file, and that file is installed in a location where Guile can automatically find it. The following session shows a simple example.

```
$ cat /usr/local/share/guile/site/foo/bar.scm

(define-module (foo bar)
  #:export (frob))

(define (frob x) (* 2 x))

$ guile
scheme@(guile-user)> (use-modules (foo bar))
scheme@(guile-user)> (frob 12)
$1 = 24
```

For more on how to install your module, see Section 4.7 [Installing Site Packages], page 55.

2.5.3 Putting Extensions into Modules

In addition to Scheme code you can also put things that are defined in C into a module.

You do this by writing a small Scheme file that defines the module and call `load-extension` directly in the body of the module.

```
$ cat /usr/local/share/guile/site/math/bessel.scm

(define-module (math bessel)
  #:export (j0))

(load-extension "libguile-bessel" "init_bessel")

$ file /usr/local/lib/guile/2.0/extensions/libguile-bessel.so
... ELF 32-bit LSB shared object ...
$ guile
scheme@(guile-user)> (use-modules (math bessel))
scheme@(guile-user)> (j0 2)
$1 = 0.223890779141236
```

See Section 6.20.4 [Modules and Extensions], page 401, for more information.

2.6 Reporting Bugs

Any problems with the installation should be reported to `bug-guile@gnu.org`.

If you find a bug in Guile, please report it to the Guile developers, so they can fix it. They may also be able to suggest workarounds when it is not possible for you to apply the bug-fix or install a new version of Guile yourself.

Before sending in bug reports, please check with the following list that you really have found a bug.

- Whenever documentation and actual behavior differ, you have certainly found a bug, either in the documentation or in the program.

- When Guile crashes, it is a bug.

- When Guile hangs or takes forever to complete a task, it is a bug.

- When calculations produce wrong results, it is a bug.

- When Guile signals an error for valid Scheme programs, it is a bug.

- When Guile does not signal an error for invalid Scheme programs, it may be a bug, unless this is explicitly documented.

- When some part of the documentation is not clear and does not make sense to you even after re-reading the section, it is a bug.

Before reporting the bug, check whether any programs you have loaded into Guile, including your `.guile` file, set any variables that may affect the functioning of Guile. Also, see whether the problem happens in a freshly started Guile without loading your `.guile` file (start Guile with the `-q` switch to prevent loading the init file). If the problem does *not* occur then, you must report the precise contents of any programs that you must load into Guile in order to cause the problem to occur.

When you write a bug report, please make sure to include as much of the information described below in the report. If you can't figure out some of the items, it is not a problem, but the more information we get, the more likely we can diagnose and fix the bug.

- The version number of Guile. You can get this information from invoking '`guile --version`' at your shell, or calling (`version`) from within Guile.

- Your machine type, as determined by the **config.guess** shell script. If you have a Guile checkout, this file is located in **build-aux**; otherwise you can fetch the latest version from http://git.savannah.gnu.org/gitweb/?p=config.git;a=blob_plain;f=config.guess;hb=HEAD.

    ```
    $ build-aux/config.guess
    x86_64-unknown-linux-gnu
    ```

- If you installed Guile from a binary package, the version of that package. On systems that use RPM, use `rpm -qa | grep guile`. On systems that use DPKG, `dpkg -l | grep guile`.

- If you built Guile yourself, the build configuration that you used:

    ```
    $ ./config.status --config
    '--enable-error-on-warning' '--disable-deprecated'...
    ```

- A complete description of how to reproduce the bug.

    If you have a Scheme program that produces the bug, please include it in the bug report. If your program is too big to include. please try to reduce your code to a minimal test case.

    If you can reproduce your problem at the REPL, that is best. Give a transcript of the expressions you typed at the REPL.

- A description of the incorrect behavior. For example, "The Guile process gets a fatal signal," or, "The resulting output is as follows, which I think is wrong."

    If the manifestation of the bug is a Guile error message, it is important to report the precise text of the error message, and a backtrace showing how the Scheme program arrived at the error. This can be done using the `,backtrace` command in Guile's debugger.

If your bug causes Guile to crash, additional information from a low-level debugger such as GDB might be helpful. If you have built Guile yourself, you can run Guile under GDB via the `meta/gdb-uninstalled-guile` script. Instead of invoking Guile as usual, invoke the wrapper script, type `run` to start the process, then `backtrace` when the crash comes. Include that backtrace in your report.

3 Hello Scheme!

In this chapter, we introduce the basic concepts that underpin the elegance and power of the Scheme language.

Readers who already possess a background knowledge of Scheme may happily skip this chapter. For the reader who is new to the language, however, the following discussions on data, procedures, expressions and closure are designed to provide a minimum level of Scheme understanding that is more or less assumed by the chapters that follow.

The style of this introductory material aims about halfway between the terse precision of R5RS and the discursiveness of existing Scheme tutorials. For pointers to useful Scheme resources on the web, please see Section 3.5 [Further Reading], page 34.

3.1 Data Types, Values and Variables

This section discusses the representation of data types and values, what it means for Scheme to be a *latently typed* language, and the role of variables. We conclude by introducing the Scheme syntaxes for defining a new variable, and for changing the value of an existing variable.

3.1.1 Latent Typing

The term *latent typing* is used to describe a computer language, such as Scheme, for which you cannot, *in general*, simply look at a program's source code and determine what type of data will be associated with a particular variable, or with the result of a particular expression.

Sometimes, of course, you *can* tell from the code what the type of an expression will be. If you have a line in your program that sets the variable x to the numeric value 1, you can be certain that, immediately after that line has executed (and in the absence of multiple threads), x has the numeric value 1. Or if you write a procedure that is designed to concatenate two strings, it is likely that the rest of your application will always invoke this procedure with two string parameters, and quite probable that the procedure would go wrong in some way if it was ever invoked with parameters that were not both strings.

Nevertheless, the point is that there is nothing in Scheme which requires the procedure parameters always to be strings, or x always to hold a numeric value, and there is no way of declaring in your program that such constraints should always be obeyed. In the same vein, there is no way to declare the expected type of a procedure's return value.

Instead, the types of variables and expressions are only known – in general – at run time. If you *need* to check at some point that a value has the expected type, Scheme provides run time procedures that you can invoke to do so. But equally, it can be perfectly valid for two separate invocations of the same procedure to specify arguments with different types, and to return values with different types.

The next subsection explains what this means in practice, for the ways that Scheme programs use data types, values and variables.

3.1.2 Values and Variables

Scheme provides many data types that you can use to represent your data. Primitive types include characters, strings, numbers and procedures. Compound types, which allow a group of primitive and compound values to be stored together, include lists, pairs, vectors and multi-dimensional arrays. In addition, Guile allows applications to define their own data types, with the same status as the built-in standard Scheme types.

As a Scheme program runs, values of all types pop in and out of existence. Sometimes values are stored in variables, but more commonly they pass seamlessly from being the result of one computation to being one of the parameters for the next.

Consider an example. A string value is created because the interpreter reads in a literal string from your program's source code. Then a numeric value is created as the result of calculating the length of the string. A second numeric value is created by doubling the calculated length. Finally the program creates a list with two elements – the doubled length and the original string itself – and stores this list in a program variable.

All of the values involved here – in fact, all values in Scheme – carry their type with them. In other words, every value "knows," at runtime, what kind of value it is. A number, a string, a list, whatever.

A variable, on the other hand, has no fixed type. A variable – x, say – is simply the name of a location – a box – in which you can store any kind of Scheme value. So the same variable in a program may hold a number at one moment, a list of procedures the next, and later a pair of strings. The "type" of a variable – insofar as the idea is meaningful at all – is simply the type of whatever value the variable happens to be storing at a particular moment.

3.1.3 Defining and Setting Variables

To define a new variable, you use Scheme's `define` syntax like this:

```
(define variable-name value)
```

This makes a new variable called *variable-name* and stores *value* in it as the variable's initial value. For example:

```
;; Make a variable 'x' with initial numeric value 1.
(define x 1)

;; Make a variable 'organization' with an initial string value.
(define organization "Free Software Foundation")
```

(In Scheme, a semicolon marks the beginning of a comment that continues until the end of the line. So the lines beginning ;; are comments.)

Changing the value of an already existing variable is very similar, except that `define` is replaced by the Scheme syntax `set!`, like this:

```
(set! variable-name new-value)
```

Remember that variables do not have fixed types, so *new-value* may have a completely different type from whatever was previously stored in the location named by *variable-name*. Both of the following examples are therefore correct.

```
;; Change the value of 'x' to 5.
(set! x 5)

;; Change the value of 'organization' to the FSF's street number.
(set! organization 545)
```

In these examples, *value* and *new-value* are literal numeric or string values. In general, however, *value* and *new-value* can be any Scheme expression. Even though we have not yet covered the forms that Scheme expressions can take (see Section 3.3 [About Expressions], page 20), you can probably guess what the following `set!` example does...

```
(set! x (+ x 1))
```

(Note: this is not a complete description of `define` and `set!`, because we need to introduce some other aspects of Scheme before the missing pieces can be filled in. If, however, you are already familiar with the structure of Scheme, you may like to read about those missing pieces immediately by jumping ahead to the following references.

- Section 3.2.4 [Lambda Alternatives], page 20, to read about an alternative form of the `define` syntax that can be used when defining new procedures.
- Section 6.9.8 [Procedures with Setters], page 255, to read about an alternative form of the `set!` syntax that helps with changing a single value in the depths of a compound data structure.)
- See Section 6.12.3 [Internal Definitions], page 289, to read about using `define` other than at top level in a Scheme program, including a discussion of when it works to use `define` rather than `set!` to change the value of an existing variable.

3.2 The Representation and Use of Procedures

This section introduces the basics of using and creating Scheme procedures. It discusses the representation of procedures as just another kind of Scheme value, and shows how procedure invocation expressions are constructed. We then explain how `lambda` is used to create new procedures, and conclude by presenting the various shorthand forms of `define` that can be used instead of writing an explicit `lambda` expression.

3.2.1 Procedures as Values

One of the great simplifications of Scheme is that a procedure is just another type of value, and that procedure values can be passed around and stored in variables in exactly the same way as, for example, strings and lists. When we talk about a built-in standard Scheme procedure such as `open-input-file`, what we actually mean is that there is a pre-defined top level variable called `open-input-file`, whose value is a procedure that implements what R5RS says that `open-input-file` should do.

Note that this is quite different from many dialects of Lisp — including Emacs Lisp — in which a program can use the same name with two quite separate meanings: one meaning identifies a Lisp function, while the other meaning identifies a Lisp variable, whose value need have nothing to do with the function that is associated with the first meaning. In these dialects, functions and variables are said to live in different *namespaces*.

In Scheme, on the other hand, all names belong to a single unified namespace, and the variables that these names identify can hold any kind of Scheme value, including procedure values.

One consequence of the "procedures as values" idea is that, if you don't happen to like the standard name for a Scheme procedure, you can change it.

For example, `call-with-current-continuation` is a very important standard Scheme procedure, but it also has a very long name! So, many programmers use the following definition to assign the same procedure value to the more convenient name `call/cc`.

```
(define call/cc call-with-current-continuation)
```

Let's understand exactly how this works. The definition creates a new variable `call/cc`, and then sets its value to the value of the variable `call-with-current-continuation`; the latter value is a procedure that implements the behaviour that R5RS specifies under the name "call-with-current-continuation". So `call/cc` ends up holding this value as well.

Now that `call/cc` holds the required procedure value, you could choose to use `call-with-current-continuation` for a completely different purpose, or just change its value so that you will get an error if you accidentally use `call-with-current-continuation` as a procedure in your program rather than `call/cc`. For example:

```
(set! call-with-current-continuation "Not a procedure any more!")
```

Or you could just leave `call-with-current-continuation` as it was. It's perfectly fine for more than one variable to hold the same procedure value.

3.2.2 Simple Procedure Invocation

A procedure invocation in Scheme is written like this:

```
(procedure [arg1 [arg2 ...]])
```

In this expression, *procedure* can be any Scheme expression whose value is a procedure. Most commonly, however, *procedure* is simply the name of a variable whose value is a procedure.

For example, `string-append` is a standard Scheme procedure whose behaviour is to concatenate together all the arguments, which are expected to be strings, that it is given. So the expression

```
(string-append "/home" "/" "andrew")
```

is a procedure invocation whose result is the string value `"/home/andrew"`.

Similarly, `string-length` is a standard Scheme procedure that returns the length of a single string argument, so

```
(string-length "abc")
```

is a procedure invocation whose result is the numeric value 3.

Each of the parameters in a procedure invocation can itself be any Scheme expression. Since a procedure invocation is itself a type of expression, we can put these two examples together to get

```
(string-length (string-append "/home" "/" "andrew"))
```

— a procedure invocation whose result is the numeric value 12.

(You may be wondering what happens if the two examples are combined the other way round. If we do this, we can make a procedure invocation expression that is *syntactically* correct:

```
(string-append "/home" (string-length "abc"))
```

but when this expression is executed, it will cause an error, because the result of (`string-length "abc"`) is a numeric value, and `string-append` is not designed to accept a numeric value as one of its arguments.)

3.2.3 Creating and Using a New Procedure

Scheme has lots of standard procedures, and Guile provides all of these via predefined top level variables. All of these standard procedures are documented in the later chapters of this reference manual.

Before very long, though, you will want to create new procedures that encapsulate aspects of your own applications' functionality. To do this, you can use the famous `lambda` syntax.

For example, the value of the following Scheme expression

```
(lambda (name address) expression ...)
```

is a newly created procedure that takes two arguments: `name` and `address`. The behaviour of the new procedure is determined by the sequence of *expression*s in the *body* of the procedure definition. (Typically, these *expression*s would use the arguments in some way, or else there wouldn't be any point in giving them to the procedure.) When invoked, the new procedure returns a value that is the value of the last *expression* in the procedure body.

To make things more concrete, let's suppose that the two arguments are both strings, and that the purpose of this procedure is to form a combined string that includes these arguments. Then the full lambda expression might look like this:

```
(lambda (name address)
  (string-append "Name=" name ":Address=" address))
```

We noted in the previous subsection that the *procedure* part of a procedure invocation expression can be any Scheme expression whose value is a procedure. But that's exactly what a lambda expression is! So we can use a lambda expression directly in a procedure invocation, like this:

```
((lambda (name address)
   (string-append "Name=" name ":Address=" address))
 "FSF"
 "Cambridge")
```

This is a valid procedure invocation expression, and its result is the string:

```
"Name=FSF:Address=Cambridge"
```

It is more common, though, to store the procedure value in a variable —

```
(define make-combined-string
  (lambda (name address)
    (string-append "Name=" name ":Address=" address)))
```

— and then to use the variable name in the procedure invocation:

```
(make-combined-string "FSF" "Cambridge")
```

Which has exactly the same result.

It's important to note that procedures created using `lambda` have exactly the same status as the standard built in Scheme procedures, and can be invoked, passed around, and stored in variables in exactly the same ways.

3.2.4 Lambda Alternatives

Since it is so common in Scheme programs to want to create a procedure and then store it in a variable, there is an alternative form of the `define` syntax that allows you to do just that.

A `define` expression of the form

```
(define (name [arg1 [arg2 ...]])
  expression ...)
```

is exactly equivalent to the longer form

```
(define name
  (lambda ([arg1 [arg2 ...]])
    expression ...))
```

So, for example, the definition of `make-combined-string` in the previous subsection could equally be written:

```
(define (make-combined-string name address)
  (string-append "Name=" name ":Address=" address))
```

This kind of procedure definition creates a procedure that requires exactly the expected number of arguments. There are two further forms of the `lambda` expression, which create a procedure that can accept a variable number of arguments:

```
(lambda (arg1 ... . args) expression ...)
```

```
(lambda args expression ...)
```

The corresponding forms of the alternative `define` syntax are:

```
(define (name arg1 ... . args) expression ...)
```

```
(define (name . args) expression ...)
```

For details on how these forms work, see See Section 6.9.1 [Lambda], page 244.

Prior to Guile 2.0, Guile provided an extension to `define` syntax that allowed you to nest the previous extension up to an arbitrary depth. These are no longer provided by default, and instead have been moved to Section 7.18 [Curried Definitions], page 693

(It could be argued that the alternative `define` forms are rather confusing, especially for newcomers to the Scheme language, as they hide both the role of `lambda` and the fact that procedures are values that are stored in variables in the some way as any other kind of value. On the other hand, they are very convenient, and they are also a good example of another of Scheme's powerful features: the ability to specify arbitrary syntactic transformations at run time, which can be applied to subsequently read input.)

3.3 Expressions and Evaluation

So far, we have met expressions that *do* things, such as the `define` expressions that create and initialize new variables, and we have also talked about expressions that have *values*, for example the value of the procedure invocation expression:

```
(string-append "/home" "/" "andrew")
```

but we haven't yet been precise about what causes an expression like this procedure invocation to be reduced to its "value", or how the processing of such expressions relates to the execution of a Scheme program as a whole.

This section clarifies what we mean by an expression's value, by introducing the idea of *evaluation*. It discusses the side effects that evaluation can have, explains how each of the various types of Scheme expression is evaluated, and describes the behaviour and use of the Guile REPL as a mechanism for exploring evaluation. The section concludes with a very brief summary of Scheme's common syntactic expressions.

3.3.1 Evaluating Expressions and Executing Programs

In Scheme, the process of executing an expression is known as *evaluation*. Evaluation has two kinds of result:

- the *value* of the evaluated expression
- the *side effects* of the evaluation, which consist of any effects of evaluating the expression that are not represented by the value.

Of the expressions that we have met so far, `define` and `set!` expressions have side effects — the creation or modification of a variable — but no value; `lambda` expressions have values — the newly constructed procedures — but no side effects; and procedure invocation expressions, in general, have either values, or side effects, or both.

It is tempting to try to define more intuitively what we mean by "value" and "side effects", and what the difference between them is. In general, though, this is extremely difficult. It is also unnecessary; instead, we can quite happily define the behaviour of a Scheme program by specifying how Scheme executes a program as a whole, and then by describing the value and side effects of evaluation for each type of expression individually.

So, some[1] definitions. . .

- A Scheme program consists of a sequence of expressions.
- A Scheme interpreter executes the program by evaluating these expressions in order, one by one.
- An expression can be
  - a piece of literal data, such as a number 2.3 or a string `"Hello world!"`
  - a variable name
  - a procedure invocation expression
  - one of Scheme's special syntactic expressions.

The following subsections describe how each of these types of expression is evaluated.

3.3.1.1 Evaluating Literal Data

When a literal data expression is evaluated, the value of the expression is simply the value that the expression describes. The evaluation of a literal data expression has no side effects.

So, for example,

- the value of the expression `"abc"` is the string value `"abc"`

---

[1] These definitions are approximate. For the whole and detailed truth, see Section "Formal syntax and semantics" in *The Revised(5) Report on the Algorithmic Language Scheme*.

- the value of the expression 3+4i is the complex number 3 + 4i
- the value of the expression #(1 2 3) is a three-element vector containing the numeric values 1, 2 and 3.

For any data type which can be expressed literally like this, the syntax of the literal data expression for that data type — in other words, what you need to write in your code to indicate a literal value of that type — is known as the data type's *read syntax*. This manual specifies the read syntax for each such data type in the section that describes that data type.

Some data types do not have a read syntax. Procedures, for example, cannot be expressed as literal data; they must be created using a `lambda` expression (see Section 3.2.3 [Creating a Procedure], page 19) or implicitly using the shorthand form of `define` (see Section 3.2.4 [Lambda Alternatives], page 20).

3.3.1.2 Evaluating a Variable Reference

When an expression that consists simply of a variable name is evaluated, the value of the expression is the value of the named variable. The evaluation of a variable reference expression has no side effects.

So, after

```
(define key "Paul Evans")
```

the value of the expression `key` is the string value `"Paul Evans"`. If *key* is then modified by

```
(set! key 3.74)
```

the value of the expression `key` is the numeric value 3.74.

If there is no variable with the specified name, evaluation of the variable reference expression signals an error.

3.3.1.3 Evaluating a Procedure Invocation Expression

This is where evaluation starts getting interesting! As already noted, a procedure invocation expression has the form

```
(procedure [arg1 [arg2 ...]])
```

where *procedure* must be an expression whose value, when evaluated, is a procedure.

The evaluation of a procedure invocation expression like this proceeds by

- evaluating individually the expressions *procedure*, *arg1*, *arg2*, and so on
- calling the procedure that is the value of the *procedure* expression with the list of values obtained from the evaluations of *arg1*, *arg2* etc. as its parameters.

For a procedure defined in Scheme, "calling the procedure with the list of values as its parameters" means binding the values to the procedure's formal parameters and then evaluating the sequence of expressions that make up the body of the procedure definition. The value of the procedure invocation expression is the value of the last evaluated expression in the procedure body. The side effects of calling the procedure are the combination of the side effects of the sequence of evaluations of expressions in the procedure body.

For a built-in procedure, the value and side-effects of calling the procedure are best described by that procedure's documentation.

Note that the complete side effects of evaluating a procedure invocation expression consist not only of the side effects of the procedure call, but also of any side effects of the preceding evaluation of the expressions *procedure*, *arg1*, *arg2*, and so on.

To illustrate this, let's look again at the procedure invocation expression:

```
(string-length (string-append "/home" "/" "andrew"))
```

In the outermost expression, *procedure* is `string-length` and *arg1* is (`string-append` `"/home"` `"/"` `"andrew"`).

- Evaluation of `string-length`, which is a variable, gives a procedure value that implements the expected behaviour for "string-length".

- Evaluation of (`string-append` `"/home"` `"/"` `"andrew"`), which is another procedure invocation expression, means evaluating each of

  - `string-append`, which gives a procedure value that implements the expected behaviour for "string-append"

  - `"/home"`, which gives the string value `"/home"`

  - `"/"`, which gives the string value `"/"`

  - `"andrew"`, which gives the string value `"andrew"`

and then invoking the procedure value with this list of string values as its arguments. The resulting value is a single string value that is the concatenation of all the arguments, namely `"/home/andrew"`.

In the evaluation of the outermost expression, the interpreter can now invoke the procedure value obtained from *procedure* with the value obtained from *arg1* as its arguments. The resulting value is a numeric value that is the length of the argument string, which is 12.

3.3.1.4 Evaluating Special Syntactic Expressions

When a procedure invocation expression is evaluated, the procedure and *all* the argument expressions must be evaluated before the procedure can be invoked. Special syntactic expressions are special because they are able to manipulate their arguments in an unevaluated form, and can choose whether to evaluate any or all of the argument expressions.

Why is this needed? Consider a program fragment that asks the user whether or not to delete a file, and then deletes the file if the user answers yes.

```
(if (string=? (read-answer "Should I delete this file?")
              "yes")
    (delete-file file))
```

If the outermost (`if` ...) expression here was a procedure invocation expression, the expression (`delete-file file`), whose side effect is to actually delete a file, would already have been evaluated before the `if` procedure even got invoked! Clearly this is no use — the whole point of an `if` expression is that the *consequent* expression is only evaluated if the condition of the `if` expression is "true".

Therefore `if` must be special syntax, not a procedure. Other special syntaxes that we have already met are `define`, `set!` and `lambda`. `define` and `set!` are syntax because they need to know the variable *name* that is given as the first argument in a `define` or `set!` expression, not that variable's value. `lambda` is syntax because it does not immediately evaluate the expressions that define the procedure body; instead it creates a procedure object that incorporates these expressions so that they can be evaluated in the future, when that procedure is invoked.

The rules for evaluating each special syntactic expression are specified individually for each special syntax. For a summary of standard special syntax, see See Section 3.3.4 [Syntax Summary], page 25.

3.3.2 Tail calls

Scheme is "properly tail recursive", meaning that tail calls or recursions from certain contexts do not consume stack space or other resources and can therefore be used on arbitrarily large data or for an arbitrarily long calculation. Consider for example,

```
(define (foo n)
  (display n)
  (newline)
  (foo (1+ n)))

(foo 1)
⊣
1
2
3
...
```

foo prints numbers infinitely, starting from the given n. It's implemented by printing n then recursing to itself to print $n + 1$ and so on. This recursion is a tail call, it's the last thing done, and in Scheme such tail calls can be made without limit.

Or consider a case where a value is returned, a version of the SRFI-1 last function (see Section 7.5.3.3 [SRFI-1 Selectors], page 554) returning the last element of a list,

```
(define (my-last lst)
  (if (null? (cdr lst))
      (car lst)
      (my-last (cdr lst))))

(my-last '(1 2 3))  ⇒ 3
```

If the list has more than one element, my-last applies itself to the cdr. This recursion is a tail call, there's no code after it, and the return value is the return value from that call. In Scheme this can be used on an arbitrarily long list argument.

A proper tail call is only available from certain contexts, namely the following special form positions,

- and — last expression
- begin — last expression
- case — last expression in each clause
- cond — last expression in each clause, and the call to a => procedure is a tail call
- do — last result expression

- `if` — "true" and "false" leg expressions
- `lambda` — last expression in body
- `let`, `let*`, `letrec`, `let-syntax`, `letrec-syntax` — last expression in body
- `or` — last expression

The following core functions make tail calls,

- `apply` — tail call to given procedure
- `call-with-current-continuation` — tail call to the procedure receiving the new continuation
- `call-with-values` — tail call to the values-receiving procedure
- `eval` — tail call to evaluate the form
- `string-any`, `string-every` — tail call to predicate on the last character (if that point is reached)

The above are just core functions and special forms. Tail calls in other modules are described with the relevant documentation, for example SRFI-1 `any` and `every` (see Section 7.5.3.7 [SRFI-1 Searching], page 560).

It will be noted there are a lot of places which could potentially be tail calls, for instance the last call in a `for-each`, but only those explicitly described are guaranteed.

3.3.3 Using the Guile REPL

If you start Guile without specifying a particular program for it to execute, Guile enters its standard Read Evaluate Print Loop — or *REPL* for short. In this mode, Guile repeatedly reads in the next Scheme expression that the user types, evaluates it, and prints the resulting value.

The REPL is a useful mechanism for exploring the evaluation behaviour described in the previous subsection. If you type `string-append`, for example, the REPL replies `#<primitive-procedure string-append>`, illustrating the relationship between the variable `string-append` and the procedure value stored in that variable.

In this manual, the notation ⇒ is used to mean "evaluates to". Wherever you see an example of the form

```
expression
⇒
result
```

feel free to try it out yourself by typing *expression* into the REPL and checking that it gives the expected *result*.

3.3.4 Summary of Common Syntax

This subsection lists the most commonly used Scheme syntactic expressions, simply so that you will recognize common special syntax when you see it. For a full description of each of these syntaxes, follow the appropriate reference.

`lambda` (see Section 6.9.1 [Lambda], page 244) is used to construct procedure objects.

`define` (see Section 6.12.1 [Top Level], page 286) is used to create a new variable and set its initial value.

`set!` (see Section 6.12.1 [Top Level], page 286) is used to modify an existing variable's value.

`let`, `let*` and `letrec` (see Section 6.12.2 [Local Bindings], page 287) create an inner lexical environment for the evaluation of a sequence of expressions, in which a specified set of local variables is bound to the values of a corresponding set of expressions. For an introduction to environments, see See Section 3.4 [About Closure], page 26.

`begin` (see Section 6.13.1 [begin], page 290) executes a sequence of expressions in order and returns the value of the last expression. Note that this is not the same as a procedure which returns its last argument, because the evaluation of a procedure invocation expression does not guarantee to evaluate the arguments in order.

`if` and `cond` (see Section 6.13.2 [Conditionals], page 292) provide conditional evaluation of argument expressions depending on whether one or more conditions evaluate to "true" or "false".

`case` (see Section 6.13.2 [Conditionals], page 292) provides conditional evaluation of argument expressions depending on whether a variable has one of a specified group of values.

`and` (see Section 6.13.3 [and or], page 293) executes a sequence of expressions in order until either there are no expressions left, or one of them evaluates to "false".

`or` (see Section 6.13.3 [and or], page 293) executes a sequence of expressions in order until either there are no expressions left, or one of them evaluates to "true".

3.4 The Concept of Closure

The concept of *closure* is the idea that a lambda expression "captures" the variable bindings that are in lexical scope at the point where the lambda expression occurs. The procedure created by the lambda expression can refer to and mutate the captured bindings, and the values of those bindings persist between procedure calls.

This section explains and explores the various parts of this idea in more detail.

3.4.1 Names, Locations, Values and Environments

We said earlier that a variable name in a Scheme program is associated with a location in which any kind of Scheme value may be stored. (Incidentally, the term "vcell" is often used in Lisp and Scheme circles as an alternative to "location".) Thus part of what we mean when we talk about "creating a variable" is in fact establishing an association between a name, or identifier, that is used by the Scheme program code, and the variable location to which that name refers. Although the value that is stored in that location may change, the location to which a given name refers is always the same.

We can illustrate this by breaking down the operation of the `define` syntax into three parts: `define`

- creates a new location

- establishes an association between that location and the name specified as the first argument of the `define` expression

- stores in that location the value obtained by evaluating the second argument of the `define` expression.

A collection of associations between names and locations is called an *environment*. When you create a top level variable in a program using `define`, the name-location association for that variable is added to the "top level" environment. The "top level" environment also includes name-location associations for all the procedures that are supplied by standard Scheme.

It is also possible to create environments other than the top level one, and to create variable bindings, or name-location associations, in those environments. This ability is a key ingredient in the concept of closure; the next subsection shows how it is done.

3.4.2 Local Variables and Environments

We have seen how to create top level variables using the `define` syntax (see Section 3.1.3 [Definition], page 16). It is often useful to create variables that are more limited in their scope, typically as part of a procedure body. In Scheme, this is done using the `let` syntax, or one of its modified forms `let*` and `letrec`. These syntaxes are described in full later in the manual (see Section 6.12.2 [Local Bindings], page 287). Here our purpose is to illustrate their use just enough that we can see how local variables work.

For example, the following code uses a local variable `s` to simplify the computation of the area of a triangle given the lengths of its three sides.

```
(define a 5.3)
(define b 4.7)
(define c 2.8)

(define area
  (let ((s (/ (+ a b c) 2)))
    (sqrt (* s (- s a) (- s b) (- s c)))))
```

The effect of the `let` expression is to create a new environment and, within this environment, an association between the name `s` and a new location whose initial value is obtained by evaluating `(/ (+ a b c) 2)`. The expressions in the body of the `let`, namely `(sqrt (* s (- s a) (- s b) (- s c)))`, are then evaluated in the context of the new environment, and the value of the last expression evaluated becomes the value of the whole `let` expression, and therefore the value of the variable `area`.

3.4.3 Environment Chaining

In the example of the previous subsection, we glossed over an important point. The body of the `let` expression in that example refers not only to the local variable `s`, but also to the top level variables `a`, `b`, `c` and `sqrt`. (`sqrt` is the standard Scheme procedure for calculating a square root.) If the body of the `let` expression is evaluated in the context of the *local* `let` environment, how does the evaluation get at the values of these top level variables?

The answer is that the local environment created by a `let` expression automatically has a reference to its containing environment — in this case the top level environment — and that the Scheme interpreter automatically looks for a variable binding in the containing environment if it doesn't find one in the local environment. More generally, every environment except for the top level one has a reference to its containing environment, and the interpreter keeps searching back up the chain of environments — from most local to top level — until it either finds a variable binding for the required identifier or exhausts the chain.

This description also determines what happens when there is more than one variable binding with the same name. Suppose, continuing the example of the previous subsection, that there was also a pre-existing top level variable s created by the expression:

```
(define s "Some beans, my lord!")
```

Then both the top level environment and the local let environment would contain bindings for the name s. When evaluating code within the let body, the interpreter looks first in the local let environment, and so finds the binding for s created by the let syntax. Even though this environment has a reference to the top level environment, which also has a binding for s, the interpreter doesn't get as far as looking there. When evaluating code outside the let body, the interpreter looks up variable names in the top level environment, so the name s refers to the top level variable.

Within the let body, the binding for s in the local environment is said to *shadow* the binding for s in the top level environment.

3.4.4 Lexical Scope

The rules that we have just been describing are the details of how Scheme implements "lexical scoping". This subsection takes a brief diversion to explain what lexical scope means in general and to present an example of non-lexical scoping.

"Lexical scope" in general is the idea that

- an identifier at a particular place in a program always refers to the same variable location — where "always" means "every time that the containing expression is executed", and that

- the variable location to which it refers can be determined by static examination of the source code context in which that identifier appears, without having to consider the flow of execution through the program as a whole.

In practice, lexical scoping is the norm for most programming languages, and probably corresponds to what you would intuitively consider to be "normal". You may even be wondering how the situation could possibly — and usefully — be otherwise. To demonstrate that another kind of scoping is possible, therefore, and to compare it against lexical scoping, the following subsection presents an example of non-lexical scoping and examines in detail how its behavior differs from the corresponding lexically scoped code.

3.4.4.1 An Example of Non-Lexical Scoping

To demonstrate that non-lexical scoping does exist and can be useful, we present the following example from Emacs Lisp, which is a "dynamically scoped" language.

```
(defvar currency-abbreviation "USD")

(defun currency-string (units hundredths)
  (concat currency-abbreviation
          (number-to-string units)
          "."
          (number-to-string hundredths)))

(defun french-currency-string (units hundredths)
  (let ((currency-abbreviation "FRF"))
```

```
(currency-string units hundredths)))
```

The question to focus on here is: what does the identifier `currency-abbreviation` refer to in the `currency-string` function? The answer, in Emacs Lisp, is that all variable bindings go onto a single stack, and that `currency-abbreviation` refers to the topmost binding from that stack which has the name "currency-abbreviation". The binding that is created by the `defvar` form, to the value `"USD"`, is only relevant if none of the code that calls `currency-string` rebinds the name "currency-abbreviation" in the meanwhile.

The second function `french-currency-string` works precisely by taking advantage of this behaviour. It creates a new binding for the name "currency-abbreviation" which overrides the one established by the `defvar` form.

```
;; Note!  This is Emacs Lisp evaluation, not Scheme!
(french-currency-string 33 44)
⇒
"FRF33.44"
```

Now let's look at the corresponding, *lexically scoped* Scheme code:

```
(define currency-abbreviation "USD")

(define (currency-string units hundredths)
  (string-append currency-abbreviation
                 (number->string units)
                 "."
                 (number->string hundredths)))

(define (french-currency-string units hundredths)
  (let ((currency-abbreviation "FRF"))
    (currency-string units hundredths)))
```

According to the rules of lexical scoping, the `currency-abbreviation` in `currency-string` refers to the variable location in the innermost environment at that point in the code which has a binding for `currency-abbreviation`, which is the variable location in the top level environment created by the preceding (`define currency-abbreviation ...`) expression.

In Scheme, therefore, the `french-currency-string` procedure does not work as intended. The variable binding that it creates for "currency-abbreviation" is purely local to the code that forms the body of the `let` expression. Since this code doesn't directly use the name "currency-abbreviation" at all, the binding is pointless.

```
(french-currency-string 33 44)
⇒
"USD33.44"
```

This begs the question of how the Emacs Lisp behaviour can be implemented in Scheme. In general, this is a design question whose answer depends upon the problem that is being addressed. In this case, the best answer may be that `currency-string` should be redesigned so that it can take an optional third argument. This third argument, if supplied, is interpreted as a currency abbreviation that overrides the default.

It is possible to change `french-currency-string` so that it mostly works without changing `currency-string`, but the fix is inelegant, and susceptible to interrupts that could leave the `currency-abbreviation` variable in the wrong state:

```
(define (french-currency-string units hundredths)
  (set! currency-abbreviation "FRF")
  (let ((result (currency-string units hundredths)))
    (set! currency-abbreviation "USD")
    result))
```

The key point here is that the code does not create any local binding for the identifier `currency-abbreviation`, so all occurrences of this identifier refer to the top level variable.

3.4.5 Closure

Consider a `let` expression that doesn't contain any `lambda`s:

```
(let ((s (/ (+ a b c) 2)))
  (sqrt (* s (- s a) (- s b) (- s c))))
```

When the Scheme interpreter evaluates this, it

- creates a new environment with a reference to the environment that was current when it encountered the `let`
- creates a variable binding for `s` in the new environment, with value given by `(/ (+ a b c) 2)`
- evaluates the expression in the body of the `let` in the context of the new local environment, and remembers the value `V`
- forgets the local environment
- continues evaluating the expression that contained the `let`, using the value `V` as the value of the `let` expression, in the context of the containing environment.

After the `let` expression has been evaluated, the local environment that was created is simply forgotten, and there is no longer any way to access the binding that was created in this environment. If the same code is evaluated again, it will follow the same steps again, creating a second new local environment that has no connection with the first, and then forgetting this one as well.

If the `let` body contains a `lambda` expression, however, the local environment is *not* forgotten. Instead, it becomes associated with the procedure that is created by the `lambda` expression, and is reinstated every time that that procedure is called. In detail, this works as follows.

- When the Scheme interpreter evaluates a `lambda` expression, to create a procedure object, it stores the current environment as part of the procedure definition.
- Then, whenever that procedure is called, the interpreter reinstates the environment that is stored in the procedure definition and evaluates the procedure body within the context of that environment.

The result is that the procedure body is always evaluated in the context of the environment that was current when the procedure was created.

This is what is meant by *closure*. The next few subsections present examples that explore the usefulness of this concept.

3.4.6 Example 1: A Serial Number Generator

This example uses closure to create a procedure with a variable binding that is private to the procedure, like a local variable, but whose value persists between procedure calls.

```
(define (make-serial-number-generator)
  (let ((current-serial-number 0))
    (lambda ()
      (set! current-serial-number (+ current-serial-number 1))
      current-serial-number)))

(define entry-sn-generator (make-serial-number-generator))

(entry-sn-generator)
⇒
1

(entry-sn-generator)
⇒
2
```

When `make-serial-number-generator` is called, it creates a local environment with a binding for `current-serial-number` whose initial value is 0, then, within this environment, creates a procedure. The local environment is stored within the created procedure object and so persists for the lifetime of the created procedure.

Every time the created procedure is invoked, it increments the value of the `current-serial-number` binding in the captured environment and then returns the current value.

Note that `make-serial-number-generator` can be called again to create a second serial number generator that is independent of the first. Every new invocation of `make-serial-number-generator` creates a new local `let` environment and returns a new procedure object with an association to this environment.

3.4.7 Example 2: A Shared Persistent Variable

This example uses closure to create two procedures, `get-balance` and `deposit`, that both refer to the same captured local environment so that they can both access the `balance` variable binding inside that environment. The value of this variable binding persists between calls to either procedure.

Note that the captured `balance` variable binding is private to these two procedures: it is not directly accessible to any other code. It can only be accessed indirectly via `get-balance` or `deposit`, as illustrated by the `withdraw` procedure.

```
(define get-balance #f)
(define deposit #f)

(let ((balance 0))
  (set! get-balance
        (lambda ()
           balance))
  (set! deposit
```

```
        (lambda (amount)
          (set! balance (+ balance amount))
          balance)))

(define (withdraw amount)
  (deposit (- amount)))

(get-balance)
⇒
0

(deposit 50)
⇒
50

(withdraw 75)
⇒
-25
```

An important detail here is that the `get-balance` and `deposit` variables must be set up by `define`ing them at top level and then `set!`ing their values inside the `let` body. Using `define` within the `let` body would not work: this would create variable bindings within the local `let` environment that would not be accessible at top level.

3.4.8 Example 3: The Callback Closure Problem

A frequently used programming model for library code is to allow an application to register a callback function for the library to call when some particular event occurs. It is often useful for the application to make several such registrations using the same callback function, for example if several similar library events can be handled using the same application code, but the need then arises to distinguish the callback function calls that are associated with one callback registration from those that are associated with different callback registrations.

In languages without the ability to create functions dynamically, this problem is usually solved by passing a `user_data` parameter on the registration call, and including the value of this parameter as one of the parameters on the callback function. Here is an example of declarations using this solution in C:

```
typedef void (event_handler_t) (int event_type,
                                void *user_data);

void register_callback (int event_type,
                        event_handler_t *handler,
                        void *user_data);
```

In Scheme, closure can be used to achieve the same functionality without requiring the library code to store a `user-data` for each callback registration.

```
;; In the library:

(define (register-callback event-type handler-proc)
  ...)
```

```
;; In the application:

(define (make-handler event-type user-data)
  (lambda ()
    ...
    <code referencing event-type and user-data>
    ...))

(register-callback event-type
                   (make-handler event-type ...))
```

As far as the library is concerned, `handler-proc` is a procedure with no arguments, and all the library has to do is call it when the appropriate event occurs. From the application's point of view, though, the handler procedure has used closure to capture an environment that includes all the context that the handler code needs — `event-type` and `user-data` — to handle the event correctly.

3.4.9 Example 4: Object Orientation

Closure is the capture of an environment, containing persistent variable bindings, within the definition of a procedure or a set of related procedures. This is rather similar to the idea in some object oriented languages of encapsulating a set of related data variables inside an "object", together with a set of "methods" that operate on the encapsulated data. The following example shows how closure can be used to emulate the ideas of objects, methods and encapsulation in Scheme.

```
(define (make-account)
  (let ((balance 0))
    (define (get-balance)
      balance)
    (define (deposit amount)
      (set! balance (+ balance amount))
      balance)
    (define (withdraw amount)
      (deposit (- amount)))

    (lambda args
      (apply
        (case (car args)
          ((get-balance) get-balance)
          ((deposit) deposit)
          ((withdraw) withdraw)
          (else (error "Invalid method!")))
        (cdr args)))))
```

Each call to `make-account` creates and returns a new procedure, created by the expression in the example code that begins "(lambda args".

```
(define my-account (make-account))
```

```
my-account
⇒
#<procedure args>
```

This procedure acts as an account object with methods `get-balance`, `deposit` and `withdraw`. To apply one of the methods to the account, you call the procedure with a symbol indicating the required method as the first parameter, followed by any other parameters that are required by that method.

```
(my-account 'get-balance)
⇒
0

(my-account 'withdraw 5)
⇒
-5

(my-account 'deposit 396)
⇒
391

(my-account 'get-balance)
⇒
391
```

Note how, in this example, both the current balance and the helper procedures `get-balance`, `deposit` and `withdraw`, used to implement the guts of the account object's methods, are all stored in variable bindings within the private local environment captured by the `lambda` expression that creates the account object procedure.

3.5 Further Reading

- The website `http://www.schemers.org/` is a good starting point for all things Scheme.

- Dorai Sitaram's online Scheme tutorial, *Teach Yourself Scheme in Fixnum Days*, at `http://www.ccs.neu.edu/home/dorai/t-y-scheme/t-y-scheme.html`. Includes a nice explanation of continuations.

- The complete text of *Structure and Interpretation of Computer Programs*, the classic introduction to computer science and Scheme by Hal Abelson, Jerry Sussman and Julie Sussman, is now available online at `http://mitpress.mit.edu/sicp/sicp.html`. This site also provides teaching materials related to the book, and all the source code used in the book, in a form suitable for loading and running.

4 Programming in Scheme

Guile's core language is Scheme, and a lot can be achieved simply by using Guile to write and run Scheme programs — as opposed to having to dive into C code. In this part of the manual, we explain how to use Guile in this mode, and describe the tools that Guile provides to help you with script writing, debugging, and packaging your programs for distribution.

For detailed reference information on the variables, functions, and so on that make up Guile's application programming interface (API), see Chapter 6 [API Reference], page 99.

4.1 Guile's Implementation of Scheme

Guile's core language is Scheme, which is specified and described in the series of reports known as *RnRS*. *RnRS* is shorthand for the *Revised^n Report on the Algorithmic Language Scheme*. Guile complies fully with R5RS (see Section "Introduction" in *R5RS*), and implements some aspects of R6RS.

Guile also has many extensions that go beyond these reports. Some of the areas where Guile extends R5RS are:

- Guile's interactive documentation system
- Guile's support for POSIX-compliant network programming
- GOOPS – Guile's framework for object oriented programming.

4.2 Invoking Guile

Many features of Guile depend on and can be changed by information that the user provides either before or when Guile is started. Below is a description of what information to provide and how to provide it.

4.2.1 Command-line Options

Here we describe Guile's command-line processing in detail. Guile processes its arguments from left to right, recognizing the switches described below. For examples, see Section 4.3.4 [Scripting Examples], page 44.

`script arg...`
`-s script arg...`

> By default, Guile will read a file named on the command line as a script. Any command-line arguments *arg...* following *script* become the script's arguments; the `command-line` function returns a list of strings of the form (`script arg...`).
>
> It is possible to name a file using a leading hyphen, for example, `-myfile.scm`. In this case, the file name must be preceded by `-s` to tell Guile that a (script) file is being named.
>
> Scripts are read and evaluated as Scheme source code just as the `load` function would. After loading *script*, Guile exits.

`-c expr arg...`

> Evaluate *expr* as Scheme code, and then exit. Any command-line arguments *arg...* following *expr* become command-line arguments; the `command-line` func-

tion returns a list of strings of the form (*guile arg...*), where *guile* is the path of the Guile executable.

-- *arg...*   Run interactively, prompting the user for expressions and evaluating them. Any command-line arguments *arg...* following the -- become command-line arguments for the interactive session; the command-line function returns a list of strings of the form (*guile arg...*), where *guile* is the path of the Guile executable.

-L *directory*

Add *directory* to the front of Guile's module load path. The given directories are searched in the order given on the command line and before any directories in the GUILE_LOAD_PATH environment variable. Paths added here are *not* in effect during execution of the user's .guile file.

-C *directory*

Like -L, but adjusts the load path for *compiled* files.

-x *extension*

Add *extension* to the front of Guile's load extension list (see Section 6.17.7 [Load Paths], page 368). The specified extensions are tried in the order given on the command line, and before the default load extensions. Extensions added here are *not* in effect during execution of the user's .guile file.

-l *file*   Load Scheme source code from *file*, and continue processing the command line.

-e *function*

Make *function* the *entry point* of the script. After loading the script file (with -s) or evaluating the expression (with -c), apply *function* to a list containing the program name and the command-line arguments—the list provided by the command-line function.

A -e switch can appear anywhere in the argument list, but Guile always invokes the *function* as the *last* action it performs. This is weird, but because of the way script invocation works under POSIX, the -s option must always come last in the list.

The *function* is most often a simple symbol that names a function that is defined in the script. It can also be of the form (@ *module-name symbol*), and in that case, the symbol is looked up in the module named *module-name*.

For compatibility with some versions of Guile 1.4, you can also use the form (symbol ...) (that is, a list of only symbols that doesn't start with @), which is equivalent to (@ (symbol ...) main), or (symbol ...) symbol (that is, a list of only symbols followed by a symbol), which is equivalent to (@ (symbol ...) symbol). We recommend to use the equivalent forms directly since they correspond to the (@ ...) read syntax that can be used in normal code. See Section 6.19.2 [Using Guile Modules], page 382 and Section 4.3.4 [Scripting Examples], page 44.

-ds   Treat a final -s option as if it occurred at this point in the command line; load the script here.

This switch is necessary because, although the POSIX script invocation mechanism effectively requires the -s option to appear last, the programmer may well want to run the script before other actions requested on the command line. For examples, see Section 4.3.4 [Scripting Examples], page 44.

\   Read more command-line arguments, starting from the second line of the script file. See Section 4.3.2 [The Meta Switch], page 41.

--use-srfi=*list*

The option **--use-srfi** expects a comma-separated list of numbers, each representing a SRFI module to be loaded into the interpreter before evaluating a script file or starting the REPL. Additionally, the feature identifier for the loaded SRFIs is recognized by the procedure **cond-expand** when this option is used.

Here is an example that loads the modules SRFI-8 ('receive') and SRFI-13 ('string library') before the GUILE interpreter is started:

```
guile --use-srfi=8,13
```

--debug   Start with the debugging virtual machine (VM) engine. Using the debugging VM will enable support for VM hooks, which are needed for tracing, breakpoints, and accurate call counts when profiling. The debugging VM is slower than the regular VM, though, by about ten percent. See Section 6.25.4.1 [VM Hooks], page 455, for more information.

By default, the debugging VM engine is only used when entering an interactive session. When executing a script with -s or -c, the normal, faster VM is used by default.

--no-debug

Do not use the debugging VM engine, even when entering an interactive session.

Note that, despite the name, Guile running with **--no-debug** *does* support the usual debugging facilities, such as printing a detailed backtrace upon error. The only difference with **--debug** is lack of support for VM hooks and the facilities that build upon it (see above).

-q   Do not load the initialization file, **.guile**. This option only has an effect when running interactively; running scripts does not load the **.guile** file. See Section 4.4.1 [Init File], page 46.

--listen[=*p*]

While this program runs, listen on a local port or a path for REPL clients. If *p* starts with a number, it is assumed to be a local port on which to listen. If it starts with a forward slash, it is assumed to be a path to a UNIX domain socket on which to listen.

If *p* is not given, the default is local port 37146. If you look at it upside down, it almost spells "Guile". If you have netcat installed, you should be able to *nc localhost 37146* and get a Guile prompt. Alternately you can fire up Emacs and connect to the process; see Section 4.5 [Using Guile in Emacs], page 54 for more details.

Note that opening a port allows anyone who can connect to that port—in the TCP case, any local user—to do anything Guile can do, as the user that the

Guile process is running as. Do not use `--listen` on multi-user machines. Of course, if you do not pass `--listen` to Guile, no port will be opened.

That said, `--listen` is great for interactive debugging and development.

`--auto-compile`

Compile source files automatically (default behavior).

`--fresh-auto-compile`

Treat the auto-compilation cache as invalid, forcing recompilation.

`--no-auto-compile`

Disable automatic source file compilation.

`--language=lang`

For the remainder of the command line arguments, assume that files mentioned with `-l` and expressions passed with `-c` are written in *lang*. *lang* must be the name of one of the languages supported by the compiler (see Section 9.4.1 [Compiler Tower], page 792). When run interactively, set the REPL's language to *lang* (see Section 4.4 [Using Guile Interactively], page 46).

The default language is `scheme`; other interesting values include `elisp` (for Emacs Lisp), and `ecmascript`.

The example below shows the evaluation of expressions in Scheme, Emacs Lisp, and ECMAScript:

```
guile -c "(apply + '(1 2))"
guile --language=elisp -c "(= (funcall (symbol-function '+) 1 2) 3)"
guile --language=ecmascript -c '(function (x) { return x * x; })(2);'
```

To load a file written in Scheme and one written in Emacs Lisp, and then start a Scheme REPL, type:

```
guile -l foo.scm --language=elisp -l foo.el --language=scheme
```

`-h`, `--help`

Display help on invoking Guile, and then exit.

`-v`, `--version`

Display the current version of Guile, and then exit.

4.2.2 Environment Variables

The *environment* is a feature of the operating system; it consists of a collection of variables with names and values. Each variable is called an *environment variable* (or, sometimes, a "shell variable"); environment variable names are case-sensitive, and it is conventional to use upper-case letters only. The values are all text strings, even those that are written as numerals. (Note that here we are referring to names and values that are defined in the operating system shell from which Guile is invoked. This is not the same as a Scheme environment that is defined within a running instance of Guile. For a description of Scheme environments, see Section 3.4.1 [About Environments], page 26.)

How to set environment variables before starting Guile depends on the operating system and, especially, the shell that you are using. For example, here is how to tell Guile to provide detailed warning messages about deprecated features by setting `GUILE_WARN_DEPRECATED` using Bash:

```
$ export GUILE_WARN_DEPRECATED="detailed"
$ guile
```

Or, detailed warnings can be turned on for a single invocation using:

```
$ env GUILE_WARN_DEPRECATED="detailed" guile
```

If you wish to retrieve or change the value of the shell environment variables that affect the run-time behavior of Guile from within a running instance of Guile, see Section 7.2.6 [Runtime Environment], page 488.

Here are the environment variables that affect the run-time behavior of Guile:

GUILE_AUTO_COMPILE

> This is a flag that can be used to tell Guile whether or not to compile Scheme source files automatically. Starting with Guile 2.0, Scheme source files will be compiled automatically, by default.

> If a compiled (.go) file corresponding to a .scm file is not found or is not newer than the .scm file, the .scm file will be compiled on the fly, and the resulting .go file stored away. An advisory note will be printed on the console.

> Compiled files will be stored in the directory $XDG_CACHE_HOME/guile/ccache, where XDG_CACHE_HOME defaults to the directory $HOME/.cache. This directory will be created if it does not already exist.

> Note that this mechanism depends on the timestamp of the .go file being newer than that of the .scm file; if the .scm or .go files are moved after installation, care should be taken to preserve their original timestamps.

> Set GUILE_AUTO_COMPILE to zero (0), to prevent Scheme files from being compiled automatically. Set this variable to "fresh" to tell Guile to compile Scheme files whether they are newer than the compiled files or not.

> See Section 6.17.5 [Compilation], page 364.

GUILE_HISTORY

> This variable names the file that holds the Guile REPL command history. You can specify a different history file by setting this environment variable. By default, the history file is $HOME/.guile_history.

GUILE_INSTALL_LOCALE

> This is a flag that can be used to tell Guile whether or not to install the current locale at startup, via a call to (setlocale LC_ALL ""). See Section 7.2.13 [Locales], page 518, for more information on locales.

> You may explicitly indicate that you do not want to install the locale by setting GUILE_INSTALL_LOCALE to 0, or explicitly enable it by setting the variable to 1.

> Usually, installing the current locale is the right thing to do. It allows Guile to correctly parse and print strings with non-ASCII characters. However, for compatibility with previous Guile 2.0 releases, this option is off by default. The next stable release series of Guile (the 2.2 series) will install locales by default.

GUILE_STACK_SIZE

> Guile currently has a limited stack size for Scheme computations. Attempting to call too many nested functions will signal an error. This is good to detect

infinite recursion, but sometimes the limit is reached for normal computations. This environment variable, if set to a positive integer, specifies the number of Scheme value slots to allocate for the stack.

In the future we will implement stacks that can grow and shrink, but for now this hack will have to do.

GUILE_LOAD_COMPILED_PATH

This variable may be used to augment the path that is searched for compiled Scheme files (`.go` files) when loading. Its value should be a colon-separated list of directories. If it contains the special path component ... (ellipsis), then the default path is put in place of the ellipsis, otherwise the default path is placed at the end. The result is stored in `%load-compiled-path` (see Section 6.17.7 [Load Paths], page 368).

Here is an example using the Bash shell that adds the current directory, `.`, and the relative directory `../my-library` to `%load-compiled-path`:

```
$ export GUILE_LOAD_COMPILED_PATH=".:../my-library"
$ guile -c '(display %load-compiled-path) (newline)'
(. ../my-library /usr/local/lib/guile/2.0/ccache)
```

GUILE_LOAD_PATH

This variable may be used to augment the path that is searched for Scheme files when loading. Its value should be a colon-separated list of directories. If it contains the special path component ... (ellipsis), then the default path is put in place of the ellipsis, otherwise the default path is placed at the end. The result is stored in `%load-path` (see Section 6.17.7 [Load Paths], page 368).

Here is an example using the Bash shell that prepends the current directory to `%load-path`, and adds the relative directory `../srfi` to the end:

```
$ env GUILE_LOAD_PATH=".:...:../srfi" \
guile -c '(display %load-path) (newline)'
(. /usr/local/share/guile/2.0 \
/usr/local/share/guile/site/2.0 \
/usr/local/share/guile/site \
/usr/local/share/guile \
../srfi)
```

(Note: The line breaks, above, are for documentation purposes only, and not required in the actual example.)

GUILE_WARN_DEPRECATED

As Guile evolves, some features will be eliminated or replaced by newer features. To help users migrate their code as this evolution occurs, Guile will issue warning messages about code that uses features that have been marked for eventual elimination. `GUILE_WARN_DEPRECATED` can be set to "no" to tell Guile not to display these warning messages, or set to "detailed" to tell Guile to display more lengthy messages describing the warning. See Section 6.2 [Deprecation], page 100.

HOME   Guile uses the environment variable `HOME`, the name of your home directory, to locate various files, such as `.guile` or `.guile_history`.

4.3 Guile Scripting

Like AWK, Perl, or any shell, Guile can interpret script files. A Guile script is simply a file of Scheme code with some extra information at the beginning which tells the operating system how to invoke Guile, and then tells Guile how to handle the Scheme code.

4.3.1 The Top of a Script File

The first line of a Guile script must tell the operating system to use Guile to evaluate the script, and then tell Guile how to go about doing that. Here is the simplest case:

- The first two characters of the file must be '#!'.

  The operating system interprets this to mean that the rest of the line is the name of an executable that can interpret the script. Guile, however, interprets these characters as the beginning of a multi-line comment, terminated by the characters '!#' on a line by themselves. (This is an extension to the syntax described in R5RS, added to support shell scripts.)

- Immediately after those two characters must come the full pathname to the Guile interpreter. On most systems, this would be '/usr/local/bin/guile'.

- Then must come a space, followed by a command-line argument to pass to Guile; this should be '-s'. This switch tells Guile to run a script, instead of soliciting the user for input from the terminal. There are more elaborate things one can do here; see Section 4.3.2 [The Meta Switch], page 41.

- Follow this with a newline.

- The second line of the script should contain only the characters '!#' — just like the top of the file, but reversed. The operating system never reads this far, but Guile treats this as the end of the comment begun on the first line by the '#!' characters.

- If this source code file is not ASCII or ISO-8859-1 encoded, a coding declaration such as coding: utf-8 should appear in a comment somewhere in the first five lines of the file: see Section 6.17.8 [Character Encoding of Source Files], page 370.

- The rest of the file should be a Scheme program.

Guile reads the program, evaluating expressions in the order that they appear. Upon reaching the end of the file, Guile exits.

4.3.2 The Meta Switch

Guile's command-line switches allow the programmer to describe reasonably complicated actions in scripts. Unfortunately, the POSIX script invocation mechanism only allows one argument to appear on the '#!' line after the path to the Guile executable, and imposes arbitrary limits on that argument's length. Suppose you wrote a script starting like this:

```
#!/usr/local/bin/guile -e main -s
!#
(define (main args)
  (map (lambda (arg) (display arg) (display " "))
       (cdr args))
  (newline))
```

The intended meaning is clear: load the file, and then call `main` on the command-line arguments. However, the system will treat everything after the Guile path as a single argument — the string `"-e main -s"` — which is not what we want.

As a workaround, the meta switch \ allows the Guile programmer to specify an arbitrary number of options without patching the kernel. If the first argument to Guile is \, Guile will open the script file whose name follows the \, parse arguments starting from the file's second line (according to rules described below), and substitute them for the \ switch.

Working in concert with the meta switch, Guile treats the characters '#!' as the beginning of a comment which extends through the next line containing only the characters '!#'. This sort of comment may appear anywhere in a Guile program, but it is most useful at the top of a file, meshing magically with the POSIX script invocation mechanism.

Thus, consider a script named /u/jimb/ekko which starts like this:

```
#!/usr/local/bin/guile \
-e main -s
!#
(define (main args)
        (map (lambda (arg) (display arg) (display " "))
             (cdr args))
        (newline))
```

Suppose a user invokes this script as follows:

```
$ /u/jimb/ekko a b c
```

Here's what happens:

- the operating system recognizes the '#!' token at the top of the file, and rewrites the command line to:

  ```
  /usr/local/bin/guile \ /u/jimb/ekko a b c
  ```

  This is the usual behavior, prescribed by POSIX.

- When Guile sees the first two arguments, \ /u/jimb/ekko, it opens /u/jimb/ekko, parses the three arguments -e, `main`, and -s from it, and substitutes them for the \ switch. Thus, Guile's command line now reads:

  ```
  /usr/local/bin/guile -e main -s /u/jimb/ekko a b c
  ```

- Guile then processes these switches: it loads /u/jimb/ekko as a file of Scheme code (treating the first three lines as a comment), and then performs the application (`main "/u/jimb/ekko" "a" "b" "c"`).

When Guile sees the meta switch \, it parses command-line argument from the script file according to the following rules:

- Each space character terminates an argument. This means that two spaces in a row introduce an argument `""`.

- The tab character is not permitted (unless you quote it with the backslash character, as described below), to avoid confusion.

- The newline character terminates the sequence of arguments, and will also terminate a final non-empty argument. (However, a newline following a space will not introduce a final empty-string argument; it only terminates the argument list.)

- The backslash character is the escape character. It escapes backslash, space, tab, and newline. The ANSI C escape sequences like \n and \t are also supported. These produce argument constituents; the two-character combination \n doesn't act like a terminating newline. The escape sequence *NNN* for exactly three octal digits reads as the character whose ASCII code is *NNN*. As above, characters produced this way are argument constituents. Backslash followed by other characters is not allowed.

4.3.3 Command Line Handling

The ability to accept and handle command line arguments is very important when writing Guile scripts to solve particular problems, such as extracting information from text files or interfacing with existing command line applications. This chapter describes how Guile makes command line arguments available to a Guile script, and the utilities that Guile provides to help with the processing of command line arguments.

When a Guile script is invoked, Guile makes the command line arguments accessible via the procedure `command-line`, which returns the arguments as a list of strings.

For example, if the script

```
#! /usr/local/bin/guile -s
!#
(write (command-line))
(newline)
```

is saved in a file `cmdline-test.scm` and invoked using the command line `./cmdline-test.scm bar.txt -o foo -frumple grob`, the output is

```
("./cmdline-test.scm" "bar.txt" "-o" "foo" "-frumple" "grob")
```

If the script invocation includes a `-e` option, specifying a procedure to call after loading the script, Guile will call that procedure with `(command-line)` as its argument. So a script that uses `-e` doesn't need to refer explicitly to `command-line` in its code. For example, the script above would have identical behaviour if it was written instead like this:

```
#! /usr/local/bin/guile \
-e main -s
!#
(define (main args)
  (write args)
  (newline))
```

(Note the use of the meta switch \ so that the script invocation can include more than one Guile option: See Section 4.3.2 [The Meta Switch], page 41.)

These scripts use the `#!` POSIX convention so that they can be executed using their own file names directly, as in the example command line `./cmdline-test.scm bar.txt -o foo -frumple grob`. But they can also be executed by typing out the implied Guile command line in full, as in:

```
$ guile -s ./cmdline-test.scm bar.txt -o foo -frumple grob
```

or

```
$ guile -e main -s ./cmdline-test2.scm bar.txt -o foo -frumple grob
```

Even when a script is invoked using this longer form, the arguments that the script receives are the same as if it had been invoked using the short form. Guile ensures that the (command-line) or -e arguments are independent of how the script is invoked, by stripping off the arguments that Guile itself processes.

A script is free to parse and handle its command line arguments in any way that it chooses. Where the set of possible options and arguments is complex, however, it can get tricky to extract all the options, check the validity of given arguments, and so on. This task can be greatly simplified by taking advantage of the module (ice-9 getopt-long), which is distributed with Guile, See Section 7.4 [getopt-long], page 546.

4.3.4 Scripting Examples

To start with, here are some examples of invoking Guile directly:

guile -- a b c
> Run Guile interactively; (command-line) will return
> ("/usr/local/bin/guile" "a" "b" "c").

guile -s /u/jimb/ex2 a b c
> Load the file /u/jimb/ex2; (command-line) will return
> ("/u/jimb/ex2" "a" "b" "c").

guile -c '(write %load-path) (newline)'
> Write the value of the variable %load-path, print a newline, and exit.

guile -e main -s /u/jimb/ex4 foo
> Load the file /u/jimb/ex4, and then call the function main, passing it the list
> ("/u/jimb/ex4" "foo").

guile -l first -ds -l last -s script
> Load the files first, script, and last, in that order. The -ds switch says
> when to process the -s switch. For a more motivated example, see the scripts
> below.

Here is a very simple Guile script:

```
#!/usr/local/bin/guile -s
!#
(display "Hello, world!")
(newline)
```

The first line marks the file as a Guile script. When the user invokes it, the system runs /usr/local/bin/guile to interpret the script, passing -s, the script's filename, and any arguments given to the script as command-line arguments. When Guile sees -s *script*, it loads *script*. Thus, running this program produces the output:

```
Hello, world!
```

Here is a script which prints the factorial of its argument:

```
#!/usr/local/bin/guile -s
!#
(define (fact n)
  (if (zero? n) 1
    (* n (fact (- n 1)))))

(display (fact (string->number (cadr (command-line)))))
```

```
(newline)
```
In action:
```
$ ./fact 5
120
$
```
However, suppose we want to use the definition of `fact` in this file from another script. We can't simply `load` the script file, and then use `fact`'s definition, because the script will try to compute and display a factorial when we load it. To avoid this problem, we might write the script this way:
```
#!/usr/local/bin/guile \
-e main -s
!#
(define (fact n)
  (if (zero? n) 1
    (* n (fact (- n 1)))))

(define (main args)
  (display (fact (string->number (cadr args))))
  (newline))
```
This version packages the actions the script should perform in a function, `main`. This allows us to load the file purely for its definitions, without any extraneous computation taking place. Then we used the meta switch \ and the entry point switch `-e` to tell Guile to call `main` after loading the script.
```
$ ./fact 50
30414093201713378043612608166064768844377641568960512000000000000
```
Suppose that we now want to write a script which computes the `choose` function: given a set of m distinct objects, (choose n m) is the number of distinct subsets containing n objects each. It's easy to write `choose` given `fact`, so we might write the script this way:
```
#!/usr/local/bin/guile \
-l fact -e main -s
!#
(define (choose n m)
  (/ (fact m) (* (fact (- m n)) (fact n))))

(define (main args)
  (let ((n (string->number (cadr args)))
        (m (string->number (caddr args))))
    (display (choose n m))
    (newline)))
```
The command-line arguments here tell Guile to first load the file `fact`, and then run the script, with `main` as the entry point. In other words, the `choose` script can use definitions made in the `fact` script. Here are some sample runs:
```
$ ./choose 0 4
1
$ ./choose 1 4
```

```
4
$ ./choose 2 4
6
$ ./choose 3 4
4
$ ./choose 4 4
1
$ ./choose 50 100
100891344545564193334812497256
```

4.4 Using Guile Interactively

When you start up Guile by typing just `guile`, without a `-c` argument or the name of a script to execute, you get an interactive interpreter where you can enter Scheme expressions, and Guile will evaluate them and print the results for you. Here are some simple examples.

```
scheme@(guile-user)> (+ 3 4 5)
$1 = 12
scheme@(guile-user)> (display "Hello world!\n")
Hello world!
scheme@(guile-user)> (values 'a 'b)
$2 = a
$3 = b
```

This mode of use is called a *REPL*, which is short for "Read-Eval-Print Loop", because the Guile interpreter first reads the expression that you have typed, then evaluates it, and then prints the result.

The prompt shows you what language and module you are in. In this case, the current language is `scheme`, and the current module is (`guile-user`). See Section 6.23 [Other Languages], page 432, for more information on Guile's support for languages other than Scheme.

4.4.1 The Init File, ~/.guile

When run interactively, Guile will load a local initialization file from ~/.guile. This file should contain Scheme expressions for evaluation.

This facility lets the user customize their interactive Guile environment, pulling in extra modules or parameterizing the REPL implementation.

To run Guile without loading the init file, use the `-q` command-line option.

4.4.2 Readline

To make it easier for you to repeat and vary previously entered expressions, or to edit the expression that you're typing in, Guile can use the GNU Readline library. This is not enabled by default because of licensing reasons, but all you need to activate Readline is the following pair of lines.

```
scheme@(guile-user)> (use-modules (ice-9 readline))
scheme@(guile-user)> (activate-readline)
```

It's a good idea to put these two lines (without the `scheme@(guile-user)>` prompts) in your `.guile` file. See Section 4.4.1 [Init File], page 46, for more on `.guile`.

4.4.3 Value History

Just as Readline helps you to reuse a previous input line, *value history* allows you to use the *result* of a previous evaluation in a new expression. When value history is enabled, each evaluation result is automatically assigned to the next in the sequence of variables $1, $2, ... You can then use these variables in subsequent expressions.

```
scheme@(guile-user)> (iota 10)
$1 = (0 1 2 3 4 5 6 7 8 9)
scheme@(guile-user)> (apply * (cdr $1))
$2 = 362880
scheme@(guile-user)> (sqrt $2)
$3 = 602.3952191045344
scheme@(guile-user)> (cons $2 $1)
$4 = (362880 0 1 2 3 4 5 6 7 8 9)
```

Value history is enabled by default, because Guile's REPL imports the (ice-9 history) module. Value history may be turned off or on within the repl, using the options interface:

```
scheme@(guile-user)> ,option value-history #f
scheme@(guile-user)> 'foo
foo
scheme@(guile-user)> ,option value-history #t
scheme@(guile-user)> 'bar
$5 = bar
```

Note that previously recorded values are still accessible, even if value history is off. In rare cases, these references to past computations can cause Guile to use too much memory. One may clear these values, possibly enabling garbage collection, via the clear-value-history! procedure, described below.

The programmatic interface to value history is in a module:

```
(use-modules (ice-9 history))
```

value-history-enabled?   [Scheme Procedure]
    Return true if value history is enabled, or false otherwise.

enable-value-history!   [Scheme Procedure]
    Turn on value history, if it was off.

disable-value-history!   [Scheme Procedure]
    Turn off value history, if it was on.

clear-value-history!   [Scheme Procedure]
    Clear the value history. If the stored values are not captured by some other data structure or closure, they may then be reclaimed by the garbage collector.

4.4.4 REPL Commands

The REPL exists to read expressions, evaluate them, and then print their results. But sometimes one wants to tell the REPL to evaluate an expression in a different way, or to do something else altogether. A user can affect the way the REPL works with a *REPL command*.

The previous section had an example of a command, in the form of ,option.

```
scheme@(guile-user)> ,option value-history #t
```
Commands are distinguished from expressions by their initial comma (','). Since a comma cannot begin an expression in most languages, it is an effective indicator to the REPL that the following text forms a command, not an expression.

REPL commands are convenient because they are always there. Even if the current module doesn't have a binding for `pretty-print`, one can always `,pretty-print`.

The following sections document the various commands, grouped together by functionality. Many of the commands have abbreviations; see the online help (`,help`) for more information.

4.4.4.1 Help Commands

When Guile starts interactively, it notifies the user that help can be had by typing ',help'. Indeed, `help` is a command, and a particularly useful one, as it allows the user to discover the rest of the commands.

help [all | *group* | [-c] *command*]   [REPL Command]
    Show help.

    With one argument, tries to look up the argument as a group name, giving help on that group if successful. Otherwise tries to look up the argument as a command, giving help on the command.

    If there is a command whose name is also a group name, use the '-c *command*' form to give help on the command instead of the group.

    Without any argument, a list of help commands and command groups are displayed.

show [*topic*]   [REPL Command]
    Gives information about Guile.

    With one argument, tries to show a particular piece of information; currently supported topics are 'warranty' (or 'w'), 'copying' (or 'c'), and 'version' (or 'v').

    Without any argument, a list of topics is displayed.

apropos *regexp*   [REPL Command]
    Find bindings/modules/packages.

describe *obj*   [REPL Command]
    Show description/documentation.

4.4.4.2 Module Commands

module [*module*]   [REPL Command]
    Change modules / Show current module.

import *module* ...   [REPL Command]
    Import modules / List those imported.

load *file*   [REPL Command]
    Load a file in the current module.

reload [*module*]   [REPL Command]
    Reload the given module, or the current module if none was given.

binding   [REPL Command]
    List current bindings.

in *module expression*   [REPL Command]
in *module command arg ...*   [REPL Command]
    Evaluate an expression, or alternatively, execute another meta-command in the con-
    text of a module. For example, ',in (foo bar) ,binding' will show the bindings in
    the module (foo bar).

4.4.4.3 Language Commands

language *language*   [REPL Command]
    Change languages.

4.4.4.4 Compile Commands

compile *exp*   [REPL Command]
    Generate compiled code.

compile-file *file*   [REPL Command]
    Compile a file.

expand *exp*   [REPL Command]
    Expand any macros in a form.

optimize *exp*   [REPL Command]
    Run the optimizer on a piece of code and print the result.

disassemble *exp*   [REPL Command]
    Disassemble a compiled procedure.

disassemble-file *file*   [REPL Command]
    Disassemble a file.

4.4.4.5 Profile Commands

time *exp*   [REPL Command]
    Time execution.

profile *exp*   [REPL Command]
    Profile execution.

trace *exp* [*#:width w*] [*#:max-indent i*]   [REPL Command]
    Trace execution.

    By default, the trace will limit its width to the width of your terminal, or *width* if
    specified. Nested procedure invocations will be printed farther to the right, though if
    the width of the indentation passes the *max-indent*, the indentation is abbreviated.

4.4.4.6 Debug Commands

These debugging commands are only available within a recursive REPL; they do not work at the top level.

backtrace [*count*] [*#:width w*] [*#:full? f*]   [REPL Command]
    Print a backtrace.

    Print a backtrace of all stack frames, or innermost *count* frames. If *count* is negative, the last *count* frames will be shown.

up [*count*]   [REPL Command]
    Select a calling stack frame.

    Select and print stack frames that called this one. An argument says how many frames up to go.

down [*count*]   [REPL Command]
    Select a called stack frame.

    Select and print stack frames called by this one. An argument says how many frames down to go.

frame [*idx*]   [REPL Command]
    Show a frame.

    Show the selected frame. With an argument, select a frame by index, then show it.

procedure   [REPL Command]
    Print the procedure for the selected frame.

locals   [REPL Command]
    Show local variables.

    Show locally-bound variables in the selected frame.

error-message   [REPL Command]
error   [REPL Command]
    Show error message.

    Display the message associated with the error that started the current debugging REPL.

registers   [REPL Command]
    Show the VM registers associated with the current frame.

    See Section 9.3.3 [Stack Layout], page 774, for more information on VM stack frames.

width [*cols*]   [REPL Command]
    Sets the number of display columns in the output of ,backtrace and ,locals to *cols*. If *cols* is not given, the width of the terminal is used.

    The next 3 commands work at any REPL.

break *proc*   [REPL Command]
    Set a breakpoint at *proc*.

break-at-source *file line*   [REPL Command]
> Set a breakpoint at the given source location.

tracepoint *proc*   [REPL Command]
> Set a tracepoint on the given procedure. This will cause all calls to the procedure to print out a tracing message. See Section 6.25.4.4 [Tracing Traps], page 460, for more information.

The rest of the commands in this subsection all apply only when the stack is *continuable* — in other words when it makes sense for the program that the stack comes from to continue running. Usually this means that the program stopped because of a trap or a breakpoint.

step   [REPL Command]
> Tell the debugged program to step to the next source location.

next   [REPL Command]
> Tell the debugged program to step to the next source location in the same frame. (See Section 6.25.4 [Traps], page 455 for the details of how this works.)

finish   [REPL Command]
> Tell the program being debugged to continue running until the completion of the current stack frame, and at that time to print the result and reenter the REPL.

4.4.4.7 Inspect Commands

inspect *exp*   [REPL Command]
> Inspect the result(s) of evaluating *exp*.

pretty-print *exp*   [REPL Command]
> Pretty-print the result(s) of evaluating *exp*.

4.4.4.8 System Commands

gc   [REPL Command]
> Garbage collection.

statistics   [REPL Command]
> Display statistics.

option [*name*] [*exp*]   [REPL Command]
> With no arguments, lists all options. With one argument, shows the current value of the *name* option. With two arguments, sets the *name* option to the result of evaluating the Scheme expression *exp*.

quit   [REPL Command]
> Quit this session.

Current REPL options include:

compile-options
> The options used when compiling expressions entered at the REPL. See Section 6.17.5 [Compilation], page 364, for more on compilation options.

interp   Whether to interpret or compile expressions given at the REPL, if such a choice
              is available. Off by default (indicating compilation).

prompt   A customized REPL prompt. #f by default, indicating the default prompt.

print   A procedure of two arguments used to print the result of evaluating each ex-
              pression. The arguments are the current REPL and the value to print. By
              default, #f, to use the default procedure.

value-history
              Whether value history is on or not. See Section 4.4.3 [Value History], page 47.

on-error   What to do when an error happens. By default, debug, meaning to enter
              the debugger. Other values include backtrace, to show a backtrace without
              entering the debugger, or report, to simply show a short error printout.

Default values for REPL options may be set using repl-default-option-set! from
(system repl common):

repl-default-option-set! *key value*   [Scheme Procedure]
       Set the default value of a REPL option. This function is particularly useful in a user's
       init file. See Section 4.4.1 [Init File], page 46.

4.4.5 Error Handling

When code being evaluated from the REPL hits an error, Guile enters a new prompt,
allowing you to inspect the context of the error.

```
scheme@(guile-user)> (map string-append '("a" "b") '("c" #\d))
ERROR: In procedure string-append:
ERROR: Wrong type (expecting string): #\d
Entering a new prompt.  Type ',bt' for a backtrace or ',q' to continue.
scheme@(guile-user) [1]>
```

The new prompt runs inside the old one, in the dynamic context of the error. It is a
recursive REPL, augmented with a reified representation of the stack, ready for debugging.

,backtrace (abbreviated ,bt) displays the Scheme call stack at the point where the
error occurred:

```
scheme@(guile-user) [1]> ,bt
           1 (map #<procedure string-append _> ("a" "b") ("c" #\d))
           0 (string-append "b" #\d)
```

In the above example, the backtrace doesn't have much source information, as map and
string-append are both primitives. But in the general case, the space on the left of the
backtrace indicates the line and column in which a given procedure calls another.

You can exit a recursive REPL in the same way that you exit any REPL: via '(quit)',
',quit' (abbreviated ',q'), or C-d, among other options.

4.4.6 Interactive Debugging

A recursive debugging REPL exposes a number of other meta-commands that inspect the
state of the computation at the time of the error. These commands allow you to

• display the Scheme call stack at the point where the error occurred;

- move up and down the call stack, to see in detail the expression being evaluated, or the procedure being applied, in each *frame*; and

- examine the values of variables and expressions in the context of each frame.

See Section 4.4.4.6 [Debug Commands], page 50, for documentation of the individual commands. This section aims to give more of a walkthrough of a typical debugging session.

First, we're going to need a good error. Let's try to macroexpand the expression (unquote foo), outside of a quasiquote form, and see how the macroexpander reports this error.

```
scheme@(guile-user)> (macroexpand '(unquote foo))
ERROR: In procedure macroexpand:
ERROR: unquote: expression not valid outside of quasiquote in (unquote foo)
Entering a new prompt.  Type ',bt' for a backtrace or ',q' to continue.
scheme@(guile-user) [1]>
```

The `backtrace` command, which can also be invoked as `bt`, displays the call stack (aka backtrace) at the point where the debugger was entered:

```
scheme@(guile-user) [1]> ,bt
In ice-9/psyntax.scm:
  1130:21  3 (chi-top (unquote foo) () ((top)) e (eval) (hygiene #))
  1071:30  2 (syntax-type (unquote foo) () ((top)) #f #f (# #) #f)
  1368:28  1 (chi-macro #<procedure de9360 at ice-9/psyntax.scm...> ...)
In unknown file:
           0 (scm-error syntax-error macroexpand "~a: ~a in ~a" # #f)
```

A call stack consists of a sequence of stack *frames*, with each frame describing one procedure which is waiting to do something with the values returned by another. Here we see that there are four frames on the stack.

Note that `macroexpand` is not on the stack – it must have made a tail call to `chi-top`, as indeed we would find if we searched `ice-9/psyntax.scm` for its definition.

When you enter the debugger, the innermost frame is selected, which means that the commands for getting information about the "current" frame, or for evaluating expressions in the context of the current frame, will do so by default with respect to the innermost frame. To select a different frame, so that these operations will apply to it instead, use the `up`, `down` and `frame` commands like this:

```
scheme@(guile-user) [1]> ,up
In ice-9/psyntax.scm:
  1368:28  1 (chi-macro #<procedure de9360 at ice-9/psyntax.scm...> ...)
scheme@(guile-user) [1]> ,frame 3
In ice-9/psyntax.scm:
  1130:21  3 (chi-top (unquote foo) () ((top)) e (eval) (hygiene #))
scheme@(guile-user) [1]> ,down
In ice-9/psyntax.scm:
  1071:30  2 (syntax-type (unquote foo) () ((top)) #f #f (# #) #f)
```

Perhaps we're interested in what's going on in frame 2, so we take a look at its local variables:

```
scheme@(guile-user) [1]> ,locals
  Local variables:
  $1 = e = (unquote foo)
  $2 = r = ()
  $3 = w = ((top))
  $4 = s = #f
  $5 = rib = #f
  $6 = mod = (hygiene guile-user)
  $7 = for-car? = #f
  $8 = first = unquote
  $9 = ftype = macro
  $10 = fval = #<procedure de9360 at ice-9/psyntax.scm:2817:2 (x)>
  $11 = fe = unquote
  $12 = fw = ((top))
  $13 = fs = #f
  $14 = fmod = (hygiene guile-user)
```

All of the values are accessible by their value-history names ($*n*):

```
scheme@(guile-user) [1]> $10
$15 = #<procedure de9360 at ice-9/psyntax.scm:2817:2 (x)>
```

We can even invoke the procedure at the REPL directly:

```
scheme@(guile-user) [1]> ($10 'not-going-to-work)
ERROR: In procedure macroexpand:
ERROR: source expression failed to match any pattern in not-going-to-work
Entering a new prompt.  Type ',bt' for a backtrace or ',q' to continue.
```

Well at this point we've caused an error within an error. Let's just quit back to the top level:

```
scheme@(guile-user) [2]> ,q
scheme@(guile-user) [1]> ,q
scheme@(guile-user)>
```

Finally, as a word to the wise: hackers close their REPL prompts with *C-d*.

4.5 Using Guile in Emacs

Any text editor can edit Scheme, but some are better than others. Emacs is the best, of course, and not just because it is a fine text editor. Emacs has good support for Scheme out of the box, with sensible indentation rules, parenthesis-matching, syntax highlighting, and even a set of keybindings for structural editing, allowing navigation, cut-and-paste, and transposition operations that work on balanced S-expressions.

As good as it is, though, two things will vastly improve your experience with Emacs and Guile.

The first is Taylor Campbell's Paredit. You should not code in any dialect of Lisp without Paredit. (They say that unopinionated writing is boring—hence this tone—but it's the truth, regardless.) Paredit is the bee's knees.

The second is José Antonio Ortega Ruiz's Geiser. Geiser complements Emacs' scheme-mode with tight integration to running Guile processes via a comint-mode REPL buffer.

Of course there are keybindings to switch to the REPL, and a good REPL environment, but Geiser goes beyond that, providing:

- Form evaluation in the context of the current file's module.
- Macro expansion.
- File/module loading and/or compilation.
- Namespace-aware identifier completion (including local bindings, names visible in the current module, and module names).
- Autodoc: the echo area shows information about the signature of the procedure/macro around point automatically.
- Jump to definition of identifier at point.
- Access to documentation (including docstrings when the implementation provides it).
- Listings of identifiers exported by a given module.
- Listings of callers/callees of procedures.
- Rudimentary support for debugging and error navigation.
- Support for multiple, simultaneous REPLs.

See Geiser's web page at `http://www.nongnu.org/geiser/`, for more information.

4.6 Using Guile Tools

Guile also comes with a growing number of command-line utilities: a compiler, a disassembler, some module inspectors, and in the future, a system to install Guile packages from the internet. These tools may be invoked using the `guild` program.

```
$ guild compile -o foo.go foo.scm
wrote 'foo.go'
```

This program used to be called `guile-tools` up to Guile version 2.0.1, and for backward compatibility it still may be called as such. However we changed the name to `guild`, not only because it is pleasantly shorter and easier to read, but also because this tool will serve to bind Guile wizards together, by allowing hackers to share code with each other using a CPAN-like system.

See Section 6.17.5 [Compilation], page 364, for more on `guild compile`.

A complete list of guild scripts can be had by invoking `guild list`, or simply `guild`.

4.7 Installing Site Packages

At some point, you will probably want to share your code with other people. To do so effectively, it is important to follow a set of common conventions, to make it easy for the user to install and use your package.

The first thing to do is to install your Scheme files where Guile can find them. When Guile goes to find a Scheme file, it will search a *load path* to find the file: first in Guile's own path, then in paths for *site packages*. A site package is any Scheme code that is installed and not part of Guile itself. See Section 6.17.7 [Load Paths], page 368, for more on load paths.

There are several site paths, for historical reasons, but the one that should generally be used can be obtained by invoking the `%site-dir` procedure. See Section 6.22.1 [Build

Config], page 427. If Guile 2.0 is installed on your system in /usr/, then (%site-dir) will be /usr/share/guile/site/2.0. Scheme files should be installed there.

If you do not install compiled .go files, Guile will compile your modules and programs when they are first used, and cache them in the user's home directory. See Section 6.17.5 [Compilation], page 364, for more on auto-compilation. However, it is better to compile the files before they are installed, and to just copy the files to a place that Guile can find them.

As with Scheme files, Guile searches a path to find compiled .go files, the %load-compiled-path. By default, this path has two entries: a path for Guile's files, and a path for site packages. You should install your .go files into the latter directory, whose value is returned by invoking the %site-ccache-dir procedure. As in the previous example, if Guile 2.0 is installed on your system in /usr/, then (%site-ccache-dir) site packages will be /usr/lib/guile/2.0/site-ccache.

Note that a .go file will only be loaded in preference to a .scm file if it is newer. For that reason, you should install your Scheme files first, and your compiled files second. Load Paths, for more on the loading process.

Finally, although this section is only about Scheme, sometimes you need to install C extensions too. Shared libraries should be installed in the *extensions dir*. This value can be had from the build config (see Section 6.22.1 [Build Config], page 427). Again, if Guile 2.0 is installed on your system in /usr/, then the extensions dir will be /usr/lib/guile/2.0/extensions.

5 Programming in C

This part of the manual explains the general concepts that you need to understand when interfacing to Guile from C. You will learn about how the latent typing of Scheme is embedded into the static typing of C, how the garbage collection of Guile is made available to C code, and how continuations influence the control flow in a C program.

This knowledge should make it straightforward to add new functions to Guile that can be called from Scheme. Adding new data types is also possible and is done by defining *smobs*.

The Section 5.7 [Programming Overview], page 83 section of this part contains general musings and guidelines about programming with Guile. It explores different ways to design a program around Guile, or how to embed Guile into existing programs.

For a pedagogical yet detailed explanation of how the data representation of Guile is implemented, See Section 9.2 [Data Representation], page 763. You don't need to know the details given there to use Guile from C, but they are useful when you want to modify Guile itself or when you are just curious about how it is all done.

For detailed reference information on the variables, functions etc. that make up Guile's application programming interface (API), See Chapter 6 [API Reference], page 99.

5.1 Parallel Installations

Guile provides strong API and ABI stability guarantees during stable series, so that if a user writes a program against Guile version 2.0.3, it will be compatible with some future version 2.0.7. We say in this case that 2.0 is the *effective version*, composed of the major and minor versions, in this case 2 and 0.

Users may install multiple effective versions of Guile, with each version's headers, libraries, and Scheme files under their own directories. This provides the necessary stability guarantee for users, while also allowing Guile developers to evolve the language and its implementation.

However, parallel installability does have a down-side, in that users need to know which version of Guile to ask for, when they build against Guile. Guile solves this problem by installing a file to be read by the `pkg-config` utility, a tool to query installed packages by name. Guile encodes the version into its pkg-config name, so that users can ask for `guile-2.0` or `guile-2.2`, as appropriate.

For effective version 2.0, for example, you would invoke `pkg-config --cflags --libs guile-2.0` to get the compilation and linking flags necessary to link to version 2.0 of Guile. You would typically run `pkg-config` during the configuration phase of your program and use the obtained information in the Makefile.

Guile's `pkg-config` file, `guile-2.0.pc`, defines additional useful variables:

sitedir   The default directory where Guile looks for Scheme source and compiled files
           (see Section 4.7 [Installing Site Packages], page 55). Run `pkg-config guile-`
           `2.0 --variable=sitedir` to see its value. See Section 5.8.2 [Autoconf Macros],
           page 94, for more on how to use it from Autoconf.

`extensiondir`

> The default directory where Guile looks for extensions—i.e., shared libraries providing additional features (see Section 6.20.4 [Modules and Extensions], page 401). Run `pkg-config guile-2.0 --variable=extensiondir` to see its value.

See the `pkg-config` man page, for more information, or its web site, `http://pkg-config.freedesktop.org/`. See Section 5.8 [Autoconf Support], page 94, for more on checking for Guile from within a `configure.ac` file.

5.2 Linking Programs With Guile

This section covers the mechanics of linking your program with Guile on a typical POSIX system.

The header file `<libguile.h>` provides declarations for all of Guile's functions and constants. You should `#include` it at the head of any C source file that uses identifiers described in this manual. Once you've compiled your source files, you need to link them against the Guile object code library, `libguile`.

As noted in the previous section, `<libguile.h>` is not in the default search path for headers. The following command lines give respectively the C compilation and link flags needed to build programs using Guile 2.0:

```
pkg-config guile-2.0 --cflags
pkg-config guile-2.0 --libs
```

5.2.1 Guile Initialization Functions

To initialize Guile, you can use one of several functions. The first, `scm_with_guile`, is the most portable way to initialize Guile. It will initialize Guile when necessary and then call a function that you can specify. Multiple threads can call `scm_with_guile` concurrently and it can also be called more than once in a given thread. The global state of Guile will survive from one call of `scm_with_guile` to the next. Your function is called from within `scm_with_guile` since the garbage collector of Guile needs to know where the stack of each thread is.

A second function, `scm_init_guile`, initializes Guile for the current thread. When it returns, you can use the Guile API in the current thread. This function employs some non-portable magic to learn about stack bounds and might thus not be available on all platforms.

One common way to use Guile is to write a set of C functions which perform some useful task, make them callable from Scheme, and then link the program with Guile. This yields a Scheme interpreter just like `guile`, but augmented with extra functions for some specific application — a special-purpose scripting language.

In this situation, the application should probably process its command-line arguments in the same manner as the stock Guile interpreter. To make that straightforward, Guile provides the `scm_boot_guile` and `scm_shell` function.

For more about these functions, see Section 6.4 [Initialization], page 101.

5.2.2 A Sample Guile Main Program

Here is `simple-guile.c`, source code for a `main` and an `inner_main` function that will produce a complete Guile interpreter.

```
/* simple-guile.c --- Start Guile from C.  */

#include <libguile.h>

static void
inner_main (void *closure, int argc, char **argv)
{
  /* preparation */
  scm_shell (argc, argv);
  /* after exit */
}

int
main (int argc, char **argv)
{
  scm_boot_guile (argc, argv, inner_main, 0);
  return 0; /* never reached, see inner_main */
}
```

The `main` function calls `scm_boot_guile` to initialize Guile, passing it `inner_main`. Once `scm_boot_guile` is ready, it invokes `inner_main`, which calls `scm_shell` to process the command-line arguments in the usual way.

5.2.3 Building the Example with Make

Here is a Makefile which you can use to compile the example program. It uses `pkg-config` to learn about the necessary compiler and linker flags.

```
# Use GCC, if you have it installed.
CC=gcc

# Tell the C compiler where to find <libguile.h>
CFLAGS=`pkg-config --cflags guile-2.0`

# Tell the linker what libraries to use and where to find them.
LIBS=`pkg-config --libs guile-2.0`

simple-guile: simple-guile.o
        ${CC} simple-guile.o ${LIBS} -o simple-guile

simple-guile.o: simple-guile.c
        ${CC} -c ${CFLAGS} simple-guile.c
```

5.2.4 Building the Example with Autoconf

If you are using the GNU Autoconf package to make your application more portable, Autoconf will settle many of the details in the Makefile automatically, making it much simpler and more portable; we recommend using Autoconf with Guile. Here is a `configure.ac` file for `simple-guile` that uses the standard `PKG_CHECK_MODULES` macro to check for Guile. Autoconf will process this file into a `configure` script. We recommend invoking Autoconf via the `autoreconf` utility.

```
AC_INIT(simple-guile.c)

# Find a C compiler.
AC_PROG_CC

# Check for Guile
PKG_CHECK_MODULES([GUILE], [guile-2.0])

# Generate a Makefile, based on the results.
AC_OUTPUT(Makefile)
```

Run `autoreconf -vif` to generate `configure`.

Here is a `Makefile.in` template, from which the `configure` script produces a Makefile customized for the host system:

```
# The configure script fills in these values.
CC=@CC@
CFLAGS=@GUILE_CFLAGS@
LIBS=@GUILE_LIBS@

simple-guile: simple-guile.o
        ${CC} simple-guile.o ${LIBS} -o simple-guile
simple-guile.o: simple-guile.c
        ${CC} -c ${CFLAGS} simple-guile.c
```

The developer should use Autoconf to generate the `configure` script from the `configure.ac` template, and distribute `configure` with the application. Here's how a user might go about building the application:

```
$ ls
Makefile.in      configure*      configure.ac      simple-guile.c
$ ./configure
checking for gcc... ccache gcc
checking whether the C compiler works... yes
checking for C compiler default output file name... a.out
checking for suffix of executables...
checking whether we are cross compiling... no
checking for suffix of object files... o
checking whether we are using the GNU C compiler... yes
checking whether ccache gcc accepts -g... yes
checking for ccache gcc option to accept ISO C89... none needed
checking for pkg-config... /usr/bin/pkg-config
checking pkg-config is at least version 0.9.0... yes
checking for GUILE... yes
configure: creating ./config.status
```

```
config.status: creating Makefile
$ make
[...]
$ ./simple-guile
guile> (+ 1 2 3)
6
guile> (getpwnam "jimb")
#("jimb" "83Z7d75W2tyJQ" 4008 10 "Jim Blandy" "/u/jimb"
  "/usr/local/bin/bash")
guile> (exit)
$
```

5.3 Linking Guile with Libraries

The previous section has briefly explained how to write programs that make use of an embedded Guile interpreter. But sometimes, all you want to do is make new primitive procedures and data types available to the Scheme programmer. Writing a new version of guile is inconvenient in this case and it would in fact make the life of the users of your new features needlessly hard.

For example, suppose that there is a program guile-db that is a version of Guile with additional features for accessing a database. People who want to write Scheme programs that use these features would have to use guile-db instead of the usual guile program. Now suppose that there is also a program guile-gtk that extends Guile with access to the popular Gtk+ toolkit for graphical user interfaces. People who want to write GUIs in Scheme would have to use guile-gtk. Now, what happens when you want to write a Scheme application that uses a GUI to let the user access a database? You would have to write a *third* program that incorporates both the database stuff and the GUI stuff. This might not be easy (because guile-gtk might be a quite obscure program, say) and taking this example further makes it easy to see that this approach can not work in practice.

It would have been much better if both the database features and the GUI feature had been provided as libraries that can just be linked with guile. Guile makes it easy to do just this, and we encourage you to make your extensions to Guile available as libraries whenever possible.

You write the new primitive procedures and data types in the normal fashion, and link them into a shared library instead of into a stand-alone program. The shared library can then be loaded dynamically by Guile.

5.3.1 A Sample Guile Extension

This section explains how to make the Bessel functions of the C library available to Scheme. First we need to write the appropriate glue code to convert the arguments and return values of the functions from Scheme to C and back. Additionally, we need a function that will add them to the set of Guile primitives. Because this is just an example, we will only implement this for the j0 function.

Consider the following file bessel.c.

```
#include <math.h>
#include <libguile.h>
```

```
SCM
j0_wrapper (SCM x)
{
  return scm_from_double (j0 (scm_to_double (x)));
}

void
init_bessel ()
{
  scm_c_define_gsubr ("j0", 1, 0, 0, j0_wrapper);
}
```

This C source file needs to be compiled into a shared library. Here is how to do it on GNU/Linux:

```
gcc `pkg-config --cflags guile-2.0` \
  -shared -o libguile-bessel.so -fPIC bessel.c
```

For creating shared libraries portably, we recommend the use of GNU Libtool (see Section "Introduction" in *GNU Libtool*).

A shared library can be loaded into a running Guile process with the function **load-extension**. In addition to the name of the library to load, this function also expects the name of a function from that library that will be called to initialize it. For our example, we are going to call the function **init_bessel** which will make **j0_wrapper** available to Scheme programs with the name j0. Note that we do not specify a filename extension such as .so when invoking **load-extension**. The right extension for the host platform will be provided automatically.

```
(load-extension "libguile-bessel" "init_bessel")
(j0 2)
⇒ 0.223890779141236
```

For this to work, **load-extension** must be able to find **libguile-bessel**, of course. It will look in the places that are usual for your operating system, and it will additionally look into the directories listed in the **LTDL_LIBRARY_PATH** environment variable.

To see how these Guile extensions via shared libraries relate to the module system, See Section 2.5.3 [Putting Extensions into Modules], page 12.

5.4 General concepts for using libguile

When you want to embed the Guile Scheme interpreter into your program or library, you need to link it against the **libguile** library (see Section 5.2 [Linking Programs With Guile], page 58). Once you have done this, your C code has access to a number of data types and functions that can be used to invoke the interpreter, or make new functions that you have written in C available to be called from Scheme code, among other things.

Scheme is different from C in a number of significant ways, and Guile tries to make the advantages of Scheme available to C as well. Thus, in addition to a Scheme interpreter, libguile also offers dynamic types, garbage collection, continuations, arithmetic on arbitrary sized numbers, and other things.

The two fundamental concepts are dynamic types and garbage collection. You need to understand how libguile offers them to C programs in order to use the rest of libguile. Also, the more general control flow of Scheme caused by continuations needs to be dealt with.

Running asynchronous signal handlers and multi-threading is known to C code already, but there are of course a few additional rules when using them together with libguile.

5.4.1 Dynamic Types

Scheme is a dynamically-typed language; this means that the system cannot, in general, determine the type of a given expression at compile time. Types only become apparent at run time. Variables do not have fixed types; a variable may hold a pair at one point, an integer at the next, and a thousand-element vector later. Instead, values, not variables, have fixed types.

In order to implement standard Scheme functions like **pair?** and **string?** and provide garbage collection, the representation of every value must contain enough information to accurately determine its type at run time. Often, Scheme systems also use this information to determine whether a program has attempted to apply an operation to an inappropriately typed value (such as taking the **car** of a string).

Because variables, pairs, and vectors may hold values of any type, Scheme implementations use a uniform representation for values — a single type large enough to hold either a complete value or a pointer to a complete value, along with the necessary typing information.

In Guile, this uniform representation of all Scheme values is the C type **SCM**. This is an opaque type and its size is typically equivalent to that of a pointer to **void**. Thus, **SCM** values can be passed around efficiently and they take up reasonably little storage on their own.

The most important rule is: You never access a **SCM** value directly; you only pass it to functions or macros defined in libguile.

As an obvious example, although a **SCM** variable can contain integers, you can of course not compute the sum of two **SCM** values by adding them with the C + operator. You must use the libguile function **scm_sum**.

Less obvious and therefore more important to keep in mind is that you also cannot directly test **SCM** values for trueness. In Scheme, the value **#f** is considered false and of course a **SCM** variable can represent that value. But there is no guarantee that the **SCM** representation of **#f** looks false to C code as well. You need to use **scm_is_true** or **scm_is_false** to test a **SCM** value for trueness or falseness, respectively.

You also can not directly compare two **SCM** values to find out whether they are identical (that is, whether they are **eq?** in Scheme terms). You need to use **scm_is_eq** for this.

The one exception is that you can directly assign a **SCM** value to a **SCM** variable by using the C = operator.

The following (contrived) example shows how to do it right. It implements a function of two arguments (*a* and *flag*) that returns *a*+1 if *flag* is true, else it returns *a* unchanged.

```
SCM
my_incrementing_function (SCM a, SCM flag)
{
  SCM result;

  if (scm_is_true (flag))
```

```
      result = scm_sum (a, scm_from_int (1));
    else
      result = a;

    return result;
  }
```

Often, you need to convert between SCM values and appropriate C values. For example, we needed to convert the integer 1 to its SCM representation in order to add it to a. Libguile provides many function to do these conversions, both from C to SCM and from SCM to C.

The conversion functions follow a common naming pattern: those that make a SCM value from a C value have names of the form `scm_from_type (...)` and those that convert a SCM value to a C value use the form `scm_to_type (...)`.

However, it is best to avoid converting values when you can. When you must combine C values and SCM values in a computation, it is often better to convert the C values to SCM values and do the computation by using libguile functions than to the other way around (converting SCM to C and doing the computation some other way).

As a simple example, consider this version of `my_incrementing_function` from above:

```
SCM
my_other_incrementing_function (SCM a, SCM flag)
{
  int result;

  if (scm_is_true (flag))
    result = scm_to_int (a) + 1;
  else
    result = scm_to_int (a);

  return scm_from_int (result);
}
```

This version is much less general than the original one: it will only work for values *A* that can fit into a `int`. The original function will work for all values that Guile can represent and that `scm_sum` can understand, including integers bigger than `long long`, floating point numbers, complex numbers, and new numerical types that have been added to Guile by third-party libraries.

Also, computing with SCM is not necessarily inefficient. Small integers will be encoded directly in the SCM value, for example, and do not need any additional memory on the heap. See Section 9.2 [Data Representation], page 763 to find out the details.

Some special SCM values are available to C code without needing to convert them from C values:

Scheme value	C representation
#f	SCM_BOOL_F
#t	SCM_BOOL_T
()	SCM_EOL

In addition to SCM, Guile also defines the related type `scm_t_bits`. This is an unsigned integral type of sufficient size to hold all information that is directly contained in a SCM value. The `scm_t_bits` type is used internally by Guile to do all the bit twiddling explained in Section 9.2 [Data Representation], page 763, but you will encounter it occasionally in low-level user code as well.

5.4.2 Garbage Collection

As explained above, the `SCM` type can represent all Scheme values. Some values fit entirely into a `SCM` value (such as small integers), but other values require additional storage in the heap (such as strings and vectors). This additional storage is managed automatically by Guile. You don't need to explicitly deallocate it when a `SCM` value is no longer used.

Two things must be guaranteed so that Guile is able to manage the storage automatically: it must know about all blocks of memory that have ever been allocated for Scheme values, and it must know about all Scheme values that are still being used. Given this knowledge, Guile can periodically free all blocks that have been allocated but are not used by any active Scheme values. This activity is called *garbage collection*.

It is easy for Guile to remember all blocks of memory that it has allocated for use by Scheme values, but you need to help it with finding all Scheme values that are in use by C code.

You do this when writing a SMOB mark function, for example (see Section 5.5.4 [Garbage Collecting Smobs], page 75). By calling this function, the garbage collector learns about all references that your SMOB has to other `SCM` values.

Other references to `SCM` objects, such as global variables of type `SCM` or other random data structures in the heap that contain fields of type `SCM`, can be made visible to the garbage collector by calling the functions `scm_gc_protect` or `scm_permanent_object`. You normally use these functions for long lived objects such as a hash table that is stored in a global variable. For temporary references in local variables or function arguments, using these functions would be too expensive.

These references are handled differently: Local variables (and function arguments) of type `SCM` are automatically visible to the garbage collector. This works because the collector scans the stack for potential references to `SCM` objects and considers all referenced objects to be alive. The scanning considers each and every word of the stack, regardless of what it is actually used for, and then decides whether it could possibly be a reference to a `SCM` object. Thus, the scanning is guaranteed to find all actual references, but it might also find words that only accidentally look like references. These 'false positives' might keep `SCM` objects alive that would otherwise be considered dead. While this might waste memory, keeping an object around longer than it strictly needs to is harmless. This is why this technique is called "conservative garbage collection". In practice, the wasted memory seems to be no problem.

The stack of every thread is scanned in this way and the registers of the CPU and all other memory locations where local variables or function parameters might show up are included in this scan as well.

The consequence of the conservative scanning is that you can just declare local variables and function parameters of type `SCM` and be sure that the garbage collector will not free the corresponding objects.

However, a local variable or function parameter is only protected as long as it is really on the stack (or in some register). As an optimization, the C compiler might reuse its location for some other value and the SCM object would no longer be protected. Normally, this leads to exactly the right behavior: the compiler will only overwrite a reference when it is no longer needed and thus the object becomes unprotected precisely when the reference disappears, just as wanted.

There are situations, however, where a SCM object needs to be around longer than its reference from a local variable or function parameter. This happens, for example, when you retrieve some pointer from a smob and work with that pointer directly. The reference to the SCM smob object might be dead after the pointer has been retrieved, but the pointer itself (and the memory pointed to) is still in use and thus the smob object must be protected. The compiler does not know about this connection and might overwrite the SCM reference too early.

To get around this problem, you can use `scm_remember_upto_here_1` and its cousins. It will keep the compiler from overwriting the reference. For a typical example of its use, see Section 5.5.5 [Remembering During Operations], page 77.

5.4.3 Control Flow

Scheme has a more general view of program flow than C, both locally and non-locally.

Controlling the local flow of control involves things like gotos, loops, calling functions and returning from them. Non-local control flow refers to situations where the program jumps across one or more levels of function activations without using the normal call or return operations.

The primitive means of C for local control flow is the `goto` statement, together with `if`. Loops done with `for`, `while` or `do` could in principle be rewritten with just `goto` and `if`. In Scheme, the primitive means for local control flow is the *function call* (together with `if`). Thus, the repetition of some computation in a loop is ultimately implemented by a function that calls itself, that is, by recursion.

This approach is theoretically very powerful since it is easier to reason formally about recursion than about gotos. In C, using recursion exclusively would not be practical, though, since it would eat up the stack very quickly. In Scheme, however, it is practical: function calls that appear in a *tail position* do not use any additional stack space (see Section 3.3.2 [Tail Calls], page 24).

A function call is in a tail position when it is the last thing the calling function does. The value returned by the called function is immediately returned from the calling function. In the following example, the call to `bar-1` is in a tail position, while the call to `bar-2` is not. (The call to `1-` in `foo-2` is in a tail position, though.)

```
(define (foo-1 x)
  (bar-1 (1- x)))

(define (foo-2 x)
  (1- (bar-2 x)))
```

Thus, when you take care to recurse only in tail positions, the recursion will only use constant stack space and will be as good as a loop constructed from gotos.

Scheme offers a few syntactic abstractions (`do` and *named* `let`) that make writing loops slightly easier.

But only Scheme functions can call other functions in a tail position: C functions can not. This matters when you have, say, two functions that call each other recursively to form a common loop. The following (unrealistic) example shows how one might go about determining whether a non-negative integer *n* is even or odd.

```
(define (my-even? n)
  (cond ((zero? n) #t)
        (else (my-odd? (1- n)))))

(define (my-odd? n)
  (cond ((zero? n) #f)
        (else (my-even? (1- n)))))
```

Because the calls to `my-even?` and `my-odd?` are in tail positions, these two procedures can be applied to arbitrary large integers without overflowing the stack. (They will still take a lot of time, of course.)

However, when one or both of the two procedures would be rewritten in C, it could no longer call its companion in a tail position (since C does not have this concept). You might need to take this consideration into account when deciding which parts of your program to write in Scheme and which in C.

In addition to calling functions and returning from them, a Scheme program can also exit non-locally from a function so that the control flow returns directly to an outer level. This means that some functions might not return at all.

Even more, it is not only possible to jump to some outer level of control, a Scheme program can also jump back into the middle of a function that has already exited. This might cause some functions to return more than once.

In general, these non-local jumps are done by invoking *continuations* that have previously been captured using `call-with-current-continuation`. Guile also offers a slightly restricted set of functions, `catch` and `throw`, that can only be used for non-local exits. This restriction makes them more efficient. Error reporting (with the function `error`) is implemented by invoking `throw`, for example. The functions `catch` and `throw` belong to the topic of *exceptions*.

Since Scheme functions can call C functions and vice versa, C code can experience the more general control flow of Scheme as well. It is possible that a C function will not return at all, or will return more than once. While C does offer `setjmp` and `longjmp` for non-local exits, it is still an unusual thing for C code. In contrast, non-local exits are very common in Scheme, mostly to report errors.

You need to be prepared for the non-local jumps in the control flow whenever you use a function from `libguile`: it is best to assume that any `libguile` function might signal an error or run a pending signal handler (which in turn can do arbitrary things).

It is often necessary to take cleanup actions when the control leaves a function non-locally. Also, when the control returns non-locally, some setup actions might be called for. For example, the Scheme function `with-output-to-port` needs to modify the global state so that `current-output-port` returns the port passed to `with-output-to-port`. The global output port needs to be reset to its previous value when `with-output-to-port` returns normally or when it is exited non-locally. Likewise, the port needs to be set again when control enters non-locally.

Scheme code can use the `dynamic-wind` function to arrange for the setting and resetting of the global state. C code can use the corresponding `scm_internal_dynamic_wind` function, or a `scm_dynwind_begin`/`scm_dynwind_end` pair together with suitable 'dynwind actions' (see Section 6.13.10 [Dynamic Wind], page 309).

Instead of coping with non-local control flow, you can also prevent it by erecting a *continuation barrier*, See Section 6.13.12 [Continuation Barriers], page 315. The function `scm_c_with_continuation_barrier`, for example, is guaranteed to return exactly once.

5.4.4 Asynchronous Signals

You can not call libguile functions from handlers for POSIX signals, but you can register Scheme handlers for POSIX signals such as `SIGINT`. These handlers do not run during the actual signal delivery. Instead, they are run when the program (more precisely, the thread that the handler has been registered for) reaches the next *safe point*.

The libguile functions themselves have many such safe points. Consequently, you must be prepared for arbitrary actions anytime you call a libguile function. For example, even `scm_cons` can contain a safe point and when a signal handler is pending for your thread, calling `scm_cons` will run this handler and anything might happen, including a non-local exit although `scm_cons` would not ordinarily do such a thing on its own.

If you do not want to allow the running of asynchronous signal handlers, you can block them temporarily with `scm_dynwind_block_asyncs`, for example. See See Section 6.21.2.1 [System asyncs], page 411.

Since signal handling in Guile relies on safe points, you need to make sure that your functions do offer enough of them. Normally, calling libguile functions in the normal course of action is all that is needed. But when a thread might spent a long time in a code section that calls no libguile function, it is good to include explicit safe points. This can allow the user to interrupt your code with `C-c`, for example.

You can do this with the macro `SCM_TICK`. This macro is syntactically a statement. That is, you could use it like this:

```
while (1)
  {
    SCM_TICK;
    do_some_work ();
  }
```

Frequent execution of a safe point is even more important in multi threaded programs, See Section 5.4.5 [Multi-Threading], page 68.

5.4.5 Multi-Threading

Guile can be used in multi-threaded programs just as well as in single-threaded ones.

Each thread that wants to use functions from libguile must put itself into *guile mode* and must then follow a few rules. If it doesn't want to honor these rules in certain situations, a thread can temporarily leave guile mode (but can no longer use libguile functions during that time, of course).

Threads enter guile mode by calling `scm_with_guile`, `scm_boot_guile`, or `scm_init_guile`. As explained in the reference documentation for these functions, Guile will then learn about the stack bounds of the thread and can protect the SCM values that are stored in local variables. When a thread puts itself into guile mode for the first time, it gets a Scheme representation and is listed by `all-threads`, for example.

Threads in guile mode can block (e.g., do blocking I/O) without causing any problems[1]; temporarily leaving guile mode with `scm_without_guile` before blocking slightly improves GC performance, though. For some common blocking operations, Guile provides convenience functions. For example, if you want to lock a pthread mutex while in guile mode, you might want to use `scm_pthread_mutex_lock` which is just like `pthread_mutex_lock` except that it leaves guile mode while blocking.

All libguile functions are (intended to be) robust in the face of multiple threads using them concurrently. This means that there is no risk of the internal data structures of libguile becoming corrupted in such a way that the process crashes.

A program might still produce nonsensical results, though. Taking hashtables as an example, Guile guarantees that you can use them from multiple threads concurrently and a hashtable will always remain a valid hashtable and Guile will not crash when you access it. It does not guarantee, however, that inserting into it concurrently from two threads will give useful results: only one insertion might actually happen, none might happen, or the table might in general be modified in a totally arbitrary manner. (It will still be a valid hashtable, but not the one that you might have expected.) Guile might also signal an error when it detects a harmful race condition.

Thus, you need to put in additional synchronizations when multiple threads want to use a single hashtable, or any other mutable Scheme object.

When writing C code for use with libguile, you should try to make it robust as well. An example that converts a list into a vector will help to illustrate. Here is a correct version:

```
SCM
my_list_to_vector (SCM list)
{
  SCM vector = scm_make_vector (scm_length (list), SCM_UNDEFINED);
  size_t len, i;

  len = scm_c_vector_length (vector);
  i = 0;
  while (i < len && scm_is_pair (list))
    {
      scm_c_vector_set_x (vector, i, scm_car (list));
      list = scm_cdr (list);
      i++;
    }

  return vector;
}
```

The first thing to note is that storing into a `SCM` location concurrently from multiple threads is guaranteed to be robust: you don't know which value wins but it will in any case be a valid `SCM` value.

---

[1] In Guile 1.8, a thread blocking in guile mode would prevent garbage collection to occur. Thus, threads had to leave guile mode whenever they could block. This is no longer needed with Guile 2.0.

But there is no guarantee that the list referenced by *list* is not modified in another thread while the loop iterates over it. Thus, while copying its elements into the vector, the list might get longer or shorter. For this reason, the loop must check both that it doesn't overrun the vector and that it doesn't overrun the list. Otherwise, `scm_c_vector_set_x` would raise an error if the index is out of range, and `scm_car` and `scm_cdr` would raise an error if the value is not a pair.

It is safe to use `scm_car` and `scm_cdr` on the local variable *list* once it is known that the variable contains a pair. The contents of the pair might change spontaneously, but it will always stay a valid pair (and a local variable will of course not spontaneously point to a different Scheme object).

Likewise, a vector such as the one returned by `scm_make_vector` is guaranteed to always stay the same length so that it is safe to only use scm_c_vector_length once and store the result. (In the example, *vector* is safe anyway since it is a fresh object that no other thread can possibly know about until it is returned from `my_list_to_vector`.)

Of course the behavior of `my_list_to_vector` is suboptimal when *list* does indeed get asynchronously lengthened or shortened in another thread. But it is robust: it will always return a valid vector. That vector might be shorter than expected, or its last elements might be unspecified, but it is a valid vector and if a program wants to rule out these cases, it must avoid modifying the list asynchronously.

Here is another version that is also correct:

```
SCM
my_pedantic_list_to_vector (SCM list)
{
  SCM vector = scm_make_vector (scm_length (list), SCM_UNDEFINED);
  size_t len, i;

  len = scm_c_vector_length (vector);
  i = 0;
  while (i < len)
    {
      scm_c_vector_set_x (vector, i, scm_car (list));
      list = scm_cdr (list);
      i++;
    }

  return vector;
}
```

This version relies on the error-checking behavior of `scm_car` and `scm_cdr`. When the list is shortened (that is, when *list* holds a non-pair), `scm_car` will throw an error. This might be preferable to just returning a half-initialized vector.

The API for accessing vectors and arrays of various kinds from C takes a slightly different approach to thread-robustness. In order to get at the raw memory that stores the elements of an array, you need to *reserve* that array as long as you need the raw memory. During the time an array is reserved, its elements can still spontaneously change their values, but the memory itself and other things like the size of the array are guaranteed to stay fixed.

Any operation that would change these parameters of an array that is currently reserved will signal an error. In order to avoid these errors, a program should of course put suitable synchronization mechanisms in place. As you can see, Guile itself is again only concerned about robustness, not about correctness: without proper synchronization, your program will likely not be correct, but the worst consequence is an error message.

Real thread-safety often requires that a critical section of code is executed in a certain restricted manner. A common requirement is that the code section is not entered a second time when it is already being executed. Locking a mutex while in that section ensures that no other thread will start executing it, blocking asyncs ensures that no asynchronous code enters the section again from the current thread, and the error checking of Guile mutexes guarantees that an error is signalled when the current thread accidentally reenters the critical section via recursive function calls.

Guile provides two mechanisms to support critical sections as outlined above. You can either use the macros `SCM_CRITICAL_SECTION_START` and `SCM_CRITICAL_SECTION_END` for very simple sections; or use a dynwind context together with a call to `scm_dynwind_critical_section`.

The macros only work reliably for critical sections that are guaranteed to not cause a non-local exit. They also do not detect an accidental reentry by the current thread. Thus, you should probably only use them to delimit critical sections that do not contain calls to libguile functions or to other external functions that might do complicated things.

The function `scm_dynwind_critical_section`, on the other hand, will correctly deal with non-local exits because it requires a dynwind context. Also, by using a separate mutex for each critical section, it can detect accidental reentries.

5.5 Defining New Types (Smobs)

Smobs are Guile's mechanism for adding new primitive types to the system. The term "smob" was coined by Aubrey Jaffer, who says it comes from "small object", referring to the fact that they are quite limited in size: they can hold just one pointer to a larger memory block plus 16 extra bits.

To define a new smob type, the programmer provides Guile with some essential information about the type — how to print it, how to garbage collect it, and so on — and Guile allocates a fresh type tag for it. The programmer can then use `scm_c_define_gsubr` to make a set of C functions visible to Scheme code that create and operate on these objects.

(You can find a complete version of the example code used in this section in the Guile distribution, in `doc/example-smob`. That directory includes a makefile and a suitable `main` function, so you can build a complete interactive Guile shell, extended with the datatypes described here.)

5.5.1 Describing a New Type

To define a new type, the programmer must write two functions to manage instances of the type:

print   Guile will apply this function to each instance of the new type to print the value, as for `display` or `write`. The default print function prints `#<NAME ADDRESS>` where NAME is the first argument passed to `scm_make_smob_type`.

equalp   If Scheme code asks the `equal?` function to compare two instances of the same
          smob type, Guile calls this function. It should return `SCM_BOOL_T` if *a* and
          b should be considered `equal?`, or `SCM_BOOL_F` otherwise. If `equalp` is `NULL`,
          `equal?` will assume that two instances of this type are never `equal?` unless they
          are `eq?`.

When the only resource associated with a smob is memory managed by the garbage
collector—i.e., memory allocated with the `scm_gc_malloc` functions—this is sufficient.
However, when a smob is associated with other kinds of resources, it may be necessary
to define one of the following functions, or both:

mark   Guile will apply this function to each instance of the new type it encounters
          during garbage collection. This function is responsible for telling the collector
          about any other `SCM` values that the object has stored, and that are in memory
          regions not already scanned by the garbage collector. See Section 5.5.4 [Garbage
          Collecting Smobs], page 75, for more details.

free   Guile will apply this function to each instance of the new type that is to be
          deallocated. The function should release all resources held by the object. This is
          analogous to the Java finalization method—it is invoked at an unspecified time
          (when garbage collection occurs) after the object is dead. See Section 5.5.4
          [Garbage Collecting Smobs], page 75, for more details.

          This function operates while the heap is in an inconsistent state and must
          therefore be careful. See Section 6.8 [Smobs], page 241, for details about what
          this function is allowed to do.

To actually register the new smob type, call `scm_make_smob_type`. It returns a value of
type `scm_t_bits` which identifies the new smob type.

The four special functions described above are registered by calling one of `scm_set_smob_mark`, `scm_set_smob_free`, `scm_set_smob_print`, or `scm_set_smob_equalp`, as appropriate. Each function is intended to be used at most once per type, and the call should
be placed immediately following the call to `scm_make_smob_type`.

There can only be at most 256 different smob types in the system. Instead of registering a
huge number of smob types (for example, one for each relevant C struct in your application),
it is sometimes better to register just one and implement a second layer of type dispatching
on top of it. This second layer might use the 16 extra bits to extend its type, for example.

Here is how one might declare and register a new type representing eight-bit gray-scale
images:

```
#include <libguile.h>

struct image {
  int width, height;
  char *pixels;

  /* The name of this image */
  SCM name;

  /* A function to call when this image is
```

```
      modified, e.g., to update the screen,
      or SCM_BOOL_F if no action necessary */
   SCM update_func;
};

static scm_t_bits image_tag;

void
init_image_type (void)
{
   image_tag = scm_make_smob_type ("image", sizeof (struct image));
   scm_set_smob_mark (image_tag, mark_image);
   scm_set_smob_free (image_tag, free_image);
   scm_set_smob_print (image_tag, print_image);
}
```

5.5.2 Creating Smob Instances

Normally, smobs can have one *immediate* word of data. This word stores either a pointer to an additional memory block that holds the real data, or it might hold the data itself when it fits. The word is large enough for a SCM value, a pointer to void, or an integer that fits into a size_t or ssize_t.

You can also create smobs that have two or three immediate words, and when these words suffice to store all data, it is more efficient to use these super-sized smobs instead of using a normal smob plus a memory block. See Section 5.5.6 [Double Smobs], page 78, for their discussion.

Guile provides functions for managing memory which are often helpful when implementing smobs. See Section 6.18.2 [Memory Blocks], page 376.

To retrieve the immediate word of a smob, you use the macro SCM_SMOB_DATA. It can be set with SCM_SET_SMOB_DATA. The 16 extra bits can be accessed with SCM_SMOB_FLAGS and SCM_SET_SMOB_FLAGS.

The two macros SCM_SMOB_DATA and SCM_SET_SMOB_DATA treat the immediate word as if it were of type scm_t_bits, which is an unsigned integer type large enough to hold a pointer to void. Thus you can use these macros to store arbitrary pointers in the smob word.

When you want to store a SCM value directly in the immediate word of a smob, you should use the macros SCM_SMOB_OBJECT and SCM_SET_SMOB_OBJECT to access it.

Creating a smob instance can be tricky when it consists of multiple steps that allocate resources. Most of the time, this is mainly about allocating memory to hold associated data structures. Using memory managed by the garbage collector simplifies things: the garbage collector will automatically scan those data structures for pointers, and reclaim them when they are no longer referenced.

Continuing the example from above, if the global variable image_tag contains a tag returned by scm_make_smob_type, here is how we could construct a smob whose immediate word contains a pointer to a freshly allocated struct image:

```
   SCM
```

```
make_image (SCM name, SCM s_width, SCM s_height)
{
  SCM smob;
  struct image *image;
  int width = scm_to_int (s_width);
  int height = scm_to_int (s_height);

  /* Step 1: Allocate the memory block.
   */
  image = (struct image *)
    scm_gc_malloc (sizeof (struct image), "image");

  /* Step 2: Initialize it with straight code.
   */
  image->width = width;
  image->height = height;
  image->pixels = NULL;
  image->name = SCM_BOOL_F;
  image->update_func = SCM_BOOL_F;

  /* Step 3: Create the smob.
   */
  smob = scm_new_smob (image_tag, image);

  /* Step 4: Finish the initialization.
   */
  image->name = name;
  image->pixels =
    scm_gc_malloc_pointerless (width * height, "image pixels");

  return smob;
}
```

We use `scm_gc_malloc_pointerless` for the pixel buffer to tell the garbage collector not to scan it for pointers. Calls to `scm_gc_malloc`, `scm_new_smob`, and `scm_gc_malloc_pointerless` raise an exception in out-of-memory conditions; the garbage collector is able to reclaim previously allocated memory if that happens.

5.5.3 Type checking

Functions that operate on smobs should check that the passed SCM value indeed is a suitable smob before accessing its data. They can do this with `scm_assert_smob_type`.

For example, here is a simple function that operates on an image smob, and checks the type of its argument.

```
SCM
clear_image (SCM image_smob)
{
  int area;
```

```
        struct image *image;

        scm_assert_smob_type (image_tag, image_smob);

        image = (struct image *) SCM_SMOB_DATA (image_smob);
        area = image->width * image->height;
        memset (image->pixels, 0, area);

        /* Invoke the image's update function.
         */
        if (scm_is_true (image->update_func))
          scm_call_0 (image->update_func);

        scm_remember_upto_here_1 (image_smob);

        return SCM_UNSPECIFIED;
      }
```

See Section 5.5.5 [Remembering During Operations], page 77 for an explanation of the call to `scm_remember_upto_here_1`.

5.5.4 Garbage Collecting Smobs

Once a smob has been released to the tender mercies of the Scheme system, it must be prepared to survive garbage collection. In the example above, all the memory associated with the smob is managed by the garbage collector because we used the `scm_gc_` allocation functions. Thus, no special care must be taken: the garbage collector automatically scans them and reclaims any unused memory.

However, when data associated with a smob is managed in some other way—e.g., `malloc`'d memory or file descriptors—it is possible to specify a *free* function to release those resources when the smob is reclaimed, and a *mark* function to mark Scheme objects otherwise invisible to the garbage collector.

As described in more detail elsewhere (see Section 9.2.4 [Conservative GC], page 767), every object in the Scheme system has a *mark bit*, which the garbage collector uses to tell live objects from dead ones. When collection starts, every object's mark bit is clear. The collector traces pointers through the heap, starting from objects known to be live, and sets the mark bit on each object it encounters. When it can find no more unmarked objects, the collector walks all objects, live and dead, frees those whose mark bits are still clear, and clears the mark bit on the others.

The two main portions of the collection are called the *mark phase*, during which the collector marks live objects, and the *sweep phase*, during which the collector frees all unmarked objects.

The mark bit of a smob lives in a special memory region. When the collector encounters a smob, it sets the smob's mark bit, and uses the smob's type tag to find the appropriate *mark* function for that smob. It then calls this *mark* function, passing it the smob as its only argument.

The *mark* function is responsible for marking any other Scheme objects the smob refers to. If it does not do so, the objects' mark bits will still be clear when the collector begins to sweep, and the collector will free them. If this occurs, it will probably break, or at least confuse, any code operating on the smob; the smob's SCM values will have become dangling references.

To mark an arbitrary Scheme object, the *mark* function calls `scm_gc_mark`.

Thus, here is how we might write `mark_image`—again this is not needed in our example since we used the `scm_gc_` allocation routines, so this is just for the sake of illustration:

```
SCM
mark_image (SCM image_smob)
{
  /* Mark the image's name and update function.  */
  struct image *image = (struct image *) SCM_SMOB_DATA (image_smob);

  scm_gc_mark (image->name);
  scm_gc_mark (image->update_func);

  return SCM_BOOL_F;
}
```

Note that, even though the image's `update_func` could be an arbitrarily complex structure (representing a procedure and any values enclosed in its environment), `scm_gc_mark` will recurse as necessary to mark all its components. Because `scm_gc_mark` sets an object's mark bit before it recurses, it is not confused by circular structures.

As an optimization, the collector will mark whatever value is returned by the *mark* function; this helps limit depth of recursion during the mark phase. Thus, the code above should really be written as:

```
SCM
mark_image (SCM image_smob)
{
  /* Mark the image's name and update function.  */
  struct image *image = (struct image *) SCM_SMOB_DATA (image_smob);

  scm_gc_mark (image->name);
  return image->update_func;
}
```

Finally, when the collector encounters an unmarked smob during the sweep phase, it uses the smob's tag to find the appropriate *free* function for the smob. It then calls that function, passing it the smob as its only argument.

The *free* function must release any resources used by the smob. However, it must not free objects managed by the collector; the collector will take care of them. For historical reasons, the return type of the *free* function should be `size_t`, an unsigned integral type; the *free* function should always return zero.

Here is how we might write the `free_image` function for the image smob type—again for the sake of illustration, since our example does not need it thanks to the use of the `scm_gc_` allocation routines:

```
size_t
free_image (SCM image_smob)
```

```
{
  struct image *image = (struct image *) SCM_SMOB_DATA (image_smob);

  scm_gc_free (image->pixels,
               image->width * image->height,
               "image pixels");
  scm_gc_free (image, sizeof (struct image), "image");

  return 0;
}
```

During the sweep phase, the garbage collector will clear the mark bits on all live objects. The code which implements a smob need not do this itself.

There is no way for smob code to be notified when collection is complete.

It is usually a good idea to minimize the amount of processing done during garbage collection; keep the *mark* and *free* functions very simple. Since collections occur at unpredictable times, it is easy for any unusual activity to interfere with normal code.

5.5.5 Remembering During Operations

It's important that a smob is visible to the garbage collector whenever its contents are being accessed. Otherwise it could be freed while code is still using it.

For example, consider a procedure to convert image data to a list of pixel values.

```
SCM
image_to_list (SCM image_smob)
{
  struct image *image;
  SCM lst;
  int i;

  scm_assert_smob_type (image_tag, image_smob);

  image = (struct image *) SCM_SMOB_DATA (image_smob);
  lst = SCM_EOL;
  for (i = image->width * image->height - 1; i >= 0; i--)
    lst = scm_cons (scm_from_char (image->pixels[i]), lst);

  scm_remember_upto_here_1 (image_smob);
  return lst;
}
```

In the loop, only the `image` pointer is used and the C compiler has no reason to keep the `image_smob` value anywhere. If `scm_cons` results in a garbage collection, `image_smob` might not be on the stack or anywhere else and could be freed, leaving the loop accessing freed data. The use of `scm_remember_upto_here_1` prevents this, by creating a reference to `image_smob` after all data accesses.

There's no need to do the same for `lst`, since that's the return value and the compiler will certainly keep it in a register or somewhere throughout the routine.

The `clear_image` example previously shown (see Section 5.5.3 [Type checking], page 74) also used `scm_remember_upto_here_1` for this reason.

It's only in quite rare circumstances that a missing `scm_remember_upto_here_1` will bite, but when it happens the consequences are serious. Fortunately the rule is simple: whenever calling a Guile library function or doing something that might, ensure that the SCM of a smob is referenced past all accesses to its insides. Do this by adding an `scm_remember_upto_here_1` if there are no other references.

In a multi-threaded program, the rule is the same. As far as a given thread is concerned, a garbage collection still only occurs within a Guile library function, not at an arbitrary time. (Guile waits for all threads to reach one of its library functions, and holds them there while the collector runs.)

5.5.6 Double Smobs

Smobs are called smob because they are small: they normally have only room for one `void*` or SCM value plus 16 bits. The reason for this is that smobs are directly implemented by using the low-level, two-word cells of Guile that are also used to implement pairs, for example. (see Section 9.2 [Data Representation], page 763 for the details.) One word of the two-word cells is used for `SCM_SMOB_DATA` (or `SCM_SMOB_OBJECT`), the other contains the 16-bit type tag and the 16 extra bits.

In addition to the fundamental two-word cells, Guile also has four-word cells, which are appropriately called *double cells*. You can use them for *double smobs* and get two more immediate words of type `scm_t_bits`.

A double smob is created with `scm_new_double_smob`. Its immediate words can be retrieved as `scm_t_bits` with `SCM_SMOB_DATA_2` and `SCM_SMOB_DATA_3` in addition to `SCM_SMOB_DATA`. Unsurprisingly, the words can be set to `scm_t_bits` values with `SCM_SET_SMOB_DATA_2` and `SCM_SET_SMOB_DATA_3`.

Of course there are also `SCM_SMOB_OBJECT_2`, `SCM_SMOB_OBJECT_3`, `SCM_SET_SMOB_OBJECT_2`, and `SCM_SET_SMOB_OBJECT_3`.

5.5.7 The Complete Example

Here is the complete text of the implementation of the image datatype, as presented in the sections above. We also provide a definition for the smob's *print* function, and make some objects and functions static, to clarify exactly what the surrounding code is using.

As mentioned above, you can find this code in the Guile distribution, in `doc/example-smob`. That directory includes a makefile and a suitable `main` function, so you can build a complete interactive Guile shell, extended with the datatypes described here.)

```
/* file "image-type.c" */

#include <stdlib.h>
#include <libguile.h>

static scm_t_bits image_tag;

struct image {
  int width, height;
```

```
    char *pixels;

    /* The name of this image */
    SCM name;

    /* A function to call when this image is
       modified, e.g., to update the screen,
       or SCM_BOOL_F if no action necessary */
    SCM update_func;
};

static SCM
make_image (SCM name, SCM s_width, SCM s_height)
{
  SCM smob;
  struct image *image;
  int width = scm_to_int (s_width);
  int height = scm_to_int (s_height);

  /* Step 1: Allocate the memory block.
   */
  image = (struct image *)
    scm_gc_malloc (sizeof (struct image), "image");

  /* Step 2: Initialize it with straight code.
   */
  image->width = width;
  image->height = height;
  image->pixels = NULL;
  image->name = SCM_BOOL_F;
  image->update_func = SCM_BOOL_F;

  /* Step 3: Create the smob.
   */
  smob = scm_new_smob (image_tag, image);

  /* Step 4: Finish the initialization.
   */
  image->name = name;
  image->pixels =
    scm_gc_malloc (width * height, "image pixels");

  return smob;
}

SCM
clear_image (SCM image_smob)
```

```
{
  int area;
  struct image *image;

  scm_assert_smob_type (image_tag, image_smob);

  image = (struct image *) SCM_SMOB_DATA (image_smob);
  area = image->width * image->height;
  memset (image->pixels, 0, area);

  /* Invoke the image's update function.
   */
  if (scm_is_true (image->update_func))
    scm_call_0 (image->update_func);

  scm_remember_upto_here_1 (image_smob);

  return SCM_UNSPECIFIED;
}

static SCM
mark_image (SCM image_smob)
{
  /* Mark the image's name and update function.  */
  struct image *image = (struct image *) SCM_SMOB_DATA (image_smob);

  scm_gc_mark (image->name);
  return image->update_func;
}

static size_t
free_image (SCM image_smob)
{
  struct image *image = (struct image *) SCM_SMOB_DATA (image_smob);

  scm_gc_free (image->pixels,
               image->width * image->height,
               "image pixels");
  scm_gc_free (image, sizeof (struct image), "image");

  return 0;
}

static int
print_image (SCM image_smob, SCM port, scm_print_state *pstate)
{
  struct image *image = (struct image *) SCM_SMOB_DATA (image_smob);
```

```
    scm_puts ("#<image ", port);
    scm_display (image->name, port);
    scm_puts (">", port);

    /* non-zero means success */
    return 1;
  }

void
init_image_type (void)
{
    image_tag = scm_make_smob_type ("image", sizeof (struct image));
    scm_set_smob_mark (image_tag, mark_image);
    scm_set_smob_free (image_tag, free_image);
    scm_set_smob_print (image_tag, print_image);

    scm_c_define_gsubr ("clear-image", 1, 0, 0, clear_image);
    scm_c_define_gsubr ("make-image", 3, 0, 0, make_image);
  }
```

Here is a sample build and interaction with the code from the example-smob directory, on the author's machine:

```
zwingli:example-smob$ make CC=gcc
gcc `pkg-config --cflags guile-2.0` -c image-type.c -o image-type.o
gcc `pkg-config --cflags guile-2.0` -c myguile.c -o myguile.o
gcc image-type.o myguile.o `pkg-config --libs guile-2.0` -o myguile
zwingli:example-smob$ ./myguile
guile> make-image
#<primitive-procedure make-image>
guile> (define i (make-image "Whistler's Mother" 100 100))
guile> i
#<image Whistler's Mother>
guile> (clear-image i)
guile> (clear-image 4)
ERROR: In procedure clear-image in expression (clear-image 4):
ERROR: Wrong type (expecting image): 4
ABORT: (wrong-type-arg)

Type "(backtrace)" to get more information.
guile>
```

5.6 Function Snarfing

When writing C code for use with Guile, you typically define a set of C functions, and then make some of them visible to the Scheme world by calling scm_c_define_gsubr or related functions. If you have many functions to publish, it can sometimes be annoying to keep the list of calls to scm_c_define_gsubr in sync with the list of function definitions.

Guile provides the `guile-snarf` program to manage this problem. Using this tool, you can keep all the information needed to define the function alongside the function definition itself; `guile-snarf` will extract this information from your source code, and automatically generate a file of calls to `scm_c_define_gsubr` which you can `#include` into an initialization function.

The snarfing mechanism works for many kind of initialization actions, not just for collecting calls to `scm_c_define_gsubr`. For a full list of what can be done, See Section 6.5 [Snarfing Macros], page 102.

The `guile-snarf` program is invoked like this:

```
guile-snarf [-o outfile] [cpp-args ...]
```

This command will extract initialization actions to *outfile*. When no *outfile* has been specified or when *outfile* is -, standard output will be used. The C preprocessor is called with *cpp-args* (which usually include an input file) and the output is filtered to extract the initialization actions.

If there are errors during processing, *outfile* is deleted and the program exits with non-zero status.

During snarfing, the pre-processor macro `SCM_MAGIC_SNARFER` is defined. You could use this to avoid including snarfer output files that don't yet exist by writing code like this:

```
#ifndef SCM_MAGIC_SNARFER
#include "foo.x"
#endif
```

Here is how you might define the Scheme function `clear-image`, implemented by the C function `clear_image`:

```
#include <libguile.h>

SCM_DEFINE (clear_image, "clear-image", 1, 0, 0,
            (SCM image_smob),
            "Clear the image.")
{
  /* C code to clear the image in image_smob... */
}

void
init_image_type ()
{
#include "image-type.x"
}
```

The `SCM_DEFINE` declaration says that the C function `clear_image` implements a Scheme function called `clear-image`, which takes one required argument (of type `SCM` and named `image_smob`), no optional arguments, and no rest argument. The string `"Clear the image."` provides a short help text for the function, it is called a *docstring*.

`SCM_DEFINE` macro also defines a static array of characters initialized to the Scheme name of the function. In this case, `s_clear_image` is set to the C string, `"clear-image"`. You might want to use this symbol when generating error messages.

Assuming the text above lives in a file named `image-type.c`, you will need to execute the following command to prepare this file for compilation:

```
guile-snarf -o image-type.x image-type.c
```

This scans `image-type.c` for `SCM_DEFINE` declarations, and writes to `image-type.x` the output:

```
scm_c_define_gsubr ("clear-image", 1, 0, 0, (SCM (*)() ) clear_image);
```

When compiled normally, `SCM_DEFINE` is a macro which expands to the function header for `clear_image`.

Note that the output file name matches the `#include` from the input file. Also, you still need to provide all the same information you would if you were using `scm_c_define_gsubr` yourself, but you can place the information near the function definition itself, so it is less likely to become incorrect or out-of-date.

If you have many files that `guile-snarf` must process, you should consider using a fragment like the following in your Makefile:

```
snarfcppopts = $(DEFS) $(INCLUDES) $(CPPFLAGS) $(CFLAGS)
.SUFFIXES: .x
.c.x:
guile-snarf -o $@ $< $(snarfcppopts)
```

This tells make to run `guile-snarf` to produce each needed `.x` file from the corresponding `.c` file.

The program `guile-snarf` passes its command-line arguments directly to the C preprocessor, which it uses to extract the information it needs from the source code. this means you can pass normal compilation flags to `guile-snarf` to define preprocessor symbols, add header file directories, and so on.

5.7 An Overview of Guile Programming

Guile is designed as an extension language interpreter that is straightforward to integrate with applications written in C (and C++). The big win here for the application developer is that Guile integration, as the Guile web page says, "lowers your project's hacktivation energy." Lowering the hacktivation energy means that you, as the application developer, *and your users*, reap the benefits that flow from being able to extend the application in a high level extension language rather than in plain old C.

In abstract terms, it's difficult to explain what this really means and what the integration process involves, so instead let's begin by jumping straight into an example of how you might integrate Guile into an existing program, and what you could expect to gain by so doing. With that example under our belts, we'll then return to a more general analysis of the arguments involved and the range of programming options available.

5.7.1 How One Might Extend Dia Using Guile

Dia is a free software program for drawing schematic diagrams like flow charts and floor plans (http://www.gnome.org/projects/dia/). This section conducts the thought experiment of adding Guile to Dia. In so doing, it aims to illustrate several of the steps and considerations involved in adding Guile to applications in general.

5.7.1.1 Deciding Why You Want to Add Guile

First off, you should understand why you want to add Guile to Dia at all, and that means forming a picture of what Dia does and how it does it. So, what are the constituents of the Dia application?

- Most importantly, the *application domain objects* — in other words, the concepts that differentiate Dia from another application such as a word processor or spreadsheet: shapes, templates, connectors, pages, plus the properties of all these things.

- The code that manages the graphical face of the application, including the layout and display of the objects above.

- The code that handles input events, which indicate that the application user is wanting to do something.

(In other words, a textbook example of the *model - view - controller* paradigm.)

Next question: how will Dia benefit once the Guile integration is complete? Several (positive!) answers are possible here, and the choice is obviously up to the application developers. Still, one answer is that the main benefit will be the ability to manipulate Dia's application domain objects from Scheme.

Suppose that Dia made a set of procedures available in Scheme, representing the most basic operations on objects such as shapes, connectors, and so on. Using Scheme, the application user could then write code that builds upon these basic operations to create more complex procedures. For example, given basic procedures to enumerate the objects on a page, to determine whether an object is a square, and to change the fill pattern of a single shape, the user can write a Scheme procedure to change the fill pattern of all squares on the current page:

```
(define (change-squares'-fill-pattern new-pattern)
  (for-each-shape current-page
    (lambda (shape)
      (if (square? shape)
          (change-fill-pattern shape new-pattern)))))
```

5.7.1.2 Four Steps Required to Add Guile

Assuming this objective, four steps are needed to achieve it.

First, you need a way of representing your application-specific objects — such as `shape` in the previous example — when they are passed into the Scheme world. Unless your objects are so simple that they map naturally into builtin Scheme data types like numbers and strings, you will probably want to use Guile's *SMOB* interface to create a new Scheme data type for your objects.

Second, you need to write code for the basic operations like `for-each-shape` and `square?` such that they access and manipulate your existing data structures correctly, and then make these operations available as *primitives* on the Scheme level.

Third, you need to provide some mechanism within the Dia application that a user can hook into to cause arbitrary Scheme code to be evaluated.

Finally, you need to restructure your top-level application C code a little so that it initializes the Guile interpreter correctly and declares your *SMOBs* and *primitives* to the Scheme world.

The following subsections expand on these four points in turn.

5.7.1.3 How to Represent Dia Data in Scheme

For all but the most trivial applications, you will probably want to allow some representation of your domain objects to exist on the Scheme level. This is where the idea of SMOBs comes in, and with it issues of lifetime management and garbage collection.

To get more concrete about this, let's look again at the example we gave earlier of how application users can use Guile to build higher-level functions from the primitives that Dia itself provides.

```
(define (change-squares'-fill-pattern new-pattern)
  (for-each-shape current-page
    (lambda (shape)
      (if (square? shape)
          (change-fill-pattern shape new-pattern)))))
```

Consider what is stored here in the variable **shape**. For each shape on the current page, the **for-each-shape** primitive calls (**lambda** (**shape**) ...) with an argument representing that shape. Question is: how is that argument represented on the Scheme level? The issues are as follows.

- Whatever the representation, it has to be decodable again by the C code for the **square?** and **change-fill-pattern** primitives. In other words, a primitive like **square?** has somehow to be able to turn the value that it receives back into something that points to the underlying C structure describing a shape.

- The representation must also cope with Scheme code holding on to the value for later use. What happens if the Scheme code stores **shape** in a global variable, but then that shape is deleted (in a way that the Scheme code is not aware of), and later on some other Scheme code uses that global variable again in a call to, say, **square?**?

- The lifetime and memory allocation of objects that exist *only* in the Scheme world is managed automatically by Guile's garbage collector using one simple rule: when there are no remaining references to an object, the object is considered dead and so its memory is freed. But for objects that exist in both C and Scheme, the picture is more complicated; in the case of Dia, where the **shape** argument passes transiently in and out of the Scheme world, it would be quite wrong the **delete** the underlying C shape just because the Scheme code has finished evaluation. How do we avoid this happening?

One resolution of these issues is for the Scheme-level representation of a shape to be a new, Scheme-specific C structure wrapped up as a SMOB. The SMOB is what is passed into and out of Scheme code, and the Scheme-specific C structure inside the SMOB points to Dia's underlying C structure so that the code for primitives like **square?** can get at it.

To cope with an underlying shape being deleted while Scheme code is still holding onto a Scheme shape value, the underlying C structure should have a new field that points to the Scheme-specific SMOB. When a shape is deleted, the relevant code chains through to the Scheme-specific structure and sets its pointer back to the underlying structure to NULL. Thus the SMOB value for the shape continues to exist, but any primitive code that tries to use it will detect that the underlying shape has been deleted because the underlying structure pointer is NULL.

So, to summarize the steps involved in this resolution of the problem (and assuming that the underlying C structure for a shape is `struct dia_shape`):

- Define a new Scheme-specific structure that *points* to the underlying C structure:

```
struct dia_guile_shape
{
  struct dia_shape * c_shape;    /* NULL => deleted */
}
```

- Add a field to `struct dia_shape` that points to its `struct dia_guile_shape` if it has one —

```
struct dia_shape
{
  ...
  struct dia_guile_shape * guile_shape;
}
```

— so that C code can set `guile_shape->c_shape` to NULL when the underlying shape is deleted.

- Wrap `struct dia_guile_shape` as a SMOB type.

- Whenever you need to represent a C shape onto the Scheme level, create a SMOB instance for it, and pass that.

- In primitive code that receives a shape SMOB instance, check the `c_shape` field when decoding it, to find out whether the underlying C shape is still there.

As far as memory management is concerned, the SMOB values and their Scheme-specific structures are under the control of the garbage collector, whereas the underlying C structures are explicitly managed in exactly the same way that Dia managed them before we thought of adding Guile.

When the garbage collector decides to free a shape SMOB value, it calls the *SMOB free* function that was specified when defining the shape SMOB type. To maintain the correctness of the `guile_shape` field in the underlying C structure, this function should chain through to the underlying C structure (if it still exists) and set its `guile_shape` field to NULL.

For full documentation on defining and using SMOB types, see Section 5.5 [Defining New Types (Smobs)], page 71.

5.7.1.4 Writing Guile Primitives for Dia

Once the details of object representation are decided, writing the primitive function code that you need is usually straightforward.

A primitive is simply a C function whose arguments and return value are all of type SCM, and whose body does whatever you want it to do. As an example, here is a possible implementation of the `square?` primitive:

```
static SCM square_p (SCM shape)
{
  struct dia_guile_shape * guile_shape;

  /* Check that arg is really a shape SMOB. */
```

```
    scm_assert_smob_type (shape_tag, shape);

    /* Access Scheme-specific shape structure. */
    guile_shape = SCM_SMOB_DATA (shape);

    /* Find out if underlying shape exists and is a
       square; return answer as a Scheme boolean. */
    return scm_from_bool (guile_shape->c_shape &&
                          (guile_shape->c_shape->type == DIA_SQUARE));
}
```

Notice how easy it is to chain through from the SCM shape parameter that square_p receives — which is a SMOB — to the Scheme-specific structure inside the SMOB, and thence to the underlying C structure for the shape.

In this code, scm_assert_smob_type, SCM_SMOB_DATA, and scm_from_bool are from the standard Guile API. We assume that shape_tag was given to us when we made the shape SMOB type, using scm_make_smob_type. The call to scm_assert_smob_type ensures that *shape* is indeed a shape. This is needed to guard against Scheme code using the square? procedure incorrectly, as in (square? "hello"); Scheme's latent typing means that usage errors like this must be caught at run time.

Having written the C code for your primitives, you need to make them available as Scheme procedures by calling the scm_c_define_gsubr function. scm_c_define_gsubr (see Section 6.9.2 [Primitive Procedures], page 245) takes arguments that specify the Scheme-level name for the primitive and how many required, optional and rest arguments it can accept. The square? primitive always requires exactly one argument, so the call to make it available in Scheme reads like this:

```
    scm_c_define_gsubr ("square?", 1, 0, 0, square_p);
```

For where to put this call, see the subsection after next on the structure of Guile-enabled code (see Section 5.7.1.6 [Dia Structure], page 87).

5.7.1.5 Providing a Hook for the Evaluation of Scheme Code

To make the Guile integration useful, you have to design some kind of hook into your application that application users can use to cause their Scheme code to be evaluated.

Technically, this is straightforward; you just have to decide on a mechanism that is appropriate for your application. Think of Emacs, for example: when you type *ESC :*, you get a prompt where you can type in any Elisp code, which Emacs will then evaluate. Or, again like Emacs, you could provide a mechanism (such as an init file) to allow Scheme code to be associated with a particular key sequence, and evaluate the code when that key sequence is entered.

In either case, once you have the Scheme code that you want to evaluate, as a null terminated string, you can tell Guile to evaluate it by calling the scm_c_eval_string function.

5.7.1.6 Top-level Structure of Guile-enabled Dia

Let's assume that the pre-Guile Dia code looks structurally like this:

- main ()

- do lots of initialization and setup stuff
- enter Gtk main loop

When you add Guile to a program, one (rather technical) requirement is that Guile's garbage collector needs to know where the bottom of the C stack is. The easiest way to ensure this is to use `scm_boot_guile` like this:

- `main ()`
    - do lots of initialization and setup stuff
    - `scm_boot_guile (argc, argv, inner_main, NULL)`
- `inner_main ()`
    - define all SMOB types
    - export primitives to Scheme using `scm_c_define_gsubr`
    - enter Gtk main loop

In other words, you move the guts of what was previously in your `main` function into a new function called `inner_main`, and then add a `scm_boot_guile` call, with `inner_main` as a parameter, to the end of `main`.

Assuming that you are using SMOBs and have written primitive code as described in the preceding subsections, you also need to insert calls to declare your new SMOBs and export the primitives to Scheme. These declarations must happen *inside* the dynamic scope of the `scm_boot_guile` call, but also *before* any code is run that could possibly use them — the beginning of `inner_main` is an ideal place for this.

5.7.1.7 Going Further with Dia and Guile

The steps described so far implement an initial Guile integration that already gives a lot of additional power to Dia application users. But there are further steps that you could take, and it's interesting to consider a few of these.

In general, you could progressively move more of Dia's source code from C into Scheme. This might make the code more maintainable and extensible, and it could open the door to new programming paradigms that are tricky to effect in C but straightforward in Scheme.

A specific example of this is that you could use the guile-gtk package, which provides Scheme-level procedures for most of the Gtk+ library, to move the code that lays out and displays Dia objects from C to Scheme.

As you follow this path, it naturally becomes less useful to maintain a distinction between Dia's original non-Guile-related source code, and its later code implementing SMOBs and primitives for the Scheme world.

For example, suppose that the original source code had a `dia_change_fill_pattern` function:

```
void dia_change_fill_pattern (struct dia_shape * shape,
                              struct dia_pattern * pattern)
{
  /* real pattern change work */
}
```

During initial Guile integration, you add a `change_fill_pattern` primitive for Scheme purposes, which accesses the underlying structures from its SMOB values and uses `dia_change_fill_pattern` to do the real work:

```
SCM change_fill_pattern (SCM shape, SCM pattern)
{
  struct dia_shape * d_shape;
  struct dia_pattern * d_pattern;

  ...

  dia_change_fill_pattern (d_shape, d_pattern);

  return SCM_UNSPECIFIED;
}
```

At this point, it makes sense to keep `dia_change_fill_pattern` and `change_fill_pattern` separate, because `dia_change_fill_pattern` can also be called without going through Scheme at all, say because the user clicks a button which causes a C-registered Gtk+ callback to be called.

But, if the code for creating buttons and registering their callbacks is moved into Scheme (using guile-gtk), it may become true that `dia_change_fill_pattern` can no longer be called other than through Scheme. In which case, it makes sense to abolish it and move its contents directly into `change_fill_pattern`, like this:

```
SCM change_fill_pattern (SCM shape, SCM pattern)
{
  struct dia_shape * d_shape;
  struct dia_pattern * d_pattern;

  ...

  /* real pattern change work */

  return SCM_UNSPECIFIED;
}
```

So further Guile integration progressively *reduces* the amount of functional C code that you have to maintain over the long term.

A similar argument applies to data representation. In the discussion of SMOBs earlier, issues arose because of the different memory management and lifetime models that normally apply to data structures in C and in Scheme. However, with further Guile integration, you can resolve this issue in a more radical way by allowing all your data structures to be under the control of the garbage collector, and kept alive by references from the Scheme world. Instead of maintaining an array or linked list of shapes in C, you would instead maintain a list in Scheme.

Rather like the coalescing of `dia_change_fill_pattern` and `change_fill_pattern`, the practical upshot of such a change is that you would no longer have to keep the `dia_shape` and `dia_guile_shape` structures separate, and so wouldn't need to worry about the pointers between them. Instead, you could change the SMOB definition to wrap the `dia_shape` structure directly, and send `dia_guile_shape` off to the scrap yard. Cut out the middle man!

Finally, we come to the holy grail of Guile's free software / extension language approach. Once you have a Scheme representation for interesting Dia data types like shapes, and a handy bunch of primitives for manipulating them, it suddenly becomes clear that you have a bundle of functionality that could have far-ranging use beyond Dia itself. In other words, the data types and primitives could now become a library, and Dia becomes just one of the many possible applications using that library — albeit, at this early stage, a rather important one!

In this model, Guile becomes just the glue that binds everything together. Imagine an application that usefully combined functionality from Dia, Gnumeric and GnuCash — it's tricky right now, because no such application yet exists; but it'll happen some day ...

5.7.2 Why Scheme is More Hackable Than C

Underlying Guile's value proposition is the assumption that programming in a high level language, specifically Guile's implementation of Scheme, is necessarily better in some way than programming in C. What do we mean by this claim, and how can we be so sure?

One class of advantages applies not only to Scheme, but more generally to any interpretable, high level, scripting language, such as Emacs Lisp, Python, Ruby, or TeX's macro language. Common features of all such languages, when compared to C, are that:

- They lend themselves to rapid and experimental development cycles, owing usually to a combination of their interpretability and the integrated development environment in which they are used.

- They free developers from some of the low level bookkeeping tasks associated with C programming, notably memory management.

- They provide high level features such as container objects and exception handling that make common programming tasks easier.

In the case of Scheme, particular features that make programming easier — and more fun! — are its powerful mechanisms for abstracting parts of programs (closures — see Section 3.4 [About Closure], page 26) and for iteration (see Section 6.13.4 [while do], page 294).

The evidence in support of this argument is empirical: the huge amount of code that has been written in extension languages for applications that support this mechanism. Most notable are extensions written in Emacs Lisp for GNU Emacs, in TeX's macro language for TeX, and in Script-Fu for the Gimp, but there is increasingly now a significant code eco-system for Guile-based applications as well, such as Lilypond and GnuCash. It is close to inconceivable that similar amounts of functionality could have been added to these applications just by writing new code in their base implementation languages.

5.7.3 Example: Using Guile for an Application Testbed

As an example of what this means in practice, imagine writing a testbed for an application that is tested by submitting various requests (via a C interface) and validating the output received. Suppose further that the application keeps an idea of its current state, and that the "correct" output for a given request may depend on the current application state. A complete "white box"[2] test plan for this application would aim to submit all pos-

---

[2] A *white box* test plan is one that incorporates knowledge of the internal design of the application under test.

sible requests in each distinguishable state, and validate the output for all request/state combinations.

To write all this test code in C would be very tedious. Suppose instead that the testbed code adds a single new C function, to submit an arbitrary request and return the response, and then uses Guile to export this function as a Scheme procedure. The rest of the testbed can then be written in Scheme, and so benefits from all the advantages of programming in Scheme that were described in the previous section.

(In this particular example, there is an additional benefit of writing most of the testbed in Scheme. A common problem for white box testing is that mistakes and mistaken assumptions in the application under test can easily be reproduced in the testbed code. It is more difficult to copy mistakes like this when the testbed is written in a different language from the application.)

5.7.4 A Choice of Programming Options

The preceding arguments and example point to a model of Guile programming that is applicable in many cases. According to this model, Guile programming involves a balance between C and Scheme programming, with the aim being to extract the greatest possible Scheme level benefit from the least amount of C level work.

The C level work required in this model usually consists of packaging and exporting functions and application objects such that they can be seen and manipulated on the Scheme level. To help with this, Guile's C language interface includes utility features that aim to make this kind of integration very easy for the application developer. These features are documented later in this part of the manual: see REFFIXME.

This model, though, is really just one of a range of possible programming options. If all of the functionality that you need is available from Scheme, you could choose instead to write your whole application in Scheme (or one of the other high level languages that Guile supports through translation), and simply use Guile as an interpreter for Scheme. (In the future, we hope that Guile will also be able to compile Scheme code, so lessening the performance gap between C and Scheme code.) Or, at the other end of the C–Scheme scale, you could write the majority of your application in C, and only call out to Guile occasionally for specific actions such as reading a configuration file or executing a user-specified extension. The choices boil down to two basic questions:

- Which parts of the application do you write in C, and which in Scheme (or another high level translated language)?

- How do you design the interface between the C and Scheme parts of your application?

These are of course design questions, and the right design for any given application will always depend upon the particular requirements that you are trying to meet. In the context of Guile, however, there are some generally applicable considerations that can help you when designing your answers.

5.7.4.1 What Functionality is Already Available?

Suppose, for the sake of argument, that you would prefer to write your whole application in Scheme. Then the API available to you consists of:

- standard Scheme

- plus the extensions to standard Scheme provided by Guile in its core distribution
- plus any additional functionality that you or others have packaged so that it can be loaded as a Guile Scheme module.

A module in the last category can either be a pure Scheme module — in other words a collection of utility procedures coded in Scheme — or a module that provides a Scheme interface to an extension library coded in C — in other words a nice package where someone else has done the work of wrapping up some useful C code for you. The set of available modules is growing quickly and already includes such useful examples as (gtk gtk), which makes Gtk+ drawing functions available in Scheme, and (database postgres), which provides SQL access to a Postgres database.

Given the growing collection of pre-existing modules, it is quite feasible that your application could be implemented by combining a selection of these modules together with new application code written in Scheme.

If this approach is not enough, because the functionality that your application needs is not already available in this form, and it is impossible to write the new functionality in Scheme, you will need to write some C code. If the required function is already available in C (e.g. in a library), all you need is a little glue to connect it to the world of Guile. If not, you need both to write the basic code and to plumb it into Guile.

In either case, two general considerations are important. Firstly, what is the interface by which the functionality is presented to the Scheme world? Does the interface consist only of function calls (for example, a simple drawing interface), or does it need to include *objects* of some kind that can be passed between C and Scheme and manipulated by both worlds. Secondly, how does the lifetime and memory management of objects in the C code relate to the garbage collection governed approach of Scheme objects? In the case where the basic C code is not already written, most of the difficulties of memory management can be avoided by using Guile's C interface features from the start.

For the full documentation on writing C code for Guile and connecting existing C code to the Guile world, see REFFIXME.

5.7.4.2 Functional and Performance Constraints

5.7.4.3 Your Preferred Programming Style

5.7.4.4 What Controls Program Execution?

5.7.5 How About Application Users?

So far we have considered what Guile programming means for an application developer. But what if you are instead *using* an existing Guile-based application, and want to know what your options are for programming and extending this application?

The answer to this question varies from one application to another, because the options available depend inevitably on whether the application developer has provided any hooks for you to hang your own code on and, if there are such hooks, what they allow you to do.[3] For example...

---

[3] Of course, in the world of free software, you always have the freedom to modify the application's source code to your own requirements. Here we are concerned with the extension options that the application has provided for without your needing to modify its source code.

- If the application permits you to load and execute any Guile code, the world is your oyster. You can extend the application in any way that you choose.

- A more cautious application might allow you to load and execute Guile code, but only in a *safe* environment, where the interface available is restricted by the application from the standard Guile API.

- Or a really fearful application might not provide a hook to really execute user code at all, but just use Scheme syntax as a convenient way for users to specify application data or configuration options.

In the last two cases, what you can do is, by definition, restricted by the application, and you should refer to the application's own manual to find out your options.

The most well known example of the first case is Emacs, with its extension language Emacs Lisp: as well as being a text editor, Emacs supports the loading and execution of arbitrary Emacs Lisp code. The result of such openness has been dramatic: Emacs now benefits from user-contributed Emacs Lisp libraries that extend the basic editing function to do everything from reading news to psychoanalysis and playing adventure games. The only limitation is that extensions are restricted to the functionality provided by Emacs's built-in set of primitive operations. For example, you can interact and display data by manipulating the contents of an Emacs buffer, but you can't pop-up and draw a window with a layout that is totally different to the Emacs standard.

This situation with a Guile application that supports the loading of arbitrary user code is similar, except perhaps even more so, because Guile also supports the loading of extension libraries written in C. This last point enables user code to add new primitive operations to Guile, and so to bypass the limitation present in Emacs Lisp.

At this point, the distinction between an application developer and an application user becomes rather blurred. Instead of seeing yourself as a user extending an application, you could equally well say that you are developing a new application of your own using some of the primitive functionality provided by the original application. As such, all the discussions of the preceding sections of this chapter are relevant to how you can proceed with developing your extension.

5.8 Autoconf Support

Autoconf, a part of the GNU build system, makes it easy for users to build your package. This section documents Guile's Autoconf support.

5.8.1 Autoconf Background

As explained in the *GNU Autoconf Manual*, any package needs configuration at build-time (see Section "Introduction" in *The GNU Autoconf Manual*). If your package uses Guile (or uses a package that in turn uses Guile), you probably need to know what specific Guile features are available and details about them.

The way to do this is to write feature tests and arrange for their execution by the `configure` script, typically by adding the tests to `configure.ac`, and running `autoconf` to create `configure`. Users of your package then run `configure` in the normal way.

Macros are a way to make common feature tests easy to express. Autoconf provides a wide range of macros (see Section "Existing Tests" in *The GNU Autoconf Manual*), and Guile installation provides Guile-specific tests in the areas of: program detection, compilation flags reporting, and Scheme module checks.

5.8.2 Autoconf Macros

As mentioned earlier in this chapter, Guile supports parallel installation, and uses `pkg-config` to let the user choose which version of Guile they are interested in. `pkg-config` has its own set of Autoconf macros that are probably installed on most every development system. The most useful of these macros is `PKG_CHECK_MODULES`.

```
PKG_CHECK_MODULES([GUILE], [guile-2.0])
```

This example looks for Guile and sets the `GUILE_CFLAGS` and `GUILE_LIBS` variables accordingly, or prints an error and exits if Guile was not found.

Guile comes with additional Autoconf macros providing more information, installed as *prefix*/share/aclocal/guile.m4. Their names all begin with `GUILE_`.

GUILE_PKG [*VERSIONS*]   [Autoconf Macro]
> This macro runs the `pkg-config` tool to find development files for an available version of Guile.
>
> By default, this macro will search for the latest stable version of Guile (e.g. 2.0), falling back to the previous stable version (e.g. 1.8) if it is available. If no guile-*VERSION*.pc file is found, an error is signalled. The found version is stored in *GUILE_EFFECTIVE_VERSION*.
>
> If `GUILE_PROGS` was already invoked, this macro ensures that the development files have the same effective version as the Guile program.
>
> *GUILE_EFFECTIVE_VERSION* is marked for substitution, as by `AC_SUBST`.

GUILE_FLAGS   [Autoconf Macro]
> This macro runs the `pkg-config` tool to find out how to compile and link programs against Guile. It sets four variables: *GUILE_CFLAGS*, *GUILE_LDFLAGS*, *GUILE_LIBS*, and *GUILE_LTLIBS*.
>
> *GUILE_CFLAGS*: flags to pass to a C or C++ compiler to build code that uses Guile header files. This is almost always just one or more `-I` flags.

GUILE_LDFLAGS: flags to pass to the compiler to link a program against Guile. This includes `-lguile-VERSION` for the Guile library itself, and may also include one or more `-L` flag to tell the compiler where to find the libraries. But it does not include flags that influence the program's runtime search path for libraries, and will therefore lead to a program that fails to start, unless all necessary libraries are installed in a standard location such as `/usr/lib`.

GUILE_LIBS and *GUILE_LTLIBS*: flags to pass to the compiler or to libtool, respectively, to link a program against Guile. It includes flags that augment the program's runtime search path for libraries, so that shared libraries will be found at the location where they were during linking, even in non-standard locations. *GUILE_LIBS* is to be used when linking the program directly with the compiler, whereas *GUILE_LTLIBS* is to be used when linking the program is done through libtool.

The variables are marked for substitution, as by `AC_SUBST`.

GUILE_SITE_DIR   [Autoconf Macro]
    This looks for Guile's "site" directory, usually something like PRE-FIX/share/guile/site, and sets var *GUILE_SITE* to the path. Note that the var name is different from the macro name.

The variable is marked for substitution, as by `AC_SUBST`.

GUILE_PROGS [*VERSION*]   [Autoconf Macro]
    This macro looks for programs `guile` and `guild`, setting variables *GUILE* and *GUILD* to their paths, respectively. If `guile` is not found, signal an error.

By default, this macro will search for the latest stable version of Guile (e.g. 2.0). x.y or x.y.z versions can be specified. If an older version is found, the macro will signal an error.

The effective version of the found `guile` is set to *GUILE_EFFECTIVE_VERSION*. This macro ensures that the effective version is compatible with the result of a previous invocation of `GUILE_FLAGS`, if any.

As a legacy interface, it also looks for `guile-config` and `guile-tools`, setting *GUILE_CONFIG* and *GUILE_TOOLS*.

The variables are marked for substitution, as by `AC_SUBST`.

GUILE_CHECK_RETVAL *var check*   [Autoconf Macro]
    var is a shell variable name to be set to the return value. *check* is a Guile Scheme expression, evaluated with "$GUILE -c", and returning either 0 or non-#f to indicate the check passed. Non-0 number or #f indicates failure. Avoid using the character "#" since that confuses autoconf.

GUILE_MODULE_CHECK *var module featuretest description*   [Autoconf Macro]
    var is a shell variable name to be set to "yes" or "no". *module* is a list of symbols, like: (ice-9 common-list). *featuretest* is an expression acceptable to GUILE_CHECK, q.v. *description* is a present-tense verb phrase (passed to AC_MSG_CHECKING).

GUILE_MODULE_AVAILABLE *var module*   [Autoconf Macro]
    var is a shell variable name to be set to "yes" or "no". *module* is a list of symbols, like: (ice-9 common-list).

`GUILE_MODULE_REQUIRED` *symlist*   [Autoconf Macro]

> *symlist* is a list of symbols, WITHOUT surrounding parens, like: ice-9 common-list.

`GUILE_MODULE_EXPORTS` *var module modvar*   [Autoconf Macro]

> *var* is a shell variable to be set to "yes" or "no". *module* is a list of symbols, like: (ice-9 common-list). *modvar* is the Guile Scheme variable to check.

`GUILE_MODULE_REQUIRED_EXPORT` *module modvar*   [Autoconf Macro]

> *module* is a list of symbols, like: (ice-9 common-list). *modvar* is the Guile Scheme variable to check.

5.8.3 Using Autoconf Macros

Using the autoconf macros is straightforward: Add the macro "calls" (actually instantiations) to `configure.ac`, run `aclocal`, and finally, run `autoconf`. If your system doesn't have guile.m4 installed, place the desired macro definitions (`AC_DEFUN` forms) in `acinclude.m4`, and `aclocal` will do the right thing.

Some of the macros can be used inside normal shell constructs: `if foo ; then GUILE_BAZ ; fi`, but this is not guaranteed. It's probably a good idea to instantiate macros at top-level.

We now include two examples, one simple and one complicated.

The first example is for a package that uses libguile, and thus needs to know how to compile and link against it. So we use `PKG_CHECK_MODULES` to set the vars `GUILE_CFLAGS` and `GUILE_LIBS`, which are automatically substituted in the Makefile.

> In `configure.ac`:

```
PKG_CHECK_MODULES([GUILE], [guile-2.0])
```

> In `Makefile.in`:

```
GUILE_CFLAGS  = @GUILE_CFLAGS@
GUILE_LIBS = @GUILE_LIBS@

myprog.o: myprog.c
        $(CC) -o $ $(GUILE_CFLAGS) $<
myprog: myprog.o
        $(CC) -o $ $< $(GUILE_LIBS)
```

The second example is for a package of Guile Scheme modules that uses an external program and other Guile Scheme modules (some might call this a "pure scheme" package). So we use the `GUILE_SITE_DIR` macro, a regular `AC_PATH_PROG` macro, and the `GUILE_MODULE_AVAILABLE` macro.

> In `configure.ac`:

```
GUILE_SITE_DIR

probably_wont_work=""
```

```
# pgtype pgtable
GUILE_MODULE_AVAILABLE(have_guile_pg, (database postgres))
test $have_guile_pg = no &&
    probably_wont_work="(my pgtype) (my pgtable) $probably_wont_work"

# gpgutils
AC_PATH_PROG(GNUPG,gpg)
test x"$GNUPG" = x &&
    probably_wont_work="(my gpgutils) $probably_wont_work"

if test ! "$probably_wont_work" = "" ; then
    p="        ***"
    echo
    echo "$p"
    echo "$p NOTE:"
    echo "$p The following modules probably won't work:"
    echo "$p   $probably_wont_work"
    echo "$p They can be installed anyway, and will work if their"
    echo "$p dependencies are installed later.  Please see README."
    echo "$p"
    echo
fi
```

In Makefile.in:

```
instdir = @GUILE_SITE@/my

install:
        $(INSTALL) my/*.scm $(instdir)
```

6 API Reference

Guile provides an application programming interface (*API*) to developers in two core languages: Scheme and C. This part of the manual contains reference documentation for all of the functionality that is available through both Scheme and C interfaces.

6.1 Overview of the Guile API

Guile's application programming interface (*API*) makes functionality available that an application developer can use in either C or Scheme programming. The interface consists of *elements* that may be macros, functions or variables in C, and procedures, variables, syntax or other types of object in Scheme.

Many elements are available to both Scheme and C, in a form that is appropriate. For example, the `assq` Scheme procedure is also available as `scm_assq` to C code. These elements are documented only once, addressing both the Scheme and C aspects of them.

The Scheme name of an element is related to its C name in a regular way. Also, a C function takes its parameters in a systematic way.

Normally, the name of a C function can be derived given its Scheme name, using some simple textual transformations:

- Replace - (hyphen) with _ (underscore).
- Replace ? (question mark) with `_p`.
- Replace ! (exclamation point) with `_x`.
- Replace internal -> with `_to_`.
- Replace <= (less than or equal) with `_leq`.
- Replace >= (greater than or equal) with `_geq`.
- Replace < (less than) with `_less`.
- Replace > (greater than) with `_gr`.
- Prefix with `scm_`.

A C function always takes a fixed number of arguments of type SCM, even when the corresponding Scheme function takes a variable number.

For some Scheme functions, some last arguments are optional; the corresponding C function must always be invoked with all optional arguments specified. To get the effect as if an argument has not been specified, pass `SCM_UNDEFINED` as its value. You can not do this for an argument in the middle; when one argument is `SCM_UNDEFINED` all the ones following it must be `SCM_UNDEFINED` as well.

Some Scheme functions take an arbitrary number of *rest* arguments; the corresponding C function must be invoked with a list of all these arguments. This list is always the last argument of the C function.

These two variants can also be combined.

The type of the return value of a C function that corresponds to a Scheme function is always SCM. In the descriptions below, types are therefore often omitted but for the return value and for the arguments.

6.2 Deprecation

From time to time functions and other features of Guile become obsolete. Guile's *deprecation* is a mechanism that can help you cope with this.

When you use a feature that is deprecated, you will likely get a warning message at runtime. Also, if you have a new enough toolchain, using a deprecated function from `libguile` will cause a link-time warning.

The primary source for information about just what interfaces are deprecated in a given release is the file `NEWS`. That file also documents what you should use instead of the obsoleted things.

The file `README` contains instructions on how to control the inclusion or removal of the deprecated features from the public API of Guile, and how to control the deprecation warning messages.

The idea behind this mechanism is that normally all deprecated interfaces are available, but you get feedback when compiling and running code that uses them, so that you can migrate to the newer APIs at your leisure.

6.3 The SCM Type

Guile represents all Scheme values with the single C type `SCM`. For an introduction to this topic, See Section 5.4.1 [Dynamic Types], page 63.

`SCM`   [C Type]
> `SCM` is the user level abstract C type that is used to represent all of Guile's Scheme objects, no matter what the Scheme object type is. No C operation except assignment is guaranteed to work with variables of type `SCM`, so you should only use macros and functions to work with `SCM` values. Values are converted between C data types and the `SCM` type with utility functions and macros.

`scm_t_bits`   [C Type]
> `scm_t_bits` is an unsigned integral data type that is guaranteed to be large enough to hold all information that is required to represent any Scheme object. While this data type is mostly used to implement Guile's internals, the use of this type is also necessary to write certain kinds of extensions to Guile.

`scm_t_signed_bits`   [C Type]
> This is a signed integral type of the same size as `scm_t_bits`.

`scm_t_bits` `SCM_UNPACK` (*SCM x*)   [C Macro]
> Transforms the `SCM` value x into its representation as an integral type. Only after applying `SCM_UNPACK` it is possible to access the bits and contents of the `SCM` value.

`SCM` `SCM_PACK` (*scm_t_bits x*)   [C Macro]
> Takes a valid integral representation of a Scheme object and transforms it into its representation as a `SCM` value.

6.4 Initializing Guile

Each thread that wants to use functions from the Guile API needs to put itself into guile mode with either `scm_with_guile` or `scm_init_guile`. The global state of Guile is initialized automatically when the first thread enters guile mode.

When a thread wants to block outside of a Guile API function, it should leave guile mode temporarily with `scm_without_guile`, See Section 6.21.5 [Blocking], page 418.

Threads that are created by `call-with-new-thread` or `scm_spawn_thread` start out in guile mode so you don't need to initialize them.

void * scm_with_guile (*void *(*func)(void *)*, *void *data*)   [C Function]
    Call *func*, passing it *data* and return what *func* returns. While *func* is running, the current thread is in guile mode and can thus use the Guile API.

    When `scm_with_guile` is called from guile mode, the thread remains in guile mode when `scm_with_guile` returns.

    Otherwise, it puts the current thread into guile mode and, if needed, gives it a Scheme representation that is contained in the list returned by `all-threads`, for example. This Scheme representation is not removed when `scm_with_guile` returns so that a given thread is always represented by the same Scheme value during its lifetime, if at all.

    When this is the first thread that enters guile mode, the global state of Guile is initialized before calling `func`.

    The function *func* is called via `scm_with_continuation_barrier`; thus, `scm_with_guile` returns exactly once.

    When `scm_with_guile` returns, the thread is no longer in guile mode (except when `scm_with_guile` was called from guile mode, see above). Thus, only `func` can store SCM variables on the stack and be sure that they are protected from the garbage collector. See `scm_init_guile` for another approach at initializing Guile that does not have this restriction.

    It is OK to call `scm_with_guile` while a thread has temporarily left guile mode via `scm_without_guile`. It will then simply temporarily enter guile mode again.

void scm_init_guile ()   [C Function]
    Arrange things so that all of the code in the current thread executes as if from within a call to `scm_with_guile`. That is, all functions called by the current thread can assume that SCM values on their stack frames are protected from the garbage collector (except when the thread has explicitly left guile mode, of course).

    When `scm_init_guile` is called from a thread that already has been in guile mode once, nothing happens. This behavior matters when you call `scm_init_guile` while the thread has only temporarily left guile mode: in that case the thread will not be in guile mode after `scm_init_guile` returns. Thus, you should not use `scm_init_guile` in such a scenario.

    When a uncaught throw happens in a thread that has been put into guile mode via `scm_init_guile`, a short message is printed to the current error port and the thread is exited via `scm_pthread_exit (NULL)`. No restrictions are placed on continuations.

The function `scm_init_guile` might not be available on all platforms since it requires some stack-bounds-finding magic that might not have been ported to all platforms that Guile runs on. Thus, if you can, it is better to use `scm_with_guile` or its variation `scm_boot_guile` instead of this function.

void **scm_boot_guile** (*int* **argc**, *char* ****argv**, *void* (***main_func**)   [C Function]
     (*void* ***data**, *int* **argc**, *char* ****argv**), *void* ***data**)

Enter guile mode as with `scm_with_guile` and call *main_func*, passing it *data*, *argc*, and *argv* as indicated. When *main_func* returns, `scm_boot_guile` calls `exit (0)`; `scm_boot_guile` never returns. If you want some other exit value, have *main_func* call `exit` itself. If you don't want to exit at all, use `scm_with_guile` instead of `scm_boot_guile`.

The function `scm_boot_guile` arranges for the Scheme `command-line` function to return the strings given by *argc* and *argv*. If *main_func* modifies *argc* or *argv*, it should call `scm_set_program_arguments` with the final list, so Scheme code will know which arguments have been processed (see Section 7.2.6 [Runtime Environment], page 488).

void **scm_shell** (*int* **argc**, *char* ****argv**)   [C Function]

Process command-line arguments in the manner of the `guile` executable. This includes loading the normal Guile initialization files, interacting with the user or running any scripts or expressions specified by `-s` or `-e` options, and then exiting. See Section 4.2 [Invoking Guile], page 35, for more details.

Since this function does not return, you must do all application-specific initialization before calling this function.

6.5 Snarfing Macros

The following macros do two different things: when compiled normally, they expand in one way; when processed during snarfing, they cause the **guile-snarf** program to pick up some initialization code, See Section 5.6 [Function Snarfing], page 81.

The descriptions below use the term 'normally' to refer to the case when the code is compiled normally, and 'while snarfing' when the code is processed by **guile-snarf**.

SCM_SNARF_INIT (*code*)   [C Macro]

Normally, **SCM_SNARF_INIT** expands to nothing; while snarfing, it causes *code* to be included in the initialization action file, followed by a semicolon.

This is the fundamental macro for snarfing initialization actions. The more specialized macros below use it internally.

SCM_DEFINE (*c_name*, *scheme_name*, *req*, *opt*, *var*, *arglist*, *docstring*)   [C Macro]

Normally, this macro expands into

```
static const char s_c_name[] = scheme_name;
SCM
c_name arglist
```

While snarfing, it causes

```
scm_c_define_gsubr (s_c_name, req, opt, var,
                    c_name);
```

to be added to the initialization actions. Thus, you can use it to declare a C function named *c_name* that will be made available to Scheme with the name *scheme_name*.

Note that the *arglist* argument must have parentheses around it.

SCM_SYMBOL (*c_name*, *scheme_name*)   [C Macro]
SCM_GLOBAL_SYMBOL (*c_name*, *scheme_name*)   [C Macro]
>   Normally, these macros expand into

```
static SCM c_name
```

>   or

```
SCM c_name
```

>   respectively. While snarfing, they both expand into the initialization code

```
c_name = scm_permanent_object (scm_from_locale_symbol (scheme_name));
```

>   Thus, you can use them declare a static or global variable of type SCM that will be initialized to the symbol named *scheme_name*.

SCM_KEYWORD (*c_name*, *scheme_name*)   [C Macro]
SCM_GLOBAL_KEYWORD (*c_name*, *scheme_name*)   [C Macro]
>   Normally, these macros expand into

```
static SCM c_name
```

>   or

```
SCM c_name
```

>   respectively. While snarfing, they both expand into the initialization code

```
c_name = scm_permanent_object (scm_c_make_keyword (scheme_name));
```

>   Thus, you can use them declare a static or global variable of type SCM that will be initialized to the keyword named *scheme_name*.

SCM_VARIABLE (*c_name*, *scheme_name*)   [C Macro]
SCM_GLOBAL_VARIABLE (*c_name*, *scheme_name*)   [C Macro]
>   These macros are equivalent to SCM_VARIABLE_INIT and SCM_GLOBAL_VARIABLE_INIT, respectively, with a *value* of SCM_BOOL_F.

SCM_VARIABLE_INIT (*c_name*, *scheme_name*, *value*)   [C Macro]
SCM_GLOBAL_VARIABLE_INIT (*c_name*, *scheme_name*, *value*)   [C Macro]
>   Normally, these macros expand into

```
static SCM c_name
```

>   or

```
SCM c_name
```

>   respectively. While snarfing, they both expand into the initialization code

```
c_name = scm_permanent_object (scm_c_define (scheme_name, value));
```

Thus, you can use them declare a static or global C variable of type SCM that will be initialized to the object representing the Scheme variable named *scheme_name* in the current module. The variable will be defined when it doesn't already exist. It is always set to *value*.

6.6 Simple Generic Data Types

This chapter describes those of Guile's simple data types which are primarily used for their role as items of generic data. By *simple* we mean data types that are not primarily used as containers to hold other data — i.e. pairs, lists, vectors and so on. For the documentation of such *compound* data types, see Section 6.7 [Compound Data Types], page 185.

6.6.1 Booleans

The two boolean values are `#t` for true and `#f` for false. They can also be written as `#true` and `#false`, as per R7RS.

Boolean values are returned by predicate procedures, such as the general equality predicates `eq?`, `eqv?` and `equal?` (see Section 6.11.1 [Equality], page 276) and numerical and string comparison operators like `string=?` (see Section 6.6.5.7 [String Comparison], page 148) and `<=` (see Section 6.6.2.8 [Comparison], page 117).

```
(<= 3 8)
⇒ #t

(<= 3 -3)
⇒ #f

(equal? "house" "houses")
⇒ #f

(eq? #f #f)
⇒
#t
```

In test condition contexts like `if` and `cond` (see Section 6.13.2 [Conditionals], page 292), where a group of subexpressions will be evaluated only if a *condition* expression evaluates to "true", "true" means any value at all except `#f`.

```
(if #t "yes" "no")
⇒ "yes"

(if 0 "yes" "no")
⇒ "yes"

(if #f "yes" "no")
⇒ "no"
```

A result of this asymmetry is that typical Scheme source code more often uses `#f` explicitly than `#t`: `#f` is necessary to represent an `if` or `cond` false value, whereas `#t` is not necessary to represent an `if` or `cond` true value.

It is important to note that `#f` is **not** equivalent to any other Scheme value. In particular, `#f` is not the same as the number 0 (like in C and C++), and not the same as the "empty list" (like in some Lisp dialects).

In C, the two Scheme boolean values are available as the two constants `SCM_BOOL_T` for `#t` and `SCM_BOOL_F` for `#f`. Care must be taken with the false value `SCM_BOOL_F`: it is not false when used in C conditionals. In order to test for it, use `scm_is_false` or `scm_is_true`.

`not` *x*   [Scheme Procedure]
`scm_not` (*x*)   [C Function]
> Return `#t` if *x* is `#f`, else return `#f`.

`boolean?` *obj*   [Scheme Procedure]
`scm_boolean_p` (*obj*)   [C Function]
> Return `#t` if *obj* is either `#t` or `#f`, else return `#f`.

`SCM SCM_BOOL_T`   [C Macro]
> The `SCM` representation of the Scheme object `#t`.

`SCM SCM_BOOL_F`   [C Macro]
> The `SCM` representation of the Scheme object `#f`.

`int scm_is_true` (*SCM obj*)   [C Function]
> Return 0 if *obj* is `#f`, else return 1.

`int scm_is_false` (*SCM obj*)   [C Function]
> Return 1 if *obj* is `#f`, else return 0.

`int scm_is_bool` (*SCM obj*)   [C Function]
> Return 1 if *obj* is either `#t` or `#f`, else return 0.

`SCM scm_from_bool` (*int val*)   [C Function]
> Return `#f` if *val* is 0, else return `#t`.

`int scm_to_bool` (*SCM val*)   [C Function]
> Return 1 if *val* is `SCM_BOOL_T`, return 0 when *val* is `SCM_BOOL_F`, else signal a 'wrong type' error.
>
> You should probably use `scm_is_true` instead of this function when you just want to test a `SCM` value for trueness.

6.6.2 Numerical data types

Guile supports a rich "tower" of numerical types — integer, rational, real and complex — and provides an extensive set of mathematical and scientific functions for operating on numerical data. This section of the manual documents those types and functions.

You may also find it illuminating to read R5RS's presentation of numbers in Scheme, which is particularly clear and accessible: see Section "Numbers" in *R5RS*.

6.6.2.1 Scheme's Numerical "Tower"

Scheme's numerical "tower" consists of the following categories of numbers:

integers   Whole numbers, positive or negative; e.g. –5, 0, 18.

rationals   The set of numbers that can be expressed as p/q where p and q are integers; e.g. 9/16 works, but pi (an irrational number) doesn't. These include integers ($n/1$).

real numbers
> The set of numbers that describes all possible positions along a one-dimensional line. This includes rationals as well as irrational numbers.

complex numbers

The set of numbers that describes all possible positions in a two dimensional space. This includes real as well as imaginary numbers ($a + bi$, where a is the *real part*, b is the *imaginary part*, and i is the square root of -1.)

It is called a tower because each category "sits on" the one that follows it, in the sense that every integer is also a rational, every rational is also real, and every real number is also a complex number (but with zero imaginary part).

In addition to the classification into integers, rationals, reals and complex numbers, Scheme also distinguishes between whether a number is represented exactly or not. For example, the result of $2\sin(\pi/4)$ is exactly $\sqrt{2}$, but Guile can represent neither $\pi/4$ nor $\sqrt{2}$ exactly. Instead, it stores an inexact approximation, using the C type `double`.

Guile can represent exact rationals of any magnitude, inexact rationals that fit into a C `double`, and inexact complex numbers with `double` real and imaginary parts.

The `number?` predicate may be applied to any Scheme value to discover whether the value is any of the supported numerical types.

`number?` *obj*   [Scheme Procedure]
`scm_number_p` (*obj*)   [C Function]
    Return `#t` if *obj* is any kind of number, else `#f`.

    For example:

    ```
    (number? 3)
    ⇒ #t

    (number? "hello there!")
    ⇒ #f

    (define pi 3.141592654)
    (number? pi)
    ⇒ #t
    ```

`int scm_is_number` (*SCM obj*)   [C Function]
    This is equivalent to `scm_is_true (scm_number_p (obj))`.

The next few subsections document each of Guile's numerical data types in detail.

6.6.2.2 Integers

Integers are whole numbers, that is numbers with no fractional part, such as 2, 83, and -3789.

Integers in Guile can be arbitrarily big, as shown by the following example.

```
(define (factorial n)
  (let loop ((n n) (product 1))
    (if (= n 0)
        product
        (loop (- n 1) (* product n)))))
```

```
(factorial 3)
⇒ 6

(factorial 20)
⇒ 2432902008176640000

(- (factorial 45))
⇒ -119622220865480194561963161495657715064383733760000000000
```

Readers whose background is in programming languages where integers are limited by the need to fit into just 4 or 8 bytes of memory may find this surprising, or suspect that Guile's representation of integers is inefficient. In fact, Guile achieves a near optimal balance of convenience and efficiency by using the host computer's native representation of integers where possible, and a more general representation where the required number does not fit in the native form. Conversion between these two representations is automatic and completely invisible to the Scheme level programmer.

C has a host of different integer types, and Guile offers a host of functions to convert between them and the SCM representation. For example, a C `int` can be handled with `scm_to_int` and `scm_from_int`. Guile also defines a few C integer types of its own, to help with differences between systems.

C integer types that are not covered can be handled with the generic `scm_to_signed_integer` and `scm_from_signed_integer` for signed types, or with `scm_to_unsigned_integer` and `scm_from_unsigned_integer` for unsigned types.

Scheme integers can be exact and inexact. For example, a number written as `3.0` with an explicit decimal-point is inexact, but it is also an integer. The functions `integer?` and `scm_is_integer` report true for such a number, but the functions `exact-integer?`, `scm_is_exact_integer`, `scm_is_signed_integer`, and `scm_is_unsigned_integer` only allow exact integers and thus report false. Likewise, the conversion functions like `scm_to_signed_integer` only accept exact integers.

The motivation for this behavior is that the inexactness of a number should not be lost silently. If you want to allow inexact integers, you can explicitly insert a call to `inexact->exact` or to its C equivalent `scm_inexact_to_exact`. (Only inexact integers will be converted by this call into exact integers; inexact non-integers will become exact fractions.)

`integer?` *x*   [Scheme Procedure]
`scm_integer_p` (*x*)   [C Function]
> Return `#t` if *x* is an exact or inexact integer number, else return `#f`.

```
(integer? 487)
⇒ #t

(integer? 3.0)
⇒ #t

(integer? -3.4)
⇒ #f
```

```
(integer? +inf.0)
⇒ #f
```

int scm_is_integer (*SCM x*)   [C Function]

>   This is equivalent to scm_is_true (scm_integer_p (x)).

exact-integer? *x*   [Scheme Procedure]
scm_exact_integer_p (*x*)   [C Function]

>   Return #t if *x* is an exact integer number, else return #f.

>    ```
>    (exact-integer? 37)
>    ⇒ #t
>    ```

>    ```
>    (exact-integer? 3.0)
>    ⇒ #f
>    ```

int scm_is_exact_integer (*SCM x*)   [C Function]

>   This is equivalent to scm_is_true (scm_exact_integer_p (x)).

scm_t_int8   [C Type]
scm_t_uint8   [C Type]
scm_t_int16   [C Type]
scm_t_uint16   [C Type]
scm_t_int32   [C Type]
scm_t_uint32   [C Type]
scm_t_int64   [C Type]
scm_t_uint64   [C Type]
scm_t_intmax   [C Type]
scm_t_uintmax   [C Type]

>   The C types are equivalent to the corresponding ISO C types but are defined on all
>   platforms, with the exception of scm_t_int64 and scm_t_uint64, which are only
>   defined when a 64-bit type is available. For example, scm_t_int8 is equivalent to
>   int8_t.

>   You can regard these definitions as a stop-gap measure until all platforms provide
>   these types. If you know that all the platforms that you are interested in already
>   provide these types, it is better to use them directly instead of the types provided by
>   Guile.

int scm_is_signed_integer (*SCM x, scm_t_intmax min,*   [C Function]
>   *scm_t_intmax max*)
int scm_is_unsigned_integer (*SCM x, scm_t_uintmax min,*   [C Function]
>   *scm_t_uintmax max*)

>   Return 1 when *x* represents an exact integer that is between *min* and *max*, inclusive.

>   These functions can be used to check whether a SCM value will fit into a given range,
>   such as the range of a given C integer type. If you just want to convert a SCM value
>   to a given C integer type, use one of the conversion functions directly.

`scm_t_intmax` **`scm_to_signed_integer`** (*SCM x, scm_t_intmax min,*   [C Function]
        scm_t_intmax max)

`scm_t_uintmax` **`scm_to_unsigned_integer`** (*SCM x, scm_t_uintmax*   [C Function]
        min, scm_t_uintmax max)

> When *x* represents an exact integer that is between *min* and *max* inclusive, return
> that integer. Else signal an error, either a 'wrong-type' error when *x* is not an exact
> integer, or an 'out-of-range' error when it doesn't fit the given range.

`SCM` **`scm_from_signed_integer`** (*scm_t_intmax x*)   [C Function]

`SCM` **`scm_from_unsigned_integer`** (*scm_t_uintmax x*)   [C Function]

> Return the SCM value that represents the integer *x*. This function will always succeed
> and will always return an exact number.

`char` **`scm_to_char`** (*SCM x*)   [C Function]
`signed char` **`scm_to_schar`** (*SCM x*)   [C Function]
`unsigned char` **`scm_to_uchar`** (*SCM x*)   [C Function]
`short` **`scm_to_short`** (*SCM x*)   [C Function]
`unsigned short` **`scm_to_ushort`** (*SCM x*)   [C Function]
`int` **`scm_to_int`** (*SCM x*)   [C Function]
`unsigned int` **`scm_to_uint`** (*SCM x*)   [C Function]
`long` **`scm_to_long`** (*SCM x*)   [C Function]
`unsigned long` **`scm_to_ulong`** (*SCM x*)   [C Function]
`long long` **`scm_to_long_long`** (*SCM x*)   [C Function]
`unsigned long long` **`scm_to_ulong_long`** (*SCM x*)   [C Function]
`size_t` **`scm_to_size_t`** (*SCM x*)   [C Function]
`ssize_t` **`scm_to_ssize_t`** (*SCM x*)   [C Function]
`scm_t_ptrdiff` **`scm_to_ptrdiff_t`** (*SCM x*)   [C Function]
`scm_t_int8` **`scm_to_int8`** (*SCM x*)   [C Function]
`scm_t_uint8` **`scm_to_uint8`** (*SCM x*)   [C Function]
`scm_t_int16` **`scm_to_int16`** (*SCM x*)   [C Function]
`scm_t_uint16` **`scm_to_uint16`** (*SCM x*)   [C Function]
`scm_t_int32` **`scm_to_int32`** (*SCM x*)   [C Function]
`scm_t_uint32` **`scm_to_uint32`** (*SCM x*)   [C Function]
`scm_t_int64` **`scm_to_int64`** (*SCM x*)   [C Function]
`scm_t_uint64` **`scm_to_uint64`** (*SCM x*)   [C Function]
`scm_t_intmax` **`scm_to_intmax`** (*SCM x*)   [C Function]
`scm_t_uintmax` **`scm_to_uintmax`** (*SCM x*)   [C Function]

> When *x* represents an exact integer that fits into the indicated C type, return that
> integer. Else signal an error, either a 'wrong-type' error when *x* is not an exact
> integer, or an 'out-of-range' error when it doesn't fit the given range.
>
> The functions `scm_to_long_long`, `scm_to_ulong_long`, `scm_to_int64`, and `scm_to_uint64` are only available when the corresponding types are.

`SCM` **`scm_from_char`** (*char x*)   [C Function]
`SCM` **`scm_from_schar`** (*signed char x*)   [C Function]
`SCM` **`scm_from_uchar`** (*unsigned char x*)   [C Function]
`SCM` **`scm_from_short`** (*short x*)   [C Function]
`SCM` **`scm_from_ushort`** (*unsigned short x*)   [C Function]

SCM `scm_from_int` (*int x*)   [C Function]
SCM `scm_from_uint` (*unsigned int x*)   [C Function]
SCM `scm_from_long` (*long x*)   [C Function]
SCM `scm_from_ulong` (*unsigned long x*)   [C Function]
SCM `scm_from_long_long` (*long long x*)   [C Function]
SCM `scm_from_ulong_long` (*unsigned long long x*)   [C Function]
SCM `scm_from_size_t` (*size_t x*)   [C Function]
SCM `scm_from_ssize_t` (*ssize_t x*)   [C Function]
SCM `scm_from_ptrdiff_t` (*scm_t_ptrdiff x*)   [C Function]
SCM `scm_from_int8` (*scm_t_int8 x*)   [C Function]
SCM `scm_from_uint8` (*scm_t_uint8 x*)   [C Function]
SCM `scm_from_int16` (*scm_t_int16 x*)   [C Function]
SCM `scm_from_uint16` (*scm_t_uint16 x*)   [C Function]
SCM `scm_from_int32` (*scm_t_int32 x*)   [C Function]
SCM `scm_from_uint32` (*scm_t_uint32 x*)   [C Function]
SCM `scm_from_int64` (*scm_t_int64 x*)   [C Function]
SCM `scm_from_uint64` (*scm_t_uint64 x*)   [C Function]
SCM `scm_from_intmax` (*scm_t_intmax x*)   [C Function]
SCM `scm_from_uintmax` (*scm_t_uintmax x*)   [C Function]
> Return the SCM value that represents the integer x. These functions will always succeed and will always return an exact number.

void `scm_to_mpz` (*SCM val, mpz_t rop*)   [C Function]
> Assign *val* to the multiple precision integer *rop*. *val* must be an exact integer, otherwise an error will be signalled. *rop* must have been initialized with `mpz_init` before this function is called. When *rop* is no longer needed the occupied space must be freed with `mpz_clear`. See Section "Initializing Integers" in *GNU MP Manual*, for details.

SCM `scm_from_mpz` (*mpz_t val*)   [C Function]
> Return the SCM value that represents *val*.

6.6.2.3 Real and Rational Numbers

Mathematically, the real numbers are the set of numbers that describe all possible points along a continuous, infinite, one-dimensional line. The rational numbers are the set of all numbers that can be written as fractions p/q, where p and q are integers. All rational numbers are also real, but there are real numbers that are not rational, for example $\sqrt{2}$, and π.

Guile can represent both exact and inexact rational numbers, but it cannot represent precise finite irrational numbers. Exact rationals are represented by storing the numerator and denominator as two exact integers. Inexact rationals are stored as floating point numbers using the C type `double`.

Exact rationals are written as a fraction of integers. There must be no whitespace around the slash:

```
1/2
-22/7
```

Even though the actual encoding of inexact rationals is in binary, it may be helpful to think of it as a decimal number with a limited number of significant figures and a decimal point somewhere, since this corresponds to the standard notation for non-whole numbers. For example:

```
0.34
-0.00000142857931198
-5648394822220000000000.0
4.0
```

The limited precision of Guile's encoding means that any finite "real" number in Guile can be written in a rational form, by multiplying and then dividing by sufficient powers of 10 (or in fact, 2). For example, '-0.00000142857931198' is the same as -142857931198 divided by 100000000000000000. In Guile's current incarnation, therefore, the `rational?` and `real?` predicates are equivalent for finite numbers.

Dividing by an exact zero leads to a error message, as one might expect. However, dividing by an inexact zero does not produce an error. Instead, the result of the division is either plus or minus infinity, depending on the sign of the divided number and the sign of the zero divisor (some platforms support signed zeroes '-0.0' and '+0.0'; '0.0' is the same as '+0.0').

Dividing zero by an inexact zero yields a NaN ('not a number') value, although they are actually considered numbers by Scheme. Attempts to compare a NaN value with any number (including itself) using =, <, >, <= or >= always returns #f. Although a NaN value is not = to itself, it is both `eqv?` and `equal?` to itself and other NaN values. However, the preferred way to test for them is by using `nan?`.

The real NaN values and infinities are written '+nan.0', '+inf.0' and '-inf.0'. This syntax is also recognized by `read` as an extension to the usual Scheme syntax. These special values are considered by Scheme to be inexact real numbers but not rational. Note that non-real complex numbers may also contain infinities or NaN values in their real or imaginary parts. To test a real number to see if it is infinite, a NaN value, or neither, use `inf?`, `nan?`, or `finite?`, respectively. Every real number in Scheme belongs to precisely one of those three classes.

On platforms that follow IEEE 754 for their floating point arithmetic, the '+inf.0', '-inf.0', and '+nan.0' values are implemented using the corresponding IEEE 754 values. They behave in arithmetic operations like IEEE 754 describes it, i.e., (= +nan.0 +nan.0) ⇒ #f.

real? *obj*   [Scheme Procedure]
scm_real_p (*obj*)   [C Function]
> Return #t if *obj* is a real number, else #f. Note that the sets of integer and rational values form subsets of the set of real numbers, so the predicate will also be fulfilled if *obj* is an integer number or a rational number.

rational? *x*   [Scheme Procedure]
scm_rational_p (*x*)   [C Function]
> Return #t if *x* is a rational number, #f otherwise. Note that the set of integer values forms a subset of the set of rational numbers, i.e. the predicate will also be fulfilled if *x* is an integer number.

`rationalize` *x eps*   [Scheme Procedure]
`scm_rationalize` (*x, eps*)   [C Function]
    Returns the *simplest* rational number differing from *x* by no more than *eps*.

    As required by R5RS, `rationalize` only returns an exact result when both its arguments are exact. Thus, you might need to use `inexact->exact` on the arguments.

```
(rationalize (inexact->exact 1.2) 1/100)
⇒ 6/5
```

`inf?` *x*   [Scheme Procedure]
`scm_inf_p` (*x*)   [C Function]
    Return `#t` if the real number *x* is '`+inf.0`' or '`-inf.0`'. Otherwise return `#f`.

`nan?` *x*   [Scheme Procedure]
`scm_nan_p` (*x*)   [C Function]
    Return `#t` if the real number *x* is '`+nan.0`', or `#f` otherwise.

`finite?` *x*   [Scheme Procedure]
`scm_finite_p` (*x*)   [C Function]
    Return `#t` if the real number *x* is neither infinite nor a NaN, `#f` otherwise.

`nan`   [Scheme Procedure]
`scm_nan` ()   [C Function]
    Return '`+nan.0`', a NaN value.

`inf`   [Scheme Procedure]
`scm_inf` ()   [C Function]
    Return '`+inf.0`', positive infinity.

`numerator` *x*   [Scheme Procedure]
`scm_numerator` (*x*)   [C Function]
    Return the numerator of the rational number *x*.

`denominator` *x*   [Scheme Procedure]
`scm_denominator` (*x*)   [C Function]
    Return the denominator of the rational number *x*.

`int scm_is_real` (*SCM val*)   [C Function]
`int scm_is_rational` (*SCM val*)   [C Function]
    Equivalent to `scm_is_true (scm_real_p (val))` and `scm_is_true (scm_rational_p (val))`, respectively.

`double scm_to_double` (*SCM val*)   [C Function]
    Returns the number closest to *val* that is representable as a `double`. Returns infinity for a *val* that is too large in magnitude. The argument *val* must be a real number.

`SCM scm_from_double` (*double val*)   [C Function]
    Return the SCM value that represents *val*. The returned value is inexact according to the predicate `inexact?`, but it will be exactly equal to *val*.

6.6.2.4 Complex Numbers

Complex numbers are the set of numbers that describe all possible points in a two-dimensional space. The two coordinates of a particular point in this space are known as the *real* and *imaginary* parts of the complex number that describes that point.

In Guile, complex numbers are written in rectangular form as the sum of their real and imaginary parts, using the symbol i to indicate the imaginary part.

```
3+4i
⇒
3.0+4.0i


(* 3-8i 2.3+0.3i)
⇒
9.3-17.5i
```

Polar form can also be used, with an '@' between magnitude and angle,

```
1@3.141592  ⇒  -1.0        (approx)
-1@1.57079  ⇒  0.0-1.0i    (approx)
```

Guile represents a complex number as a pair of inexact reals, so the real and imaginary parts of a complex number have the same properties of inexactness and limited precision as single inexact real numbers.

Note that each part of a complex number may contain any inexact real value, including the special values '+nan.0', '+inf.0' and '-inf.0', as well as either of the signed zeroes '0.0' or '-0.0'.

complex? *z*   [Scheme Procedure]
scm_complex_p (*z*)   [C Function]
> Return #t if *z* is a complex number, #f otherwise. Note that the sets of real, rational and integer values form subsets of the set of complex numbers, i.e. the predicate will also be fulfilled if *z* is a real, rational or integer number.

int scm_is_complex (*SCM val*)   [C Function]
> Equivalent to scm_is_true (scm_complex_p (val)).

6.6.2.5 Exact and Inexact Numbers

R5RS requires that, with few exceptions, a calculation involving inexact numbers always produces an inexact result. To meet this requirement, Guile distinguishes between an exact integer value such as '5' and the corresponding inexact integer value which, to the limited precision available, has no fractional part, and is printed as '5.0'. Guile will only convert the latter value to the former when forced to do so by an invocation of the inexact->exact procedure.

The only exception to the above requirement is when the values of the inexact numbers do not affect the result. For example (expt n 0) is '1' for any value of n, therefore (expt 5.0 0) is permitted to return an exact '1'.

exact? *z*   [Scheme Procedure]
scm_exact_p (*z*)   [C Function]
> Return #t if the number *z* is exact, #f otherwise.

```
(exact? 2)
⇒ #t

(exact? 0.5)
⇒ #f

(exact? (/ 2))
⇒ #t
```

int scm_is_exact (*SCM z*) [C Function]

Return a 1 if the number *z* is exact, and 0 otherwise. This is equivalent to `scm_is_true (scm_exact_p (z))`.

An alternate approch to testing the exactness of a number is to use `scm_is_signed_integer` or `scm_is_unsigned_integer`.

inexact? *z* [Scheme Procedure]
scm_inexact_p (*z*) [C Function]

Return `#t` if the number *z* is inexact, `#f` else.

int scm_is_inexact (*SCM z*) [C Function]

Return a 1 if the number *z* is inexact, and 0 otherwise. This is equivalent to `scm_is_true (scm_inexact_p (z))`.

inexact->exact *z* [Scheme Procedure]
scm_inexact_to_exact (*z*) [C Function]

Return an exact number that is numerically closest to *z*, when there is one. For inexact rationals, Guile returns the exact rational that is numerically equal to the inexact rational. Inexact complex numbers with a non-zero imaginary part can not be made exact.

```
(inexact->exact 0.5)
⇒ 1/2
```

The following happens because 12/10 is not exactly representable as a `double` (on most platforms). However, when reading a decimal number that has been marked exact with the "#e" prefix, Guile is able to represent it correctly.

```
(inexact->exact 1.2)
⇒ 5404319552844595/4503599627370496

#e1.2
⇒ 6/5
```

exact->inexact *z* [Scheme Procedure]
scm_exact_to_inexact (*z*) [C Function]

Convert the number *z* to its inexact representation.

6.6.2.6 Read Syntax for Numerical Data

The read syntax for integers is a string of digits, optionally preceded by a minus or plus character, a code indicating the base in which the integer is encoded, and a code indicating whether the number is exact or inexact. The supported base codes are:

```
#b
#B          the integer is written in binary (base 2)

#o
#O          the integer is written in octal (base 8)

#d
#D          the integer is written in decimal (base 10)

#x
#X          the integer is written in hexadecimal (base 16)
```

If the base code is omitted, the integer is assumed to be decimal. The following examples show how these base codes are used.

```
    -13
    ⇒ -13

    #d-13
    ⇒ -13

    #x-13
    ⇒ -19

    #b+1101
    ⇒ 13

    #o377
    ⇒ 255
```

The codes for indicating exactness (which can, incidentally, be applied to all numerical values) are:

```
#e
#E          the number is exact

#i
#I          the number is inexact.
```

If the exactness indicator is omitted, the number is exact unless it contains a radix point. Since Guile can not represent exact complex numbers, an error is signalled when asking for them.

```
    (exact? 1.2)
    ⇒ #f

    (exact? #e1.2)
    ⇒ #t

    (exact? #e+1i)
    ERROR: Wrong type argument
```

Guile also understands the syntax '+inf.0' and '-inf.0' for plus and minus infinity, respectively. The value must be written exactly as shown, that is, they always must have

a sign and exactly one zero digit after the decimal point. It also understands '+nan.0' and
'-nan.0' for the special 'not-a-number' value. The sign is ignored for 'not-a-number' and
the value is always printed as '+nan.0'.

6.6.2.7 Operations on Integer Values

odd? n [Scheme Procedure]
scm_odd_p (n)   [C Function]
> Return #t if n is an odd number, #f otherwise.

even? n [Scheme Procedure]
scm_even_p (n)   [C Function]
> Return #t if n is an even number, #f otherwise.

quotient n d [Scheme Procedure]
remainder n d [Scheme Procedure]
scm_quotient (n, d)   [C Function]
scm_remainder (n, d)   [C Function]
> Return the quotient or remainder from n divided by d. The quotient is rounded
> towards zero, and the remainder will have the same sign as n. In all cases quotient
> and remainder satisfy $n = q * d + r$.
>
>> (remainder 13 4) $\Rightarrow$ 1
>> (remainder -13 4) $\Rightarrow$ -1
>
> See also truncate-quotient, truncate-remainder and related operations in
> Section 6.6.2.11 [Arithmetic], page 119.

modulo n d [Scheme Procedure]
scm_modulo (n, d)   [C Function]
> Return the remainder from n divided by d, with the same sign as d.
>
>> (modulo 13 4) $\Rightarrow$ 1
>> (modulo -13 4) $\Rightarrow$ 3
>> (modulo 13 -4) $\Rightarrow$ -3
>> (modulo -13 -4) $\Rightarrow$ -1
>
> See also floor-quotient, floor-remainder and related operations in
> Section 6.6.2.11 [Arithmetic], page 119.

gcd x...   [Scheme Procedure]
scm_gcd (x, y)   [C Function]
> Return the greatest common divisor of all arguments. If called without arguments, 0
> is returned.
>
> The C function scm_gcd always takes two arguments, while the Scheme function can
> take an arbitrary number.

lcm x...   [Scheme Procedure]
scm_lcm (x, y)   [C Function]
> Return the least common multiple of the arguments. If called without arguments, 1
> is returned.
>
> The C function scm_lcm always takes two arguments, while the Scheme function can
> take an arbitrary number.

modulo-expt n k m [Scheme Procedure]
scm_modulo_expt (n, k, m) [C Function]
> Return n raised to the integer exponent k, modulo m.

> > (modulo-expt 2 3 5)
> > $\Rightarrow$ 3

exact-integer-sqrt k [Scheme Procedure]
void scm_exact_integer_sqrt (SCM k, SCM *s, SCM *r)   [C Function]
> Return two exact non-negative integers s and r such that $k = s^2 + r$ and $s^2 <= k < (s+1)^2$. An error is raised if k is not an exact non-negative integer.

> > (exact-integer-sqrt 10) $\Rightarrow$ 3 and 1

6.6.2.8 Comparison Predicates

The C comparison functions below always takes two arguments, while the Scheme functions can take an arbitrary number. Also keep in mind that the C functions return one of the Scheme boolean values SCM_BOOL_T or SCM_BOOL_F which are both true as far as C is concerned. Thus, always write scm_is_true (scm_num_eq_p (x, y)) when testing the two Scheme numbers x and y for equality, for example.

=   [Scheme Procedure]
scm_num_eq_p (x, y) [C Function]
> Return #t if all parameters are numerically equal.

<   [Scheme Procedure]
scm_less_p (x, y) [C Function]
> Return #t if the list of parameters is monotonically increasing.

>   [Scheme Procedure]
scm_gr_p (x, y) [C Function]
> Return #t if the list of parameters is monotonically decreasing.

<=   [Scheme Procedure]
scm_leq_p (x, y) [C Function]
> Return #t if the list of parameters is monotonically non-decreasing.

>=   [Scheme Procedure]
scm_geq_p (x, y) [C Function]
> Return #t if the list of parameters is monotonically non-increasing.

zero? z [Scheme Procedure]
scm_zero_p (z) [C Function]
> Return #t if z is an exact or inexact number equal to zero.

positive? x [Scheme Procedure]
scm_positive_p (x) [C Function]
> Return #t if x is an exact or inexact number greater than zero.

negative? x [Scheme Procedure]
scm_negative_p (x) [C Function]
> Return #t if x is an exact or inexact number less than zero.

6.6.2.9 Converting Numbers To and From Strings

The following procedures read and write numbers according to their external representation as defined by R5RS (see Section "Lexical structure" in *The Revised^5 Report on the Algorithmic Language Scheme*). See Section 6.24.4 [Number Input and Output], page 439, for locale-dependent number parsing.

number->string *n* [*radix*]   [Scheme Procedure]
scm_number_to_string (*n*, *radix*)   [C Function]
> Return a string holding the external representation of the number *n* in the given *radix*. If *n* is inexact, a radix of 10 will be used.

string->number *string* [*radix*]   [Scheme Procedure]
scm_string_to_number (*string*, *radix*)   [C Function]
> Return a number of the maximally precise representation expressed by the given *string*. *radix* must be an exact integer, either 2, 8, 10, or 16. If supplied, *radix* is a default radix that may be overridden by an explicit radix prefix in *string* (e.g. "#o177"). If *radix* is not supplied, then the default radix is 10. If string is not a syntactically valid notation for a number, then string->number returns #f.

SCM scm_c_locale_stringn_to_number (*const char *string, size_t*   [C Function]
> *len, unsigned radix*)
> As per string->number above, but taking a C string, as pointer and length. The string characters should be in the current locale encoding (locale in the name refers only to that, there's no locale-dependent parsing).

6.6.2.10 Complex Number Operations

make-rectangular *real_part imaginary_part*   [Scheme Procedure]
scm_make_rectangular (*real_part, imaginary_part*)   [C Function]
> Return a complex number constructed of the given *real-part* and *imaginary-part* parts.

make-polar *mag ang*   [Scheme Procedure]
scm_make_polar (*mag, ang*)   [C Function]
> Return the complex number *mag* * e^(i * *ang*).

real-part *z*   [Scheme Procedure]
scm_real_part (*z*)   [C Function]
> Return the real part of the number *z*.

imag-part *z*   [Scheme Procedure]
scm_imag_part (*z*)   [C Function]
> Return the imaginary part of the number *z*.

magnitude *z*   [Scheme Procedure]
scm_magnitude (*z*)   [C Function]
> Return the magnitude of the number *z*. This is the same as abs for real arguments, but also allows complex numbers.

angle *z*   [Scheme Procedure]
scm_angle (*z*)   [C Function]
> Return the angle of the complex number *z*.

SCM `scm_c_make_rectangular` (*double re, double im*)   [C Function]
SCM `scm_c_make_polar` (*double x, double y*)   [C Function]
> Like `scm_make_rectangular` or `scm_make_polar`, respectively, but these functions take `doubles` as their arguments.

`double scm_c_real_part` (*z*)   [C Function]
`double scm_c_imag_part` (*z*)   [C Function]
> Returns the real or imaginary part of *z* as a `double`.

`double scm_c_magnitude` (*z*)   [C Function]
`double scm_c_angle` (*z*)   [C Function]
> Returns the magnitude or angle of *z* as a `double`.

6.6.2.11 Arithmetic Functions

The C arithmetic functions below always takes two arguments, while the Scheme functions can take an arbitrary number. When you need to invoke them with just one argument, for example to compute the equivalent of (- x), pass `SCM_UNDEFINED` as the second one: `scm_difference (x, SCM_UNDEFINED)`.

`+` *z1* ...   [Scheme Procedure]
`scm_sum` (*z1, z2*)   [C Function]
> Return the sum of all parameter values. Return 0 if called without any parameters.

`-` *z1 z2* ...   [Scheme Procedure]
`scm_difference` (*z1, z2*)   [C Function]
> If called with one argument *z1*, *-z1* is returned. Otherwise the sum of all but the first argument are subtracted from the first argument.

`*` *z1* ...   [Scheme Procedure]
`scm_product` (*z1, z2*)   [C Function]
> Return the product of all arguments. If called without arguments, 1 is returned.

`/` *z1 z2* ...   [Scheme Procedure]
`scm_divide` (*z1, z2*)   [C Function]
> Divide the first argument by the product of the remaining arguments. If called with one argument *z1*, $1/z1$ is returned.

`1+` *z*   [Scheme Procedure]
`scm_oneplus` (*z*)   [C Function]
> Return $z + 1$.

`1-` *z*   [Scheme Procedure]
`scm_oneminus` (*z*)   [C function]
> Return $z - 1$.

`abs` *x*   [Scheme Procedure]
`scm_abs` (*x*)   [C Function]
> Return the absolute value of *x*.

> *x* must be a number with zero imaginary part. To calculate the magnitude of a complex number, use `magnitude` instead.

`max` *x1 x2* ...   [Scheme Procedure]
`scm_max` (*x1, x2*)   [C Function]
> Return the maximum of all parameter values.

`min` *x1 x2* ...   [Scheme Procedure]
`scm_min` (*x1, x2*)   [C Function]
> Return the minimum of all parameter values.

`truncate` *x*   [Scheme Procedure]
`scm_truncate_number` (*x*)   [C Function]
> Round the inexact number *x* towards zero.

`round` *x*   [Scheme Procedure]
`scm_round_number` (*x*)   [C Function]
> Round the inexact number *x* to the nearest integer. When exactly halfway between
> two integers, round to the even one.

`floor` *x*   [Scheme Procedure]
`scm_floor` (*x*)   [C Function]
> Round the number *x* towards minus infinity.

`ceiling` *x*   [Scheme Procedure]
`scm_ceiling` (*x*)   [C Function]
> Round the number *x* towards infinity.

`double scm_c_truncate` (*double x*)   [C Function]
`double scm_c_round` (*double x*)   [C Function]
> Like `scm_truncate_number` or `scm_round_number`, respectively, but these functions
> take and return `double` values.

`euclidean/` *x y*   [Scheme Procedure]
`euclidean-quotient` *x y*   [Scheme Procedure]
`euclidean-remainder` *x y*   [Scheme Procedure]
`void scm_euclidean_divide` (*SCM x, SCM y, SCM *q, SCM *r*)   [C Function]
`SCM scm_euclidean_quotient` (*SCM x, SCM y*)   [C Function]
`SCM scm_euclidean_remainder` (*SCM x, SCM y*)   [C Function]
> These procedures accept two real numbers *x* and *y*, where the divisor *y* must be non-
> zero. `euclidean-quotient` returns the integer *q* and `euclidean-remainder` returns
> the real number *r* such that $x = q * y + r$ and $0 <= r < |y|$. `euclidean/` returns
> both *q* and *r*, and is more efficient than computing each separately. Note that when
> $y > 0$, `euclidean-quotient` returns $floor(x/y)$, otherwise it returns $ceiling(x/y)$.
>
> Note that these operators are equivalent to the R6RS operators `div`, `mod`, and `div-and-mod`.
>
> ```
> (euclidean-quotient 123 10)  ⇒ 12
> (euclidean-remainder 123 10)  ⇒ 3
> (euclidean/ 123 10)  ⇒ 12 and 3
> (euclidean/ 123 -10)  ⇒ -12 and 3
> (euclidean/ -123 10)  ⇒ -13 and 7
> (euclidean/ -123 -10)  ⇒ 13 and 7
> ```

```
(euclidean/ -123.2 -63.5) ⇒ 2.0 and 3.8
(euclidean/ 16/3 -10/7) ⇒ -3 and 22/21
```

floor/ *x y*   [Scheme Procedure]
floor-quotient *x y*   [Scheme Procedure]
floor-remainder *x y*   [Scheme Procedure]
void scm_floor_divide (*SCM x, SCM y, SCM *q, SCM *r*)   [C Function]
SCM scm_floor_quotient (*x, y*)   [C Function]
SCM scm_floor_remainder (*x, y*)   [C Function]

These procedures accept two real numbers x and y, where the divisor y must be non-zero. floor-quotient returns the integer q and floor-remainder returns the real number r such that $q = floor(x/y)$ and $x = q * y + r$. floor/ returns both q and r, and is more efficient than computing each separately. Note that r, if non-zero, will have the same sign as y.

When x and y are integers, floor-remainder is equivalent to the R5RS integer-only operator modulo.

```
(floor-quotient 123 10) ⇒ 12
(floor-remainder 123 10) ⇒ 3
(floor/ 123 10) ⇒ 12 and 3
(floor/ 123 -10) ⇒ -13 and -7
(floor/ -123 10) ⇒ -13 and 7
(floor/ -123 -10) ⇒ 12 and -3
(floor/ -123.2 -63.5) ⇒ 1.0 and -59.7
(floor/ 16/3 -10/7) ⇒ -4 and -8/21
```

ceiling/ *x y*   [Scheme Procedure]
ceiling-quotient *x y*   [Scheme Procedure]
ceiling-remainder *x y*   [Scheme Procedure]
void scm_ceiling_divide (*SCM x, SCM y, SCM *q, SCM *r*)   [C Function]
SCM scm_ceiling_quotient (*x, y*)   [C Function]
SCM scm_ceiling_remainder (*x, y*)   [C Function]

These procedures accept two real numbers x and y, where the divisor y must be non-zero. ceiling-quotient returns the integer q and ceiling-remainder returns the real number r such that $q = ceiling(x/y)$ and $x = q * y + r$. ceiling/ returns both q and r, and is more efficient than computing each separately. Note that r, if non-zero, will have the opposite sign of y.

```
(ceiling-quotient 123 10) ⇒ 13
(ceiling-remainder 123 10) ⇒ -7
(ceiling/ 123 10) ⇒ 13 and -7
(ceiling/ 123 -10) ⇒ -12 and 3
(ceiling/ -123 10) ⇒ -12 and -3
(ceiling/ -123 -10) ⇒ 13 and 7
(ceiling/ -123.2 -63.5) ⇒ 2.0 and 3.8
(ceiling/ 16/3 -10/7) ⇒ -3 and 22/21
```

truncate/ *x y*   [Scheme Procedure]
truncate-quotient *x y*   [Scheme Procedure]

truncate-remainder *x y*   [Scheme Procedure]
void scm_truncate_divide (*SCM x, SCM y, SCM *q, SCM *r*)   [C Function]
SCM scm_truncate_quotient (*x, y*)   [C Function]
SCM scm_truncate_remainder (*x, y*)   [C Function]

These procedures accept two real numbers x and y, where the divisor y must be non-zero. truncate-quotient returns the integer q and truncate-remainder returns the real number r such that q is x/y rounded toward zero, and $x = q*y+r$. truncate/ returns both q and r, and is more efficient than computing each separately. Note that r, if non-zero, will have the same sign as x.

When x and y are integers, these operators are equivalent to the R5RS integer-only operators quotient and remainder.

```
(truncate-quotient 123 10) ⇒ 12
(truncate-remainder 123 10) ⇒ 3
(truncate/ 123 10) ⇒ 12 and 3
(truncate/ 123 -10) ⇒ -12 and 3
(truncate/ -123 10) ⇒ -12 and -3
(truncate/ -123 -10) ⇒ 12 and -3
(truncate/ -123.2 -63.5) ⇒ 1.0 and -59.7
(truncate/ 16/3 -10/7) ⇒ -3 and 22/21
```

centered/ *x y*   [Scheme Procedure]
centered-quotient *x y*   [Scheme Procedure]
centered-remainder *x y*   [Scheme Procedure]
void scm_centered_divide (*SCM x, SCM y, SCM *q, SCM *r*)   [C Function]
SCM scm_centered_quotient (*SCM x, SCM y*)   [C Function]
SCM scm_centered_remainder (*SCM x, SCM y*)   [C Function]

These procedures accept two real numbers x and y, where the divisor y must be non-zero. centered-quotient returns the integer q and centered-remainder returns the real number r such that $x = q*y+r$ and $-|y/2| <= r < |y/2|$. centered/ returns both q and r, and is more efficient than computing each separately.

Note that centered-quotient returns x/y rounded to the nearest integer. When x/y lies exactly half-way between two integers, the tie is broken according to the sign of y. If $y > 0$, ties are rounded toward positive infinity, otherwise they are rounded toward negative infinity. This is a consequence of the requirement that $-|y/2| <= r < |y/2|$.

Note that these operators are equivalent to the R6RS operators div0, mod0, and div0-and-mod0.

```
(centered-quotient 123 10) ⇒ 12
(centered-remainder 123 10) ⇒ 3
(centered/ 123 10) ⇒ 12 and 3
(centered/ 123 -10) ⇒ -12 and 3
(centered/ -123 10) ⇒ -12 and -3
(centered/ -123 -10) ⇒ 12 and -3
(centered/ 125 10) ⇒ 13 and -5
(centered/ 127 10) ⇒ 13 and -3
(centered/ 135 10) ⇒ 14 and -5
(centered/ -123.2 -63.5) ⇒ 2.0 and 3.8
```

(centered/ 16/3 -10/7) ⇒ -4 and -8/21

round/ *x y*	[Scheme Procedure]
round-quotient *x y*	[Scheme Procedure]
round-remainder *x y*	[Scheme Procedure]
void scm_round_divide (*SCM x, SCM y, SCM *q, SCM *r*)	[C Function]
SCM scm_round_quotient (*x, y*)	[C Function]
SCM scm_round_remainder (*x, y*)	[C Function]

These procedures accept two real numbers x and y, where the divisor y must be non-zero. round-quotient returns the integer q and round-remainder returns the real number r such that $x = q * y + r$ and q is x/y rounded to the nearest integer, with ties going to the nearest even integer. round/ returns both q and r, and is more efficient than computing each separately.

Note that round/ and centered/ are almost equivalent, but their behavior differs when x/y lies exactly half-way between two integers. In this case, round/ chooses the nearest even integer, whereas centered/ chooses in such a way to satisfy the constraint $-|y/2| <= r < |y/2|$, which is stronger than the corresponding constraint for round/, $-|y/2| <= r <= |y/2|$. In particular, when x and y are integers, the number of possible remainders returned by centered/ is $|y|$, whereas the number of possible remainders returned by round/ is $|y| + 1$ when y is even.

```
(round-quotient 123 10) ⇒ 12
(round-remainder 123 10) ⇒ 3
(round/ 123 10) ⇒ 12 and 3
(round/ 123 -10) ⇒ -12 and 3
(round/ -123 10) ⇒ -12 and -3
(round/ -123 -10) ⇒ 12 and -3
(round/ 125 10) ⇒ 12 and 5
(round/ 127 10) ⇒ 13 and -3
(round/ 135 10) ⇒ 14 and -5
(round/ -123.2 -63.5) ⇒ 2.0 and 3.8
(round/ 16/3 -10/7) ⇒ -4 and -8/21
```

6.6.2.12 Scientific Functions

The following procedures accept any kind of number as arguments, including complex numbers.

sqrt *z*	[Scheme Procedure]

Return the square root of z. Of the two possible roots (positive and negative), the one with a positive real part is returned, or if that's zero then a positive imaginary part. Thus,

```
(sqrt 9.0)       ⇒ 3.0
(sqrt -9.0)      ⇒ 0.0+3.0i
(sqrt 1.0+1.0i)  ⇒ 1.09868411346781+0.455089860562227i
(sqrt -1.0-1.0i) ⇒ 0.455089860562227-1.09868411346781i
```

expt *z1 z2*	[Scheme Procedure]

Return $z1$ raised to the power of $z2$.

sin *z*   [Scheme Procedure]
> Return the sine of *z*.

cos *z*   [Scheme Procedure]
> Return the cosine of *z*.

tan *z*   [Scheme Procedure]
> Return the tangent of *z*.

asin *z*   [Scheme Procedure]
> Return the arcsine of *z*.

acos *z*   [Scheme Procedure]
> Return the arccosine of *z*.

atan *z*   [Scheme Procedure]
atan *y x*   [Scheme Procedure]
> Return the arctangent of *z*, or of *y/x*.

exp *z*   [Scheme Procedure]
> Return e to the power of *z*, where e is the base of natural logarithms (2.71828...).

log *z*   [Scheme Procedure]
> Return the natural logarithm of *z*.

log10 *z*   [Scheme Procedure]
> Return the base 10 logarithm of *z*.

sinh *z*   [Scheme Procedure]
> Return the hyperbolic sine of *z*.

cosh *z*   [Scheme Procedure]
> Return the hyperbolic cosine of *z*.

tanh *z*   [Scheme Procedure]
> Return the hyperbolic tangent of *z*.

asinh *z*   [Scheme Procedure]
> Return the hyperbolic arcsine of *z*.

acosh *z*   [Scheme Procedure]
> Return the hyperbolic arccosine of *z*.

atanh *z*   [Scheme Procedure]
> Return the hyperbolic arctangent of *z*.

6.6.2.13 Bitwise Operations

For the following bitwise functions, negative numbers are treated as infinite precision twos-complements. For instance −6 is bits . . . 111010, with infinitely many ones on the left. It can be seen that adding 6 (binary 110) to such a bit pattern gives all zeros.

logand *n1 n2* . . .   [Scheme Procedure]
scm_logand (*n1, n2*)   [C Function]
>   Return the bitwise AND of the integer arguments.
>
>   (logand) ⇒ -1
>   (logand 7) ⇒ 7
>   (logand #b111 #b011 #b001) ⇒ 1

logior *n1 n2* . . .   [Scheme Procedure]
scm_logior (*n1, n2*)   [C Function]
>   Return the bitwise OR of the integer arguments.
>
>   (logior) ⇒ 0
>   (logior 7) ⇒ 7
>   (logior #b000 #b001 #b011) ⇒ 3

logxor *n1 n2* . . .   [Scheme Procedure]
scm_loxor (*n1, n2*)   [C Function]
>   Return the bitwise XOR of the integer arguments. A bit is set in the result if it is set
>   in an odd number of arguments.
>
>   (logxor) ⇒ 0
>   (logxor 7) ⇒ 7
>   (logxor #b000 #b001 #b011) ⇒ 2
>   (logxor #b000 #b001 #b011 #b011) ⇒ 1

lognot *n*   [Scheme Procedure]
scm_lognot (*n*)   [C Function]
>   Return the integer which is the ones-complement of the integer argument, ie. each 0
>   bit is changed to 1 and each 1 bit to 0.
>
>   (number->string (lognot #b10000000) 2)
>   ⇒ "-10000001"
>   (number->string (lognot #b0) 2)
>   ⇒ "-1"

logtest *j k*   [Scheme Procedure]
scm_logtest (*j, k*)   [C Function]
>   Test whether *j* and *k* have any 1 bits in common. This is equivalent to (not (zero?
>   (logand j k))), but without actually calculating the logand, just testing for non-
>   zero.
>
>   (logtest #b0100 #b1011) ⇒ #f
>   (logtest #b0100 #b0111) ⇒ #t

logbit? *index j*   [Scheme Procedure]
scm_logbit_p (*index, j*)   [C Function]
>   Test whether bit number *index* in *j* is set. *index* starts from 0 for the least significant
>   bit.

```
(logbit? 0 #b1101) ⇒ #t
(logbit? 1 #b1101) ⇒ #f
(logbit? 2 #b1101) ⇒ #t
(logbit? 3 #b1101) ⇒ #t
(logbit? 4 #b1101) ⇒ #f
```

ash *n count*   [Scheme Procedure]
scm_ash (*n, count*)   [C Function]

Return $floor(n * 2^count)$. *n* and *count* must be exact integers.

With *n* viewed as an infinite-precision twos-complement integer, **ash** means a left shift introducing zero bits when *count* is positive, or a right shift dropping bits when *count* is negative. This is an "arithmetic" shift.

```
(number->string (ash #b1 3) 2)    ⇒ "1000"
(number->string (ash #b1010 -1) 2) ⇒ "101"


;; -23 is bits ...11101001, -6 is bits ...111010
(ash -23 -2) ⇒ -6
```

round-ash *n count*   [Scheme Procedure]
scm_round_ash (*n, count*)   [C Function]

Return $round(n * 2^count)$. *n* and *count* must be exact integers.

With *n* viewed as an infinite-precision twos-complement integer, **round-ash** means a left shift introducing zero bits when *count* is positive, or a right shift rounding to the nearest integer (with ties going to the nearest even integer) when *count* is negative. This is a rounded "arithmetic" shift.

```
(number->string (round-ash #b1 3) 2)    ⇒ \"1000\"
(number->string (round-ash #b1010 -1) 2) ⇒ \"101\"
(number->string (round-ash #b1010 -2) 2) ⇒ \"10\"
(number->string (round-ash #b1011 -2) 2) ⇒ \"11\"
(number->string (round-ash #b1101 -2) 2) ⇒ \"11\"
(number->string (round-ash #b1110 -2) 2) ⇒ \"100\"
```

logcount *n*   [Scheme Procedure]
scm_logcount (*n*)   [C Function]

Return the number of bits in integer *n*. If *n* is positive, the 1-bits in its binary representation are counted. If negative, the 0-bits in its two's-complement binary representation are counted. If zero, 0 is returned.

```
(logcount #b10101010)
   ⇒ 4
(logcount 0)
   ⇒ 0
(logcount -2)
   ⇒ 1
```

integer-length *n*   [Scheme Procedure]
scm_integer_length (*n*)   [C Function]

Return the number of bits necessary to represent *n*.

For positive n this is how many bits to the most significant one bit. For negative n it's how many bits to the most significant zero bit in twos complement form.

```
(integer-length #b10101010)  ⇒ 8
(integer-length #b1111)      ⇒ 4
(integer-length 0)           ⇒ 0
(integer-length -1)          ⇒ 0
(integer-length -256)        ⇒ 8
(integer-length -257)        ⇒ 9
```

integer-expt n k [Scheme Procedure]
scm_integer_expt (n, k)   [C Function]

    Return n raised to the power k. k must be an exact integer, n can be any number.

    Negative k is supported, and results in $1/n^{|k|}$ in the usual way. n^0 is 1, as usual, and that includes 0^0 is 1.

```
(integer-expt 2 5)   ⇒ 32
(integer-expt -3 3)  ⇒ -27
(integer-expt 5 -3)  ⇒ 1/125
(integer-expt 0 0)   ⇒ 1
```

bit-extract n $start$ end [Scheme Procedure]
scm_bit_extract (n, $start$, end)   [C Function]

    Return the integer composed of the $start$ (inclusive) through end (exclusive) bits of n. The $start$th bit becomes the 0-th bit in the result.

```
(number->string (bit-extract #b1101101010 0 4) 2)
   ⇒ "1010"
(number->string (bit-extract #b1101101010 4 9) 2)
   ⇒ "10110"
```

6.6.2.14 Random Number Generation

Pseudo-random numbers are generated from a random state object, which can be created with seed->random-state or datum->random-state. An external representation (i.e. one which can written with write and read with read) of a random state object can be obtained via random-state->datum. The $state$ parameter to the various functions below is optional, it defaults to the state object in the *random-state* variable.

copy-random-state [$state$]   [Scheme Procedure]
scm_copy_random_state ($state$)   [C Function]

    Return a copy of the random state $state$.

random n [$state$]   [Scheme Procedure]
scm_random (n, $state$)   [C Function]

    Return a number in $[0, n)$.

    Accepts a positive integer or real n and returns a number of the same type between zero (inclusive) and n (exclusive). The values returned have a uniform distribution.

`random:exp` [*state*]   [Scheme Procedure]
`scm_random_exp` (*state*)   [C Function]
> Return an inexact real in an exponential distribution with mean 1. For an exponential
> distribution with mean *u* use (`* u (random:exp)`).

`random:hollow-sphere!` *vect* [*state*]   [Scheme Procedure]
`scm_random_hollow_sphere_x` (*vect, state*)   [C Function]
> Fills *vect* with inexact real random numbers the sum of whose squares is equal to 1.0.
> Thinking of *vect* as coordinates in space of dimension n = (`vector-length vect`),
> the coordinates are uniformly distributed over the surface of the unit n-sphere.

`random:normal` [*state*]   [Scheme Procedure]
`scm_random_normal` (*state*)   [C Function]
> Return an inexact real in a normal distribution. The distribution used has mean
> 0 and standard deviation 1. For a normal distribution with mean *m* and standard
> deviation *d* use (`+ m (* d (random:normal))`).

`random:normal-vector!` *vect* [*state*]   [Scheme Procedure]
`scm_random_normal_vector_x` (*vect, state*)   [C Function]
> Fills *vect* with inexact real random numbers that are independent and standard nor-
> mally distributed (i.e., with mean 0 and variance 1).

`random:solid-sphere!` *vect* [*state*]   [Scheme Procedure]
`scm_random_solid_sphere_x` (*vect, state*)   [C Function]
> Fills *vect* with inexact real random numbers the sum of whose squares is less than 1.0.
> Thinking of *vect* as coordinates in space of dimension n = (`vector-length vect`),
> the coordinates are uniformly distributed within the unit *n*-sphere.

`random:uniform` [*state*]   [Scheme Procedure]
`scm_random_uniform` (*state*)   [C Function]
> Return a uniformly distributed inexact real random number in [0,1).

`seed->random-state` *seed*   [Scheme Procedure]
`scm_seed_to_random_state` (*seed*)   [C Function]
> Return a new random state using *seed*.

`datum->random-state` *datum*   [Scheme Procedure]
`scm_datum_to_random_state` (*datum*)   [C Function]
> Return a new random state from *datum*, which should have been obtained by `random-`
> `state->datum`.

`random-state->datum` *state*   [Scheme Procedure]
`scm_random_state_to_datum` (*state*)   [C Function]
> Return a datum representation of *state* that may be written out and read back with
> the Scheme reader.

`random-state-from-platform`   [Scheme Procedure]
`scm_random_state_from_platform` ()   [C Function]
> Construct a new random state seeded from a platform-specific source of entropy,
> appropriate for use in non-security-critical applications. Currently `/dev/urandom` is

tried first, or else the seed is based on the time, date, process ID, an address from a
freshly allocated heap cell, an address from the local stack frame, and a high-resolution
timer if available.

random-state   [Variable]
> The global random state used by the above functions when the *state* parameter is
> not given.

Note that the initial value of *random-state* is the same every time Guile starts up.
Therefore, if you don't pass a *state* parameter to the above procedures, and you don't
set *random-state* to (seed->random-state your-seed), where your-seed is something
that *isn't* the same every time, you'll get the same sequence of "random" numbers on every
run.

For example, unless the relevant source code has changed, (map random (cdr (iota
30))), if the first use of random numbers since Guile started up, will always give:

```
(map random (cdr (iota 19)))
⇒
(0 1 1 2 2 2 1 2 6 7 10 0 5 3 12 5 5 12)
```

To seed the random state in a sensible way for non-security-critical applications, do this
during initialization of your program:

```
(set! *random-state* (random-state-from-platform))
```

6.6.3 Characters

In Scheme, there is a data type to describe a single character.

Defining what exactly a character *is* can be more complicated than it seems. Guile
follows the advice of R6RS and uses The Unicode Standard to help define what a character
is. So, for Guile, a character is anything in the Unicode Character Database.

The Unicode Character Database is basically a table of characters indexed using integers
called 'code points'. Valid code points are in the ranges 0 to #xD7FF inclusive or #xE000 to
#x10FFFF inclusive, which is about 1.1 million code points.

Any code point that has been assigned to a character or that has otherwise been given a
meaning by Unicode is called a 'designated code point'. Most of the designated code points,
about 200,000 of them, indicate characters, accents or other combining marks that modify
other characters, symbols, whitespace, and control characters. Some are not characters but
indicators that suggest how to format or display neighboring characters.

If a code point is not a designated code point – if it has not been assigned to a character
by The Unicode Standard – it is a 'reserved code point', meaning that they are reserved for
future use. Most of the code points, about 800,000, are 'reserved code points'.

By convention, a Unicode code point is written as "U+XXXX" where "XXXX" is a
hexadecimal number. Please note that this convenient notation is not valid code. Guile
does not interpret "U+XXXX" as a character.

In Scheme, a character literal is written as #*name* where *name* is the name of the
character that you want. Printable characters have their usual single character name; for
example, #\a is a lower case a.

Some of the code points are 'combining characters' that are not meant to be printed by themselves but are instead meant to modify the appearance of the previous character. For combining characters, an alternate form of the character literal is #\ followed by U+25CC (a small, dotted circle), followed by the combining character. This allows the combining character to be drawn on the circle, not on the backslash of #\.

Many of the non-printing characters, such as whitespace characters and control characters, also have names.

The most commonly used non-printing characters have long character names, described in the table below.

Character Name	Codepoint
#\nul	U+0000
#\alarm	u+0007
#\backspace	U+0008
#\tab	U+0009
#\linefeed	U+000A
#\newline	U+000A
#\vtab	U+000B
#\page	U+000C
#\return	U+000D
#\esc	U+001B
#\space	U+0020
#\delete	U+007F

There are also short names for all of the "C0 control characters" (those with code points below 32). The following table lists the short name for each character.

0 = #\nul	1 = #\soh	2 = #\stx	3 = #\etx
4 = #\eot	5 = #\enq	6 = #\ack	7 = #\bel
8 = #\bs	9 = #\ht	10 = #\lf	11 = #\vt
12 = #\ff	13 = #\cr	14 = #\so	15 = #\si
16 = #\dle	17 = #\dc1	18 = #\dc2	19 = #\dc3
20 = #\dc4	21 = #\nak	22 = #\syn	23 = #\etb
24 = #\can	25 = #\em	26 = #\sub	27 = #\esc
28 = #\fs	29 = #\gs	30 = #\rs	31 = #\us
32 = #\sp			

The short name for the "delete" character (code point U+007F) is #\del.

The R7RS name for the "escape" character (code point U+001B) is #\escape.

There are also a few alternative names left over for compatibility with previous versions of Guile.

Alternate	Standard
#\nl	#\newline
#\np	#\page
#\null	#\nul

Characters may also be written using their code point values. They can be written with as an octal number, such as #\10 for #\bs or #\177 for #\del.

If one prefers hex to octal, there is an additional syntax for character escapes: `#\xHHHH`
– the letter 'x' followed by a hexadecimal number of one to eight digits.

`char?` *x*   [Scheme Procedure]
`scm_char_p` (*x*)   [C Function]
    Return `#t` if *x* is a character, else `#f`.

Fundamentally, the character comparison operations below are numeric comparisons of
the character's code points.

`char=?` *x y*   [Scheme Procedure]
    Return `#t` if code point of *x* is equal to the code point of *y*, else `#f`.

`char<?` *x y*   [Scheme Procedure]
    Return `#t` if the code point of *x* is less than the code point of *y*, else `#f`.

`char<=?` *x y*   [Scheme Procedure]
    Return `#t` if the code point of *x* is less than or equal to the code point of *y*, else `#f`.

`char>?` *x y*   [Scheme Procedure]
    Return `#t` if the code point of *x* is greater than the code point of *y*, else `#f`.

`char>=?` *x y*   [Scheme Procedure]
    Return `#t` if the code point of *x* is greater than or equal to the code point of *y*, else
    `#f`.

Case-insensitive character comparisons use *Unicode case folding*. In case folding comparisons, if a character is lowercase and has an uppercase form that can be expressed as a single
character, it is converted to uppercase before comparison. All other characters undergo no
conversion before the comparison occurs. This includes the German sharp S (Eszett) which
is not uppercased before conversion because its uppercase form has two characters. Unicode
case folding is language independent: it uses rules that are generally true, but, it cannot
cover all cases for all languages.

`char-ci=?` *x y*   [Scheme Procedure]
    Return `#t` if the case-folded code point of *x* is the same as the case-folded code point
    of *y*, else `#f`.

`char-ci<?` *x y*   [Scheme Procedure]
    Return `#t` if the case-folded code point of *x* is less than the case-folded code point of
    y, else `#f`.

`char-ci<=?` *x y*   [Scheme Procedure]
    Return `#t` if the case-folded code point of *x* is less than or equal to the case-folded
    code point of *y*, else `#f`.

`char-ci>?` *x y*   [Scheme Procedure]
    Return `#t` if the case-folded code point of *x* is greater than the case-folded code point
    of *y*, else `#f`.

`char-ci>=?` *x y*   [Scheme Procedure]

> Return #t if the case-folded code point of *x* is greater than or equal to the case-folded code point of *y*, else #f.

`char-alphabetic?` *chr*   [Scheme Procedure]
`scm_char_alphabetic_p` (*chr*)   [C Function]

> Return #t if *chr* is alphabetic, else #f.

`char-numeric?` *chr*   [Scheme Procedure]
`scm_char_numeric_p` (*chr*)   [C Function]

> Return #t if *chr* is numeric, else #f.

`char-whitespace?` *chr*   [Scheme Procedure]
`scm_char_whitespace_p` (*chr*)   [C Function]

> Return #t if *chr* is whitespace, else #f.

`char-upper-case?` *chr*   [Scheme Procedure]
`scm_char_upper_case_p` (*chr*)   [C Function]

> Return #t if *chr* is uppercase, else #f.

`char-lower-case?` *chr*   [Scheme Procedure]
`scm_char_lower_case_p` (*chr*)   [C Function]

> Return #t if *chr* is lowercase, else #f.

`char-is-both?` *chr*   [Scheme Procedure]
`scm_char_is_both_p` (*chr*)   [C Function]

> Return #t if *chr* is either uppercase or lowercase, else #f.

`char-general-category` *chr*   [Scheme Procedure]
`scm_char_general_category` (*chr*)   [C Function]

> Return a symbol giving the two-letter name of the Unicode general category assigned to *chr* or #f if no named category is assigned. The following table provides a list of category names along with their meanings.

Lu	Uppercase letter	Pf	Final quote punctuation
Ll	Lowercase letter	Po	Other punctuation
Lt	Titlecase letter	Sm	Math symbol
Lm	Modifier letter	Sc	Currency symbol
Lo	Other letter	Sk	Modifier symbol
Mn	Non-spacing mark	So	Other symbol
Mc	Combining spacing mark	Zs	Space separator
Me	Enclosing mark	Zl	Line separator
Nd	Decimal digit number	Zp	Paragraph separator
Nl	Letter number	Cc	Control
No	Other number	Cf	Format
Pc	Connector punctuation	Cs	Surrogate
Pd	Dash punctuation	Co	Private use
Ps	Open punctuation	Cn	Unassigned
Pe	Close punctuation		
Pi	Initial quote punctuation		

`char->integer` *chr*   [Scheme Procedure]
`scm_char_to_integer` (*chr*)   [C Function]
> Return the code point of *chr*.

`integer->char` *n*   [Scheme Procedure]
`scm_integer_to_char` (*n*)   [C Function]
> Return the character that has code point *n*. The integer *n* must be a valid code point.
> Valid code points are in the ranges 0 to `#xD7FF` inclusive or `#xE000` to `#x10FFFF`
> inclusive.

`char-upcase` *chr*   [Scheme Procedure]
`scm_char_upcase` (*chr*)   [C Function]
> Return the uppercase character version of *chr*.

`char-downcase` *chr*   [Scheme Procedure]
`scm_char_downcase` (*chr*)   [C Function]
> Return the lowercase character version of *chr*.

`char-titlecase` *chr*   [Scheme Procedure]
`scm_char_titlecase` (*chr*)   [C Function]
> Return the titlecase character version of *chr* if one exists; otherwise return the up-
> percase version.
>
> For most characters these will be the same, but the Unicode Standard includes cer-
> tain digraph compatibility characters, such as U+01F3 "dz", for which the uppercase
> and titlecase characters are different (U+01F1 "DZ" and U+01F2 "Dz" in this case,
> respectively).

`scm_t_wchar scm_c_upcase` (*scm_t_wchar* **c**)   [C Function]
`scm_t_wchar scm_c_downcase` (*scm_t_wchar* **c**)   [C Function]
`scm_t_wchar scm_c_titlecase` (*scm_t_wchar* **c**)   [C Function]
> These C functions take an integer representation of a Unicode codepoint and return
> the codepoint corresponding to its uppercase, lowercase, and titlecase forms respec-
> tively. The type `scm_t_wchar` is a signed, 32-bit integer.

6.6.4 Character Sets

The features described in this section correspond directly to SRFI-14.

The data type *charset* implements sets of characters (see Section 6.6.3 [Characters],
page 129). Because the internal representation of character sets is not visible to the user, a
lot of procedures for handling them are provided.

Character sets can be created, extended, tested for the membership of a characters and
be compared to other character sets.

6.6.4.1 Character Set Predicates/Comparison

Use these procedures for testing whether an object is a character set, or whether several
character sets are equal or subsets of each other. `char-set-hash` can be used for calculating
a hash value, maybe for usage in fast lookup procedures.

char-set? *obj*   [Scheme Procedure]
scm_char_set_p (*obj*)   [C Function]
    Return #t if *obj* is a character set, #f otherwise.

char-set= *char_set* ...   [Scheme Procedure]
scm_char_set_eq (*char_sets*)   [C Function]
    Return #t if all given character sets are equal.

char-set<= *char_set* ...   [Scheme Procedure]
scm_char_set_leq (*char_sets*)   [C Function]
    Return #t if every character set *char_set*i is a subset of character set *char_set*i+1.

char-set-hash *cs* [*bound*]   [Scheme Procedure]
scm_char_set_hash (*cs, bound*)   [C Function]
    Compute a hash value for the character set *cs*. If *bound* is given and non-zero, it
    restricts the returned value to the range 0 ... *bound* - 1.

6.6.4.2 Iterating Over Character Sets

Character set cursors are a means for iterating over the members of a character sets. After
creating a character set cursor with char-set-cursor, a cursor can be dereferenced with
char-set-ref, advanced to the next member with char-set-cursor-next. Whether a
cursor has passed past the last element of the set can be checked with end-of-char-set?.

    Additionally, mapping and (un-)folding procedures for character sets are provided.

char-set-cursor *cs*   [Scheme Procedure]
scm_char_set_cursor (*cs*)   [C Function]
    Return a cursor into the character set *cs*.

char-set-ref *cs cursor*   [Scheme Procedure]
scm_char_set_ref (*cs, cursor*)   [C Function]
    Return the character at the current cursor position *cursor* in the character set *cs*. It
    is an error to pass a cursor for which end-of-char-set? returns true.

char-set-cursor-next *cs cursor*   [Scheme Procedure]
scm_char_set_cursor_next (*cs, cursor*)   [C Function]
    Advance the character set cursor *cursor* to the next character in the character set *cs*.
    It is an error if the cursor given satisfies end-of-char-set?.

end-of-char-set? *cursor*   [Scheme Procedure]
scm_end_of_char_set_p (*cursor*)   [C Function]
    Return #t if *cursor* has reached the end of a character set, #f otherwise.

char-set-fold *kons knil cs*   [Scheme Procedure]
scm_char_set_fold (*kons, knil, cs*)   [C Function]
    Fold the procedure *kons* over the character set *cs*, initializing it with *knil*.

char-set-unfold *p f g seed* [*base_cs*]   [Scheme Procedure]
scm_char_set_unfold (*p, f, g, seed, base_cs*)   [C Function]
    This is a fundamental constructor for character sets.

- *g* is used to generate a series of "seed" values from the initial seed: *seed*, (*g seed*), (*g^2 seed*), (*g^3 seed*), ...

- *p* tells us when to stop – when it returns true when applied to one of the seed values.

- *f* maps each seed value to a character. These characters are added to the base character set *base_cs* to form the result; *base_cs* defaults to the empty set.

char-set-unfold! *p f g seed base_cs*   [Scheme Procedure]
scm_char_set_unfold_x (*p, f, g, seed, base_cs*)   [C Function]
    This is a fundamental constructor for character sets.

- *g* is used to generate a series of "seed" values from the initial seed: *seed*, (*g seed*), (*g^2 seed*), (*g^3 seed*), ...

- *p* tells us when to stop – when it returns true when applied to one of the seed values.

- *f* maps each seed value to a character. These characters are added to the base character set *base_cs* to form the result; *base_cs* defaults to the empty set.

char-set-for-each *proc cs*   [Scheme Procedure]
scm_char_set_for_each (*proc, cs*)   [C Function]
    Apply *proc* to every character in the character set *cs*. The return value is not specified.

char-set-map *proc cs*   [Scheme Procedure]
scm_char_set_map (*proc, cs*)   [C Function]
    Map the procedure *proc* over every character in *cs*. *proc* must be a character -> character procedure.

6.6.4.3 Creating Character Sets

New character sets are produced with these procedures.

char-set-copy *cs*   [Scheme Procedure]
scm_char_set_copy (*cs*)   [C Function]
    Return a newly allocated character set containing all characters in *cs*.

char-set *chr* ...   [Scheme Procedure]
scm_char_set (*chrs*)   [C Function]
    Return a character set containing all given characters.

list->char-set *list* [*base_cs*]   [Scheme Procedure]
scm_list_to_char_set (*list, base_cs*)   [C Function]
    Convert the character list *list* to a character set. If the character set *base_cs* is given, the character in this set are also included in the result.

list->char-set! *list base_cs*   [Scheme Procedure]
scm_list_to_char_set_x (*list, base_cs*)   [C Function]
    Convert the character list *list* to a character set. The characters are added to *base_cs* and *base_cs* is returned.

`string->char-set` *str* [*base_cs*]   [Scheme Procedure]
`scm_string_to_char_set` (*str*, *base_cs*)   [C Function]
> Convert the string *str* to a character set. If the character set *base_cs* is given, the characters in this set are also included in the result.

`string->char-set!` *str base_cs*   [Scheme Procedure]
`scm_string_to_char_set_x` (*str*, *base_cs*)   [C Function]
> Convert the string *str* to a character set. The characters from the string are added to *base_cs*, and *base_cs* is returned.

`char-set-filter` *pred cs* [*base_cs*]   [Scheme Procedure]
`scm_char_set_filter` (*pred*, *cs*, *base_cs*)   [C Function]
> Return a character set containing every character from *cs* so that it satisfies *pred*. If provided, the characters from *base_cs* are added to the result.

`char-set-filter!` *pred cs base_cs*   [Scheme Procedure]
`scm_char_set_filter_x` (*pred*, *cs*, *base_cs*)   [C Function]
> Return a character set containing every character from *cs* so that it satisfies *pred*. The characters are added to *base_cs* and *base_cs* is returned.

`ucs-range->char-set` *lower upper* [*error* [*base_cs*]]   [Scheme Procedure]
`scm_ucs_range_to_char_set` (*lower*, *upper*, *error*, *base_cs*)   [C Function]
> Return a character set containing all characters whose character codes lie in the half-open range [*lower*,*upper*).
>
> If *error* is a true value, an error is signalled if the specified range contains characters which are not contained in the implemented character range. If *error* is `#f`, these characters are silently left out of the resulting character set.
>
> The characters in *base_cs* are added to the result, if given.

`ucs-range->char-set!` *lower upper error base_cs*   [Scheme Procedure]
`scm_ucs_range_to_char_set_x` (*lower*, *upper*, *error*, *base_cs*)   [C Function]
> Return a character set containing all characters whose character codes lie in the half-open range [*lower*,*upper*).
>
> If *error* is a true value, an error is signalled if the specified range contains characters which are not contained in the implemented character range. If *error* is `#f`, these characters are silently left out of the resulting character set.
>
> The characters are added to *base_cs* and *base_cs* is returned.

`->char-set` *x*   [Scheme Procedure]
`scm_to_char_set` (*x*)   [C Function]
> Coerces x into a char-set. x may be a string, character or char-set. A string is converted to the set of its constituent characters; a character is converted to a singleton set; a char-set is returned as-is.

6.6.4.4 Querying Character Sets

Access the elements and other information of a character set with these procedures.

`%char-set-dump` *cs*   [Scheme Procedure]

> Returns an association list containing debugging information for *cs*. The association
> list has the following entries.
>
> `char-set`   The char-set itself
>
> `len`   The number of groups of contiguous code points the char-set contains
>
> `ranges`   A list of lists where each sublist is a range of code points and their asso-
>   ciated characters
>
> The return value of this function cannot be relied upon to be consistent between
> versions of Guile and should not be used in code.

`char-set-size` *cs*   [Scheme Procedure]
`scm_char_set_size` (*cs*)   [C Function]

> Return the number of elements in character set *cs*.

`char-set-count` *pred cs*   [Scheme Procedure]
`scm_char_set_count` (*pred, cs*)   [C Function]

> Return the number of the elements int the character set *cs* which satisfy the predicate
> *pred*.

`char-set->list` *cs*   [Scheme Procedure]
`scm_char_set_to_list` (*cs*)   [C Function]

> Return a list containing the elements of the character set *cs*.

`char-set->string` *cs*   [Scheme Procedure]
`scm_char_set_to_string` (*cs*)   [C Function]

> Return a string containing the elements of the character set *cs*. The order in which
> the characters are placed in the string is not defined.

`char-set-contains?` *cs ch*   [Scheme Procedure]
`scm_char_set_contains_p` (*cs, ch*)   [C Function]

> Return `#t` if the character *ch* is contained in the character set *cs*, or `#f` otherwise.

`char-set-every` *pred cs*   [Scheme Procedure]
`scm_char_set_every` (*pred, cs*)   [C Function]

> Return a true value if every character in the character set *cs* satisfies the predicate
> *pred*.

`char-set-any` *pred cs*   [Scheme Procedure]
`scm_char_set_any` (*pred, cs*)   [C Function]

> Return a true value if any character in the character set *cs* satisfies the predicate
> *pred*.

6.6.4.5 Character-Set Algebra

Character sets can be manipulated with the common set algebra operation, such as union,
complement, intersection etc. All of these procedures provide side-effecting variants, which
modify their character set argument(s).

`char-set-adjoin` *cs chr* ...   [Scheme Procedure]
`scm_char_set_adjoin` (*cs, chrs*)   [C Function]
  Add all character arguments to the first argument, which must be a character set.

`char-set-delete` *cs chr* ...   [Scheme Procedure]
`scm_char_set_delete` (*cs, chrs*)   [C Function]
  Delete all character arguments from the first argument, which must be a character
  set.

`char-set-adjoin!` *cs chr* ...   [Scheme Procedure]
`scm_char_set_adjoin_x` (*cs, chrs*)   [C Function]
  Add all character arguments to the first argument, which must be a character set.

`char-set-delete!` *cs chr* ...   [Scheme Procedure]
`scm_char_set_delete_x` (*cs, chrs*)   [C Function]
  Delete all character arguments from the first argument, which must be a character
  set.

`char-set-complement` *cs*   [Scheme Procedure]
`scm_char_set_complement` (*cs*)   [C Function]
  Return the complement of the character set *cs*.

Note that the complement of a character set is likely to contain many reserved code
points (code points that are not associated with characters). It may be helpful to modify
the output of `char-set-complement` by computing its intersection with the set of designated
code points, `char-set:designated`.

`char-set-union` *cs* ...   [Scheme Procedure]
`scm_char_set_union` (*char_sets*)   [C Function]
  Return the union of all argument character sets.

`char-set-intersection` *cs* ...   [Scheme Procedure]
`scm_char_set_intersection` (*char_sets*)   [C Function]
  Return the intersection of all argument character sets.

`char-set-difference` *cs1 cs* ...   [Scheme Procedure]
`scm_char_set_difference` (*cs1, char_sets*)   [C Function]
  Return the difference of all argument character sets.

`char-set-xor` *cs* ...   [Scheme Procedure]
`scm_char_set_xor` (*char_sets*)   [C Function]
  Return the exclusive-or of all argument character sets.

`char-set-diff+intersection` *cs1 cs* ...   [Scheme Procedure]
`scm_char_set_diff_plus_intersection` (*cs1, char_sets*)   [C Function]
  Return the difference and the intersection of all argument character sets.

`char-set-complement!` *cs*   [Scheme Procedure]
`scm_char_set_complement_x` (*cs*)   [C Function]
  Return the complement of the character set *cs*.

char-set-union! *cs1 cs* ...   [Scheme Procedure]
scm_char_set_union_x (*cs1, char_sets*)   [C Function]
    Return the union of all argument character sets.

char-set-intersection! *cs1 cs* ...   [Scheme Procedure]
scm_char_set_intersection_x (*cs1, char_sets*)   [C Function]
    Return the intersection of all argument character sets.

char-set-difference! *cs1 cs* ...   [Scheme Procedure]
scm_char_set_difference_x (*cs1, char_sets*)   [C Function]
    Return the difference of all argument character sets.

char-set-xor! *cs1 cs* ...   [Scheme Procedure]
scm_char_set_xor_x (*cs1, char_sets*)   [C Function]
    Return the exclusive-or of all argument character sets.

char-set-diff+intersection! *cs1 cs2 cs* ...   [Scheme Procedure]
scm_char_set_diff_plus_intersection_x (*cs1, cs2, char_sets*)   [C Function]
    Return the difference and the intersection of all argument character sets.

6.6.4.6 Standard Character Sets

In order to make the use of the character set data type and procedures useful, several
predefined character set variables exist.

These character sets are locale independent and are not recomputed upon a `setlocale`
call. They contain characters from the whole range of Unicode code points. For instance,
`char-set:letter` contains about 100,000 characters.

char-set:lower-case   [Scheme Variable]
scm_char_set_lower_case   [C Variable]
    All lower-case characters.

char-set:upper-case   [Scheme Variable]
scm_char_set_upper_case   [C Variable]
    All upper-case characters.

char-set:title-case   [Scheme Variable]
scm_char_set_title_case   [C Variable]
    All single characters that function as if they were an upper-case letter followed by a
    lower-case letter.

char-set:letter   [Scheme Variable]
scm_char_set_letter   [C Variable]
    All letters. This includes `char-set:lower-case`, `char-set:upper-case`,
    `char-set:title-case`, and many letters that have no case at all. For example,
    Chinese and Japanese characters typically have no concept of case.

char-set:digit   [Scheme Variable]
scm_char_set_digit   [C Variable]
    All digits.

`char-set:letter+digit`   [Scheme Variable]
`scm_char_set_letter_and_digit`   [C Variable]
> The union of `char-set:letter` and `char-set:digit`.

`char-set:graphic`   [Scheme Variable]
`scm_char_set_graphic`   [C Variable]
> All characters which would put ink on the paper.

`char-set:printing`   [Scheme Variable]
`scm_char_set_printing`   [C Variable]
> The union of `char-set:graphic` and `char-set:whitespace`.

`char-set:whitespace`   [Scheme Variable]
`scm_char_set_whitespace`   [C Variable]
> All whitespace characters.

`char-set:blank`   [Scheme Variable]
`scm_char_set_blank`   [C Variable]
> All horizontal whitespace characters, which notably includes `#\space` and `#\tab`.

`char-set:iso-control`   [Scheme Variable]
`scm_char_set_iso_control`   [C Variable]
> The ISO control characters are the C0 control characters (U+0000 to U+001F), delete (U+007F), and the C1 control characters (U+0080 to U+009F).

`char-set:punctuation`   [Scheme Variable]
`scm_char_set_punctuation`   [C Variable]
> All punctuation characters, such as the characters `!"#%&'()*,-./:;?@[\\]_{}`

`char-set:symbol`   [Scheme Variable]
`scm_char_set_symbol`   [C Variable]
> All symbol characters, such as the characters `$+<=>^`|~`.

`char-set:hex-digit`   [Scheme Variable]
`scm_char_set_hex_digit`   [C Variable]
> The hexadecimal digits `0123456789abcdefABCDEF`.

`char-set:ascii`   [Scheme Variable]
`scm_char_set_ascii`   [C Variable]
> All ASCII characters.

`char-set:empty`   [Scheme Variable]
`scm_char_set_empty`   [C Variable]
> The empty character set.

`char-set:designated`   [Scheme Variable]
`scm_char_set_designated`   [C Variable]
> This character set contains all designated code points. This includes all the code points to which Unicode has assigned a character or other meaning.

char-set:full   [Scheme Variable]
scm_char_set_full   [C Variable]
> This character set contains all possible code points. This includes both designated
> and reserved code points.

6.6.5 Strings

Strings are fixed-length sequences of characters. They can be created by calling constructor
procedures, but they can also literally get entered at the REPL or in Scheme source files.

Strings always carry the information about how many characters they are composed of
with them, so there is no special end-of-string character, like in C. That means that Scheme
strings can contain any character, even the '#\nul' character '\0'.

To use strings efficiently, you need to know a bit about how Guile implements them. In
Guile, a string consists of two parts, a head and the actual memory where the characters
are stored. When a string (or a substring of it) is copied, only a new head gets created, the
memory is usually not copied. The two heads start out pointing to the same memory.

When one of these two strings is modified, as with **string-set!**, their common memory does get copied so that each string has its own memory and modifying one does not
accidentally modify the other as well. Thus, Guile's strings are 'copy on write'; the actual
copying of their memory is delayed until one string is written to.

This implementation makes functions like **substring** very efficient in the common case
that no modifications are done to the involved strings.

If you do know that your strings are getting modified right away, you can use
substring/copy instead of **substring**. This function performs the copy immediately at
the time of creation. This is more efficient, especially in a multi-threaded program. Also,
substring/copy can avoid the problem that a short substring holds on to the memory of
a very large original string that could otherwise be recycled.

If you want to avoid the copy altogether, so that modifications of one string show up in
the other, you can use **substring/shared**. The strings created by this procedure are called
mutation sharing substrings since the substring and the original string share modifications
to each other.

If you want to prevent modifications, use **substring/read-only**.

Guile provides all procedures of SRFI-13 and a few more.

6.6.5.1 String Read Syntax

The read syntax for strings is an arbitrarily long sequence of characters enclosed in double
quotes (").

Backslash is an escape character and can be used to insert the following special charac-
ters. \" and \\ are R5RS standard, \| is R7RS standard, the next seven are R6RS standard
— notice they follow C syntax — and the remaining four are Guile extensions.

\\   Backslash character.

\"   Double quote character (an unescaped " is otherwise the end of the string).

\| Vertical bar character.

\a   Bell character (ASCII 7).

\f   Formfeed character (ASCII 12).

\n   Newline character (ASCII 10).

\r   Carriage return character (ASCII 13).

\t   Tab character (ASCII 9).

\v   Vertical tab character (ASCII 11).

\b   Backspace character (ASCII 8).

\0   NUL character (ASCII 0).

\ followed by newline (ASCII 10)

Nothing. This way if \ is the last character in a line, the string will continue with the first character from the next line, without a line break.

If the `hungry-eol-escapes` reader option is enabled, which is not the case by default, leading whitespace on the next line is discarded.

```
"foo\
  bar"
⇒ "foo  bar"
(read-enable 'hungry-eol-escapes)
"foo\
  bar"
⇒ "foobar"
```

\xHH   Character code given by two hexadecimal digits. For example \x7f for an ASCII DEL (127).

\uHHHH   Character code given by four hexadecimal digits. For example \u0100 for a capital A with macron (U+0100).

\UHHHHHH   Character code given by six hexadecimal digits. For example \U010402.

The following are examples of string literals:

```
"foo"
"bar plonk"
"Hello World"
"\"Hi\", he said."
```

The three escape sequences \xHH, \uHHHH and \UHHHHHH were chosen to not break compatibility with code written for previous versions of Guile. The R6RS specification suggests a different, incompatible syntax for hex escapes: \xHHHH; – a character code followed by one to eight hexadecimal digits terminated with a semicolon. If this escape format is desired instead, it can be enabled with the reader option `r6rs-hex-escapes`.

```
(read-enable 'r6rs-hex-escapes)
```

For more on reader options, See Section 6.17.2 [Scheme Read], page 360.

6.6.5.2 String Predicates

The following procedures can be used to check whether a given string fulfills some specified property.

string? *obj*   [Scheme Procedure]
scm_string_p (*obj*)   [C Function]
>   Return #t if *obj* is a string, else #f.

int scm_is_string (*SCM obj*)   [C Function]
>   Returns 1 if *obj* is a string, 0 otherwise.

string-null? *str*   [Scheme Procedure]
scm_string_null_p (*str*)   [C Function]
>   Return #t if *str*'s length is zero, and #f otherwise.
>
>    ```
>    (string-null? "")   ⇒ #t
>    y                   ⇒ "foo"
>    (string-null? y)    ⇒ #f
>    ```

string-any *char_pred s* [*start* [*end*]]   [Scheme Procedure]
scm_string_any (*char_pred, s, start, end*)   [C Function]
>   Check if *char_pred* is true for any character in string *s*.
>
>   *char_pred* can be a character to check for any equal to that, or a character set (see
>   Section 6.6.4 [Character Sets], page 133) to check for any in that set, or a predicate
>   procedure to call.
>
>   For a procedure, calls (`char_pred c`) are made successively on the characters from
>   *start* to *end*. If *char_pred* returns true (ie. non-#f), string-any stops and that return
>   value is the return from string-any. The call on the last character (ie. at *end* − 1),
>   if that point is reached, is a tail call.
>
>   If there are no characters in *s* (ie. *start* equals *end*) then the return is #f.

string-every *char_pred s* [*start* [*end*]]   [Scheme Procedure]
scm_string_every (*char_pred, s, start, end*)   [C Function]
>   Check if *char_pred* is true for every character in string *s*.
>
>   *char_pred* can be a character to check for every character equal to that, or a character
>   set (see Section 6.6.4 [Character Sets], page 133) to check for every character being
>   in that set, or a predicate procedure to call.
>
>   For a procedure, calls (`char_pred c`) are made successively on the characters from
>   *start* to *end*. If *char_pred* returns #f, string-every stops and returns #f. The call
>   on the last character (ie. at *end* − 1), if that point is reached, is a tail call and the
>   return from that call is the return from string-every.
>
>   If there are no characters in *s* (ie. *start* equals *end*) then the return is #t.

6.6.5.3 String Constructors

The string constructor procedures create new string objects, possibly initializing them with
some specified character data. See also See Section 6.6.5.5 [String Selection], page 145, for
ways to create strings from existing strings.

string *char*...   [Scheme Procedure]
>   Return a newly allocated string made from the given character arguments.
>
>    ```
>    (string #\x #\y #\z) ⇒ "xyz"
>    (string)             ⇒ ""
>    ```

`list->string` *lst*   [Scheme Procedure]
`scm_string` (*lst*)   [C Function]
> Return a newly allocated string made from a list of characters.
>
>   (list->string '(#\a #\b #\c)) ⇒ "abc"

`reverse-list->string` *lst*   [Scheme Procedure]
`scm_reverse_list_to_string` (*lst*)   [C Function]
> Return a newly allocated string made from a list of characters, in reverse order.
>
>   (reverse-list->string '(#\a #\B #\c)) ⇒ "cBa"

`make-string` *k* [*chr*]   [Scheme Procedure]
`scm_make_string` (*k*, *chr*)   [C Function]
> Return a newly allocated string of length *k*. If *chr* is given, then all elements of the
> string are initialized to *chr*, otherwise the contents of the string are unspecified.

`SCM scm_c_make_string` (*size_t len*, *SCM chr*)   [C Function]
> Like `scm_make_string`, but expects the length as a `size_t`.

`string-tabulate` *proc len*   [Scheme Procedure]
`scm_string_tabulate` (*proc*, *len*)   [C Function]
> *proc* is an integer->char procedure. Construct a string of size *len* by applying *proc* to
> each index to produce the corresponding string element. The order in which *proc* is
> applied to the indices is not specified.

`string-join` *ls* [*delimiter* [*grammar*]]   [Scheme Procedure]
`scm_string_join` (*ls*, *delimiter*, *grammar*)   [C Function]
> Append the string in the string list *ls*, using the string *delimiter* as a delimiter between
> the elements of *ls*. *grammar* is a symbol which specifies how the delimiter is placed
> between the strings, and defaults to the symbol `infix`.
>
> `infix`   Insert the separator between list elements. An empty string will produce
>   an empty list.
>
> `strict-infix`
>   Like `infix`, but will raise an error if given the empty list.
>
> `suffix`   Insert the separator after every list element.
>
> `prefix`   Insert the separator before each list element.

6.6.5.4 List/String conversion

When processing strings, it is often convenient to first convert them into a list representation
by using the procedure `string->list`, work with the resulting list, and then convert it back
into a string. These procedures are useful for similar tasks.

`string->list` *str* [*start* [*end*]]   [Scheme Procedure]
`scm_substring_to_list` (*str*, *start*, *end*)   [C Function]
`scm_string_to_list` (*str*)   [C Function]
> Convert the string *str* into a list of characters.

`string-split` *str char_pred*   [Scheme Procedure]
`scm_string_split` (*str, char_pred*)   [C Function]

> Split the string *str* into a list of substrings delimited by appearances of characters that

- equal *char_pred*, if it is a character,

- satisfy the predicate *char_pred*, if it is a procedure,

- are in the set *char_pred*, if it is a character set.

> Note that an empty substring between separator characters will result in an empty string in the result list.

```
(string-split "root:x:0:0:root:/root:/bin/bash" #\:)
⇒
("root" "x" "0" "0" "root" "/root" "/bin/bash")

(string-split "::" #\:)
⇒
("" "" "")

(string-split "" #\:)
⇒
("")
```

6.6.5.5 String Selection

Portions of strings can be extracted by these procedures. `string-ref` delivers individual characters whereas `substring` can be used to extract substrings from longer strings.

`string-length` *string*   [Scheme Procedure]
`scm_string_length` (*string*)   [C Function]

> Return the number of characters in *string*.

`size_t scm_c_string_length` (*SCM str*)   [C Function]

> Return the number of characters in *str* as a `size_t`.

`string-ref` *str k*   [Scheme Procedure]
`scm_string_ref` (*str, k*)   [C Function]

> Return character *k* of *str* using zero-origin indexing. *k* must be a valid index of *str*.

`SCM scm_c_string_ref` (*SCM str, size_t k*)   [C Function]

> Return character *k* of *str* using zero-origin indexing. *k* must be a valid index of *str*.

`string-copy` *str* [*start* [*end*]]   [Scheme Procedure]
`scm_substring_copy` (*str, start, end*)   [C Function]
`scm_string_copy` (*str*)   [C Function]

> Return a copy of the given string *str*.

> The returned string shares storage with *str* initially, but it is copied as soon as one of the two strings is modified.

`substring` *str start* [*end*]   [Scheme Procedure]
`scm_substring` (*str, start, end*)   [C Function]
> Return a new string formed from the characters of *str* beginning with index *start* (inclusive) and ending with index *end* (exclusive). *str* must be a string, *start* and *end* must be exact integers satisfying:
>
> 0 <= *start* <= *end* <= (`string-length str`).
>
> The returned string shares storage with *str* initially, but it is copied as soon as one of the two strings is modified.

`substring/shared` *str start* [*end*]   [Scheme Procedure]
`scm_substring_shared` (*str, start, end*)   [C Function]
> Like `substring`, but the strings continue to share their storage even if they are modified. Thus, modifications to *str* show up in the new string, and vice versa.

`substring/copy` *str start* [*end*]   [Scheme Procedure]
`scm_substring_copy` (*str, start, end*)   [C Function]
> Like `substring`, but the storage for the new string is copied immediately.

`substring/read-only` *str start* [*end*]   [Scheme Procedure]
`scm_substring_read_only` (*str, start, end*)   [C Function]
> Like `substring`, but the resulting string can not be modified.

SCM `scm_c_substring` (*SCM str, size_t start, size_t end*)   [C Function]
SCM `scm_c_substring_shared` (*SCM str, size_t start, size_t end*) [C Function]
SCM `scm_c_substring_copy` (*SCM str, size_t start, size_t end*) [C Function]
SCM `scm_c_substring_read_only` (*SCM str, size_t start, size_t end*) [C Function]
> Like `scm_substring`, etc. but the bounds are given as a `size_t`.

`string-take` *s n*   [Scheme Procedure]
`scm_string_take` (*s, n*)   [C Function]
> Return the *n* first characters of *s*.

`string-drop` *s n*   [Scheme Procedure]
`scm_string_drop` (*s, n*)   [C Function]
> Return all but the first *n* characters of *s*.

`string-take-right` *s n*   [Scheme Procedure]
`scm_string_take_right` (*s, n*)   [C Function]
> Return the *n* last characters of *s*.

`string-drop-right` *s n*   [Scheme Procedure]
`scm_string_drop_right` (*s, n*)   [C Function]
> Return all but the last *n* characters of *s*.

`string-pad` *s len* [*chr* [*start* [*end*]]]   [Scheme Procedure]
`string-pad-right` *s len* [*chr* [*start* [*end*]]]   [Scheme Procedure]
`scm_string_pad` (*s, len, chr, start, end*)   [C Function]
`scm_string_pad_right` (*s, len, chr, start, end*)   [C Function]
> Take characters *start* to *end* from the string *s* and either pad with *chr* or truncate them to give *len* characters.
>
> `string-pad` pads or truncates on the left, so for example

```
(string-pad "x" 3)     ⇒ "  x"
(string-pad "abcde" 3) ⇒ "cde"
```

string-pad-right pads or truncates on the right, so for example

```
(string-pad-right "x" 3)     ⇒ "x  "
(string-pad-right "abcde" 3) ⇒ "abc"
```

string-trim *s [char_pred [start [end]]]*   [Scheme Procedure]
string-trim-right *s [char_pred [start [end]]]*   [Scheme Procedure]
string-trim-both *s [char_pred [start [end]]]*   [Scheme Procedure]
scm_string_trim *(s, char_pred, start, end)*   [C Function]
scm_string_trim_right *(s, char_pred, start, end)*   [C Function]
scm_string_trim_both *(s, char_pred, start, end)*   [C Function]

> Trim occurrences of *char_pred* from the ends of *s*.
>
> string-trim trims *char_pred* characters from the left (start) of the string, string-trim-right trims them from the right (end) of the string, string-trim-both trims from both ends.
>
> *char_pred* can be a character, a character set, or a predicate procedure to call on each character. If *char_pred* is not given the default is whitespace as per char-set:whitespace (see Section 6.6.4.6 [Standard Character Sets], page 139).
>
> ```
> (string-trim " x ")                     ⇒ "x "
> (string-trim-right "banana" #\a) ⇒ "banan"
> (string-trim-both ".,xy:;" char-set:punctuation)
>                          ⇒ "xy"
> (string-trim-both "xyzzy" (lambda (c)
>                            (or (eqv? c #\x)
>                                (eqv? c #\y))))
>                          ⇒ "zz"
> ```

6.6.5.6 String Modification

These procedures are for modifying strings in-place. This means that the result of the operation is not a new string; instead, the original string's memory representation is modified.

string-set! *str k chr*   [Scheme Procedure]
scm_string_set_x *(str, k, chr)*   [C Function]

> Store *chr* in element *k* of *str* and return an unspecified value. *k* must be a valid index of *str*.

void scm_c_string_set_x *(SCM str, size_t k, SCM chr)*   [C Function]

> Like scm_string_set_x, but the index is given as a size_t.

string-fill! *str chr [start [end]]*   [Scheme Procedure]
scm_substring_fill_x *(str, chr, start, end)*   [C Function]
scm_string_fill_x *(str, chr)*   [C Function]

> Stores *chr* in every element of the given *str* and returns an unspecified value.

substring-fill! *str start end fill*   [Scheme Procedure]
scm_substring_fill_x *(str, start, end, fill)*   [C Function]

> Change every character in *str* between *start* and *end* to *fill*.

```
(define y (string-copy "abcdefg"))
(substring-fill! y 1 3 #\r)
y
⇒ "arrdefg"
```

substring-move! *str1 start1 end1 str2 start2*   [Scheme Procedure]
scm_substring_move_x (*str1, start1, end1, str2, start2*)   [C Function]
    Copy the substring of *str1* bounded by *start1* and *end1* into *str2* beginning at position *start2*. *str1* and *str2* can be the same string.

string-copy! *target tstart s* [*start* [*end*]]   [Scheme Procedure]
scm_string_copy_x (*target, tstart, s, start, end*)   [C Function]
    Copy the sequence of characters from index range [*start, end*) in string *s* to string *target*, beginning at index *tstart*. The characters are copied left-to-right or right-to-left as needed – the copy is guaranteed to work, even if *target* and *s* are the same string. It is an error if the copy operation runs off the end of the target string.

6.6.5.7 String Comparison

The procedures in this section are similar to the character ordering predicates (see Section 6.6.3 [Characters], page 129), but are defined on character sequences.

The first set is specified in R5RS and has names that end in **?**. The second set is specified in SRFI-13 and the names have not ending **?**.

The predicates ending in **-ci** ignore the character case when comparing strings. For now, case-insensitive comparison is done using the R5RS rules, where every lower-case character that has a single character upper-case form is converted to uppercase before comparison. See See Section 6.24.2 [Text Collation], page 437, for locale-dependent string comparison.

string=? *s1 s2 s3 ...*   [Scheme Procedure]
    Lexicographic equality predicate; return **#t** if all strings are the same length and contain the same characters in the same positions, otherwise return **#f**.

    The procedure **string-ci=?** treats upper and lower case letters as though they were the same character, but **string=?** treats upper and lower case as distinct characters.

string<? *s1 s2 s3 ...*   [Scheme Procedure]
    Lexicographic ordering predicate; return **#t** if, for every pair of consecutive string arguments *str_i* and *str_i+1*, *str_i* is lexicographically less than *str_i+1*.

string<=? *s1 s2 s3 ...*   [Scheme Procedure]
    Lexicographic ordering predicate; return **#t** if, for every pair of consecutive string arguments *str_i* and *str_i+1*, *str_i* is lexicographically less than or equal to *str_i+1*.

string>? *s1 s2 s3 ...*   [Scheme Procedure]
    Lexicographic ordering predicate; return **#t** if, for every pair of consecutive string arguments *str_i* and *str_i+1*, *str_i* is lexicographically greater than *str_i+1*.

string>=? *s1 s2 s3 ...*   [Scheme Procedure]
    Lexicographic ordering predicate; return **#t** if, for every pair of consecutive string arguments *str_i* and *str_i+1*, *str_i* is lexicographically greater than or equal to *str_i+1*.

`string-ci=?` *s1 s2 s3 ...*   [Scheme Procedure]
> Case-insensitive string equality predicate; return `#t` if all strings are the same length and their component characters match (ignoring case) at each position; otherwise return `#f`.

`string-ci<?` *s1 s2 s3 ...*   [Scheme Procedure]
> Case insensitive lexicographic ordering predicate; return `#t` if, for every pair of consecutive string arguments *str_i* and *str_i+1*, *str_i* is lexicographically less than *str_i+1* regardless of case.

`string-ci<=?` *s1 s2 s3 ...*   [Scheme Procedure]
> Case insensitive lexicographic ordering predicate; return `#t` if, for every pair of consecutive string arguments *str_i* and *str_i+1*, *str_i* is lexicographically less than or equal to *str_i+1* regardless of case.

`string-ci>?` *s1 s2 s3 ...*   [Scheme Procedure]
> Case insensitive lexicographic ordering predicate; return `#t` if, for every pair of consecutive string arguments *str_i* and *str_i+1*, *str_i* is lexicographically greater than *str_i+1* regardless of case.

`string-ci>=?` *s1 s2 s3 ...*   [Scheme Procedure]
> Case insensitive lexicographic ordering predicate; return `#t` if, for every pair of consecutive string arguments *str_i* and *str_i+1*, *str_i* is lexicographically greater than or equal to *str_i+1* regardless of case.

`string-compare` *s1 s2 proc_lt proc_eq proc_gt [start1 [end1*   [Scheme Procedure]
       [start2 [end2]]]]
`scm_string_compare` *(s1, s2, proc_lt, proc_eq, proc_gt, start1, end1,*   [C Function]
       start2, end2)
> Apply *proc_lt*, *proc_eq*, *proc_gt* to the mismatch index, depending upon whether *s1* is less than, equal to, or greater than *s2*. The mismatch index is the largest index *i* such that for every $0 <= j < i$, $s1[j] = s2[j]$ – that is, *i* is the first position that does not match.

`string-compare-ci` *s1 s2 proc_lt proc_eq proc_gt [start1 [end1*   [Scheme Procedure]
       [start2 [end2]]]]
`scm_string_compare_ci` *(s1, s2, proc_lt, proc_eq, proc_gt, start1,*   [C Function]
       end1, start2, end2)
> Apply *proc_lt*, *proc_eq*, *proc_gt* to the mismatch index, depending upon whether *s1* is less than, equal to, or greater than *s2*. The mismatch index is the largest index *i* such that for every $0 <= j < i$, $s1[j] = s2[j]$ – that is, *i* is the first position where the lowercased letters do not match.

`string=` *s1 s2 [start1 [end1 [start2 [end2]]]]*   [Scheme Procedure]
`scm_string_eq` *(s1, s2, start1, end1, start2, end2)*   [C Function]
> Return `#f` if *s1* and *s2* are not equal, a true value otherwise.

`string<>` *s1 s2 [start1 [end1 [start2 [end2]]]]*   [Scheme Procedure]
`scm_string_neq` *(s1, s2, start1, end1, start2, end2)*   [C Function]
> Return `#f` if *s1* and *s2* are equal, a true value otherwise.

`string< ` *s1 s2* [*start1* [*end1* [*start2* [*end2*]]]]   [Scheme Procedure]
`scm_string_lt ` (*s1, s2, start1, end1, start2, end2*)   [C Function]
> Return #f if *s1* is greater or equal to *s2*, a true value otherwise.

`string> ` *s1 s2* [*start1* [*end1* [*start2* [*end2*]]]]   [Scheme Procedure]
`scm_string_gt ` (*s1, s2, start1, end1, start2, end2*)   [C Function]
> Return #f if *s1* is less or equal to *s2*, a true value otherwise.

`string<= ` *s1 s2* [*start1* [*end1* [*start2* [*end2*]]]]   [Scheme Procedure]
`scm_string_le ` (*s1, s2, start1, end1, start2, end2*)   [C Function]
> Return #f if *s1* is greater to *s2*, a true value otherwise.

`string>= ` *s1 s2* [*start1* [*end1* [*start2* [*end2*]]]]   [Scheme Procedure]
`scm_string_ge ` (*s1, s2, start1, end1, start2, end2*)   [C Function]
> Return #f if *s1* is less to *s2*, a true value otherwise.

`string-ci= ` *s1 s2* [*start1* [*end1* [*start2* [*end2*]]]]   [Scheme Procedure]
`scm_string_ci_eq ` (*s1, s2, start1, end1, start2, end2*)   [C Function]
> Return #f if *s1* and *s2* are not equal, a true value otherwise. The character comparison is done case-insensitively.

`string-ci<> ` *s1 s2* [*start1* [*end1* [*start2* [*end2*]]]]   [Scheme Procedure]
`scm_string_ci_neq ` (*s1, s2, start1, end1, start2, end2*)   [C Function]
> Return #f if *s1* and *s2* are equal, a true value otherwise. The character comparison is done case-insensitively.

`string-ci< ` *s1 s2* [*start1* [*end1* [*start2* [*end2*]]]]   [Scheme Procedure]
`scm_string_ci_lt ` (*s1, s2, start1, end1, start2, end2*)   [C Function]
> Return #f if *s1* is greater or equal to *s2*, a true value otherwise. The character comparison is done case-insensitively.

`string-ci> ` *s1 s2* [*start1* [*end1* [*start2* [*end2*]]]]   [Scheme Procedure]
`scm_string_ci_gt ` (*s1, s2, start1, end1, start2, end2*)   [C Function]
> Return #f if *s1* is less or equal to *s2*, a true value otherwise. The character comparison is done case-insensitively.

`string-ci<= ` *s1 s2* [*start1* [*end1* [*start2* [*end2*]]]]   [Scheme Procedure]
`scm_string_ci_le ` (*s1, s2, start1, end1, start2, end2*)   [C Function]
> Return #f if *s1* is greater to *s2*, a true value otherwise. The character comparison is done case-insensitively.

`string-ci>= ` *s1 s2* [*start1* [*end1* [*start2* [*end2*]]]]   [Scheme Procedure]
`scm_string_ci_ge ` (*s1, s2, start1, end1, start2, end2*)   [C Function]
> Return #f if *s1* is less to *s2*, a true value otherwise. The character comparison is done case-insensitively.

`string-hash ` *s* [*bound* [*start* [*end*]]]   [Scheme Procedure]
`scm_substring_hash ` (*s, bound, start, end*)   [C Function]
> Compute a hash value for *s*. The optional argument *bound* is a non-negative exact integer specifying the range of the hash function. A positive value restricts the return value to the range [0,bound).

`string-hash-ci` *s* [*bound* [*start* [*end*]]]   [Scheme Procedure]
`scm_substring_hash_ci` (*s, bound, start, end*)   [C Function]
    Compute a hash value for *s*. The optional argument *bound* is a non-negative exact
    integer specifying the range of the hash function. A positive value restricts the return
    value to the range [0,bound).

Because the same visual appearance of an abstract Unicode character can be obtained
via multiple sequences of Unicode characters, even the case-insensitive string comparison
functions described above may return `#f` when presented with strings containing different
representations of the same character. For example, the Unicode character "LATIN SMALL
LETTER S WITH DOT BELOW AND DOT ABOVE" can be represented with a single
character (U+1E69) or by the character "LATIN SMALL LETTER S" (U+0073) followed by
the combining marks "COMBINING DOT BELOW" (U+0323) and "COMBINING DOT
ABOVE" (U+0307).

For this reason, it is often desirable to ensure that the strings to be compared are using
a mutually consistent representation for every character. The Unicode standard defines two
methods of normalizing the contents of strings: Decomposition, which breaks composite
characters into a set of constituent characters with an ordering defined by the Unicode
Standard; and composition, which performs the converse.

There are two decomposition operations. "Canonical decomposition" produces character
sequences that share the same visual appearance as the original characters, while "compatibility decomposition" produces ones whose visual appearances may differ from the originals
but which represent the same abstract character.

These operations are encapsulated in the following set of normalization forms:

NFD   Characters are decomposed to their canonical forms.

NFKD   Characters are decomposed to their compatibility forms.

NFC   Characters are decomposed to their canonical forms, then composed.

NFKC   Characters are decomposed to their compatibility forms, then composed.

The functions below put their arguments into one of the forms described above.

`string-normalize-nfd` *s*   [Scheme Procedure]
`scm_string_normalize_nfd` (*s*)   [C Function]
    Return the `NFD` normalized form of *s*.

`string-normalize-nfkd` *s*   [Scheme Procedure]
`scm_string_normalize_nfkd` (*s*)   [C Function]
    Return the `NFKD` normalized form of *s*.

`string-normalize-nfc` *s*   [Scheme Procedure]
`scm_string_normalize_nfc` (*s*)   [C Function]
    Return the `NFC` normalized form of *s*.

`string-normalize-nfkc` *s*   [Scheme Procedure]
`scm_string_normalize_nfkc` (*s*)   [C Function]
    Return the `NFKC` normalized form of *s*.

6.6.5.8 String Searching

string-index *s char_pred* [*start* [*end*]]   [Scheme Procedure]
scm_string_index (*s, char_pred, start, end*)   [C Function]
    Search through the string *s* from left to right, returning the index of the first occur-
    rence of a character which

- equals *char_pred*, if it is character,
- satisfies the predicate *char_pred*, if it is a procedure,
- is in the set *char_pred*, if it is a character set.

    Return **#f** if no match is found.

string-rindex *s char_pred* [*start* [*end*]]   [Scheme Procedure]
scm_string_rindex (*s, char_pred, start, end*)   [C Function]
    Search through the string *s* from right to left, returning the index of the last occurrence
    of a character which

- equals *char_pred*, if it is character,
- satisfies the predicate *char_pred*, if it is a procedure,
- is in the set if *char_pred* is a character set.

    Return **#f** if no match is found.

string-prefix-length *s1 s2* [*start1* [*end1* [*start2* [*end2*]]]]   [Scheme Procedure]
scm_string_prefix_length (*s1, s2, start1, end1, start2, end2*)   [C Function]
    Return the length of the longest common prefix of the two strings.

string-prefix-length-ci *s1 s2* [*start1* [*end1* [*start2* [*end2*]]]]   [Scheme Procedure]
scm_string_prefix_length_ci (*s1, s2, start1, end1, start2, end2*)   [C Function]
    Return the length of the longest common prefix of the two strings, ignoring character
    case.

string-suffix-length *s1 s2* [*start1* [*end1* [*start2* [*end2*]]]]   [Scheme Procedure]
scm_string_suffix_length (*s1, s2, start1, end1, start2, end2*)   [C Function]
    Return the length of the longest common suffix of the two strings.

string-suffix-length-ci *s1 s2* [*start1* [*end1* [*start2* [*end2*]]]]   [Scheme Procedure]
scm_string_suffix_length_ci (*s1, s2, start1, end1, start2, end2*)   [C Function]
    Return the length of the longest common suffix of the two strings, ignoring character
    case.

string-prefix? *s1 s2* [*start1* [*end1* [*start2* [*end2*]]]]   [Scheme Procedure]
scm_string_prefix_p (*s1, s2, start1, end1, start2, end2*)   [C Function]
    Is *s1* a prefix of *s2*?

string-prefix-ci? *s1 s2* [*start1* [*end1* [*start2* [*end2*]]]]   [Scheme Procedure]
scm_string_prefix_ci_p (*s1, s2, start1, end1, start2, end2*)   [C Function]
    Is *s1* a prefix of *s2*, ignoring character case?

string-suffix? *s1 s2* [*start1* [*end1* [*start2* [*end2*]]]]   [Scheme Procedure]
scm_string_suffix_p (*s1, s2, start1, end1, start2, end2*)   [C Function]
    Is *s1* a suffix of *s2*?

`string-suffix-ci?` *s1 s2* [*start1* [*end1* [*start2* [*end2*]]]]   [Scheme Procedure]
`scm_string_suffix_ci_p` (*s1, s2, start1, end1, start2, end2*)   [C Function]
> Is *s1* a suffix of *s2*, ignoring character case?

`string-index-right` *s char_pred* [*start* [*end*]]   [Scheme Procedure]
`scm_string_index_right` (*s, char_pred, start, end*)   [C Function]
> Search through the string *s* from right to left, returning the index of the last occurrence of a character which
>
> - equals *char_pred*, if it is character,
> - satisfies the predicate *char_pred*, if it is a procedure,
> - is in the set if *char_pred* is a character set.
>
> Return #f if no match is found.

`string-skip` *s char_pred* [*start* [*end*]]   [Scheme Procedure]
`scm_string_skip` (*s, char_pred, start, end*)   [C Function]
> Search through the string *s* from left to right, returning the index of the first occurrence of a character which
>
> - does not equal *char_pred*, if it is character,
> - does not satisfy the predicate *char_pred*, if it is a procedure,
> - is not in the set if *char_pred* is a character set.

`string-skip-right` *s char_pred* [*start* [*end*]]   [Scheme Procedure]
`scm_string_skip_right` (*s, char_pred, start, end*)   [C Function]
> Search through the string *s* from right to left, returning the index of the last occurrence of a character which
>
> - does not equal *char_pred*, if it is character,
> - does not satisfy the predicate *char_pred*, if it is a procedure,
> - is not in the set if *char_pred* is a character set.

`string-count` *s char_pred* [*start* [*end*]]   [Scheme Procedure]
`scm_string_count` (*s, char_pred, start, end*)   [C Function]
> Return the count of the number of characters in the string *s* which
>
> - equals *char_pred*, if it is character,
> - satisfies the predicate *char_pred*, if it is a procedure.
> - is in the set *char_pred*, if it is a character set.

`string-contains` *s1 s2* [*start1* [*end1* [*start2* [*end2*]]]]   [Scheme Procedure]
`scm_string_contains` (*s1, s2, start1, end1, start2, end2*)   [C Function]
> Does string *s1* contain string *s2*? Return the index in *s1* where *s2* occurs as a substring, or false. The optional start/end indices restrict the operation to the indicated substrings.

`string-contains-ci` *s1 s2* [*start1* [*end1* [*start2* [*end2*]]]]   [Scheme Procedure]
`scm_string_contains_ci` (*s1, s2, start1, end1, start2, end2*)   [C Function]
> Does string *s1* contain string *s2*? Return the index in *s1* where *s2* occurs as a substring, or false. The optional start/end indices restrict the operation to the indicated substrings. Character comparison is done case-insensitively.

6.6.5.9 Alphabetic Case Mapping

These are procedures for mapping strings to their upper- or lower-case equivalents, respectively, or for capitalizing strings.

They use the basic case mapping rules for Unicode characters. No special language or context rules are considered. The resulting strings are guaranteed to be the same length as the input strings.

See Section 6.24.3 [Character Case Mapping], page 438, for locale-dependent case conversions.

string-upcase *str* [*start* [*end*]]   [Scheme Procedure]
scm_substring_upcase (*str*, *start*, *end*)   [C Function]
scm_string_upcase (*str*)   [C Function]
    Upcase every character in `str`.

string-upcase! *str* [*start* [*end*]]   [Scheme Procedure]
scm_substring_upcase_x (*str*, *start*, *end*)   [C Function]
scm_string_upcase_x (*str*)   [C Function]
    Destructively upcase every character in `str`.

```
(string-upcase! y)
⇒ "ARRDEFG"
y
⇒ "ARRDEFG"
```

string-downcase *str* [*start* [*end*]]   [Scheme Procedure]
scm_substring_downcase (*str*, *start*, *end*)   [C Function]
scm_string_downcase (*str*)   [C Function]
    Downcase every character in *str*.

string-downcase! *str* [*start* [*end*]]   [Scheme Procedure]
scm_substring_downcase_x (*str*, *start*, *end*)   [C Function]
scm_string_downcase_x (*str*)   [C Function]
    Destructively downcase every character in *str*.

```
y
⇒ "ARRDEFG"
(string-downcase! y)
⇒ "arrdefg"
y
⇒ "arrdefg"
```

string-capitalize *str*   [Scheme Procedure]
scm_string_capitalize (*str*)   [C Function]
    Return a freshly allocated string with the characters in *str*, where the first character of every word is capitalized.

string-capitalize! *str*   [Scheme Procedure]
scm_string_capitalize_x (*str*)   [C Function]
    Upcase the first character of every word in *str* destructively and return *str*.

```
y                           ⇒ "hello world"
(string-capitalize! y)  ⇒ "Hello World"
y                           ⇒ "Hello World"
```

string-titlecase *str* [*start* [*end*]]   [Scheme Procedure]
scm_string_titlecase (*str, start, end*)   [C Function]
>   Titlecase every first character in a word in *str*.

string-titlecase! *str* [*start* [*end*]]   [Scheme Procedure]
scm_string_titlecase_x (*str, start, end*)   [C Function]
>   Destructively titlecase every first character in a word in *str*.

6.6.5.10 Reversing and Appending Strings

string-reverse *str* [*start* [*end*]]   [Scheme Procedure]
scm_string_reverse (*str, start, end*)   [C Function]
>   Reverse the string *str*. The optional arguments *start* and *end* delimit the region of
>   *str* to operate on.

string-reverse! *str* [*start* [*end*]]   [Scheme Procedure]
scm_string_reverse_x (*str, start, end*)   [C Function]
>   Reverse the string *str* in-place. The optional arguments *start* and *end* delimit the
>   region of *str* to operate on. The return value is unspecified.

string-append *arg* ...   [Scheme Procedure]
scm_string_append (*args*)   [C Function]
>   Return a newly allocated string whose characters form the concatenation of the given
>   strings, *arg* ....
>
>   (let ((h "hello "))
>   (string-append h "world"))
>   ⇒ "hello world"

string-append/shared *arg* ...   [Scheme Procedure]
scm_string_append_shared (*args*)   [C Function]
>   Like string-append, but the result may share memory with the argument strings.

string-concatenate *ls*   [Scheme Procedure]
scm_string_concatenate (*ls*)   [C Function]
>   Append the elements (which must be strings) of *ls* together into a single string.
>   Guaranteed to return a freshly allocated string.

string-concatenate-reverse *ls* [*final_string* [*end*]]   [Scheme Procedure]
scm_string_concatenate_reverse (*ls, final_string, end*)   [C Function]
>   Without optional arguments, this procedure is equivalent to
>
>   (string-concatenate (reverse ls))
>
>   If the optional argument *final_string* is specified, it is consed onto the beginning to *ls*
>   before performing the list-reverse and string-concatenate operations. If *end* is given,
>   only the characters of *final_string* up to index *end* are used.
>
>   Guaranteed to return a freshly allocated string.

`string-concatenate/shared` *ls*   [Scheme Procedure]
`scm_string_concatenate_shared` (*ls*)   [C Function]
> Like `string-concatenate`, but the result may share memory with the strings in the
> list *ls*.

`string-concatenate-reverse/shared` *ls* [*final_string* [*end*]]   [Scheme Procedure]
`scm_string_concatenate_reverse_shared` (*ls, final_string, end*)   [C Function]
> Like `string-concatenate-reverse`, but the result may share memory with the
> strings in the *ls* arguments.

6.6.5.11 Mapping, Folding, and Unfolding

`string-map` *proc s* [*start* [*end*]]   [Scheme Procedure]
`scm_string_map` (*proc, s, start, end*)   [C Function]
> *proc* is a char->char procedure, it is mapped over *s*. The order in which the procedure
> is applied to the string elements is not specified.

`string-map!` *proc s* [*start* [*end*]]   [Scheme Procedure]
`scm_string_map_x` (*proc, s, start, end*)   [C Function]
> *proc* is a char->char procedure, it is mapped over *s*. The order in which the procedure
> is applied to the string elements is not specified. The string *s* is modified in-place,
> the return value is not specified.

`string-for-each` *proc s* [*start* [*end*]]   [Scheme Procedure]
`scm_string_for_each` (*proc, s, start, end*)   [C Function]
> *proc* is mapped over *s* in left-to-right order. The return value is not specified.

`string-for-each-index` *proc s* [*start* [*end*]]   [Scheme Procedure]
`scm_string_for_each_index` (*proc, s, start, end*)   [C Function]
> Call (`proc` i) for each index i in *s*, from left to right.
>
> For example, to change characters to alternately upper and lower case,

```
(define str (string-copy "studly"))
(string-for-each-index
    (lambda (i)
      (string-set! str i
        ((if (even? i) char-upcase char-downcase)
         (string-ref str i))))
    str)
str ⇒ "StUdLy"
```

`string-fold` *kons knil s* [*start* [*end*]]   [Scheme Procedure]
`scm_string_fold` (*kons, knil, s, start, end*)   [C Function]
> Fold *kons* over the characters of *s*, with *knil* as the terminating element, from left to
> right. *kons* must expect two arguments: The actual character and the last result of
> *kons*' application.

string-fold-right *kons knil s* [*start* [*end*]]   [Scheme Procedure]
scm_string_fold_right (*kons, knil, s, start, end*)   [C Function]

Fold *kons* over the characters of *s*, with *knil* as the terminating element, from right to left. *kons* must expect two arguments: The actual character and the last result of *kons*' application.

string-unfold *p f g seed* [*base* [*make_final*]]   [Scheme Procedure]
scm_string_unfold (*p, f, g, seed, base, make_final*)   [C Function]

- *g* is used to generate a series of *seed* values from the initial *seed*: *seed*, (*g seed*), (*g^2 seed*), (*g^3 seed*), ...

- *p* tells us when to stop – when it returns true when applied to one of these seed values.

- *f* maps each seed value to the corresponding character in the result string. These chars are assembled into the string in a left-to-right order.

- *base* is the optional initial/leftmost portion of the constructed string; it default to the empty string.

- *make_final* is applied to the terminal seed value (on which *p* returns true) to produce the final/rightmost portion of the constructed string. The default is nothing extra.

string-unfold-right *p f g seed* [*base* [*make_final*]]   [Scheme Procedure]
scm_string_unfold_right (*p, f, g, seed, base, make_final*)   [C Function]

- *g* is used to generate a series of *seed* values from the initial *seed*: *seed*, (*g seed*), (*g^2 seed*), (*g^3 seed*), ...

- *p* tells us when to stop – when it returns true when applied to one of these seed values.

- *f* maps each seed value to the corresponding character in the result string. These chars are assembled into the string in a right-to-left order.

- *base* is the optional initial/rightmost portion of the constructed string; it default to the empty string.

- *make_final* is applied to the terminal seed value (on which *p* returns true) to produce the final/leftmost portion of the constructed string. It defaults to (`lambda (x)`).

6.6.5.12 Miscellaneous String Operations

xsubstring *s from* [*to* [*start* [*end*]]]   [Scheme Procedure]
scm_xsubstring (*s, from, to, start, end*)   [C Function]

This is the *extended substring* procedure that implements replicated copying of a substring of some string.

s is a string, *start* and *end* are optional arguments that demarcate a substring of *s*, defaulting to 0 and the length of *s*. Replicate this substring up and down index space, in both the positive and negative directions. **xsubstring** returns the substring of this string beginning at index *from*, and ending at *to*, which defaults to *from* + (*end* - *start*).

`string-xcopy!` *target tstart s sfrom* [*sto* [*start* [*end*]]]   [Scheme Procedure]

`scm_string_xcopy_x` (*target, tstart, s, sfrom, sto, start, end*)   [C Function]

> Exactly the same as `xsubstring`, but the extracted text is written into the string *target* starting at index *tstart*. The operation is not defined if (`eq? target s`) or these arguments share storage – you cannot copy a string on top of itself.

`string-replace` *s1 s2* [*start1* [*end1* [*start2* [*end2*]]]]   [Scheme Procedure]

`scm_string_replace` (*s1, s2, start1, end1, start2, end2*)   [C Function]

> Return the string *s1*, but with the characters *start1* ... *end1* replaced by the characters *start2* ... *end2* from *s2*.

`string-tokenize` *s* [*token_set* [*start* [*end*]]]   [Scheme Procedure]

`scm_string_tokenize` (*s, token_set, start, end*)   [C Function]

> Split the string *s* into a list of substrings, where each substring is a maximal non-empty contiguous sequence of characters from the character set *token_set*, which defaults to `char-set:graphic`. If *start* or *end* indices are provided, they restrict `string-tokenize` to operating on the indicated substring of *s*.

`string-filter` *char_pred s* [*start* [*end*]]   [Scheme Procedure]

`scm_string_filter` (*char_pred, s, start, end*)   [C Function]

> Filter the string *s*, retaining only those characters which satisfy *char_pred*.
>
> If *char_pred* is a procedure, it is applied to each character as a predicate, if it is a character, it is tested for equality and if it is a character set, it is tested for membership.

`string-delete` *char_pred s* [*start* [*end*]]   [Scheme Procedure]

`scm_string_delete` (*char_pred, s, start, end*)   [C Function]

> Delete characters satisfying *char_pred* from *s*.
>
> If *char_pred* is a procedure, it is applied to each character as a predicate, if it is a character, it is tested for equality and if it is a character set, it is tested for membership.

6.6.5.13 Representing Strings as Bytes

Out in the cold world outside of Guile, not all strings are treated in the same way. Out there there are only bytes, and there are many ways of representing a strings (sequences of characters) as binary data (sequences of bytes).

As a user, usually you don't have to think about this very much. When you type on your keyboard, your system encodes your keystrokes as bytes according to the locale that you have configured on your computer. Guile uses the locale to decode those bytes back into characters – hopefully the same characters that you typed in.

All is not so clear when dealing with a system with multiple users, such as a web server. Your web server might get a request from one user for data encoded in the ISO-8859-1 character set, and then another request from a different user for UTF-8 data.

Guile provides an *iconv* module for converting between strings and sequences of bytes. See Section 6.6.6 [Bytevectors], page 163, for more on how Guile represents raw byte sequences. This module gets its name from the common UNIX command of the same name.

Note that often it is sufficient to just read and write strings from ports instead of using these functions. To do this, specify the port encoding using `set-port-encoding!`. See Section 6.14.1 [Ports], page 316, for more on ports and character encodings.

Unlike the rest of the procedures in this section, you have to load the `iconv` module before having access to these procedures:

```
(use-modules (ice-9 iconv))
```

`string->bytevector` *string encoding* [*conversion-strategy*]   [Scheme Procedure]
    Encode *string* as a sequence of bytes.

    The string will be encoded in the character set specified by the *encoding* string. If the string has characters that cannot be represented in the encoding, by default this procedure raises an `encoding-error`. Pass a *conversion-strategy* argument to specify other behaviors.

    The return value is a bytevector. See Section 6.6.6 [Bytevectors], page 163, for more on bytevectors. See Section 6.14.1 [Ports], page 316, for more on character encodings and conversion strategies.

`bytevector->string` *bytevector encoding* [*conversion-strategy*]   [Scheme Procedure]
    Decode *bytevector* into a string.

    The bytes will be decoded from the character set by the *encoding* string. If the bytes do not form a valid encoding, by default this procedure raises an `decoding-error`. As with `string->bytevector`, pass the optional *conversion-strategy* argument to modify this behavior. See Section 6.14.1 [Ports], page 316, for more on character encodings and conversion strategies.

`call-with-output-encoded-string` *encoding proc*   [Scheme Procedure]
        [*conversion-strategy*]
    Like `call-with-output-string`, but instead of returning a string, returns a encoding of the string according to *encoding*, as a bytevector. This procedure can be more efficient than collecting a string and then converting it via `string->bytevector`.

6.6.5.14 Conversion to/from C

When creating a Scheme string from a C string or when converting a Scheme string to a C string, the concept of character encoding becomes important.

In C, a string is just a sequence of bytes, and the character encoding describes the relation between these bytes and the actual characters that make up the string. For Scheme strings, character encoding is not an issue (most of the time), since in Scheme you usually treat strings as character sequences, not byte sequences.

Converting to C and converting from C each have their own challenges.

When converting from C to Scheme, it is important that the sequence of bytes in the C string be valid with respect to its encoding. ASCII strings, for example, can't have any bytes greater than 127. An ASCII byte greater than 127 is considered *ill-formed* and cannot be converted into a Scheme character.

Problems can occur in the reverse operation as well. Not all character encodings can hold all possible Scheme characters. Some encodings, like ASCII for example, can only describe a small subset of all possible characters. So, when converting to C, one must first decide what to do with Scheme characters that can't be represented in the C string.

Converting a Scheme string to a C string will often allocate fresh memory to hold the result. You must take care that this memory is properly freed eventually. In many cases, this can be achieved by using `scm_dynwind_free` inside an appropriate dynwind context, See Section 6.13.10 [Dynamic Wind], page 309.

SCM `scm_from_locale_string` (*const char *str*)   [C Function]
SCM `scm_from_locale_stringn` (*const char *str, size_t len*)   [C Function]
> Creates a new Scheme string that has the same contents as *str* when interpreted in the character encoding of the current locale.
>
> For `scm_from_locale_string`, *str* must be null-terminated.
>
> For `scm_from_locale_stringn`, *len* specifies the length of *str* in bytes, and *str* does not need to be null-terminated. If *len* is (`size_t`)-1, then *str* does need to be null-terminated and the real length will be found with `strlen`.
>
> If the C string is ill-formed, an error will be raised.
>
> Note that these functions should *not* be used to convert C string constants, because there is no guarantee that the current locale will match that of the execution character set, used for string and character constants. Most modern C compilers use UTF-8 by default, so to convert C string constants we recommend `scm_from_utf8_string`.

SCM `scm_take_locale_string` (*char *str*)   [C Function]
SCM `scm_take_locale_stringn` (*char *str, size_t len*)   [C Function]
> Like `scm_from_locale_string` and `scm_from_locale_stringn`, respectively, but also frees *str* with `free` eventually. Thus, you can use this function when you would free *str* anyway immediately after creating the Scheme string. In certain cases, Guile can then use *str* directly as its internal representation.

char * `scm_to_locale_string` (*SCM str*)   [C Function]
char * `scm_to_locale_stringn` (*SCM str, size_t *lenp*)   [C Function]
> Returns a C string with the same contents as *str* in the character encoding of the current locale. The C string must be freed with `free` eventually, maybe by using `scm_dynwind_free`, See Section 6.13.10 [Dynamic Wind], page 309.
>
> For `scm_to_locale_string`, the returned string is null-terminated and an error is signalled when *str* contains `#\nul` characters.
>
> For `scm_to_locale_stringn` and *lenp* not NULL, *str* might contain `#\nul` characters and the length of the returned string in bytes is stored in *`*lenp`*. The returned string will not be null-terminated in this case. If *lenp* is NULL, `scm_to_locale_stringn` behaves like `scm_to_locale_string`.
>
> If a character in *str* cannot be represented in the character encoding of the current locale, the default port conversion strategy is used. See Section 6.14.1 [Ports], page 316, for more on conversion strategies.
>
> If the conversion strategy is `error`, an error will be raised. If it is `substitute`, a replacement character, such as a question mark, will be inserted in its place. If it is `escape`, a hex escape will be inserted in its place.

size_t scm_to_locale_stringbuf (*SCM str, char *buf, size_t*   [C Function]
max_len)

> Puts *str* as a C string in the current locale encoding into the memory pointed to by *buf*. The buffer at *buf* has room for *max_len* bytes and `scm_to_local_stringbuf` will never store more than that. No terminating '\0' will be stored.

> The return value of `scm_to_locale_stringbuf` is the number of bytes that are needed for all of *str*, regardless of whether *buf* was large enough to hold them. Thus, when the return value is larger than *max_len*, only *max_len* bytes have been stored and you probably need to try again with a larger buffer.

For most situations, string conversion should occur using the current locale, such as with the functions above. But there may be cases where one wants to convert strings from a character encoding other than the locale's character encoding. For these cases, the lower-level functions `scm_to_stringn` and `scm_from_stringn` are provided. These functions should seldom be necessary if one is properly using locales.

scm_t_string_failed_conversion_handler   [C Type]

> This is an enumerated type that can take one of three values: `SCM_FAILED_CONVERSION_ERROR`, `SCM_FAILED_CONVERSION_QUESTION_MARK`, and `SCM_FAILED_CONVERSION_ESCAPE_SEQUENCE`. They are used to indicate a strategy for handling characters that cannot be converted to or from a given character encoding. `SCM_FAILED_CONVERSION_ERROR` indicates that a conversion should throw an error if some characters cannot be converted. `SCM_FAILED_CONVERSION_QUESTION_MARK` indicates that a conversion should replace unconvertable characters with the question mark character. And, `SCM_FAILED_CONVERSION_ESCAPE_SEQUENCE` requests that a conversion should replace an unconvertable character with an escape sequence.

> While all three strategies apply when converting Scheme strings to C, only `SCM_FAILED_CONVERSION_ERROR` and `SCM_FAILED_CONVERSION_QUESTION_MARK` can be used when converting C strings to Scheme.

char *scm_to_stringn (*SCM str, size_t *lenp, const char *encoding,*   [C Function]
scm_t_string_failed_conversion_handler handler)

> This function returns a newly allocated C string from the Guile string *str*. The length of the returned string in bytes will be returned in *lenp*. The character encoding of the C string is passed as the ASCII, null-terminated C string *encoding*. The *handler* parameter gives a strategy for dealing with characters that cannot be converted into *encoding*.

> If *lenp* is `NULL`, this function will return a null-terminated C string. It will throw an error if the string contains a null character.

> The Scheme interface to this function is `string->bytevector`, from the `ice-9 iconv` module. See Section 6.6.5.13 [Representing Strings as Bytes], page 158.

SCM scm_from_stringn (*const char *str, size_t len, const char*   [C Function]
encoding, scm_t_string_failed_conversion_handler handler)

> This function returns a scheme string from the C string *str*. The length in bytes of the C string is input as *len*. The encoding of the C string is passed as the ASCII,

null-terminated C string encoding. The *handler* parameters suggests a strategy for dealing with unconvertable characters.

The Scheme interface to this function is `bytevector->string`. See Section 6.6.5.13 [Representing Strings as Bytes], page 158.

The following conversion functions are provided as a convenience for the most commonly used encodings.

SCM `scm_from_latin1_string` (*const char *str*)   [C Function]
SCM `scm_from_utf8_string` (*const char *str*)   [C Function]
SCM `scm_from_utf32_string` (*const scm_t_wchar *str*)   [C Function]
> Return a scheme string from the null-terminated C string *str*, which is ISO-8859-1-, UTF-8-, or UTF-32-encoded. These functions should be used to convert hard-coded C string constants into Scheme strings.

SCM `scm_from_latin1_stringn` (*const char *str, size_t len*)   [C Function]
SCM `scm_from_utf8_stringn` (*const char *str, size_t len*)   [C Function]
SCM `scm_from_utf32_stringn` (*const scm_t_wchar *str, size_t len*)   [C Function]
> Return a scheme string from C string *str*, which is ISO-8859-1-, UTF-8-, or UTF-32-encoded, of length *len*. *len* is the number of bytes pointed to by *str* for `scm_from_latin1_stringn` and `scm_from_utf8_stringn`; it is the number of elements (code points) in *str* in the case of `scm_from_utf32_stringn`.

char `*scm_to_latin1_stringn` (*SCM str, size_t *lenp*)   [C function]
char `*scm_to_utf8_stringn` (*SCM str, size_t *lenp*)   [C function]
`scm_t_wchar *scm_to_utf32_stringn` (*SCM str, size_t *lenp*)   [C function]
> Return a newly allocated, ISO-8859-1-, UTF-8-, or UTF-32-encoded C string from Scheme string *str*. An error is thrown when *str* cannot be converted to the specified encoding. If *lenp* is NULL, the returned C string will be null terminated, and an error will be thrown if the C string would otherwise contain null characters. If *lenp* is not NULL, the string is not null terminated, and the length of the returned string is returned in *lenp*. The length returned is the number of bytes for `scm_to_latin1_stringn` and `scm_to_utf8_stringn`; it is the number of elements (code points) for `scm_to_utf32_stringn`.

6.6.5.15 String Internals

Guile stores each string in memory as a contiguous array of Unicode code points along with an associated set of attributes. If all of the code points of a string have an integer range between 0 and 255 inclusive, the code point array is stored as one byte per code point: it is stored as an ISO-8859-1 (aka Latin-1) string. If any of the code points of the string has an integer value greater that 255, the code point array is stored as four bytes per code point: it is stored as a UTF-32 string.

Conversion between the one-byte-per-code-point and four-bytes-per-code-point representations happens automatically as necessary.

No API is provided to set the internal representation of strings; however, there are pair of procedures available to query it. These are debugging procedures. Using them in production code is discouraged, since the details of Guile's internal representation of strings may change from release to release.

```
string-bytes-per-char str                                      [Scheme Procedure]
scm_string_bytes_per_char (str)                                    [C Function]
```
> Return the number of bytes used to encode a Unicode code point in string *str*. The
> result is one or four.

```
%string-dump str                                               [Scheme Procedure]
scm_sys_string_dump (str)                                          [C Function]
```
> Returns an association list containing debugging information for *str*. The association
> list has the following entries.

> `string`   The string itself.

> `start`   The start index of the string into its stringbuf

> `length`   The length of the string

> `shared`   If this string is a substring, it returns its parent string. Otherwise, it
> returns `#f`

> `read-only`
> > `#t` if the string is read-only

> `stringbuf-chars`
> > A new string containing this string's stringbuf's characters

> `stringbuf-length`
> > The number of characters in this stringbuf

> `stringbuf-shared`
> > `#t` if this stringbuf is shared

> `stringbuf-wide`
> > `#t` if this stringbuf's characters are stored in a 32-bit buffer, or `#f` if they
> > are stored in an 8-bit buffer

6.6.6 Bytevectors

A *bytevector* is a raw bit string. The (`rnrs bytevectors`) module provides the programming interface specified by the Revised^6 Report on the Algorithmic Language Scheme
(R6RS). It contains procedures to manipulate bytevectors and interpret their contents in
a number of ways: bytevector contents can be accessed as signed or unsigned integer of
various sizes and endianness, as IEEE-754 floating point numbers, or as strings. It is a
useful tool to encode and decode binary data.

The R6RS (Section 4.3.4) specifies an external representation for bytevectors, whereby
the octets (integers in the range 0–255) contained in the bytevector are represented as a list
prefixed by #vu8:

```
#vu8(1 53 204)
```

denotes a 3-byte bytevector containing the octets 1, 53, and 204. Like string literals,
booleans, etc., bytevectors are "self-quoting", i.e., they do not need to be quoted:

```
#vu8(1 53 204)
⇒ #vu8(1 53 204)
```

Bytevectors can be used with the binary input/output primitives of the R6RS (see
Section 6.14.10 [R6RS I/O Ports], page 332).

6.6.6.1 Endianness

Some of the following procedures take an *endianness* parameter. The *endianness* is defined as the order of bytes in multi-byte numbers: numbers encoded in *big endian* have their most significant bytes written first, whereas numbers encoded in *little endian* have their least significant bytes first[1].

Little-endian is the native endianness of the IA32 architecture and its derivatives, while big-endian is native to SPARC and PowerPC, among others. The `native-endianness` procedure returns the native endianness of the machine it runs on.

`native-endianness`   [Scheme Procedure]
`scm_native_endianness ()`   [C Function]
    Return a value denoting the native endianness of the host machine.

`endianness` *symbol*   [Scheme Macro]
    Return an object denoting the endianness specified by *symbol*. If *symbol* is neither `big` nor `little` then an error is raised at expand-time.

`scm_endianness_big`   [C Variable]
`scm_endianness_little`   [C Variable]
    The objects denoting big- and little-endianness, respectively.

6.6.6.2 Manipulating Bytevectors

Bytevectors can be created, copied, and analyzed with the following procedures and C functions.

`make-bytevector` *len* [*fill*]   [Scheme Procedure]
`scm_make_bytevector (len, fill)`   [C Function]
`scm_c_make_bytevector (size_t len)`   [C Function]
    Return a new bytevector of *len* bytes. Optionally, if *fill* is given, fill it with *fill*; *fill* must be in the range [-128,255].

`bytevector?` *obj*   [Scheme Procedure]
`scm_bytevector_p (obj)`   [C Function]
    Return true if *obj* is a bytevector.

`int scm_is_bytevector (SCM obj)`   [C Function]
    Equivalent to `scm_is_true (scm_bytevector_p (obj))`.

`bytevector-length` *bv*   [Scheme Procedure]
`scm_bytevector_length (bv)`   [C Function]
    Return the length in bytes of bytevector *bv*.

`size_t scm_c_bytevector_length (SCM bv)`   [C Function]
    Likewise, return the length in bytes of bytevector *bv*.

---

[1] Big-endian and little-endian are the most common "endiannesses", but others do exist. For instance, the GNU MP library allows *word order* to be specified independently of *byte order* (see Section "Integer Import and Export" in *The GNU Multiple Precision Arithmetic Library Manual*).

`bytevector=?` *bv1 bv2*   [Scheme Procedure]
`scm_bytevector_eq_p` (*bv1, bv2*)   [C Function]
>   Return is *bv1* equals to *bv2*—i.e., if they have the same length and contents.

`bytevector-fill!` *bv fill*   [Scheme Procedure]
`scm_bytevector_fill_x` (*bv, fill*)   [C Function]
>   Fill bytevector *bv* with *fill*, a byte.

`bytevector-copy!` *source source-start target target-start len*   [Scheme Procedure]
`scm_bytevector_copy_x` (*source, source_start, target, target_start,*   [C Function]
>   *len*)
>   Copy *len* bytes from *source* into *target*, starting reading from *source-start* (a positive
>   index within *source*) and start writing at *target-start*. It is permitted for the *source*
>   and *target* regions to overlap.

`bytevector-copy` *bv*   [Scheme Procedure]
`scm_bytevector_copy` (*bv*)   [C Function]
>   Return a newly allocated copy of *bv*.

`scm_t_uint8 scm_c_bytevector_ref` (*SCM bv, size_t index*)   [C Function]
>   Return the byte at *index* in bytevector *bv*.

`void scm_c_bytevector_set_x` (*SCM bv, size_t index, scm_t_uint8*   [C Function]
>   *value*)
>   Set the byte at *index* in *bv* to *value*.

Low-level C macros are available. They do not perform any type-checking; as such they
should be used with care.

`size_t SCM_BYTEVECTOR_LENGTH` (*bv*)   [C Macro]
>   Return the length in bytes of bytevector *bv*.

`signed char * SCM_BYTEVECTOR_CONTENTS` (*bv*)   [C Macro]
>   Return a pointer to the contents of bytevector *bv*.

6.6.6.3 Interpreting Bytevector Contents as Integers

The contents of a bytevector can be interpreted as a sequence of integers of any given size,
sign, and endianness.

```
(let ((bv (make-bytevector 4)))
  (bytevector-u8-set! bv 0 #x12)
  (bytevector-u8-set! bv 1 #x34)
  (bytevector-u8-set! bv 2 #x56)
  (bytevector-u8-set! bv 3 #x78)

  (map (lambda (number)
         (number->string number 16))
       (list (bytevector-u8-ref bv 0)
             (bytevector-u16-ref bv 0 (endianness big))
             (bytevector-u32-ref bv 0 (endianness little)))))
```

$\Rightarrow$ ("12" "1234" "78563412")

The most generic procedures to interpret bytevector contents as integers are described below.

bytevector-uint-ref *bv index endianness size* [Scheme Procedure]
scm_bytevector_uint_ref (*bv, index, endianness, size*) [C Function]
> Return the *size*-byte long unsigned integer at index *index* in *bv*, decoded according to *endianness*.

bytevector-sint-ref *bv index endianness size* [Scheme Procedure]
scm_bytevector_sint_ref (*bv, index, endianness, size*) [C Function]
> Return the *size*-byte long signed integer at index *index* in *bv*, decoded according to *endianness*.

bytevector-uint-set! *bv index value endianness size* [Scheme Procedure]
scm_bytevector_uint_set_x (*bv, index, value, endianness, size*) [C Function]
> Set the *size*-byte long unsigned integer at *index* to *value*, encoded according to *endianness*.

bytevector-sint-set! *bv index value endianness size* [Scheme Procedure]
scm_bytevector_sint_set_x (*bv, index, value, endianness, size*) [C Function]
> Set the *size*-byte long signed integer at *index* to *value*, encoded according to *endianness*.

The following procedures are similar to the ones above, but specialized to a given integer size:

bytevector-u8-ref *bv index* [Scheme Procedure]
bytevector-s8-ref *bv index* [Scheme Procedure]
bytevector-u16-ref *bv index endianness* [Scheme Procedure]
bytevector-s16-ref *bv index endianness* [Scheme Procedure]
bytevector-u32-ref *bv index endianness* [Scheme Procedure]
bytevector-s32-ref *bv index endianness* [Scheme Procedure]
bytevector-u64-ref *bv index endianness* [Scheme Procedure]
bytevector-s64-ref *bv index endianness* [Scheme Procedure]
scm_bytevector_u8_ref (*bv, index*) [C Function]
scm_bytevector_s8_ref (*bv, index*) [C Function]
scm_bytevector_u16_ref (*bv, index, endianness*) [C Function]
scm_bytevector_s16_ref (*bv, index, endianness*) [C Function]
scm_bytevector_u32_ref (*bv, index, endianness*) [C Function]
scm_bytevector_s32_ref (*bv, index, endianness*) [C Function]
scm_bytevector_u64_ref (*bv, index, endianness*) [C Function]
scm_bytevector_s64_ref (*bv, index, endianness*) [C Function]
> Return the unsigned *n*-bit (signed) integer (where *n* is 8, 16, 32 or 64) from *bv* at *index*, decoded according to *endianness*.

bytevector-u8-set! *bv index value* [Scheme Procedure]
bytevector-s8-set! *bv index value* [Scheme Procedure]

`bytevector-u16-set!`	*bv index value endianness*	[Scheme Procedure]
`bytevector-s16-set!`	*bv index value endianness*	[Scheme Procedure]
`bytevector-u32-set!`	*bv index value endianness*	[Scheme Procedure]
`bytevector-s32-set!`	*bv index value endianness*	[Scheme Procedure]
`bytevector-u64-set!`	*bv index value endianness*	[Scheme Procedure]
`bytevector-s64-set!`	*bv index value endianness*	[Scheme Procedure]
`scm_bytevector_u8_set_x`	(*bv, index, value*)	[C Function]
`scm_bytevector_s8_set_x`	(*bv, index, value*)	[C Function]
`scm_bytevector_u16_set_x`	(*bv, index, value, endianness*)	[C Function]
`scm_bytevector_s16_set_x`	(*bv, index, value, endianness*)	[C Function]
`scm_bytevector_u32_set_x`	(*bv, index, value, endianness*)	[C Function]
`scm_bytevector_s32_set_x`	(*bv, index, value, endianness*)	[C Function]
`scm_bytevector_u64_set_x`	(*bv, index, value, endianness*)	[C Function]
`scm_bytevector_s64_set_x`	(*bv, index, value, endianness*)	[C Function]

Store *value* as an *n*-bit (signed) integer (where *n* is 8, 16, 32 or 64) in *bv* at *index*, encoded according to *endianness*.

Finally, a variant specialized for the host's endianness is available for each of these functions (with the exception of the u8 accessors, for obvious reasons):

`bytevector-u16-native-ref`	*bv index*	[Scheme Procedure]
`bytevector-s16-native-ref`	*bv index*	[Scheme Procedure]
`bytevector-u32-native-ref`	*bv index*	[Scheme Procedure]
`bytevector-s32-native-ref`	*bv index*	[Scheme Procedure]
`bytevector-u64-native-ref`	*bv index*	[Scheme Procedure]
`bytevector-s64-native-ref`	*bv index*	[Scheme Procedure]
`scm_bytevector_u16_native_ref`	(*bv, index*)	[C Function]
`scm_bytevector_s16_native_ref`	(*bv, index*)	[C Function]
`scm_bytevector_u32_native_ref`	(*bv, index*)	[C Function]
`scm_bytevector_s32_native_ref`	(*bv, index*)	[C Function]
`scm_bytevector_u64_native_ref`	(*bv, index*)	[C Function]
`scm_bytevector_s64_native_ref`	(*bv, index*)	[C Function]

Return the unsigned *n*-bit (signed) integer (where *n* is 8, 16, 32 or 64) from *bv* at *index*, decoded according to the host's native endianness.

`bytevector-u16-native-set!`	*bv index value*	[Scheme Procedure]
`bytevector-s16-native-set!`	*bv index value*	[Scheme Procedure]
`bytevector-u32-native-set!`	*bv index value*	[Scheme Procedure]
`bytevector-s32-native-set!`	*bv index value*	[Scheme Procedure]
`bytevector-u64-native-set!`	*bv index value*	[Scheme Procedure]
`bytevector-s64-native-set!`	*bv index value*	[Scheme Procedure]
`scm_bytevector_u16_native_set_x`	(*bv, index, value*)	[C Function]
`scm_bytevector_s16_native_set_x`	(*bv, index, value*)	[C Function]
`scm_bytevector_u32_native_set_x`	(*bv, index, value*)	[C Function]
`scm_bytevector_s32_native_set_x`	(*bv, index, value*)	[C Function]
`scm_bytevector_u64_native_set_x`	(*bv, index, value*)	[C Function]

`scm_bytevector_s64_native_set_x` (*bv, index, value*)   [C Function]
> Store *value* as an *n*-bit (signed) integer (where *n* is 8, 16, 32 or 64) in *bv* at *index*, encoded according to the host's native endianness.

6.6.6.4 Converting Bytevectors to/from Integer Lists

Bytevector contents can readily be converted to/from lists of signed or unsigned integers:

```
(bytevector->sint-list (u8-list->bytevector (make-list 4 255))
                       (endianness little) 2)
⇒ (-1 -1)
```

`bytevector->u8-list` *bv*   [Scheme Procedure]
`scm_bytevector_to_u8_list` (*bv*)   [C Function]
> Return a newly allocated list of unsigned 8-bit integers from the contents of *bv*.

`u8-list->bytevector` *lst*   [Scheme Procedure]
`scm_u8_list_to_bytevector` (*lst*)   [C Function]
> Return a newly allocated bytevector consisting of the unsigned 8-bit integers listed in *lst*.

`bytevector->uint-list` *bv endianness size*   [Scheme Procedure]
`scm_bytevector_to_uint_list` (*bv, endianness, size*)   [C Function]
> Return a list of unsigned integers of *size* bytes representing the contents of *bv*, decoded according to *endianness*.

`bytevector->sint-list` *bv endianness size*   [Scheme Procedure]
`scm_bytevector_to_sint_list` (*bv, endianness, size*)   [C Function]
> Return a list of signed integers of *size* bytes representing the contents of *bv*, decoded according to *endianness*.

`uint-list->bytevector` *lst endianness size*   [Scheme Procedure]
`scm_uint_list_to_bytevector` (*lst, endianness, size*)   [C Function]
> Return a new bytevector containing the unsigned integers listed in *lst* and encoded on *size* bytes according to *endianness*.

`sint-list->bytevector` *lst endianness size*   [Scheme Procedure]
`scm_sint_list_to_bytevector` (*lst, endianness, size*)   [C Function]
> Return a new bytevector containing the signed integers listed in *lst* and encoded on *size* bytes according to *endianness*.

6.6.6.5 Interpreting Bytevector Contents as Floating Point Numbers

Bytevector contents can also be accessed as IEEE-754 single- or double-precision floating point numbers (respectively 32 and 64-bit long) using the procedures described here.

`bytevector-ieee-single-ref` *bv index endianness*   [Scheme Procedure]
`bytevector-ieee-double-ref` *bv index endianness*   [Scheme Procedure]
`scm_bytevector_ieee_single_ref` (*bv, index, endianness*)   [C Function]
`scm_bytevector_ieee_double_ref` (*bv, index, endianness*)   [C Function]
> Return the IEEE-754 single-precision floating point number from *bv* at *index* according to *endianness*.

bytevector-ieee-single-set! *bv index value endianness*	[Scheme Procedure]
bytevector-ieee-double-set! *bv index value endianness*	[Scheme Procedure]
scm_bytevector_ieee_single_set_x (*bv*, *index*, *value*, *endianness*)	[C Function]
scm_bytevector_ieee_double_set_x (*bv*, *index*, *value*, *endianness*)	[C Function]

Store real number *value* in *bv* at *index* according to *endianness*.

Specialized procedures are also available:

bytevector-ieee-single-native-ref *bv index*	[Scheme Procedure]
bytevector-ieee-double-native-ref *bv index*	[Scheme Procedure]
scm_bytevector_ieee_single_native_ref (*bv*, *index*)	[C Function]
scm_bytevector_ieee_double_native_ref (*bv*, *index*)	[C Function]

Return the IEEE-754 single-precision floating point number from *bv* at *index* according to the host's native endianness.

bytevector-ieee-single-native-set! *bv index value*	[Scheme Procedure]
bytevector-ieee-double-native-set! *bv index value*	[Scheme Procedure]
scm_bytevector_ieee_single_native_set_x (*bv*, *index*, *value*)	[C Function]
scm_bytevector_ieee_double_native_set_x (*bv*, *index*, *value*)	[C Function]

Store real number *value* in *bv* at *index* according to the host's native endianness.

6.6.6.6 Interpreting Bytevector Contents as Unicode Strings

Bytevector contents can also be interpreted as Unicode strings encoded in one of the most commonly available encoding formats. See Section 6.6.5.13 [Representing Strings as Bytes], page 158, for a more generic interface.

```
(utf8->string (u8-list->bytevector '(99 97 102 101)))
⇒ "cafe"

(string->utf8 "café")  ;; SMALL LATIN LETTER E WITH ACUTE ACCENT
⇒ #vu8(99 97 102 195 169)
```

string->utf8 *str*	[Scheme Procedure]
string->utf16 *str* [*endianness*]	[Scheme Procedure]
string->utf32 *str* [*endianness*]	[Scheme Procedure]
scm_string_to_utf8 (*str*)	[C Function]
scm_string_to_utf16 (*str*, *endianness*)	[C Function]
scm_string_to_utf32 (*str*, *endianness*)	[C Function]

Return a newly allocated bytevector that contains the UTF-8, UTF-16, or UTF-32 (aka. UCS-4) encoding of *str*. For UTF-16 and UTF-32, *endianness* should be the symbol big or little; when omitted, it defaults to big endian.

utf8->string *utf*	[Scheme Procedure]
utf16->string *utf* [*endianness*]	[Scheme Procedure]
utf32->string *utf* [*endianness*]	[Scheme Procedure]
scm_utf8_to_string (*utf*)	[C Function]
scm_utf16_to_string (*utf*, *endianness*)	[C Function]

`scm_utf32_to_string` (*utf*, *endianness*)   [C Function]
>   Return a newly allocated string that contains from the UTF-8-, UTF-16-, or UTF-
>   32-decoded contents of bytevector *utf*. For UTF-16 and UTF-32, *endianness* should
>   be the symbol `big` or `little`; when omitted, it defaults to big endian.

6.6.6.7 Accessing Bytevectors with the Array API

As an extension to the R6RS, Guile allows bytevectors to be manipulated with the *array*
procedures (see Section 6.7.5 [Arrays], page 200). When using these APIs, bytes are accessed
one at a time as 8-bit unsigned integers:

```
(define bv #vu8(0 1 2 3))

(array? bv)
⇒ #t

(array-rank bv)
⇒ 1

(array-ref bv 2)
⇒ 2

;; Note the different argument order on array-set!.
(array-set! bv 77 2)
(array-ref bv 2)
⇒ 77

(array-type bv)
⇒ vu8
```

6.6.6.8 Accessing Bytevectors with the SRFI-4 API

Bytevectors may also be accessed with the SRFI-4 API. See Section 7.5.5.3 [SRFI-4 and
Bytevectors], page 574, for more information.

6.6.7 Symbols

Symbols in Scheme are widely used in three ways: as items of discrete data, as lookup keys
for alists and hash tables, and to denote variable references.

A *symbol* is similar to a string in that it is defined by a sequence of characters. The
sequence of characters is known as the symbol's *name*. In the usual case — that is, where the
symbol's name doesn't include any characters that could be confused with other elements
of Scheme syntax — a symbol is written in a Scheme program by writing the sequence of
characters that make up the name, *without* any quotation marks or other special syntax.
For example, the symbol whose name is "multiply-by-2" is written, simply:

```
multiply-by-2
```

Notice how this differs from a *string* with contents "multiply-by-2", which is written
with double quotation marks, like this:

```
"multiply-by-2"
```

Looking beyond how they are written, symbols are different from strings in two important respects.

The first important difference is uniqueness. If the same-looking string is read twice from two different places in a program, the result is two *different* string objects whose contents just happen to be the same. If, on the other hand, the same-looking symbol is read twice from two different places in a program, the result is the *same* symbol object both times.

Given two read symbols, you can use `eq?` to test whether they are the same (that is, have the same name). `eq?` is the most efficient comparison operator in Scheme, and comparing two symbols like this is as fast as comparing, for example, two numbers. Given two strings, on the other hand, you must use `equal?` or `string=?`, which are much slower comparison operators, to determine whether the strings have the same contents.

```
(define sym1 (quote hello))
(define sym2 (quote hello))
(eq? sym1 sym2) ⇒ #t

(define str1 "hello")
(define str2 "hello")
(eq? str1 str2) ⇒ #f
(equal? str1 str2) ⇒ #t
```

The second important difference is that symbols, unlike strings, are not self-evaluating. This is why we need the `(quote ...)`s in the example above: `(quote hello)` evaluates to the symbol named "hello" itself, whereas an unquoted `hello` is *read* as the symbol named "hello" and evaluated as a variable reference ... about which more below (see Section 6.6.7.3 [Symbol Variables], page 173).

6.6.7.1 Symbols as Discrete Data

Numbers and symbols are similar to the extent that they both lend themselves to `eq?` comparison. But symbols are more descriptive than numbers, because a symbol's name can be used directly to describe the concept for which that symbol stands.

For example, imagine that you need to represent some colours in a computer program. Using numbers, you would have to choose arbitrarily some mapping between numbers and colours, and then take care to use that mapping consistently:

```
;; 1=red, 2=green, 3=purple

(if (eq? (colour-of car) 1)
    ...)
```

You can make the mapping more explicit and the code more readable by defining constants:

```
(define red 1)
(define green 2)
(define purple 3)

(if (eq? (colour-of car) red)
    ...)
```

But the simplest and clearest approach is not to use numbers at all, but symbols whose names specify the colours that they refer to:

```
(if (eq? (colour-of car) 'red)
    ...)
```

The descriptive advantages of symbols over numbers increase as the set of concepts that you want to describe grows. Suppose that a car object can have other properties as well, such as whether it has or uses:

- automatic or manual transmission
- leaded or unleaded fuel
- power steering (or not).

Then a car's combined property set could be naturally represented and manipulated as a list of symbols:

```
(properties-of car1)
⇒
(red manual unleaded power-steering)

(if (memq 'power-steering (properties-of car1))
    (display "Unfit people can drive this car.\n")
    (display "You'll need strong arms to drive this car!\n"))
⊣
Unfit people can drive this car.
```

Remember, the fundamental property of symbols that we are relying on here is that an occurrence of 'red in one part of a program is an *indistinguishable* symbol from an occurrence of 'red in another part of a program; this means that symbols can usefully be compared using eq?. At the same time, symbols have naturally descriptive names. This combination of efficiency and descriptive power makes them ideal for use as discrete data.

6.6.7.2 Symbols as Lookup Keys

Given their efficiency and descriptive power, it is natural to use symbols as the keys in an association list or hash table.

To illustrate this, consider a more structured representation of the car properties example from the preceding subsection. Rather than mixing all the properties up together in a flat list, we could use an association list like this:

```
(define car1-properties '((colour . red)
                          (transmission . manual)
                          (fuel . unleaded)
                          (steering . power-assisted)))
```

Notice how this structure is more explicit and extensible than the flat list. For example it makes clear that manual refers to the transmission rather than, say, the windows or the locking of the car. It also allows further properties to use the same symbols among their possible values without becoming ambiguous:

```
(define car1-properties '((colour . red)
                          (transmission . manual)
                          (fuel . unleaded)
                          (steering . power-assisted)
                          (seat-colour . red)
```

```
(locking . manual)))
```

With a representation like this, it is easy to use the efficient assq-XXX family of procedures (see Section 6.7.12 [Association Lists], page 228) to extract or change individual pieces of information:

```
(assq-ref car1-properties 'fuel) ⇒ unleaded
(assq-ref car1-properties 'transmission) ⇒ manual

(assq-set! car1-properties 'seat-colour 'black)
⇒
((colour . red)
 (transmission . manual)
 (fuel . unleaded)
 (steering . power-assisted)
 (seat-colour . black)
 (locking . manual)))
```

Hash tables also have keys, and exactly the same arguments apply to the use of symbols in hash tables as in association lists. The hash value that Guile uses to decide where to add a symbol-keyed entry to a hash table can be obtained by calling the symbol-hash procedure:

symbol-hash *symbol*   [Scheme Procedure]
scm_symbol_hash (*symbol*)   [C Function]
    Return a hash value for *symbol*.

See Section 6.7.14 [Hash Tables], page 236 for information about hash tables in general, and for why you might choose to use a hash table rather than an association list.

6.6.7.3 Symbols as Denoting Variables

When an unquoted symbol in a Scheme program is evaluated, it is interpreted as a variable reference, and the result of the evaluation is the appropriate variable's value.

For example, when the expression (string-length "abcd") is read and evaluated, the sequence of characters string-length is read as the symbol whose name is "string-length". This symbol is associated with a variable whose value is the procedure that implements string length calculation. Therefore evaluation of the string-length symbol results in that procedure.

The details of the connection between an unquoted symbol and the variable to which it refers are explained elsewhere. See Section 6.12 [Binding Constructs], page 286, for how associations between symbols and variables are created, and Section 6.19 [Modules], page 381, for how those associations are affected by Guile's module system.

6.6.7.4 Operations Related to Symbols

Given any Scheme value, you can determine whether it is a symbol using the symbol? primitive:

symbol? *obj*   [Scheme Procedure]
scm_symbol_p (*obj*)   [C Function]
    Return #t if *obj* is a symbol, otherwise return #f.

`int scm_is_symbol` (*SCM val*)   [C Function]
      Equivalent to `scm_is_true (scm_symbol_p (val))`.

Once you know that you have a symbol, you can obtain its name as a string by calling `symbol->string`. Note that Guile differs by default from R5RS on the details of `symbol->string` as regards case-sensitivity:

`symbol->string` *s*   [Scheme Procedure]
`scm_symbol_to_string` (*s*)   [C Function]
      Return the name of symbol *s* as a string. By default, Guile reads symbols case-sensitively, so the string returned will have the same case variation as the sequence of characters that caused *s* to be created.

      If Guile is set to read symbols case-insensitively (as specified by R5RS), and *s* comes into being as part of a literal expression (see Section "Literal expressions" in *The Revised^5 Report on Scheme*) or by a call to the `read` or `string-ci->symbol` procedures, Guile converts any alphabetic characters in the symbol's name to lower case before creating the symbol object, so the string returned here will be in lower case.

      If *s* was created by `string->symbol`, the case of characters in the string returned will be the same as that in the string that was passed to `string->symbol`, regardless of Guile's case-sensitivity setting at the time *s* was created.

      It is an error to apply mutation procedures like `string-set!` to strings returned by this procedure.

Most symbols are created by writing them literally in code. However it is also possible to create symbols programmatically using the following procedures:

`symbol` *char...*   [Scheme Procedure]
      Return a newly allocated symbol made from the given character arguments.

            `(symbol #\x #\y #\z)` ⇒ `xyz`

`list->symbol` *lst*   [Scheme Procedure]
      Return a newly allocated symbol made from a list of characters.

            `(list->symbol '(#\a #\b #\c))` ⇒ `abc`

`symbol-append` *arg* ...   [Scheme Procedure]
      Return a newly allocated symbol whose characters form the concatenation of the given symbols, *arg* ....

            `(let ((h 'hello))`
              `(symbol-append h 'world))`
            `⇒ helloworld`

`string->symbol` *string*   [Scheme Procedure]
`scm_string_to_symbol` (*string*)   [C Function]
      Return the symbol whose name is *string*. This procedure can create symbols with names containing special characters or letters in the non-standard case, but it is usually a bad idea to create such symbols because in some implementations of Scheme they cannot be read as themselves.

```
string-ci->symbol str                                          [Scheme Procedure]
scm_string_ci_to_symbol (str)                                        [C Function]
```
Return the symbol whose name is *str*. If Guile is currently reading symbols case-insensitively, *str* is converted to lowercase before the returned symbol is looked up or created.

The following examples illustrate Guile's detailed behaviour as regards the case-sensitivity of symbols:

```
(read-enable 'case-insensitive)    ; R5RS compliant behaviour

(symbol->string 'flying-fish)     ⇒ "flying-fish"
(symbol->string 'Martin)          ⇒ "martin"
(symbol->string
    (string->symbol "Malvina"))   ⇒ "Malvina"

(eq? 'mISSISSIppi 'mississippi)   ⇒ #t
(string->symbol "mISSISSIppi")    ⇒ mISSISSIppi
(eq? 'bitBlt (string->symbol "bitBlt")) ⇒ #f
(eq? 'LolliPop
   (string->symbol (symbol->string 'LolliPop))) ⇒ #t
(string=? "K. Harper, M.D."
    (symbol->string
       (string->symbol "K. Harper, M.D."))) ⇒ #t


(read-disable 'case-insensitive)   ; Guile default behaviour

(symbol->string 'flying-fish)     ⇒ "flying-fish"
(symbol->string 'Martin)          ⇒ "Martin"
(symbol->string
    (string->symbol "Malvina"))   ⇒ "Malvina"

(eq? 'mISSISSIppi 'mississippi)   ⇒ #f
(string->symbol "mISSISSIppi")    ⇒ mISSISSIppi
(eq? 'bitBlt (string->symbol "bitBlt")) ⇒ #t
(eq? 'LolliPop
   (string->symbol (symbol->string 'LolliPop))) ⇒ #t
(string=? "K. Harper, M.D."
    (symbol->string
       (string->symbol "K. Harper, M.D."))) ⇒ #t
```

From C, there are lower level functions that construct a Scheme symbol from a C string in the current locale encoding.

When you want to do more from C, you should convert between symbols and strings using `scm_symbol_to_string` and `scm_string_to_symbol` and work with the strings.

SCM **scm_from_latin1_symbol** (*const char *name*)   [C Function]
SCM **scm_from_utf8_symbol** (*const char *name*)   [C Function]
    Construct and return a Scheme symbol whose name is specified by the null-terminated
    C string *name*. These are appropriate when the C string is hard-coded in the source
    code.

SCM **scm_from_locale_symbol** (*const char *name*)   [C Function]
SCM **scm_from_locale_symboln** (*const char *name, size_t len*)   [C Function]
    Construct and return a Scheme symbol whose name is specified by *name*. For `scm_from_locale_symbol`, *name* must be null terminated; for `scm_from_locale_symboln` the length of *name* is specified explicitly by *len*.

    Note that these functions should *not* be used when *name* is a C string constant, because there is no guarantee that the current locale will match that of the execution character set, used for string and character constants. Most modern C compilers use UTF-8 by default, so in such cases we recommend `scm_from_utf8_symbol`.

SCM **scm_take_locale_symbol** (*char *str*)   [C Function]
SCM **scm_take_locale_symboln** (*char *str, size_t len*)   [C Function]
    Like `scm_from_locale_symbol` and `scm_from_locale_symboln`, respectively, but also frees *str* with `free` eventually. Thus, you can use this function when you would free *str* anyway immediately after creating the Scheme string. In certain cases, Guile can then use *str* directly as its internal representation.

    The size of a symbol can also be obtained from C:

size_t **scm_c_symbol_length** (*SCM sym*)   [C Function]
    Return the number of characters in *sym*.

Finally, some applications, especially those that generate new Scheme code dynamically, need to generate symbols for use in the generated code. The **gensym** primitive meets this need:

gensym [*prefix*]   [Scheme Procedure]
scm_gensym (*prefix*)   [C Function]
    Create a new symbol with a name constructed from a prefix and a counter value. The string *prefix* can be specified as an optional argument. Default prefix is ' **g**'. The counter is increased by 1 at each call. There is no provision for resetting the counter.

The symbols generated by **gensym** are *likely* to be unique, since their names begin with a space and it is only otherwise possible to generate such symbols if a programmer goes out of their way to do so. Uniqueness can be guaranteed by instead using uninterned symbols (see Section 6.6.7.7 [Symbol Uninterned], page 178), though they can't be usefully written out and read back in.

6.6.7.5 Function Slots and Property Lists

In traditional Lisp dialects, symbols are often understood as having three kinds of value at once:

- a *variable* value, which is used when the symbol appears in code in a variable reference context

- a *function* value, which is used when the symbol appears in code in a function name position (i.e. as the first element in an unquoted list)

- a *property list* value, which is used when the symbol is given as the first argument to Lisp's `put` or `get` functions.

Although Scheme (as one of its simplifications with respect to Lisp) does away with the distinction between variable and function namespaces, Guile currently retains some elements of the traditional structure in case they turn out to be useful when implementing translators for other languages, in particular Emacs Lisp.

Specifically, Guile symbols have two extra slots, one for a symbol's property list, and one for its "function value." The following procedures are provided to access these slots.

`symbol-fref` *symbol*   [Scheme Procedure]
`scm_symbol_fref` (*symbol*)   [C Function]
    Return the contents of *symbol*'s *function slot*.

`symbol-fset!` *symbol value*   [Scheme Procedure]
`scm_symbol_fset_x` (*symbol, value*)   [C Function]
    Set the contents of *symbol*'s function slot to *value*.

`symbol-pref` *symbol*   [Scheme Procedure]
`scm_symbol_pref` (*symbol*)   [C Function]
    Return the *property list* currently associated with *symbol*.

`symbol-pset!` *symbol value*   [Scheme Procedure]
`scm_symbol_pset_x` (*symbol, value*)   [C Function]
    Set *symbol*'s property list to *value*.

`symbol-property` *sym prop*   [Scheme Procedure]
    From *sym*'s property list, return the value for property *prop*. The assumption is that *sym*'s property list is an association list whose keys are distinguished from each other using `equal?`; *prop* should be one of the keys in that list. If the property list has no entry for *prop*, `symbol-property` returns `#f`.

`set-symbol-property!` *sym prop val*   [Scheme Procedure]
    In *sym*'s property list, set the value for property *prop* to *val*, or add a new entry for *prop*, with value *val*, if none already exists. For the structure of the property list, see `symbol-property`.

`symbol-property-remove!` *sym prop*   [Scheme Procedure]
    From *sym*'s property list, remove the entry for property *prop*, if there is one. For the structure of the property list, see `symbol-property`.

Support for these extra slots may be removed in a future release, and it is probably better to avoid using them. For a more modern and Schemely approach to properties, see Section 6.11.2 [Object Properties], page 278.

6.6.7.6 Extended Read Syntax for Symbols

The read syntax for a symbol is a sequence of letters, digits, and *extended alphabetic characters*, beginning with a character that cannot begin a number. In addition, the special cases of +, -, and ... are read as symbols even though numbers can begin with +, - or ..

Extended alphabetic characters may be used within identifiers as if they were letters. The set of extended alphabetic characters is:

```
! $ % & * + - . / : < = > ? @ ^ _ ~
```

In addition to the standard read syntax defined above (which is taken from R5RS (see Section "Formal syntax" in *The Revised^5 Report on Scheme*)), Guile provides an extended symbol read syntax that allows the inclusion of unusual characters such as space characters, newlines and parentheses. If (for whatever reason) you need to write a symbol containing characters not mentioned above, you can do so as follows.

- Begin the symbol with the characters #{,

- write the characters of the symbol and

- finish the symbol with the characters }#.

Here are a few examples of this form of read syntax. The first symbol needs to use extended syntax because it contains a space character, the second because it contains a line break, and the last because it looks like a number.

```
#{foo bar}#
```

```
#{what
ever}#
```

```
#{4242}#
```

Although Guile provides this extended read syntax for symbols, widespread usage of it is discouraged because it is not portable and not very readable.

Alternatively, if you enable the **r7rs-symbols** read option (see see Section 6.17.2 [Scheme Read], page 360), you can write arbitrary symbols using the same notation used for strings, except delimited by vertical bars instead of double quotes.

```
|foo bar|
|\x3BB; is a greek lambda|
|\| is a vertical bar|
```

Note that there's also an **r7rs-symbols** print option (see Section 6.17.3 [Scheme Write], page 361). To enable the use of this notation, evaluate one or both of the following expressions:

```
(read-enable  'r7rs-symbols)
(print-enable 'r7rs-symbols)
```

6.6.7.7 Uninterned Symbols

What makes symbols useful is that they are automatically kept unique. There are no two symbols that are distinct objects but have the same name. But of course, there is no rule without exception. In addition to the normal symbols that have been discussed up to now, you can also create special *uninterned* symbols that behave slightly differently.

To understand what is different about them and why they might be useful, we look at how normal symbols are actually kept unique.

Whenever Guile wants to find the symbol with a specific name, for example during `read` or when executing `string->symbol`, it first looks into a table of all existing symbols to find out whether a symbol with the given name already exists. When this is the case, Guile just returns that symbol. When not, a new symbol with the name is created and entered into the table so that it can be found later.

Sometimes you might want to create a symbol that is guaranteed 'fresh', i.e. a symbol that did not exist previously. You might also want to somehow guarantee that no one else will ever unintentionally stumble across your symbol in the future. These properties of a symbol are often needed when generating code during macro expansion. When introducing new temporary variables, you want to guarantee that they don't conflict with variables in other people's code.

The simplest way to arrange for this is to create a new symbol but not enter it into the global table of all symbols. That way, no one will ever get access to your symbol by chance. Symbols that are not in the table are called *uninterned*. Of course, symbols that *are* in the table are called *interned*.

You create new uninterned symbols with the function `make-symbol`. You can test whether a symbol is interned or not with `symbol-interned?`.

Uninterned symbols break the rule that the name of a symbol uniquely identifies the symbol object. Because of this, they can not be written out and read back in like interned symbols. Currently, Guile has no support for reading uninterned symbols. Note that the function `gensym` does not return uninterned symbols for this reason.

`make-symbol` *name*   [Scheme Procedure]
`scm_make_symbol` (*name*)   [C Function]
> Return a new uninterned symbol with the name *name*. The returned symbol is guaranteed to be unique and future calls to `string->symbol` will not return it.

`symbol-interned?` *symbol*   [Scheme Procedure]
`scm_symbol_interned_p` (*symbol*)   [C Function]
> Return `#t` if *symbol* is interned, otherwise return `#f`.

For example:

```
(define foo-1 (string->symbol "foo"))
(define foo-2 (string->symbol "foo"))
(define foo-3 (make-symbol "foo"))
(define foo-4 (make-symbol "foo"))

(eq? foo-1 foo-2)
⇒ #t
; Two interned symbols with the same name are the same object,

(eq? foo-1 foo-3)
⇒ #f
; but a call to make-symbol with the same name returns a
```

```
; distinct object.

(eq? foo-3 foo-4)
⇒ #f
; A call to make-symbol always returns a new object, even for
; the same name.

foo-3
⇒ #<uninterned-symbol foo 8085290>
; Uninterned symbols print differently from interned symbols,

(symbol? foo-3)
⇒ #t
; but they are still symbols,

(symbol-interned? foo-3)
⇒ #f
; just not interned.
```

6.6.8 Keywords

Keywords are self-evaluating objects with a convenient read syntax that makes them easy to type.

Guile's keyword support conforms to R5RS, and adds a (switchable) read syntax extension to permit keywords to begin with : as well as #:, or to end with :.

6.6.8.1 Why Use Keywords?

Keywords are useful in contexts where a program or procedure wants to be able to accept a large number of optional arguments without making its interface unmanageable.

To illustrate this, consider a hypothetical `make-window` procedure, which creates a new window on the screen for drawing into using some graphical toolkit. There are many parameters that the caller might like to specify, but which could also be sensibly defaulted, for example:

- color depth – Default: the color depth for the screen
- background color – Default: white
- width – Default: 600
- height – Default: 400

If `make-window` did not use keywords, the caller would have to pass in a value for each possible argument, remembering the correct argument order and using a special value to indicate the default value for that argument:

```
(make-window 'default            ;; Color depth
             'default            ;; Background color
             800                 ;; Width
             100                 ;; Height
             ...)                ;; More make-window arguments
```

With keywords, on the other hand, defaulted arguments are omitted, and non-default arguments are clearly tagged by the appropriate keyword. As a result, the invocation becomes much clearer:

```
(make-window #:width 800 #:height 100)
```

On the other hand, for a simpler procedure with few arguments, the use of keywords would be a hindrance rather than a help. The primitive procedure cons, for example, would not be improved if it had to be invoked as

```
(cons #:car x #:cdr y)
```

So the decision whether to use keywords or not is purely pragmatic: use them if they will clarify the procedure invocation at point of call.

6.6.8.2 Coding With Keywords

If a procedure wants to support keywords, it should take a rest argument and then use whatever means is convenient to extract keywords and their corresponding arguments from the contents of that rest argument.

The following example illustrates the principle: the code for make-window uses a helper procedure called get-keyword-value to extract individual keyword arguments from the rest argument.

```
(define (get-keyword-value args keyword default)
  (let ((kv (memq keyword args)))
    (if (and kv (>= (length kv) 2))
        (cadr kv)
        default)))

(define (make-window . args)
  (let ((depth  (get-keyword-value args #:depth  screen-depth))
        (bg     (get-keyword-value args #:bg     "white"))
        (width  (get-keyword-value args #:width  800))
        (height (get-keyword-value args #:height 100))
        ...)
    ...))
```

But you don't need to write get-keyword-value. The (ice-9 optargs) module provides a set of powerful macros that you can use to implement keyword-supporting procedures like this:

```
(use-modules (ice-9 optargs))

(define (make-window . args)
  (let-keywords args #f ((depth  screen-depth)
                         (bg     "white")
                         (width  800)
                         (height 100))
    ...))
```

Or, even more economically, like this:

```
(use-modules (ice-9 optargs))
```

```
(define* (make-window #:key (depth   screen-depth)
                            (bg      "white")
                            (width   800)
                            (height  100))
  ...)
```

For further details on `let-keywords`, `define*` and other facilities provided by the `(ice-9 optargs)` module, see Section 6.9.4 [Optional Arguments], page 248.

To handle keyword arguments from procedures implemented in C, use `scm_c_bind_keyword_arguments` (see Section 6.6.8.4 [Keyword Procedures], page 183).

6.6.8.3 Keyword Read Syntax

Guile, by default, only recognizes a keyword syntax that is compatible with R5RS. A token of the form `#:NAME`, where `NAME` has the same syntax as a Scheme symbol (see Section 6.6.7.6 [Symbol Read Syntax], page 178), is the external representation of the keyword named `NAME`. Keyword objects print using this syntax as well, so values containing keyword objects can be read back into Guile. When used in an expression, keywords are self-quoting objects.

If the `keyword` read option is set to `'prefix`, Guile also recognizes the alternative read syntax `:NAME`. Otherwise, tokens of the form `:NAME` are read as symbols, as required by R5RS.

If the `keyword` read option is set to `'postfix`, Guile recognizes the SRFI-88 read syntax `NAME:` (see Section 7.5.40 [SRFI-88], page 620). Otherwise, tokens of this form are read as symbols.

To enable and disable the alternative non-R5RS keyword syntax, you use the `read-set!` procedure documented Section 6.17.2 [Scheme Read], page 360. Note that the `prefix` and `postfix` syntax are mutually exclusive.

```
(read-set! keywords 'prefix)

#:type
⇒
#:type

:type
⇒
#:type

(read-set! keywords 'postfix)

type:
⇒
#:type

:type
⇒
:type
```

```
(read-set! keywords #f)

#:type
⇒
#:type

:type
⊣
ERROR: In expression :type:
ERROR: Unbound variable: :type
ABORT: (unbound-variable)
```

6.6.8.4 Keyword Procedures

`keyword?` *obj*   [Scheme Procedure]
`scm_keyword_p` *(obj)*   [C Function]
> Return `#t` if the argument *obj* is a keyword, else `#f`.

`keyword->symbol` *keyword*   [Scheme Procedure]
`scm_keyword_to_symbol` *(keyword)*   [C Function]
> Return the symbol with the same name as *keyword*.

`symbol->keyword` *symbol*   [Scheme Procedure]
`scm_symbol_to_keyword` *(symbol)*   [C Function]
> Return the keyword with the same name as *symbol*.

`int scm_is_keyword` *(SCM obj)*   [C Function]
> Equivalent to `scm_is_true (scm_keyword_p (obj))`.

`SCM scm_from_locale_keyword` *(const char *name)*   [C Function]
`SCM scm_from_locale_keywordn` *(const char *name, size_t len)*   [C Function]
> Equivalent to `scm_symbol_to_keyword (scm_from_locale_symbol (name))` and
> `scm_symbol_to_keyword (scm_from_locale_symboln (name, len))`, respectively.
>
> Note that these functions should *not* be used when *name* is a C string constant,
> because there is no guarantee that the current locale will match that of the execution
> character set, used for string and character constants. Most modern C compilers use
> UTF-8 by default, so in such cases we recommend `scm_from_utf8_keyword`.

`SCM scm_from_latin1_keyword` *(const char *name)*   [C Function]
`SCM scm_from_utf8_keyword` *(const char *name)*   [C Function]
> Equivalent to `scm_symbol_to_keyword (scm_from_latin1_symbol (name))` and
> `scm_symbol_to_keyword (scm_from_utf8_symbol (name))`, respectively.

`void scm_c_bind_keyword_arguments` *(const char *subr, SCM rest,*   [C Function]
> *scm_t_keyword_arguments_flags flags, SCM keyword1, SCM *argp1, ..., SCM*
> *keywordN, SCM *argpN, SCM_UNDEFINED)*
> Extract the specified keyword arguments from *rest*, which is not modified. If the
> keyword argument *keyword1* is present in *rest* with an associated value, that value is

stored in the variable pointed to by *argp1*, otherwise the variable is left unchanged. Similarly for the other keywords and argument pointers up to *keywordN* and *argpN*. The argument list to `scm_c_bind_keyword_arguments` must be terminated by `SCM_UNDEFINED`.

Note that since the variables pointed to by *argp1* through *argpN* are left unchanged if the associated keyword argument is not present, they should be initialized to their default values before calling `scm_c_bind_keyword_arguments`. Alternatively, you can initialize them to `SCM_UNDEFINED` before the call, and then use `SCM_UNBNDP` after the call to see which ones were provided.

If an unrecognized keyword argument is present in *rest* and *flags* does not contain `SCM_ALLOW_OTHER_KEYS`, or if non-keyword arguments are present and *flags* does not contain `SCM_ALLOW_NON_KEYWORD_ARGUMENTS`, an exception is raised. *subr* should be the name of the procedure receiving the keyword arguments, for purposes of error reporting.

For example:

```
SCM k_delimiter;
SCM k_grammar;
SCM sym_infix;

SCM my_string_join (SCM strings, SCM rest)
{
  SCM delimiter = SCM_UNDEFINED;
  SCM grammar   = sym_infix;

  scm_c_bind_keyword_arguments ("my-string-join", rest, 0,
                                k_delimiter, &delimiter,
                                k_grammar, &grammar,
                                SCM_UNDEFINED);

  if (SCM_UNBNDP (delimiter))
    delimiter = scm_from_utf8_string (" ");

  return scm_string_join (strings, delimiter, grammar);
}

void my_init ()
{
  k_delimiter = scm_from_utf8_keyword ("delimiter");
  k_grammar   = scm_from_utf8_keyword ("grammar");
  sym_infix   = scm_from_utf8_symbol  ("infix");
  scm_c_define_gsubr ("my-string-join", 1, 0, 1, my_string_join);
}
```

6.6.9 "Functionality-Centric" Data Types

Procedures and macros are documented in their own sections: see Section 6.9 [Procedures], page 244 and Section 6.10 [Macros], page 257.

Variable objects are documented as part of the description of Guile's module system: see Section 6.19.7 [Variables], page 390.

Asyncs, dynamic roots and fluids are described in the section on scheduling: see Section 6.21 [Scheduling], page 410.

Hooks are documented in the section on general utility functions: see Section 6.11.6 [Hooks], page 281.

Ports are described in the section on I/O: see Section 6.14 [Input and Output], page 316.

Regular expressions are described in their own section: see Section 6.15 [Regular Expressions], page 349.

6.7 Compound Data Types

This chapter describes Guile's compound data types. By *compound* we mean that the primary purpose of these data types is to act as containers for other kinds of data (including other compound objects). For instance, a (non-uniform) vector with length 5 is a container that can hold five arbitrary Scheme objects.

The various kinds of container object differ from each other in how their memory is allocated, how they are indexed, and how particular values can be looked up within them.

6.7.1 Pairs

Pairs are used to combine two Scheme objects into one compound object. Hence the name: A pair stores a pair of objects.

The data type *pair* is extremely important in Scheme, just like in any other Lisp dialect. The reason is that pairs are not only used to make two values available as one object, but that pairs are used for constructing lists of values. Because lists are so important in Scheme, they are described in a section of their own (see Section 6.7.2 [Lists], page 188).

Pairs can literally get entered in source code or at the REPL, in the so-called *dotted list* syntax. This syntax consists of an opening parentheses, the first element of the pair, a dot, the second element and a closing parentheses. The following example shows how a pair consisting of the two numbers 1 and 2, and a pair containing the symbols `foo` and `bar` can be entered. It is very important to write the whitespace before and after the dot, because otherwise the Scheme parser would not be able to figure out where to split the tokens.

```
(1 . 2)
(foo . bar)
```

But beware, if you want to try out these examples, you have to *quote* the expressions. More information about quotation is available in the section Section 6.17.1.1 [Expression Syntax], page 357. The correct way to try these examples is as follows.

```
'(1 . 2)
⇒
(1 . 2)
'(foo . bar)
⇒
(foo . bar)
```

A new pair is made by calling the procedure `cons` with two arguments. Then the argument values are stored into a newly allocated pair, and the pair is returned. The name `cons` stands for "construct". Use the procedure `pair?` to test whether a given Scheme object is a pair or not.

`cons` *x* *y*   [Scheme Procedure]
`scm_cons` (*x*, *y*)   [C Function]
    Return a newly allocated pair whose car is *x* and whose cdr is *y*. The pair is guaranteed to be different (in the sense of `eq?`) from every previously existing object.

`pair?` *x*   [Scheme Procedure]
`scm_pair_p` (*x*)   [C Function]
    Return `#t` if *x* is a pair; otherwise return `#f`.

`int scm_is_pair` (*SCM x*)   [C Function]
    Return 1 when *x* is a pair; otherwise return 0.

The two parts of a pair are traditionally called *car* and *cdr*. They can be retrieved with procedures of the same name (`car` and `cdr`), and can be modified with the procedures `set-car!` and `set-cdr!`.

Since a very common operation in Scheme programs is to access the car of a car of a pair, or the car of the cdr of a pair, etc., the procedures called `caar`, `cadr` and so on are also predefined. However, using these procedures is often detrimental to readability, and error-prone. Thus, accessing the contents of a list is usually better achieved using pattern matching techniques (see Section 7.7 [Pattern Matching], page 657).

`car` *pair*   [Scheme Procedure]
`cdr` *pair*   [Scheme Procedure]
`scm_car` (*pair*)   [C Function]
`scm_cdr` (*pair*)   [C Function]
    Return the car or the cdr of *pair*, respectively.

`SCM SCM_CAR` (*SCM pair*)   [C Macro]
`SCM SCM_CDR` (*SCM pair*)   [C Macro]
    These two macros are the fastest way to access the car or cdr of a pair; they can be thought of as compiling into a single memory reference.

    These macros do no checking at all. The argument *pair* must be a valid pair.

`cddr` *pair*   [Scheme Procedure]
`cdar` *pair*   [Scheme Procedure]
`cadr` *pair*   [Scheme Procedure]
`caar` *pair*   [Scheme Procedure]
`cdddr` *pair*   [Scheme Procedure]
`cddar` *pair*   [Scheme Procedure]
`cdadr` *pair*   [Scheme Procedure]
`cdaar` *pair*   [Scheme Procedure]
`caddr` *pair*   [Scheme Procedure]
`cadar` *pair*   [Scheme Procedure]
`caadr` *pair*   [Scheme Procedure]
`caaar` *pair*   [Scheme Procedure]
`cddddr` *pair*   [Scheme Procedure]

cdddar *pair*	[Scheme Procedure]
cddadr *pair*	[Scheme Procedure]
cddaar *pair*	[Scheme Procedure]
cdaddr *pair*	[Scheme Procedure]
cdadar *pair*	[Scheme Procedure]
cdaadr *pair*	[Scheme Procedure]
cdaaar *pair*	[Scheme Procedure]
cadddr *pair*	[Scheme Procedure]
caddar *pair*	[Scheme Procedure]
cadadr *pair*	[Scheme Procedure]
cadaar *pair*	[Scheme Procedure]
caaddr *pair*	[Scheme Procedure]
caadar *pair*	[Scheme Procedure]
caaadr *pair*	[Scheme Procedure]
caaaar *pair*	[Scheme Procedure]
scm_cddr (*pair*)	[C Function]
scm_cdar (*pair*)	[C Function]
scm_cadr (*pair*)	[C Function]
scm_caar (*pair*)	[C Function]
scm_cdddr (*pair*)	[C Function]
scm_cddar (*pair*)	[C Function]
scm_cdadr (*pair*)	[C Function]
scm_cdaar (*pair*)	[C Function]
scm_caddr (*pair*)	[C Function]
scm_cadar (*pair*)	[C Function]
scm_caadr (*pair*)	[C Function]
scm_caaar (*pair*)	[C Function]
scm_cddddr (*pair*)	[C Function]
scm_cdddar (*pair*)	[C Function]
scm_cddadr (*pair*)	[C Function]
scm_cddaar (*pair*)	[C Function]
scm_cdaddr (*pair*)	[C Function]
scm_cdadar (*pair*)	[C Function]
scm_cdaadr (*pair*)	[C Function]
scm_cdaaar (*pair*)	[C Function]
scm_cadddr (*pair*)	[C Function]
scm_caddar (*pair*)	[C Function]
scm_cadadr (*pair*)	[C Function]
scm_cadaar (*pair*)	[C Function]
scm_caaddr (*pair*)	[C Function]
scm_caadar (*pair*)	[C Function]
scm_caaadr (*pair*)	[C Function]
scm_caaaar (*pair*)	[C Function]

These procedures are compositions of `car` and `cdr`, where for example `caddr` could be defined by

```
(define caddr (lambda (x) (car (cdr (cdr x)))))
```

cadr, caddr and cadddr pick out the second, third or fourth elements of a list, respectively. SRFI-1 provides the same under the names second, third and fourth (see Section 7.5.3.3 [SRFI-1 Selectors], page 554).

set-car! *pair value*   [Scheme Procedure]
scm_set_car_x (*pair, value*)   [C Function]
    Stores *value* in the car field of *pair*. The value returned by set-car! is unspecified.

set-cdr! *pair value*   [Scheme Procedure]
scm_set_cdr_x (*pair, value*)   [C Function]
    Stores *value* in the cdr field of *pair*. The value returned by set-cdr! is unspecified.

6.7.2 Lists

A very important data type in Scheme—as well as in all other Lisp dialects—is the data type *list*.[2]

This is the short definition of what a list is:

- Either the empty list (),

- or a pair which has a list in its cdr.

6.7.2.1 List Read Syntax

The syntax for lists is an opening parentheses, then all the elements of the list (separated by whitespace) and finally a closing parentheses.[3].

```
(1 2 3)              ;  a list of the numbers 1, 2 and 3
("foo" bar 3.1415)   ;  a string, a symbol and a real number
()                   ;  the empty list
```

The last example needs a bit more explanation. A list with no elements, called the *empty list*, is special in some ways. It is used for terminating lists by storing it into the cdr of the last pair that makes up a list. An example will clear that up:

```
(car '(1))
⇒
1
(cdr '(1))
⇒
()
```

This example also shows that lists have to be quoted when written (see Section 6.17.1.1 [Expression Syntax], page 357), because they would otherwise be mistakingly taken as procedure applications (see Section 3.2.2 [Simple Invocation], page 18).

6.7.2.2 List Predicates

Often it is useful to test whether a given Scheme object is a list or not. List-processing procedures could use this information to test whether their input is valid, or they could do different things depending on the datatype of their arguments.

---

[2] Strictly speaking, Scheme does not have a real datatype *list*. Lists are made up of *chained pairs*, and only exist by definition—a list is a chain of pairs which looks like a list.

[3] Note that there is no separation character between the list elements, like a comma or a semicolon.

list? *x*   [Scheme Procedure]
scm_list_p (*x*)   [C Function]
> Return #t if *x* is a proper list, else #f.

The predicate null? is often used in list-processing code to tell whether a given list has run out of elements. That is, a loop somehow deals with the elements of a list until the list satisfies null?. Then, the algorithm terminates.

null? *x*   [Scheme Procedure]
scm_null_p (*x*)   [C Function]
> Return #t if *x* is the empty list, else #f.

int scm_is_null (*SCM x*)   [C Function]
> Return 1 when *x* is the empty list; otherwise return 0.

6.7.2.3 List Constructors

This section describes the procedures for constructing new lists. list simply returns a list where the elements are the arguments, cons* is similar, but the last argument is stored in the cdr of the last pair of the list.

list *elem* ...   [Scheme Procedure]
scm_list_1 (*elem1*)   [C Function]
scm_list_2 (*elem1*, *elem2*)   [C Function]
scm_list_3 (*elem1*, *elem2*, *elem3*)   [C Function]
scm_list_4 (*elem1*, *elem2*, *elem3*, *elem4*)   [C Function]
scm_list_5 (*elem1*, *elem2*, *elem3*, *elem4*, *elem5*)   [C Function]
scm_list_n (*elem1*, ..., *elemN*, SCM_UNDEFINED)   [C Function]
> Return a new list containing elements *elem* ....
>
> scm_list_n takes a variable number of arguments, terminated by the special SCM_UNDEFINED. That final SCM_UNDEFINED is not included in the list. None of *elem* ... can themselves be SCM_UNDEFINED, or scm_list_n will terminate at that point.

cons* *arg1 arg2* ...   [Scheme Procedure]
> Like list, but the last arg provides the tail of the constructed list, returning (cons *arg1* (cons *arg2* (cons ... *argn*))). Requires at least one argument. If given one argument, that argument is returned as result. This function is called list* in some other Schemes and in Common LISP.

list-copy *lst*   [Scheme Procedure]
scm_list_copy (*lst*)   [C Function]
> Return a (newly-created) copy of *lst*.

make-list *n* [*init*]   [Scheme Procedure]
> Create a list containing of *n* elements, where each element is initialized to *init*. *init* defaults to the empty list () if not given.

Note that list-copy only makes a copy of the pairs which make up the spine of the lists. The list elements are not copied, which means that modifying the elements of the new list also modifies the elements of the old list. On the other hand, applying procedures like `set-cdr!` or `delv!` to the new list will not alter the old list. If you also need to copy the list elements (making a deep copy), use the procedure `copy-tree` (see Section 6.11.4 [Copying], page 280).

6.7.2.4 List Selection

These procedures are used to get some information about a list, or to retrieve one or more elements of a list.

length *lst*   [Scheme Procedure]
scm_length (*lst*)   [C Function]
    Return the number of elements in list *lst*.

last-pair *lst*   [Scheme Procedure]
scm_last_pair (*lst*)   [C Function]
    Return the last pair in *lst*, signalling an error if *lst* is circular.

list-ref *list k*   [Scheme Procedure]
scm_list_ref (*list, k*)   [C Function]
    Return the kth element from *list*.

list-tail *lst k*   [Scheme Procedure]
list-cdr-ref *lst k*   [Scheme Procedure]
scm_list_tail (*lst, k*)   [C Function]
    Return the "tail" of *lst* beginning with its kth element. The first element of the list is considered to be element 0.

    `list-tail` and `list-cdr-ref` are identical. It may help to think of `list-cdr-ref` as accessing the kth cdr of the list, or returning the results of cdring k times down *lst*.

list-head *lst k*   [Scheme Procedure]
scm_list_head (*lst, k*)   [C Function]
    Copy the first k elements from *lst* into a new list, and return it.

6.7.2.5 Append and Reverse

`append` and `append!` are used to concatenate two or more lists in order to form a new list. `reverse` and `reverse!` return lists with the same elements as their arguments, but in reverse order. The procedure variants with an ! directly modify the pairs which form the list, whereas the other procedures create new pairs. This is why you should be careful when using the side-effecting variants.

append *lst ... obj*   [Scheme Procedure]
append   [Scheme Procedure]
append! *lst ... obj*   [Scheme Procedure]
append!   [Scheme Procedure]
scm_append (*lstlst*)   [C Function]
scm_append_x (*lstlst*)   [C Function]
    Return a list comprising all the elements of lists *lst ... obj*. If called with no arguments, return the empty list.

```
(append '(x) '(y))           ⇒  (x y)
(append '(a) '(b c d))       ⇒  (a b c d)
(append '(a (b)) '((c)))     ⇒  (a (b) (c))
```

The last argument *obj* may actually be any object; an improper list results if the last argument is not a proper list.

```
(append '(a b) '(c . d))     ⇒  (a b c . d)
(append '() 'a)              ⇒  a
```

append doesn't modify the given lists, but the return may share structure with the final *obj*. append! is permitted, but not required, to modify the given lists to form its return.

For scm_append and scm_append_x, *lstlst* is a list of the list operands *lst ... obj*. That *lstlst* itself is not modified or used in the return.

---

reverse *lst*   [Scheme Procedure]
reverse! *lst* [*newtail*]   [Scheme Procedure]
scm_reverse (*lst*)   [C Function]
scm_reverse_x (*lst, newtail*)   [C Function]
> Return a list comprising the elements of *lst*, in reverse order.
>
> reverse constructs a new list. reverse! is permitted, but not required, to modify *lst* in constructing its return.
>
> For reverse!, the optional *newtail* is appended to the result. *newtail* isn't reversed, it simply becomes the list tail. For scm_reverse_x, the *newtail* parameter is mandatory, but can be SCM_EOL if no further tail is required.

6.7.2.6 List Modification

The following procedures modify an existing list, either by changing elements of the list, or by changing the list structure itself.

list-set! *list k val*   [Scheme Procedure]
scm_list_set_x (*list, k, val*)   [C Function]
> Set the *k*th element of *list* to *val*.

list-cdr-set! *list k val*   [Scheme Procedure]
scm_list_cdr_set_x (*list, k, val*)   [C Function]
> Set the *k*th cdr of *list* to *val*.

delq *item lst*   [Scheme Procedure]
scm_delq (*item, lst*)   [C Function]
> Return a newly-created copy of *lst* with elements eq? to *item* removed. This procedure mirrors memq: delq compares elements of *lst* against *item* with eq?.

delv *item lst*   [Scheme Procedure]
scm_delv (*item, lst*)   [C Function]
> Return a newly-created copy of *lst* with elements eqv? to *item* removed. This procedure mirrors memv: delv compares elements of *lst* against *item* with eqv?.

`delete` *item lst*   [Scheme Procedure]

`scm_delete` (*item*, *lst*)   [C Function]

> Return a newly-created copy of *lst* with elements `equal?` to *item* removed. This procedure mirrors `member`: `delete` compares elements of *lst* against *item* with `equal?`.
>
> See also SRFI-1 which has an extended `delete` (Section 7.5.3.8 [SRFI-1 Deleting], page 561), and also an `lset-difference` which can delete multiple *items* in one call (Section 7.5.3.10 [SRFI-1 Set Operations], page 563).

`delq!` *item lst*   [Scheme Procedure]

`delv!` *item lst*   [Scheme Procedure]

`delete!` *item lst*   [Scheme Procedure]

`scm_delq_x` (*item*, *lst*)   [C Function]

`scm_delv_x` (*item*, *lst*)   [C Function]

`scm_delete_x` (*item*, *lst*)   [C Function]

> These procedures are destructive versions of `delq`, `delv` and `delete`: they modify the pointers in the existing *lst* rather than creating a new list. Caveat evaluator: Like other destructive list functions, these functions cannot modify the binding of *lst*, and so cannot be used to delete the first element of *lst* destructively.

`delq1!` *item lst*   [Scheme Procedure]

`scm_delq1_x` (*item*, *lst*)   [C Function]

> Like `delq!`, but only deletes the first occurrence of *item* from *lst*. Tests for equality using `eq?`. See also `delv1!` and `delete1!`.

`delv1!` *item lst*   [Scheme Procedure]

`scm_delv1_x` (*item*, *lst*)   [C Function]

> Like `delv!`, but only deletes the first occurrence of *item* from *lst*. Tests for equality using `eqv?`. See also `delq1!` and `delete1!`.

`delete1!` *item lst*   [Scheme Procedure]

`scm_delete1_x` (*item*, *lst*)   [C Function]

> Like `delete!`, but only deletes the first occurrence of *item* from *lst*. Tests for equality using `equal?`. See also `delq1!` and `delv1!`.

`filter` *pred lst*   [Scheme Procedure]

`filter!` *pred lst*   [Scheme Procedure]

> Return a list containing all elements from *lst* which satisfy the predicate *pred*. The elements in the result list have the same order as in *lst*. The order in which *pred* is applied to the list elements is not specified.
>
> `filter` does not change *lst*, but the result may share a tail with it. `filter!` may modify *lst* to construct its return.

6.7.2.7 List Searching

The following procedures search lists for particular elements. They use different comparison predicates for comparing list elements with the object to be searched. When they fail, they return `#f`, otherwise they return the sublist whose car is equal to the search object, where equality depends on the equality predicate used.

`memq` *x lst*   [Scheme Procedure]

`scm_memq` (*x, lst*)   [C Function]

> Return the first sublist of *lst* whose car is `eq?` to *x* where the sublists of *lst* are the non-empty lists returned by (`list-tail` *lst* *k*) for *k* less than the length of *lst*. If *x* does not occur in *lst*, then `#f` (not the empty list) is returned.

`memv` *x lst*   [Scheme Procedure]

`scm_memv` (*x, lst*)   [C Function]

> Return the first sublist of *lst* whose car is `eqv?` to *x* where the sublists of *lst* are the non-empty lists returned by (`list-tail` *lst* *k*) for *k* less than the length of *lst*. If *x* does not occur in *lst*, then `#f` (not the empty list) is returned.

`member` *x lst*   [Scheme Procedure]

`scm_member` (*x, lst*)   [C Function]

> Return the first sublist of *lst* whose car is `equal?` to *x* where the sublists of *lst* are the non-empty lists returned by (`list-tail` *lst* *k*) for *k* less than the length of *lst*. If *x* does not occur in *lst*, then `#f` (not the empty list) is returned.
>
> See also SRFI-1 which has an extended `member` function (Section 7.5.3.7 [SRFI-1 Searching], page 560).

6.7.2.8 List Mapping

List processing is very convenient in Scheme because the process of iterating over the elements of a list can be highly abstracted. The procedures in this section are the most basic iterating procedures for lists. They take a procedure and one or more lists as arguments, and apply the procedure to each element of the list. They differ in their return value.

`map` *proc arg1 arg2 ...*   [Scheme Procedure]

`map-in-order` *proc arg1 arg2 ...*   [Scheme Procedure]

`scm_map` (*proc, arg1, args*)   [C Function]

> Apply *proc* to each element of the list *arg1* (if only two arguments are given), or to the corresponding elements of the argument lists (if more than two arguments are given). The result(s) of the procedure applications are saved and returned in a list. For `map`, the order of procedure applications is not specified, `map-in-order` applies the procedure from left to right to the list elements.

`for-each` *proc arg1 arg2 ...*   [Scheme Procedure]

> Like `map`, but the procedure is always applied from left to right, and the result(s) of the procedure applications are thrown away. The return value is not specified.
>
> See also SRFI-1 which extends these functions to take lists of unequal lengths (Section 7.5.3.5 [SRFI-1 Fold and Map], page 556).

6.7.3 Vectors

Vectors are sequences of Scheme objects. Unlike lists, the length of a vector, once the vector is created, cannot be changed. The advantage of vectors over lists is that the time required to access one element of a vector given its *position* (synonymous with *index*), a zero-origin number, is constant, whereas lists have an access time linear to the position of the accessed element in the list.

Vectors can contain any kind of Scheme object; it is even possible to have different types of objects in the same vector. For vectors containing vectors, you may wish to use arrays, instead. Note, too, that vectors are the special case of one dimensional non-uniform arrays and that most array procedures operate happily on vectors (see Section 6.7.5 [Arrays], page 200).

Also see Section 7.5.29 [SRFI-43], page 609, for a comprehensive vector library.

6.7.3.1 Read Syntax for Vectors

Vectors can literally be entered in source code, just like strings, characters or some of the other data types. The read syntax for vectors is as follows: A sharp sign (#), followed by an opening parentheses, all elements of the vector in their respective read syntax, and finally a closing parentheses. Like strings, vectors do not have to be quoted.

The following are examples of the read syntax for vectors; where the first vector only contains numbers and the second three different object types: a string, a symbol and a number in hexadecimal notation.

```
#(1 2 3)
#("Hello" foo #xdeadbeef)
```

6.7.3.2 Dynamic Vector Creation and Validation

Instead of creating a vector implicitly by using the read syntax just described, you can create a vector dynamically by calling one of the `vector` and `list->vector` primitives with the list of Scheme values that you want to place into a vector. The size of the vector thus created is determined implicitly by the number of arguments given.

`vector` *arg . . .* [Scheme Procedure]
`list->vector` *l* [Scheme Procedure]
`scm_vector` (*l*) [C Function]

> Return a newly allocated vector composed of the given arguments. Analogous to `list`.
>
> > (vector 'a 'b 'c) ⇒ #(a b c)

The inverse operation is `vector->list`:

`vector->list` *v* [Scheme Procedure]
`scm_vector_to_list` (*v*) [C Function]

> Return a newly allocated list composed of the elements of *v*.
>
> > (vector->list #(dah dah didah)) ⇒ (dah dah didah)
> > (list->vector '(dididit dah)) ⇒ #(dididit dah)

To allocate a vector with an explicitly specified size, use `make-vector`. With this primitive you can also specify an initial value for the vector elements (the same value for all elements, that is):

`make-vector` *len* [*fill*] [Scheme Procedure]
`scm_make_vector` (*len, fill*) [C Function]

> Return a newly allocated vector of *len* elements. If a second argument is given, then each position is initialized to *fill*. Otherwise the initial contents of each position is unspecified.

SCM `scm_c_make_vector` (*size_t k, SCM fill*)   [C Function]
> Like `scm_make_vector`, but the length is given as a `size_t`.

To check whether an arbitrary Scheme value *is* a vector, use the `vector?` primitive:

`vector?` *obj*   [Scheme Procedure]
`scm_vector_p` (*obj*)   [C Function]
> Return `#t` if *obj* is a vector, otherwise return `#f`.

`int scm_is_vector` (*SCM obj*)   [C Function]
> Return non-zero when *obj* is a vector, otherwise return `zero`.

6.7.3.3 Accessing and Modifying Vector Contents

`vector-length` and `vector-ref` return information about a given vector, respectively its size and the elements that are contained in the vector.

`vector-length` *vector*   [Scheme Procedure]
`scm_vector_length` (*vector*)   [C Function]
> Return the number of elements in *vector* as an exact integer.

`size_t scm_c_vector_length` (*SCM vec*)   [C Function]
> Return the number of elements in *vec* as a `size_t`.

`vector-ref` *vec k*   [Scheme Procedure]
`scm_vector_ref` (*vec, k*)   [C Function]
> Return the contents of position *k* of *vec*. *k* must be a valid index of *vec*.
>
> ```
>         (vector-ref #(1 1 2 3 5 8 13 21) 5)  ⇒ 8
>         (vector-ref #(1 1 2 3 5 8 13 21)
>             (let ((i (round (* 2 (acos -1)))))
>               (if (inexact? i)
>                 (inexact->exact i)
>                   i)))  ⇒ 13
> ```

SCM `scm_c_vector_ref` (*SCM vec, size_t k*)   [C Function]
> Return the contents of position *k* (a `size_t`) of *vec*.

A vector created by one of the dynamic vector constructor procedures (see Section 6.7.3.2 [Vector Creation], page 194) can be modified using the following procedures.

NOTE: According to R5RS, it is an error to use any of these procedures on a literally read vector, because such vectors should be considered as constants. Currently, however, Guile does not detect this error.

`vector-set!` *vec k obj*   [Scheme Procedure]
`scm_vector_set_x` (*vec, k, obj*)   [C Function]
> Store *obj* in position *k* of *vec*. *k* must be a valid index of *vec*. The value returned by `'vector-set!'` is unspecified.
>
> ```
>         (let ((vec (vector 0 '(2 2 2 2) "Anna")))
>           (vector-set! vec 1 '("Sue" "Sue"))
>             vec)  ⇒  #(0 ("Sue" "Sue") "Anna")
> ```

void **scm_c_vector_set_x** (*SCM vec, size_t k, SCM obj*)   [C Function]
>   Store *obj* in position *k* (a `size_t`) of *vec*.

vector-fill! *vec fill*   [Scheme Procedure]
scm_vector_fill_x (*vec, fill*)   [C Function]
>   Store *fill* in every position of *vec*. The value returned by `vector-fill!` is unspecified.

vector-copy *vec*   [Scheme Procedure]
scm_vector_copy (*vec*)   [C Function]
>   Return a copy of *vec*.

vector-move-left! *vec1 start1 end1 vec2 start2*   [Scheme Procedure]
scm_vector_move_left_x (*vec1, start1, end1, vec2, start2*)   [C Function]
>   Copy elements from *vec1*, positions *start1* to *end1*, to *vec2* starting at position *start2*. *start1* and *start2* are inclusive indices; *end1* is exclusive.
>
>   `vector-move-left!` copies elements in leftmost order. Therefore, in the case where *vec1* and *vec2* refer to the same vector, `vector-move-left!` is usually appropriate when *start1* is greater than *start2*.

vector-move-right! *vec1 start1 end1 vec2 start2*   [Scheme Procedure]
scm_vector_move_right_x (*vec1, start1, end1, vec2, start2*)   [C Function]
>   Copy elements from *vec1*, positions *start1* to *end1*, to *vec2* starting at position *start2*. *start1* and *start2* are inclusive indices; *end1* is exclusive.
>
>   `vector-move-right!` copies elements in rightmost order. Therefore, in the case where *vec1* and *vec2* refer to the same vector, `vector-move-right!` is usually appropriate when *start1* is less than *start2*.

6.7.3.4 Vector Accessing from C

A vector can be read and modified from C with the functions `scm_c_vector_ref` and `scm_c_vector_set_x`, for example. In addition to these functions, there are two more ways to access vectors from C that might be more efficient in certain situations: you can restrict yourself to *simple vectors* and then use the very fast *simple vector macros*; or you can use the very general framework for accessing all kinds of arrays (see Section 6.7.5.4 [Accessing Arrays from C], page 208), which is more verbose, but can deal efficiently with all kinds of vectors (and arrays). For vectors, you can use the `scm_vector_elements` and `scm_vector_writable_elements` functions as shortcuts.

int **scm_is_simple_vector** (*SCM obj*)   [C Function]
>   Return non-zero if *obj* is a simple vector, else return zero. A simple vector is a vector that can be used with the `SCM_SIMPLE_*` macros below.
>
>   The following functions are guaranteed to return simple vectors: `scm_make_vector`, `scm_c_make_vector`, `scm_vector`, `scm_list_to_vector`.

size_t **SCM_SIMPLE_VECTOR_LENGTH** (*SCM vec*)   [C Macro]
>   Evaluates to the length of the simple vector *vec*. No type checking is done.

SCM **SCM_SIMPLE_VECTOR_REF** (*SCM vec, size_t idx*)   [C Macro]
>   Evaluates to the element at position *idx* in the simple vector *vec*. No type or range checking is done.

void SCM_SIMPLE_VECTOR_SET (*SCM vec, size_t idx, SCM val*)   [C Macro]
> Sets the element at position *idx* in the simple vector *vec* to *val*. No type or range checking is done.

const SCM * scm_vector_elements (*SCM vec, scm_t_array_handle*   [C Function]
> *handle, size_t *lenp, ssize_t *incp*)
> Acquire a handle for the vector *vec* and return a pointer to the elements of it. This pointer can only be used to read the elements of *vec*. When *vec* is not a vector, an error is signaled. The handle must eventually be released with `scm_array_handle_release`.
>
> The variables pointed to by *lenp* and *incp* are filled with the number of elements of the vector and the increment (number of elements) between successive elements, respectively. Successive elements of *vec* need not be contiguous in their underlying "root vector" returned here; hence the increment is not necessarily equal to 1 and may well be negative too (see Section 6.7.5.3 [Shared Arrays], page 206).
>
> The following example shows the typical way to use this function. It creates a list of all elements of *vec* (in reverse order).

```
scm_t_array_handle handle;
size_t i, len;
ssize_t inc;
const SCM *elt;
SCM list;

elt = scm_vector_elements (vec, &handle, &len, &inc);
list = SCM_EOL;
for (i = 0; i < len; i++, elt += inc)
  list = scm_cons (*elt, list);
scm_array_handle_release (&handle);
```

SCM * scm_vector_writable_elements (*SCM vec,*   [C Function]
> *scm_t_array_handle *handle, size_t *lenp, ssize_t *incp*)
> Like `scm_vector_elements` but the pointer can be used to modify the vector.
>
> The following example shows the typical way to use this function. It fills a vector with #t.

```
scm_t_array_handle handle;
size_t i, len;
ssize_t inc;
SCM *elt;

elt = scm_vector_writable_elements (vec, &handle, &len, &inc);
for (i = 0; i < len; i++, elt += inc)
  *elt = SCM_BOOL_T;
scm_array_handle_release (&handle);
```

6.7.3.5 Uniform Numeric Vectors

A uniform numeric vector is a vector whose elements are all of a single numeric type. Guile offers uniform numeric vectors for signed and unsigned 8-bit, 16-bit, 32-bit, and 64-bit integers, two sizes of floating point values, and complex floating-point numbers of these two sizes. See Section 7.5.5 [SRFI-4], page 566, for more information.

For many purposes, bytevectors work just as well as uniform vectors, and have the advantage that they integrate well with binary input and output. See Section 6.6.6 [Bytevectors], page 163, for more information on bytevectors.

6.7.4 Bit Vectors

Bit vectors are zero-origin, one-dimensional arrays of booleans. They are displayed as a sequence of 0s and 1s prefixed by #*, e.g.,

```
(make-bitvector 8 #f) ⇒
#*00000000
```

Bit vectors are the special case of one dimensional bit arrays, and can thus be used with the array procedures, See Section 6.7.5 [Arrays], page 200.

bitvector? *obj*   [Scheme Procedure]
scm_bitvector_p (*obj*)   [C Function]
> Return #t when *obj* is a bitvector, else return #f.

int scm_is_bitvector (*SCM obj*)   [C Function]
> Return 1 when *obj* is a bitvector, else return 0.

make-bitvector *len* [*fill*]   [Scheme Procedure]
scm_make_bitvector (*len, fill*)   [C Function]
> Create a new bitvector of length *len* and optionally initialize all elements to *fill*.

SCM scm_c_make_bitvector (*size_t len, SCM fill*)   [C Function]
> Like scm_make_bitvector, but the length is given as a size_t.

bitvector *bit ...*   [Scheme Procedure]
scm_bitvector (*bits*)   [C Function]
> Create a new bitvector with the arguments as elements.

bitvector-length *vec*   [Scheme Procedure]
scm_bitvector_length (*vec*)   [C Function]
> Return the length of the bitvector *vec*.

size_t scm_c_bitvector_length (*SCM vec*)   [C Function]
> Like scm_bitvector_length, but the length is returned as a size_t.

bitvector-ref *vec idx*   [Scheme Procedure]
scm_bitvector_ref (*vec, idx*)   [C Function]
> Return the element at index *idx* of the bitvector *vec*.

SCM scm_c_bitvector_ref (*SCM vec, size_t idx*)   [C Function]
> Return the element at index *idx* of the bitvector *vec*.

bitvector-set! *vec idx val*   [Scheme Procedure]
scm_bitvector_set_x (*vec, idx, val*)   [C Function]
> Set the element at index *idx* of the bitvector *vec* when *val* is true, else clear it.

SCM `scm_c_bitvector_set_x` (*SCM vec, size_t idx, SCM val*)   [C Function]
>   Set the element at index *idx* of the bitvector *vec* when *val* is true, else clear it.

`bitvector-fill!` *vec val*   [Scheme Procedure]
`scm_bitvector_fill_x` (*vec, val*)   [C Function]
>   Set all elements of the bitvector *vec* when *val* is true, else clear them.

`list->bitvector` *list*   [Scheme Procedure]
`scm_list_to_bitvector` (*list*)   [C Function]
>   Return a new bitvector initialized with the elements of *list*.

`bitvector->list` *vec*   [Scheme Procedure]
`scm_bitvector_to_list` (*vec*)   [C Function]
>   Return a new list initialized with the elements of the bitvector *vec*.

`bit-count` *bool bitvector*   [Scheme Procedure]
`scm_bit_count` (*bool, bitvector*)   [C Function]
>   Return a count of how many entries in *bitvector* are equal to *bool*. For example,

>   `(bit-count #f #*000111000)` $\Rightarrow$ `6`

`bit-position` *bool bitvector start*   [Scheme Procedure]
`scm_bit_position` (*bool, bitvector, start*)   [C Function]
>   Return the index of the first occurrence of *bool* in *bitvector*, starting from *start*. If
>   there is no *bool* entry between *start* and the end of *bitvector*, then return `#f`. For
>   example,

>   `(bit-position #t #*000101 0)` $\Rightarrow$ `3`
>   `(bit-position #f #*0001111 3)` $\Rightarrow$ `#f`

`bit-invert!` *bitvector*   [Scheme Procedure]
`scm_bit_invert_x` (*bitvector*)   [C Function]
>   Modify *bitvector* by replacing each element with its negation.

`bit-set*!` *bitvector uvec bool*   [Scheme Procedure]
`scm_bit_set_star_x` (*bitvector, uvec, bool*)   [C Function]
>   Set entries of *bitvector* to *bool*, with *uvec* selecting the entries to change. The return
>   value is unspecified.

>   If *uvec* is a bit vector, then those entries where it has `#t` are the ones in *bitvector*
>   which are set to *bool*. *uvec* and *bitvector* must be the same length. When *bool* is
>   `#t` it's like *uvec* is OR'ed into *bitvector*. Or when *bool* is `#f` it can be seen as an
>   ANDNOT.

>   `(define bv #*01000010)`
>   `(bit-set*! bv #*10010001 #t)`
>   `bv`
> $\Rightarrow$ `#*11010011`

>   If *uvec* is a uniform vector of unsigned long integers, then they're indexes into *bitvector* which are set to *bool*.

```
(define bv #*01000010)
(bit-set*! bv #u(5 2 7) #t)
bv
⇒ #*01100111
```

bit-count* *bitvector uvec bool*   [Scheme Procedure]
scm_bit_count_star (*bitvector, uvec, bool*)   [C Function]
> Return a count of how many entries in *bitvector* are equal to *bool*, with *uvec* selecting the entries to consider.
>
> *uvec* is interpreted in the same way as for bit-set*! above. Namely, if *uvec* is a bit vector then entries which have #t there are considered in *bitvector*. Or if *uvec* is a uniform vector of unsigned long integers then it's the indexes in *bitvector* to consider.
>
> For example,
>
> > (bit-count* #*01110111 #*11001101 #t) ⇒ 3
> > (bit-count* #*01110111 #u(7 0 4) #f) ⇒ 2

const scm_t_uint32 * scm_bitvector_elements (*SCM vec*,   [C Function]
> *scm_t_array_handle *handle, size_t *offp, size_t *lenp, ssize_t *incp*)
> Like scm_vector_elements (see Section 6.7.3.4 [Vector Accessing from C], page 196), but for bitvectors. The variable pointed to by *offp* is set to the value returned by scm_array_handle_bit_elements_offset. See scm_array_handle_bit_elements for how to use the returned pointer and the offset.

scm_t_uint32 * scm_bitvector_writable_elements (*SCM vec*,   [C Function]
> *scm_t_array_handle *handle, size_t *offp, size_t *lenp, ssize_t *incp*)
> Like scm_bitvector_elements, but the pointer is good for reading and writing.

6.7.5 Arrays

Arrays are a collection of cells organized into an arbitrary number of dimensions. Each cell can be accessed in constant time by supplying an index for each dimension.

In the current implementation, an array uses a vector of some kind for the actual storage of its elements. Any kind of vector will do, so you can have arrays of uniform numeric values, arrays of characters, arrays of bits, and of course, arrays of arbitrary Scheme values. For example, arrays with an underlying c64vector might be nice for digital signal processing, while arrays made from a u8vector might be used to hold gray-scale images.

The number of dimensions of an array is called its *rank*. Thus, a matrix is an array of rank 2, while a vector has rank 1. When accessing an array element, you have to specify one exact integer for each dimension. These integers are called the *indices* of the element. An array specifies the allowed range of indices for each dimension via an inclusive lower and upper bound. These bounds can well be negative, but the upper bound must be greater than or equal to the lower bound minus one. When all lower bounds of an array are zero, it is called a *zero-origin* array.

Arrays can be of rank 0, which could be interpreted as a scalar. Thus, a zero-rank array can store exactly one object and the list of indices of this element is the empty list.

Arrays contain zero elements when one of their dimensions has a zero length. These empty arrays maintain information about their shape: a matrix with zero columns and 3 rows is different from a matrix with 3 columns and zero rows, which again is different from a vector of length zero.

The array procedures are all polymorphic, treating strings, uniform numeric vectors, bytevectors, bit vectors and ordinary vectors as one dimensional arrays.

6.7.5.1 Array Syntax

An array is displayed as `#` followed by its rank, followed by a tag that describes the underlying vector, optionally followed by information about its shape, and finally followed by the cells, organized into dimensions using parentheses.

In more words, the array tag is of the form

```
#<rank><vectag><@lower><:len><@lower><:len>...
```

where `<rank>` is a positive integer in decimal giving the rank of the array. It is omitted when the rank is 1 and the array is non-shared and has zero-origin (see below). For shared arrays and for a non-zero origin, the rank is always printed even when it is 1 to distinguish them from ordinary vectors.

The `<vectag>` part is the tag for a uniform numeric vector, like `u8`, `s16`, etc, `b` for bitvectors, or `a` for strings. It is empty for ordinary vectors.

The `<@lower>` part is a '`@`' character followed by a signed integer in decimal giving the lower bound of a dimension. There is one `<@lower>` for each dimension. When all lower bounds are zero, all `<@lower>` parts are omitted.

The `<:len>` part is a '`:`' character followed by an unsigned integer in decimal giving the length of a dimension. Like for the lower bounds, there is one `<:len>` for each dimension, and the `<:len>` part always follows the `<@lower>` part for a dimension. Lengths are only then printed when they can't be deduced from the nested lists of elements of the array literal, which can happen when at least one length is zero.

As a special case, an array of rank 0 is printed as `#0<vectag>(<scalar>)`, where `<scalar>` is the result of printing the single element of the array.

Thus,

`#(1 2 3)`　　is an ordinary array of rank 1 with lower bound 0 in dimension 0. (I.e., a regular vector.)

`#@2(1 2 3)`

　　　　is an ordinary array of rank 1 with lower bound 2 in dimension 0.

`#2((1 2 3) (4 5 6))`

　　　　is a non-uniform array of rank 2; a 3×3 matrix with index ranges 0..2 and 0..2.

`#u32(0 1 2)`

　　　　is a uniform u8 array of rank 1.

`#2u32@2@3((1 2) (2 3))`

　　　　is a uniform u8 array of rank 2 with index ranges 2..3 and 3..4.

`#2()`　　is a two-dimensional array with index ranges 0..-1 and 0..-1, i.e. both dimensions have length zero.

`#2:0:2()`　　is a two-dimensional array with index ranges 0..-1 and 0..1, i.e. the first dimension has length zero, but the second has length 2.

`#0(12)`   is a rank-zero array with contents 12.

In addition, bytevectors are also arrays, but use a different syntax (see Section 6.6.6 [Bytevectors], page 163):

`#vu8(1 2 3)`
        is a 3-byte long bytevector, with contents 1, 2, 3.

6.7.5.2 Array Procedures

When an array is created, the range of each dimension must be specified, e.g., to create a 2×3 array with a zero-based index:

    `(make-array 'ho 2 3)` $\Rightarrow$ `#2((ho ho ho) (ho ho ho))`

The range of each dimension can also be given explicitly, e.g., another way to create the same array:

    `(make-array 'ho '(0 1) '(0 2))` $\Rightarrow$ `#2((ho ho ho) (ho ho ho))`

The following procedures can be used with arrays (or vectors). An argument shown as *idx*... means one parameter for each dimension in the array. A *idxlist* argument means a list of such values, one for each dimension.

`array?` *obj*   [Scheme Procedure]
`scm_array_p` (*obj, unused*)   [C Function]
    Return `#t` if the *obj* is an array, and `#f` if not.

    The second argument to `scm_array_p` is there for historical reasons, but it is not used. You should always pass `SCM_UNDEFINED` as its value.

`typed-array?` *obj type*   [Scheme Procedure]
`scm_typed_array_p` (*obj, type*)   [C Function]
    Return `#t` if the *obj* is an array of type *type*, and `#f` if not.

`int scm_is_array` (*SCM obj*)   [C Function]
    Return 1 if the *obj* is an array and 0 if not.

`int scm_is_typed_array` (*SCM obj, SCM type*)   [C Function]
    Return 0 if the *obj* is an array of type *type*, and 1 if not.

`make-array` *fill bound* ...   [Scheme Procedure]
`scm_make_array` (*fill, bounds*)   [C Function]
    Equivalent to (`make-typed-array #t` *fill bound* ...).

`make-typed-array` *type fill bound* ...   [Scheme Procedure]
`scm_make_typed_array` (*type, fill, bounds*)   [C Function]
    Create and return an array that has as many dimensions as there are *bound*s and (maybe) fill it with *fill*.

    The underlying storage vector is created according to *type*, which must be a symbol whose name is the 'vectag' of the array as explained above, or `#t` for ordinary, non-specialized arrays.

    For example, using the symbol `f64` for *type* will create an array that uses a `f64vector` for storing its elements, and `a` will use a string.

When *fill* is not the special *unspecified* value, the new array is filled with *fill*. Otherwise, the initial contents of the array is unspecified. The special *unspecified* value is stored in the variable *unspecified* so that for example (make-typed-array 'u32 *unspecified* 4) creates a uninitialized u32 vector of length 4.

Each *bound* may be a positive non-zero integer *n*, in which case the index for that dimension can range from 0 through *n*-1; or an explicit index range specifier in the form (LOWER UPPER), where both *lower* and *upper* are integers, possibly less than zero, and possibly the same number (however, *lower* cannot be greater than *upper*).

list->array *dimspec list*   [Scheme Procedure]
    Equivalent to (list->typed-array #t *dimspec list*).

list->typed-array *type dimspec list*   [Scheme Procedure]
scm_list_to_typed_array (*type, dimspec, list*)   [C Function]
    Return an array of the type indicated by *type* with elements the same as those of *list*.

    The argument *dimspec* determines the number of dimensions of the array and their lower bounds. When *dimspec* is an exact integer, it gives the number of dimensions directly and all lower bounds are zero. When it is a list of exact integers, then each element is the lower index bound of a dimension, and there will be as many dimensions as elements in the list.

array-type *array*   [Scheme Procedure]
scm_array_type (*array*)   [C Function]
    Return the type of *array*. This is the 'vectag' used for printing *array* (or #t for ordinary arrays) and can be used with make-typed-array to create an array of the same kind as *array*.

array-ref *array idx* ...   [Scheme Procedure]
scm_array_ref (*array, idxlist*)   [C Function]
    Return the element at (idx ...) in *array*.

```
(define a (make-array 999 '(1 2) '(3 4)))
(array-ref a 2 4) ⇒ 999
```

array-in-bounds? *array idx* ...   [Scheme Procedure]
scm_array_in_bounds_p (*array, idxlist*)   [C Function]
    Return #t if the given indices would be acceptable to array-ref.

```
(define a (make-array #f '(1 2) '(3 4)))
(array-in-bounds? a 2 3) ⇒ #t
(array-in-bounds? a 0 0) ⇒ #f
```

array-set! *array obj idx* ...   [Scheme Procedure]
scm_array_set_x (*array, obj, idxlist*)   [C Function]
    Set the element at (idx ...) in *array* to *obj*. The return value is unspecified.

```
(define a (make-array #f '(0 1) '(0 1)))
(array-set! a #t 1 1)
a ⇒ #2((#f #f) (#f #t))
```

`array-shape` *array*   [Scheme Procedure]
`array-dimensions` *array*   [Scheme Procedure]
`scm_array_dimensions` (*array*)   [C Function]
> Return a list of the bounds for each dimension of *array*.
>
> `array-shape` gives (`lower upper`) for each dimension. `array-dimensions` instead returns just *upper* + 1 for dimensions with a 0 lower bound. Both are suitable as input to `make-array`.
>
> For example,
>
> ```
> (define a (make-array 'foo '(-1 3) 5))
> (array-shape a)      ⇒ ((-1 3) (0 4))
> (array-dimensions a) ⇒ ((-1 3) 5)
> ```

`array-length` *array*   [Scheme Procedure]
`scm_array_length` (*array*)   [C Function]
`size_t` *scm_c_array_length* (*array*)   [C Function]
> Return the length of an array: its first dimension. It is an error to ask for the length of an array of rank 0.

`array-rank` *array*   [Scheme Procedure]
`scm_array_rank` (*array*)   [C Function]
> Return the rank of *array*.

`size_t scm_c_array_rank` (*SCM array*)   [C Function]
> Return the rank of *array* as a `size_t`.

`array->list` *array*   [Scheme Procedure]
`scm_array_to_list` (*array*)   [C Function]
> Return a list consisting of all the elements, in order, of *array*.

`array-copy!` *src dst*   [Scheme Procedure]
`array-copy-in-order!` *src dst*   [Scheme Procedure]
`scm_array_copy_x` (*src, dst*)   [C Function]
> Copy every element from vector or array *src* to the corresponding element of *dst*. *dst* must have the same rank as *src*, and be at least as large in each dimension. The return value is unspecified.

`array-fill!` *array fill*   [Scheme Procedure]
`scm_array_fill_x` (*array, fill*)   [C Function]
> Store *fill* in every element of *array*. The value returned is unspecified.

`array-equal?` *array . . .*   [Scheme Procedure]
> Return #t if all arguments are arrays with the same shape, the same type, and have corresponding elements which are either `equal?` or `array-equal?`. This function differs from `equal?` (see Section 6.11.1 [Equality], page 276) in that all arguments must be arrays.

`array-map!` *dst proc src . . .*   [Scheme Procedure]
`array-map-in-order!` *dst proc src1 . . . srcN*   [Scheme Procedure]

`scm_array_map_x` (*dst*, *proc*, *srclist*)   [C Function]

> Set each element of the *dst* array to values obtained from calls to *proc*. The value returned is unspecified.
>
> Each call is (`proc elem1 ... elemN`), where each *elem* is from the corresponding *src* array, at the *dst* index. `array-map-in-order!` makes the calls in row-major order, `array-map!` makes them in an unspecified order.
>
> The *src* arrays must have the same number of dimensions as *dst*, and must have a range for each dimension which covers the range in *dst*. This ensures all *dst* indices are valid in each *src*.

`array-for-each` *proc src1 src2* ...   [Scheme Procedure]
`scm_array_for_each` (*proc*, *src1*, *srclist*)   [C Function]

> Apply *proc* to each tuple of elements of *src1 src2* ..., in row-major order. The value returned is unspecified.

`array-index-map!` *dst proc*   [Scheme Procedure]
`scm_array_index_map_x` (*dst*, *proc*)   [C Function]

> Set each element of the *dst* array to values returned by calls to *proc*. The value returned is unspecified.
>
> Each call is (`proc i1 ... iN`), where *i1...iN* is the destination index, one parameter for each dimension. The order in which the calls are made is unspecified.
>
> For example, to create a 4×4 matrix representing a cyclic group,
> $$\begin{pmatrix} 0 & 1 & 2 & 3 \\ 1 & 2 & 3 & 0 \\ 2 & 3 & 0 & 1 \\ 3 & 0 & 1 & 2 \end{pmatrix}$$
> ```
> (define a (make-array #f 4 4))
> (array-index-map! a (lambda (i j)
>                       (modulo (+ i j) 4)))
> ```

`uniform-array-read!` *ra* [*port_or_fd* [*start* [*end*]]]   [Scheme Procedure]
`scm_uniform_array_read_x` (*ra*, *port_or_fd*, *start*, *end*)   [C Function]

> Attempt to read all elements of array *ra*, in lexicographic order, as binary objects from *port_or_fd*. If an end of file is encountered, the objects up to that point are put into *ra* (starting at the beginning) and the remainder of the array is unchanged.
>
> The optional arguments *start* and *end* allow a specified region of a vector (or linearized array) to be read, leaving the remainder of the vector unchanged.
>
> `uniform-array-read!` returns the number of objects read. *port_or_fd* may be omitted, in which case it defaults to the value returned by (`current-input-port`).

`uniform-array-write` *ra* [*port_or_fd* [*start* [*end*]]]   [Scheme Procedure]
`scm_uniform_array_write` (*ra*, *port_or_fd*, *start*, *end*)   [C Function]

> Writes all elements of *ra* as binary objects to *port_or_fd*.
>
> The optional arguments *start* and *end* allow a specified region of a vector (or linearized array) to be written.
>
> The number of objects actually written is returned. *port_or_fd* may be omitted, in which case it defaults to the value returned by (`current-output-port`).

6.7.5.3 Shared Arrays

make-shared-array *oldarray mapfunc bound ...* [Scheme Procedure]
scm_make_shared_array (*oldarray, mapfunc, boundlist*) [C Function]

Return a new array which shares the storage of *oldarray*. Changes made through either affect the same underlying storage. The *bound ...* arguments are the shape of the new array, the same as **make-array** (see Section 6.7.5.2 [Array Procedures], page 202).

mapfunc translates coordinates from the new array to the *oldarray*. It's called as (*mapfunc* newidx1 ...) with one parameter for each dimension of the new array, and should return a list of indices for *oldarray*, one for each dimension of *oldarray*.

mapfunc must be affine linear, meaning that each *oldarray* index must be formed by adding integer multiples (possibly negative) of some or all of *newidx1* etc, plus a possible integer offset. The multiples and offset must be the same in each call.

One good use for a shared array is to restrict the range of some dimensions, so as to apply say **array-for-each** or **array-fill!** to only part of an array. The plain **list** function can be used for *mapfunc* in this case, making no changes to the index values. For example,

```
(make-shared-array #2((a b c) (d e f) (g h i)) list 3 2)
⇒ #2((a b) (d e) (g h))
```

The new array can have fewer dimensions than *oldarray*, for example to take a column from an array.

```
(make-shared-array #2((a b c) (d e f) (g h i))
                   (lambda (i) (list i 2))
                   '(0 2))
⇒ #1(c f i)
```

A diagonal can be taken by using the single new array index for both row and column in the old array. For example,

```
(make-shared-array #2((a b c) (d e f) (g h i))
                   (lambda (i) (list i i))
                   '(0 2))
⇒ #1(a e i)
```

Dimensions can be increased by for instance considering portions of a one dimensional array as rows in a two dimensional array. (**array-contents** below can do the opposite, flattening an array.)

```
(make-shared-array #1(a b c d e f g h i j k l)
                   (lambda (i j) (list (+ (* i 3) j)))
                   4 3)
⇒ #2((a b c) (d e f) (g h i) (j k l))
```

By negating an index the order that elements appear can be reversed. The following just reverses the column order,

```
(make-shared-array #2((a b c) (d e f) (g h i))
                   (lambda (i j) (list i (- 2 j)))
```

```
                              3 3)
    ⇒ #2((c b a) (f e d) (i h g))
```
A fixed offset on indexes allows for instance a change from a 0 based to a 1 based array,

```
    (define x #2((a b c) (d e f) (g h i)))
    (define y (make-shared-array x
                              (lambda (i j) (list (1- i) (1- j)))
                              '(1 3) '(1 3)))
    (array-ref x 0 0) ⇒ a
    (array-ref y 1 1) ⇒ a
```
A multiple on an index allows every Nth element of an array to be taken. The following is every third element,

```
    (make-shared-array #1(a b c d e f g h i j k l)
                      (lambda (i) (list (* i 3)))
                      4)
    ⇒ #1(a d g j)
```
The above examples can be combined to make weird and wonderful selections from an array, but it's important to note that because *mapfunc* must be affine linear, arbitrary permutations are not possible.

In the current implementation, *mapfunc* is not called for every access to the new array but only on some sample points to establish a base and stride for new array indices in *oldarray* data. A few sample points are enough because *mapfunc* is linear.

shared-array-increments *array*   [Scheme Procedure]
scm_shared_array_increments (*array*)   [C Function]
>   For each dimension, return the distance between elements in the root vector.

shared-array-offset *array*   [Scheme Procedure]
scm_shared_array_offset (*array*)   [C Function]
>   Return the root vector index of the first element in the array.

shared-array-root *array*   [Scheme Procedure]
scm_shared_array_root (*array*)   [C Function]
>   Return the root vector of a shared array.

array-contents *array* [*strict*]   [Scheme Procedure]
scm_array_contents (*array, strict*)   [C Function]
>   If *array* may be *unrolled* into a one dimensional shared array without changing their order (last subscript changing fastest), then **array-contents** returns that shared array, otherwise it returns #f. All arrays made by **make-array** and **make-typed-array** may be unrolled, some arrays made by **make-shared-array** may not be.
>
>   If the optional argument *strict* is provided, a shared array will be returned only if its elements are stored internally contiguous in memory.

transpose-array *array dim1 dim2 . . .*   [Scheme Procedure]
scm_transpose_array (*array, dimlist*)   [C Function]
>   Return an array sharing contents with *array*, but with dimensions arranged in a different order. There must be one *dim* argument for each dimension of *array*. *dim1,*

dim2, ... should be integers between 0 and the rank of the array to be returned. Each integer in that range must appear at least once in the argument list.

The values of *dim1*, *dim2*, ... correspond to dimensions in the array to be returned, and their positions in the argument list to dimensions of *array*. Several *dims* may have the same value, in which case the returned array will have smaller rank than *array*.

```
(transpose-array '#2((a b) (c d)) 1 0) ⇒ #2((a c) (b d))
(transpose-array '#2((a b) (c d)) 0 0) ⇒ #1(a d)
(transpose-array '#3(((a b c) (d e f)) ((1 2 3) (4 5 6))) 1 1 0) ⇒
                  #2((a 4) (b 5) (c 6))
```

6.7.5.4 Accessing Arrays from C

For interworking with external C code, Guile provides an API to allow C code to access the elements of a Scheme array. In particular, for uniform numeric arrays, the API exposes the underlying uniform data as a C array of numbers of the relevant type.

While pointers to the elements of an array are in use, the array itself must be protected so that the pointer remains valid. Such a protected array is said to be *reserved*. A reserved array can be read but modifications to it that would cause the pointer to its elements to become invalid are prevented. When you attempt such a modification, an error is signalled.

(This is similar to locking the array while it is in use, but without the danger of a deadlock. In a multi-threaded program, you will need additional synchronization to avoid modifying reserved arrays.)

You must take care to always unreserve an array after reserving it, even in the presence of non-local exits. If a non-local exit can happen between these two calls, you should install a dynwind context that releases the array when it is left (see Section 6.13.10 [Dynamic Wind], page 309).

In addition, array reserving and unreserving must be properly paired. For instance, when reserving two or more arrays in a certain order, you need to unreserve them in the opposite order.

Once you have reserved an array and have retrieved the pointer to its elements, you must figure out the layout of the elements in memory. Guile allows slices to be taken out of arrays without actually making a copy, such as making an alias for the diagonal of a matrix that can be treated as a vector. Arrays that result from such an operation are not stored contiguously in memory and when working with their elements directly, you need to take this into account.

The layout of array elements in memory can be defined via a *mapping function* that computes a scalar position from a vector of indices. The scalar position then is the offset of the element with the given indices from the start of the storage block of the array.

In Guile, this mapping function is restricted to be *affine*: all mapping functions of Guile arrays can be written as `p = b + c[0]*i[0] + c[1]*i[1] + ... + c[n-1]*i[n-1]` where `i[k]` is the kth index and `n` is the rank of the array. For example, a matrix of size 3x3 would have `b == 0`, `c[0] == 3` and `c[1] == 1`. When you transpose this matrix (with **transpose-array**, say), you will get an array whose mapping function has `b == 0`, `c[0] == 1` and `c[1] == 3`.

The function `scm_array_handle_dims` gives you (indirect) access to the coefficients
c[k].

Note that there are no functions for accessing the elements of a character array yet.
Once the string implementation of Guile has been changed to use Unicode, we will provide
them.

`scm_t_array_handle`   [C Type]
> This is a structure type that holds all information necessary to manage the reservation
> of arrays as explained above. Structures of this type must be allocated on the stack
> and must only be accessed by the functions listed below.

void `scm_array_get_handle` (*SCM array, scm_t_array_handle*   [C Function]
> **handle*)
> Reserve *array*, which must be an array, and prepare *handle* to be used with the
> functions below. You must eventually call `scm_array_handle_release` on *handle*,
> and do this in a properly nested fashion, as explained above. The structure pointed
> to by *handle* does not need to be initialized before calling this function.

void `scm_array_handle_release` (*scm_t_array_handle *handle*)   [C Function]
> End the array reservation represented by *handle*. After a call to this function, *handle*
> might be used for another reservation.

size_t `scm_array_handle_rank` (*scm_t_array_handle *handle*)   [C Function]
> Return the rank of the array represented by *handle*.

`scm_t_array_dim`   [C Type]
> This structure type holds information about the layout of one dimension of an array.
> It includes the following fields:

> `ssize_t lbnd`
> `ssize_t ubnd`
>> The lower and upper bounds (both inclusive) of the permissible index
>> range for the given dimension. Both values can be negative, but *lbnd* is
>> always less than or equal to *ubnd*.

> `ssize_t inc`
>> The distance from one element of this dimension to the next. Note, too,
>> that this can be negative.

const scm_t_array_dim * `scm_array_handle_dims`   [C Function]
> (*scm_t_array_handle *handle*)
> Return a pointer to a C vector of information about the dimensions of the array
> represented by *handle*. This pointer is valid as long as the array remains reserved.
> As explained above, the `scm_t_array_dim` structures returned by this function can
> be used calculate the position of an element in the storage block of the array from its
> indices.

> This position can then be used as an index into the C array pointer returned by the
> various `scm_array_handle_<foo>_elements` functions, or with `scm_array_handle_`
> `ref` and `scm_array_handle_set`.

Here is how one can compute the position *pos* of an element given its indices in the vector *indices*:

```
ssize_t indices[RANK];
scm_t_array_dim *dims;
ssize_t pos;
size_t i;

pos = 0;
for (i = 0; i < RANK; i++)
  {
    if (indices[i] < dims[i].lbnd || indices[i] > dims[i].ubnd)
      out_of_range ();
    pos += (indices[i] - dims[i].lbnd) * dims[i].inc;
  }
```

ssize_t scm_array_handle_pos (*scm_t_array_handle *handle, SCM*   [C Function]
    indices)

Compute the position corresponding to *indices*, a list of indices. The position is computed as described above for scm_array_handle_dims. The number of the indices and their range is checked and an appropriate error is signalled for invalid indices.

SCM scm_array_handle_ref (*scm_t_array_handle *handle, ssize_t pos*)   [C Function]

Return the element at position *pos* in the storage block of the array represented by *handle*. Any kind of array is acceptable. No range checking is done on *pos*.

void scm_array_handle_set (*scm_t_array_handle *handle, ssize_t*   [C Function]
    pos, SCM val)

Set the element at position *pos* in the storage block of the array represented by *handle* to *val*. Any kind of array is acceptable. No range checking is done on *pos*. An error is signalled when the array can not store *val*.

const SCM * scm_array_handle_elements (*scm_t_array_handle*   [C Function]
    handle)

Return a pointer to the elements of a ordinary array of general Scheme values (i.e., a non-uniform array) for reading. This pointer is valid as long as the array remains reserved.

SCM * scm_array_handle_writable_elements (*scm_t_array_handle*   [C Function]
    handle)

Like scm_array_handle_elements, but the pointer is good for reading and writing.

const void * scm_array_handle_uniform_elements   [C Function]
    (*scm_t_array_handle *handle*)

Return a pointer to the elements of a uniform numeric array for reading. This pointer is valid as long as the array remains reserved. The size of each element is given by scm_array_handle_uniform_element_size.

`void * scm_array_handle_uniform_writable_elements`   [C Function]
      (*scm_t_array_handle *handle*)

    Like `scm_array_handle_uniform_elements`, but the pointer is good reading and writing.

`size_t scm_array_handle_uniform_element_size`   [C Function]
      (*scm_t_array_handle *handle*)

    Return the size of one element of the uniform numeric array represented by *handle*.

`const scm_t_uint8 * scm_array_handle_u8_elements`   [C Function]
      (*scm_t_array_handle *handle*)
`const scm_t_int8 * scm_array_handle_s8_elements`   [C Function]
      (*scm_t_array_handle *handle*)
`const scm_t_uint16 * scm_array_handle_u16_elements`   [C Function]
      (*scm_t_array_handle *handle*)
`const scm_t_int16 * scm_array_handle_s16_elements`   [C Function]
      (*scm_t_array_handle *handle*)
`const scm_t_uint32 * scm_array_handle_u32_elements`   [C Function]
      (*scm_t_array_handle *handle*)
`const scm_t_int32 * scm_array_handle_s32_elements`   [C Function]
      (*scm_t_array_handle *handle*)
`const scm_t_uint64 * scm_array_handle_u64_elements`   [C Function]
      (*scm_t_array_handle *handle*)
`const scm_t_int64 * scm_array_handle_s64_elements`   [C Function]
      (*scm_t_array_handle *handle*)
`const float * scm_array_handle_f32_elements`   [C Function]
      (*scm_t_array_handle *handle*)
`const double * scm_array_handle_f64_elements`   [C Function]
      (*scm_t_array_handle *handle*)
`const float * scm_array_handle_c32_elements`   [C Function]
      (*scm_t_array_handle *handle*)
`const double * scm_array_handle_c64_elements`   [C Function]
      (*scm_t_array_handle *handle*)

    Return a pointer to the elements of a uniform numeric array of the indicated kind for reading. This pointer is valid as long as the array remains reserved.

    The pointers for `c32` and `c64` uniform numeric arrays point to pairs of floating point numbers. The even index holds the real part, the odd index the imaginary part of the complex number.

`scm_t_uint8 * scm_array_handle_u8_writable_elements`   [C Function]
      (*scm_t_array_handle *handle*)
`scm_t_int8 * scm_array_handle_s8_writable_elements`   [C Function]
      (*scm_t_array_handle *handle*)
`scm_t_uint16 * scm_array_handle_u16_writable_elements`   [C Function]
      (*scm_t_array_handle *handle*)
`scm_t_int16 * scm_array_handle_s16_writable_elements`   [C Function]
      (*scm_t_array_handle *handle*)

scm_t_uint32 * scm_array_handle_u32_writable_elements   [C Function]
       (*scm_t_array_handle *handle*)
scm_t_int32 * scm_array_handle_s32_writable_elements   [C Function]
       (*scm_t_array_handle *handle*)
scm_t_uint64 * scm_array_handle_u64_writable_elements   [C Function]
       (*scm_t_array_handle *handle*)
scm_t_int64 * scm_array_handle_s64_writable_elements   [C Function]
       (*scm_t_array_handle *handle*)
float * scm_array_handle_f32_writable_elements   [C Function]
       (*scm_t_array_handle *handle*)
double * scm_array_handle_f64_writable_elements   [C Function]
       (*scm_t_array_handle *handle*)
float * scm_array_handle_c32_writable_elements   [C Function]
       (*scm_t_array_handle *handle*)
double * scm_array_handle_c64_writable_elements   [C Function]
       (*scm_t_array_handle *handle*)

> Like scm_array_handle_<kind>_elements, but the pointer is good for reading and writing.

const scm_t_uint32 * scm_array_handle_bit_elements   [C Function]
       (*scm_t_array_handle *handle*)

> Return a pointer to the words that store the bits of the represented array, which must be a bit array.
>
> Unlike other arrays, bit arrays have an additional offset that must be figured into index calculations. That offset is returned by scm_array_handle_bit_elements_offset.
>
> To find a certain bit you first need to calculate its position as explained above for scm_array_handle_dims and then add the offset. This gives the absolute position of the bit, which is always a non-negative integer.
>
> Each word of the bit array storage block contains exactly 32 bits, with the least significant bit in that word having the lowest absolute position number. The next word contains the next 32 bits.
>
> Thus, the following code can be used to access a bit whose position according to scm_array_handle_dims is given in *pos*:

```
SCM bit_array;
scm_t_array_handle handle;
scm_t_uint32 *bits;
ssize_t pos;
size_t abs_pos;
size_t word_pos, mask;

scm_array_get_handle (&bit_array, &handle);
bits = scm_array_handle_bit_elements (&handle);

pos = ...
abs_pos = pos + scm_array_handle_bit_elements_offset (&handle);
word_pos = abs_pos / 32;
```

```
          mask = 1L << (abs_pos % 32);

          if (bits[word_pos] & mask)
            /* bit is set. */

          scm_array_handle_release (&handle);
```

scm_t_uint32 * scm_array_handle_bit_writable_elements   [C Function]
        (*scm_t_array_handle *handle*)
     Like `scm_array_handle_bit_elements` but the pointer is good for reading and writ-
     ing. You must take care not to modify bits outside of the allowed index range of the
     array, even for contiguous arrays.

6.7.6 VLists

The (`ice-9 vlist`) module provides an implementation of the *VList* data structure designed by Phil Bagwell in 2002. VLists are immutable lists, which can contain any Scheme
object. They improve on standard Scheme linked lists in several areas:

  - Random access has typically constant-time complexity.

  - Computing the length of a VList has time complexity logarithmic in the number of
    elements.

  - VLists use less storage space than standard lists.

  - VList elements are stored in contiguous regions, which improves memory locality and
    leads to more efficient use of hardware caches.

The idea behind VLists is to store vlist elements in increasingly large contiguous blocks
(implemented as vectors here). These blocks are linked to one another using a pointer to
the next block and an offset within that block. The size of these blocks form a geometric
series with ratio `block-growth-factor` (2 by default).

The VList structure also serves as the basis for the *VList-based hash lists* or "vhashes",
an immutable dictionary type (see Section 6.7.13 [VHashes], page 234).

However, the current implementation in (`ice-9 vlist`) has several noteworthy short-
comings:

  - It is *not* thread-safe. Although operations on vlists are all *referentially transparent*
    (i.e., purely functional), adding elements to a vlist with `vlist-cons` mutates part of
    its internal structure, which makes it non-thread-safe. This could be fixed, but it would
    slow down `vlist-cons`.

  - `vlist-cons` always allocates at least as much memory as `cons`. Again, Phil Bagwell
    describes how to fix it, but that would require tuning the garbage collector in a way
    that may not be generally beneficial.

  - `vlist-cons` is a Scheme procedure compiled to bytecode, and it does not compete with
    the straightforward C implementation of `cons`, and with the fact that the VM has a
    special `cons` instruction.

We hope to address these in the future.

The programming interface exported by (`ice-9 vlist`) is defined below. Most of it is
the same as SRFI-1 with an added `vlist-` prefix to function names.

`vlist?` *obj*   [Scheme Procedure]
> Return true if *obj* is a VList.

`vlist-null`   [Scheme Variable]
> The empty VList. Note that it's possible to create an empty VList not `eq?` to `vlist-null`; thus, callers should always use `vlist-null?` when testing whether a VList is empty.

`vlist-null?` *vlist*   [Scheme Procedure]
> Return true if *vlist* is empty.

`vlist-cons` *item vlist*   [Scheme Procedure]
> Return a new vlist with *item* as its head and *vlist* as its tail.

`vlist-head` *vlist*   [Scheme Procedure]
> Return the head of *vlist*.

`vlist-tail` *vlist*   [Scheme Procedure]
> Return the tail of *vlist*.

`block-growth-factor`   [Scheme Variable]
> A fluid that defines the growth factor of VList blocks, 2 by default.

The functions below provide the usual set of higher-level list operations.

`vlist-fold` *proc init vlist*   [Scheme Procedure]
`vlist-fold-right` *proc init vlist*   [Scheme Procedure]
> Fold over *vlist*, calling *proc* for each element, as for SRFI-1 `fold` and `fold-right` (see Section 7.5.3 [SRFI-1], page 552).

`vlist-ref` *vlist index*   [Scheme Procedure]
> Return the element at index *index* in *vlist*. This is typically a constant-time operation.

`vlist-length` *vlist*   [Scheme Procedure]
> Return the length of *vlist*. This is typically logarithmic in the number of elements in *vlist*.

`vlist-reverse` *vlist*   [Scheme Procedure]
> Return a new *vlist* whose content are those of *vlist* in reverse order.

`vlist-map` *proc vlist*   [Scheme Procedure]
> Map *proc* over the elements of *vlist* and return a new vlist.

`vlist-for-each` *proc vlist*   [Scheme Procedure]
> Call *proc* on each element of *vlist*. The result is unspecified.

`vlist-drop` *vlist count*   [Scheme Procedure]
> Return a new vlist that does not contain the *count* first elements of *vlist*. This is typically a constant-time operation.

`vlist-take` *vlist count*   [Scheme Procedure]
> Return a new vlist that contains only the *count* first elements of *vlist*.

vlist-filter *pred vlist*   [Scheme Procedure]
>   Return a new vlist containing all the elements from *vlist* that satisfy *pred*.

vlist-delete *x vlist* [*equal?*]   [Scheme Procedure]
>   Return a new vlist corresponding to *vlist* without the elements *equal?* to *x*.

vlist-unfold *p f g seed* [*tail-gen*]   [Scheme Procedure]
vlist-unfold-right *p f g seed* [*tail*]   [Scheme Procedure]
>   Return a new vlist, as for SRFI-1 **unfold** and **unfold-right** (see Section 7.5.3 [SRFI-1], page 552).

vlist-append *vlist* ...   [Scheme Procedure]
>   Append the given vlists and return the resulting vlist.

list->vlist *lst*   [Scheme Procedure]
>   Return a new vlist whose contents correspond to *lst*.

vlist->list *vlist*   [Scheme Procedure]
>   Return a new list whose contents match those of *vlist*.

6.7.7 Record Overview

Records, also called *structures*, are Scheme's primary mechanism to define new disjoint types. A *record type* defines a list of *fields* that instances of the type consist of. This is like C's **struct**.

Historically, Guile has offered several different ways to define record types and to create records, offering different features, and making different trade-offs. Over the years, each "standard" has also come with its own new record interface, leading to a maze of record APIs.

At the highest level is SRFI-9, a high-level record interface implemented by most Scheme implementations (see Section 6.7.8 [SRFI-9 Records], page 216). It defines a simple and efficient syntactic abstraction of record types and their associated type predicate, fields, and field accessors. SRFI-9 is suitable for most uses, and this is the recommended way to create record types in Guile. Similar high-level record APIs include SRFI-35 (see Section 7.5.23 [SRFI-35], page 594) and R6RS records (see Section 7.6.2.9 [rnrs records syntactic], page 635).

Then comes Guile's historical "records" API (see Section 6.7.9 [Records], page 219). Record types defined this way are first-class objects. Introspection facilities are available, allowing users to query the list of fields or the value of a specific field at run-time, without prior knowledge of the type.

Finally, the common denominator of these interfaces is Guile's *structure* API (see Section 6.7.10 [Structures], page 220). Guile's structures are the low-level building block for all other record APIs. Application writers will normally not need to use it.

Records created with these APIs may all be pattern-matched using Guile's standard pattern matcher (see Section 7.7 [Pattern Matching], page 657).

6.7.8 SRFI-9 Records

SRFI-9 standardizes a syntax for defining new record types and creating predicate, constructor, and field getter and setter functions. In Guile this is the recommended option to create new record types (see Section 6.7.7 [Record Overview], page 215). It can be used with:

```
(use-modules (srfi srfi-9))
```

define-record-type *type*   [Scheme Syntax]
        (*constructor fieldname* . . .)
        predicate
        (*fieldname accessor* [*modifier*]) . . .

    Create a new record type, and make various **defines** for using it. This syntax can only occur at the top-level, not nested within some other form.

    type is bound to the record type, which is as per the return from the core **make-record-type**. *type* also provides the name for the record, as per **record-type-name**.

    constructor is bound to a function to be called as (*constructor* fieldval ...) to create a new record of this type. The arguments are initial values for the fields, one argument for each field, in the order they appear in the **define-record-type** form.

    The *fieldnames* provide the names for the record fields, as per the core **record-type-fields** etc, and are referred to in the subsequent accessor/modifier forms.

    predicate is bound to a function to be called as (*predicate* obj). It returns #t or #f according to whether *obj* is a record of this type.

    Each *accessor* is bound to a function to be called (*accessor* record) to retrieve the respective field from a *record*. Similarly each *modifier* is bound to a function to be called (*modifier* record val) to set the respective field in a *record*.

An example will illustrate typical usage,

```
(define-record-type <employee>
  (make-employee name age salary)
  employee?
  (name    employee-name)
  (age     employee-age    set-employee-age!)
  (salary  employee-salary set-employee-salary!))
```

This creates a new employee data type, with name, age and salary fields. Accessor functions are created for each field, but no modifier function for the name (the intention in this example being that it's established only when an employee object is created). These can all then be used as for example,

```
<employee> ⇒ #<record-type <employee>>

(define fred (make-employee "Fred" 45 20000.00))

(employee? fred)        ⇒ #t
(employee-age fred)     ⇒ 45
(set-employee-salary! fred 25000.00)  ;; pay rise
```

The functions created by `define-record-type` are ordinary top-level `defines`. They can be redefined or `set!` as desired, exported from a module, etc.

Non-toplevel Record Definitions

The SRFI-9 specification explicitly disallows record definitions in a non-toplevel context, such as inside `lambda` body or inside a *let* block. However, Guile's implementation does not enforce that restriction.

Custom Printers

You may use `set-record-type-printer!` to customize the default printing behavior of records. This is a Guile extension and is not part of SRFI-9. It is located in the (`srfi srfi-9 gnu`) module.

`set-record-type-printer!` *name proc*   [Scheme Syntax]

> Where *type* corresponds to the first argument of `define-record-type`, and *proc* is a procedure accepting two arguments, the record to print, and an output port.

This example prints the employee's name in brackets, for instance [Fred].

```
(set-record-type-printer! <employee>
  (lambda (record port)
    (write-char #\[ port)
    (display (employee-name record) port)
    (write-char #\] port)))
```

Functional "Setters"

When writing code in a functional style, it is desirable to never alter the contents of records. For such code, a simple way to return new record instances based on existing ones is highly desirable.

The (`srfi srfi-9 gnu`) module extends SRFI-9 with facilities to return new record instances based on existing ones, only with one or more field values changed—*functional setters*. First, the `define-immutable-record-type` works like `define-record-type`, except that fields are immutable and setters are defined as functional setters.

`define-immutable-record-type` *type*   [Scheme Syntax]
> > (*constructor fieldname* ...)
> > *predicate*
> > (*fieldname accessor* [*modifier*]) ...

> Define *type* as a new record type, like `define-record-type`. However, the record type is made *immutable* (records may not be mutated, even with `struct-set!`), and any *modifier* is defined to be a functional setter—a procedure that returns a new record instance with the specified field changed, and leaves the original unchanged (see example below.)

In addition, the generic `set-field` and `set-fields` macros may be applied to any SRFI-9 record.

`set-field` *record* (*field sub-fields* ...) *value*   [Scheme Syntax]
> Return a new record of *record*'s type whose fields are equal to the corresponding fields of *record* except for the one specified by *field*.

field must be the name of the getter corresponding to the field of *record* being "set". Subsequent *sub-fields* must be record getters designating sub-fields within that field value to be set (see example below.)

set-fields *record* ((*field sub-fields ...*) *value*) ...   [Scheme Syntax]
   Like **set-field**, but can be used to set more than one field at a time. This expands to code that is more efficient than a series of single **set-field** calls.

To illustrate the use of functional setters, let's assume these two record type definitions:

```
(define-record-type <address>
  (address street city country)
  address?
  (street   address-street)
  (city     address-city)
  (country address-country))

(define-immutable-record-type <person>
  (person age email address)
  person?
  (age       person-age set-person-age)
  (email     person-email set-person-email)
  (address person-address set-person-address))
```

First, note that the **<person>** record type definition introduces named functional setters. These may be used like this:

```
(define fsf-address
  (address "Franklin Street" "Boston" "USA"))

(define rms
  (person 30 "rms@gnu.org" fsf-address))

(and (equal? (set-person-age rms 60)
             (person 60 "rms@gnu.org" fsf-address))
     (= (person-age rms) 30))
⇒ #t
```

Here, the original **<person>** record, to which *rms* is bound, is left unchanged.

Now, suppose we want to change both the street and age of *rms*. This can be achieved using **set-fields**:

```
(set-fields rms
  ((person-age) 60)
  ((person-address address-street) "Temple Place"))
⇒ #<<person> age: 60 email: "rms@gnu.org"
   address: #<<address> street: "Temple Place" city: "Boston" country: "USA">>
```

Notice how the above changed two fields of *rms*, including the **street** field of its **address** field, in a concise way. Also note that **set-fields** works equally well for types defined with just **define-record-type**.

6.7.9 Records

A *record type* is a first class object representing a user-defined data type. A *record* is an instance of a record type.

Note that in many ways, this interface is too low-level for every-day use. Most uses of records are better served by SRFI-9 records. See Section 6.7.8 [SRFI-9 Records], page 216.

record? *obj*   [Scheme Procedure]

>   Return #t if *obj* is a record of any type and #f otherwise.

>   Note that **record?** may be true of any Scheme value; there is no promise that records are disjoint with other Scheme types.

make-record-type *type-name field-names* [*print*]   [Scheme Procedure]

>   Create and return a new *record-type descriptor*.

>   *type-name* is a string naming the type. Currently it's only used in the printed representation of records, and in diagnostics. *field-names* is a list of symbols naming the fields of a record of the type. Duplicates are not allowed among these symbols.

>   ```
>   (make-record-type "employee" '(name age salary))
>   ```

>   The optional *print* argument is a function used by **display**, **write**, etc, for printing a record of the new type. It's called as (**print** *record port*) and should look at *record* and write to *port*.

record-constructor *rtd* [*field-names*]   [Scheme Procedure]

>   Return a procedure for constructing new members of the type represented by *rtd*. The returned procedure accepts exactly as many arguments as there are symbols in the given list, *field-names*; these are used, in order, as the initial values of those fields in a new record, which is returned by the constructor procedure. The values of any fields not named in that list are unspecified. The *field-names* argument defaults to the list of field names in the call to **make-record-type** that created the type represented by *rtd*; if the *field-names* argument is provided, it is an error if it contains any duplicates or any symbols not in the default list.

record-predicate *rtd*   [Scheme Procedure]

>   Return a procedure for testing membership in the type represented by *rtd*. The returned procedure accepts exactly one argument and returns a true value if the argument is a member of the indicated record type; it returns a false value otherwise.

record-accessor *rtd field-name*   [Scheme Procedure]

>   Return a procedure for reading the value of a particular field of a member of the type represented by *rtd*. The returned procedure accepts exactly one argument which must be a record of the appropriate type; it returns the current value of the field named by the symbol *field-name* in that record. The symbol *field-name* must be a member of the list of field-names in the call to **make-record-type** that created the type represented by *rtd*.

record-modifier *rtd field-name*   [Scheme Procedure]

>   Return a procedure for writing the value of a particular field of a member of the type represented by *rtd*. The returned procedure accepts exactly two arguments: first, a

record of the appropriate type, and second, an arbitrary Scheme value; it modifies the field named by the symbol *field-name* in that record to contain the given value. The returned value of the modifier procedure is unspecified. The symbol *field-name* must be a member of the list of field-names in the call to `make-record-type` that created the type represented by *rtd*.

`record-type-descriptor` *record*   [Scheme Procedure]
　　Return a record-type descriptor representing the type of the given record. That is, for example, if the returned descriptor were passed to `record-predicate`, the resulting predicate would return a true value when passed the given record. Note that it is not necessarily the case that the returned descriptor is the one that was passed to `record-constructor` in the call that created the constructor procedure that created the given record.

`record-type-name` *rtd*   [Scheme Procedure]
　　Return the type-name associated with the type represented by rtd. The returned value is `eqv?` to the *type-name* argument given in the call to `make-record-type` that created the type represented by *rtd*.

`record-type-fields` *rtd*   [Scheme Procedure]
　　Return a list of the symbols naming the fields in members of the type represented by *rtd*. The returned value is `equal?` to the field-names argument given in the call to `make-record-type` that created the type represented by *rtd*.

6.7.10 Structures

A *structure* is a first class data type which holds Scheme values or C words in fields numbered 0 upwards. A *vtable* is a structure that represents a structure type, giving field types and permissions, and an optional print function for `write` etc.

　　Structures are lower level than records (see Section 6.7.9 [Records], page 219). Usually, when you need to represent structured data, you just want to use records. But sometimes you need to implement new kinds of structured data abstractions, and for that purpose structures are useful. Indeed, records in Guile are implemented with structures.

6.7.10.1 Vtables

A vtable is a structure type, specifying its layout, and other information. A vtable is actually itself a structure, but there's no need to worry about that initially (see Section 6.7.10.3 [Vtable Contents], page 222.)

`make-vtable` *fields* [*print*]   [Scheme Procedure]
　　Create a new vtable.

　　fields is a string describing the fields in the structures to be created. Each field is represented by two characters, a type letter and a permissions letter, for example `"pw"`. The types are as follows.

- p – a Scheme value. "p" stands for "protected" meaning it's protected against garbage collection.

- u – an arbitrary word of data (an `scm_t_bits`). At the Scheme level it's read and written as an unsigned integer. "u" stands for "uninterpreted" (it's not treated as a Scheme value), or "unprotected" (it's not marked during GC), or "unsigned long" (its size), or all of these things.

- **s** – a self-reference. Such a field holds the **SCM** value of the structure itself (a circular reference). This can be useful in C code where you might have a pointer to the data array, and want to get the Scheme **SCM** handle for the structure. In Scheme code it has no use.

The second letter for each field is a permission code,

- **w** – writable, the field can be read and written.

- **r** – read-only, the field can be read but not written.

- **o** – opaque, the field can be neither read nor written at the Scheme level. This can be used for fields which should only be used from C code.

Here are some examples. See Section 6.7.10.6 [Tail Arrays], page 227, for information on the legacy tail array facility.

```
(make-vtable "pw")       ;; one writable field
(make-vtable "prpw")     ;; one read-only and one writable
(make-vtable "pwuwuw")   ;; one scheme and two uninterpreted
```

The optional *print* argument is a function called by `display` and `write` (etc) to give a printed representation of a structure created from this vtable. It's called (*print struct port*) and should look at *struct* and write to *port*. The default print merely gives a form like '`#<struct ADDR:ADDR>`' with a pair of machine addresses.

The following print function for example shows the two fields of its structure.

```
(make-vtable "prpw"
             (lambda (struct port)
               (format port "#<~a and ~a>"
                       (struct-ref struct 0)
                       (struct-ref struct 1))))
```

6.7.10.2 Structure Basics

This section describes the basic procedures for working with structures. `make-struct` creates a structure, and `struct-ref` and `struct-set!` access its fields.

`make-struct` *vtable tail-size init ...*	[Scheme Procedure]
`make-struct/no-tail` *vtable init ...*	[Scheme Procedure]

Create a new structure, with layout per the given *vtable* (see Section 6.7.10.1 [Vtables], page 220).

The optional *init...* arguments are initial values for the fields of the structure. This is the only way to put values in read-only fields. If there are fewer *init* arguments than fields then the defaults are `#f` for a Scheme field (type **p**) or 0 for an uninterpreted field (type **u**).

Structures also have the ability to allocate a variable number of additional cells at the end, at their tails. However, this legacy *tail array* facilty is confusing and inefficient, and so we do not recommend it. See Section 6.7.10.6 [Tail Arrays], page 227, for more on the legacy tail array interface.

Type **s** self-reference fields, permission **o** opaque fields, and the count field of a tail array are all ignored for the *init* arguments, ie. an argument is not consumed by such a field. An **s** is always set to the structure itself, an **o** is always set to #f or 0 (with the intention that C code will do something to it later), and the tail count is always the given *tail-size*.

For example,

```
(define v (make-vtable "prpwpw"))
(define s (make-struct v 0 123 "abc" 456))
(struct-ref s 0) ⇒ 123
(struct-ref s 1) ⇒ "abc"
```

SCM **scm_make_struct** (*SCM vtable, SCM tail_size, SCM init_list*)   [C Function]
SCM **scm_c_make_struct** (*SCM vtable, SCM tail_size, SCM init, ...*)   [C Function]
SCM **scm_c_make_structv** (*SCM vtable, SCM tail_size, size_t n_inits,*   [C Function]
    scm_t_bits init[])

> There are a few ways to make structures from C. **scm_make_struct** takes a list, **scm_c_make_struct** takes variable arguments terminated with SCM_UNDEFINED, and **scm_c_make_structv** takes a packed array.

struct? *obj*   [Scheme Procedure]
scm_struct_p (*obj*)   [C Function]
> Return #t if *obj* is a structure, or #f if not.

struct-ref *struct n*   [Scheme Procedure]
scm_struct_ref (*struct, n*)   [C Function]
> Return the contents of field number *n* in *struct*. The first field is number 0.
>
> An error is thrown if *n* is out of range, or if the field cannot be read because it's **o** opaque.

struct-set! *struct n value*   [Scheme Procedure]
scm_struct_set_x (*struct, n, value*)   [C Function]
> Set field number *n* in *struct* to *value*. The first field is number 0.
>
> An error is thrown if *n* is out of range, or if the field cannot be written because it's **r** read-only or **o** opaque.

struct-vtable *struct*   [Scheme Procedure]
scm_struct_vtable (*struct*)   [C Function]
> Return the vtable that describes *struct*.
>
> The vtable is effectively the type of the structure. See Section 6.7.10.3 [Vtable Contents], page 222, for more on vtables.

6.7.10.3 Vtable Contents

A vtable is itself a structure. It has a specific set of fields describing various aspects of its *instances*: the structures created from a vtable. Some of the fields are internal to Guile, some of them are part of the public interface, and there may be additional fields added on by the user.

Every vtable has a field for the layout of their instances, a field for the procedure used to print its instances, and a field for the name of the vtable itself. Access to the layout and printer is exposed directly via field indexes. Access to the vtable name is exposed via accessor procedures.

vtable-index-layout   [Scheme Variable]
scm_vtable_index_layout   [C Macro]
> The field number of the layout specification in a vtable. The layout specification is a
> symbol like pwpw formed from the fields string passed to make-vtable, or created by
> make-struct-layout (see Section 6.7.10.4 [Meta-Vtables], page 223).
>
>   (define v (make-vtable "pwpw" 0))
>   (struct-ref v vtable-index-layout) ⇒ pwpw
>
> This field is read-only, since the layout of structures using a vtable cannot be changed.

vtable-index-printer   [Scheme Variable]
scm_vtable_index_printer   [C Macro]
> The field number of the printer function. This field contains #f if the default print
> function should be used.
>
>   (define (my-print-func struct port)
>   ...)
>   (define v (make-vtable "pwpw" my-print-func))
>   (struct-ref v vtable-index-printer) ⇒ my-print-func
>
> This field is writable, allowing the print function to be changed dynamically.

struct-vtable-name *vtable*   [Scheme Procedure]
set-struct-vtable-name! *vtable name*   [Scheme Procedure]
scm_struct_vtable_name (*vtable*)   [C Function]
scm_set_struct_vtable_name_x (*vtable*, *name*)   [C Function]
> Get or set the name of *vtable*. *name* is a symbol and is used in the default print
> function when printing structures created from *vtable*.
>
>   (define v (make-vtable "pw"))
>   (set-struct-vtable-name! v 'my-name)
>
>   (define s (make-struct v 0))
>   (display s) ⊣ #<my-name b7ab3ae0:b7ab3730>

6.7.10.4 Meta-Vtables

As a structure, a vtable also has a vtable, which is also a structure. Structures, their vtables, the vtables of the vtables, and so on form a tree of structures. Making a new structure adds a leaf to the tree, and if that structure is a vtable, it may be used to create other leaves.

If you traverse up the tree of vtables, via calling struct-vtable, eventually you reach a root which is the vtable of itself:

```
scheme@(guile-user)> (current-module)
$1 = #<directory (guile-user) 221b090>
scheme@(guile-user)> (struct-vtable $1)
$2 = #<record-type module>
scheme@(guile-user)> (struct-vtable $2)
$3 = #<<standard-vtable> 12c30a0>
```

```
scheme@(guile-user)> (struct-vtable $3)
$4 = #<<standard-vtable> 12c3fa0>
scheme@(guile-user)> (struct-vtable $4)
$5 = #<<standard-vtable> 12c3fa0>
scheme@(guile-user)> <standard-vtable>
$6 = #<<standard-vtable> 12c3fa0>
```

In this example, we can say that $1 is an instance of $2, $2 is an instance of $3, $3 is an instance of $4, and $4, strangely enough, is an instance of itself. The value bound to $4 in this console session also bound to `<standard-vtable>` in the default environment.

`<standard-vtable>`   [Scheme Variable]
     A meta-vtable, useful for making new vtables.

All of these values are structures. All but $1 are vtables. As $2 is an instance of $3, and $3 is a vtable, we can say that $3 is a *meta-vtable*: a vtable that can create vtables.

With this definition, we can specify more precisely what a vtable is: a vtable is a structure made from a meta-vtable. Making a structure from a meta-vtable runs some special checks to ensure that the first field of the structure is a valid layout. Additionally, if these checks see that the layout of the child vtable contains all the required fields of a vtable, in the correct order, then the child vtable will also be a meta-table, inheriting a magical bit from the parent.

`struct-vtable?` *obj*   [Scheme Procedure]
`scm_struct_vtable_p` (*obj*)   [C Function]
     Return #t if *obj* is a vtable structure: an instance of a meta-vtable.

`<standard-vtable>` is a root of the vtable tree. (Normally there is only one root in a given Guile process, but due to some legacy interfaces there may be more than one.)

The set of required fields of a vtable is the set of fields in the `<standard-vtable>`, and is bound to `standard-vtable-fields` in the default environment. It is possible to create a meta-vtable that with additional fields in its layout, which can be used to create vtables with additional data:

```
scheme@(guile-user)> (struct-ref $3 vtable-index-layout)
$6 = pruhsruhpwphuhuhprprpw
scheme@(guile-user)> (struct-ref $4 vtable-index-layout)
$7 = pruhsruhpwphuhuh
scheme@(guile-user)> standard-vtable-fields
$8 = "pruhsruhpwphuhuh"
scheme@(guile-user)> (struct-ref $2 vtable-offset-user)
$9 = module
```

In this continuation of our earlier example, $2 is a vtable that has extra fields, because its vtable, $3, was made from a meta-vtable with an extended layout. `vtable-offset-user` is a convenient definition that indicates the number of fields in `standard-vtable-fields`.

`standard-vtable-fields`   [Scheme Variable]
     A string containing the orderedq set of fields that a vtable must have.

`vtable-offset-user`   [Scheme Variable]
>   The first index in a vtable that is available for a user.

`make-struct-layout` *fields*   [Scheme Procedure]
`scm_make_struct_layout` (*fields*)   [C Function]
>   Return a structure layout symbol, from a *fields* string. *fields* is as described under
>   `make-vtable` (see Section 6.7.10.1 [Vtables], page 220). An invalid *fields* string is an
>   error.

With these definitions, one can define `make-vtable` in this way:

```
(define* (make-vtable fields #:optional printer)
  (make-struct/no-tail <standard-vtable>
    (make-struct-layout fields)
    printer))
```

6.7.10.5 Vtable Example

Let us bring these points together with an example. Consider a simple object system with
single inheritance. Objects will be normal structures, and classes will be vtables with three
extra class fields: the name of the class, the parent class, and the list of fields.

So, first we need a meta-vtable that allocates instances with these extra class fields.

```
(define <class>
  (make-vtable
   (string-append standard-vtable-fields "pwpwpw")
   (lambda (x port)
     (format port "<<class> ~a>" (class-name x)))))

(define (class? x)
  (and (struct? x)
       (eq? (struct-vtable x) <class>)))
```

To make a structure with a specific meta-vtable, we will use `make-struct/no-tail`,
passing it the computed instance layout and printer, as with `make-vtable`, and additionally
the extra three class fields.

```
(define (make-class name parent fields)
  (let* ((fields (compute-fields parent fields))
         (layout (compute-layout fields)))
    (make-struct/no-tail <class>
      layout
      (lambda (x port)
        (print-instance x port))
      name
      parent
      fields)))
```

Instances will store their associated data in slots in the structure: as many slots as there
are fields. The `compute-layout` procedure below can compute a layout, and `field-index`
returns the slot corresponding to a field.

```
(define-syntax-rule (define-accessor name n)
  (define (name obj)
    (struct-ref obj n)))

;; Accessors for classes
(define-accessor class-name (+ vtable-offset-user 0))
(define-accessor class-parent (+ vtable-offset-user 1))
(define-accessor class-fields (+ vtable-offset-user 2))

(define (compute-fields parent fields)
  (if parent
      (append (class-fields parent) fields)
      fields))

(define (compute-layout fields)
  (make-struct-layout
   (string-concatenate (make-list (length fields) "pw"))))

(define (field-index class field)
  (list-index (class-fields class) field))

(define (print-instance x port)
  (format port "<~a" (class-name (struct-vtable x)))
  (for-each (lambda (field idx)
              (format port " ~a: ~a" field (struct-ref x idx)))
            (class-fields (struct-vtable x))
            (iota (length (class-fields (struct-vtable x)))))
  (format port ">"))
```

So, at this point we can actually make a few classes:

```
(define-syntax-rule (define-class name parent field ...)
  (define name (make-class 'name parent '(field ...))))

(define-class <surface> #f
  width height)

(define-class <window> <surface>
  x y)
```

And finally, make an instance:

```
(make-struct/no-tail <window> 400 300 10 20)
⇒ <<window> width: 400 height: 300 x: 10 y: 20>
```

And that's that. Note that there are many possible optimizations and feature enhancements that can be made to this object system, and the included GOOPS system does make most of them. For more simple use cases, the records facility is usually sufficient. But sometimes you need to make new kinds of data abstractions, and for that purpose, structs are here.

6.7.10.6 Tail Arrays

Guile's structures have a facility whereby each instance of a vtable can contain a variable-length tail array of values. The length of the tail array is stored in the structure. This facility was originally intended to allow C code to expose raw C structures with word-sized tail arrays to Scheme.

However, the tail array facility is confusing and doesn't work very well. It is very rarely used, but it insinuates itself into all invocations of `make-struct`. For this reason the clumsily-named `make-struct/no-tail` procedure can actually be more elegant in actual use, because it doesn't have a random 0 argument stuck in the middle.

Tail arrays also inhibit optimization by allowing instances to affect their shapes. In the absence of tail arrays, all instances of a given vtable have the same number and kinds of fields. This uniformity can be exploited by the runtime and the optimizer. The presence of tail arrays make some of these optimizations more difficult.

Finally, the tail array facility is ad-hoc and does not compose with the rest of Guile. If a Guile user wants an array with user-specified length, it's best to use a vector. It is more clear in the code, and the standard optimization techniques will do a good job with it.

That said, we should mention some details about the interface. A vtable that has tail array has upper-case permission descriptors: `W`, `R` or `O`, correspoding to tail arrays of writable, read-only, or opaque elements. A tail array permission descriptor may only appear in the last element of a vtable layout.

For exampple, 'pW' indicates a tail of writable Scheme-valued fields. The 'pW' field itself holds the tail size, and the tail fields come after it.

```
(define v (make-vtable "prpW")) ;; one fixed then a tail array
(define s (make-struct v 6 "fixed field" 'x 'y))
(struct-ref s 0) ⇒ "fixed field"
(struct-ref s 1) ⇒ 2     ;; tail size
(struct-ref s 2) ⇒ x     ;; tail array ...
(struct-ref s 3) ⇒ y
(struct-ref s 4) ⇒ #f
```

6.7.11 Dictionary Types

A *dictionary* object is a data structure used to index information in a user-defined way. In standard Scheme, the main aggregate data types are lists and vectors. Lists are not really indexed at all, and vectors are indexed only by number (e.g. `(vector-ref foo 5)`). Often you will find it useful to index your data on some other type; for example, in a library catalog you might want to look up a book by the name of its author. Dictionaries are used to help you organize information in such a way.

An *association list* (or *alist* for short) is a list of key-value pairs. Each pair represents a single quantity or object; the `car` of the pair is a key which is used to identify the object, and the `cdr` is the object's value.

A *hash table* also permits you to index objects with arbitrary keys, but in a way that makes looking up any one object extremely fast. A well-designed hash system makes hash table lookups almost as fast as conventional array or vector references.

Alists are popular among Lisp programmers because they use only the language's primitive operations (lists, *car*, *cdr* and the equality primitives). No changes to the language core are necessary. Therefore, with Scheme's built-in list manipulation facilities, it is very convenient to handle data stored in an association list. Also, alists are highly portable and can be easily implemented on even the most minimal Lisp systems.

However, alists are inefficient, especially for storing large quantities of data. Because we want Guile to be useful for large software systems as well as small ones, Guile provides a rich set of tools for using either association lists or hash tables.

6.7.12 Association Lists

An association list is a conventional data structure that is often used to implement simple key-value databases. It consists of a list of entries in which each entry is a pair. The *key* of each entry is the `car` of the pair and the *value* of each entry is the `cdr`.

```
ASSOCIATION LIST ::=   '( (KEY1 . VALUE1)
                          (KEY2 . VALUE2)
                          (KEY3 . VALUE3)
                          ...
                        )
```

Association lists are also known, for short, as *alists*.

The structure of an association list is just one example of the infinite number of possible structures that can be built using pairs and lists. As such, the keys and values in an association list can be manipulated using the general list structure procedures `cons`, `car`, `cdr`, `set-car!`, `set-cdr!` and so on. However, because association lists are so useful, Guile also provides specific procedures for manipulating them.

6.7.12.1 Alist Key Equality

All of Guile's dedicated association list procedures, apart from `acons`, come in three flavours, depending on the level of equality that is required to decide whether an existing key in the association list is the same as the key that the procedure call uses to identify the required entry.

- Procedures with *assq* in their name use `eq?` to determine key equality.
- Procedures with *assv* in their name use `eqv?` to determine key equality.
- Procedures with *assoc* in their name use `equal?` to determine key equality.

`acons` is an exception because it is used to build association lists which do not require their entries' keys to be unique.

6.7.12.2 Adding or Setting Alist Entries

`acons` adds a new entry to an association list and returns the combined association list. The combined alist is formed by consing the new entry onto the head of the alist specified in the `acons` procedure call. So the specified alist is not modified, but its contents become shared with the tail of the combined alist that `acons` returns.

In the most common usage of `acons`, a variable holding the original association list is updated with the combined alist:

```
(set! address-list (acons name address address-list))
```

In such cases, it doesn't matter that the old and new values of `address-list` share some of their contents, since the old value is usually no longer independently accessible.

Note that `acons` adds the specified new entry regardless of whether the alist may already contain entries with keys that are, in some sense, the same as that of the new entry. Thus `acons` is ideal for building alists where there is no concept of key uniqueness.

```
(set! task-list (acons 3 "pay gas bill" '()))
task-list
⇒
((3 . "pay gas bill"))

(set! task-list (acons 3 "tidy bedroom" task-list))
task-list
⇒
((3 . "tidy bedroom") (3 . "pay gas bill"))
```

`assq-set!`, `assv-set!` and `assoc-set!` are used to add or replace an entry in an association list where there *is* a concept of key uniqueness. If the specified association list already contains an entry whose key is the same as that specified in the procedure call, the existing entry is replaced by the new one. Otherwise, the new entry is consed onto the head of the old association list to create the combined alist. In all cases, these procedures return the combined alist.

`assq-set!` and friends *may* destructively modify the structure of the old association list in such a way that an existing variable is correctly updated without having to `set!` it to the value returned:

```
address-list
⇒
(("mary" . "34 Elm Road") ("james" . "16 Bow Street"))

(assoc-set! address-list "james" "1a London Road")
⇒
(("mary" . "34 Elm Road") ("james" . "1a London Road"))

address-list
⇒
(("mary" . "34 Elm Road") ("james" . "1a London Road"))
```

Or they may not:

```
(assoc-set! address-list "bob" "11 Newington Avenue")
⇒
(("bob" . "11 Newington Avenue") ("mary" . "34 Elm Road")
 ("james" . "1a London Road"))

address-list
⇒
(("mary" . "34 Elm Road") ("james" . "1a London Road"))
```

The only safe way to update an association list variable when adding or replacing an entry like this is to `set!` the variable to the returned value:

```
(set! address-list
      (assoc-set! address-list "bob" "11 Newington Avenue"))
```

```
address-list
⇒
(("bob" . "11 Newington Avenue") ("mary" . "34 Elm Road")
 ("james" . "1a London Road"))
```

Because of this slight inconvenience, you may find it more convenient to use hash tables to store dictionary data. If your application will not be modifying the contents of an alist very often, this may not make much difference to you.

If you need to keep the old value of an association list in a form independent from the list that results from modification by `acons`, `assq-set!`, `assv-set!` or `assoc-set!`, use `list-copy` to copy the old association list before modifying it.

`acons` *key value alist*	[Scheme Procedure]
`scm_acons` (*key, value, alist*)	[C Function]

> Add a new key-value pair to *alist*. A new pair is created whose car is *key* and whose cdr is *value*, and the pair is consed onto *alist*, and the new list is returned. This function is *not* destructive; *alist* is not modified.

`assq-set!` *alist key val*	[Scheme Procedure]
`assv-set!` *alist key value*	[Scheme Procedure]
`assoc-set!` *alist key value*	[Scheme Procedure]
`scm_assq_set_x` (*alist, key, val*)	[C Function]
`scm_assv_set_x` (*alist, key, val*)	[C Function]
`scm_assoc_set_x` (*alist, key, val*)	[C Function]

> Reassociate *key* in *alist* with *value*: find any existing *alist* entry for *key* and associate it with the new *value*. If *alist* does not contain an entry for *key*, add a new one. Return the (possibly new) alist.
>
> These functions do not attempt to verify the structure of *alist*, and so may cause unusual results if passed an object that is not an association list.

6.7.12.3 Retrieving Alist Entries

`assq`, `assv` and `assoc` find the entry in an alist for a given key, and return the (*key . value*) pair. `assq-ref`, `assv-ref` and `assoc-ref` do a similar lookup, but return just the *value*.

`assq` *key alist*	[Scheme Procedure]
`assv` *key alist*	[Scheme Procedure]
`assoc` *key alist*	[Scheme Procedure]
`scm_assq` (*key, alist*)	[C Function]
`scm_assv` (*key, alist*)	[C Function]
`scm_assoc` (*key, alist*)	[C Function]

> Return the first entry in *alist* with the given *key*. The return is the pair (KEY . VALUE) from *alist*. If there's no matching entry the return is #f.
>
> `assq` compares keys with `eq?`, `assv` uses `eqv?` and `assoc` uses `equal?`. See also SRFI-1 which has an extended `assoc` (Section 7.5.3.9 [SRFI-1 Association Lists], page 562).

`assq-ref` *alist key*	[Scheme Procedure]
`assv-ref` *alist key*	[Scheme Procedure]

`assoc-ref` *alist key*	[Scheme Procedure]
`scm_assq_ref` (*alist*, *key*)	[C Function]
`scm_assv_ref` (*alist*, *key*)	[C Function]
`scm_assoc_ref` (*alist*, *key*)	[C Function]

Return the value from the first entry in *alist* with the given *key*, or `#f` if there's no such entry.

`assq-ref` compares keys with `eq?`, `assv-ref` uses `eqv?` and `assoc-ref` uses `equal?`.

Notice these functions have the *key* argument last, like other `-ref` functions, but this is opposite to what `assq` etc above use.

When the return is `#f` it can be either *key* not found, or an entry which happens to have value `#f` in the `cdr`. Use `assq` etc above if you need to differentiate these cases.

6.7.12.4 Removing Alist Entries

To remove the element from an association list whose key matches a specified key, use `assq-remove!`, `assv-remove!` or `assoc-remove!` (depending, as usual, on the level of equality required between the key that you specify and the keys in the association list).

As with `assq-set!` and friends, the specified alist may or may not be modified destructively, and the only safe way to update a variable containing the alist is to `set!` it to the value that `assq-remove!` and friends return.

```
address-list
⇒
(("bob" . "11 Newington Avenue") ("mary" . "34 Elm Road")
 ("james" . "1a London Road"))

(set! address-list (assoc-remove! address-list "mary"))
address-list
⇒
(("bob" . "11 Newington Avenue") ("james" . "1a London Road"))
```

Note that, when `assq/v/oc-remove!` is used to modify an association list that has been constructed only using the corresponding `assq/v/oc-set!`, there can be at most one matching entry in the alist, so the question of multiple entries being removed in one go does not arise. If `assq/v/oc-remove!` is applied to an association list that has been constructed using `acons`, or an `assq/v/oc-set!` with a different level of equality, or any mixture of these, it removes only the first matching entry from the alist, even if the alist might contain further matching entries. For example:

```
(define address-list '())
(set! address-list (assq-set! address-list "mary" "11 Elm Street"))
(set! address-list (assq-set! address-list "mary" "57 Pine Drive"))
address-list
⇒
(("mary" . "57 Pine Drive") ("mary" . "11 Elm Street"))

(set! address-list (assoc-remove! address-list "mary"))
address-list
⇒
```

```
(("mary" . "11 Elm Street"))
```

In this example, the two instances of the string "mary" are not the same when compared using eq?, so the two `assq-set!` calls add two distinct entries to `address-list`. When compared using equal?, both "mary"s in `address-list` are the same as the "mary" in the `assoc-remove!` call, but `assoc-remove!` stops after removing the first matching entry that it finds, and so one of the "mary" entries is left in place.

`assq-remove!` *alist key*	[Scheme Procedure]
`assv-remove!` *alist key*	[Scheme Procedure]
`assoc-remove!` *alist key*	[Scheme Procedure]
`scm_assq_remove_x` (*alist, key*)	[C Function]
`scm_assv_remove_x` (*alist, key*)	[C Function]
`scm_assoc_remove_x` (*alist, key*)	[C Function]

Delete the first entry in *alist* associated with *key*, and return the resulting alist.

6.7.12.5 Sloppy Alist Functions

`sloppy-assq`, `sloppy-assv` and `sloppy-assoc` behave like the corresponding non-`sloppy-` procedures, except that they return `#f` when the specified association list is not well-formed, where the non-`sloppy-` versions would signal an error.

Specifically, there are two conditions for which the non-`sloppy-` procedures signal an error, which the `sloppy-` procedures handle instead by returning `#f`. Firstly, if the specified alist as a whole is not a proper list:

```
(assoc "mary" '((1 . 2) ("key" . "door") . "open sesame"))
⇒
ERROR: In procedure assoc in expression (assoc "mary" (quote #)):
ERROR: Wrong type argument in position 2 (expecting
    association list): ((1 . 2) ("key" . "door") . "open sesame")

(sloppy-assoc "mary" '((1 . 2) ("key" . "door") . "open sesame"))
⇒
#f
```

Secondly, if one of the entries in the specified alist is not a pair:

```
(assoc 2 '((1 . 1) 2 (3 . 9)))
⇒
ERROR: In procedure assoc in expression (assoc 2 (quote #)):
ERROR: Wrong type argument in position 2 (expecting
    association list): ((1 . 1) 2 (3 . 9))

(sloppy-assoc 2 '((1 . 1) 2 (3 . 9)))
⇒
#f
```

Unless you are explicitly working with badly formed association lists, it is much safer to use the non-`sloppy-` procedures, because they help to highlight coding and data errors that the `sloppy-` versions would silently cover up.

sloppy-assq *key alist*   [Scheme Procedure]
scm_sloppy_assq (*key, alist*)   [C Function]
>   Behaves like `assq` but does not do any error checking. Recommended only for use in
>   Guile internals.

sloppy-assv *key alist*   [Scheme Procedure]
scm_sloppy_assv (*key, alist*)   [C Function]
>   Behaves like `assv` but does not do any error checking. Recommended only for use in
>   Guile internals.

sloppy-assoc *key alist*   [Scheme Procedure]
scm_sloppy_assoc (*key, alist*)   [C Function]
>   Behaves like `assoc` but does not do any error checking. Recommended only for use
>   in Guile internals.

6.7.12.6 Alist Example

Here is a longer example of how alists may be used in practice.

```
(define capitals '(("New York" . "Albany")
                   ("Oregon"   . "Salem")
                   ("Florida"  . "Miami")))


;; What's the capital of Oregon?
(assoc "Oregon" capitals)      ⇒ ("Oregon" . "Salem")
(assoc-ref capitals "Oregon")  ⇒ "Salem"


;; We left out South Dakota.
(set! capitals
      (assoc-set! capitals "South Dakota" "Pierre"))
capitals
⇒ (("South Dakota" . "Pierre")
   ("New York" . "Albany")
   ("Oregon" . "Salem")
   ("Florida" . "Miami"))


;; And we got Florida wrong.
(set! capitals
      (assoc-set! capitals "Florida" "Tallahassee"))
capitals
⇒ (("South Dakota" . "Pierre")
   ("New York" . "Albany")
   ("Oregon" . "Salem")
   ("Florida" . "Tallahassee"))


;; After Oregon secedes, we can remove it.
(set! capitals
      (assoc-remove! capitals "Oregon"))
capitals
```

```
⇒ (("South Dakota" . "Pierre")
   ("New York" . "Albany")
   ("Florida" . "Tallahassee"))
```

6.7.13 VList-Based Hash Lists or "VHashes"

The (ice-9 vlist) module provides an implementation of *VList-based hash lists* (see Section 6.7.6 [VLists], page 213). VList-based hash lists, or *vhashes*, are an immutable dictionary type similar to association lists that maps *keys* to *values*. However, unlike association lists, accessing a value given its key is typically a constant-time operation.

The VHash programming interface of (ice-9 vlist) is mostly the same as that of association lists found in SRFI-1, with procedure names prefixed by vhash- instead of alist- (see Section 7.5.3.9 [SRFI-1 Association Lists], page 562).

In addition, vhashes can be manipulated using VList operations:

```
(vlist-head (vhash-consq 'a 1 vlist-null))
⇒ (a . 1)


(define vh1 (vhash-consq 'b 2 (vhash-consq 'a 1 vlist-null)))
(define vh2 (vhash-consq 'c 3 (vlist-tail vh1)))


(vhash-assq 'a vh2)
⇒ (a . 1)
(vhash-assq 'b vh2)
⇒ #f
(vhash-assq 'c vh2)
⇒ (c . 3)
(vlist->list vh2)
⇒ ((c . 3) (a . 1))
```

However, keep in mind that procedures that construct new VLists (vlist-map, vlist-filter, etc.) return raw VLists, not vhashes:

```
(define vh (alist->vhash '((a . 1) (b . 2) (c . 3)) hashq))
(vhash-assq 'a vh)
⇒ (a . 1)


(define vl
  ;; This will create a raw vlist.
  (vlist-filter (lambda (key+value) (odd? (cdr key+value))) vh))
(vhash-assq 'a vl)
⇒ ERROR: Wrong type argument in position 2


(vlist->list vl)
⇒ ((a . 1) (c . 3))
```

vhash? *obj*   [Scheme Procedure]
    Return true if *obj* is a vhash.

vhash-cons *key value vhash [hash-proc]*   [Scheme Procedure]
vhash-consq *key value vhash*   [Scheme Procedure]

`vhash-consv` *key value vhash*   [Scheme Procedure]

> Return a new hash list based on *vhash* where *key* is associated with *value*, using *hash-proc* to compute the hash of *key*. *vhash* must be either `vlist-null` or a vhash returned by a previous call to `vhash-cons`. *hash-proc* defaults to `hash` (see Section 6.7.14.2 [Hash Table Reference], page 237). With `vhash-consq`, the `hashq` hash function is used; with `vhash-consv` the `hashv` hash function is used.
>
> All `vhash-cons` calls made to construct a vhash should use the same *hash-proc*. Failing to do that, the result is undefined.

`vhash-assoc` *key vhash* [*equal?* [*hash-proc*]]   [Scheme Procedure]
`vhash-assq` *key vhash*   [Scheme Procedure]
`vhash-assv` *key vhash*   [Scheme Procedure]

> Return the first key/value pair from *vhash* whose key is equal to *key* according to the *equal?* equality predicate (which defaults to `equal?`), and using *hash-proc* (which defaults to `hash`) to compute the hash of *key*. The second form uses `eq?` as the equality predicate and `hashq` as the hash function; the last form uses `eqv?` and `hashv`.
>
> Note that it is important to consistently use the same hash function for *hash-proc* as was passed to `vhash-cons`. Failing to do that, the result is unpredictable.

`vhash-delete` *key vhash* [*equal?* [*hash-proc*]]   [Scheme Procedure]
`vhash-delq` *key vhash*   [Scheme Procedure]
`vhash-delv` *key vhash*   [Scheme Procedure]

> Remove all associations from *vhash* with *key*, comparing keys with *equal?* (which defaults to `equal?`), and computing the hash of *key* using *hash-proc* (which defaults to `hash`). The second form uses `eq?` as the equality predicate and `hashq` as the hash function; the last one uses `eqv?` and `hashv`.
>
> Again the choice of *hash-proc* must be consistent with previous calls to `vhash-cons`.

`vhash-fold` *proc init vhash*   [Scheme Procedure]
`vhash-fold-right` *proc init vhash*   [Scheme Procedure]

> Fold over the key/value elements of *vhash* in the given direction, with each call to *proc* having the form (`proc key value result`), where *result* is the result of the previous call to *proc* and *init* the value of *result* for the first call to *proc*.

`vhash-fold*` *proc init key vhash* [*equal?* [*hash*]]   [Scheme Procedure]
`vhash-foldq*` *proc init key vhash*   [Scheme Procedure]
`vhash-foldv*` *proc init key vhash*   [Scheme Procedure]

> Fold over all the values associated with *key* in *vhash*, with each call to *proc* having the form (`proc value result`), where *result* is the result of the previous call to *proc* and *init* the value of *result* for the first call to *proc*.
>
> Keys in *vhash* are hashed using *hash* are compared using *equal?*. The second form uses `eq?` as the equality predicate and `hashq` as the hash function; the third one uses `eqv?` and `hashv`.
>
> Example:

```
(define vh
  (alist->vhash '((a . 1) (a . 2) (z . 0) (a . 3))))
```

```
(vhash-fold* cons '() 'a vh)
⇒ (3 2 1)

(vhash-fold* cons '() 'z vh)
⇒ (0)
```

alist->vhash *alist* [*hash-proc*]   [Scheme Procedure]
    Return the vhash corresponding to *alist*, an association list, using *hash-proc* to com-
    pute key hashes. When omitted, *hash-proc* defaults to `hash`.

6.7.14 Hash Tables

Hash tables are dictionaries which offer similar functionality as association lists: They
provide a mapping from keys to values. The difference is that association lists need time
linear in the size of elements when searching for entries, whereas hash tables can normally
search in constant time. The drawback is that hash tables require a little bit more memory,
and that you can not use the normal list procedures (see Section 6.7.2 [Lists], page 188) for
working with them.

6.7.14.1 Hash Table Examples

For demonstration purposes, this section gives a few usage examples of some hash table
procedures, together with some explanation what they do.

First we start by creating a new hash table with 31 slots, and populate it with two
key/value pairs.

```
(define h (make-hash-table 31))

;; This is an opaque object
h
⇒
#<hash-table 0/31>

;; Inserting into a hash table can be done with hashq-set!
(hashq-set! h 'foo "bar")
⇒
"bar"

(hashq-set! h 'braz "zonk")
⇒
"zonk"

;; Or with hash-create-handle!
(hashq-create-handle! h 'frob #f)
⇒
(frob . #f)
```

You can get the value for a given key with the procedure `hashq-ref`, but the problem
with this procedure is that you cannot reliably determine whether a key does exists in the
table. The reason is that the procedure returns `#f` if the key is not in the table, but it will

return the same value if the key is in the table and just happens to have the value #f, as you can see in the following examples.

```
(hashq-ref h 'foo)
⇒
"bar"

(hashq-ref h 'frob)
⇒
#f

(hashq-ref h 'not-there)
⇒
#f
```

Better is to use the procedure `hashq-get-handle`, which makes a distinction between the two cases. Just like `assq`, this procedure returns a key/value-pair on success, and #f if the key is not found.

```
(hashq-get-handle h 'foo)
⇒
(foo . "bar")

(hashq-get-handle h 'not-there)
⇒
#f
```

Interesting results can be computed by using `hash-fold` to work through each element. This example will count the total number of elements:

```
(hash-fold (lambda (key value seed) (+ 1 seed)) 0 h)
⇒
3
```

The same thing can be done with the procedure `hash-count`, which can also count the number of elements matching a particular predicate. For example, count the number of elements with string values:

```
(hash-count (lambda (key value) (string? value)) h)
⇒
2
```

Counting all the elements is a simple task using `const`:

```
(hash-count (const #t) h)
⇒
3
```

6.7.14.2 Hash Table Reference

Like the association list functions, the hash table functions come in several varieties, according to the equality test used for the keys. Plain `hash-` functions use `equal?`, `hashq-` functions use `eq?`, `hashv-` functions use `eqv?`, and the `hashx-` functions use an application supplied test.

A single `make-hash-table` creates a hash table suitable for use with any set of functions, but it's imperative that just one set is then used consistently, or results will be unpredictable.

Hash tables are implemented as a vector indexed by a hash value formed from the key, with an association list of key/value pairs for each bucket in case distinct keys hash together. Direct access to the pairs in those lists is provided by the `-handle-` functions.

When the number of entries in a hash table goes above a threshold, the vector is made larger and the entries are rehashed, to prevent the bucket lists from becoming too long and slowing down accesses. When the number of entries goes below a threshold, the vector is shrunk to save space.

For the `hashx-` "extended" routines, an application supplies a *hash* function producing an integer index like `hashq` etc below, and an *assoc* alist search function like `assq` etc (see Section 6.7.12.3 [Retrieving Alist Entries], page 230). Here's an example of such functions implementing case-insensitive hashing of string keys,

```
(use-modules (srfi srfi-1)
             (srfi srfi-13))

(define (my-hash str size)
  (remainder (string-hash-ci str) size))
(define (my-assoc str alist)
  (find (lambda (pair) (string-ci=? str (car pair))) alist))

(define my-table (make-hash-table))
(hashx-set! my-hash my-assoc my-table "foo" 123)

(hashx-ref my-hash my-assoc my-table "FOO")
⇒ 123
```

In a `hashx-` *hash* function the aim is to spread keys across the vector, so bucket lists don't become long. But the actual values are arbitrary as long as they're in the range 0 to $size - 1$. Helpful functions for forming a hash value, in addition to `hashq` etc below, include `symbol-hash` (see Section 6.6.7.2 [Symbol Keys], page 172), `string-hash` and `string-hash-ci` (see Section 6.6.5.7 [String Comparison], page 148), and `char-set-hash` (see Section 6.6.4.1 [Character Set Predicates/Comparison], page 133).

`make-hash-table` [*size*]   [Scheme Procedure]

> Create a new hash table object, with an optional minimum vector *size*.
>
> When *size* is given, the table vector will still grow and shrink automatically, as described above, but with *size* as a minimum. If an application knows roughly how many entries the table will hold then it can use *size* to avoid rehashing when initial entries are added.

`alist->hash-table` *alist*   [Scheme Procedure]
`alist->hashq-table` *alist*   [Scheme Procedure]
`alist->hashv-table` *alist*   [Scheme Procedure]
`alist->hashx-table` *hash assoc alist*   [Scheme Procedure]

> Convert *alist* into a hash table. When keys are repeated in *alist*, the leftmost association takes precedence.

```
(use-modules (ice-9 hash-table))
(alist->hash-table '((foo . 1) (bar . 2)))
```

When converting to an extended hash table, custom *hash* and *assoc* procedures must be provided.

```
(alist->hashx-table hash assoc '((foo . 1) (bar . 2)))
```

hash-table? *obj*   [Scheme Procedure]
scm_hash_table_p (*obj*)   [C Function]
    Return #t if *obj* is a abstract hash table object.

hash-clear! *table*   [Scheme Procedure]
scm_hash_clear_x (*table*)   [C Function]
    Remove all items from *table* (without triggering a resize).

hash-ref *table key* [*dflt*]   [Scheme Procedure]
hashq-ref *table key* [*dflt*]   [Scheme Procedure]
hashv-ref *table key* [*dflt*]   [Scheme Procedure]
hashx-ref *hash assoc table key* [*dflt*]   [Scheme Procedure]
scm_hash_ref (*table, key, dflt*)   [C Function]
scm_hashq_ref (*table, key, dflt*)   [C Function]
scm_hashv_ref (*table, key, dflt*)   [C Function]
scm_hashx_ref (*hash, assoc, table, key, dflt*)   [C Function]
    Lookup *key* in the given hash *table*, and return the associated value. If *key* is not found, return *dflt*, or #f if *dflt* is not given.

hash-set! *table key val*   [Scheme Procedure]
hashq-set! *table key val*   [Scheme Procedure]
hashv-set! *table key val*   [Scheme Procedure]
hashx-set! *hash assoc table key val*   [Scheme Procedure]
scm_hash_set_x (*table, key, val*)   [C Function]
scm_hashq_set_x (*table, key, val*)   [C Function]
scm_hashv_set_x (*table, key, val*)   [C Function]
scm_hashx_set_x (*hash, assoc, table, key, val*)   [C Function]
    Associate *val* with *key* in the given hash *table*. If *key* is already present then it's associated value is changed. If it's not present then a new entry is created.

hash-remove! *table key*   [Scheme Procedure]
hashq-remove! *table key*   [Scheme Procedure]
hashv-remove! *table key*   [Scheme Procedure]
hashx-remove! *hash assoc table key*   [Scheme Procedure]
scm_hash_remove_x (*table, key*)   [C Function]
scm_hashq_remove_x (*table, key*)   [C Function]
scm_hashv_remove_x (*table, key*)   [C Function]
scm_hashx_remove_x (*hash, assoc, table, key*)   [C Function]
    Remove any association for *key* in the given hash *table*. If *key* is not in *table* then nothing is done.

hash *key size*   [Scheme Procedure]
hashq *key size*   [Scheme Procedure]

`hashv` *key size*	[Scheme Procedure]
`scm_hash` (*key, size*)	[C Function]
`scm_hashq` (*key, size*)	[C Function]
`scm_hashv` (*key, size*)	[C Function]

Return a hash value for *key*. This is a number in the range 0 to *size* − 1, which is suitable for use in a hash table of the given *size*.

Note that `hashq` and `hashv` may use internal addresses of objects, so if an object is garbage collected and re-created it can have a different hash value, even when the two are notionally `eq?`. For instance with symbols,

```
(hashq 'something 123)   ⇒ 19
(gc)
(hashq 'something 123)   ⇒ 62
```

In normal use this is not a problem, since an object entered into a hash table won't be garbage collected until removed. It's only if hashing calculations are somehow separated from normal references that its lifetime needs to be considered.

`hash-get-handle` *table key*	[Scheme Procedure]
`hashq-get-handle` *table key*	[Scheme Procedure]
`hashv-get-handle` *table key*	[Scheme Procedure]
`hashx-get-handle` *hash assoc table key*	[Scheme Procedure]
`scm_hash_get_handle` (*table, key*)	[C Function]
`scm_hashq_get_handle` (*table, key*)	[C Function]
`scm_hashv_get_handle` (*table, key*)	[C Function]
`scm_hashx_get_handle` (*hash, assoc, table, key*)	[C Function]

Return the (`key . value`) pair for *key* in the given hash *table*, or `#f` if *key* is not in *table*.

`hash-create-handle!` *table key init*	[Scheme Procedure]
`hashq-create-handle!` *table key init*	[Scheme Procedure]
`hashv-create-handle!` *table key init*	[Scheme Procedure]
`hashx-create-handle!` *hash assoc table key init*	[Scheme Procedure]
`scm_hash_create_handle_x` (*table, key, init*)	[C Function]
`scm_hashq_create_handle_x` (*table, key, init*)	[C Function]
`scm_hashv_create_handle_x` (*table, key, init*)	[C Function]
`scm_hashx_create_handle_x` (*hash, assoc, table, key, init*)	[C Function]

Return the (`key . value`) pair for *key* in the given hash *table*. If *key* is not in *table* then create an entry for it with *init* as the value, and return that pair.

`hash-map->list` *proc table*	[Scheme Procedure]
`hash-for-each` *proc table*	[Scheme Procedure]
`scm_hash_map_to_list` (*proc, table*)	[C Function]
`scm_hash_for_each` (*proc, table*)	[C Function]

Apply *proc* to the entries in the given hash *table*. Each call is (`proc key value`). `hash-map->list` returns a list of the results from these calls, `hash-for-each` discards the results and returns an unspecified value.

Calls are made over the table entries in an unspecified order, and for `hash-map->list` the order of the values in the returned list is unspecified. Results will be unpredictable if *table* is modified while iterating.

For example the following returns a new alist comprising all the entries from `mytable`, in no particular order.

```
(hash-map->list cons mytable)
```

`hash-for-each-handle` *proc table*   [Scheme Procedure]
`scm_hash_for_each_handle` (*proc, table*)   [C Function]

Apply *proc* to the entries in the given hash *table*. Each call is (`proc handle`), where *handle* is a (`key . value`) pair. Return an unspecified value.

`hash-for-each-handle` differs from `hash-for-each` only in the argument list of *proc*.

`hash-fold` *proc init table*   [Scheme Procedure]
`scm_hash_fold` (*proc, init, table*)   [C Function]

Accumulate a result by applying *proc* to the elements of the given hash *table*. Each call is (`proc key value prior-result`), where *key* and *value* are from the *table* and *prior-result* is the return from the previous *proc* call. For the first call, *prior-result* is the given *init* value.

Calls are made over the table entries in an unspecified order. Results will be unpredictable if *table* is modified while `hash-fold` is running.

For example, the following returns a count of how many keys in `mytable` are strings.

```
(hash-fold (lambda (key value prior)
              (if (string? key) (1+ prior) prior))
           0 mytable)
```

`hash-count` *pred table*   [Scheme Procedure]
`scm_hash_count` (*pred, table*)   [C Function]

Return the number of elements in the given hash *table* that cause (`pred key value`) to return true. To quickly determine the total number of elements, use (`const #t`) for *pred*.

6.8 Smobs

This chapter contains reference information related to defining and working with smobs. See Section 5.5 [Defining New Types (Smobs)], page 71 for a tutorial-like introduction to smobs.

`scm_t_bits scm_make_smob_type` (*const char *name, size_t size*)   [Function]

This function adds a new smob type, named *name*, with instance size *size*, to the system. The return value is a tag that is used in creating instances of the type.

If *size* is 0, the default *free* function will do nothing.

If *size* is not 0, the default *free* function will deallocate the memory block pointed to by `SCM_SMOB_DATA` with `scm_gc_free`. The *what* parameter in the call to `scm_gc_free` will be *name*.

Default values are provided for the *mark*, *free*, *print*, and *equalp* functions, as described in Section 5.5 [Defining New Types (Smobs)], page 71. If you want to customize any of these functions, the call to `scm_make_smob_type` should be immediately followed by calls to one or several of `scm_set_smob_mark`, `scm_set_smob_free`, `scm_set_smob_print`, and/or `scm_set_smob_equalp`.

void scm_set_smob_free (*scm_t_bits tc, size_t* (*free*) (*SCM obj*))   [C Function]
> This function sets the smob freeing procedure (sometimes referred to as a *finalizer*) for the smob type specified by the tag *tc*. *tc* is the tag returned by `scm_make_smob_type`.
>
> The *free* procedure must deallocate all resources that are directly associated with the smob instance *obj*. It must assume that all SCM values that it references have already been freed and are thus invalid.
>
> It must also not call any libguile function or macro except `scm_gc_free`, `SCM_SMOB_FLAGS`, `SCM_SMOB_DATA`, `SCM_SMOB_DATA_2`, and `SCM_SMOB_DATA_3`.
>
> The *free* procedure must return 0.
>
> Note that defining a freeing procedure is not necessary if the resources associated with *obj* consists only of memory allocated with `scm_gc_malloc` or `scm_gc_malloc_pointerless` because this memory is automatically reclaimed by the garbage collector when it is no longer needed (see Section 6.18.2 [Memory Blocks], page 376).

void scm_set_smob_mark (*scm_t_bits tc, SCM* (*mark*) (*SCM obj*))   [C Function]
> This function sets the smob marking procedure for the smob type specified by the tag *tc*. *tc* is the tag returned by `scm_make_smob_type`.
>
> Defining a marking procedure may sometimes be unnecessary because large parts of the process' memory (with the exception of `scm_gc_malloc_pointerless` regions, and `malloc`- or `scm_malloc`-allocated memory) are scanned for live pointers[4].
>
> The *mark* procedure must cause `scm_gc_mark` to be called for every SCM value that is directly referenced by the smob instance *obj*. One of these SCM values can be returned from the procedure and Guile will call `scm_gc_mark` for it. This can be used to avoid deep recursions for smob instances that form a list.
>
> It must not call any libguile function or macro except `scm_gc_mark`, `SCM_SMOB_FLAGS`, `SCM_SMOB_DATA`, `SCM_SMOB_DATA_2`, and `SCM_SMOB_DATA_3`.

void scm_set_smob_print (*scm_t_bits tc, int* (*print*) (*SCM obj,*   [C Function]
> *SCM port, scm_print_state* pstate*))
> This function sets the smob printing procedure for the smob type specified by the tag *tc*. *tc* is the tag returned by `scm_make_smob_type`.
>
> The *print* procedure should output a textual representation of the smob instance *obj* to *port*, using information in *pstate*.
>
> The textual representation should be of the form `#<name ...>`. This ensures that `read` will not interpret it as some other Scheme value.
>
> It is often best to ignore *pstate* and just print to *port* with `scm_display`, `scm_write`, `scm_simple_format`, and `scm_puts`.

void scm_set_smob_equalp (*scm_t_bits tc, SCM* (*equalp*) (*SCM*   [C Function]
> *obj1, SCM obj2*))
> This function sets the smob equality-testing predicate for the smob type specified by the tag *tc*. *tc* is the tag returned by `scm_make_smob_type`.

---

[4] Conversely, in Guile up to the 1.8 series, the marking procedure was always required. The reason is that Guile's GC would only look for pointers in the memory area used for built-in types (the *cell heap*), not in user-allocated or statically allocated memory. This approach is often referred to as *precise marking*.

The *equalp* procedure should return `SCM_BOOL_T` when *obj1* is `equal?` to *obj2*. Else it should return `SCM_BOOL_F`. Both *obj1* and *obj2* are instances of the smob type *tc*.

void **scm_assert_smob_type** (*scm_t_bits tag, SCM val*)   [C Function]
> When *val* is a smob of the type indicated by *tag*, do nothing. Else, signal an error.

int **SCM_SMOB_PREDICATE** (*scm_t_bits tag, SCM exp*)   [C Macro]
> Return true if *exp* is a smob instance of the type indicated by *tag*, or false otherwise. The expression *exp* can be evaluated more than once, so it shouldn't contain any side effects.

SCM **scm_new_smob** (*scm_t_bits tag, void *data*)   [C Function]
SCM **scm_new_double_smob** (*scm_t_bits tag, void *data, void *data2,*   [C Function]
> *void *data3*)
>
> Make a new smob of the type with tag *tag* and smob data *data*, *data2*, and *data3*, as appropriate.
>
> The *tag* is what has been returned by `scm_make_smob_type`. The initial values *data*, *data2*, and *data3* are of type `scm_t_bits`; when you want to use them for SCM values, these values need to be converted to a `scm_t_bits` first by using `SCM_UNPACK`.
>
> The flags of the smob instance start out as zero.

scm_t_bits **SCM_SMOB_FLAGS** (*SCM obj*)   [C Macro]
> Return the 16 extra bits of the smob *obj*. No meaning is predefined for these bits, you can use them freely.

scm_t_bits **SCM_SET_SMOB_FLAGS** (*SCM obj, scm_t_bits flags*)   [C Macro]
> Set the 16 extra bits of the smob *obj* to *flags*. No meaning is predefined for these bits, you can use them freely.

scm_t_bits **SCM_SMOB_DATA** (*SCM obj*)   [C Macro]
scm_t_bits **SCM_SMOB_DATA_2** (*SCM obj*)   [C Macro]
scm_t_bits **SCM_SMOB_DATA_3** (*SCM obj*)   [C Macro]
> Return the first (second, third) immediate word of the smob *obj* as a `scm_t_bits` value. When the word contains a SCM value, use `SCM_SMOB_OBJECT` (etc.) instead.

void **SCM_SET_SMOB_DATA** (*SCM obj, scm_t_bits val*)   [C Macro]
void **SCM_SET_SMOB_DATA_2** (*SCM obj, scm_t_bits val*)   [C Macro]
void **SCM_SET_SMOB_DATA_3** (*SCM obj, scm_t_bits val*)   [C Macro]
> Set the first (second, third) immediate word of the smob *obj* to *val*. When the word should be set to a SCM value, use `SCM_SMOB_SET_OBJECT` (etc.) instead.

SCM **SCM_SMOB_OBJECT** (*SCM obj*)   [C Macro]
SCM **SCM_SMOB_OBJECT_2** (*SCM obj*)   [C Macro]
SCM **SCM_SMOB_OBJECT_3** (*SCM obj*)   [C Macro]
> Return the first (second, third) immediate word of the smob *obj* as a SCM value. When the word contains a `scm_t_bits` value, use `SCM_SMOB_DATA` (etc.) instead.

void **SCM_SET_SMOB_OBJECT** (*SCM obj, SCM val*)   [C Macro]
void **SCM_SET_SMOB_OBJECT_2** (*SCM obj, SCM val*)   [C Macro]

`void SCM_SET_SMOB_OBJECT_3` (*SCM obj, SCM val*)   [C Macro]

Set the first (second, third) immediate word of the smob *obj* to *val*. When the word should be set to a `scm_t_bits` value, use `SCM_SMOB_SET_DATA` (etc.) instead.

`SCM * SCM_SMOB_OBJECT_LOC` (*SCM obj*)   [C Macro]
`SCM * SCM_SMOB_OBJECT_2_LOC` (*SCM obj*)   [C Macro]
`SCM * SCM_SMOB_OBJECT_3_LOC` (*SCM obj*)   [C Macro]

Return a pointer to the first (second, third) immediate word of the smob *obj*. Note that this is a pointer to `SCM`. If you need to work with `scm_t_bits` values, use `SCM_PACK` and `SCM_UNPACK`, as appropriate.

`SCM scm_markcdr` (*SCM x*)   [Function]

Mark the references in the smob *x*, assuming that *x*'s first data word contains an ordinary Scheme object, and *x* refers to no other objects. This function simply returns *x*'s first data word.

6.9 Procedures

6.9.1 Lambda: Basic Procedure Creation

A `lambda` expression evaluates to a procedure. The environment which is in effect when a `lambda` expression is evaluated is enclosed in the newly created procedure, this is referred to as a *closure* (see Section 3.4 [About Closure], page 26).

When a procedure created by `lambda` is called with some actual arguments, the environment enclosed in the procedure is extended by binding the variables named in the formal argument list to new locations and storing the actual arguments into these locations. Then the body of the `lambda` expression is evaluated sequentially. The result of the last expression in the procedure body is then the result of the procedure invocation.

The following examples will show how procedures can be created using `lambda`, and what you can do with these procedures.

```
(lambda (x) (+ x x))        ⇒ a procedure
((lambda (x) (+ x x)) 4)    ⇒ 8
```

The fact that the environment in effect when creating a procedure is enclosed in the procedure is shown with this example:

```
(define add4
  (let ((x 4))
    (lambda (y) (+ x y))))
(add4 6)                    ⇒ 10
```

`lambda` *formals body*   [syntax]

formals should be a formal argument list as described in the following table.

(*variable1* ...)

The procedure takes a fixed number of arguments; when the procedure is called, the arguments will be stored into the newly created location for the formal variables.

variable   The procedure takes any number of arguments; when the procedure is called, the sequence of actual arguments will converted into a list and stored into the newly created location for the formal variable.

(*variable1* ... *variablen* . *variablen+1*)

> If a space-delimited period precedes the last variable, then the procedure takes *n* or more variables where *n* is the number of formal arguments before the period. There must be at least one argument before the period. The first *n* actual arguments will be stored into the newly allocated locations for the first *n* formal arguments and the sequence of the remaining actual arguments is converted into a list and the stored into the location for the last formal argument. If there are exactly *n* actual arguments, the empty list is stored into the location of the last formal argument.

The list in *variable* or *variablen+1* is always newly created and the procedure can modify it if desired. This is the case even when the procedure is invoked via **apply**, the required part of the list argument there will be copied (see Section 6.17.4 [Procedures for On the Fly Evaluation], page 362).

body is a sequence of Scheme expressions which are evaluated in order when the procedure is invoked.

6.9.2 Primitive Procedures

Procedures written in C can be registered for use from Scheme, provided they take only arguments of type SCM and return SCM values. **scm_c_define_gsubr** is likely to be the most useful mechanism, combining the process of registration (**scm_c_make_gsubr**) and definition (**scm_define**).

SCM **scm_c_make_gsubr** (*const char *name, int req, int opt, int rst, fcn*)   [Function]
> Register a C procedure *fcn* as a "subr" — a primitive subroutine that can be called from Scheme. It will be associated with the given *name* but no environment binding will be created. The arguments *req*, *opt* and *rst* specify the number of required, optional and "rest" arguments respectively. The total number of these arguments should match the actual number of arguments to *fcn*, but may not exceed 10. The number of rest arguments should be 0 or 1. **scm_c_make_gsubr** returns a value of type SCM which is a "handle" for the procedure.

SCM **scm_c_define_gsubr** (*const char *name, int req, int opt, int rst,*   [Function]
    fcn)
> Register a C procedure *fcn*, as for **scm_c_make_gsubr** above, and additionally create a top-level Scheme binding for the procedure in the "current environment" using **scm_define**. **scm_c_define_gsubr** returns a handle for the procedure in the same way as **scm_c_make_gsubr**, which is usually not further required.

6.9.3 Compiled Procedures

The evaluation strategy given in Section 6.9.1 [Lambda], page 244 describes how procedures are *interpreted*. Interpretation operates directly on expanded Scheme source code, recursively calling the evaluator to obtain the value of nested expressions.

Most procedures are compiled, however. This means that Guile has done some pre-computation on the procedure, to determine what it will need to do each time the procedure runs. Compiled procedures run faster than interpreted procedures.

Loading files is the normal way that compiled procedures come to being. If Guile sees that a file is uncompiled, or that its compiled file is out of date, it will attempt to compile the file when it is loaded, and save the result to disk. Procedures can be compiled at runtime as well. See Section 6.17 [Read/Load/Eval/Compile], page 357, for more information on runtime compilation.

Compiled procedures, also known as *programs*, respond all procedures that operate on procedures. In addition, there are a few more accessors for low-level details on programs.

Most people won't need to use the routines described in this section, but it's good to have them documented. You'll have to include the appropriate module first, though:

```
(use-modules (system vm program))
```

program? *obj*   [Scheme Procedure]
scm_program_p (*obj*)   [C Function]
> Returns #t if *obj* is a compiled procedure, or #f otherwise.

program-objcode *program*   [Scheme Procedure]
scm_program_objcode (*program*)   [C Function]
> Returns the object code associated with this program. See Section 9.4.6 [Bytecode and Objcode], page 803, for more information.

program-objects *program*   [Scheme Procedure]
scm_program_objects (*program*)   [C Function]
> Returns the "object table" associated with this program, as a vector. See Section 9.3.5 [VM Programs], page 776, for more information.

program-module *program*   [Scheme Procedure]
scm_program_module (*program*)   [C Function]
> Returns the module that was current when this program was created. Can return #f if the compiler could determine that this information was unnecessary.

program-free-variables *program*   [Scheme Procedure]
scm_program_free_variables (*program*)   [C Function]
> Returns the set of free variables that this program captures in its closure, as a vector. If a closure is code with data, you can get the code from program-objcode, and the data via program-free-variables.
>
> Some of the values captured are actually in variable "boxes". See Section 9.3.4 [Variables and the VM], page 775, for more information.
>
> Users must not modify the returned value unless they think they're really clever.

program-meta *program*   [Scheme Procedure]
scm_program_meta (*program*)   [C Function]
> Return the metadata thunk of *program*, or #f if it has no metadata.
>
> When called, a metadata thunk returns a list of the following form: (**bindings sources arities . properties**). The format of each of these elements is discussed below.

`program-bindings` *program*	[Scheme Procedure]
`make-binding` *name boxed? index start end*	[Scheme Procedure]
`binding:name` *binding*	[Scheme Procedure]
`binding:boxed?` *binding*	[Scheme Procedure]
`binding:index` *binding*	[Scheme Procedure]
`binding:start` *binding*	[Scheme Procedure]
`binding:end` *binding*	[Scheme Procedure]

Bindings annotations for programs, along with their accessors.

Bindings declare names and liveness extents for block-local variables. The best way to see what these are is to play around with them at a REPL. See Section 9.3.2 [VM Concepts], page 773, for more information.

Note that bindings information is stored in a program as part of its metadata thunk, so including it in the generated object code does not impose a runtime performance penalty.

`program-sources` *program*	[Scheme Procedure]
`source:addr` *source*	[Scheme Procedure]
`source:line` *source*	[Scheme Procedure]
`source:column` *source*	[Scheme Procedure]
`source:file` *source*	[Scheme Procedure]

Source location annotations for programs, along with their accessors.

Source location information propagates through the compiler and ends up being serialized to the program's metadata. This information is keyed by the offset of the instruction pointer within the object code of the program. Specifically, it is keyed on the ip *just following* an instruction, so that backtraces can find the source location of a call that is in progress.

`program-arities` *program*	[Scheme Procedure]
`scm_program_arities` (*program*)	[C Function]
`program-arity` *program ip*	[Scheme Procedure]
`arity:start` *arity*	[Scheme Procedure]
`arity:end` *arity*	[Scheme Procedure]
`arity:nreq` *arity*	[Scheme Procedure]
`arity:nopt` *arity*	[Scheme Procedure]
`arity:rest?` *arity*	[Scheme Procedure]
`arity:kw` *arity*	[Scheme Procedure]
`arity:allow-other-keys?` *arity*	[Scheme Procedure]

Accessors for a representation of the "arity" of a program.

The normal case is that a procedure has one arity. For example, (`lambda (x) x`), takes one required argument, and that's it. One could access that number of required arguments via (`arity:nreq (program-arities (lambda (x) x))`). Similarly, `arity:nopt` gets the number of optional arguments, and `arity:rest?` returns a true value if the procedure has a rest arg.

`arity:kw` returns a list of (`kw . idx`) pairs, if the procedure has keyword arguments. The *idx* refers to the *idx*th local variable; See Section 9.3.4 [Variables and the VM], page 775, for more information. Finally `arity:allow-other-keys?` returns a true value if other keys are allowed. See Section 6.9.4 [Optional Arguments], page 248, for more information.

So what about `arity:start` and `arity:end`, then? They return the range of bytes in the program's bytecode for which a given arity is valid. You see, a procedure can actually have more than one arity. The question, "what is a procedure's arity" only really makes sense at certain points in the program, delimited by these `arity:start` and `arity:end` values.

`program-arguments-alist` *program* [*ip*]   [Scheme Procedure]
> Return an association list describing the arguments that *program* accepts, or `#f` if the information cannot be obtained.
>
> The alist keys that are currently defined are 'required', 'optional', 'keyword', 'allow-other-keys?', and 'rest'. For example:
>
> ```
> (program-arguments-alist
>  (lambda* (a b #:optional c #:key (d 1) #:rest e)
>    #t)) ⇒
> ((required . (a b))
>  (optional . (c))
>  (keyword . ((#:d . 4)))
>  (allow-other-keys? . #f)
>  (rest . d))
> ```

`program-lambda-list` *program* [*ip*]   [Scheme Procedure]
> Return a representation of the arguments of *program* as a lambda list, or `#f` if this information is not available.
>
> For example:
>
> ```
> (program-lambda-list
>  (lambda* (a b #:optional c #:key (d 1) #:rest e)
>    #t)) ⇒
> ```

6.9.4 Optional Arguments

Scheme procedures, as defined in R5RS, can either handle a fixed number of actual arguments, or a fixed number of actual arguments followed by arbitrarily many additional arguments. Writing procedures of variable arity can be useful, but unfortunately, the syntactic means for handling argument lists of varying length is a bit inconvenient. It is possible to give names to the fixed number of arguments, but the remaining (optional) arguments can be only referenced as a list of values (see Section 6.9.1 [Lambda], page 244).

For this reason, Guile provides an extension to `lambda`, `lambda*`, which allows the user to define procedures with optional and keyword arguments. In addition, Guile's virtual machine has low-level support for optional and keyword argument dispatch. Calls to procedures with optional and keyword arguments can be made cheaply, without allocating a rest list.

6.9.4.1 lambda* and define*.

`lambda*` is like `lambda`, except with some extensions to allow optional and keyword arguments.

lambda* ([*var*...]   [library syntax]
      [*#:optional vardef*...]
      [*#:key vardef*... [*#:allow-other-keys*]]
      [*#:rest var* | . *var*])
      body1 body2 ...

Create a procedure which takes optional and/or keyword arguments specified with `#:optional` and `#:key`. For example,

```
(lambda* (a b #:optional c d . e) '())
```

is a procedure with fixed arguments *a* and *b*, optional arguments *c* and *d*, and rest argument *e*. If the optional arguments are omitted in a call, the variables for them are bound to `#f`.

Likewise, `define*` is syntactic sugar for defining procedures using `lambda*`.

`lambda*` can also make procedures with keyword arguments. For example, a procedure defined like this:

```
(define* (sir-yes-sir #:key action how-high)
  (list action how-high))
```

can be called as `(sir-yes-sir #:action 'jump)`, `(sir-yes-sir #:how-high 13)`, `(sir-yes-sir #:action 'lay-down #:how-high 0)`, or just `(sir-yes-sir)`. Whichever arguments are given as keywords are bound to values (and those not given are `#f`).

Optional and keyword arguments can also have default values to take when not present in a call, by giving a two-element list of variable name and expression. For example in

```
(define* (frob foo #:optional (bar 42) #:key (baz 73))
  (list foo bar baz))
```

foo is a fixed argument, *bar* is an optional argument with default value 42, and baz is a keyword argument with default value 73. Default value expressions are not evaluated unless they are needed, and until the procedure is called.

Normally it's an error if a call has keywords other than those specified by `#:key`, but adding `#:allow-other-keys` to the definition (after the keyword argument declarations) will ignore unknown keywords.

If a call has a keyword given twice, the last value is used. For example,

```
(define* (flips #:key (heads 0) (tails 0))
  (display (list heads tails)))

(flips #:heads 37 #:tails 42 #:heads 99)
⊣ (99 42)
```

`#:rest` is a synonym for the dotted syntax rest argument. The argument lists `(a . b)` and `(a #:rest b)` are equivalent in all respects. This is provided for more similarity to DSSSL, MIT-Scheme and Kawa among others, as well as for refugees from other Lisp dialects.

When `#:key` is used together with a rest argument, the keyword parameters in a call all remain in the rest list. This is the same as Common Lisp. For example,

```
((lambda* (#:key (x 0) #:allow-other-keys #:rest r)
   (display r))
 #:x 123 #:y 456)
⊣ (#:x 123 #:y 456)
```

`#:optional` and `#:key` establish their bindings successively, from left to right. This means default expressions can refer back to prior parameters, for example

```
(lambda* (start #:optional (end (+ 10 start)))
  (do ((i start (1+ i)))
      ((> i end))
    (display i)))
```

The exception to this left-to-right scoping rule is the rest argument. If there is a rest argument, it is bound after the optional arguments, but before the keyword arguments.

6.9.4.2 (ice-9 optargs)

Before Guile 2.0, `lambda*` and `define*` were implemented using macros that processed rest list arguments. This was not optimal, as calling procedures with optional arguments had to allocate rest lists at every procedure invocation. Guile 2.0 improved this situation by bringing optional and keyword arguments into Guile's core.

However there are occasions in which you have a list and want to parse it for optional or keyword arguments. Guile's (ice-9 optargs) provides some macros to help with that task.

The syntax `let-optional` and `let-optional*` are for destructuring rest argument lists and giving names to the various list elements. `let-optional` binds all variables simultaneously, while `let-optional*` binds them sequentially, consistent with `let` and `let*` (see Section 6.12.2 [Local Bindings], page 287).

`let-optional` *rest-arg* (*binding ...*) *body1 body2 ...*   [library syntax]
`let-optional*` *rest-arg* (*binding ...*) *body1 body2 ...*   [library syntax]

These two macros give you an optional argument interface that is very *Schemey* and introduces no fancy syntax. They are compatible with the scsh macros of the same name, but are slightly extended. Each of *binding* may be of one of the forms *var* or (*var default-value*). *rest-arg* should be the rest-argument of the procedures these are used from. The items in *rest-arg* are sequentially bound to the variable names are given. When *rest-arg* runs out, the remaining vars are bound either to the default values or `#f` if no default value was specified. *rest-arg* remains bound to whatever may have been left of *rest-arg*.

After binding the variables, the expressions *body1 body2 ...* are evaluated in order.

Similarly, `let-keywords` and `let-keywords*` extract values from keyword style argument lists, binding local variables to those values or to defaults.

`let-keywords` *args allow-other-keys?* (*binding ...*) *body1 body2 ...*   [library syntax]
`let-keywords*` *args allow-other-keys?* (*binding ...*) *body1 body2*   [library syntax]
        . . .

args is evaluated and should give a list of the form (#:keyword1 value1 #:keyword2 value2 ...). The *binding*s are variables and default expressions, with the variables to be set (by name) from the keyword values. The *body1 body2 ...* forms are then evaluated and the last is the result. An example will make the syntax clearest,

```
(define args '(#:xyzzy "hello" #:foo "world"))


(let-keywords args #t
      ((foo  "default for foo")
       (bar  (string-append "default" "for" "bar")))
   (display foo)
   (display ", ")
   (display bar))
⊣ world, defaultforbar
```

The binding for `foo` comes from the `#:foo` keyword in `args`. But the binding for `bar` is the default in the `let-keywords`, since there's no `#:bar` in the args.

allow-other-keys? is evaluated and controls whether unknown keywords are allowed in the *args* list. When true other keys are ignored (such as `#:xyzzy` in the example), when `#f` an error is thrown for anything unknown.

`(ice-9 optargs)` also provides some more `define*` sugar, which is not so useful with modern Guile coding, but still supported: `define*-public` is the `lambda*` version of `define-public`; `defmacro*` and `defmacro*-public` exist for defining macros with the improved argument list handling possibilities. The `-public` versions not only define the procedures/macros, but also export them from the current module.

define*-public *formals body1 body2 ...*   [library syntax]
>   Like a mix of `define*` and `define-public`.

defmacro* *name formals body1 body2 ...*   [library syntax]
defmacro*-public *name formals body1 body2 ...*   [library syntax]
>   These are just like `defmacro` and `defmacro-public` except that they take `lambda*`-style extended parameter lists, where `#:optional`, `#:key`, `#:allow-other-keys` and `#:rest` are allowed with the usual semantics. Here is an example of a macro with an optional argument:
>
>   ```
>   (defmacro* transmogrify (a #:optional b)
>     (a 1))
>   ```

6.9.5 Case-lambda

R5RS's rest arguments are indeed useful and very general, but they often aren't the most appropriate or efficient means to get the job done. For example, `lambda*` is a much better solution to the optional argument problem than `lambda` with rest arguments.

Likewise, `case-lambda` works well for when you want one procedure to do double duty (or triple, or ...), without the penalty of consing a rest list.

For example:

```
(define (make-accum n)
  (case-lambda
    (() n)
    ((m) (set! n (+ n m)) n)))
```

```
(define a (make-accum 20))
(a) ⇒ 20
(a 10) ⇒ 30
(a) ⇒ 30
```

The value returned by a `case-lambda` form is a procedure which matches the number of actual arguments against the formals in the various clauses, in order. The first matching clause is selected, the corresponding values from the actual parameter list are bound to the variable names in the clauses and the body of the clause is evaluated. If no clause matches, an error is signalled.

The syntax of the `case-lambda` form is defined in the following EBNF grammar. *Formals* means a formal argument list just like with `lambda` (see Section 6.9.1 [Lambda], page 244).

```
<case-lambda>
  --> (case-lambda <case-lambda-clause>*)
  --> (case-lambda <docstring> <case-lambda-clause>*)
<case-lambda-clause>
  --> (<formals> <definition-or-command>*)
<formals>
  --> (<identifier>*)
   | (<identifier>* . <identifier>)
   | <identifier>
```

Rest lists can be useful with `case-lambda`:

```
(define plus
  (case-lambda
    "Return the sum of all arguments."
    (() 0)
    ((a) a)
    ((a b) (+ a b))
    ((a b . rest) (apply plus (+ a b) rest))))
(plus 1 2 3) ⇒ 6
```

Also, for completeness. Guile defines `case-lambda*` as well, which is like `case-lambda`, except with `lambda*` clauses. A `case-lambda*` clause matches if the arguments fill the required arguments, but are not too many for the optional and/or rest arguments.

Keyword arguments are possible with `case-lambda*` as well, but they do not contribute to the "matching" behavior, and their interactions with required, optional, and rest arguments can be surprising.

For the purposes of `case-lambda*` (and of `case-lambda`, as a special case), a clause *matches* if it has enough required arguments, and not too many positional arguments. The required arguments are any arguments before the `#:optional`, `#:key`, and `#:rest` arguments. *Positional* arguments are the required arguments, together with the optional arguments.

In the absence of `#:key` or `#:rest` arguments, it's easy to see how there could be too many positional arguments: you pass 5 arguments to a function that only takes 4 arguments, including optional arguments. If there is a `#:rest` argument, there can never be too many positional arguments: any application with enough required arguments for a clause will match that clause, even if there are also `#:key` arguments.

Otherwise, for applications to a clause with `#:key` arguments (and without a `#:rest` argument), a clause will match there only if there are enough required arguments and if the next argument after binding required and optional arguments, if any, is a keyword. For efficiency reasons, Guile is currently unable to include keyword arguments in the matching algorithm. Clauses match on positional arguments only, not by comparing a given keyword to the available set of keyword arguments that a function has.

Some examples follow.

```
(define f
  (case-lambda*
    ((a #:optional b) 'clause-1)
    ((a #:optional b #:key c) 'clause-2)
    ((a #:key d) 'clause-3)
    ((#:key e #:rest f) 'clause-4)))

(f)  ⇒ clause-4
(f 1)  ⇒ clause-1
(f)  ⇒ clause-4
(f #:e 10) clause-1
(f 1 #:foo) clause-1
(f 1 #:c 2) clause-2
(f #:a #:b #:c #:d #:e) clause-4

;; clause-2 will match anything that clause-3 would match.
(f 1 #:d 2) ⇒ error: bad keyword args in clause 2
```

Don't forget that the clauses are matched in order, and the first matching clause will be taken. This can result in a keyword being bound to a required argument, as in the case of `f #:e 10`.

6.9.6 Higher-Order Functions

As a functional programming language, Scheme allows the definition of *higher-order functions*, i.e., functions that take functions as arguments and/or return functions. Utilities to derive procedures from other procedures are provided and described below.

const *value*   [Scheme Procedure]
    Return a procedure that accepts any number of arguments and returns *value*.

```
(procedure? (const 3))    ⇒ #t
((const 'hello))          ⇒ hello
((const 'hello) 'world)   ⇒ hello
```

negate *proc*   [Scheme Procedure]
    Return a procedure with the same arity as *proc* that returns the **not** of *proc*'s result.

```
(procedure? (negate number?)) ⇒ #t
((negate odd?) 2)             ⇒ #t
((negate real?) 'dream)       ⇒ #t
```

```
((negate string-prefix?) "GNU" "GNU Guile")
                              ⇒ #f
(filter (negate number?) '(a 2 "b"))
                              ⇒ (a "b")
```

compose *proc1 proc2 ...*   [Scheme Procedure]

Compose *proc1* with the procedures *proc2 ...* such that the last *proc* argument is applied first and *proc1* last, and return the resulting procedure. The given procedures must have compatible arity.

```
(procedure? (compose 1+ 1-)) ⇒ #t
((compose sqrt 1+ 1+) 2)     ⇒ 2.0
((compose 1+ sqrt) 3)        ⇒ 2.73205080756888
(eq? (compose 1+) 1+)        ⇒ #t

((compose zip unzip2) '((1 2) (a b)))
                              ⇒ ((1 2) (a b))
```

identity *x*   [Scheme Procedure]

Return X.

and=> *value proc*   [Scheme Procedure]

When *value* is #f, return #f. Otherwise, return (`proc value`).

6.9.7 Procedure Properties and Meta-information

In addition to the information that is strictly necessary to run, procedures may have other associated information. For example, the name of a procedure is information not for the procedure, but about the procedure. This meta-information can be accessed via the procedure properties interface.

The first group of procedures in this meta-interface are predicates to test whether a Scheme object is a procedure, or a special procedure, respectively. procedure? is the most general predicates, it returns #t for any kind of procedure.

procedure? *obj*   [Scheme Procedure]
scm_procedure_p (*obj*)   [C Function]

Return #t if *obj* is a procedure.

thunk? *obj*   [Scheme Procedure]
scm_thunk_p (*obj*)   [C Function]

Return #t if *obj* is a thunk—a procedure that does not accept arguments.

Procedure properties are general properties associated with procedures. These can be the name of a procedure or other relevant information, such as debug hints.

procedure-name *proc*   [Scheme Procedure]
scm_procedure_name (*proc*)   [C Function]

Return the name of the procedure *proc*

procedure-source *proc*   [Scheme Procedure]
scm_procedure_source (*proc*)   [C Function]

Return the source of the procedure *proc*. Returns #f if the source code is not available.

procedure-properties *proc*   [Scheme Procedure]
scm_procedure_properties (*proc*)   [C Function]
>   Return the properties associated with *proc*, as an association list.

procedure-property *proc key*   [Scheme Procedure]
scm_procedure_property (*proc, key*)   [C Function]
>   Return the property of *proc* with name *key*.

set-procedure-properties! *proc alist*   [Scheme Procedure]
scm_set_procedure_properties_x (*proc, alist*)   [C Function]
>   Set *proc*'s property list to *alist*.

set-procedure-property! *proc key value*   [Scheme Procedure]
scm_set_procedure_property_x (*proc, key, value*)   [C Function]
>   In *proc*'s property list, set the property named *key* to *value*.

Documentation for a procedure can be accessed with the procedure **procedure-documentation**.

procedure-documentation *proc*   [Scheme Procedure]
scm_procedure_documentation (*proc*)   [C Function]
>   Return the documentation string associated with **proc**. By convention, if a procedure
>   contains more than one expression and the first expression is a string constant, that
>   string is assumed to contain documentation for that procedure.

6.9.8 Procedures with Setters

A *procedure with setter* is a special kind of procedure which normally behaves like any
accessor procedure, that is a procedure which accesses a data structure. The difference is
that this kind of procedure has a so-called *setter* attached, which is a procedure for storing
something into a data structure.

Procedures with setters are treated specially when the procedure appears in the special
form **set!** (REFFIXME). How it works is best shown by example.

Suppose we have a procedure called **foo-ref**, which accepts two arguments, a value of
type **foo** and an integer. The procedure returns the value stored at the given index in the
foo object. Let **f** be a variable containing such a **foo** data structure.[5]

```
(foo-ref f 0)      ⇒ bar
(foo-ref f 1)      ⇒ braz
```

Also suppose that a corresponding setter procedure called **foo-set!** does exist.

```
(foo-set! f 0 'bla)
(foo-ref f 0)      ⇒ bla
```

Now we could create a new procedure called **foo**, which is a procedure with setter, by
calling **make-procedure-with-setter** with the accessor and setter procedures **foo-ref** and
foo-set!. Let us call this new procedure **foo**.

---

[5] Working definitions would be:

```
(define foo-ref vector-ref)
(define foo-set! vector-set!)
(define f (make-vector 2 #f))
```

```
(define foo (make-procedure-with-setter foo-ref foo-set!))
```

foo can from now an be used to either read from the data structure stored in f, or to write into the structure.

```
(set! (foo f 0) 'dum)
(foo f 0)                ⇒ dum
```

make-procedure-with-setter *procedure setter*   [Scheme Procedure]
scm_make_procedure_with_setter (*procedure, setter*)   [C Function]
> Create a new procedure which behaves like *procedure*, but with the associated setter *setter*.

procedure-with-setter? *obj*   [Scheme Procedure]
scm_procedure_with_setter_p (*obj*)   [C Function]
> Return #t if *obj* is a procedure with an associated setter procedure.

procedure *proc*   [Scheme Procedure]
scm_procedure (*proc*)   [C Function]
> Return the procedure of *proc*, which must be an applicable struct.

setter *proc*   [Scheme Procedure]
> Return the setter of *proc*, which must be either a procedure with setter or an operator struct.

6.9.9 Inlinable Procedures

You can define an *inlinable procedure* by using define-inlinable instead of define. An inlinable procedure behaves the same as a regular procedure, but direct calls will result in the procedure body being inlined into the caller.

Bear in mind that starting from version 2.0.3, Guile has a partial evaluator that can inline the body of inner procedures when deemed appropriate:

```
scheme@(guile-user)> ,optimize (define (foo x)
                                 (define (bar) (+ x 3))
                                 (* (bar) 2))
$1 = (define foo
       (lambda (#{x 94}#) (* (+ #{x 94}# 3) 2)))
```

The partial evaluator does not inline top-level bindings, though, so this is a situation where you may find it interesting to use define-inlinable.

Procedures defined with define-inlinable are *always* inlined, at all direct call sites. This eliminates function call overhead at the expense of an increase in code size. Additionally, the caller will not transparently use the new definition if the inline procedure is redefined. It is not possible to trace an inlined procedures or install a breakpoint in it (see Section 6.25.4 [Traps], page 455). For these reasons, you should not make a procedure inlinable unless it demonstrably improves performance in a crucial way.

In general, only small procedures should be considered for inlining, as making large procedures inlinable will probably result in an increase in code size. Additionally, the elimination of the call overhead rarely matters for large procedures.

`define-inlinable` (*name parameter* ...) *body1 body2* ...   [Scheme Syntax]
>   Define *name* as a procedure with parameters *parameters* and bodies *body1*, *body2*,
>   . . . .

6.10 Macros

At its best, programming in Lisp is an iterative process of building up a language appropriate
to the problem at hand, and then solving the problem in that language. Defining new
procedures is part of that, but Lisp also allows the user to extend its syntax, with its
famous *macros*.

Macros are syntactic extensions which cause the expression that they appear in to be
transformed in some way *before* being evaluated. In expressions that are intended for
macro transformation, the identifier that names the relevant macro must appear as the first
element, like this:

>   (*macro-name macro-args* ...)

Macro expansion is a separate phase of evaluation, run before code is interpreted or
compiled. A macro is a program that runs on programs, translating an embedded language
into core Scheme[6].

6.10.1 Defining Macros

A macro is a binding between a keyword and a syntax transformer. Since it's difficult to
discuss **define-syntax** without discussing the format of transformers, consider the following
example macro definition:

```
(define-syntax when
  (syntax-rules ()
    ((when condition exp ...)
     (if condition
         (begin exp ...)))))

(when #t
  (display "hey ho\n")
  (display "let's go\n"))
⊣ hey ho
⊣ let's go
```

In this example, the **when** binding is bound with **define-syntax**. Syntax transformers
are discussed in more depth in Section 6.10.2 [Syntax Rules], page 258 and Section 6.10.3
[Syntax Case], page 263.

define-syntax *keyword transformer*   [Syntax]
>   Bind *keyword* to the syntax transformer obtained by evaluating *transformer*.
>
>   After a macro has been defined, further instances of *keyword* in Scheme source code
>   will invoke the syntax transformer defined by *transformer*.
>
>   One can also establish local syntactic bindings with **let-syntax**.

---

[6] These days such embedded languages are often referred to as *embedded domain-specific languages*, or
EDSLs.

let-syntax ((*keyword transformer*) ...) *exp1 exp2* ...   [Syntax]
    Bind each *keyword* to its corresponding *transformer* while expanding *exp1 exp2* ....

    A `let-syntax` binding only exists at expansion-time.

```
(let-syntax ((unless
                (syntax-rules ()
                  ((unless condition exp ...)
                   (if (not condition)
                       (begin exp ...))))))
  (unless #t
    (primitive-exit 1))
  "rock rock rock")
⇒ "rock rock rock"
```

A `define-syntax` form is valid anywhere a definition may appear: at the top-level, or locally. Just as a local `define` expands out to an instance of `letrec`, a local `define-syntax` expands out to `letrec-syntax`.

letrec-syntax ((*keyword transformer*) ...) *exp1 exp2* ...   [Syntax]
    Bind each *keyword* to its corresponding *transformer* while expanding *exp1 exp2* ....

    In the spirit of `letrec` versus `let`, an expansion produced by *transformer* may reference a *keyword* bound by the same *letrec-syntax*.

```
(letrec-syntax ((my-or
                  (syntax-rules ()
                    ((my-or)
                     #t)
                    ((my-or exp)
                     exp)
                    ((my-or exp rest ...)
                     (let ((t exp))
                       (if t
                           t
                           (my-or rest ...)))))))
  (my-or #f "rockaway beach"))
⇒ "rockaway beach"
```

6.10.2 Syntax-rules Macros

`syntax-rules` macros are simple, pattern-driven syntax transformers, with a beauty worthy of Scheme.

syntax-rules *literals* (*pattern template*) ...   [Syntax]
    Create a syntax transformer that will rewrite an expression using the rules embodied in the *pattern* and *template* clauses.

A `syntax-rules` macro consists of three parts: the literals (if any), the patterns, and as many templates as there are patterns.

When the syntax expander sees the invocation of a `syntax-rules` macro, it matches the expression against the patterns, in order, and rewrites the expression using the template from the first matching pattern. If no pattern matches, a syntax error is signalled.

6.10.2.1 Patterns

We have already seen some examples of patterns in the previous section: (unless condition exp ...), (my-or exp), and so on. A pattern is structured like the expression that it is to match. It can have nested structure as well, like (let ((var val) ...) exp exp* ...). Broadly speaking, patterns are made of lists, improper lists, vectors, identifiers, and datums. Users can match a sequence of patterns using the ellipsis (...).

Identifiers in a pattern are called *literals* if they are present in the syntax-rules literals list, and *pattern variables* otherwise. When building up the macro output, the expander replaces instances of a pattern variable in the template with the matched subexpression.

```
(define-syntax kwote
  (syntax-rules ()
    ((kwote exp)
     (quote exp))))
(kwote (foo . bar))
⇒ (foo . bar)
```

An improper list of patterns matches as rest arguments do:

```
(define-syntax let1
  (syntax-rules ()
    ((_ (var val) . exps)
     (let ((var val)) . exps))))
```

However this definition of let1 probably isn't what you want, as the tail pattern *exps* will match non-lists, like (let1 (foo 'bar) . baz). So often instead of using improper lists as patterns, ellipsized patterns are better. Instances of a pattern variable in the template must be followed by an ellipsis.

```
(define-syntax let1
  (syntax-rules ()
    ((_ (var val) exp ...)
     (let ((var val)) exp ...))))
```

This let1 probably still doesn't do what we want, because the body matches sequences of zero expressions, like (let1 (foo 'bar)). In this case we need to assert we have at least one body expression. A common idiom for this is to name the ellipsized pattern variable with an asterisk:

```
(define-syntax let1
  (syntax-rules ()
    ((_ (var val) exp exp* ...)
     (let ((var val)) exp exp* ...))))
```

A vector of patterns matches a vector whose contents match the patterns, including ellipsizing and tail patterns.

```
(define-syntax letv
  (syntax-rules ()
    ((_ #((var val) ...) exp exp* ...)
     (let ((var val) ...) exp exp* ...))))
(letv #((foo 'bar)) foo)
⇒ bar
```

Literals are used to match specific datums in an expression, like the use of => and else in cond expressions.

```
(define-syntax cond1
  (syntax-rules (=> else)
    ((cond1 test => fun)
     (let ((exp test))
       (if exp (fun exp) #f)))
    ((cond1 test exp exp* ...)
     (if test (begin exp exp* ...)))
    ((cond1 else exp exp* ...)
     (begin exp exp* ...))))

(define (square x) (* x x))
(cond1 10 => square)
⇒ 100
(let ((=> #t))
  (cond1 10 => square))
⇒ #<procedure square (x)>
```

A literal matches an input expression if the input expression is an identifier with the same name as the literal, and both are unbound[7].

If a pattern is not a list, vector, or an identifier, it matches as a literal, with equal?.

```
(define-syntax define-matcher-macro
  (syntax-rules ()
    ((_ name lit)
     (define-syntax name
       (syntax-rules ()
         ((_ lit) #t)
         ((_ else) #f))))))

(define-matcher-macro is-literal-foo? "foo")

(is-literal-foo? "foo")
⇒ #t
(is-literal-foo? "bar")
⇒ #f
(let ((foo "foo"))
  (is-literal-foo? foo))
⇒ #f
```

The last example indicates that matching happens at expansion-time, not at run-time.

Syntax-rules macros are always used as (*macro* . *args*), and the *macro* will always be a symbol. Correspondingly, a syntax-rules pattern must be a list (proper or improper), and the first pattern in that list must be an identifier. Incidentally it can be any identifier – it doesn't have to actually be the name of the macro. Thus the following three are equivalent:

---

[7] Language lawyers probably see the need here for use of literal-identifier=? rather than free-identifier=?, and would probably be correct. Patches accepted.

```
(define-syntax when
  (syntax-rules ()
    ((when c e ...)
     (if c (begin e ...)))))

(define-syntax when
  (syntax-rules ()
    ((_ c e ...)
     (if c (begin e ...)))))

(define-syntax when
  (syntax-rules ()
    ((something-else-entirely c e ...)
     (if c (begin e ...)))))
```

For clarity, use one of the first two variants. Also note that since the pattern variable will always match the macro itself (e.g., `cond1`), it is actually left unbound in the template.

6.10.2.2 Hygiene

`syntax-rules` macros have a magical property: they preserve referential transparency. When you read a macro definition, any free bindings in that macro are resolved relative to the macro definition; and when you read a macro instantiation, all free bindings in that expression are resolved relative to the expression.

This property is sometimes known as *hygiene*, and it does aid in code cleanliness. In your macro definitions, you can feel free to introduce temporary variables, without worrying about inadvertently introducing bindings into the macro expansion.

Consider the definition of `my-or` from the previous section:

```
(define-syntax my-or
  (syntax-rules ()
    ((my-or)
     #t)
    ((my-or exp)
     exp)
    ((my-or exp rest ...)
     (let ((t exp))
       (if t
           t
           (my-or rest ...))))))
```

A naive expansion of `(let ((t #t)) (my-or #f t))` would yield:

```
(let ((t #t))
  (let ((t #f))
    (if t t t)))
⇒ #f
```

Which clearly is not what we want. Somehow the `t` in the definition is distinct from the `t` at the site of use; and it is indeed this distinction that is maintained by the syntax expander, when expanding hygienic macros.

This discussion is mostly relevant in the context of traditional Lisp macros (see Section 6.10.5 [Defmacros], page 270), which do not preserve referential transparency. Hygiene adds to the expressive power of Scheme.

6.10.2.3 Shorthands

One often ends up writing simple one-clause `syntax-rules` macros. There is a convenient shorthand for this idiom, in the form of `define-syntax-rule`.

define-syntax-rule (*keyword . pattern*) [*docstring*] *template*   [Syntax]
  Define *keyword* as a new `syntax-rules` macro with one clause.

Cast into this form, our `when` example is significantly shorter:

```
(define-syntax-rule (when c e ...)
  (if c (begin e ...)))
```

6.10.2.4 Reporting Syntax Errors in Macros

syntax-error *message* [*arg ...*]   [Syntax]
  Report an error at macro-expansion time. *message* must be a string literal, and the optional *arg* operands can be arbitrary expressions providing additional information.

`syntax-error` is intended to be used within `syntax-rules` templates. For example:

```
(define-syntax simple-let
  (syntax-rules ()
    ((_ (head ... ((x . y) val) . tail)
        body1 body2 ...)
     (syntax-error
      "expected an identifier but got"
      (x . y)))
    ((_ ((name val) ...) body1 body2 ...)
     ((lambda (name ...) body1 body2 ...)
      val ...))))
```

6.10.2.5 Specifying a Custom Ellipsis Identifier

When writing macros that generate macro definitions, it is convenient to use a different ellipsis identifier at each level. Guile allows the desired ellipsis identifier to be specified as the first operand to `syntax-rules`, as specified by SRFI-46 and R7RS. For example:

```
(define-syntax define-quotation-macros
  (syntax-rules ()
    ((_ (macro-name head-symbol) ...)
     (begin (define-syntax macro-name
              (syntax-rules ::: ()
                ((_ x :::)
                 (quote (head-symbol x :::)))))
            ...))))
(define-quotation-macros (quote-a a) (quote-b b) (quote-c c))
(quote-a 1 2 3) ⇒ (a 1 2 3)
```

6.10.2.6 Further Information

For a formal definition of `syntax-rules` and its pattern language, see See Section "Macros" in *Revised(5) Report on the Algorithmic Language Scheme*.

`syntax-rules` macros are simple and clean, but do they have limitations. They do not lend themselves to expressive error messages: patterns either match or they don't. Their ability to generate code is limited to template-driven expansion; often one needs to define a number of helper macros to get real work done. Sometimes one wants to introduce a binding into the lexical context of the generated code; this is impossible with `syntax-rules`. Relatedly, they cannot programmatically generate identifiers.

The solution to all of these problems is to use `syntax-case` if you need its features. But if for some reason you're stuck with `syntax-rules`, you might enjoy Joe Marshall's `syntax-rules` Primer for the Merely Eccentric.

6.10.3 Support for the `syntax-case` System

`syntax-case` macros are procedural syntax transformers, with a power worthy of Scheme.

`syntax-case` *syntax literals* (*pattern* [*guard*] *exp*) ...   [Syntax]
>   Match the syntax object *syntax* against the given patterns, in order. If a *pattern* matches, return the result of evaluating the associated *exp*.

Compare the following definitions of `when`:

```
(define-syntax when
  (syntax-rules ()
    ((_ test e e* ...)
     (if test (begin e e* ...)))))

(define-syntax when
  (lambda (x)
    (syntax-case x ()
      ((_ test e e* ...)
       #'(if test (begin e e* ...))))))
```

Clearly, the `syntax-case` definition is similar to its `syntax-rules` counterpart, and equally clearly there are some differences. The `syntax-case` definition is wrapped in a `lambda`, a function of one argument; that argument is passed to the `syntax-case` invocation; and the "return value" of the macro has a `#'` prefix.

All of these differences stem from the fact that `syntax-case` does not define a syntax transformer itself – instead, `syntax-case` expressions provide a way to destructure a *syntax object*, and to rebuild syntax objects as output.

So the `lambda` wrapper is simply a leaky implementation detail, that syntax transformers are just functions that transform syntax to syntax. This should not be surprising, given that we have already described macros as "programs that write programs". `syntax-case` is simply a way to take apart and put together program text, and to be a valid syntax transformer it needs to be wrapped in a procedure.

Unlike traditional Lisp macros (see Section 6.10.5 [Defmacros], page 270), `syntax-case` macros transform syntax objects, not raw Scheme forms. Recall the naive expansion of `my-or` given in the previous section:

```
(let ((t #t))
  (my-or #f t))
;; naive expansion:
(let ((t #t))
  (let ((t #f))
    (if t t t)))
```

Raw Scheme forms simply don't have enough information to distinguish the first two t instances in (if t t t) from the third t. So instead of representing identifiers as symbols, the syntax expander represents identifiers as annotated syntax objects, attaching such information to those syntax objects as is needed to maintain referential transparency.

syntax *form*   [Syntax]
  Create a syntax object wrapping *form* within the current lexical context.

Syntax objects are typically created internally to the process of expansion, but it is possible to create them outside of syntax expansion:

```
(syntax (foo bar baz))
⇒ #<some representation of that syntax>
```

However it is more common, and useful, to create syntax objects when building output from a syntax-case expression.

```
(define-syntax add1
  (lambda (x)
    (syntax-case x ()
      ((_ exp)
       (syntax (+ exp 1))))))
```

It is not strictly necessary for a syntax-case expression to return a syntax object, because syntax-case expressions can be used in helper functions, or otherwise used outside of syntax expansion itself. However a syntax transformer procedure must return a syntax object, so most uses of syntax-case do end up returning syntax objects.

Here in this case, the form that built the return value was (syntax (+ exp 1)). The interesting thing about this is that within a syntax expression, any appearance of a pattern variable is substituted into the resulting syntax object, carrying with it all relevant metadata from the source expression, such as lexical identity and source location.

Indeed, a pattern variable may only be referenced from inside a syntax form. The syntax expander would raise an error when defining add1 if it found *exp* referenced outside a syntax form.

Since syntax appears frequently in macro-heavy code, it has a special reader macro: #'. #'foo is transformed by the reader into (syntax foo), just as 'foo is transformed into (quote foo).

The pattern language used by syntax-case is conveniently the same language used by syntax-rules. Given this, Guile actually defines syntax-rules in terms of syntax-case:

```
(define-syntax syntax-rules
  (lambda (x)
    (syntax-case x ()
      ((_ (k ...) ((keyword . pattern) template) ...)
```

```
#'(lambda (x)
    (syntax-case x (k ...)
      ((dummy . pattern) #'template)
      ...))))))
```

And that's that.

6.10.3.1 Why `syntax-case`?

The examples we have shown thus far could just as well have been expressed with **syntax-rules**, and have just shown that **syntax-case** is more verbose, which is true. But there is a difference: **syntax-case** creates *procedural* macros, giving the full power of Scheme to the macro expander. This has many practical applications.

A common desire is to be able to match a form only if it is an identifier. This is impossible with **syntax-rules**, given the datum matching forms. But with **syntax-case** it is easy:

identifier? *syntax-object*   [Scheme Procedure]
      Returns **#t** if *syntax-object* is an identifier, or **#f** otherwise.

```
;; relying on previous add1 definition
(define-syntax add1!
  (lambda (x)
    (syntax-case x ()
      ((_ var) (identifier? #'var)
       #'(set! var (add1 var))))))
```

```
(define foo 0)
(add1! foo)
foo ⇒ 1
(add1! "not-an-identifier") ⇒ error
```

With **syntax-rules**, the error for (add1! "not-an-identifier") would be something like "invalid **set!**". With **syntax-case**, it will say something like "invalid **add1!**", because we attach the *guard clause* to the pattern: (identifier? #'var). This becomes more important with more complicated macros. It is necessary to use **identifier?**, because to the expander, an identifier is more than a bare symbol.

Note that even in the guard clause, we reference the *var* pattern variable within a **syntax** form, via #'var.

Another common desire is to introduce bindings into the lexical context of the output expression. One example would be in the so-called "anaphoric macros", like **aif**. Anaphoric macros bind some expression to a well-known identifier, often **it**, within their bodies. For example, in (aif (foo) (bar it)), **it** would be bound to the result of (foo).

To begin with, we should mention a solution that doesn't work:

```
;; doesn't work
(define-syntax aif
  (lambda (x)
    (syntax-case x ()
      ((_ test then else)
       #'(let ((it test))
```

```
(if it then else))))))
```

The reason that this doesn't work is that, by default, the expander will preserve referential transparency; the *then* and *else* expressions won't have access to the binding of it.

But they can, if we explicitly introduce a binding via `datum->syntax`.

`datum->syntax` *for-syntax datum*   [Scheme Procedure]
> Create a syntax object that wraps *datum*, within the lexical context corresponding to the syntax object *for-syntax*.

For completeness, we should mention that it is possible to strip the metadata from a syntax object, returning a raw Scheme datum:

`syntax->datum` *syntax-object*   [Scheme Procedure]
> Strip the metadata from *syntax-object*, returning its contents as a raw Scheme datum.

In this case we want to introduce it in the context of the whole expression, so we can create a syntax object as `(datum->syntax x 'it)`, where x is the whole expression, as passed to the transformer procedure.

Here's another solution that doesn't work:

```
;; doesn't work either
(define-syntax aif
  (lambda (x)
    (syntax-case x ()
      ((_ test then else)
       (let ((it (datum->syntax x 'it)))
         #'(let ((it test))
             (if it then else)))))))
```

The reason that this one doesn't work is that there are really two environments at work here – the environment of pattern variables, as bound by `syntax-case`, and the environment of lexical variables, as bound by normal Scheme. The outer let form establishes a binding in the environment of lexical variables, but the inner let form is inside a syntax form, where only pattern variables will be substituted. Here we need to introduce a piece of the lexical environment into the pattern variable environment, and we can do so using `syntax-case` itself:

```
;; works, but is obtuse
(define-syntax aif
  (lambda (x)
    (syntax-case x ()
      ((_ test then else)
       ;; invoking syntax-case on the generated
       ;; syntax object to expose it to 'syntax'
       (syntax-case (datum->syntax x 'it) ()
         (it
          #'(let ((it test))
              (if it then else)))))))))
```

```
(aif (getuid) (display it) (display "none")) (newline)
⊣ 500
```

However there are easier ways to write this. `with-syntax` is often convenient:

with-syntax ((*pat val*) ...) *exp* ...   [Syntax]

> Bind patterns *pat* from their corresponding values *val*, within the lexical context of *exp* ....

```
;; better
(define-syntax aif
  (lambda (x)
    (syntax-case x ()
      ((_ test then else)
       (with-syntax ((it (datum->syntax x 'it)))
         #'(let ((it test))
             (if it then else)))))))
```

As you might imagine, `with-syntax` is defined in terms of `syntax-case`. But even that might be off-putting to you if you are an old Lisp macro hacker, used to building macro output with `quasiquote`. The issue is that `with-syntax` creates a separation between the point of definition of a value and its point of substitution.

So for cases in which a `quasiquote` style makes more sense, `syntax-case` also defines `quasisyntax`, and the related `unsyntax` and `unsyntax-splicing`, abbreviated by the reader as `#'`, `#,`, and `#,@`, respectively.

For example, to define a macro that inserts a compile-time timestamp into a source file, one may write:

```
(define-syntax display-compile-timestamp
  (lambda (x)
    (syntax-case x ()
      ((_)
       #'(begin
           (display "The compile timestamp was: ")
           (display #,(current-time))
           (newline))))))
```

Readers interested in further information on `syntax-case` macros should see R. Kent Dybvig's excellent *The Scheme Programming Language*, either edition 3 or 4, in the chapter on syntax. Dybvig was the primary author of the `syntax-case` system. The book itself is available online at `http://scheme.com/tspl4/`.

6.10.3.2 Custom Ellipsis Identifiers for syntax-case Macros

When writing procedural macros that generate macro definitions, it is convenient to use a different ellipsis identifier at each level. Guile supports this for procedural macros using the `with-ellipsis` special form:

with-ellipsis *ellipsis body* ...   [Syntax]

> *ellipsis* must be an identifier. Evaluate *body* in a special lexical environment such that all macro patterns and templates within *body* will use *ellipsis* as the ellipsis identifier instead of the usual three dots (...).

For example:

```
(define-syntax define-quotation-macros
  (lambda (x)
    (syntax-case x ()
      ((_ (macro-name head-symbol) ...)
       #'(begin (define-syntax macro-name
                  (lambda (x)
                    (with-ellipsis :::
                      (syntax-case x ()
                        ((_ x :::)
                         #'(quote (head-symbol x :::)))))))
                ...)))))
(define-quotation-macros (quote-a a) (quote-b b) (quote-c c))
(quote-a 1 2 3) ⇒ (a 1 2 3)
```

Note that `with-ellipsis` does not affect the ellipsis identifier of the generated code, unless `with-ellipsis` is included around the generated code.

6.10.4 Syntax Transformer Helpers

As noted in the previous section, Guile's syntax expander operates on syntax objects. Procedural macros consume and produce syntax objects. This section describes some of the auxiliary helpers that procedural macros can use to compare, generate, and query objects of this data type.

bound-identifier=? *a b*   [Scheme Procedure]
    Return `#t` if the syntax objects *a* and *b* refer to the same lexically-bound identifier, or `#f` otherwise.

free-identifier=? *a b*   [Scheme Procedure]
    Return `#t` if the syntax objects *a* and *b* refer to the same free identifier, or `#f` otherwise.

generate-temporaries *ls*   [Scheme Procedure]
    Return a list of temporary identifiers as long as *ls* is long.

syntax-source *x*   [Scheme Procedure]
    Return the source properties that correspond to the syntax object *x*. See Section 6.25.2 [Source Properties], page 447, for more information.

Guile also offers some more experimental interfaces in a separate module. As was the case with the Large Hadron Collider, it is unclear to our senior macrologists whether adding these interfaces will result in awesomeness or in the destruction of Guile via the creation of a singularity. We will preserve their functionality through the 2.0 series, but we reserve the right to modify them in a future stable series, to a more than usual degree.

```
(use-modules (system syntax))
```

syntax-module *id*   [Scheme Procedure]
    Return the name of the module whose source contains the identifier *id*.

`syntax-local-binding` *id*   [Scheme Procedure]

Resolve the identifer *id*, a syntax object, within the current lexical environment, and return two values, the binding type and a binding value. The binding type is a symbol, which may be one of the following:

lexical   A lexically-bound variable. The value is a unique token (in the sense of `eq?`) identifying this binding.

macro   A syntax transformer, either local or global. The value is the transformer procedure.

pattern-variable
        A pattern variable, bound via `syntax-case`. The value is an opaque object, internal to the expander.

ellipsis   An internal binding, bound via `with-ellipsis`. The value is the (anti-marked) local ellipsis identifier.

displaced-lexical
        A lexical variable that has gone out of scope. This can happen if a badly-written procedural macro saves a syntax object, then attempts to introduce it in a context in which it is unbound. The value is `#f`.

global   A global binding. The value is a pair, whose head is the symbol, and whose tail is the name of the module in which to resolve the symbol.

other   Some other binding, like `lambda` or other core bindings. The value is `#f`.

This is a very low-level procedure, with limited uses. One case in which it is useful is to build abstractions that associate auxiliary information with macros:

```
(define aux-property (make-object-property))
(define-syntax-rule (with-aux aux value)
  (let ((trans value))
    (set! (aux-property trans) aux)
    trans))
(define-syntax retrieve-aux
  (lambda (x)
    (syntax-case x ()
      ((x id)
       (call-with-values (lambda () (syntax-local-binding #'id))
         (lambda (type val)
           (with-syntax ((aux (datum->syntax #'here
                                             (and (eq? type 'macro)
                                                  (aux-property val)))))
             #''aux)))))))
(define-syntax foo
  (with-aux 'bar
    (syntax-rules () ((_) 'foo))))
(foo)
⇒ foo
(retrieve-aux foo)
```

$\Rightarrow$ `bar`

`syntax-local-binding` must be called within the dynamic extent of a syntax transformer; to call it otherwise will signal an error.

`syntax-locally-bound-identifiers` *id*   [Scheme Procedure]

Return a list of identifiers that were visible lexically when the identifier *id* was created, in order from outermost to innermost.

This procedure is intended to be used in specialized procedural macros, to provide a macro with the set of bound identifiers that the macro can reference.

As a technical implementation detail, the identifiers returned by `syntax-locally-bound-identifiers` will be anti-marked, like the syntax object that is given as input to a macro. This is to signal to the macro expander that these bindings were present in the original source, and do not need to be hygienically renamed, as would be the case with other introduced identifiers. See the discussion of hygiene in section 12.1 of the R6RS, for more information on marks.

```
(define (local-lexicals id)
  (filter (lambda (x)
            (eq? (syntax-local-binding x) 'lexical))
          (syntax-locally-bound-identifiers id)))
(define-syntax lexicals
  (lambda (x)
    (syntax-case x ()
      ((lexicals) #'(lexicals lexicals))
      ((lexicals scope)
       (with-syntax (((id ...) (local-lexicals #'scope)))
         #'(list (cons 'id id) ...))))))

(let* ((x 10) (x 20)) (lexicals))
⇒ ((x . 10) (x . 20))
```

6.10.5 Lisp-style Macro Definitions

The traditional way to define macros in Lisp is very similar to procedure definitions. The key differences are that the macro definition body should return a list that describes the transformed expression, and that the definition is marked as a macro definition (rather than a procedure definition) by the use of a different definition keyword: in Lisp, `defmacro` rather than `defun`, and in Scheme, `define-macro` rather than `define`.

Guile supports this style of macro definition using both `defmacro` and `define-macro`. The only difference between them is how the macro name and arguments are grouped together in the definition:

```
(defmacro name (args ...) body ...)
```

is the same as

```
(define-macro (name args ...) body ...)
```

The difference is analogous to the corresponding difference between Lisp's `defun` and Scheme's `define`.

Having read the previous section on `syntax-case`, it's probably clear that Guile actually implements defmacros in terms of `syntax-case`, applying the transformer on the expression between invocations of `syntax->datum` and `datum->syntax`. This realization leads us to the problem with defmacros, that they do not preserve referential transparency. One can be careful to not introduce bindings into expanded code, via liberal use of `gensym`, but there is no getting around the lack of referential transparency for free bindings in the macro itself.

Even a macro as simple as our `when` from before is difficult to get right:

```
(define-macro (when cond exp . rest)
  `(if ,cond
       (begin ,exp . ,rest)))

(when #f (display "Launching missiles!\n"))
⇒ #f

(let ((if list))
  (when #f (display "Launching missiles!\n")))
⊣ Launching missiles!
⇒ (#f #<unspecified>)
```

Guile's perspective is that defmacros have had a good run, but that modern macros should be written with `syntax-rules` or `syntax-case`. There are still many uses of defmacros within Guile itself, but we will be phasing them out over time. Of course we won't take away `defmacro` or `define-macro` themselves, as there is lots of code out there that uses them.

6.10.6 Identifier Macros

When the syntax expander sees a form in which the first element is a macro, the whole form gets passed to the macro's syntax transformer. One may visualize this as:

```
(define-syntax foo foo-transformer)
(foo arg...)
;; expands via
(foo-transformer #'(foo arg...))
```

If, on the other hand, a macro is referenced in some other part of a form, the syntax transformer is invoked with only the macro reference, not the whole form.

```
(define-syntax foo foo-transformer)
foo
;; expands via
(foo-transformer #'foo)
```

This allows bare identifier references to be replaced programmatically via a macro. `syntax-rules` provides some syntax to effect this transformation more easily.

`identifier-syntax` *exp*   [Syntax]
     Returns a macro transformer that will replace occurrences of the macro with *exp*.

For example, if you are importing external code written in terms of `fx+`, the fixnum addition operator, but Guile doesn't have `fx+`, you may use the following to replace `fx+` with `+`:

```
(define-syntax fx+ (identifier-syntax +))
```

There is also special support for recognizing identifiers on the left-hand side of a `set!` expression, as in the following:

```
(define-syntax foo foo-transformer)
(set! foo val)
;; expands via
(foo-transformer #'(set! foo val))
;; if foo-transformer is a "variable transformer"
```

As the example notes, the transformer procedure must be explicitly marked as being a "variable transformer", as most macros aren't written to discriminate on the form in the operator position.

make-variable-transformer *transformer*   [Scheme Procedure]
Mark the *transformer* procedure as being a "variable transformer". In practice this means that, when bound to a syntactic keyword, it may detect references to that keyword on the left-hand-side of a `set!`.

```
(define bar 10)
(define-syntax bar-alias
  (make-variable-transformer
    (lambda (x)
      (syntax-case x (set!)
        ((set! var val) #'(set! bar val))
        ((var arg ...) #'(bar arg ...))
        (var (identifier? #'var) #'bar)))))

bar-alias ⇒ 10
(set! bar-alias 20)
bar ⇒ 20
(set! bar 30)
bar-alias ⇒ 30
```

There is an extension to identifier-syntax which allows it to handle the `set!` case as well:

identifier-syntax (*var exp1*) ((*set! var val*) *exp2*)   [Syntax]
Create a variable transformer. The first clause is used for references to the variable in operator or operand position, and the second for appearances of the variable on the left-hand-side of an assignment.

For example, the previous `bar-alias` example could be expressed more succinctly like this:

```
(define-syntax bar-alias
  (identifier-syntax
    (var bar)
    ((set! var val) (set! bar val))))
```

As before, the templates in `identifier-syntax` forms do not need wrapping in `#'` syntax forms.

6.10.7 Syntax Parameters

Syntax parameters[8] are a mechanism for rebinding a macro definition within the dynamic extent of a macro expansion. This provides a convenient solution to one of the most common types of unhygienic macro: those that introduce a unhygienic binding each time the macro is used. Examples include a `lambda` form with a `return` keyword, or class macros that introduce a special `self` binding.

With syntax parameters, instead of introducing the binding unhygienically each time, we instead create one binding for the keyword, which we can then adjust later when we want the keyword to have a different meaning. As no new bindings are introduced, hygiene is preserved. This is similar to the dynamic binding mechanisms we have at run-time (see Section 7.5.26 [SRFI-39], page 599), except that the dynamic binding only occurs during macro expansion. The code after macro expansion remains lexically scoped.

define-syntax-parameter *keyword transformer*   [Syntax]

> Binds *keyword* to the value obtained by evaluating *transformer*. The *transformer* provides the default expansion for the syntax parameter, and in the absence of **syntax-parameterize**, is functionally equivalent to **define-syntax**. Usually, you will just want to have the *transformer* throw a syntax error indicating that the *keyword* is supposed to be used in conjunction with another macro, for example:

```
(define-syntax-parameter return
  (lambda (stx)
    (syntax-violation 'return "return used outside of a lambda^" stx)))
```

syntax-parameterize ((*keyword transformer*) ...) *exp* ...   [Syntax]

> Adjusts *keyword* ... to use the values obtained by evaluating their *transformer* ..., in the expansion of the *exp* ... forms. Each *keyword* must be bound to a syntax-parameter. **syntax-parameterize** differs from **let-syntax**, in that the binding is not shadowed, but adjusted, and so uses of the keyword in the expansion of *exp* ... use the new transformers. This is somewhat similar to how **parameterize** adjusts the values of regular parameters, rather than creating new bindings.

```
(define-syntax lambda^
  (syntax-rules ()
    [(lambda^ argument-list body body* ...)
     (lambda argument-list
       (call-with-current-continuation
        (lambda (escape)
          ;; In the body we adjust the 'return' keyword so that calls
          ;; to 'return' are replaced with calls to the escape
          ;; continuation.
          (syntax-parameterize ([return (syntax-rules ()
                                          [(return vals (... ...))
                                           (escape vals (... ...))])])
            body body* ...))))]))

;; Now we can write functions that return early.  Here, 'product' will
```

---

[8] Described in the paper *Keeping it Clean with Syntax Parameters* by Barzilay, Culpepper and Flatt.

```
;; return immediately if it sees any 0 element.
(define product
  (lambda^ (list)
           (fold (lambda (n o)
                    (if (zero? n)
                        (return 0)
                        (* n o)))
                 1
                 list)))
```

6.10.8 Eval-when

As `syntax-case` macros have the whole power of Scheme available to them, they present a problem regarding time: when a macro runs, what parts of the program are available for the macro to use?

The default answer to this question is that when you import a module (via `define-module` or `use-modules`), that module will be loaded up at expansion-time, as well as at run-time. Additionally, top-level syntactic definitions within one compilation unit made by `define-syntax` are also evaluated at expansion time, in the order that they appear in the compilation unit (file).

But if a syntactic definition needs to call out to a normal procedure at expansion-time, it might well need need special declarations to indicate that the procedure should be made available at expansion-time.

For example, the following code will work at a REPL, but not in a file:

```
;; incorrect
(use-modules (srfi srfi-19))
(define (date) (date->string (current-date)))
(define-syntax %date (identifier-syntax (date)))
(define *compilation-date* %date)
```

It works at a REPL because the expressions are evaluated one-by-one, in order, but if placed in a file, the expressions are expanded one-by-one, but not evaluated until the compiled file is loaded.

The fix is to use `eval-when`.

```
;; correct: using eval-when
(use-modules (srfi srfi-19))
(eval-when (expand load eval)
  (define (date) (date->string (current-date))))
(define-syntax %date (identifier-syntax (date)))
(define *compilation-date* %date)
```

eval-when *conditions exp...*   [Syntax]
> Evaluate *exp...* under the given *conditions*. Valid conditions include:

expand   Evaluate during macro expansion, whether compiling or not.

load   Evaluate during the evaluation phase of compiled code, e.g. when loading a compiled module or running compiled code at the REPL.

eval   Evaluate during the evaluation phase of non-compiled code.

compile   Evaluate during macro expansion, but only when compiling.

In other words, when using the primitive evaluator, `eval-when` expressions with `expand` are run during macro expansion, and those with `eval` are run during the evaluation phase.

When using the compiler, `eval-when` expressions with either `expand` or `compile` are run during macro expansion, and those with `load` are run during the evaluation phase.

When in doubt, use the three conditions (`expand load eval`), as in the example above. Other uses of `eval-when` may void your warranty or poison your cat.

6.10.9 Internal Macros

`make-syntax-transformer` *name type binding*   [Scheme Procedure]
   Construct a syntax transformer object. This is part of Guile's low-level support for syntax-case.

`macro?` *obj*   [Scheme Procedure]
`scm_macro_p` (*obj*)   [C Function]
   Return `#t` if *obj* is a syntax transformer, or `#f` otherwise.

   Note that it's a bit difficult to actually get a macro as a first-class object; simply naming it (like `case`) will produce a syntax error. But it is possible to get these objects using `module-ref`:

```
(macro? (module-ref (current-module) 'case))
⇒ #t
```

`macro-type` *m*   [Scheme Procedure]
`scm_macro_type` (*m*)   [C Function]
   Return the *type* that was given when *m* was constructed, via `make-syntax-transformer`.

`macro-name` *m*   [Scheme Procedure]
`scm_macro_name` (*m*)   [C Function]
   Return the name of the macro *m*.

`macro-binding` *m*   [Scheme Procedure]
`scm_macro_binding` (*m*)   [C Function]
   Return the binding of the macro *m*.

`macro-transformer` *m*   [Scheme Procedure]
`scm_macro_transformer` (*m*)   [C Function]
   Return the transformer of the macro *m*. This will return a procedure, for which one may ask the docstring. That's the whole reason this section is documented. Actually a part of the result of `macro-binding`.

6.11 General Utility Functions

This chapter contains information about procedures which are not cleanly tied to a specific data type. Because of their wide range of applications, they are collected in a *utility* chapter.

6.11.1 Equality

There are three kinds of core equality predicates in Scheme, described below. The same kinds of comparisons arise in other functions, like memq and friends (see Section 6.7.2.7 [List Searching], page 192).

For all three tests, objects of different types are never equal. So for instance a list and a vector are not equal?, even if their contents are the same. Exact and inexact numbers are considered different types too, and are hence not equal even if their values are the same.

eq? tests just for the same object (essentially a pointer comparison). This is fast, and can be used when searching for a particular object, or when working with symbols or keywords (which are always unique objects).

eqv? extends eq? to look at the value of numbers and characters. It can for instance be used somewhat like = (see Section 6.6.2.8 [Comparison], page 117) but without an error if one operand isn't a number.

equal? goes further, it looks (recursively) into the contents of lists, vectors, etc. This is good for instance on lists that have been read or calculated in various places and are the same, just not made up of the same pairs. Such lists look the same (when printed), and equal? will consider them the same.

eq? *x y*   [Scheme Procedure]
scm_eq_p (*x, y*)   [C Function]
>   Return #t if *x* and *y* are the same object, except for numbers and characters. For
>   example,
>
>   (define x (vector 1 2 3))
>   (define y (vector 1 2 3))
>
>   (eq? x x)   ⇒ #t
>   (eq? x y)   ⇒ #f

Numbers and characters are not equal to any other object, but the problem is they're not necessarily eq? to themselves either. This is even so when the number comes directly from a variable,

            (let ((n (+ 2 3)))
              (eq? n n))   ⇒ *unspecified*

Generally eqv? below should be used when comparing numbers or characters. = (see Section 6.6.2.8 [Comparison], page 117) or char=? (see Section 6.6.3 [Characters], page 129) can be used too.

It's worth noting that end-of-list (), #t, #f, a symbol of a given name, and a keyword of a given name, are unique objects. There's just one of each, so for instance no matter how () arises in a program, it's the same object and can be compared with eq?,

```
(define x (cdr '(123)))
(define y (cdr '(456)))
(eq? x y) ⇒ #t

(define x (string->symbol "foo"))
(eq? x 'foo) ⇒ #t
```

`int scm_is_eq (SCM x, SCM y)`   [C Function]
>   Return 1 when x and y are equal in the sense of eq?, otherwise return 0.
>
>   The == operator should not be used on SCM values, an SCM is a C type which cannot
>   necessarily be compared using == (see Section 6.3 [The SCM Type], page 100).

`eqv? x y`   [Scheme Procedure]
`scm_eqv_p (x, y)`   [C Function]
>   Return #t if x and y are the same object, or for characters and numbers the same
>   value.
>
>   On objects except characters and numbers, eqv? is the same as eq? above, it's true
>   if x and y are the same object.
>
>   If x and y are numbers or characters, eqv? compares their type and value. An exact
>   number is not eqv? to an inexact number (even if their value is the same).

```
(eqv? 3 (+ 1 2)) ⇒ #t
(eqv? 1 1.0)     ⇒ #f
```

`equal? x y`   [Scheme Procedure]
`scm_equal_p (x, y)`   [C Function]
>   Return #t if x and y are the same type, and their contents or value are equal.
>
>   For a pair, string, vector, array or structure, equal? compares the contents, and does
>   so using the same equal? recursively, so a deep structure can be traversed.

```
(equal? (list 1 2 3) (list 1 2 3))   ⇒ #t
(equal? (list 1 2 3) (vector 1 2 3)) ⇒ #f
```

>   For other objects, equal? compares as per eqv? above, which means characters and
>   numbers are compared by type and value (and like eqv?, exact and inexact numbers
>   are not equal?, even if their value is the same).

```
(equal? 3 (+ 1 2)) ⇒ #t
(equal? 1 1.0)     ⇒ #f
```

>   Hash tables are currently only compared as per eq?, so two different tables are not
>   equal?, even if their contents are the same.
>
>   equal? does not support circular data structures, it may go into an infinite loop if
>   asked to compare two circular lists or similar.
>
>   New application-defined object types (see Section 5.5 [Defining New Types (Smobs)],
>   page 71) have an equalp handler which is called by equal?. This lets an application
>   traverse the contents or control what is considered equal? for two objects of such a
>   type. If there's no such handler, the default is to just compare as per eq?.

6.11.2 Object Properties

It's often useful to associate a piece of additional information with a Scheme object even though that object does not have a dedicated slot available in which the additional information could be stored. Object properties allow you to do just that.

Guile's representation of an object property is a procedure-with-setter (see Section 6.9.8 [Procedures with Setters], page 255) that can be used with the generalized form of `set!` (REFFIXME) to set and retrieve that property for any Scheme object. So, setting a property looks like this:

```
(set! (my-property obj1) value-for-obj1)
(set! (my-property obj2) value-for-obj2)
```

And retrieving values of the same property looks like this:

```
(my-property obj1)
⇒
value-for-obj1

(my-property obj2)
⇒
value-for-obj2
```

To create an object property in the first place, use the `make-object-property` procedure:

```
(define my-property (make-object-property))
```

`make-object-property`   [Scheme Procedure]
> Create and return an object property. An object property is a procedure-with-setter that can be called in two ways. `(set! (property obj) val)` sets *obj*'s *property* to *val*. `(property obj)` returns the current setting of *obj*'s *property*.

A single object property created by `make-object-property` can associate distinct property values with all Scheme values that are distinguishable by `eq?` (including, for example, integers).

Internally, object properties are implemented using a weak key hash table. This means that, as long as a Scheme value with property values is protected from garbage collection, its property values are also protected. When the Scheme value is collected, its entry in the property table is removed and so the (ex-) property values are no longer protected by the table.

Guile also implements a more traditional Lispy interface to properties, in which each object has an list of key-value pairs associated with it. Properties in that list are keyed by symbols. This is a legacy interface; you should use weak hash tables or object properties instead.

`object-properties` *obj*   [Scheme Procedure]
`scm_object_properties` (*obj*)   [C Function]
> Return *obj*'s property list.

`set-object-properties!` *obj alist*   [Scheme Procedure]
`scm_set_object_properties_x` (*obj*, *alist*)   [C Function]
> Set *obj*'s property list to *alist*.

`object-property` *obj key*   [Scheme Procedure]
`scm_object_property` (*obj*, *key*)   [C Function]
> Return the property of *obj* with name *key*.

`set-object-property!` *obj key value*   [Scheme Procedure]
`scm_set_object_property_x` (*obj*, *key*, *value*)   [C Function]
> In *obj*'s property list, set the property named *key* to *value*.

6.11.3 Sorting

Sorting is very important in computer programs. Therefore, Guile comes with several sorting procedures built-in. As always, procedures with names ending in ! are side-effecting, that means that they may modify their parameters in order to produce their results.

The first group of procedures can be used to merge two lists (which must be already sorted on their own) and produce sorted lists containing all elements of the input lists.

`merge` *alist blist less*   [Scheme Procedure]
`scm_merge` (*alist*, *blist*, *less*)   [C Function]
> Merge two already sorted lists into one. Given two lists *alist* and *blist*, such that `(sorted? alist less?)` and `(sorted? blist less?)`, return a new list in which the elements of *alist* and *blist* have been stably interleaved so that `(sorted? (merge alist blist less?) less?)`. Note: this does _not_ accept vectors.

`merge!` *alist blist less*   [Scheme Procedure]
`scm_merge_x` (*alist*, *blist*, *less*)   [C Function]
> Takes two lists *alist* and *blist* such that `(sorted? alist less?)` and `(sorted? blist less?)` and returns a new list in which the elements of *alist* and *blist* have been stably interleaved so that `(sorted? (merge alist blist less?) less?)`. This is the destructive variant of `merge` Note: this does _not_ accept vectors.

The following procedures can operate on sequences which are either vectors or list. According to the given arguments, they return sorted vectors or lists, respectively. The first of the following procedures determines whether a sequence is already sorted, the other sort a given sequence. The variants with names starting with `stable-` are special in that they maintain a special property of the input sequences: If two or more elements are the same according to the comparison predicate, they are left in the same order as they appeared in the input.

`sorted?` *items less*   [Scheme Procedure]
`scm_sorted_p` (*items*, *less*)   [C Function]
> Return `#t` if *items* is a list or vector such that, for each element *x* and the next element *y* of *items*, (`less y x`) returns `#f`. Otherwise return `#f`.

`sort` *items less*   [Scheme Procedure]
`scm_sort` (*items*, *less*)   [C Function]
> Sort the sequence *items*, which may be a list or a vector. *less* is used for comparing the sequence elements. This is not a stable sort.

`sort!` *items less*   [Scheme Procedure]
`scm_sort_x` (*items, less*)   [C Function]
> Sort the sequence *items*, which may be a list or a vector. *less* is used for comparing
> the sequence elements. The sorting is destructive, that means that the input sequence
> is modified to produce the sorted result. This is not a stable sort.

`stable-sort` *items less*   [Scheme Procedure]
`scm_stable_sort` (*items, less*)   [C Function]
> Sort the sequence *items*, which may be a list or a vector. *less* is used for comparing
> the sequence elements. This is a stable sort.

`stable-sort!` *items less*   [Scheme Procedure]
`scm_stable_sort_x` (*items, less*)   [C Function]
> Sort the sequence *items*, which may be a list or a vector. *less* is used for comparing
> the sequence elements. The sorting is destructive, that means that the input sequence
> is modified to produce the sorted result. This is a stable sort.

The procedures in the last group only accept lists or vectors as input, as their names
indicate.

`sort-list` *items less*   [Scheme Procedure]
`scm_sort_list` (*items, less*)   [C Function]
> Sort the list *items*, using *less* for comparing the list elements. This is a stable sort.

`sort-list!` *items less*   [Scheme Procedure]
`scm_sort_list_x` (*items, less*)   [C Function]
> Sort the list *items*, using *less* for comparing the list elements. The sorting is destruc-
> tive, that means that the input list is modified to produce the sorted result. This is
> a stable sort.

`restricted-vector-sort!` *vec less startpos endpos*   [Scheme Procedure]
`scm_restricted_vector_sort_x` (*vec, less, startpos, endpos*)   [C Function]
> Sort the vector *vec*, using *less* for comparing the vector elements. *startpos* (inclu-
> sively) and *endpos* (exclusively) delimit the range of the vector which gets sorted.
> The return value is not specified.

6.11.4 Copying Deep Structures

The procedures for copying lists (see Section 6.7.2 [Lists], page 188) only produce a flat
copy of the input list, and currently Guile does not even contain procedures for copying
vectors. `copy-tree` can be used for these application, as it does not only copy the spine of
a list, but also copies any pairs in the cars of the input lists.

`copy-tree` *obj*   [Scheme Procedure]
`scm_copy_tree` (*obj*)   [C Function]
> Recursively copy the data tree that is bound to *obj*, and return the new data structure.
> `copy-tree` recurses down the contents of both pairs and vectors (since both cons cells
> and vector cells may point to arbitrary objects), and stops recursing when it hits any
> other object.

6.11.5 General String Conversion

When debugging Scheme programs, but also for providing a human-friendly interface, a procedure for converting any Scheme object into string format is very useful. Conversion from/to strings can of course be done with specialized procedures when the data type of the object to convert is known, but with this procedure, it is often more comfortable.

`object->string` converts an object by using a print procedure for writing to a string port, and then returning the resulting string. Converting an object back from the string is only possible if the object type has a read syntax and the read syntax is preserved by the printing procedure.

`object->string` *obj* [*printer*]   [Scheme Procedure]
`scm_object_to_string` (*obj, printer*)   [C Function]
>   Return a Scheme string obtained by printing *obj*. Printing function can be specified by the optional second argument *printer* (default: `write`).

6.11.6 Hooks

A hook is a list of procedures to be called at well defined points in time. Typically, an application provides a hook *h* and promises its users that it will call all of the procedures in *h* at a defined point in the application's processing. By adding its own procedure to *h*, an application user can tap into or even influence the progress of the application.

Guile itself provides several such hooks for debugging and customization purposes: these are listed in a subsection below.

When an application first creates a hook, it needs to know how many arguments will be passed to the hook's procedures when the hook is run. The chosen number of arguments (which may be none) is declared when the hook is created, and all the procedures that are added to that hook must be capable of accepting that number of arguments.

A hook is created using `make-hook`. A procedure can be added to or removed from a hook using `add-hook!` or `remove-hook!`, and all of a hook's procedures can be removed together using `reset-hook!`. When an application wants to run a hook, it does so using `run-hook`.

6.11.6.1 Hook Usage by Example

Hook usage is shown by some examples in this section. First, we will define a hook of arity 2 — that is, the procedures stored in the hook will have to accept two arguments.

```
(define hook (make-hook 2))
hook
⇒ #<hook 2 40286c90>
```

Now we are ready to add some procedures to the newly created hook with `add-hook!`. In the following example, two procedures are added, which print different messages and do different things with their arguments.

```
(add-hook! hook (lambda (x y)
                  (display "Foo: ")
                  (display (+ x y))
                  (newline)))
(add-hook! hook (lambda (x y)
```

```
              (display "Bar: ")
              (display (* x y))
              (newline)))
```

Once the procedures have been added, we can invoke the hook using `run-hook`.

```
(run-hook hook 3 4)
⊣ Bar: 12
⊣ Foo: 7
```

Note that the procedures are called in the reverse of the order with which they were added. This is because the default behaviour of `add-hook!` is to add its procedure to the *front* of the hook's procedure list. You can force `add-hook!` to add its procedure to the *end* of the list instead by providing a third `#t` argument on the second call to `add-hook!`.

```
(add-hook! hook (lambda (x y)
                  (display "Foo: ")
                  (display (+ x y))
                  (newline)))
(add-hook! hook (lambda (x y)
                  (display "Bar: ")
                  (display (* x y))
                  (newline))
                  #t)                    ; <- Change here!

(run-hook hook 3 4)
⊣ Foo: 7
⊣ Bar: 12
```

6.11.6.2 Hook Reference

When you create a hook with `make-hook`, you must specify the arity of the procedures which can be added to the hook. If the arity is not given explicitly as an argument to `make-hook`, it defaults to zero. All procedures of a given hook must have the same arity, and when the procedures are invoked using `run-hook`, the number of arguments passed must match the arity specified at hook creation time.

The order in which procedures are added to a hook matters. If the third parameter to `add-hook!` is omitted or is equal to `#f`, the procedure is added in front of the procedures which might already be on that hook, otherwise the procedure is added at the end. The procedures are always called from the front to the end of the list when they are invoked via `run-hook`.

The ordering of the list of procedures returned by `hook->list` matches the order in which those procedures would be called if the hook was run using `run-hook`.

Note that the C functions in the following entries are for handling *Scheme-level* hooks in C. There are also *C-level* hooks which have their own interface (see Section 6.11.6.4 [C Hooks], page 284).

make-hook [*n_args*]   [Scheme Procedure]
scm_make_hook (*n_args*)   [C Function]

Create a hook for storing procedure of arity *n_args*. *n_args* defaults to zero. The returned value is a hook object to be used with the other hook procedures.

hook? *x*   [Scheme Procedure]
scm_hook_p (*x*)   [C Function]
> Return #t if *x* is a hook, #f otherwise.

hook-empty? *hook*   [Scheme Procedure]
scm_hook_empty_p (*hook*)   [C Function]
> Return #t if *hook* is an empty hook, #f otherwise.

add-hook! *hook proc* [*append_p*]   [Scheme Procedure]
scm_add_hook_x (*hook, proc, append_p*)   [C Function]
> Add the procedure *proc* to the hook *hook*. The procedure is added to the end if
> *append_p* is true, otherwise it is added to the front. The return value of this procedure
> is not specified.

remove-hook! *hook proc*   [Scheme Procedure]
scm_remove_hook_x (*hook, proc*)   [C Function]
> Remove the procedure *proc* from the hook *hook*. The return value of this procedure
> is not specified.

reset-hook! *hook*   [Scheme Procedure]
scm_reset_hook_x (*hook*)   [C Function]
> Remove all procedures from the hook *hook*. The return value of this procedure is not
> specified.

hook->list *hook*   [Scheme Procedure]
scm_hook_to_list (*hook*)   [C Function]
> Convert the procedure list of *hook* to a list.

run-hook *hook arg* ...   [Scheme Procedure]
scm_run_hook (*hook, args*)   [C Function]
> Apply all procedures from the hook *hook* to the arguments *arg* .... The order of
> the procedure application is first to last. The return value of this procedure is not
> specified.

If, in C code, you are certain that you have a hook object and well formed argument list
for that hook, you can also use **scm_c_run_hook**, which is identical to **scm_run_hook** but
does no type checking.

void scm_c_run_hook (*SCM hook, SCM args*)   [C Function]
> The same as **scm_run_hook** but without any type checking to confirm that *hook* is
> actually a hook object and that *args* is a well-formed list matching the arity of the
> hook.

For C code, SCM_HOOKP is a faster alternative to **scm_hook_p**:

int SCM_HOOKP (*x*)   [C Macro]
> Return 1 if *x* is a Scheme-level hook, 0 otherwise.

6.11.6.3 Handling Scheme-level hooks from C code

Here is an example of how to handle Scheme-level hooks from C code using the above functions.

```
if (scm_is_true (scm_hook_p (obj)))
  /* handle Scheme-level hook using C functions */
  scm_reset_hook_x (obj);
else
  /* do something else (obj is not a hook) */
```

6.11.6.4 Hooks For C Code.

The hooks already described are intended to be populated by Scheme-level procedures. In addition to this, the Guile library provides an independent set of interfaces for the creation and manipulation of hooks that are designed to be populated by functions implemented in C.

The original motivation here was to provide a kind of hook that could safely be invoked at various points during garbage collection. Scheme-level hooks are unsuitable for this purpose as running them could itself require memory allocation, which would then invoke garbage collection recursively ... However, it is also the case that these hooks are easier to work with than the Scheme-level ones if you only want to register C functions with them. So if that is mainly what your code needs to do, you may prefer to use this interface.

To create a C hook, you should allocate storage for a structure of type `scm_t_c_hook` and then initialize it using `scm_c_hook_init`.

`scm_t_c_hook`   [C Type]

> Data type for a C hook. The internals of this type should be treated as opaque.

`scm_t_c_hook_type`   [C Enum]

> Enumeration of possible hook types, which are:

> `SCM_C_HOOK_NORMAL`

> > Type of hook for which all the registered functions will always be called.

> `SCM_C_HOOK_OR`

> > Type of hook for which the sequence of registered functions will be called only until one of them returns C true (a non-NULL pointer).

> `SCM_C_HOOK_AND`

> > Type of hook for which the sequence of registered functions will be called only until one of them returns C false (a NULL pointer).

`void scm_c_hook_init` (*scm_t_c_hook *hook, void *hook_data,*   [C Function]
    scm_t_c_hook_type type)

> Initialize the C hook at memory pointed to by *hook*. *type* should be one of the values of the `scm_t_c_hook_type` enumeration, and controls how the hook functions will be called. *hook_data* is a closure parameter that will be passed to all registered hook functions when they are called.

To add or remove a C function from a C hook, use `scm_c_hook_add` or `scm_c_hook_remove`. A hook function must expect three `void *` parameters which are, respectively:

hook_data   The hook closure data that was specified at the time the hook was initialized by `scm_c_hook_init`.

func_data   The function closure data that was specified at the time that that function was registered with the hook by `scm_c_hook_add`.

data   The call closure data specified by the `scm_c_hook_run` call that runs the hook.

`scm_t_c_hook_function`   [C Type]

> Function type for a C hook function: takes three **void** * parameters and returns a **void** * result.

void `scm_c_hook_add` (*scm_t_c_hook *hook, scm_t_c_hook_function*   [C Function]
> *func, void *func_data, int appendp*)
> Add function *func*, with function closure data *func_data*, to the C hook *hook*. The new function is appended to the hook's list of functions if *appendp* is non-zero, otherwise prepended.

void `scm_c_hook_remove` (*scm_t_c_hook *hook,*   [C Function]
> *scm_t_c_hook_function func, void *func_data*)
> Remove function *func*, with function closure data *func_data*, from the C hook *hook*. `scm_c_hook_remove` checks both *func* and *func_data* so as to allow for the same *func* being registered multiple times with different closure data.

Finally, to invoke a C hook, call the `scm_c_hook_run` function specifying the hook and the call closure data for this run:

void * `scm_c_hook_run` (*scm_t_c_hook *hook, void *data*)   [C Function]
> Run the C hook *hook* will call closure data *data*. Subject to the variations for hook types `SCM_C_HOOK_OR` and `SCM_C_HOOK_AND`, `scm_c_hook_run` calls *hook*'s registered functions in turn, passing them the hook's closure data, each function's closure data, and the call closure data.
>
> `scm_c_hook_run`'s return value is the return value of the last function to be called.

6.11.6.5 Hooks for Garbage Collection

Whenever Guile performs a garbage collection, it calls the following hooks in the order shown.

`scm_before_gc_c_hook`   [C Hook]

> C hook called at the very start of a garbage collection, after setting `scm_gc_running_p` to 1, but before entering the GC critical section.
>
> If garbage collection is blocked because `scm_block_gc` is non-zero, GC exits early soon after calling this hook, and no further hooks will be called.

`scm_before_mark_c_hook`   [C Hook]

> C hook called before beginning the mark phase of garbage collection, after the GC thread has entered a critical section.

`scm_before_sweep_c_hook`   [C Hook]

> C hook called before beginning the sweep phase of garbage collection. This is the same as at the end of the mark phase, since nothing else happens between marking and sweeping.

`scm_after_sweep_c_hook`   [C Hook]

> C hook called after the end of the sweep phase of garbage collection, but while the GC thread is still inside its critical section.

`scm_after_gc_c_hook`   [C Hook]

> C hook called at the very end of a garbage collection, after the GC thread has left its critical section.

`after-gc-hook`   [Scheme Hook]

> Scheme hook with arity 0. This hook is run asynchronously (see Section 6.21.2 [Asyncs], page 411) soon after the GC has completed and any other events that were deferred during garbage collection have been processed. (Also accessible from C with the name `scm_after_gc_hook`.)

All the C hooks listed here have type `SCM_C_HOOK_NORMAL`, are initialized with hook closure data NULL, are invoked by `scm_c_hook_run` with call closure data NULL.

The Scheme hook `after-gc-hook` is particularly useful in conjunction with guardians (see Section 6.18.4 [Guardians], page 380). Typically, if you are using a guardian, you want to call the guardian after garbage collection to see if any of the objects added to the guardian have been collected. By adding a thunk that performs this call to `after-gc-hook`, you can ensure that your guardian is tested after every garbage collection cycle.

6.11.6.6 Hooks into the Guile REPL

6.12 Definitions and Variable Bindings

Scheme supports the definition of variables in different contexts. Variables can be defined at the top level, so that they are visible in the entire program, and variables can be defined locally to procedures and expressions. This is important for modularity and data abstraction.

6.12.1 Top Level Variable Definitions

At the top level of a program (i.e., not nested within any other expression), a definition of the form

```
(define a value)
```

defines a variable called `a` and sets it to the value *value*.

If the variable already exists in the current module, because it has already been created by a previous **define** expression with the same name, its value is simply changed to the new *value*. In this case, then, the above form is completely equivalent to

```
(set! a value)
```

This equivalence means that **define** can be used interchangeably with **set!** to change the value of variables at the top level of the REPL or a Scheme source file. It is useful during interactive development when reloading a Scheme file that you have modified, because it allows the **define** expressions in that file to work as expected both the first time that the file is loaded and on subsequent occasions.

Note, though, that **define** and **set!** are not always equivalent. For example, a **set!** is not allowed if the named variable does not already exist, and the two expressions can behave differently in the case where there are imported variables visible from another module.

define *name value*   [Scheme Syntax]

> Create a top level variable named *name* with value *value*. If the named variable already exists, just change its value. The return value of a **define** expression is unspecified.

The C API equivalents of **define** are **scm_define** and **scm_c_define**, which differ from each other in whether the variable name is specified as a SCM symbol or as a null-terminated C string.

scm_define (*sym, value*)   [C Function]

scm_c_define (*const char *name, value*)   [C Function]

> C equivalents of **define**, with variable name specified either by *sym*, a symbol, or by *name*, a null-terminated C string. Both variants return the new or preexisting variable object.

define (when it occurs at top level), **scm_define** and **scm_c_define** all create or set the value of a variable in the top level environment of the current module. If there was not already a variable with the specified name belonging to the current module, but a similarly named variable from another module was visible through having been imported, the newly created variable in the current module will shadow the imported variable, such that the imported variable is no longer visible.

Attention: Scheme definitions inside local binding constructs (see Section 6.12.2 [Local Bindings], page 287) act differently (see Section 6.12.3 [Internal Definitions], page 289).

Many people end up in a development style of adding and changing definitions at runtime, building out their program without restarting it. (You can do this using **reload-module**, the **reload** REPL command, the **load** procedure, or even just pasting code into a REPL.) If you are one of these people, you will find that sometimes you there are some variables that you *don't* want to redefine all the time. For these, use **define-once**.

define-once *name value*   [Scheme Syntax]

> Create a top level variable named *name* with value *value*, but only if *name* is not already bound in the current module.

Old Lispers probably know **define-once** under its Lisp name, **defvar**.

6.12.2 Local Variable Bindings

As opposed to definitions at the top level, which creates bindings that are visible to all code in a module, it is also possible to define variables which are only visible in a well-defined part of the program. Normally, this part of a program will be a procedure or a subexpression of a procedure.

With the constructs for local binding (**let**, **let***, **letrec**, and **letrec***), the Scheme language has a block structure like most other programming languages since the days of AL-GOL 60. Readers familiar to languages like C or Java should already be used to this concept, but the family of **let** expressions has a few properties which are well worth knowing.

The most basic local binding construct is **let**.

let *bindings body*   [syntax]

> *bindings* has the form

```
((variable1 init1) ...)
```

that is zero or more two-element lists of a variable and an arbitrary expression each. All *variable* names must be distinct.

A `let` expression is evaluated as follows.

- All *init* expressions are evaluated.
- New storage is allocated for the *variables*.
- The values of the *init* expressions are stored into the variables.
- The expressions in *body* are evaluated in order, and the value of the last expression is returned as the value of the `let` expression.

The *init* expressions are not allowed to refer to any of the *variables*.

The other binding constructs are variations on the same theme: making new values, binding them to variables, and executing a body in that new, extended lexical context.

`let*` *bindings body*   [syntax]

Similar to `let`, but the variable bindings are performed sequentially, that means that all *init* expression are allowed to use the variables defined on their left in the binding list.

A `let*` expression can always be expressed with nested `let` expressions.

```
(let* ((a 1) (b a))
   b)
≡
(let ((a 1))
  (let ((b a))
    b))
```

`letrec` *bindings body*   [syntax]

Similar to `let`, but it is possible to refer to the *variable* from lambda expression created in any of the *inits*. That is, procedures created in the *init* expression can recursively refer to the defined variables.

```
(letrec ((even? (lambda (n)
                   (if (zero? n)
                       #t
                       (odd? (- n 1)))))
          (odd? (lambda (n)
                   (if (zero? n)
                       #f
                       (even? (- n 1))))))
  (even? 88))
⇒
#t
```

Note that while the *init* expressions may refer to the new variables, they may not access their values. For example, making the **even?** function above creates a closure (see Section 3.4 [About Closure], page 26) referencing the **odd?** variable. But **odd?** can't be called until after execution has entered the body.

`letrec*` *bindings body*   [syntax]
>   Similar to `letrec`, except the *init* expressions are bound to their variables in order.
>
>   `letrec*` thus relaxes the letrec restriction, in that later *init* expressions may refer to
>   the values of previously bound variables.
>
> ```
> (letrec ((a 42)
>          (b (+ a 10)))  ;; Illegal access
>   (* a b))
> ;; The behavior of the expression above is unspecified
>
> (letrec* ((a 42)
>           (b (+ a 10)))
>   (* a b))
> ⇒ 2184
> ```

There is also an alternative form of the `let` form, which is used for expressing iteration.
Because of the use as a looping construct, this form (the *named let*) is documented in the
section about iteration (see Section 6.13.4 [while do], page 294)

6.12.3 Internal definitions

A `define` form which appears inside the body of a `lambda`, `let`, `let*`, `letrec`, `letrec*`
or equivalent expression is called an *internal definition*. An internal definition differs from
a top level definition (see Section 6.12.1 [Top Level], page 286), because the definition is
only visible inside the complete body of the enclosing form. Let us examine the following
example.

```
(let ((frumble "froz"))
   (define banana (lambda () (apple 'peach)))
   (define apple (lambda (x) x))
   (banana))
⇒
peach
```

Here the enclosing form is a `let`, so the `define`s in the `let`-body are internal definitions.
Because the scope of the internal definitions is the **complete** body of the `let`-expression,
the `lambda`-expression which gets bound to the variable `banana` may refer to the variable
`apple`, even though its definition appears lexically *after* the definition of `banana`. This is
because a sequence of internal definition acts as if it were a `letrec*` expression.

```
(let ()
   (define a 1)
   (define b 2)
   (+ a b))
```

is equivalent to

```
(let ()
   (letrec* ((a 1) (b 2))
      (+ a b)))
```

Internal definitions are only allowed at the beginning of the body of an enclosing expression. They may not be mixed with other expressions.

Another noteworthy difference to top level definitions is that within one group of internal definitions all variable names must be distinct. That means where on the top level a second define for a given variable acts like a `set!`, an exception is thrown for internal definitions with duplicate bindings.

As a historical note, it used to be that internal bindings were expanded in terms of `letrec`, not `letrec*`. This was the situation for the R5RS report and before. However with the R6RS, it was recognized that sequential definition was a more intuitive expansion, as in the following case:

```
(let ()
  (define a 1)
  (define b (+ a a))
  (+ a b))
```

Guile decided to follow the R6RS in this regard, and now expands internal definitions using `letrec*`.

6.12.4 Querying variable bindings

Guile provides a procedure for checking whether a symbol is bound in the top level environment.

defined? *sym* [*module*]   [Scheme Procedure]
scm_defined_p (*sym, module*)   [C Function]
    Return `#t` if *sym* is defined in the module *module* or the current module when *module* is not specified; otherwise return `#f`.

6.12.5 Binding multiple return values

define-values *formals expression*   [Syntax]
    The *expression* is evaluated, and the *formals* are bound to the return values in the same way that the formals in a `lambda` expression are matched to the arguments in a procedure call.

```
(define-values (q r) (floor/ 10 3))
(list q r) ⇒ (3 1)

(define-values (x . y) (values 1 2 3))
x ⇒ 1
y ⇒ (2 3)

(define-values x (values 1 2 3))
x ⇒ (1 2 3)
```

6.13 Controlling the Flow of Program Execution

See Section 5.4.3 [Control Flow], page 66 for a discussion of how the more general control flow of Scheme affects C code.

6.13.1 Sequencing and Splicing

As an expression, the `begin` syntax is used to evaluate a sequence of sub-expressions in order. Consider the conditional expression below:

```
(if (> x 0)
    (begin (display "greater") (newline)))
```

If the test is true, we want to display "greater" to the current output port, then display a newline. We use `begin` to form a compound expression out of this sequence of subexpressions.

`begin` *expr* . . .   [syntax]

> The expression(s) are evaluated in left-to-right order and the value of the last expression is returned as the value of the `begin`-expression. This expression type is used when the expressions before the last one are evaluated for their side effects.

The `begin` syntax has another role in definition context (see Section 6.12.3 [Internal Definitions], page 289). A `begin` form in a definition context *splices* its subforms into its place. For example, consider the following procedure:

```
(define (make-seal)
  (define-sealant seal open)
  (values seal open))
```

Let us assume the existence of a `define-sealant` macro that expands out to some definitions wrapped in a `begin`, like so:

```
(define (make-seal)
  (begin
    (define seal-tag
      (list 'seal))
    (define (seal x)
      (cons seal-tag x))
    (define (sealed? x)
      (and (pair? x) (eq? (car x) seal-tag)))
    (define (open x)
      (if (sealed? x)
          (cdr x)
          (error "Expected a sealed value:" x))))
  (values seal open))
```

Here, because the `begin` is in definition context, its subforms are *spliced* into the place of the `begin`. This allows the definitions created by the macro to be visible to the following expression, the `values` form.

It is a fine point, but splicing and sequencing are different. It can make sense to splice zero forms, because it can make sense to have zero internal definitions before the expressions in a procedure or lexical binding form. However it does not make sense to have a sequence of zero expressions, because in that case it would not be clear what the value of the sequence would be, because in a sequence of zero expressions, there can be no last value. Sequencing zero expressions is an error.

It would be more elegant in some ways to eliminate splicing from the Scheme language, and without macros (see Section 6.10 [Macros], page 257), that would be a good idea. But it is useful to be able to write macros that expand out to multiple definitions, as in `define-sealant` above, so Scheme abuses the `begin` form for these two tasks.

6.13.2 Simple Conditional Evaluation

Guile provides three syntactic constructs for conditional evaluation. if is the normal if-then-else expression (with an optional else branch), **cond** is a conditional expression with multiple branches and **case** branches if an expression has one of a set of constant values.

if *test consequent* [*alternate*]   [syntax]

All arguments may be arbitrary expressions. First, *test* is evaluated. If it returns a true value, the expression *consequent* is evaluated and *alternate* is ignored. If *test* evaluates to #f, *alternate* is evaluated instead. The values of the evaluated branch (*consequent* or *alternate*) are returned as the values of the if expression.

When *alternate* is omitted and the *test* evaluates to #f, the value of the expression is not specified.

When you go to write an if without an alternate (a *one-armed* if), part of what you are expressing is that you don't care about the return value (or values) of the expression. As such, you are more interested in the *effect* of evaluating the consequent expression. (By convention, we use the word *statement* to refer to an expression that is evaluated for effect, not for value).

In such a case, it is considered more clear to express these intentions with these special forms, **when** and **unless**. As an added bonus, these forms accept multiple statements to evaluate, which are implicitly wrapped in a **begin**.

when *test statement1 statement2 ...*   [Scheme Syntax]
unless *test statement1 statement2 ...*   [Scheme Syntax]

The actual definitions of these forms are in many ways their most clear documentation:

```
(define-syntax-rule (when test stmt stmt* ...)
  (if test (begin stmt stmt* ...)))

(define-syntax-rule (unless condition stmt stmt* ...)
  (if (not test) (begin stmt stmt* ...)))
```

That is to say, **when** evaluates its consequent statements in order if *test* is true. **unless** is the opposite: it evaluates the statements if *test* is false.

cond *clause1 clause2 ...*   [syntax]

Each **cond**-clause must look like this:

```
(test expression ...)
```

where *test* and *expression* are arbitrary expression, or like this

```
(test => expression)
```

where *expression* must evaluate to a procedure.

The *tests* of the clauses are evaluated in order and as soon as one of them evaluates to a true values, the corresponding *expressions* are evaluated in order and the last value is returned as the value of the **cond**-expression. For the => clause type, *expression* is evaluated and the resulting procedure is applied to the value of *test*. The result of this procedure application is then the result of the **cond**-expression.

One additional **cond**-clause is available as an extension to standard Scheme:

```
(test guard => expression)
```

where *guard* and *expression* must evaluate to procedures. For this clause type, *test* may return multiple values, and `cond` ignores its boolean state; instead, `cond` evaluates *guard* and applies the resulting procedure to the value(s) of *test*, as if *guard* were the *consumer* argument of `call-with-values`. If the result of that procedure call is a true value, it evaluates *expression* and applies the resulting procedure to the value(s) of *test*, in the same manner as the *guard* was called.

The *test* of the last *clause* may be the symbol `else`. Then, if none of the preceding *tests* is true, the *expressions* following the `else` are evaluated to produce the result of the `cond`-expression.

case *key clause1 clause2 ...*   [syntax]

key may be any expression, and the *clauses* must have the form

```
((datum1 ...) expr1 expr2 ...)
```

or

```
((datum1 ...) => expression)
```

and the last *clause* may have the form

```
(else expr1 expr2 ...)
```

or

```
(else => expression)
```

All *datums* must be distinct. First, *key* is evaluated. The result of this evaluation is compared against all *datum* values using `eqv?`. When this comparison succeeds, the expression(s) following the *datum* are evaluated from left to right, returning the value of the last expression as the result of the `case` expression.

If the *key* matches no *datum* and there is an `else`-clause, the expressions following the `else` are evaluated. If there is no such clause, the result of the expression is unspecified.

For the `=>` clause types, *expression* is evaluated and the resulting procedure is applied to the value of *key*. The result of this procedure application is then the result of the `case`-expression.

6.13.3 Conditional Evaluation of a Sequence of Expressions

`and` and `or` evaluate all their arguments in order, similar to `begin`, but evaluation stops as soon as one of the expressions evaluates to false or true, respectively.

and *expr ...*   [syntax]

Evaluate the *exprs* from left to right and stop evaluation as soon as one expression evaluates to `#f`; the remaining expressions are not evaluated. The value of the last evaluated expression is returned. If no expression evaluates to `#f`, the value of the last expression is returned.

If used without expressions, `#t` is returned.

or *expr ...*   [syntax]

Evaluate the *exprs* from left to right and stop evaluation as soon as one expression evaluates to a true value (that is, a value different from `#f`); the remaining expressions are not evaluated. The value of the last evaluated expression is returned. If all expressions evaluate to #f, #f is returned.

If used without expressions, #f is returned.

6.13.4 Iteration mechanisms

Scheme has only few iteration mechanisms, mainly because iteration in Scheme programs is normally expressed using recursion. Nevertheless, R5RS defines a construct for programming loops, calling do. In addition, Guile has an explicit looping syntax called while.

do ((*variable init* [*step*]) ...) (*test expr* ...) *body* ...   [syntax]
> Bind *variables* and evaluate *body* until *test* is true. The return value is the last *expr* after *test*, if given. A simple example will illustrate the basic form,
>
> ```
> (do ((i 1 (1+ i)))
>     ((> i 4))
>   (display i))
> ⊣ 1234
> ```
>
> Or with two variables and a final return value,
>
> ```
> (do ((i 1 (1+ i))
>      (p 3 (* 3 p)))
>     ((> i 4)
>      p)
>   (format #t "3**~s is ~s\n" i p))
> ⊣
> 3**1 is 3
> 3**2 is 9
> 3**3 is 27
> 3**4 is 81
> ⇒
> 789
> ```
>
> The *variable* bindings are established like a let, in that the expressions are all evaluated and then all bindings made. When iterating, the optional *step* expressions are evaluated with the previous bindings in scope, then new bindings all made.
>
> The *test* expression is a termination condition. Looping stops when the *test* is true. It's evaluated before running the *body* each time, so if it's true the first time then *body* is not run at all.
>
> The optional *exprs* after the *test* are evaluated at the end of looping, with the final *variable* bindings available. The last *expr* gives the return value, or if there are no *exprs* the return value is unspecified.
>
> Each iteration establishes bindings to fresh locations for the *variables*, like a new let for each iteration. This is done for *variables* without *step* expressions too. The following illustrates this, showing how a new i is captured by the lambda in each iteration (see Section 3.4 [The Concept of Closure], page 26).
>
> ```
> (define lst '())
> (do ((i 1 (1+ i)))
>     ((> i 4))
> ```

```
(set! lst (cons (lambda () i) lst)))
(map (lambda (proc) (proc)) lst)
⇒
(4 3 2 1)
```

while *cond body ...*   [syntax]

Run a loop executing the *body* forms while *cond* is true. *cond* is tested at the start of each iteration, so if it's **#f** the first time then *body* is not executed at all.

Within **while**, two extra bindings are provided, they can be used from both *cond* and *body*.

> **break** *break-arg ...*   [Scheme Procedure]
>   Break out of the **while** form.

> **continue**   [Scheme Procedure]
>   Abandon the current iteration, go back to the start and test *cond* again, etc.

If the loop terminates normally, by the *cond* evaluating to **#f**, then the **while** expression as a whole evaluates to **#f**. If it terminates by a call to **break** with some number of arguments, those arguments are returned from the **while** expression, as multiple values. Otherwise if it terminates by a call to **break** with no arguments, then return value is **#t**.

```
(while #f (error "not reached")) ⇒ #f
(while #t (break)) ⇒ #t
(while #t (break 1 2 3)) ⇒ 1 2 3
```

Each **while** form gets its own **break** and **continue** procedures, operating on that **while**. This means when loops are nested the outer **break** can be used to escape all the way out. For example,

```
(while (test1)
  (let ((outer-break break))
    (while (test2)
      (if (something)
        (outer-break #f))
      ...)))
```

Note that each **break** and **continue** procedure can only be used within the dynamic extent of its **while**. Outside the **while** their behaviour is unspecified.

Another very common way of expressing iteration in Scheme programs is the use of the so-called *named let*.

Named let is a variant of **let** which creates a procedure and calls it in one step. Because of the newly created procedure, named let is more powerful than **do**–it can be used for iteration, but also for arbitrary recursion.

let *variable bindings body*   [syntax]

For the definition of *bindings* see the documentation about **let** (see Section 6.12.2 [Local Bindings], page 287).

Named **let** works as follows:

- A new procedure which accepts as many arguments as are in *bindings* is created and bound locally (using `let`) to *variable*. The new procedure's formal argument names are the name of the *variables*.

- The *body* expressions are inserted into the newly created procedure.

- The procedure is called with the *init* expressions as the formal arguments.

The next example implements a loop which iterates (by recursion) 1000 times.

```
(let lp ((x 1000))
  (if (positive? x)
      (lp (- x 1))
      x))
⇒
0
```

6.13.5 Prompts

Prompts are control-flow barriers between different parts of a program. In the same way that a user sees a shell prompt (e.g., the Bash prompt) as a barrier between the operating system and her programs, Scheme prompts allow the Scheme programmer to treat parts of programs as if they were running in different operating systems.

We use this roundabout explanation because, unless you're a functional programming junkie, you probably haven't heard the term, "delimited, composable continuation". That's OK; it's a relatively recent topic, but a very useful one to know about.

6.13.5.1 Prompt Primitives

Guile's primitive delimited control operators are `call-with-prompt` and `abort-to-prompt`.

call-with-prompt *tag thunk handler*   [Scheme Procedure]
    Set up a prompt, and call *thunk* within that prompt.

    During the dynamic extent of the call to *thunk*, a prompt named *tag* will be present in the dynamic context, such that if a user calls `abort-to-prompt` (see below) with that tag, control rewinds back to the prompt, and the *handler* is run.

    handler must be a procedure. The first argument to *handler* will be the state of the computation begun when *thunk* was called, and ending with the call to `abort-to-prompt`. The remaining arguments to *handler* are those passed to `abort-to-prompt`.

make-prompt-tag [*stem*]   [Scheme Procedure]
    Make a new prompt tag. Currently prompt tags are generated symbols. This may change in some future Guile version.

default-prompt-tag   [Scheme Procedure]
    Return the default prompt tag. Having a distinguished default prompt tag allows some useful prompt and abort idioms, discussed in the next section.

abort-to-prompt *tag val1 val2 . . .*   [Scheme Procedure]
    Unwind the dynamic and control context to the nearest prompt named *tag*, also passing the given values.

C programmers may recognize `call-with-prompt` and `abort-to-prompt` as a fancy kind of `setjmp` and `longjmp`, respectively. Prompts are indeed quite useful as non-local escape mechanisms. Guile's `catch` and `throw` are implemented in terms of prompts. Prompts are more convenient than `longjmp`, in that one has the opportunity to pass multiple values to the jump target.

Also unlike `longjmp`, the prompt handler is given the full state of the process that was aborted, as the first argument to the prompt's handler. That state is the *continuation* of the computation wrapped by the prompt. It is a *delimited continuation*, because it is not the whole continuation of the program; rather, just the computation initiated by the call to `call-with-prompt`.

The continuation is a procedure, and may be reinstated simply by invoking it, with any number of values. Here's where things get interesting, and complicated as well. Besides being described as delimited, continuations reified by prompts are also *composable*, because invoking a prompt-saved continuation composes that continuation with the current one.

Imagine you have saved a continuation via call-with-prompt:

```
(define cont
  (call-with-prompt
    ;; tag
    'foo
    ;; thunk
    (lambda ()
      (+ 34 (abort-to-prompt 'foo)))
    ;; handler
    (lambda (k) k)))
```

The resulting continuation is the addition of 34. It's as if you had written:

```
(define cont
  (lambda (x)
    (+ 34 x)))
```

So, if we call `cont` with one numeric value, we get that number, incremented by 34:

```
(cont 8)
⇒ 42
(* 2 (cont 8))
⇒ 84
```

The last example illustrates what we mean when we say, "composes with the current continuation". We mean that there is a current continuation – some remaining things to compute, like `(lambda (x) (* x 2))` – and that calling the saved continuation doesn't wipe out the current continuation, it composes the saved continuation with the current one.

We're belaboring the point here because traditional Scheme continuations, as discussed in the next section, aren't composable, and are actually less expressive than continuations captured by prompts. But there's a place for them both.

Before moving on, we should mention that if the handler of a prompt is a `lambda` expression, and the first argument isn't referenced, an abort to that prompt will not cause a continuation to be reified. This can be an important efficiency consideration to keep in mind.

One example where this optimization matters is *escape continuations*. Escape continuations are delimited continuations whose only use is to make a non-local exit—i.e., to escape from the current continuation. Such continuations are invoked only once, and for this reason they are sometimes called *one-shot continuations*. A common use of escape continuations is when throwing an exception (see Section 6.13.8 [Exceptions], page 303).

The constructs below are syntactic sugar atop prompts to simplify the use of escape continuations.

call-with-escape-continuation *proc*   [Scheme Procedure]
call/ec *proc*   [Scheme Procedure]
> Call *proc* with an escape continuation.
>
> In the example below, the *return* continuation is used to escape the continuation of the call to fold.

```
(use-modules (ice-9 control)
             (srfi srfi-1))


(define (prefix x lst)
  ;; Return all the elements before the first occurrence
  ;; of X in LST.
  (call/ec
    (lambda (return)
      (fold (lambda (element prefix)
              (if (equal? element x)
                  (return (reverse prefix))  ; escape 'fold'
                  (cons element prefix)))
            '()
            lst))))


(prefix 'a '(0 1 2 a 3 4 5))
⇒ (0 1 2)
```

let-escape-continuation *k body* ...   [Scheme Syntax]
let/ec *k body* ...   [Scheme Syntax]
> Bind *k* within *body* to an escape continuation.
>
> This is equivalent to (call/ec (lambda (*k*) *body* ...)).

6.13.5.2 Shift, Reset, and All That

There is a whole zoo of delimited control operators, and as it does not seem to be a bounded set, Guile implements support for them in a separate module:

```
(use-modules (ice-9 control))
```

Firstly, we have a helpful abbreviation for the call-with-prompt operator.

% *expr*   [Scheme Syntax]
% *expr handler*   [Scheme Syntax]
% *tag expr handler*   [Scheme Syntax]
> Evaluate *expr* in a prompt, optionally specifying a tag and a handler. If no tag is given, the default prompt tag is used.

If no handler is given, a default handler is installed. The default handler accepts a procedure of one argument, which will called on the captured continuation, within a prompt.

Sometimes it's easier just to show code, as in this case:

```
(define (default-prompt-handler k proc)
  (% (default-prompt-tag)
     (proc k)
     default-prompt-handler))
```

The % symbol is chosen because it looks like a prompt.

Likewise there is an abbreviation for `abort-to-prompt`, which assumes the default prompt tag:

`abort` *val1 val2 ...*   [Scheme Procedure]
    Abort to the default prompt tag, passing *val1 val2 ...* to the handler.

As mentioned before, (`ice-9 control`) also provides other delimited control operators. This section is a bit technical, and first-time users of delimited continuations should probably come back to it after some practice with %.

Still here? So, when one implements a delimited control operator like `call-with-prompt`, one needs to make two decisions. Firstly, does the handler run within or outside the prompt? Having the handler run within the prompt allows an abort inside the handler to return to the same prompt handler, which is often useful. However it prevents tail calls from the handler, so it is less general.

Similarly, does invoking a captured continuation reinstate a prompt? Again we have the tradeoff of convenience versus proper tail calls.

These decisions are captured in the Felleisen F operator. If neither the continuations nor the handlers implicitly add a prompt, the operator is known as $-F-$. This is the case for Guile's `call-with-prompt` and `abort-to-prompt`.

If both continuation and handler implicitly add prompts, then the operator is $+F+$. `shift` and `reset` are such operators.

`reset` *body1 body2 ...*   [Scheme Syntax]
    Establish a prompt, and evaluate *body1 body2 ...* within that prompt.

    The prompt handler is designed to work with `shift`, described below.

`shift` *cont body1 body2 ...*   [Scheme Syntax]
    Abort to the nearest `reset`, and evaluate *body1 body2 ...* in a context in which the captured continuation is bound to *cont*.

    As mentioned above, taken together, the *body1 body2 ...* expressions and the invocations of *cont* implicitly establish a prompt.

Interested readers are invited to explore Oleg Kiselyov's wonderful web site at `http://okmij.org/ftp/`, for more information on these operators.

6.13.6 Continuations

A "continuation" is the code that will execute when a given function or expression returns.
For example, consider

```
(define (foo)
  (display "hello\n")
  (display (bar)) (newline)
  (exit))
```

The continuation from the call to `bar` comprises a `display` of the value returned, a
`newline` and an `exit`. This can be expressed as a function of one argument.

```
(lambda (r)
  (display r) (newline)
  (exit))
```

In Scheme, continuations are represented as special procedures just like this. The special
property is that when a continuation is called it abandons the current program location and
jumps directly to that represented by the continuation.

A continuation is like a dynamic label, capturing at run-time a point in program execution, including all the nested calls that have lead to it (or rather the code that will execute
when those calls return).

Continuations are created with the following functions.

call-with-current-continuation *proc*   [Scheme Procedure]
call/cc *proc*   [Scheme Procedure]
>   Capture the current continuation and call (*proc cont*) with it. The return value is
>   the value returned by *proc*, or when (*cont value*) is later invoked, the return is the
>   *value* passed.
>
>   Normally *cont* should be called with one argument, but when the location resumed is
>   expecting multiple values (see Section 6.13.7 [Multiple Values], page 301) then they
>   should be passed as multiple arguments, for instance (*cont x y z*).
>
>   *cont* may only be used from the same side of a continuation barrier as it was cre-
>   ated (see Section 6.13.12 [Continuation Barriers], page 315), and in a multi-threaded
>   program only from the thread in which it was created.
>
>   The call to *proc* is not part of the continuation captured, it runs only when the
>   continuation is created. Often a program will want to store *cont* somewhere for later
>   use; this can be done in *proc*.
>
>   The `call` in the name `call-with-current-continuation` refers to the way a call to
>   *proc* gives the newly created continuation. It's not related to the way a call is used
>   later to invoke that continuation.
>
>   `call/cc` is an alias for `call-with-current-continuation`. This is in common use
>   since the latter is rather long.

Here is a simple example,

```
(define kont #f)
(format #t "the return is ~a\n"
```

```
      (call/cc (lambda (k)
                 (set! kont k)
                 1)))
  ⇒ the return is 1


  (kont 2)
  ⇒ the return is 2
```

`call/cc` captures a continuation in which the value returned is going to be displayed by `format`. The `lambda` stores this in `kont` and gives an initial return `1` which is displayed. The later invocation of `kont` resumes the captured point, but this time returning `2`, which is displayed.

When Guile is run interactively, a call to `format` like this has an implicit return back to the read-eval-print loop. `call/cc` captures that like any other return, which is why interactively `kont` will come back to read more input.

C programmers may note that `call/cc` is like `setjmp` in the way it records at runtime a point in program execution. A call to a continuation is like a `longjmp` in that it abandons the present location and goes to the recorded one. Like `longjmp`, the value passed to the continuation is the value returned by `call/cc` on resuming there. However `longjmp` can only go up the program stack, but the continuation mechanism can go anywhere.

When a continuation is invoked, `call/cc` and subsequent code effectively "returns" a second time. It can be confusing to imagine a function returning more times than it was called. It may help instead to think of it being stealthily re-entered and then program flow going on as normal.

`dynamic-wind` (see Section 6.13.10 [Dynamic Wind], page 309) can be used to ensure setup and cleanup code is run when a program locus is resumed or abandoned through the continuation mechanism.

Continuations are a powerful mechanism, and can be used to implement almost any sort of control structure, such as loops, coroutines, or exception handlers.

However the implementation of continuations in Guile is not as efficient as one might hope, because Guile is designed to cooperate with programs written in other languages, such as C, which do not know about continuations. Basically continuations are captured by a block copy of the stack, and resumed by copying back.

For this reason, continuations captured by `call/cc` should be used only when there is no other simple way to achieve the desired result, or when the elegance of the continuation mechanism outweighs the need for performance.

Escapes upwards from loops or nested functions are generally best handled with prompts (see Section 6.13.5 [Prompts], page 296). Coroutines can be efficiently implemented with cooperating threads (a thread holds a full program stack but doesn't copy it around the way continuations do).

6.13.7 Returning and Accepting Multiple Values

Scheme allows a procedure to return more than one value to its caller. This is quite different to other languages which only allow single-value returns. Returning multiple values is different from returning a list (or pair or vector) of values to the caller, because conceptually not *one* compound object is returned, but several distinct values.

The primitive procedures for handling multiple values are `values` and `call-with-values`. `values` is used for returning multiple values from a procedure. This is done by placing a call to `values` with zero or more arguments in tail position in a procedure body. `call-with-values` combines a procedure returning multiple values with a procedure which accepts these values as parameters.

`values` *arg* . . .   [Scheme Procedure]
`scm_values` (*args*)   [C Function]
> Delivers all of its arguments to its continuation. Except for continuations created by the `call-with-values` procedure, all continuations take exactly one value. The effect of passing no value or more than one value to continuations that were not created by `call-with-values` is unspecified.
>
> For `scm_values`, *args* is a list of arguments and the return is a multiple-values object which the caller can return. In the current implementation that object shares structure with *args*, so *args* should not be modified subsequently.

SCM `scm_c_values` (*SCM *base, size_t n*)   [C Function]
> `scm_c_values` is an alternative to `scm_values`. It creates a new values object, and copies into it the *n* values starting from *base*.
>
> Currently this creates a list and passes it to `scm_values`, but we expect that in the future we will be able to use more a efficient representation.

size_t `scm_c_nvalues` (*SCM obj*)   [C Function]
> If *obj* is a multiple-values object, returns the number of values it contains. Otherwise returns 1.

SCM `scm_c_value_ref` (*SCM obj, size_t idx*)   [C Function]
> Returns the value at the position specified by *idx* in *obj*. Note that *obj* will ordinarily be a multiple-values object, but it need not be. Any other object represents a single value (itself), and is handled appropriately.

`call-with-values` *producer consumer*   [Scheme Procedure]
> Calls its *producer* argument with no values and a continuation that, when passed some values, calls the *consumer* procedure with those values as arguments. The continuation for the call to *consumer* is the continuation of the call to `call-with-values`.
>
> ```
> (call-with-values (lambda () (values 4 5))
>                   (lambda (a b) b))
> ⇒ 5
>
>
> (call-with-values * -)
> ⇒ -1
> ```

In addition to the fundamental procedures described above, Guile has a module which exports a syntax called `receive`, which is much more convenient. This is in the `(ice-9 receive)` and is the same as specified by SRFI-8 (see Section 7.5.7 [SRFI-8], page 575).

```
(use-modules (ice-9 receive))
```

receive *formals expr body* ...   [library syntax]
> Evaluate the expression *expr*, and bind the result values (zero or more) to the formal arguments in *formals*. *formals* is a list of symbols, like the argument list in a `lambda` (see Section 6.9.1 [Lambda], page 244). After binding the variables, the expressions in *body* ... are evaluated in order, the return value is the result from the last expression.

> For example getting results from `partition` in SRFI-1 (see Section 7.5.3 [SRFI-1], page 552),

```
(receive (odds evens)
    (partition odd? '(7 4 2 8 3))
  (display odds)
  (display " and ")
  (display evens))
⊣ (7 3) and (4 2 8)
```

6.13.8 Exceptions

A common requirement in applications is to want to jump *non-locally* from the depths of a computation back to, say, the application's main processing loop. Usually, the place that is the target of the jump is somewhere in the calling stack of procedures that called the procedure that wants to jump back. For example, typical logic for a key press driven application might look something like this:

```
main-loop:
  read the next key press and call dispatch-key

dispatch-key:
  lookup the key in a keymap and call an appropriate procedure,
  say find-file

find-file:
  interactively read the required file name, then call
  find-specified-file

find-specified-file:
  check whether file exists; if not, jump back to main-loop
  ...
```

The jump back to `main-loop` could be achieved by returning through the stack one procedure at a time, using the return value of each procedure to indicate the error condition, but Guile (like most modern programming languages) provides an additional mechanism called *exception handling* that can be used to implement such jumps much more conveniently.

6.13.8.1 Exception Terminology

There are several variations on the terminology for dealing with non-local jumps. It is useful to be aware of them, and to realize that they all refer to the same basic mechanism.

- Actually making a non-local jump may be called *raising an exception, raising a signal, throwing an exception* or *doing a long jump.* When the jump indicates an error condition, people may talk about *signalling, raising* or *throwing an error.*

- Handling the jump at its target may be referred to as *catching* or *handling* the *exception, signal* or, where an error condition is involved, *error.*

Where *signal* and *signalling* are used, special care is needed to avoid the risk of confusion with POSIX signals.

This manual prefers to speak of throwing and catching exceptions, since this terminology matches the corresponding Guile primitives.

The exception mechanism described in this section has connections with *delimited continuations* (see Section 6.13.5 [Prompts], page 296). In particular, throwing an exception is akin to invoking an *escape continuation* (see Section 6.13.5.1 [Prompt Primitives], page 296).

6.13.8.2 Catching Exceptions

`catch` is used to set up a target for a possible non-local jump. The arguments of a `catch` expression are a *key*, which restricts the set of exceptions to which this `catch` applies, a thunk that specifies the code to execute and one or two *handler* procedures that say what to do if an exception is thrown while executing the code. If the execution thunk executes *normally*, which means without throwing any exceptions, the handler procedures are not called at all.

When an exception is thrown using the `throw` function, the first argument of the `throw` is a symbol that indicates the type of the exception. For example, Guile throws an exception using the symbol `numerical-overflow` to indicate numerical overflow errors such as division by zero:

```
(/ 1 0)
⇒
ABORT: (numerical-overflow)
```

The *key* argument in a `catch` expression corresponds to this symbol. *key* may be a specific symbol, such as `numerical-overflow`, in which case the `catch` applies specifically to exceptions of that type; or it may be `#t`, which means that the `catch` applies to all exceptions, irrespective of their type.

The second argument of a `catch` expression should be a thunk (i.e. a procedure that accepts no arguments) that specifies the normal case code. The `catch` is active for the execution of this thunk, including any code called directly or indirectly by the thunk's body. Evaluation of the `catch` expression activates the catch and then calls this thunk.

The third argument of a `catch` expression is a handler procedure. If an exception is thrown, this procedure is called with exactly the arguments specified by the `throw`. Therefore, the handler procedure must be designed to accept a number of arguments that corresponds to the number of arguments in all `throw` expressions that can be caught by this `catch`.

The fourth, optional argument of a `catch` expression is another handler procedure, called the *pre-unwind* handler. It differs from the third argument in that if an exception is thrown, it is called, *before* the third argument handler, in exactly the dynamic context of the `throw` expression that threw the exception. This means that it is useful for capturing or displaying the stack at the point of the **throw**, or for examining other aspects of the dynamic context, such as fluid values, before the context is unwound back to that of the prevailing **catch**.

catch *key thunk handler* [*pre-unwind-handler*]   [Scheme Procedure]
scm_catch_with_pre_unwind_handler (*key, thunk, handler,*   [C Function]
        pre_unwind_handler)
scm_catch (*key, thunk, handler*)   [C Function]

    Invoke *thunk* in the dynamic context of *handler* for exceptions matching *key*. If thunk throws to the symbol *key*, then *handler* is invoked this way:

        `(handler key args ...)`

    key is a symbol or **#t**.

    thunk takes no arguments. If *thunk* returns normally, that is the return value of **catch**.

    Handler is invoked outside the scope of its own **catch**. If *handler* again throws to the same key, a new handler from further up the call chain is invoked.

    If the key is **#t**, then a throw to *any* symbol will match this call to **catch**.

    If a *pre-unwind-handler* is given and *thunk* throws an exception that matches *key*, Guile calls the *pre-unwind-handler* before unwinding the dynamic state and invoking the main *handler*. *pre-unwind-handler* should be a procedure with the same signature as *handler*, that is (**lambda (key . args)**). It is typically used to save the stack at the point where the exception occurred, but can also query other parts of the dynamic state at that point, such as fluid values.

    A *pre-unwind-handler* can exit either normally or non-locally. If it exits normally, Guile unwinds the stack and dynamic context and then calls the normal (third argument) handler. If it exits non-locally, that exit determines the continuation.

If a handler procedure needs to match a variety of **throw** expressions with varying numbers of arguments, you should write it like this:

    `(lambda (key . args)`
      `...)`

The *key* argument is guaranteed always to be present, because a **throw** without a *key* is not valid. The number and interpretation of the *args* varies from one type of exception to another, but should be specified by the documentation for each exception type.

Note that, once the normal (post-unwind) handler procedure is invoked, the catch that led to the handler procedure being called is no longer active. Therefore, if the handler procedure itself throws an exception, that exception can only be caught by another active catch higher up the call stack, if there is one.

SCM scm_c_catch (*SCM tag, scm_t_catch_body body, void *body_data,*   [C Function]
      *scm_t_catch_handler handler, void *handler_data, scm_t_catch_handler*
      *pre_unwind_handler, void *pre_unwind_handler_data*)
SCM scm_internal_catch (*SCM tag, scm_t_catch_body body, void*   [C Function]
      **body_data, scm_t_catch_handler handler, void *handler_data*)

    The above **scm_catch_with_pre_unwind_handler** and **scm_catch** take Scheme procedures as body and handler arguments. **scm_c_catch** and **scm_internal_catch** are equivalents taking C functions.

body is called as *body* (*body_data*) with a catch on exceptions of the given *tag* type. If an exception is caught, *pre_unwind_handler* and *handler* are called as `handler` (*handler_data*, *key*, *args*). *key* and *args* are the SCM key and argument list from the `throw`.

body and *handler* should have the following prototypes. `scm_t_catch_body` and `scm_t_catch_handler` are pointer typedefs for these.

```
SCM body (void *data);
SCM handler (void *data, SCM key, SCM args);
```

The *body_data* and *handler_data* parameters are passed to the respective calls so an application can communicate extra information to those functions.

If the data consists of an SCM object, care should be taken that it isn't garbage collected while still required. If the SCM is a local C variable, one way to protect it is to pass a pointer to that variable as the data parameter, since the C compiler will then know the value must be held on the stack. Another way is to use `scm_remember_upto_here_1` (see Section 5.5.5 [Remembering During Operations], page 77).

6.13.8.3 Throw Handlers

It's sometimes useful to be able to intercept an exception that is being thrown before the stack is unwound. This could be to clean up some related state, to print a backtrace, or to pass information about the exception to a debugger, for example. The `with-throw-handler` procedure provides a way to do this.

`with-throw-handler` *key thunk handler*   [Scheme Procedure]
`scm_with_throw_handler` (*key, thunk, handler*)   [C Function]

> Add *handler* to the dynamic context as a throw handler for key *key*, then invoke *thunk*.
>
> This behaves exactly like `catch`, except that it does not unwind the stack before invoking *handler*. If the *handler* procedure returns normally, Guile rethrows the same exception again to the next innermost catch or throw handler. *handler* may exit nonlocally, of course, via an explicit throw or via invoking a continuation.

Typically *handler* is used to display a backtrace of the stack at the point where the corresponding `throw` occurred, or to save off this information for possible display later.

Not unwinding the stack means that throwing an exception that is handled via a throw handler is equivalent to calling the throw handler handler inline instead of each `throw`, and then omitting the surrounding `with-throw-handler`. In other words,

```
(with-throw-handler 'key
  (lambda () ... (throw 'key args ...) ...)
  handler)
```

is mostly equivalent to

```
((lambda () ... (handler 'key args ...) ...))
```

In particular, the dynamic context when *handler* is invoked is that of the site where `throw` is called. The examples are not quite equivalent, because the body of a `with-throw-handler` is not in tail position with respect to the `with-throw-handler`, and if *handler* exits normally, Guile arranges to rethrow the error, but hopefully the intention is clear.

(For an introduction to what is meant by dynamic context, See Section 6.13.10 [Dynamic Wind], page 309.)

SCM **scm_c_with_throw_handler** (*SCM tag, scm_t_catch_body body,*   [C Function]
        void *body_data, scm_t_catch_handler handler, void *handler_data, int
        lazy_catch_p)
    The above `scm_with_throw_handler` takes Scheme procedures as body (thunk) and handler arguments. `scm_c_with_throw_handler` is an equivalent taking C functions. See `scm_c_catch` (see Section 6.13.8.2 [Catch], page 304) for a description of the parameters, the behaviour however of course follows `with-throw-handler`.

If *thunk* throws an exception, Guile handles that exception by invoking the innermost `catch` or throw handler whose key matches that of the exception. When the innermost thing is a throw handler, Guile calls the specified handler procedure using (`apply` *handler* `key args`). The handler procedure may either return normally or exit non-locally. If it returns normally, Guile passes the exception on to the next innermost `catch` or throw handler. If it exits non-locally, that exit determines the continuation.

The behaviour of a throw handler is very similar to that of a `catch` expression's optional pre-unwind handler. In particular, a throw handler's handler procedure is invoked in the exact dynamic context of the `throw` expression, just as a pre-unwind handler is. `with-throw-handler` may be seen as a half-`catch`: it does everything that a `catch` would do until the point where `catch` would start unwinding the stack and dynamic context, but then it rethrows to the next innermost `catch` or throw handler instead.

Note also that since the dynamic context is not unwound, if a `with-throw-handler` handler throws to a key that does not match the `with-throw-handler` expression's *key*, the new throw may be handled by a `catch` or throw handler that is *closer* to the throw than the first `with-throw-handler`.

Here is an example to illustrate this behavior:

```
(catch 'a
  (lambda ()
    (with-throw-handler 'b
      (lambda ()
        (catch 'a
          (lambda ()
            (throw 'b))
          inner-handler))
      (lambda (key . args)
        (throw 'a))))
  outer-handler)
```

This code will call `inner-handler` and then continue with the continuation of the inner `catch`.

6.13.8.4 Throwing Exceptions

The `throw` primitive is used to throw an exception. One argument, the *key*, is mandatory, and must be a symbol; it indicates the type of exception that is being thrown. Following the *key*, `throw` accepts any number of additional arguments, whose meaning depends on the exception type. The documentation for each possible type of exception should specify the additional arguments that are expected for that kind of exception.

throw *key arg* ...   [Scheme Procedure]
scm_throw (*key*, *args*)   [C Function]

> Invoke the catch form matching *key*, passing *arg* ... to the *handler*.
>
> *key* is a symbol. It will match catches of the same symbol or of `#t`.
>
> If there is no handler at all, Guile prints an error and then exits.

When an exception is thrown, it will be caught by the innermost `catch` or throw handler that applies to the type of the thrown exception; in other words, whose *key* is either `#t` or the same symbol as that used in the `throw` expression. Once Guile has identified the appropriate `catch` or throw handler, it handles the exception by applying the relevant handler procedure(s) to the arguments of the `throw`.

If there is no appropriate `catch` or throw handler for a thrown exception, Guile prints an error to the current error port indicating an uncaught exception, and then exits. In practice, it is quite difficult to observe this behaviour, because Guile when used interactively installs a top level `catch` handler that will catch all exceptions and print an appropriate error message *without* exiting. For example, this is what happens if you try to throw an unhandled exception in the standard Guile REPL; note that Guile's command loop continues after the error message:

```
guile> (throw 'badex)
<unnamed port>:3:1: In procedure gsubr-apply ...
<unnamed port>:3:1: unhandled-exception: badex
ABORT: (misc-error)
guile>
```

The default uncaught exception behaviour can be observed by evaluating a `throw` expression from the shell command line:

```
$ guile -c "(begin (throw 'badex) (display \"here\\n\"))"
guile: uncaught throw to badex: ()
$
```

That Guile exits immediately following the uncaught exception is shown by the absence of any output from the `display` expression, because Guile never gets to the point of evaluating that expression.

6.13.8.5 How Guile Implements Exceptions

It is traditional in Scheme to implement exception systems using `call-with-current-continuation`. Continuations (see Section 6.13.6 [Continuations], page 300) are such a powerful concept that any other control mechanism — including `catch` and `throw` — can be implemented in terms of them.

Guile does not implement `catch` and `throw` like this, though. Why not? Because Guile is specifically designed to be easy to integrate with applications written in C. In a mixed Scheme/C environment, the concept of *continuation* must logically include "what happens next" in the C parts of the application as well as the Scheme parts, and it turns out that the only reasonable way of implementing continuations like this is to save and restore the complete C stack.

So Guile's implementation of `call-with-current-continuation` is a stack copying one. This allows it to interact well with ordinary C code, but means that creating and calling a continuation is slowed down by the time that it takes to copy the C stack.

The more targeted mechanism provided by `catch` and `throw` does not need to save and restore the C stack because the `throw` always jumps to a location higher up the stack of the code that executes the `throw`. Therefore Guile implements the `catch` and `throw` primitives independently of `call-with-current-continuation`, in a way that takes advantage of this *upwards only* nature of exceptions.

6.13.9 Procedures for Signaling Errors

Guile provides a set of convenience procedures for signaling error conditions that are implemented on top of the exception primitives just described.

error *msg arg ...*   [Scheme Procedure]
> Raise an error with key `misc-error` and a message constructed by displaying *msg* and writing *arg* ....

scm-error *key subr message args data*   [Scheme Procedure]
scm_error_scm (*key, subr, message, args, data*)   [C Function]
> Raise an error with key *key*. *subr* can be a string naming the procedure associated with the error, or `#f`. *message* is the error message string, possibly containing `~S` and `~A` escapes. When an error is reported, these are replaced by formatting the corresponding members of *args*: `~A` (was `%s` in older versions of Guile) formats using `display` and `~S` (was `%S`) formats using `write`. *data* is a list or `#f` depending on *key*: if *key* is `system-error` then it should be a list containing the Unix `errno` value; If *key* is `signal` then it should be a list containing the Unix signal number; If *key* is `out-of-range`, `wrong-type-arg`, or `keyword-argument-error`, it is a list containing the bad value; otherwise it will usually be `#f`.

strerror *err*   [Scheme Procedure]
scm_strerror (*err*)   [C Function]
> Return the Unix error message corresponding to *err*, an integer `errno` value.
>
> When `setlocale` has been called (see Section 7.2.13 [Locales], page 518), the message is in the language and charset of `LC_MESSAGES`. (This is done by the C library.)

false-if-exception *expr*   [syntax]
> Returns the result of evaluating its argument; however if an exception occurs then `#f` is returned instead.

6.13.10 Dynamic Wind

For Scheme code, the fundamental procedure to react to non-local entry and exits of dynamic contexts is `dynamic-wind`. C code could use `scm_internal_dynamic_wind`, but since C does not allow the convenient construction of anonymous procedures that close over lexical variables, this will be, well, inconvenient.

Therefore, Guile offers the functions `scm_dynwind_begin` and `scm_dynwind_end` to delimit a dynamic extent. Within this dynamic extent, which is called a *dynwind context*, you can perform various *dynwind actions* that control what happens when the dynwind context is entered or left. For example, you can register a cleanup routine with `scm_dynwind_unwind_handler` that is executed when the context is left. There are several other more specialized dynwind actions as well, for example to temporarily block the execution of asyncs or to temporarily change the current output port. They are described elsewhere in this manual.

Here is an example that shows how to prevent memory leaks.

```
/* Suppose there is a function called FOO in some library that you
   would like to make available to Scheme code (or to C code that
   follows the Scheme conventions).

   FOO takes two C strings and returns a new string.  When an error has
   occurred in FOO, it returns NULL.
*/

char *foo (char *s1, char *s2);

/* SCM_FOO interfaces the C function FOO to the Scheme way of life.
   It takes care to free up all temporary strings in the case of
   non-local exits.
 */

SCM
scm_foo (SCM s1, SCM s2)
{
  char *c_s1, *c_s2, *c_res;

  scm_dynwind_begin (0);

  c_s1 = scm_to_locale_string (s1);

  /* Call 'free (c_s1)' when the dynwind context is left.
  */
  scm_dynwind_unwind_handler (free, c_s1, SCM_F_WIND_EXPLICITLY);

  c_s2 = scm_to_locale_string (s2);

  /* Same as above, but more concisely.
  */
  scm_dynwind_free (c_s2);

  c_res = foo (c_s1, c_s2);
  if (c_res == NULL)
    scm_memory_error ("foo");

  scm_dynwind_end ();
```

```
        return scm_take_locale_string (res);
    }
```

dynamic-wind *in_guard thunk out_guard*   [Scheme Procedure]
scm_dynamic_wind (*in_guard, thunk, out_guard*)   [C Function]

All three arguments must be 0-argument procedures. *in_guard* is called, then *thunk*, then *out_guard*.

If, any time during the execution of *thunk*, the dynamic extent of the `dynamic-wind` expression is escaped non-locally, *out_guard* is called. If the dynamic extent of the dynamic-wind is re-entered, *in_guard* is called. Thus *in_guard* and *out_guard* may be called any number of times.

```
        (define x 'normal-binding)
        ⇒ x
        (define a-cont
          (call-with-current-continuation
            (lambda (escape)
              (let ((old-x x))
                (dynamic-wind
                    ;; in-guard:
                    ;;
                    (lambda () (set! x 'special-binding))

                    ;; thunk
                    ;;
                    (lambda () (display x) (newline)
                            (call-with-current-continuation escape)
                            (display x) (newline)
                            x)

                    ;; out-guard:
                    ;;
                    (lambda () (set! x old-x)))))))
      ;; Prints:
      special-binding
      ;; Evaluates to:
      ⇒ a-cont
      x
      ⇒ normal-binding
      (a-cont #f)
      ;; Prints:
      special-binding
      ;; Evaluates to:
      ⇒ a-cont   ;; the value of the (define a-cont...)
      x
      ⇒ normal-binding
      a-cont
```

⇒ `special-binding`

`scm_t_dynwind_flags`   [C Type]

> This is an enumeration of several flags that modify the behavior of `scm_dynwind_begin`. The flags are listed in the following table.

`SCM_F_DYNWIND_REWINDABLE`

> > The dynamic context is *rewindable*. This means that it can be reentered non-locally (via the invocation of a continuation). The default is that a dynwind context can not be reentered non-locally.

`void scm_dynwind_begin` (*scm_t_dynwind_flags flags*)   [C Function]

> The function `scm_dynwind_begin` starts a new dynamic context and makes it the 'current' one.
>
> The *flags* argument determines the default behavior of the context. Normally, use 0. This will result in a context that can not be reentered with a captured continuation. When you are prepared to handle reentries, include `SCM_F_DYNWIND_REWINDABLE` in *flags*.
>
> Being prepared for reentry means that the effects of unwind handlers can be undone on reentry. In the example above, we want to prevent a memory leak on non-local exit and thus register an unwind handler that frees the memory. But once the memory is freed, we can not get it back on reentry. Thus reentry can not be allowed.
>
> The consequence is that continuations become less useful when non-reentrant contexts are captured, but you don't need to worry about that too much.
>
> The context is ended either implicitly when a non-local exit happens, or explicitly with `scm_dynwind_end`. You must make sure that a dynwind context is indeed ended properly. If you fail to call `scm_dynwind_end` for each `scm_dynwind_begin`, the behavior is undefined.

`void scm_dynwind_end ()`   [C Function]

> End the current dynamic context explicitly and make the previous one current.

`scm_t_wind_flags`   [C Type]

> This is an enumeration of several flags that modify the behavior of `scm_dynwind_unwind_handler` and `scm_dynwind_rewind_handler`. The flags are listed in the following table.

`SCM_F_WIND_EXPLICITLY`

> > The registered action is also carried out when the dynwind context is entered or left locally.

`void scm_dynwind_unwind_handler` (*void (*func)(void *), void*   [C Function]
      **data, scm_t_wind_flags flags*)

`void scm_dynwind_unwind_handler_with_scm` (*void (*func)(SCM),*   [C Function]
      SCM data, scm_t_wind_flags flags)

> Arranges for *func* to be called with *data* as its arguments when the current context ends implicitly. If *flags* contains `SCM_F_WIND_EXPLICITLY`, *func* is also called when the context ends explicitly with `scm_dynwind_end`.
>
> The function `scm_dynwind_unwind_handler_with_scm` takes care that *data* is protected from garbage collection.

`void scm_dynwind_rewind_handler` (*void* (**func*)(*void **), *void*   [C Function]
       *data, scm_t_wind_flags flags)
`void scm_dynwind_rewind_handler_with_scm` (*void* (**func*)(*SCM*),   [C Function]
       SCM data, scm_t_wind_flags flags)

> Arrange for *func* to be called with *data* as its argument when the current context
> is restarted by rewinding the stack. When *flags* contains `SCM_F_WIND_EXPLICITLY`,
> *func* is called immediately as well.
>
> The function `scm_dynwind_rewind_handler_with_scm` takes care that *data* is pro-
> tected from garbage collection.

`void scm_dynwind_free` (*void *mem*)   [C Function]

> Arrange for *mem* to be freed automatically whenever the current context is exited,
> whether normally or non-locally. `scm_dynwind_free` (mem) is an equivalent short-
> hand for `scm_dynwind_unwind_handler` (free, mem, SCM_F_WIND_EXPLICITLY).

6.13.11 How to Handle Errors

Error handling is based on `catch` and `throw`. Errors are always thrown with a *key* and four
arguments:

- *key*: a symbol which indicates the type of error. The symbols used by libguile are
  listed below.

- *subr*: the name of the procedure from which the error is thrown, or `#f`.

- *message*: a string (possibly language and system dependent) describing the error. The
  tokens `~A` and `~S` can be embedded within the message: they will be replaced with
  members of the *args* list when the message is printed. `~A` indicates an argument printed
  using `display`, while `~S` indicates an argument printed using `write`. *message* can also
  be `#f`, to allow it to be derived from the *key* by the error handler (may be useful if the
  key is to be thrown from both C and Scheme).

- *args*: a list of arguments to be used to expand `~A` and `~S` tokens in *message*. Can also
  be `#f` if no arguments are required.

- *rest*: a list of any additional objects required. e.g., when the key is `'system-error`,
  this contains the C errno value. Can also be `#f` if no additional objects are required.

In addition to `catch` and `throw`, the following Scheme facilities are available:

`display-error` *frame port subr message args rest*   [Scheme Procedure]
`scm_display_error` (*frame, port, subr, message, args, rest*)   [C Function]

> Display an error message to the output port *port*. *frame* is the frame in which the error
> occurred, *subr* is the name of the procedure in which the error occurred and *message*
> is the actual error message, which may contain formatting instructions. These will
> format the arguments in the list *args* accordingly. *rest* is currently ignored.

The following are the error keys defined by libguile and the situations in which they are
used:

- `error-signal`: thrown after receiving an unhandled fatal signal such as SIGSEGV,
  SIGBUS, SIGFPE etc. The *rest* argument in the throw contains the coded signal
  number (at present this is not the same as the usual Unix signal number).

- `system-error`: thrown after the operating system indicates an error condition. The *rest* argument in the throw contains the errno value.

- `numerical-overflow`: numerical overflow.

- `out-of-range`: the arguments to a procedure do not fall within the accepted domain.

- `wrong-type-arg`: an argument to a procedure has the wrong type.

- `wrong-number-of-args`: a procedure was called with the wrong number of arguments.

- `memory-allocation-error`: memory allocation error.

- `stack-overflow`: stack overflow error.

- `regular-expression-syntax`: errors generated by the regular expression library.

- `misc-error`: other errors.

6.13.11.1 C Support

In the following C functions, *SUBR* and *MESSAGE* parameters can be `NULL` to give the effect of `#f` described above.

SCM **scm_error** (*SCM key, char *subr, char *message, SCM args,*   [C Function]
    SCM rest)

> Throw an error, as per `scm-error` (see Section 6.13.9 [Error Reporting], page 309).

void **scm_syserror** (*char *subr*)   [C Function]
void **scm_syserror_msg** (*char *subr, char *message, SCM args*)   [C Function]

> Throw an error with key `system-error` and supply `errno` in the *rest* argument. For `scm_syserror` the message is generated using `strerror`.

> Care should be taken that any code in between the failing operation and the call to these routines doesn't change `errno`.

void **scm_num_overflow** (*char *subr*)   [C Function]
void **scm_out_of_range** (*char *subr, SCM bad_value*)   [C Function]
void **scm_wrong_num_args** (*SCM proc*)   [C Function]
void **scm_wrong_type_arg** (*char *subr, int argnum, SCM*   [C Function]
    bad_value)
void **scm_wrong_type_arg_msg** (*char *subr, int argnum, SCM*   [C Function]
    bad_value, const char *expected)
void **scm_memory_error** (*char *subr*)   [C Function]
void **scm_misc_error** (*const char *subr, const char *message, SCM*   [C Function]
    args)

> Throw an error with the various keys described above.

> In `scm_wrong_num_args`, *proc* should be a Scheme symbol which is the name of the procedure incorrectly invoked. The other routines take the name of the invoked procedure as a C string.

> In `scm_wrong_type_arg_msg`, *expected* is a C string describing the type of argument that was expected.

> In `scm_misc_error`, *message* is the error message string, possibly containing **simple-format** escapes (see Section 6.14.3 [Writing], page 320), and the corresponding arguments in the *args* list.

6.13.11.2 Signalling Type Errors

Every function visible at the Scheme level should aggressively check the types of its arguments, to avoid misinterpreting a value, and perhaps causing a segmentation fault. Guile provides some macros to make this easier.

void **SCM_ASSERT** (*int* ***test***, *SCM* ***obj***, *unsigned int* ***position***, *const char*   [Macro]
      *subr)
void **SCM_ASSERT_TYPE** (*int* ***test***, *SCM* ***obj***, *unsigned int* ***position***,   [Macro]
      const char ****subr***, *const char* ****expected***)
    If *test* is zero, signal a "wrong type argument" error, attributed to the subroutine
    named *subr*, operating on the value *obj*, which is the *position*'th argument of *subr*.

    In SCM_ASSERT_TYPE, *expected* is a C string describing the type of argument that was
    expected.

int SCM_ARG1   [Macro]
int SCM_ARG2   [Macro]
int SCM_ARG3   [Macro]
int SCM_ARG4   [Macro]
int SCM_ARG5   [Macro]
int SCM_ARG6   [Macro]
int SCM_ARG7   [Macro]
    One of the above values can be used for *position* to indicate the number of the
    argument of *subr* which is being checked. Alternatively, a positive integer number can
    be used, which allows to check arguments after the seventh. However, for parameter
    numbers up to seven it is preferable to use SCM_ARGN instead of the corresponding
    raw number, since it will make the code easier to understand.

int SCM_ARGn   [Macro]
    Passing a value of zero or SCM_ARGn for *position* allows to leave it unspecified which
    argument's type is incorrect. Again, SCM_ARGn should be preferred over a raw zero
    constant.

6.13.12 Continuation Barriers

The non-local flow of control caused by continuations might sometimes not be wanted. You can use with-continuation-barrier to erect fences that continuations can not pass.

with-continuation-barrier *proc*   [Scheme Procedure]
scm_with_continuation_barrier (*proc*)   [C Function]
    Call *proc* and return its result. Do not allow the invocation of continuations that
    would leave or enter the dynamic extent of the call to with-continuation-barrier.
    Such an attempt causes an error to be signaled.

    Throws (such as errors) that are not caught from within *proc* are caught by with-
    continuation-barrier. In that case, a short message is printed to the current error
    port and #f is returned.

    Thus, with-continuation-barrier returns exactly once.

`void * scm_c_with_continuation_barrier` (*void *(*func)* (*void*   [C Function]
        *), void *data)
> Like `scm_with_continuation_barrier` but call *func* on *data*. When an error is
> caught, `NULL` is returned.

6.14 Input and Output

6.14.1 Ports

Sequential input/output in Scheme is represented by operations on a *port*. This chapter
explains the operations that Guile provides for working with ports.

Ports are created by opening, for instance `open-file` for a file (see Section 6.14.9.1 [File
Ports], page 326). Characters can be read from an input port and written to an output
port, or both on an input/output port. A port can be closed (see Section 6.14.4 [Closing],
page 321) when no longer required, after which any attempt to read or write is an error.

The formal definition of a port is very generic: an input port is simply "an object which
can deliver characters on demand," and an output port is "an object which can accept
characters." Because this definition is so loose, it is easy to write functions that simulate
ports in software. *Soft ports* and *string ports* are two interesting and powerful examples
of this technique. (see Section 6.14.9.3 [Soft Ports], page 331, and Section 6.14.9.2 [String
Ports], page 329.)

Ports are garbage collected in the usual way (see Section 6.18 [Memory Management],
page 374), and will be closed at that time if not already closed. In this case any errors
occurring in the close will not be reported. Usually a program will want to explicitly
close so as to be sure all its operations have been successful. Of course if a program has
abandoned something due to an error or other condition then closing problems are probably
not of interest.

It is strongly recommended that file ports be closed explicitly when no longer required.
Most systems have limits on how many files can be open, both on a per-process and a
system-wide basis. A program that uses many files should take care not to hit those limits.
The same applies to similar system resources such as pipes and sockets.

Note that automatic garbage collection is triggered only by memory consumption, not
by file or other resource usage, so a program cannot rely on that to keep it away from system
limits. An explicit call to `gc` can of course be relied on to pick up unreferenced ports. If
program flow makes it hard to be certain when to close then this may be an acceptable way
to control resource usage.

All file access uses the "LFS" large file support functions when available, so files bigger
than 2 Gbytes (2^31 bytes) can be read and written on a 32-bit system.

Each port has an associated character encoding that controls how bytes read from the
port are converted to characters and string and controls how characters and strings written
to the port are converted to bytes. When ports are created, they inherit their character
encoding from the current locale, but, that can be modified after the port is created.

Currently, the ports only work with *non-modal* encodings. Most encodings are non-
modal, meaning that the conversion of bytes to a string doesn't depend on its context: the
same byte sequence will always return the same string. A couple of modal encodings are in
common use, like ISO-2022-JP and ISO-2022-KR, and they are not yet supported.

Each port also has an associated conversion strategy: what to do when a Guile character can't be converted to the port's encoded character representation for output. There are three possible strategies: to raise an error, to replace the character with a hex escape, or to replace the character with a substitute character.

input-port? *x*   [Scheme Procedure]
scm_input_port_p (*x*)   [C Function]
    Return #t if *x* is an input port, otherwise return #f. Any object satisfying this predicate also satisfies **port?**.

output-port? *x*   [Scheme Procedure]
scm_output_port_p (*x*)   [C Function]
    Return #t if *x* is an output port, otherwise return #f. Any object satisfying this predicate also satisfies **port?**.

port? *x*   [Scheme Procedure]
scm_port_p (*x*)   [C Function]
    Return a boolean indicating whether *x* is a port. Equivalent to (or (input-port? *x*) (output-port? *x*)).

set-port-encoding! *port enc*   [Scheme Procedure]
scm_set_port_encoding_x (*port, enc*)   [C Function]
    Sets the character encoding that will be used to interpret all port I/O. *enc* is a string containing the name of an encoding. Valid encoding names are those defined by IANA.

%default-port-encoding   [Scheme Variable]
    A fluid containing #f or the name of the encoding to be used by default for newly created ports (see Section 6.21.7 [Fluids and Dynamic States], page 419). The value #f is equivalent to "ISO-8859-1".

    New ports are created with the encoding appropriate for the current locale if **setlocale** has been called or the value specified by this fluid otherwise.

port-encoding *port*   [Scheme Procedure]
scm_port_encoding (*port*)   [C Function]
    Returns, as a string, the character encoding that *port* uses to interpret its input and output. The value #f is equivalent to "ISO-8859-1".

set-port-conversion-strategy! *port sym*   [Scheme Procedure]
scm_set_port_conversion_strategy_x (*port, sym*)   [C Function]
    Sets the behavior of the interpreter when outputting a character that is not representable in the port's current encoding. *sym* can be either 'error, 'substitute, or 'escape. If it is 'error, an error will be thrown when an nonconvertible character is encountered. If it is 'substitute, then nonconvertible characters will be replaced with approximate characters, or with question marks if no approximately correct character is available. If it is 'escape, it will appear as a hex escape when output.

    If *port* is an open port, the conversion error behavior is set for that port. If it is #f, it is set as the default behavior for any future ports that get created in this thread.

`port-conversion-strategy` *port* [Scheme Procedure]

`scm_port_conversion_strategy` (*port*) [C Function]

Returns the behavior of the port when outputting a character that is not representable in the port's current encoding. It returns the symbol `error` if unrepresentable characters should cause exceptions, `substitute` if the port should try to replace unrepresentable characters with question marks or approximate characters, or `escape` if unrepresentable characters should be converted to string escapes.

If *port* is `#f`, then the current default behavior will be returned. New ports will have this default behavior when they are created.

`%default-port-conversion-strategy` [Scheme Variable]

The fluid that defines the conversion strategy for newly created ports, and for other conversion routines such as `scm_to_stringn`, `scm_from_stringn`, `string->pointer`, and `pointer->string`.

Its value must be one of the symbols described above, with the same semantics: `'error`, `'substitute`, or `'escape`.

When Guile starts, its value is `'substitute`.

Note that (`set-port-conversion-strategy!` `#f` *sym*) is equivalent to (`fluid-set!` `%default-port-conversion-strategy` *sym*).

6.14.2 Reading

[Generic procedures for reading from ports.]

These procedures pertain to reading characters and strings from ports. To read general S-expressions from ports, See Section 6.17.2 [Scheme Read], page 360.

`eof-object?` *x* [Scheme Procedure]

`scm_eof_object_p` (*x*) [C Function]

Return `#t` if *x* is an end-of-file object; otherwise return `#f`.

`char-ready?` [*port*] [Scheme Procedure]

`scm_char_ready_p` (*port*) [C Function]

Return `#t` if a character is ready on input *port* and return `#f` otherwise. If `char-ready?` returns `#t` then the next `read-char` operation on *port* is guaranteed not to hang. If *port* is a file port at end of file then `char-ready?` returns `#t`.

`char-ready?` exists to make it possible for a program to accept characters from interactive ports without getting stuck waiting for input. Any input editors associated with such ports must make sure that characters whose existence has been asserted by `char-ready?` cannot be rubbed out. If `char-ready?` were to return `#f` at end of file, a port at end of file would be indistinguishable from an interactive port that has no ready characters.

`read-char` [*port*] [Scheme Procedure]

`scm_read_char` (*port*) [C Function]

Return the next character available from *port*, updating *port* to point to the following character. If no more characters are available, the end-of-file object is returned.

When *port*'s data cannot be decoded according to its character encoding, a `decoding-error` is raised and *port* points past the erroneous byte sequence.

`size_t scm_c_read` (*SCM port, void *buffer, size_t size*)   [C Function]
>   Read up to *size* bytes from *port* and store them in *buffer*. The return value is the
>   number of bytes actually read, which can be less than *size* if end-of-file has been
>   reached.
>
>   Note that this function does not update `port-line` and `port-column` below.

`peek-char` [*port*]   [Scheme Procedure]
`scm_peek_char` (*port*)   [C Function]
>   Return the next character available from *port*, *without* updating *port* to point to
>   the following character. If no more characters are available, the end-of-file object is
>   returned.
>
>   The value returned by a call to `peek-char` is the same as the value that would have
>   been returned by a call to `read-char` on the same port. The only difference is that
>   the very next call to `read-char` or `peek-char` on that *port* will return the value
>   returned by the preceding call to `peek-char`. In particular, a call to `peek-char` on
>   an interactive port will hang waiting for input whenever a call to `read-char` would
>   have hung.
>
>   As for `read-char`, a `decoding-error` may be raised if such a situation occurs. How-
>   ever, unlike with `read-char`, *port* still points at the beginning of the erroneous byte
>   sequence when the error is raised.

`unread-char` *cobj* [*port*]   [Scheme Procedure]
`scm_unread_char` (*cobj, port*)   [C Function]
>   Place character *cobj* in *port* so that it will be read by the next read operation. If
>   called multiple times, the unread characters will be read again in last-in first-out
>   order. If *port* is not supplied, the current input port is used.

`unread-string` *str port*   [Scheme Procedure]
`scm_unread_string` (*str, port*)   [C Function]
>   Place the string *str* in *port* so that its characters will be read from left-to-right as
>   the next characters from *port* during subsequent read operations. If called multiple
>   times, the unread characters will be read again in last-in first-out order. If *port* is
>   not supplied, the `current-input-port` is used.

`drain-input` *port*   [Scheme Procedure]
`scm_drain_input` (*port*)   [C Function]
>   This procedure clears a port's input buffers, similar to the way that force-output
>   clears the output buffer. The contents of the buffers are returned as a single string,
>   e.g.,
>
>    ```
>    (define p (open-input-file ...))
>    (drain-input p) => empty string, nothing buffered yet.
>    (unread-char (read-char p) p)
>    (drain-input p) => initial chars from p, up to the buffer size.
>    ```
>
>   Draining the buffers may be useful for cleanly finishing buffered I/O so that the file
>   descriptor can be used directly for further input.

`port-column` *port*   [Scheme Procedure]
`port-line` *port*   [Scheme Procedure]

`scm_port_column` (*port*)   [C Function]
`scm_port_line` (*port*)   [C Function]
>   Return the current column number or line number of *port*. If the number is unknown,
>   the result is #f. Otherwise, the result is a 0-origin integer - i.e. the first character
>   of the first line is line 0, column 0. (However, when you display a file position, for
>   example in an error message, we recommend you add 1 to get 1-origin integers. This
>   is because lines and column numbers traditionally start with 1, and that is what
>   non-programmers will find most natural.)

`set-port-column!` *port column*   [Scheme Procedure]
`set-port-line!` *port line*   [Scheme Procedure]
`scm_set_port_column_x` (*port, column*)   [C Function]
`scm_set_port_line_x` (*port, line*)   [C Function]
>   Set the current column or line number of *port*.

6.14.3 Writing

[Generic procedures for writing to ports.]

These procedures are for writing characters and strings to ports. For more information
on writing arbitrary Scheme objects to ports, See Section 6.17.3 [Scheme Write], page 361.

`get-print-state` *port*   [Scheme Procedure]
`scm_get_print_state` (*port*)   [C Function]
>   Return the print state of the port *port*. If *port* has no associated print state, #f is
>   returned.

`newline` [*port*]   [Scheme Procedure]
`scm_newline` (*port*)   [C Function]
>   Send a newline to *port*. If *port* is omitted, send to the current output port.

`port-with-print-state` *port* [*pstate*]   [Scheme Procedure]
`scm_port_with_print_state` (*port, pstate*)   [C Function]
>   Create a new port which behaves like *port*, but with an included print state *pstate*.
>   *pstate* is optional. If *pstate* isn't supplied and *port* already has a print state, the old
>   print state is reused.

`simple-format` *destination message . args*   [Scheme Procedure]
`scm_simple_format` (*destination, message, args*)   [C Function]
>   Write *message* to *destination*, defaulting to the current output port. *message* can
>   contain ~A (was %s) and ~S (was %S) escapes. When printed, the escapes are replaced
>   with corresponding members of *args*: ~A formats using `display` and ~S formats using
>   `write`. If *destination* is #t, then use the current output port, if *destination* is #f,
>   then return a string containing the formatted text. Does not add a trailing newline.

`write-char` *chr* [*port*]   [Scheme Procedure]
`scm_write_char` (*chr, port*)   [C Function]
>   Send character *chr* to *port*.

`void scm_c_write` (*SCM port, const void *buffer, size_t size*)   [C Function]
>   Write *size* bytes at *buffer* to *port*.

Note that this function does not update `port-line` and `port-column` (see Section 6.14.2 [Reading], page 318).

`force-output` [*port*]   [Scheme Procedure]
`scm_force_output` (*port*)   [C Function]
> Flush the specified output port, or the current output port if *port* is omitted. The current output buffer contents are passed to the underlying port implementation (e.g., in the case of fports, the data will be written to the file and the output buffer will be cleared.) It has no effect on an unbuffered port.
>
> The return value is unspecified.

`flush-all-ports`   [Scheme Procedure]
`scm_flush_all_ports` ()   [C Function]
> Equivalent to calling `force-output` on all open output ports. The return value is unspecified.

6.14.4 Closing

`close-port` *port*   [Scheme Procedure]
`scm_close_port` (*port*)   [C Function]
> Close the specified port object. Return `#t` if it successfully closes a port or `#f` if it was already closed. An exception may be raised if an error occurs, for example when flushing buffered output. See also Section 7.2.2 [Ports and File Descriptors], page 469, for a procedure which can close file descriptors.

`close-input-port` *port*   [Scheme Procedure]
`close-output-port` *port*   [Scheme Procedure]
`scm_close_input_port` (*port*)   [C Function]
`scm_close_output_port` (*port*)   [C Function]
> Close the specified input or output *port*. An exception may be raised if an error occurs while closing. If *port* is already closed, nothing is done. The return value is unspecified.
>
> See also Section 7.2.2 [Ports and File Descriptors], page 469, for a procedure which can close file descriptors.

`port-closed?` *port*   [Scheme Procedure]
`scm_port_closed_p` (*port*)   [C Function]
> Return `#t` if *port* is closed or `#f` if it is open.

6.14.5 Random Access

`seek` *fd_port offset whence*   [Scheme Procedure]
`scm_seek` (*fd_port, offset, whence*)   [C Function]
> Sets the current position of *fd_port* to the integer *offset*, which is interpreted according to the value of *whence*.
>
> One of the following variables should be supplied for *whence*:

`SEEK_SET`   [Variable]
> Seek from the beginning of the file.

SEEK_CUR   [Variable]
> Seek from the current position.

SEEK_END   [Variable]
> Seek from the end of the file.

If *fd_port* is a file descriptor, the underlying system call is `lseek`. *port* may be a string port.

The value returned is the new position in the file. This means that the current position of a port can be obtained using:

```
(seek port 0 SEEK_CUR)
```

ftell *fd_port*   [Scheme Procedure]
scm_ftell (*fd_port*)   [C Function]
> Return an integer representing the current position of *fd_port*, measured from the beginning. Equivalent to:
>
> ```
> (seek port 0 SEEK_CUR)
> ```

truncate-file *file* [*length*]   [Scheme Procedure]
scm_truncate_file (*file, length*)   [C Function]
> Truncate *file* to *length* bytes. *file* can be a filename string, a port object, or an integer file descriptor. The return value is unspecified.
>
> For a port or file descriptor *length* can be omitted, in which case the file is truncated at the current position (per `ftell` above).
>
> On most systems a file can be extended by giving a length greater than the current size, but this is not mandatory in the POSIX standard.

6.14.6 Line Oriented and Delimited Text

The delimited-I/O module can be accessed with:

```
(use-modules (ice-9 rdelim))
```

It can be used to read or write lines of text, or read text delimited by a specified set of characters. It's similar to the (`scsh rdelim`) module from guile-scsh, but does not use multiple values or character sets and has an extra procedure `write-line`.

read-line [*port*] [*handle-delim*]   [Scheme Procedure]
> Return a line of text from *port* if specified, otherwise from the value returned by (`current-input-port`). Under Unix, a line of text is terminated by the first end-of-line character or by end-of-file.
>
> If *handle-delim* is specified, it should be one of the following symbols:
>
> trim   Discard the terminating delimiter. This is the default, but it will be impossible to tell whether the read terminated with a delimiter or end-of-file.
>
> concat   Append the terminating delimiter (if any) to the returned string.
>
> peek   Push the terminating delimiter (if any) back on to the port.

split   Return a pair containing the string read from the port and the terminating
         delimiter or end-of-file object.

Like **read-char**, this procedure can throw to **decoding-error** (see Section 6.14.2
[Reading], page 318).

read-line! *buf* [*port*]   [Scheme Procedure]
    Read a line of text into the supplied string *buf* and return the number of characters
    added to *buf*. If *buf* is filled, then **#f** is returned. Read from *port* if specified,
    otherwise from the value returned by (**current-input-port**).

read-delimited *delims* [*port*] [*handle-delim*]   [Scheme Procedure]
    Read text until one of the characters in the string *delims* is found or end-of-file is
    reached. Read from *port* if supplied, otherwise from the value returned by (**current-
    input-port**). *handle-delim* takes the same values as described for **read-line**.

read-delimited! *delims buf* [*port*] [*handle-delim*] [*start*] [*end*]   [Scheme Procedure]
    Read text into the supplied string *buf*.

    If a delimiter was found, return the number of characters written, except if *handle-
    delim* is **split**, in which case the return value is a pair, as noted above.

    As a special case, if *port* was already at end-of-stream, the EOF object is returned.
    Also, if no characters were written because the buffer was full, **#f** is returned.

    It's something of a wacky interface, to be honest.

write-line *obj* [*port*]   [Scheme Procedure]
scm_write_line (*obj, port*)   [C Function]
    Display *obj* and a newline character to *port*. If *port* is not specified, (**current-
    output-port**) is used. This function is equivalent to:

```
(display obj [port])
(newline [port])
```

In the past, Guile did not have a procedure that would just read out all of the characters
from a port. As a workaround, many people just called **read-delimited** with no delimiters,
knowing that would produce the behavior they wanted. This prompted Guile developers to
add some routines that would read all characters from a port. So it is that (**ice-9 rdelim**)
is also the home for procedures that can reading undelimited text:

read-string [*port*] [*count*]   [Scheme Procedure]
    Read all of the characters out of *port* and return them as a string. If the *count* is
    present, treat it as a limit to the number of characters to read.

    By default, read from the current input port, with no size limit on the result. This
    procedure always returns a string, even if no characters were read.

read-string! *buf* [*port*] [*start*] [*end*]   [Scheme Procedure]
    Fill *buf* with characters read from *port*, defaulting to the current input port. Return
    the number of characters read.

    If *start* or *end* are specified, store data only into the substring of *str* bounded by *start*
    and *end* (which default to the beginning and end of the string, respectively).

Some of the aforementioned I/O functions rely on the following C primitives. These will mainly be of interest to people hacking Guile internals.

%read-delimited! *delims str gobble* [*port* [*start* [*end*]]]   [Scheme Procedure]
scm_read_delimited_x (*delims, str, gobble, port, start, end*)   [C Function]
> Read characters from *port* into *str* until one of the characters in the *delims* string is encountered. If *gobble* is true, discard the delimiter character; otherwise, leave it in the input stream for the next read. If *port* is not specified, use the value of (current-input-port). If *start* or *end* are specified, store data only into the substring of *str* bounded by *start* and *end* (which default to the beginning and end of the string, respectively).

> Return a pair consisting of the delimiter that terminated the string and the number of characters read. If reading stopped at the end of file, the delimiter returned is the *eof-object*; if the string was filled without encountering a delimiter, this value is #f.

%read-line [*port*]   [Scheme Procedure]
scm_read_line (*port*)   [C Function]
> Read a newline-terminated line from *port*, allocating storage as necessary. The new-line terminator (if any) is removed from the string, and a pair consisting of the line and its delimiter is returned. The delimiter may be either a newline or the *eof-object*; if %read-line is called at the end of file, it returns the pair (#<eof> . #<eof>).

6.14.7 Block reading and writing

The Block-string-I/O module can be accessed with:

```
(use-modules (ice-9 rw))
```

It currently contains procedures that help to implement the (scsh rw) module in guile-scsh.

read-string!/partial *str* [*port_or_fdes* [*start* [*end*]]]   [Scheme Procedure]
scm_read_string_x_partial (*str, port_or_fdes, start, end*)   [C Function]
> Read characters from a port or file descriptor into a string *str*. A port must have an underlying file descriptor — a so-called fport. This procedure is scsh-compatible and can efficiently read large strings. It will:

> - attempt to fill the entire string, unless the *start* and/or *end* arguments are supplied. i.e., *start* defaults to 0 and *end* defaults to (string-length str)
> - use the current input port if *port_or_fdes* is not supplied.
> - return fewer than the requested number of characters in some cases, e.g., on end of file, if interrupted by a signal, or if not all the characters are immediately available.
> - wait indefinitely for some input if no characters are currently available, unless the port is in non-blocking mode.
> - read characters from the port's input buffers if available, instead from the underlying file descriptor.
> - return #f if end-of-file is encountered before reading any characters, otherwise return the number of characters read.

- return 0 if the port is in non-blocking mode and no characters are immediately available.

- return 0 if the request is for 0 bytes, with no end-of-file check.

write-string/partial *str* [*port_or_fdes* [*start* [*end*]]]   [Scheme Procedure]
scm_write_string_partial (*str*, *port_or_fdes*, *start*, *end*)   [C Function]
    Write characters from a string *str* to a port or file descriptor. A port must have an underlying file descriptor — a so-called fport. This procedure is scsh-compatible and can efficiently write large strings. It will:

- attempt to write the entire string, unless the *start* and/or *end* arguments are supplied. i.e., *start* defaults to 0 and *end* defaults to (`string-length str`)

- use the current output port if *port_of_fdes* is not supplied.

- in the case of a buffered port, store the characters in the port's output buffer, if all will fit. If they will not fit then any existing buffered characters will be flushed before attempting to write the new characters directly to the underlying file descriptor. If the port is in non-blocking mode and buffered characters can not be flushed immediately, then an `EAGAIN` system-error exception will be raised (Note: scsh does not support the use of non-blocking buffered ports.)

- write fewer than the requested number of characters in some cases, e.g., if interrupted by a signal or if not all of the output can be accepted immediately.

- wait indefinitely for at least one character from *str* to be accepted by the port, unless the port is in non-blocking mode.

- return the number of characters accepted by the port.

- return 0 if the port is in non-blocking mode and can not accept at least one character from *str* immediately

- return 0 immediately if the request size is 0 bytes.

6.14.8 Default Ports for Input, Output and Errors

current-input-port   [Scheme Procedure]
scm_current_input_port ()   [C Function]
    Return the current input port. This is the default port used by many input procedures.

    Initially this is the *standard input* in Unix and C terminology. When the standard input is a tty the port is unbuffered, otherwise it's fully buffered.

    Unbuffered input is good if an application runs an interactive subprocess, since any type-ahead input won't go into Guile's buffer and be unavailable to the subprocess.

    Note that Guile buffering is completely separate from the tty "line discipline". In the usual cooked mode on a tty Guile only sees a line of input once the user presses `Return`.

current-output-port   [Scheme Procedure]
scm_current_output_port ()   [C Function]
    Return the current output port. This is the default port used by many output procedures.

Initially this is the *standard output* in Unix and C terminology. When the standard output is a tty this port is unbuffered, otherwise it's fully buffered.

Unbuffered output to a tty is good for ensuring progress output or a prompt is seen. But an application which always prints whole lines could change to line buffered, or an application with a lot of output could go fully buffered and perhaps make explicit `force-output` calls (see Section 6.14.3 [Writing], page 320) at selected points.

`current-error-port`   [Scheme Procedure]
`scm_current_error_port ()`   [C Function]
> Return the port to which errors and warnings should be sent.
>
> Initially this is the *standard error* in Unix and C terminology. When the standard error is a tty this port is unbuffered, otherwise it's fully buffered.

`set-current-input-port` *port*   [Scheme Procedure]
`set-current-output-port` *port*   [Scheme Procedure]
`set-current-error-port` *port*   [Scheme Procedure]
`scm_set_current_input_port` (*port*)   [C Function]
`scm_set_current_output_port` (*port*)   [C Function]
`scm_set_current_error_port` (*port*)   [C Function]
> Change the ports returned by `current-input-port`, `current-output-port` and `current-error-port`, respectively, so that they use the supplied *port* for input or output.

`void scm_dynwind_current_input_port` (*SCM port*)   [C Function]
`void scm_dynwind_current_output_port` (*SCM port*)   [C Function]
`void scm_dynwind_current_error_port` (*SCM port*)   [C Function]
> These functions must be used inside a pair of calls to `scm_dynwind_begin` and `scm_dynwind_end` (see Section 6.13.10 [Dynamic Wind], page 309). During the dynwind context, the indicated port is set to *port*.
>
> More precisely, the current port is swapped with a 'backup' value whenever the dynwind context is entered or left. The backup value is initialized with the *port* argument.

6.14.9 Types of Port

[Types of port; how to make them.]

6.14.9.1 File Ports

The following procedures are used to open file ports. See also Section 7.2.2 [Ports and File Descriptors], page 469, for an interface to the Unix `open` system call.

Most systems have limits on how many files can be open, so it's strongly recommended that file ports be closed explicitly when no longer required (see Section 6.14.1 [Ports], page 316).

`open-file` *filename mode* [*#:guess-encoding=#f*]   [Scheme Procedure]
    [*#:encoding=#f*]
`scm_open_file_with_encoding` (*filename, mode, guess_encoding,*   [C Function]
    encoding)

scm_open_file (*filename, mode*)   [C Function]

Open the file whose name is *filename*, and return a port representing that file. The attributes of the port are determined by the *mode* string. The way in which this is interpreted is similar to C stdio. The first character must be one of the following:

'r'   Open an existing file for input.

'w'   Open a file for output, creating it if it doesn't already exist or removing its contents if it does.

'a'   Open a file for output, creating it if it doesn't already exist. All writes to the port will go to the end of the file. The "append mode" can be turned off while the port is in use see Section 7.2.2 [Ports and File Descriptors], page 469

The following additional characters can be appended:

'+'   Open the port for both input and output. E.g., **r+**: open an existing file for both input and output.

'0'   Create an "unbuffered" port. In this case input and output operations are passed directly to the underlying port implementation without additional buffering. This is likely to slow down I/O operations. The buffering mode can be changed while a port is in use see Section 7.2.2 [Ports and File Descriptors], page 469

'l'   Add line-buffering to the port. The port output buffer will be automatically flushed whenever a newline character is written.

'b'   Use binary mode, ensuring that each byte in the file will be read as one Scheme character.

                To provide this property, the file will be opened with the 8-bit character encoding "ISO-8859-1", ignoring the default port encoding. See Section 6.14.1 [Ports], page 316, for more information on port encodings.

                Note that while it is possible to read and write binary data as characters or strings, it is usually better to treat bytes as octets, and byte sequences as bytevectors. See Section 6.14.10.8 [R6RS Binary Input], page 339, and Section 6.14.10.11 [R6RS Binary Output], page 344, for more.

                This option had another historical meaning, for DOS compatibility: in the default (textual) mode, DOS reads a CR-LF sequence as one LF byte. The **b** flag prevents this from happening, adding **O_BINARY** to the underlying **open** call. Still, the flag is generally useful because of its port encoding ramifications.

Unless binary mode is requested, the character encoding of the new port is determined as follows: First, if *guess-encoding* is true, the **file-encoding** procedure is used to guess the encoding of the file (see Section 6.17.8 [Character Encoding of Source Files], page 370). If *guess-encoding* is false or if **file-encoding** fails, *encoding* is used unless it is also false. As a last resort, the default port encoding is used. See Section 6.14.1 [Ports], page 316, for more information on port encodings. It is an error to pass a non-false *guess-encoding* or *encoding* if binary mode is requested.

If a file cannot be opened with the access requested, `open-file` throws an exception.

When the file is opened, its encoding is set to the current `%default-port-encoding`, unless the b flag was supplied. Sometimes it is desirable to honor Emacs-style coding declarations in files[9]. When that is the case, the `file-encoding` procedure can be used as follows (see Section 6.17.8 [Character Encoding of Source Files], page 370):

```
(let* ((port     (open-input-file file))
       (encoding (file-encoding port)))
    (set-port-encoding! port (or encoding (port-encoding port))))
```

In theory we could create read/write ports which were buffered in one direction only. However this isn't included in the current interfaces.

`open-input-file` *filename* [*#:guess-encoding=#f*]   [Scheme Procedure]
          [*#:encoding=#f*] [*#:binary=#f*]
> Open *filename* for input. If *binary* is true, open the port in binary mode, otherwise use text mode. *encoding* and *guess-encoding* determine the character encoding as described above for `open-file`. Equivalent to
>
> ```
> (open-file filename
>            (if binary "rb" "r")
>            #:guess-encoding guess-encoding
>            #:encoding encoding)
> ```

`open-output-file` *filename* [*#:encoding=#f*] [*#:binary=#f*]   [Scheme Procedure]
> Open *filename* for output. If *binary* is true, open the port in binary mode, otherwise use text mode. *encoding* specifies the character encoding as described above for `open-file`. Equivalent to
>
> ```
> (open-file filename
>            (if binary "wb" "w")
>            #:encoding encoding)
> ```

`call-with-input-file` *filename proc* [*#:guess-encoding=#f*]   [Scheme Procedure]
          [*#:encoding=#f*] [*#:binary=#f*]
`call-with-output-file` *filename proc* [*#:encoding=#f*]   [Scheme Procedure]
          [*#:binary=#f*]
> Open *filename* for input or output, and call (*proc* port) with the resulting port. Return the value returned by *proc*. *filename* is opened as per `open-input-file` or `open-output-file` respectively, and an error is signaled if it cannot be opened.
>
> When *proc* returns, the port is closed. If *proc* does not return (e.g. if it throws an error), then the port might not be closed automatically, though it will be garbage collected in the usual way if not otherwise referenced.

`with-input-from-file` *filename thunk* [*#:guess-encoding=#f*]   [Scheme Procedure]
          [*#:encoding=#f*] [*#:binary=#f*]
`with-output-to-file` *filename thunk* [*#:encoding=#f*]   [Scheme Procedure]
          [*#:binary=#f*]

---

[9] Guile 2.0.0 to 2.0.7 would do this by default. This behavior was deemed inappropriate and disabled starting from Guile 2.0.8.

with-error-to-file *filename thunk* [#:encoding=#f]   [Scheme Procedure]
      [#:binary=#f]
    Open *filename* and call (`thunk`) with the new port setup as respectively the `current-`
    `input-port`, `current-output-port`, or `current-error-port`. Return the value re-
    turned by *thunk*. *filename* is opened as per `open-input-file` or `open-output-file`
    respectively, and an error is signaled if it cannot be opened.

    When *thunk* returns, the port is closed and the previous setting of the respective
    current port is restored.

    The current port setting is managed with `dynamic-wind`, so the previous value is
    restored no matter how *thunk* exits (eg. an exception), and if *thunk* is re-entered (via
    a captured continuation) then it's set again to the *filename* port.

    The port is closed when *thunk* returns normally, but not when exited via an exception
    or new continuation. This ensures it's still ready for use if *thunk* is re-entered by a
    captured continuation. Of course the port is always garbage collected and closed in
    the usual way when no longer referenced anywhere.

port-mode *port*   [Scheme Procedure]
scm_port_mode (*port*)   [C Function]
    Return the port modes associated with the open port *port*. These will not necessar-
    ily be identical to the modes used when the port was opened, since modes such as
    "append" which are used only during port creation are not retained.

port-filename *port*   [Scheme Procedure]
scm_port_filename (*port*)   [C Function]
    Return the filename associated with *port*, or #f if no filename is associated with the
    port.

    port must be open, `port-filename` cannot be used once the port is closed.

set-port-filename! *port filename*   [Scheme Procedure]
scm_set_port_filename_x (*port, filename*)   [C Function]
    Change the filename associated with *port*, using the current input port if none is
    specified. Note that this does not change the port's source of data, but only the value
    that is returned by `port-filename` and reported in diagnostic output.

file-port? *obj*   [Scheme Procedure]
scm_file_port_p (*obj*)   [C Function]
    Determine whether *obj* is a port that is related to a file.

6.14.9.2 String Ports

The following allow string ports to be opened by analogy to R4RS file port facilities:

    With string ports, the port-encoding is treated differently than other types of ports.
When string ports are created, they do not inherit a character encoding from the current
locale. They are given a default locale that allows them to handle all valid string characters.
Typically one should not modify a string port's character encoding away from its default.

call-with-output-string *proc*   [Scheme Procedure]
scm_call_with_output_string (*proc*)   [C Function]

> Calls the one-argument procedure *proc* with a newly created output port. When the function returns, the string composed of the characters written into the port is returned. *proc* should not close the port.
>
> Note that which characters can be written to a string port depend on the port's encoding. The default encoding of string ports is specified by the `%default-port-encoding` fluid (see Section 6.14.1 [Ports], page 316). For instance, it is an error to write Greek letter alpha to an ISO-8859-1-encoded string port since this character cannot be represented with ISO-8859-1:
>
> ```
> (define alpha (integer->char #x03b1)) ; GREEK SMALL LETTER ALPHA
>
>
> (with-fluids ((%default-port-encoding "ISO-8859-1"))
>   (call-with-output-string
>     (lambda (p)
>       (display alpha p))))
>
>
> ⇒
> Throw to key 'encoding-error'
> ```
>
> Changing the string port's encoding to a Unicode-capable encoding such as UTF-8 solves the problem.

call-with-input-string *string proc*   [Scheme Procedure]
scm_call_with_input_string (*string, proc*)   [C Function]

> Calls the one-argument procedure *proc* with a newly created input port from which *string*'s contents may be read. The value yielded by the *proc* is returned.

with-output-to-string *thunk*   [Scheme Procedure]

> Calls the zero-argument procedure *thunk* with the current output port set temporarily to a new string port. It returns a string composed of the characters written to the current output.
>
> See `call-with-output-string` above for character encoding considerations.

with-input-from-string *string thunk*   [Scheme Procedure]

> Calls the zero-argument procedure *thunk* with the current input port set temporarily to a string port opened on the specified *string*. The value yielded by *thunk* is returned.

open-input-string *str*   [Scheme Procedure]
scm_open_input_string (*str*)   [C Function]

> Take a string and return an input port that delivers characters from the string. The port can be closed by `close-input-port`, though its storage will be reclaimed by the garbage collector if it becomes inaccessible.

open-output-string   [Scheme Procedure]
scm_open_output_string ()   [C Function]

> Return an output port that will accumulate characters for retrieval by `get-output-string`. The port can be closed by the procedure `close-output-port`, though its storage will be reclaimed by the garbage collector if it becomes inaccessible.

get-output-string *port*   [Scheme Procedure]
scm_get_output_string (*port*)   [C Function]
>   Given an output port created by open-output-string, return a string consisting of
>   the characters that have been output to the port so far.
>
>   get-output-string must be used before closing *port*, once closed the string cannot
>   be obtained.

A string port can be used in many procedures which accept a port but which are not
dependent on implementation details of fports. E.g., seeking and truncating will work on a
string port, but trying to extract the file descriptor number will fail.

6.14.9.3 Soft Ports

A *soft-port* is a port based on a vector of procedures capable of accepting or delivering
characters. It allows emulation of I/O ports.

make-soft-port *pv modes*   [Scheme Procedure]
scm_make_soft_port (*pv, modes*)   [C Function]
>   Return a port capable of receiving or delivering characters as specified by the *modes*
>   string (see Section 6.14.9.1 [File Ports], page 326). *pv* must be a vector of length 5
>   or 6. Its components are as follows:
>
>   0. procedure accepting one character for output
>
>   1. procedure accepting a string for output
>
>   2. thunk for flushing output
>
>   3. thunk for getting one character
>
>   4. thunk for closing port (not by garbage collection)
>
>   5. (if present and not #f) thunk for computing the number of characters that can
>   be read from the port without blocking.

For an output-only port only elements 0, 1, 2, and 4 need be procedures. For an
input-only port only elements 3 and 4 need be procedures. Thunks 2 and 4 can
instead be #f if there is no useful operation for them to perform.

If thunk 3 returns #f or an eof-object (see Section "Input" in *The Revised^5 Report
on Scheme*) it indicates that the port has reached end-of-file. For example:

```
(define stdout (current-output-port))
(define p (make-soft-port
           (vector
            (lambda (c) (write c stdout))
            (lambda (s) (display s stdout))
            (lambda () (display "." stdout))
            (lambda () (char-upcase (read-char)))
            (lambda () (display "@" stdout)))
           "rw"))

(write p p) ⇒ #<input-output: soft 8081e20>
```

6.14.9.4 Void Ports

This kind of port causes any data to be discarded when written to, and always returns the
end-of-file object when read from.

`%make-void-port` *mode*   [Scheme Procedure]
`scm_sys_make_void_port` (*mode*)   [C Function]
> Create and return a new void port. A void port acts like `/dev/null`. The *mode*
> argument specifies the input/output modes for this port: see the documentation for
> `open-file` in Section 6.14.9.1 [File Ports], page 326.

6.14.10 R6RS I/O Ports

The I/O port API of the Revised Report^6 on the Algorithmic Language Scheme (R6RS)
is provided by the `(rnrs io ports)` module. It provides features, such as binary I/O and
Unicode string I/O, that complement or refine Guile's historical port API presented above
(see Section 6.14 [Input and Output], page 316). Note that R6RS ports are not disjoint
from Guile's native ports, so Guile-specific procedures will work on ports created using the
R6RS API, and vice versa.

The text in this section is taken from the R6RS standard libraries document, with only
minor adaptions for inclusion in this manual. The Guile developers offer their thanks to
the R6RS editors for having provided the report's text under permissive conditions making
this possible.

Note: The implementation of this R6RS API is not complete yet.

A subset of the `(rnrs io ports)` module, plus one non-standard procedure `unget-
bytevector` (see Section 6.14.10.8 [R6RS Binary Input], page 339), is provided by the
`(ice-9 binary-ports)` module. It contains binary input/output procedures and does not
rely on R6RS support.

6.14.10.1 File Names

Some of the procedures described in this chapter accept a file name as an argument. Valid
values for such a file name include strings that name a file using the native notation of
file system paths on an implementation's underlying operating system, and may include
implementation-dependent values as well.

A *filename* parameter name means that the corresponding argument must be a file name.

6.14.10.2 File Options

When opening a file, the various procedures in this library accept a `file-options` object
that encapsulates flags to specify how the file is to be opened. A `file-options` object is an
enum-set (see Section 7.6.2.24 [rnrs enums], page 654) over the symbols constituting valid
file options.

A *file-options* parameter name means that the corresponding argument must be a file-
options object.

`file-options` *file-options-symbol ...*   [Scheme Syntax]
> Each *file-options-symbol* must be a symbol.
>
> The `file-options` syntax returns a file-options object that encapsulates the specified
> options.

When supplied to an operation that opens a file for output, the file-options object returned by (`file-options`) specifies that the file is created if it does not exist and an exception with condition type `&i/o-file-already-exists` is raised if it does exist. The following standard options can be included to modify the default behavior.

`no-create`

> If the file does not already exist, it is not created; instead, an exception with condition type `&i/o-file-does-not-exist` is raised. If the file already exists, the exception with condition type `&i/o-file-already-exists` is not raised and the file is truncated to zero length.

`no-fail`   If the file already exists, the exception with condition type `&i/o-file-already-exists` is not raised, even if `no-create` is not included, and the file is truncated to zero length.

`no-truncate`

> If the file already exists and the exception with condition type `&i/o-file-already-exists` has been inhibited by inclusion of `no-create` or `no-fail`, the file is not truncated, but the port's current position is still set to the beginning of the file.

These options have no effect when a file is opened only for input. Symbols other than those listed above may be used as *file-options-symbols*; they have implementation-specific meaning, if any.

> **Note:** Only the name of *file-options-symbol* is significant.

6.14.10.3 Buffer Modes

Each port has an associated buffer mode. For an output port, the buffer mode defines when an output operation flushes the buffer associated with the output port. For an input port, the buffer mode defines how much data will be read to satisfy read operations. The possible buffer modes are the symbols `none` for no buffering, `line` for flushing upon line endings and reading up to line endings, or other implementation-dependent behavior, and `block` for arbitrary buffering. This section uses the parameter name *buffer-mode* for arguments that must be buffer-mode symbols.

If two ports are connected to the same mutable source, both ports are unbuffered, and reading a byte or character from that shared source via one of the two ports would change the bytes or characters seen via the other port, a lookahead operation on one port will render the peeked byte or character inaccessible via the other port, while a subsequent read operation on the peeked port will see the peeked byte or character even though the port is otherwise unbuffered.

In other words, the semantics of buffering is defined in terms of side effects on shared mutable sources, and a lookahead operation has the same side effect on the shared source as a read operation.

`buffer-mode` *buffer-mode-symbol*   [Scheme Syntax]

> *buffer-mode-symbol* must be a symbol whose name is one of `none`, `line`, and `block`. The result is the corresponding symbol, and specifies the associated buffer mode.
>
> **Note:** Only the name of *buffer-mode-symbol* is significant.

`buffer-mode?` *obj*   [Scheme Procedure]
 Returns `#t` if the argument is a valid buffer-mode symbol, and returns `#f` otherwise.

6.14.10.4 Transcoders

Several different Unicode encoding schemes describe standard ways to encode characters and strings as byte sequences and to decode those sequences. Within this document, a *codec* is an immutable Scheme object that represents a Unicode or similar encoding scheme.

An *end-of-line style* is a symbol that, if it is not `none`, describes how a textual port transcodes representations of line endings.

A *transcoder* is an immutable Scheme object that combines a codec with an end-of-line style and a method for handling decoding errors. Each transcoder represents some specific bidirectional (but not necessarily lossless), possibly stateful translation between byte sequences and Unicode characters and strings. Every transcoder can operate in the input direction (bytes to characters) or in the output direction (characters to bytes). A *transcoder* parameter name means that the corresponding argument must be a transcoder.

A *binary port* is a port that supports binary I/O, does not have an associated transcoder and does not support textual I/O. A *textual port* is a port that supports textual I/O, and does not support binary I/O. A textual port may or may not have an associated transcoder.

`latin-1-codec`   [Scheme Procedure]
`utf-8-codec`   [Scheme Procedure]
`utf-16-codec`   [Scheme Procedure]
 These are predefined codecs for the ISO 8859-1, UTF-8, and UTF-16 encoding schemes.

 A call to any of these procedures returns a value that is equal in the sense of `eqv?` to the result of any other call to the same procedure.

`eol-style` *eol-style-symbol*   [Scheme Syntax]
 eol-style-symbol should be a symbol whose name is one of `lf`, `cr`, `crlf`, `nel`, `crnel`, `ls`, and `none`.

 The form evaluates to the corresponding symbol. If the name of *eol-style-symbol* is not one of these symbols, the effect and result are implementation-dependent; in particular, the result may be an eol-style symbol acceptable as an *eol-style* argument to `make-transcoder`. Otherwise, an exception is raised.

 All eol-style symbols except `none` describe a specific line-ending encoding:

`lf`	linefeed
`cr`	carriage return
`crlf`	carriage return, linefeed
`nel`	next line
`crnel`	carriage return, next line
`ls`	line separator

 For a textual port with a transcoder, and whose transcoder has an eol-style symbol `none`, no conversion occurs. For a textual input port, any eol-style symbol other than **none** means that all of the above line-ending encodings are recognized and are translated into a single linefeed. For a textual output port, **none** and **lf** are equivalent. Linefeed characters are encoded according to the specified eol-style symbol, and all other characters that participate in possible line endings are encoded as is.

> **Note:** Only the name of *eol-style-symbol* is significant.

native-eol-style   [Scheme Procedure]
> Returns the default end-of-line style of the underlying platform, e.g., **lf** on Unix and **crlf** on Windows.

&i/o-decoding   [Condition Type]
make-i/o-decoding-error *port*   [Scheme Procedure]
i/o-decoding-error? *obj*   [Scheme Procedure]
> This condition type could be defined by

```
(define-condition-type &i/o-decoding &i/o-port
  make-i/o-decoding-error i/o-decoding-error?)
```

An exception with this type is raised when one of the operations for textual input from a port encounters a sequence of bytes that cannot be translated into a character or string by the input direction of the port's transcoder.

When such an exception is raised, the port's position is past the invalid encoding.

&i/o-encoding   [Condition Type]
make-i/o-encoding-error *port char*   [Scheme Procedure]
i/o-encoding-error? *obj*   [Scheme Procedure]
i/o-encoding-error-char *condition*   [Scheme Procedure]
> This condition type could be defined by

```
(define-condition-type &i/o-encoding &i/o-port
  make-i/o-encoding-error i/o-encoding-error?
  (char i/o-encoding-error-char))
```

An exception with this type is raised when one of the operations for textual output to a port encounters a character that cannot be translated into bytes by the output direction of the port's transcoder. *char* is the character that could not be encoded.

error-handling-mode *error-handling-mode-symbol*   [Scheme Syntax]
> *error-handling-mode-symbol* should be a symbol whose name is one of **ignore**, **raise**, and **replace**. The form evaluates to the corresponding symbol. If *error-handling-mode-symbol* is not one of these identifiers, effect and result are implementation-dependent: The result may be an error-handling-mode symbol acceptable as a *handling-mode* argument to **make-transcoder**. If it is not acceptable as a *handling-mode* argument to **make-transcoder**, an exception is raised.

> **Note:** Only the name of *error-handling-mode-symbol* is significant.

The error-handling mode of a transcoder specifies the behavior of textual I/O operations in the presence of encoding or decoding errors.

If a textual input operation encounters an invalid or incomplete character encoding, and the error-handling mode is **ignore**, an appropriate number of bytes of the invalid encoding are ignored and decoding continues with the following bytes.

If the error-handling mode is `replace`, the replacement character U+FFFD is injected into the data stream, an appropriate number of bytes are ignored, and decoding continues with the following bytes.

If the error-handling mode is `raise`, an exception with condition type `&i/o-decoding` is raised.

If a textual output operation encounters a character it cannot encode, and the error-handling mode is `ignore`, the character is ignored and encoding continues with the next character. If the error-handling mode is `replace`, a codec-specific replacement character is emitted by the transcoder, and encoding continues with the next character. The replacement character is U+FFFD for transcoders whose codec is one of the Unicode encodings, but is the ? character for the Latin-1 encoding. If the error-handling mode is `raise`, an exception with condition type `&i/o-encoding` is raised.

make-transcoder *codec*   [Scheme Procedure]
make-transcoder *codec eol-style*   [Scheme Procedure]
make-transcoder *codec eol-style handling-mode*   [Scheme Procedure]
> *codec* must be a codec; *eol-style*, if present, an eol-style symbol; and *handling-mode*, if present, an error-handling-mode symbol.
>
> *eol-style* may be omitted, in which case it defaults to the native end-of-line style of the underlying platform. *handling-mode* may be omitted, in which case it defaults to `replace`. The result is a transcoder with the behavior specified by its arguments.

native-transcoder   [Scheme procedure]
> Returns an implementation-dependent transcoder that represents a possibly locale-dependent "native" transcoding.

transcoder-codec *transcoder*   [Scheme Procedure]
transcoder-eol-style *transcoder*   [Scheme Procedure]
transcoder-error-handling-mode *transcoder*   [Scheme Procedure]
> These are accessors for transcoder objects; when applied to a transcoder returned by `make-transcoder`, they return the *codec*, *eol-style*, and *handling-mode* arguments, respectively.

bytevector->string *bytevector transcoder*   [Scheme Procedure]
> Returns the string that results from transcoding the *bytevector* according to the input direction of the transcoder.

string->bytevector *string transcoder*   [Scheme Procedure]
> Returns the bytevector that results from transcoding the *string* according to the output direction of the transcoder.

6.14.10.5 The End-of-File Object

R5RS' eof-object? procedure is provided by the (`rnrs io ports`) module:

eof-object? *obj*   [Scheme Procedure]
scm_eof_object_p (*obj*)   [C Function]
> Return true if *obj* is the end-of-file (EOF) object.

In addition, the following procedure is provided:

```
eof-object                                           [Scheme Procedure]
scm_eof_object ()                                        [C Function]
```
    Return the end-of-file (EOF) object.

```
(eof-object? (eof-object))
⇒ #t
```

6.14.10.6 Port Manipulation

The procedures listed below operate on any kind of R6RS I/O port.

```
port? obj                                            [Scheme Procedure]
```
    Returns #t if the argument is a port, and returns #f otherwise.

```
port-transcoder port                                 [Scheme Procedure]
```
    Returns the transcoder associated with *port* if *port* is textual and has an associated transcoder, and returns #f if *port* is binary or does not have an associated transcoder.

```
binary-port? port                                    [Scheme Procedure]
```
    Return #t if *port* is a *binary port*, suitable for binary data input/output.

    Note that internally Guile does not differentiate between binary and textual ports, unlike the R6RS. Thus, this procedure returns true when *port* does not have an associated encoding—i.e., when (port-encoding *port*) is #f (see Section 6.14.1 [Ports], page 316). This is the case for ports returned by R6RS procedures such as open-bytevector-input-port and make-custom-binary-output-port.

    However, Guile currently does not prevent use of textual I/O procedures such as display or read-char with binary ports. Doing so "upgrades" the port from binary to textual, under the ISO-8859-1 encoding. Likewise, Guile does not prevent use of set-port-encoding! on a binary port, which also turns it into a "textual" port.

```
textual-port? port                                   [Scheme Procedure]
```
    Always return #t, as all ports can be used for textual I/O in Guile.

```
transcoded-port binary-port transcoder               [Scheme Procedure]
```
    The transcoded-port procedure returns a new textual port with the specified *transcoder*. Otherwise the new textual port's state is largely the same as that of *binary-port*. If *binary-port* is an input port, the new textual port will be an input port and will transcode the bytes that have not yet been read from *binary-port*. If *binary-port* is an output port, the new textual port will be an output port and will transcode output characters into bytes that are written to the byte sink represented by *binary-port*.

    As a side effect, however, transcoded-port closes *binary-port* in a special way that allows the new textual port to continue to use the byte source or sink represented by *binary-port*, even though *binary-port* itself is closed and cannot be used by the input and output operations described in this chapter.

`port-position` *port*   [Scheme Procedure]

> If *port* supports it (see below), return the offset (an integer) indicating where the next octet will be read from/written to in *port*. If *port* does not support this operation, an error condition is raised.
>
> This is similar to Guile's `seek` procedure with the `SEEK_CUR` argument (see Section 6.14.5 [Random Access], page 321).

`port-has-port-position?` *port*   [Scheme Procedure]

> Return `#t` is *port* supports `port-position`.

`set-port-position!` *port offset*   [Scheme Procedure]

> If *port* supports it (see below), set the position where the next octet will be read from/written to *port* to *offset* (an integer). If *port* does not support this operation, an error condition is raised.
>
> This is similar to Guile's `seek` procedure with the `SEEK_SET` argument (see Section 6.14.5 [Random Access], page 321).

`port-has-set-port-position!?` *port*   [Scheme Procedure]

> Return `#t` is *port* supports `set-port-position!`.

`call-with-port` *port proc*   [Scheme Procedure]

> Call *proc*, passing it *port* and closing *port* upon exit of *proc*. Return the return values of *proc*.

6.14.10.7 Input Ports

`input-port?` *obj*   [Scheme Procedure]

> Returns `#t` if the argument is an input port (or a combined input and output port), and returns `#f` otherwise.

`port-eof?` *input-port*   [Scheme Procedure]

> Returns `#t` if the `lookahead-u8` procedure (if *input-port* is a binary port) or the `lookahead-char` procedure (if *input-port* is a textual port) would return the end-of-file object, and `#f` otherwise. The operation may block indefinitely if no data is available but the port cannot be determined to be at end of file.

`open-file-input-port` *filename*   [Scheme Procedure]
`open-file-input-port` *filename file-options*   [Scheme Procedure]
`open-file-input-port` *filename file-options buffer-mode*   [Scheme Procedure]
`open-file-input-port` *filename file-options buffer-mode*   [Scheme Procedure]
>   *maybe-transcoder*
>
> *maybe-transcoder* must be either a transcoder or `#f`.
>
> The `open-file-input-port` procedure returns an input port for the named file. The *file-options* and *maybe-transcoder* arguments are optional.
>
> The *file-options* argument, which may determine various aspects of the returned port (see Section 6.14.10.2 [R6RS File Options], page 332), defaults to the value of `(file-options)`.
>
> The *buffer-mode* argument, if supplied, must be one of the symbols that name a buffer mode. The *buffer-mode* argument defaults to `block`.

If *maybe-transcoder* is a transcoder, it becomes the transcoder associated with the returned port.

If *maybe-transcoder* is #f or absent, the port will be a binary port and will support the `port-position` and `set-port-position!` operations. Otherwise the port will be a textual port, and whether it supports the `port-position` and `set-port-position!` operations is implementation-dependent (and possibly transcoder-dependent).

`standard-input-port`   [Scheme Procedure]

Returns a fresh binary input port connected to standard input. Whether the port supports the `port-position` and `set-port-position!` operations is implementation-dependent.

`current-input-port`   [Scheme Procedure]

This returns a default textual port for input. Normally, this default port is associated with standard input, but can be dynamically re-assigned using the `with-input-from-file` procedure from the `io simple (6)` library (see Section 7.6.2.16 [rnrs io simple], page 643). The port may or may not have an associated transcoder; if it does, the transcoder is implementation-dependent.

6.14.10.8 Binary Input

R6RS binary input ports can be created with the procedures described below.

`open-bytevector-input-port` *bv* [*transcoder*]   [Scheme Procedure]
`scm_open_bytevector_input_port` (*bv*, *transcoder*)   [C Function]

Return an input port whose contents are drawn from bytevector *bv* (see Section 6.6.6 [Bytevectors], page 163).

The *transcoder* argument is currently not supported.

`make-custom-binary-input-port` *id read! get-position*   [Scheme Procedure]
        set-position! close
`scm_make_custom_binary_input_port` (*id*, *read!*, *get-position*,   [C Function]
        set-position!, *close*)

Return a new custom binary input port[10] named *id* (a string) whose input is drained by invoking *read!* and passing it a bytevector, an index where bytes should be written, and the number of bytes to read. The `read!` procedure must return an integer indicating the number of bytes read, or 0 to indicate the end-of-file.

Optionally, if *get-position* is not #f, it must be a thunk that will be called when `port-position` is invoked on the custom binary port and should return an integer indicating the position within the underlying data stream; if *get-position* was not supplied, the returned port does not support `port-position`.

Likewise, if *set-position!* is not #f, it should be a one-argument procedure. When `set-port-position!` is invoked on the custom binary input port, *set-position!* is passed an integer indicating the position of the next byte is to read.

Finally, if *close* is not #f, it must be a thunk. It is invoked when the custom binary input port is closed.

---

[10] This is similar in spirit to Guile's *soft ports* (see Section 6.14.9.3 [Soft Ports], page 331).

The returned port is fully buffered by default, but its buffering mode can be changed using `setvbuf` (see Section 7.2.2 [Ports and File Descriptors], page 469).

Using a custom binary input port, the `open-bytevector-input-port` procedure could be implemented as follows:

```
(define (open-bytevector-input-port source)
  (define position 0)
  (define length (bytevector-length source))

  (define (read! bv start count)
    (let ((count (min count (- length position))))
      (bytevector-copy! source position
                        bv start count)
      (set! position (+ position count))
      count))

  (define (get-position) position)

  (define (set-position! new-position)
    (set! position new-position))

  (make-custom-binary-input-port "the port" read!
                                 get-position
                                 set-position!))

(read (open-bytevector-input-port (string->utf8 "hello")))
⇒ hello
```

Binary input is achieved using the procedures below:

get-u8 *port*   [Scheme Procedure]
scm_get_u8 (*port*)   [C Function]
   Return an octet read from *port*, a binary input port, blocking as necessary, or the end-of-file object.

lookahead-u8 *port*   [Scheme Procedure]
scm_lookahead_u8 (*port*)   [C Function]
   Like `get-u8` but does not update *port*'s position to point past the octet.

get-bytevector-n *port count*   [Scheme Procedure]
scm_get_bytevector_n (*port, count*)   [C Function]
   Read *count* octets from *port*, blocking as necessary and return a bytevector containing the octets read. If fewer bytes are available, a bytevector smaller than *count* is returned.

get-bytevector-n! *port bv start count*   [Scheme Procedure]
scm_get_bytevector_n_x (*port, bv, start, count*)   [C Function]
   Read *count* bytes from *port* and store them in *bv* starting at index *start*. Return either the number of bytes actually read or the end-of-file object.

`get-bytevector-some` *port*   [Scheme Procedure]
`scm_get_bytevector_some` (*port*)   [C Function]
> Read from *port*, blocking as necessary, until bytes are available or an end-of-file is reached. Return either the end-of-file object or a new bytevector containing some of the available bytes (at least one), and update the port position to point just past these bytes.

`get-bytevector-all` *port*   [Scheme Procedure]
`scm_get_bytevector_all` (*port*)   [C Function]
> Read from *port*, blocking as necessary, until the end-of-file is reached. Return either a new bytevector containing the data read or the end-of-file object (if no data were available).

The (`ice-9 binary-ports`) module provides the following procedure as an extension to (`rnrs io ports`):

`unget-bytevector` *port bv* [*start* [*count*]]   [Scheme Procedure]
`scm_unget_bytevector` (*port, bv, start, count*)   [C Function]
> Place the contents of *bv* in *port*, optionally starting at index *start* and limiting to *count* octets, so that its bytes will be read from left-to-right as the next bytes from *port* during subsequent read operations. If called multiple times, the unread bytes will be read again in last-in first-out order.

6.14.10.9 Textual Input

`get-char` *textual-input-port*   [Scheme Procedure]
> Reads from *textual-input-port*, blocking as necessary, until a complete character is available from *textual-input-port*, or until an end of file is reached.

> If a complete character is available before the next end of file, `get-char` returns that character and updates the input port to point past the character. If an end of file is reached before any character is read, `get-char` returns the end-of-file object.

`lookahead-char` *textual-input-port*   [Scheme Procedure]
> The `lookahead-char` procedure is like `get-char`, but it does not update *textual-input-port* to point past the character.

`get-string-n` *textual-input-port count*   [Scheme Procedure]
> *count* must be an exact, non-negative integer object, representing the number of characters to be read.

> The `get-string-n` procedure reads from *textual-input-port*, blocking as necessary, until *count* characters are available, or until an end of file is reached.

> If *count* characters are available before end of file, `get-string-n` returns a string consisting of those *count* characters. If fewer characters are available before an end of file, but one or more characters can be read, `get-string-n` returns a string containing those characters. In either case, the input port is updated to point just past the characters read. If no characters can be read before an end of file, the end-of-file object is returned.

get-string-n! *textual-input-port string start count*   [Scheme Procedure]
    start and *count* must be exact, non-negative integer objects, with *count* representing
    the number of characters to be read. *string* must be a string with at least $start +
    count$ characters.

    The **get-string-n!** procedure reads from *textual-input-port* in the same manner
    as **get-string-n**. If *count* characters are available before an end of file, they are
    written into *string* starting at index *start*, and *count* is returned. If fewer characters
    are available before an end of file, but one or more can be read, those characters are
    written into *string* starting at index *start* and the number of characters actually read
    is returned as an exact integer object. If no characters can be read before an end of
    file, the end-of-file object is returned.

get-string-all *textual-input-port*   [Scheme Procedure]
    Reads from *textual-input-port* until an end of file, decoding characters in the same
    manner as **get-string-n** and **get-string-n!**.

    If characters are available before the end of file, a string containing all the characters
    decoded from that data are returned. If no character precedes the end of file, the
    end-of-file object is returned.

get-line *textual-input-port*   [Scheme Procedure]
    Reads from *textual-input-port* up to and including the linefeed character or end of
    file, decoding characters in the same manner as **get-string-n** and **get-string-n!**.

    If a linefeed character is read, a string containing all of the text up to (but not
    including) the linefeed character is returned, and the port is updated to point just past
    the linefeed character. If an end of file is encountered before any linefeed character
    is read, but some characters have been read and decoded as characters, a string
    containing those characters is returned. If an end of file is encountered before any
    characters are read, the end-of-file object is returned.

>   **Note:** The end-of-line style, if not **none**, will cause all line endings to be
>   read as linefeed characters. See Section 6.14.10.4 [R6RS Transcoders],
>   page 334.

get-datum *textual-input-port count*   [Scheme Procedure]
    Reads an external representation from *textual-input-port* and returns the datum it
    represents. The **get-datum** procedure returns the next datum that can be parsed
    from the given *textual-input-port*, updating *textual-input-port* to point exactly past
    the end of the external representation of the object.

    Any *interlexeme space* (comment or whitespace, see Section 6.17.1 [Scheme Syntax],
    page 357) in the input is first skipped. If an end of file occurs after the interlexeme
    space, the end-of-file object (see Section 6.14.10.5 [R6RS End-of-File], page 336) is
    returned.

    If a character inconsistent with an external representation is encountered in the input,
    an exception with condition types **&lexical** and **&i/o-read** is raised. Also, if the
    end of file is encountered after the beginning of an external representation, but the
    external representation is incomplete and therefore cannot be parsed, an exception
    with condition types **&lexical** and **&i/o-read** is raised.

6.14.10.10 Output Ports

output-port? *obj*   [Scheme Procedure]
> Returns #t if the argument is an output port (or a combined input and output port),
> #f otherwise.

flush-output-port *port*   [Scheme Procedure]
> Flushes any buffered output from the buffer of *output-port* to the underlying file,
> device, or object. The flush-output-port procedure returns an unspecified values.

open-file-output-port *filename*   [Scheme Procedure]
open-file-output-port *filename file-options*   [Scheme Procedure]
open-file-output-port *filename file-options buffer-mode*   [Scheme Procedure]
open-file-output-port *filename file-options buffer-mode*   [Scheme Procedure]
> *maybe-transcoder*
> *maybe-transcoder* must be either a transcoder or #f.

> The open-file-output-port procedure returns an output port for the named file.

> The *file-options* argument, which may determine various aspects of the returned port
> (see Section 6.14.10.2 [R6RS File Options], page 332), defaults to the value of (file-
> options).

> The *buffer-mode* argument, if supplied, must be one of the symbols that name a
> buffer mode. The *buffer-mode* argument defaults to block.

> If *maybe-transcoder* is a transcoder, it becomes the transcoder associated with the
> port.

> If *maybe-transcoder* is #f or absent, the port will be a binary port and will support
> the port-position and set-port-position! operations. Otherwise the port will be
> a textual port, and whether it supports the port-position and set-port-position!
> operations is implementation-dependent (and possibly transcoder-dependent).

standard-output-port   [Scheme Procedure]
standard-error-port   [Scheme Procedure]
> Returns a fresh binary output port connected to the standard output or standard
> error respectively. Whether the port supports the port-position and set-port-
> position! operations is implementation-dependent.

current-output-port   [Scheme Procedure]
current-error-port   [Scheme Procedure]
> These return default textual ports for regular output and error output. Normally,
> these default ports are associated with standard output, and standard error,
> respectively. The return value of current-output-port can be dynamically
> re-assigned using the with-output-to-file procedure from the io simple (6)
> library (see Section 7.6.2.16 [rnrs io simple], page 643). A port returned by one
> of these procedures may or may not have an associated transcoder; if it does, the
> transcoder is implementation-dependent.

6.14.10.11 Binary Output

Binary output ports can be created with the procedures below.

open-bytevector-output-port [*transcoder*]   [Scheme Procedure]
scm_open_bytevector_output_port (*transcoder*)   [C Function]

    Return two values: a binary output port and a procedure. The latter should be called
    with zero arguments to obtain a bytevector containing the data accumulated by the
    port, as illustrated below.

```
(call-with-values
  (lambda ()
    (open-bytevector-output-port))
  (lambda (port get-bytevector)
    (display "hello" port)
    (get-bytevector)))

⇒ #vu8(104 101 108 108 111)
```

    The *transcoder* argument is currently not supported.

make-custom-binary-output-port *id write! get-position*   [Scheme Procedure]
        set-position! close
scm_make_custom_binary_output_port (*id, write!, get-position,*   [C Function]
        set-position!, close)

    Return a new custom binary output port named *id* (a string) whose output is sunk
    by invoking *write!* and passing it a bytevector, an index where bytes should be read
    from this bytevector, and the number of bytes to be "written". The `write!` procedure
    must return an integer indicating the number of bytes actually written; when it is
    passed 0 as the number of bytes to write, it should behave as though an end-of-file
    was sent to the byte sink.

    The other arguments are as for `make-custom-binary-input-port` (see
    Section 6.14.10.8 [R6RS Binary Input], page 339).

Writing to a binary output port can be done using the following procedures:

put-u8 *port octet*   [Scheme Procedure]
scm_put_u8 (*port, octet*)   [C Function]

    Write *octet*, an integer in the 0–255 range, to *port*, a binary output port.

put-bytevector *port bv* [*start* [*count*]]   [Scheme Procedure]
scm_put_bytevector (*port, bv, start, count*)   [C Function]

    Write the contents of *bv* to *port*, optionally starting at index *start* and limiting to
    count octets.

6.14.10.12 Textual Output

put-char *port char*   [Scheme Procedure]

    Writes *char* to the port. The `put-char` procedure returns an unspecified value.

`put-string` *port string* [Scheme Procedure]

`put-string` *port string start* [Scheme Procedure]

`put-string` *port string start count* [Scheme Procedure]

> *start* and *count* must be non-negative exact integer objects. *string* must have a length of at least *start* + *count*. *start* defaults to 0. *count* defaults to (`string` − `lengthstring`) − *start*$. The `put-string` procedure writes the *count* characters of *string* starting at index *start* to the port. The `put-string` procedure returns an unspecified value.

`put-datum` *textual-output-port datum* [Scheme Procedure]

> *datum* should be a datum value. The `put-datum` procedure writes an external representation of *datum* to *textual-output-port*. The specific external representation is implementation-dependent. However, whenever possible, an implementation should produce a representation for which `get-datum`, when reading the representation, will return an object equal (in the sense of `equal?`) to *datum*.

>> **Note:** Not all datums may allow producing an external representation for which `get-datum` will produce an object that is equal to the original. Specifically, NaNs contained in *datum* may make this impossible.

>> **Note:** The `put-datum` procedure merely writes the external representation, but no trailing delimiter. If `put-datum` is used to write several subsequent external representations to an output port, care should be taken to delimit them properly so they can be read back in by subsequent calls to `get-datum`.

6.14.11 Using and Extending Ports in C

6.14.11.1 C Port Interface

This section describes how to use Scheme ports from C.

Port basics

There are two main data structures. A port type object (ptob) is of type `scm_ptob_descriptor`. A port instance is of type `scm_port`. Given an SCM variable which points to a port, the corresponding C port object can be obtained using the `SCM_PTAB_ENTRY` macro. The ptob can be obtained by using `SCM_PTOBNUM` to give an index into the `scm_ptobs` global array.

Port buffers

An input port always has a read buffer and an output port always has a write buffer. However the size of these buffers is not guaranteed to be more than one byte (e.g., the `shortbuf` field in `scm_port` which is used when no other buffer is allocated). The way in which the buffers are allocated depends on the implementation of the ptob. For example in the case of an fport, buffers may be allocated with malloc when the port is created, but in the case of an strport the underlying string is used as the buffer.

The `rw_random` flag

Special treatment is required for ports which can be seeked at random. Before various operations, such as seeking the port or changing from input to output on a bidirectional port or vice versa, the port implementation must be given a chance to update its state. The write buffer is updated by calling the **flush** ptob procedure and the input buffer is updated by calling the **end_input** ptob procedure. In the case of an fport, **flush** causes buffered output to be written to the file descriptor, while **end_input** causes the descriptor position to be adjusted to account for buffered input which was never read.

The special treatment must be performed if the **rw_random** flag in the port is non-zero.

The rw_active variable

The **rw_active** variable in the port is only used if **rw_random** is set. It's defined as an enum with the following values:

SCM_PORT_READ
> the read buffer may have unread data.

SCM_PORT_WRITE
> the write buffer may have unwritten data.

SCM_PORT_NEITHER
> neither the write nor the read buffer has data.

Reading from a port.

To read from a port, it's possible to either call existing libguile procedures such as **scm_getc** and **scm_read_line** or to read data from the read buffer directly. Reading from the buffer involves the following steps:

1. Flush output on the port, if **rw_active** is SCM_PORT_WRITE.

2. Fill the read buffer, if it's empty, using **scm_fill_input**.

3. Read the data from the buffer and update the read position in the buffer. Steps 2) and 3) may be repeated as many times as required.

4. Set rw_active to SCM_PORT_READ if **rw_random** is set.

5. update the port's line and column counts.

Writing to a port.

To write data to a port, calling **scm_lfwrite** should be sufficient for most purposes. This takes care of the following steps:

1. End input on the port, if **rw_active** is SCM_PORT_READ.

2. Pass the data to the ptob implementation using the **write** ptob procedure. The advantage of using the ptob **write** instead of manipulating the write buffer directly is that it allows the data to be written in one operation even if the port is using the single-byte **shortbuf**.

3. Set **rw_active** to SCM_PORT_WRITE if **rw_random** is set.

6.14.11.2 Port Implementation

This section describes how to implement a new port type in C.

As described in the previous section, a port type object (ptob) is a structure of type **scm_ptob_descriptor**. A ptob is created by calling **scm_make_port_type**.

`scm_t_bits scm_make_port_type` (*char *name, int (*fill_input) (SCM*   [Function]
        port), void (*write) (SCM port, const void *data, size_t size))
    Return a new port type object. The *name*, *fill_input* and *write* parameters are initial
    values for those port type fields, as described below. The other fields are initialized
    with default values and can be changed later.

All of the elements of the ptob, apart from **name**, are procedures which collectively
implement the port behaviour. Creating a new port type mostly involves writing these
procedures.

name
    A pointer to a NUL terminated string: the name of the port type. This is the
    only element of `scm_ptob_descriptor` which is not a procedure. Set via the
    first argument to `scm_make_port_type`.

mark
    Called during garbage collection to mark any SCM objects that a port object
    may contain. It doesn't need to be set unless the port has SCM components. Set
    using

    `void scm_set_port_mark` (*scm_t_bits tc, SCM (*mark)*   [Function]
        (SCM port))

free
    Called when the port is collected during gc. It should free any resources used
    by the port. Set using

    `void scm_set_port_free` (*scm_t_bits tc, size_t (*free)*   [Function]
        (SCM port))

print
    Called when **write** is called on the port object, to print a port description.
    E.g., for an fport it may produce something like: `#<input: /etc/passwd 3>`.
    Set using

    `void scm_set_port_print` (*scm_t_bits tc, int (*print) (SCM*   [Function]
        port, SCM dest_port, scm_print_state *pstate))
        The first argument *port* is the object being printed, the second argument
        dest_port is where its description should go.

equalp
    Not used at present. Set using

    `void scm_set_port_equalp` (*scm_t_bits tc, SCM (*equalp)*   [Function]
        (SCM, SCM))

close
    Called when the port is closed, unless it was collected during gc. It should free
    any resources used by the port. Set using

    `void scm_set_port_close` (*scm_t_bits tc, int (*close) (SCM*   [Function]
        port))

write
    Accept data which is to be written using the port. The port implementation
    may choose to buffer the data instead of processing it directly. Set via the third
    argument to `scm_make_port_type`.

flush
    Complete the processing of buffered output data. Reset the value of `rw_active`
    to `SCM_PORT_NEITHER`. Set using

> void scm_set_port_flush (*scm_t_bits tc, void (*flush)*   [Function]
>   (*SCM port*))

end_input

> Perform any synchronization required when switching from input to output on
> the port. Reset the value of `rw_active` to `SCM_PORT_NEITHER`. Set using

> void scm_set_port_end_input (*scm_t_bits tc, void*   [Function]
>   (**end_input) (SCM port, int offset*))

fill_input

> Read new data into the read buffer and return the first character. It can be
> assumed that the read buffer is empty when this procedure is called. Set via
> the second argument to `scm_make_port_type`.

input_waiting

> Return a lower bound on the number of bytes that could be read from the port
> without blocking. It can be assumed that the current state of `rw_active` is
> `SCM_PORT_NEITHER`. Set using

> void scm_set_port_input_waiting (*scm_t_bits tc, int*   [Function]
>   (**input_waiting) (SCM port*))

seek

> Set the current position of the port. The procedure can not make any assump-
> tions about the value of `rw_active` when it's called. It can reset the buffers
> first if desired by using something like:

```
if (pt->rw_active == SCM_PORT_READ)
  scm_end_input (port);
else if (pt->rw_active == SCM_PORT_WRITE)
  ptob->flush (port);
```

> However note that this will have the side effect of discarding any data in the
> unread-char buffer, in addition to any side effects from the `end_input` and
> `flush` ptob procedures. This is undesirable when seek is called to measure the
> current position of the port, i.e., (seek p 0 SEEK_CUR). The libguile fport and
> string port implementations take care to avoid this problem.

> The procedure is set using

> void scm_set_port_seek (*scm_t_bits tc, scm_t_off (*seek)*   [Function]
>   (*SCM port, scm_t_off offset, int whence*))

truncate   Truncate the port data to be specified length. It can be assumed that the
> current state of `rw_active` is `SCM_PORT_NEITHER`. Set using

> void scm_set_port_truncate (*scm_t_bits tc, void*   [Function]
>   (**truncate) (SCM port, scm_t_off length*))

6.14.12 Handling of Unicode byte order marks.

This section documents the finer points of Guile's handling of Unicode byte order marks
(BOMs). A byte order mark (U+FEFF) is typically found at the start of a UTF-16 or UTF-
32 stream, to allow readers to reliably determine the byte order. Occasionally, a BOM is
found at the start of a UTF-8 stream, but this is much less common and not generally
recommended.

Guile attempts to handle BOMs automatically, and in accordance with the recommendations of the Unicode Standard, when the port encoding is set to UTF-8, UTF-16, or UTF-32. In brief, Guile automatically writes a BOM at the start of a UTF-16 or UTF-32 stream, and automatically consumes one from the start of a UTF-8, UTF-16, or UTF-32 stream.

As specified in the Unicode Standard, a BOM is only handled specially at the start of a stream, and only if the port encoding is set to UTF-8, UTF-16 or UTF-32. If the port encoding is set to UTF-16BE, UTF-16LE, UTF-32BE, or UTF-32LE, then BOMs are *not* handled specially, and none of the special handling described in this section applies.

- To ensure that Guile will properly detect the byte order of a UTF-16 or UTF-32 stream, you must perform a textual read before any writes, seeks, or binary I/O. Guile will not attempt to read a BOM unless a read is explicitly requested at the start of the stream.

- If a textual write is performed before the first read, then an arbitrary byte order will be chosen. Currently, big endian is the default on all platforms, but that may change in the future. If you wish to explicitly control the byte order of an output stream, set the port encoding to UTF-16BE, UTF-16LE, UTF-32BE, or UTF-32LE, and explicitly write a BOM (#\xFEFF) if desired.

- If set-port-encoding! is called in the middle of a stream, Guile treats this as a new logical "start of stream" for purposes of BOM handling, and will forget about any BOMs that had previously been seen. Therefore, it may choose a different byte order than had been used previously. This is intended to support multiple logical text streams embedded within a larger binary stream.

- Binary I/O operations are not guaranteed to update Guile's notion of whether the port is at the "start of the stream", nor are they guaranteed to produce or consume BOMs.

- For ports that support seeking (e.g. normal files), the input and output streams are considered linked: if the user reads first, then a BOM will be consumed (if appropriate), but later writes will *not* produce a BOM. Similarly, if the user writes first, then later reads will *not* consume a BOM.

- For ports that do not support seeking (e.g. pipes, sockets, and terminals), the input and output streams are considered *independent* for purposes of BOM handling: the first read will consume a BOM (if appropriate), and the first write will *also* produce a BOM (if appropriate). However, the input and output streams will always use the same byte order.

- Seeks to the beginning of a file will set the "start of stream" flags. Therefore, a subsequent textual read or write will consume or produce a BOM. However, unlike set-port-encoding!, if a byte order had already been chosen for the port, it will remain in effect after a seek, and cannot be changed by the presence of a BOM. Seeks anywhere other than the beginning of a file clear the "start of stream" flags.

6.15 Regular Expressions

A *regular expression* (or *regexp*) is a pattern that describes a whole class of strings. A full description of regular expressions and their syntax is beyond the scope of this manual; an introduction can be found in the Emacs manual (see Section "Syntax of Regular Expressions" in *The GNU Emacs Manual*), or in many general Unix reference books.

If your system does not include a POSIX regular expression library, and you have not linked Guile with a third-party regexp library such as Rx, these functions will not be available. You can tell whether your Guile installation includes regular expression support by checking whether (provided? 'regex) returns true.

The following regexp and string matching features are provided by the (ice-9 regex) module. Before using the described functions, you should load this module by executing (use-modules (ice-9 regex)).

6.15.1 Regexp Functions

By default, Guile supports POSIX extended regular expressions. That means that the characters '(', ')', '+' and '?' are special, and must be escaped if you wish to match the literal characters.

This regular expression interface was modeled after that implemented by SCSH, the Scheme Shell. It is intended to be upwardly compatible with SCSH regular expressions.

Zero bytes (#\nul) cannot be used in regex patterns or input strings, since the underlying C functions treat that as the end of string. If there's a zero byte an error is thrown.

Internally, patterns and input strings are converted to the current locale's encoding, and then passed to the C library's regular expression routines (see Section "Regular Expressions" in The GNU C Library Reference Manual). The returned match structures always point to characters in the strings, not to individual bytes, even in the case of multi-byte encodings.

string-match *pattern str* [*start*]   [Scheme Procedure]
> Compile the string *pattern* into a regular expression and compare it with *str*. The optional numeric argument *start* specifies the position of *str* at which to begin matching.
>
> **string-match** returns a *match structure* which describes what, if anything, was matched by the regular expression. See Section 6.15.2 [Match Structures], page 354. If *str* does not match *pattern* at all, **string-match** returns #f.

Two examples of a match follow. In the first example, the pattern matches the four digits in the match string. In the second, the pattern matches nothing.

```
(string-match "[0-9][0-9][0-9][0-9]" "blah2002")
⇒ #("blah2002" (4 . 8))

(string-match "[A-Za-z]" "123456")
⇒ #f
```

Each time **string-match** is called, it must compile its *pattern* argument into a regular expression structure. This operation is expensive, which makes **string-match** inefficient if the same regular expression is used several times (for example, in a loop). For better performance, you can compile a regular expression in advance and then match strings against the compiled regexp.

make-regexp *pat flag...*   [Scheme Procedure]
scm_make_regexp (*pat, flaglst*)   [C Function]
> Compile the regular expression described by *pat*, and return the compiled regexp structure. If *pat* does not describe a legal regular expression, **make-regexp** throws a **regular-expression-syntax** error.
>
> The *flag* arguments change the behavior of the compiled regular expression. The following values may be supplied:

regexp/icase   [Variable]

Consider uppercase and lowercase letters to be the same when matching.

regexp/newline   [Variable]

If a newline appears in the target string, then permit the '`^`' and '`$`' operators to match immediately after or immediately before the newline, respectively. Also, the '`.`' and '`[^...]`' operators will never match a newline character. The intent of this flag is to treat the target string as a buffer containing many lines of text, and the regular expression as a pattern that may match a single one of those lines.

regexp/basic   [Variable]

Compile a basic ("obsolete") regexp instead of the extended ("modern") regexps that are the default. Basic regexps do not consider '`|`', '`+`' or '`?`' to be special characters, and require the '`{...}`' and '`(...)`' metacharacters to be backslash-escaped (see Section 6.15.3 [Backslash Escapes], page 355). There are several other differences between basic and extended regular expressions, but these are the most significant.

regexp/extended   [Variable]

Compile an extended regular expression rather than a basic regexp. This is the default behavior; this flag will not usually be needed. If a call to `make-regexp` includes both `regexp/basic` and `regexp/extended` flags, the one which comes last will override the earlier one.

regexp-exec *rx str* [*start* [*flags*]]   [Scheme Procedure]
scm_regexp_exec (*rx*, *str*, *start*, *flags*)   [C Function]

Match the compiled regular expression *rx* against `str`. If the optional integer *start* argument is provided, begin matching from that position in the string. Return a match structure describing the results of the match, or `#f` if no match could be found.

The *flags* argument changes the matching behavior. The following flag values may be supplied, use `logior` (see Section 6.6.2.13 [Bitwise Operations], page 125) to combine them,

regexp/notbol   [Variable]

Consider that the *start* offset into *str* is not the beginning of a line and should not match operator '`^`'.

If *rx* was created with the `regexp/newline` option above, '`^`' will still match after a newline in *str*.

regexp/noteol   [Variable]

Consider that the end of *str* is not the end of a line and should not match operator '`$`'.

If *rx* was created with the `regexp/newline` option above, '`$`' will still match before a newline in *str*.

```
;; Regexp to match uppercase letters
(define r (make-regexp "[A-Z]*"))

;; Regexp to match letters, ignoring case
(define ri (make-regexp "[A-Z]*" regexp/icase))

;; Search for bob using regexp r
(match:substring (regexp-exec r "bob"))
⇒ ""                      ; no match

;; Search for bob using regexp ri
(match:substring (regexp-exec ri "Bob"))
⇒ "Bob"                   ; matched case insensitive
```

regexp? *obj*   [Scheme Procedure]
scm_regexp_p *(obj)*   [C Function]
    Return #t if *obj* is a compiled regular expression, or #f otherwise.

list-matches *regexp str* [*flags*]   [Scheme Procedure]
    Return a list of match structures which are the non-overlapping matches of *regexp* in
str. *regexp* can be either a pattern string or a compiled regexp. The *flags* argument
is as per **regexp-exec** above.

```
(map match:substring (list-matches "[a-z]+" "abc 42 def 78"))
⇒ ("abc" "def")
```

fold-matches *regexp str init proc* [*flags*]   [Scheme Procedure]
    Apply *proc* to the non-overlapping matches of *regexp* in *str*, to build a result. *regexp*
can be either a pattern string or a compiled regexp. The *flags* argument is as per
regexp-exec above.

    proc is called as **(proc match prev)** where *match* is a match structure and *prev* is
the previous return from *proc*. For the first call *prev* is the given *init* parameter.
fold-matches returns the final value from *proc*.

    For example to count matches,

```
(fold-matches "[a-z][0-9]" "abc x1 def y2" 0
              (lambda (match count)
                (1+ count)))
⇒ 2
```

    Regular expressions are commonly used to find patterns in one string and replace them
with the contents of another string. The following functions are convenient ways to do this.

regexp-substitute *port match item . . .*   [Scheme Procedure]
    Write to *port* selected parts of the match structure *match*. Or if *port* is #f then form
a string from those parts and return that.

    Each *item* specifies a part to be written, and may be one of the following,

- A string. String arguments are written out verbatim.

- An integer. The submatch with that number is written (`match:substring`). Zero is the entire match.

- The symbol 'pre'. The portion of the matched string preceding the regexp match is written (`match:prefix`).

- The symbol 'post'. The portion of the matched string following the regexp match is written (`match:suffix`).

For example, changing a match and retaining the text before and after,

```
(regexp-substitute #f (string-match "[0-9]+" "number 25 is good")
                   'pre "37" 'post)
⇒ "number 37 is good"
```

Or matching a YYYYMMDD format date such as '20020828' and re-ordering and hyphenating the fields.

```
(define date-regex
   "([0-9][0-9][0-9][0-9])([0-9][0-9])([0-9][0-9])")
(define s "Date 20020429 12am.")
(regexp-substitute #f (string-match date-regex s)
                   'pre 2 "-" 3 "-" 1 'post " (" 0 ")")
⇒ "Date 04-29-2002 12am. (20020429)"
```

regexp-substitute/global *port regexp target item...*   [Scheme Procedure]
Write to *port* selected parts of matches of *regexp* in *target*. If *port* is #f then form a string from those parts and return that. *regexp* can be a string or a compiled regex.

This is similar to `regexp-substitute`, but allows global substitutions on *target*. Each *item* behaves as per `regexp-substitute`, with the following differences,

- A function. Called as (*item* match) with the match structure for the *regexp* match, it should return a string to be written to *port*.

- The symbol 'post'. This doesn't output anything, but instead causes `regexp-substitute/global` to recurse on the unmatched portion of *target*.

  This *must* be supplied to perform a global search and replace on *target*; without it `regexp-substitute/global` returns after a single match and output.

For example, to collapse runs of tabs and spaces to a single hyphen each,

```
(regexp-substitute/global #f "[ \t]+" "this   is   the text"
                          'pre "-" 'post)
⇒ "this-is-the-text"
```

Or using a function to reverse the letters in each word,

```
(regexp-substitute/global #f "[a-z]+" "to do and not-do"
  'pre (lambda (m) (string-reverse (match:substring m))) 'post)
⇒ "ot od dna ton-od"
```

Without the `post` symbol, just one regexp match is made. For example the following is the date example from `regexp-substitute` above, without the need for the separate `string-match` call.

```
(define date-regex
  "([0-9][0-9][0-9][0-9])([0-9][0-9])([0-9][0-9])")
(define s "Date 20020429 12am.")
(regexp-substitute/global #f date-regex s
                          'pre 2 "-" 3 "-" 1 'post " (" 0 ")")
```

⇒ "Date 04-29-2002 12am. (20020429)"

6.15.2 Match Structures

A *match structure* is the object returned by **string-match** and **regexp-exec**. It describes which portion of a string, if any, matched the given regular expression. Match structures include: a reference to the string that was checked for matches; the starting and ending positions of the regexp match; and, if the regexp included any parenthesized subexpressions, the starting and ending positions of each submatch.

In each of the regexp match functions described below, the **match** argument must be a match structure returned by a previous call to **string-match** or **regexp-exec**. Most of these functions return some information about the original target string that was matched against a regular expression; we will call that string *target* for easy reference.

regexp-match? *obj*   [Scheme Procedure]
    Return **#t** if *obj* is a match structure returned by a previous call to **regexp-exec**, or **#f** otherwise.

match:substring *match* [*n*]   [Scheme Procedure]
    Return the portion of *target* matched by subexpression number *n*. Submatch 0 (the default) represents the entire regexp match. If the regular expression as a whole matched, but the subexpression number *n* did not match, return **#f**.

```
(define s (string-match "[0-9][0-9][0-9][0-9]" "blah2002foo"))
(match:substring s)
⇒ "2002"

;; match starting at offset 6 in the string
(match:substring
  (string-match "[0-9][0-9][0-9][0-9]" "blah987654" 6))
⇒ "7654"
```

match:start *match* [*n*]   [Scheme Procedure]
    Return the starting position of submatch number *n*.

In the following example, the result is 4, since the match starts at character index 4:

```
(define s (string-match "[0-9][0-9][0-9][0-9]" "blah2002foo"))
(match:start s)
⇒ 4
```

match:end *match* [*n*]   [Scheme Procedure]
    Return the ending position of submatch number *n*.

In the following example, the result is 8, since the match runs between characters 4 and 8 (i.e. the "2002").

```
(define s (string-match "[0-9][0-9][0-9][0-9]" "blah2002foo"))
(match:end s)
⇒ 8
```

`match:prefix` *match*   [Scheme Procedure]

Return the unmatched portion of *target* preceding the regexp match.

```
(define s (string-match "[0-9][0-9][0-9][0-9]" "blah2002foo"))
(match:prefix s)
⇒ "blah"
```

`match:suffix` *match*   [Scheme Procedure]

Return the unmatched portion of *target* following the regexp match.

```
(define s (string-match "[0-9][0-9][0-9][0-9]" "blah2002foo"))
(match:suffix s)
⇒ "foo"
```

`match:count` *match*   [Scheme Procedure]

Return the number of parenthesized subexpressions from *match*. Note that the entire regular expression match itself counts as a subexpression, and failed submatches are included in the count.

`match:string` *match*   [Scheme Procedure]

Return the original *target* string.

```
(define s (string-match "[0-9][0-9][0-9][0-9]" "blah2002foo"))
(match:string s)
⇒ "blah2002foo"
```

6.15.3 Backslash Escapes

Sometimes you will want a regexp to match characters like '*' or '$' exactly. For example, to check whether a particular string represents a menu entry from an Info node, it would be useful to match it against a regexp like '^* [^:]*::'. However, this won't work; because the asterisk is a metacharacter, it won't match the '*' at the beginning of the string. In this case, we want to make the first asterisk un-magic.

You can do this by preceding the metacharacter with a backslash character '\'. (This is also called *quoting* the metacharacter, and is known as a *backslash escape*.) When Guile sees a backslash in a regular expression, it considers the following glyph to be an ordinary character, no matter what special meaning it would ordinarily have. Therefore, we can make the above example work by changing the regexp to '^* [^:]*::'. The '*' sequence tells the regular expression engine to match only a single asterisk in the target string.

Since the backslash is itself a metacharacter, you may force a regexp to match a backslash in the target string by preceding the backslash with itself. For example, to find variable references in a TeX program, you might want to find occurrences of the string '\let\' followed by any number of alphabetic characters. The regular expression '\\let\\[A-Za-z]*' would do this: the double backslashes in the regexp each match a single backslash in the target string.

regexp-quote *str*   [Scheme Procedure]
>   Quote each special character found in *str* with a backslash, and return the resulting string.

Very important: Using backslash escapes in Guile source code (as in Emacs Lisp or C) can be tricky, because the backslash character has special meaning for the Guile reader. For example, if Guile encounters the character sequence '\n' in the middle of a string while processing Scheme code, it replaces those characters with a newline character. Similarly, the character sequence '\t' is replaced by a horizontal tab. Several of these *escape sequences* are processed by the Guile reader before your code is executed. Unrecognized escape sequences are ignored: if the characters '*' appear in a string, they will be translated to the single character '*'.

This translation is obviously undesirable for regular expressions, since we want to be able to include backslashes in a string in order to escape regexp metacharacters. Therefore, to make sure that a backslash is preserved in a string in your Guile program, you must use *two* consecutive backslashes:

```
(define Info-menu-entry-pattern (make-regexp "^\\* [^:]*"))
```

The string in this example is preprocessed by the Guile reader before any code is executed. The resulting argument to `make-regexp` is the string '^* [^:]*', which is what we really want.

This also means that in order to write a regular expression that matches a single backslash character, the regular expression string in the source code must include *four* backslashes. Each consecutive pair of backslashes gets translated by the Guile reader to a single backslash, and the resulting double-backslash is interpreted by the regexp engine as matching a single backslash character. Hence:

```
(define tex-variable-pattern (make-regexp "\\\\let\\\\=[A-Za-z]*"))
```

The reason for the unwieldiness of this syntax is historical. Both regular expression pattern matchers and Unix string processing systems have traditionally used backslashes with the special meanings described above. The POSIX regular expression specification and ANSI C standard both require these semantics. Attempting to abandon either convention would cause other kinds of compatibility problems, possibly more severe ones. Therefore, without extending the Scheme reader to support strings with different quoting conventions (an ungainly and confusing extension when implemented in other languages), we must adhere to this cumbersome escape syntax.

6.16 LALR(1) Parsing

The (`system base lalr`) module provides the `lalr-scm` LALR(1) parser generator by Dominique Boucher. `lalr-scm` uses the same algorithm as GNU Bison (see Section "Introduction" in *Bison, The Yacc-compatible Parser Generator*). Parsers are defined using the `lalr-parser` macro.

lalr-parser [*options*] *tokens rules...*   [Scheme Syntax]
>   Generate an LALR(1) syntax analyzer. *tokens* is a list of symbols representing the terminal symbols of the grammar. *rules* are the grammar production rules.

Each rule has the form (*non-terminal* (*rhs* ...) : *action* ...), where *non-terminal* is the name of the rule, *rhs* are the right-hand sides, i.e., the production rule, and *action* is a semantic action associated with the rule.

The generated parser is a two-argument procedure that takes a *tokenizer* and a *syntax error procedure*. The tokenizer should be a thunk that returns lexical tokens as produced by `make-lexical-token`. The syntax error procedure may be called with at least an error message (a string), and optionally the lexical token that caused the error.

Please refer to the `lalr-scm` documentation for details.

6.17 Reading and Evaluating Scheme Code

This chapter describes Guile functions that are concerned with reading, loading, evaluating, and compiling Scheme code at run time.

6.17.1 Scheme Syntax: Standard and Guile Extensions

6.17.1.1 Expression Syntax

An expression to be evaluated takes one of the following forms.

symbol   A symbol is evaluated by dereferencing. A binding of that symbol is sought and the value there used. For example,

```
(define x 123)
x ⇒ 123
```

(*proc args...*)

A parenthesised expression is a function call. *proc* and each argument are evaluated, then the function (which *proc* evaluated to) is called with those arguments.

The order in which *proc* and the arguments are evaluated is unspecified, so be careful when using expressions with side effects.

```
(max 1 2 3) ⇒ 3
```

```
(define (get-some-proc)  min)
((get-some-proc) 1 2 3) ⇒ 1
```

The same sort of parenthesised form is used for a macro invocation, but in that case the arguments are not evaluated. See the descriptions of macros for more on this (see Section 6.10 [Macros], page 257, and see Section 6.10.2 [Syntax Rules], page 258).

constant Number, string, character and boolean constants evaluate "to themselves", so can appear as literals.

```
123     ⇒ 123
99.9    ⇒ 99.9
"hello" ⇒ "hello"
#\z     ⇒ #\z
#t      ⇒ #t
```

Note that an application must not attempt to modify literal strings, since they may be in read-only memory.

(quote *data*)

'*data* Quoting is used to obtain a literal symbol (instead of a variable reference), a literal list (instead of a function call), or a literal vector. ' is simply a shorthand for a quote form. For example,

```
'x                    ⇒ x
'(1 2 3)              ⇒ (1 2 3)
'#(1 (2 3) 4)         ⇒ #(1 (2 3) 4)
(quote x)             ⇒ x
(quote (1 2 3))       ⇒ (1 2 3)
(quote #(1 (2 3) 4))  ⇒ #(1 (2 3) 4)
```

Note that an application must not attempt to modify literal lists or vectors obtained from a quote form, since they may be in read-only memory.

(quasiquote *data*)

'*data* Backquote quasi-quotation is like quote, but selected sub-expressions are evaluated. This is a convenient way to construct a list or vector structure most of which is constant, but at certain points should have expressions substituted.

The same effect can always be had with suitable list, cons or vector calls, but quasi-quoting is often easier.

(unquote *expr*)

,*expr* Within the quasiquote *data*, unquote or , indicates an expression to be evaluated and inserted. The comma syntax , is simply a shorthand for an unquote form. For example,

```
'(1 2 ,(* 9 9) 3 4)      ⇒ (1 2 81 3 4)
'(1 (unquote (+ 1 1)) 3) ⇒ (1 2 3)
'#(1 ,(/ 12 2))          ⇒ #(1 6)
```

(unquote-splicing *expr*)

,@*expr* Within the quasiquote *data*, unquote-splicing or ,@ indicates an expression to be evaluated and the elements of the returned list inserted. *expr* must evaluate to a list. The "comma-at" syntax ,@ is simply a shorthand for an unquote-splicing form.

```
(define x '(2 3))
'(1 ,@x 4)                      ⇒ (1 2 3 4)
'(1 (unquote-splicing (map 1+ x))) ⇒ (1 3 4)
'#(9 ,@x 9)                     ⇒ #(9 2 3 9)
```

Notice ,@ differs from plain , in the way one level of nesting is stripped. For ,@ the elements of a returned list are inserted, whereas with , it would be the list itself inserted.

6.17.1.2 Comments

Comments in Scheme source files are written by starting them with a semicolon character (;). The comment then reaches up to the end of the line. Comments can begin at any column, and the may be inserted on the same line as Scheme code.

```
; Comment
;; Comment too
(define x 1)          ; Comment after expression
(let ((y 1))
  ;; Display something.
  (display y)
;;; Comment at left margin.
  (display (+ y 1)))
```

It is common to use a single semicolon for comments following expressions on a line, to use two semicolons for comments which are indented like code, and three semicolons for comments which start at column 0, even if they are inside an indented code block. This convention is used when indenting code in Emacs' Scheme mode.

6.17.1.3 Block Comments

In addition to the standard line comments defined by R5RS, Guile has another comment type for multiline comments, called *block comments*. This type of comment begins with the character sequence #! and ends with the characters !#, which must appear on a line of their own. These comments are compatible with the block comments in the Scheme Shell **scsh** (see Section 7.17 [The Scheme shell (scsh)], page 693). The characters #! were chosen because they are the magic characters used in shell scripts for indicating that the name of the program for executing the script follows on the same line.

Thus a Guile script often starts like this.

```
#! /usr/local/bin/guile -s
!#
```

More details on Guile scripting can be found in the scripting section (see Section 4.3 [Guile Scripting], page 41).

Similarly, Guile (starting from version 2.0) supports nested block comments as specified by R6RS and SRFI-30:

```
(+ 1 #| this is a #| nested |# block comment |# 2)
⇒ 3
```

For backward compatibility, this syntax can be overridden with **read-hash-extend** (see Section 6.17.1.6 [Reader Extensions], page 360).

There is one special case where the contents of a comment can actually affect the interpretation of code. When a character encoding declaration, such as **coding: utf-8** appears in one of the first few lines of a source file, it indicates to Guile's default reader that this source code file is not ASCII. For details see Section 6.17.8 [Character Encoding of Source Files], page 370.

6.17.1.4 Case Sensitivity

Scheme as defined in R5RS is not case sensitive when reading symbols. Guile, on the contrary is case sensitive by default, so the identifiers

```
guile-whuzzy
Guile-Whuzzy
```

are the same in R5RS Scheme, but are different in Guile.

It is possible to turn off case sensitivity in Guile by setting the reader option **case-insensitive**. For more information on reader options, See Section 6.17.2 [Scheme Read], page 360.

```
(read-enable 'case-insensitive)
```

It is also possible to disable (or enable) case sensitivity within a single file by placing the reader directives #!fold-case (or #!no-fold-case) within the file itself.

6.17.1.5 Keyword Syntax

6.17.1.6 Reader Extensions

read-hash-extend *chr proc*   [Scheme Procedure]
scm_read_hash_extend (*chr, proc*)   [C Function]
> Install the procedure *proc* for reading expressions starting with the character sequence # and *chr*. *proc* will be called with two arguments: the character *chr* and the port to read further data from. The object returned will be the return value of **read**. Passing #f for *proc* will remove a previous setting.

6.17.2 Reading Scheme Code

read [*port*]   [Scheme Procedure]
scm_read (*port*)   [C Function]
> Read an s-expression from the input port *port*, or from the current input port if *port* is not specified. Any whitespace before the next token is discarded.

The behaviour of Guile's Scheme reader can be modified by manipulating its read options.

read-options [*setting*]   [Scheme Procedure]
> Display the current settings of the global read options. If *setting* is omitted, only a short form of the current read options is printed. Otherwise if *setting* is the symbol **help**, a complete options description is displayed.

The set of available options, and their default values, may be had by invoking **read-options** at the prompt.

```
scheme@(guile-user)> (read-options)
(square-brackets keywords #f positions)
scheme@(guile-user)> (read-options 'help)
copy                no    Copy source code expressions.
positions           yes   Record positions of source code expressions.
case-insensitive    no    Convert symbols to lower case.
keywords            #f    Style of keyword recognition: #f, 'prefix or 'postfix.
r6rs-hex-escapes    no    Use R6RS variable-length character and string hex escapes.
square-brackets     yes   Treat '[' and ']' as parentheses, for R6RS compatibility.
hungry-eol-escapes  no    In strings, consume leading whitespace after an
                          escaped end-of-line.
curly-infix         no    Support SRFI-105 curly infix expressions.
r7rs-symbols        no    Support R7RS |...| symbol notation.
```

Note that Guile also includes a preliminary mechanism for setting read options on a per-port basis. For instance, the **case-insensitive** read option is set (or unset) on the port when the reader encounters the #!fold-case or #!no-fold-case reader directives. Similarly, the #!curly-infix reader directive sets the **curly-infix** read option on the port, and `#!curly-infix-and-bracket-lists` sets `curly-infix` and unsets `square-brackets` on the port (see Section 7.5.42 [SRFI-105], page 621). There is currently no other way to access or set the per-port read options.

The boolean options may be toggled with `read-enable` and `read-disable`. The non-boolean `keywords` option must be set using `read-set!`.

read-enable *option-name*   [Scheme Procedure]
read-disable *option-name*   [Scheme Procedure]
read-set! *option-name value*   [Scheme Syntax]
>   Modify the read options. `read-enable` should be used with boolean options and switches them on, `read-disable` switches them off.
>
>   `read-set!` can be used to set an option to a specific value. Due to historical oddities, it is a macro that expects an unquoted option name.

For example, to make `read` fold all symbols to their lower case (perhaps for compatibility with older Scheme code), you can enter:

```
(read-enable 'case-insensitive)
```

For more information on the effect of the `r6rs-hex-escapes` and `hungry-eol-escapes` options, see (see Section 6.6.5.1 [String Syntax], page 141).

For more information on the `r7rs-symbols` option, see (see Section 6.6.7.6 [Symbol Read Syntax], page 178).

6.17.3 Writing Scheme Values

Any scheme value may be written to a port. Not all values may be read back in (see Section 6.17.2 [Scheme Read], page 360), however.

write *obj* [*port*]   [Scheme Procedure]
>   Send a representation of *obj* to *port* or to the current output port if not given.
>
>   The output is designed to be machine readable, and can be read back with `read` (see Section 6.17.2 [Scheme Read], page 360). Strings are printed in double quotes, with escapes if necessary, and characters are printed in '#\' notation.

display *obj* [*port*]   [Scheme Procedure]
>   Send a representation of *obj* to *port* or to the current output port if not given.
>
>   The output is designed for human readability, it differs from `write` in that strings are printed without double quotes and escapes, and characters are printed as per `write-char`, not in '#\' form.

As was the case with the Scheme reader, there are a few options that affect the behavior of the Scheme printer.

print-options [*setting*]   [Scheme Procedure]
>   Display the current settings of the read options. If *setting* is omitted, only a short form of the current read options is printed. Otherwise if *setting* is the symbol `help`, a complete options description is displayed.

The set of available options, and their default values, may be had by invoking print-options at the prompt.

```
scheme@(guile-user)> (print-options)
(quote-keywordish-symbols reader highlight-suffix "}" highlight-prefix "{")
scheme@(guile-user)> (print-options 'help)
highlight-prefix         {       The string to print before highlighted values.
highlight-suffix         }       The string to print after highlighted values.
quote-keywordish-symbols reader  How to print symbols that have a colon
                                 as their first or last character. The
                                 value '#f' does not quote the colons;
                                 '#t' quotes them; 'reader' quotes them
                                 when the reader option 'keywords' is
                                 not '#f'.
escape-newlines          yes     Render newlines as \n when printing
                                 using 'write'.
r7rs-symbols             no      Escape symbols using R7RS |...| symbol
                                 notation.
```

These options may be modified with the print-set! syntax.

print-set! *option-name value*   [Scheme Syntax]
  Modify the print options. Due to historical oddities, print-set! is a macro that
  expects an unquoted option name.

6.17.4 Procedures for On the Fly Evaluation

Scheme has the lovely property that its expressions may be represented as data. The eval
procedure takes a Scheme datum and evaluates it as code.

eval *exp module_or_state*   [Scheme Procedure]
scm_eval (*exp, module_or_state*)   [C Function]
  Evaluate *exp*, a list representing a Scheme expression, in the top-level environment
  specified by *module_or_state*. While *exp* is evaluated (using primitive-eval), *module_or_state* is made the current module. The current module is reset to its previous
  value when eval returns. XXX - dynamic states. Example: (eval '(+ 1 2) (interaction-
  environment))

interaction-environment   [Scheme Procedure]
scm_interaction_environment ()   [C Function]
  Return a specifier for the environment that contains implementation–defined bindings,
  typically a superset of those listed in the report. The intent is that this procedure
  will return the environment in which the implementation would evaluate expressions
  dynamically typed by the user.

See Section 6.19.11 [Environments], page 395, for other environments.

One does not always receive code as Scheme data, of course, and this is especially the case
for Guile's other language implementations (see Section 6.23 [Other Languages], page 432).
For the case in which all you have is a string, we have eval-string. There is a legacy
version of this procedure in the default environment, but you really want the one from
(ice-9 eval-string), so load it up:

```
(use-modules (ice-9 eval-string))
```

`eval-string` *string* [*#:module=#f*] [*#:file=#f*] [*#:line=#f*]   [Scheme Procedure]
    [*#:column=#f*] [*#:lang=(current-language)*] [*#:compile?=#f*]

    Parse *string* according to the current language, normally Scheme. Evaluate or compile
    the expressions it contains, in order, returning the last expression.

    If the *module* keyword argument is set, save a module excursion (see Section 6.19.8
    [Module System Reflection], page 391) and set the current module to *module* before
    evaluation.

    The *file*, *line*, and *column* keyword arguments can be used to indicate that the source
    string begins at a particular source location.

    Finally, *lang* is a language, defaulting to the current language, and the expression is
    compiled if *compile?* is true or there is no evaluator for the given language.

`scm_eval_string` (*string*)   [C Function]
`scm_eval_string_in_module` (*string, module*)   [C Function]
    These C bindings call `eval-string` from (`ice-9 eval-string`), evaluating within
    module or the current module.

`SCM scm_c_eval_string` (*const char *string*)   [C Function]
    `scm_eval_string`, but taking a C string in locale encoding instead of an `SCM`.

`apply` *proc arg ... arglst*   [Scheme Procedure]
`scm_apply_0` (*proc, arglst*)   [C Function]
`scm_apply_1` (*proc, arg1, arglst*)   [C Function]
`scm_apply_2` (*proc, arg1, arg2, arglst*)   [C Function]
`scm_apply_3` (*proc, arg1, arg2, arg3, arglst*)   [C Function]
`scm_apply` (*proc, arg, rest*)   [C Function]
    Call *proc* with arguments *arg* ... and the elements of the *arglst* list.

    `scm_apply` takes parameters corresponding to a Scheme level (`lambda (proc arg1 .`
    `rest) ...`). So *arg1* and all but the last element of the *rest* list make up *arg* ...,
    and the last element of *rest* is the *arglst* list. Or if *rest* is the empty list `SCM_EOL` then
    there's no *arg* ..., and (*arg1*) is the *arglst*.

    arglst is not modified, but the *rest* list passed to `scm_apply` is modified.

`scm_call_0` (*proc*)   [C Function]
`scm_call_1` (*proc, arg1*)   [C Function]
`scm_call_2` (*proc, arg1, arg2*)   [C Function]
`scm_call_3` (*proc, arg1, arg2, arg3*)   [C Function]
`scm_call_4` (*proc, arg1, arg2, arg3, arg4*)   [C Function]
`scm_call_5` (*proc, arg1, arg2, arg3, arg4, arg5*)   [C Function]
`scm_call_6` (*proc, arg1, arg2, arg3, arg4, arg5, arg6*)   [C Function]
`scm_call_7` (*proc, arg1, arg2, arg3, arg4, arg5, arg6, arg7*)   [C Function]
`scm_call_8` (*proc, arg1, arg2, arg3, arg4, arg5, arg6, arg7, arg8*)   [C Function]
`scm_call_9` (*proc, arg1, arg2, arg3, arg4, arg5, arg6, arg7, arg8, arg9*)   [C Function]
    Call *proc* with the given arguments.

`scm_call` (*proc, ...*)   [C Function]
    Call *proc* with any number of arguments. The argument list must be terminated by
    `SCM_UNDEFINED`. For example:

```
scm_call (scm_c_public_ref ("guile", "+"),
          scm_from_int (1),
          scm_from_int (2),
          SCM_UNDEFINED);
```

scm_call_n (*proc, argv, nargs*)   [C Function]
> Call *proc* with the array of arguments *argv*, as a SCM*. The length of the arguments
> should be passed in *nargs*, as a `size_t`.

apply:nconc2last *lst*   [Scheme Procedure]
scm_nconc2last (*lst*)   [C Function]
> *lst* should be a list (*arg1 ... argN arglst*), with *arglst* being a list. This function
> returns a list comprising *arg1* to *argN* plus the elements of *arglst*. *lst* is modified to
> form the return. *arglst* is not modified, though the return does share structure with
> it.
>
> This operation collects up the arguments from a list which is `apply` style parameters.

primitive-eval *exp*   [Scheme Procedure]
scm_primitive_eval (*exp*)   [C Function]
> Evaluate *exp* in the top-level environment specified by the current module.

6.17.5 Compiling Scheme Code

The `eval` procedure directly interprets the S-expression representation of Scheme. An
alternate strategy for evaluation is to determine ahead of time what computations will be
necessary to evaluate the expression, and then use that recipe to produce the desired results.
This is known as *compilation*.

While it is possible to compile simple Scheme expressions such as (+ 2 2) or even "Hello
world!", compilation is most interesting in the context of procedures. Compiling a lambda
expression produces a compiled procedure, which is just like a normal procedure except
typically much faster, because it can bypass the generic interpreter.

Functions from system modules in a Guile installation are normally compiled already,
so they load and run quickly.

Note that well-written Scheme programs will not typically call the procedures in this
section, for the same reason that it is often bad taste to use `eval`. By default, Guile automatically compiles any files it encounters that have not been compiled yet (see Section 4.2
[Invoking Guile], page 35). The compiler can also be invoked explicitly from the shell as
`guild compile foo.scm`.

(Why are calls to `eval` and `compile` usually in bad taste? Because they are limited, in
that they can only really make sense for top-level expressions. Also, most needs for "compile-
time" computation are fulfilled by macros and closures. Of course one good counterexample
is the REPL itself, or any code that reads expressions from a port.)

Automatic compilation generally works transparently, without any need for user inter-
vention. However Guile does not yet do proper dependency tracking, so that if file `a.scm`
uses macros from `b.scm`, and *b.scm* changes, `a.scm` would not be automatically recompiled.
To forcibly invalidate the auto-compilation cache, pass the `--fresh-auto-compile` option
to Guile, or set the `GUILE_AUTO_COMPILE` environment variable to `fresh` (instead of to 0 or
1).

For more information on the compiler itself, see Section 9.4 [Compiling to the Virtual Machine], page 791. For information on the virtual machine, see Section 9.3 [A Virtual Machine for Guile], page 772.

The command-line interface to Guile's compiler is the `guild compile` command:

`guild compile [option...] file...`   [Command]

Compile *file*, a source file, and store bytecode in the compilation cache or in the file specified by the `-o` option. The following options are available:

`-L dir`
`--load-path=dir`

Add *dir* to the front of the module load path.

`-o ofile`
`--output=ofile`

Write output bytecode to *ofile*. By convention, bytecode file names end in `.go`. When `-o` is omitted, the output file name is as for `compile-file` (see below).

`-W warning`
`--warn=warning`

Emit warnings of type *warning*; use `--warn=help` for a list of available warnings and their description. Currently recognized warnings include `unused-variable`, `unused-toplevel`, `unbound-variable`, `arity-mismatch`, `format`, `duplicate-case-datum`, and `bad-case-datum`.

`-f lang`
`--from=lang`

Use *lang* as the source language of *file*. If this option is omitted, `scheme` is assumed.

`-t lang`
`--to=lang`

Use *lang* as the target language of *file*. If this option is omitted, `objcode` is assumed.

`-T target`
`--target=target`

Produce bytecode for *target* instead of %*host-type* (see Section 6.22.1 [Build Config], page 427). Target must be a valid GNU triplet, such as `armv5tel-unknown-linux-gnueabi` (see Section "Specifying Target Triplets" in *GNU Autoconf Manual*).

Each *file* is assumed to be UTF-8-encoded, unless it contains a coding declaration as recognized by `file-encoding` (see Section 6.17.8 [Character Encoding of Source Files], page 370).

The compiler can also be invoked directly by Scheme code using the procedures below:

`compile` *exp* [#:env=#f] [#:from=(current-language)]   [Scheme Procedure]
      [#:to=value] [#:opts=()]

Compile the expression *exp* in the environment *env*. If *exp* is a procedure, the result will be a compiled procedure; otherwise `compile` is mostly equivalent to `eval`.

For a discussion of languages and compiler options, See Section 9.4 [Compiling to the Virtual Machine], page 791.

compile-file *file* [*#:output-file=#f*]   [Scheme Procedure]
      [*#:from=(current-language)*] [*#:to='objcode*] [*#:env=(default-environment from)*] [*#:opts='()*] [*#:canonicalization='relative*]
Compile the file named *file*.

      Output will be written to a *output-file*. If you do not supply an output file name, output is written to a file in the cache directory, as computed by (**compiled-file-name** *file*).

      from and *to* specify the source and target languages. See Section 9.4 [Compiling to the Virtual Machine], page 791, for more information on these options, and on *env* and *opts*.

      As with **guild compile**, *file* is assumed to be UTF-8-encoded unless it contains a coding declaration.

compiled-file-name *file*   [Scheme Procedure]
      Compute a cached location for a compiled version of a Scheme file named *file*.

      This file will usually be below the **$HOME/.cache/guile/ccache** directory, depending on the value of the **XDG_CACHE_HOME** environment variable. The intention is that **compiled-file-name** provides a fallback location for caching auto-compiled files. If you want to place a compile file in the **%load-compiled-path**, you should pass the *output-file* option to **compile-file**, explicitly.

%auto-compilation-options   [Scheme Variable]
      This variable contains the options passed to the **compile-file** procedure when auto-compiling source files. By default, it enables useful compilation warnings. It can be customized from `~/.guile`.

6.17.6 Loading Scheme Code from File

load *filename* [*reader*]   [Scheme Procedure]
      Load *filename* and evaluate its contents in the top-level environment.

      reader if provided should be either **#f**, or a procedure with the signature (**lambda (port) ...**) which reads the next expression from *port*. If *reader* is **#f** or absent, Guile's built-in **read** procedure is used (see Section 6.17.2 [Scheme Read], page 360).

      The *reader* argument takes effect by setting the value of the **current-reader** fluid (see below) before loading the file, and restoring its previous value when loading is complete. The Scheme code inside *filename* can itself change the current reader procedure on the fly by setting **current-reader** fluid.

      If the variable **%load-hook** is defined, it should be bound to a procedure that will be called before any code is loaded. See documentation for **%load-hook** later in this section.

load-compiled *filename*   [Scheme Procedure]
      Load the compiled file named *filename*.

Compiling a source file (see Section 6.17 [Read/Load/Eval/Compile], page 357) and then calling `load-compiled` on the resulting file is equivalent to calling `load` on the source file.

`primitive-load` *filename*   [Scheme Procedure]

`scm_primitive_load` (*filename*)   [C Function]

> Load the file named *filename* and evaluate its contents in the top-level environment. *filename* must either be a full pathname or be a pathname relative to the current directory. If the variable `%load-hook` is defined, it should be bound to a procedure that will be called before any code is loaded. See the documentation for `%load-hook` later in this section.

`SCM scm_c_primitive_load` (*const char *filename*)   [C Function]

> `scm_primitive_load`, but taking a C string instead of an SCM.

`current-reader`   [Variable]

> `current-reader` holds the read procedure that is currently being used by the above loading procedures to read expressions (from the file that they are loading). **current-reader** is a fluid, so it has an independent value in each dynamic root and should be read and set using `fluid-ref` and `fluid-set!` (see Section 6.21.7 [Fluids and Dynamic States], page 419).
>
> Changing `current-reader` is typically useful to introduce local syntactic changes, such that code following the `fluid-set!` call is read using the newly installed reader. The `current-reader` change should take place at evaluation time when the code is evaluated, or at compilation time when the code is compiled:
>
> ```
> (eval-when (compile eval)
>   (fluid-set! current-reader my-own-reader))
> ```
>
> The `eval-when` form above ensures that the `current-reader` change occurs at the right time.

`%load-hook`   [Variable]

> A procedure to be called (`%load-hook filename`) whenever a file is loaded, or `#f` for no such call. `%load-hook` is used by all of the loading functions (`load` and `primitive-load`, and `load-from-path` and `primitive-load-path` documented in the next section).
>
> For example an application can set this to show what's loaded,
>
> ```
> (set! %load-hook (lambda (filename)
>                    (format #t "Loading ~a ...\n" filename)))
> (load-from-path "foo.scm")
> ⊣ Loading /usr/local/share/guile/site/foo.scm ...
> ```

`current-load-port`   [Scheme Procedure]

`scm_current_load_port` ()   [C Function]

> Return the current-load-port. The load port is used internally by `primitive-load`.

6.17.7 Load Paths

The procedure in the previous section look for Scheme code in the file system at specific location. Guile also has some procedures to search the load path for code.

`%load-path`   [Variable]

> List of directories which should be searched for Scheme modules and libraries. When Guile starts up, `%load-path` is initialized to the default load path (`list` (`%library-dir`) (`%site-dir`) (`%global-site-dir`) (`%package-data-dir`)). The `GUILE_LOAD_PATH` environment variable can be used to prepend or append additional directories (see Section 4.2.2 [Environment Variables], page 38).
>
> See Section 6.22.1 [Build Config], page 427, for more on `%site-dir` and related procedures.

`load-from-path` *filename*   [Scheme Procedure]

> Similar to `load`, but searches for *filename* in the load paths. Preferentially loads a compiled version of the file, if it is available and up-to-date.

A user can extend the load path by calling `add-to-load-path`.

`add-to-load-path` *dir*   [Scheme Syntax]

> Add *dir* to the load path.

For example, a script might include this form to add the directory that it is in to the load path:

```
(add-to-load-path (dirname (current-filename)))
```

It's better to use `add-to-load-path` than to modify `%load-path` directly, because `add-to-load-path` takes care of modifying the path both at compile-time and at run-time.

`primitive-load-path` *filename* [*exception-on-not-found*]   [Scheme Procedure]
`scm_primitive_load_path` (*filename*)   [C Function]

> Search `%load-path` for the file named *filename* and load it into the top-level environment. If *filename* is a relative pathname and is not found in the list of search paths, an error is signalled. Preferentially loads a compiled version of the file, if it is available and up-to-date.
>
> If *filename* is a relative pathname and is not found in the list of search paths, one of three things may happen, depending on the optional second argument, *exception-on-not-found*. If it is `#f`, `#f` will be returned. If it is a procedure, it will be called with no arguments. (This allows a distinction to be made between exceptions raised by loading a file, and exceptions related to the loader itself.) Otherwise an error is signalled.
>
> For compatibility with Guile 1.8 and earlier, the C function takes only one argument, which can be either a string (the file name) or an argument list.

`%search-load-path` *filename*   [Scheme Procedure]
`scm_sys_search_load_path` (*filename*)   [C Function]

> Search `%load-path` for the file named *filename*, which must be readable by the current user. If *filename* is found in the list of paths to search or is an absolute pathname, return its full pathname. Otherwise, return `#f`. Filenames may have any of the

optional extensions in the `%load-extensions` list; `%search-load-path` will try each extension automatically.

`%load-extensions`   [Variable]
> A list of default file extensions for files containing Scheme code. `%search-load-path` tries each of these extensions when looking for a file to load. By default, `%load-extensions` is bound to the list (`""` `".scm"`).

As mentioned above, when Guile searches the `%load-path` for a source file, it will also search the `%load-compiled-path` for a corresponding compiled file. If the compiled file is as new or newer than the source file, it will be loaded instead of the source file, using `load-compiled`.

`%load-compiled-path`   [Variable]
> Like `%load-path`, but for compiled files. By default, this path has two entries: one for compiled files from Guile itself, and one for site packages. The `GUILE_LOAD_COMPILED_PATH` environment variable can be used to prepend or append additional directories (see Section 4.2.2 [Environment Variables], page 38).

When `primitive-load-path` searches the `%load-compiled-path` for a corresponding compiled file for a relative path it does so by appending `.go` to the relative path. For example, searching for `ice-9/popen` could find `/usr/lib/guile/2.0/ccache/ice-9/popen.go`, and use it instead of `/usr/share/guile/2.0/ice-9/popen.scm`.

If `primitive-load-path` does not find a corresponding `.go` file in the `%load-compiled-path`, or the `.go` file is out of date, it will search for a corresponding auto-compiled file in the fallback path, possibly creating one if one does not exist.

See Section 4.7 [Installing Site Packages], page 55, for more on how to correctly install site packages. See Section 6.19.4 [Modules and the File System], page 386, for more on the relationship between load paths and modules. See Section 6.17.5 [Compilation], page 364, for more on the fallback path and auto-compilation.

Finally, there are a couple of helper procedures for general path manipulation.

`parse-path` *path* [*tail*]   [Scheme Procedure]
`scm_parse_path` (*path, tail*)   [C Function]
> Parse *path*, which is expected to be a colon-separated string, into a list and return the resulting list with *tail* appended. If *path* is `#f`, *tail* is returned.

`parse-path-with-ellipsis` *path base*   [Scheme Procedure]
`scm_parse_path_with_ellipsis` (*path, base*)   [C Function]
> Parse *path*, which is expected to be a colon-separated string, into a list and return the resulting list with *base* (a list) spliced in place of the ... path component, if present, or else *base* is added to the end. If *path* is `#f`, *base* is returned.

`search-path` *path filename* [*extensions* [*require-exts?*]]   [Scheme Procedure]
`scm_search_path` (*path, filename, rest*)   [C Function]
> Search *path* for a directory containing a file named *filename*. The file must be readable, and not a directory. If we find one, return its full filename; otherwise, return `#f`. If *filename* is absolute, return it unchanged. If given, *extensions* is a list of strings;

for each directory in *path*, we search for *filename* concatenated with each *extension*. If *require-exts?* is true, require that the returned file name have one of the given extensions; if *require-exts?* is not given, it defaults to `#f`.

For compatibility with Guile 1.8 and earlier, the C function takes only three arguments.

6.17.8 Character Encoding of Source Files

Scheme source code files are usually encoded in ASCII or UTF-8, but the built-in reader can interpret other character encodings as well. When Guile loads Scheme source code, it uses the `file-encoding` procedure (described below) to try to guess the encoding of the file. In the absence of any hints, UTF-8 is assumed. One way to provide a hint about the encoding of a source file is to place a coding declaration in the top 500 characters of the file.

A coding declaration has the form `coding: XXXXXX`, where `XXXXXX` is the name of a character encoding in which the source code file has been encoded. The coding declaration must appear in a scheme comment. It can either be a semicolon-initiated comment, or the first block `#!` comment in the file.

The name of the character encoding in the coding declaration is typically lower case and containing only letters, numbers, and hyphens, as recognized by `set-port-encoding!` (see Section 6.14.1 [Ports], page 316). Common examples of character encoding names are `utf-8` and `iso-8859-1`, as defined by IANA. Thus, the coding declaration is mostly compatible with Emacs.

However, there are some differences in encoding names recognized by Emacs and encoding names defined by IANA, the latter being essentially a subset of the former. For instance, `latin-1` is a valid encoding name for Emacs, but it's not according to the IANA standard, which Guile follows; instead, you should use `iso-8859-1`, which is both understood by Emacs and dubbed by IANA (IANA writes it uppercase but Emacs wants it lowercase and Guile is case insensitive.)

For source code, only a subset of all possible character encodings can be interpreted by the built-in source code reader. Only those character encodings in which ASCII text appears unmodified can be used. This includes `UTF-8` and `ISO-8859-1` through `ISO-8859-15`. The multi-byte character encodings `UTF-16` and `UTF-32` may not be used because they are not compatible with ASCII.

There might be a scenario in which one would want to read non-ASCII code from a port, such as with the function `read`, instead of with `load`. If the port's character encoding is the same as the encoding of the code to be read by the port, not other special handling is necessary. The port will automatically do the character encoding conversion. The functions `setlocale` or by `set-port-encoding!` are used to set port encodings (see Section 6.14.1 [Ports], page 316).

If a port is used to read code of unknown character encoding, it can accomplish this in three steps. First, the character encoding of the port should be set to ISO-8859-1 using `set-port-encoding!`. Then, the procedure `file-encoding`, described below, is used to scan for a coding declaration when reading from the port. As a side effect, it rewinds the port after its scan is complete. After that, the port's character encoding should be set to the encoding returned by `file-encoding`, if any, again by using `set-port-encoding!`. Then the code can be read as normal.

Alternatively, one can use the `#:guess-encoding` keyword argument of `open-file` and related procedures. See Section 6.14.9.1 [File Ports], page 326.

`file-encoding` *port*   [Scheme Procedure]
`scm_file_encoding` (*port*)   [C Function]
>   Attempt to scan the first few hundred bytes from the *port* for hints about its character encoding. Return a string containing the encoding name or `#f` if the encoding cannot be determined. The port is rewound.
>
>   Currently, the only supported method is to look for an Emacs-like character coding declaration (see Section "Recognize Coding" in *The GNU Emacs Reference Manual*). The coding declaration is of the form `coding: XXXXX` and must appear in a Scheme comment. Additional heuristics may be added in the future.

6.17.9 Delayed Evaluation

Promises are a convenient way to defer a calculation until its result is actually needed, and to run such a calculation only once. Also see Section 7.5.30 [SRFI-45], page 614.

`delay` *expr*   [syntax]
>   Return a promise object which holds the given *expr* expression, ready to be evaluated by a later `force`.

`promise?` *obj*   [Scheme Procedure]
`scm_promise_p` (*obj*)   [C Function]
>   Return true if *obj* is a promise.

`force` *p*   [Scheme Procedure]
`scm_force` (*p*)   [C Function]
>   Return the value obtained from evaluating the *expr* in the given promise *p*. If *p* has previously been forced then its *expr* is not evaluated again, instead the value obtained at that time is simply returned.
>
>   During a `force`, an *expr* can call `force` again on its own promise, resulting in a recursive evaluation of that *expr*. The first evaluation to return gives the value for the promise. Higher evaluations run to completion in the normal way, but their results are ignored, `force` always returns the first value.

6.17.10 Local Evaluation

Guile includes a facility to capture a lexical environment, and later evaluate a new expression within that environment. This code is implemented in a module.

```
(use-modules (ice-9 local-eval))
```

`the-environment`   [syntax]
>   Captures and returns a lexical environment for use with `local-eval` or `local-compile`.

`local-eval` *exp env*   [Scheme Procedure]
`scm_local_eval` (*exp, env*)   [C Function]
`local-compile` *exp env* [*opts=()*]   [Scheme Procedure]
    Evaluate or compile the expression *exp* in the lexical environment *env*.

Here is a simple example, illustrating that it is the variable that gets captured, not just
its value at one point in time.

```
(define e (let ((x 100)) (the-environment)))
(define fetch-x (local-eval '(lambda () x) e))
(fetch-x)
⇒ 100
(local-eval '(set! x 42) e)
(fetch-x)
⇒ 42
```

While *exp* is evaluated within the lexical environment of (`the-environment`), it has the
dynamic environment of the call to `local-eval`.

`local-eval` and `local-compile` can only evaluate expressions, not definitions.

```
(local-eval '(define foo 42)
            (let ((x 100)) (the-environment)))
⇒ syntax error: definition in expression context
```

Note that the current implementation of (`the-environment`) only captures "normal"
lexical bindings, and pattern variables bound by `syntax-case`. It does not currently capture
local syntax transformers bound by `let-syntax`, `letrec-syntax` or non-top-level `define-syntax` forms. Any attempt to reference such captured syntactic keywords via `local-eval`
or `local-compile` produces an error.

6.17.11 Local Inclusion

This section has discussed various means of linking Scheme code together: fundamentally,
loading up files at run-time using `load` and `load-compiled`. Guile provides another option
to compose parts of programs together at expansion-time instead of at run-time.

`include` *file-name*   [Scheme Syntax]
    Open *file-name*, at expansion-time, and read the Scheme forms that it contains, splic-
    ing them into the location of the `include`, within a `begin`.

    If *file-name* is a relative path, it is searched for relative to the path that contains the
    file that the `include` for appears in.

If you are a C programmer, if `load` in Scheme is like `dlopen` in C, consider `include` to
be like the C preprocessor's `#include`. When you use `include`, it is as if the contents of
the included file were typed in instead of the `include` form.

Because the code is included at compile-time, it is available to the macroexpander.
Syntax definitions in the included file are available to later code in the form in which
the `include` appears, without the need for `eval-when`. (See Section 6.10.8 [Eval When],
page 274.)

For the same reason, compiling a form that uses `include` results in one compilation
unit, composed of multiple files. Loading the compiled file is one `stat` operation for the

compilation unit, instead of 2*n in the case of load (once for each loaded source file, and once each corresponding compiled file, in the best case).

Unlike load, include also works within nested lexical contexts. It so happens that the optimizer works best within a lexical context, because all of the uses of bindings in a lexical context are visible, so composing files by including them within a (let () ...) can sometimes lead to important speed improvements.

On the other hand, include does have all the disadvantages of early binding: once the code with the include is compiled, no change to the included file is reflected in the future behavior of the including form.

Also, the particular form of include, which requires an absolute path, or a path relative to the current directory at compile-time, is not very amenable to compiling the source in one place, but then installing the source to another place. For this reason, Guile provides another form, include-from-path, which looks for the source file to include within a load path.

include-from-path *file-name*   [Scheme Syntax]
> Like include, but instead of expecting file-name to be an absolute file name, it is
> expected to be a relative path to search in the %load-path.

include-from-path is more useful when you want to install all of the source files for a package (as you should!). It makes it possible to evaluate an installed file from source, instead of relying on the .go file being up to date.

6.17.12 REPL Servers

The procedures in this section are provided by

> (use-modules (system repl server))

When an application is written in Guile, it is often convenient to allow the user to be able to interact with it by evaluating Scheme expressions in a REPL.

The procedures of this module allow you to spawn a *REPL server*, which permits interaction over a local or TCP connection. Guile itself uses them internally to implement the --listen switch, Section 4.2.1 [Command-line Options], page 35.

make-tcp-server-socket [#:host=#f] [#:addr]   [Scheme Procedure]
> [#:port=37146]
> Return a stream socket bound to a given address *addr* and port number *port*. If the
> host is given, and *addr* is not, then the *host* string is converted to an address. If
> neither is given, we use the loopback address.

make-unix-domain-server-socket   [Scheme Procedure]
> [#:path="/tmp/guile-socket"]
> Return a UNIX domain socket, bound to a given *path*.

run-server [*server-socket*]   [Scheme Procedure]
spawn-server [*server-socket*]   [Scheme Procedure]
> Create and run a REPL, making it available over the given *server-socket*. If *server-socket* is not provided, it defaults to the socket created by calling make-tcp-server-socket with no arguments.

run-server runs the server in the current thread, whereas spawn-server runs the server in a new thread.

stop-server-and-clients!   [Scheme Procedure]
Closes the connection on all running server sockets.

Please note that in the current implementation, the REPL threads are cancelled without unwinding their stacks. If any of them are holding mutexes or are within a critical section, the results are unspecified.

6.17.13 Cooperative REPL Servers

The procedures in this section are provided by

        (use-modules (system repl coop-server))

Whereas ordinary REPL servers run in their own threads (see Section 6.17.12 [REPL Servers], page 373), sometimes it is more convenient to provide REPLs that run at specified times within an existing thread, for example in programs utilizing an event loop or in single-threaded programs. This allows for safe access and mutation of a program's data structures from the REPL, without concern for thread synchronization.

Although the REPLs are run in the thread that calls spawn-coop-repl-server and poll-coop-repl-server, dedicated threads are spawned so that the calling thread is not blocked. The spawned threads read input for the REPLs and to listen for new connections.

Cooperative REPL servers must be polled periodically to evaluate any pending expressions by calling poll-coop-repl-server with the object returned from spawn-coop-repl-server. The thread that calls poll-coop-repl-server will be blocked for as long as the expression takes to be evaluated or if the debugger is entered.

spawn-coop-repl-server [server-socket]   [Scheme Procedure]
Create and return a new cooperative REPL server object, and spawn a new thread to listen for connections on server-socket. Proper functioning of the REPL server requires that poll-coop-repl-server be called periodically on the returned server object.

poll-coop-repl-server coop-server   [Scheme Procedure]
Poll the cooperative REPL server coop-server and apply a pending operation if there is one, such as evaluating an expression typed at the REPL prompt. This procedure must be called from the same thread that called spawn-coop-repl-server.

6.18 Memory Management and Garbage Collection

Guile uses a *garbage collector* to manage most of its objects. While the garbage collector is designed to be mostly invisible, you sometimes need to interact with it explicitly.

See Section 5.4.2 [Garbage Collection], page 65 for a general discussion of how garbage collection relates to using Guile from C.

6.18.1 Function related to Garbage Collection

gc   [Scheme Procedure] `scm_gc ()`   [C Function]

> Scans all of SCM objects and reclaims for further use those that are no longer accessible. You normally don't need to call this function explicitly. It is called automatically when appropriate.

`SCM scm_gc_protect_object (SCM obj)`   [C Function]

> Protects *obj* from being freed by the garbage collector, when it otherwise might be. When you are done with the object, call `scm_gc_unprotect_object` on the object. Calls to `scm_gc_protect/scm_gc_unprotect_object` can be nested, and the object remains protected until it has been unprotected as many times as it was protected. It is an error to unprotect an object more times than it has been protected. Returns the SCM object it was passed.
>
> Note that storing *obj* in a C global variable has the same effect[11].

`SCM scm_gc_unprotect_object (SCM obj)`   [C Function]

> Unprotects an object from the garbage collector which was protected by `scm_gc_unprotect_object`. Returns the SCM object it was passed.

`SCM scm_permanent_object (SCM obj)`   [C Function]

> Similar to `scm_gc_protect_object` in that it causes the collector to always mark the object, except that it should not be nested (only call `scm_permanent_object` on an object once), and it has no corresponding unpermanent function. Once an object is declared permanent, it will never be freed. Returns the SCM object it was passed.

`void scm_remember_upto_here_1 (SCM obj)`   [C Macro]
`void scm_remember_upto_here_2 (SCM obj1, SCM obj2)`   [C Macro]

> Create a reference to the given object or objects, so they're certain to be present on the stack or in a register and hence will not be freed by the garbage collector before this point.
>
> Note that these functions can only be applied to ordinary C local variables (ie. "automatics"). Objects held in global or static variables or some malloced block or the like cannot be protected with this mechanism.

`gc-stats`   [Scheme Procedure]
`scm_gc_stats ()`   [C Function]

> Return an association list of statistics about Guile's current use of storage.

`gc-live-object-stats`   [Scheme Procedure]
`scm_gc_live_object_stats ()`   [C Function]

> Return an alist of statistics of the current live objects.

`void scm_gc_mark (SCM x)`   [Function]

> Mark the object *x*, and recurse on any objects *x* refers to. If *x*'s mark bit is already set, return immediately. This function must only be called during the mark-phase of garbage collection, typically from a smob *mark* function.

---

[11] In Guile up to version 1.8, C global variables were not scanned by the garbage collector; hence, `scm_gc_protect_object` was the only way in C to prevent a Scheme object from being freed.

6.18.2 Memory Blocks

In C programs, dynamic management of memory blocks is normally done with the functions malloc, realloc, and free. Guile has additional functions for dynamic memory allocation that are integrated into the garbage collector and the error reporting system.

Memory blocks that are associated with Scheme objects (for example a smob) should be allocated with scm_gc_malloc or scm_gc_malloc_pointerless. These two functions will either return a valid pointer or signal an error. Memory blocks allocated this way can be freed with scm_gc_free; however, this is not strictly needed: memory allocated with scm_gc_malloc or scm_gc_malloc_pointerless is automatically reclaimed when the garbage collector no longer sees any live reference to it[12].

Memory allocated with scm_gc_malloc is scanned for live pointers. This means that if scm_gc_malloc-allocated memory contains a pointer to some other part of the memory, the garbage collector notices it and prevents it from being reclaimed[13]. Conversely, memory allocated with scm_gc_malloc_pointerless is assumed to be "pointer-less" and is not scanned.

For memory that is not associated with a Scheme object, you can use scm_malloc instead of malloc. Like scm_gc_malloc, it will either return a valid pointer or signal an error. However, it will not assume that the new memory block can be freed by a garbage collection. The memory must be explicitly freed with free.

There is also scm_gc_realloc and scm_realloc, to be used in place of realloc when appropriate, and scm_gc_calloc and scm_calloc, to be used in place of calloc when appropriate.

The function scm_dynwind_free can be useful when memory should be freed with libc's free when leaving a dynwind context, See Section 6.13.10 [Dynamic Wind], page 309.

void * scm_malloc (size_t size)   [C Function]
void * scm_calloc (size_t size)   [C Function]
> Allocate size bytes of memory and return a pointer to it. When size is 0, return NULL. When not enough memory is available, signal an error. This function runs the GC to free up some memory when it deems it appropriate.
>
> The memory is allocated by the libc malloc function and can be freed with free. There is no scm_free function to go with scm_malloc to make it easier to pass memory back and forth between different modules.
>
> The function scm_calloc is similar to scm_malloc, but initializes the block of memory to zero as well.
>
> These functions will (indirectly) call scm_gc_register_allocation.

void * scm_realloc (void *mem, size_t new_size)   [C Function]
> Change the size of the memory block at mem to new_size and return its new location. When new_size is 0, this is the same as calling free on mem and NULL is returned.

---

[12] In Guile up to version 1.8, memory allocated with scm_gc_malloc *had* to be freed with scm_gc_free.

[13] In Guile up to 1.8, memory allocated with scm_gc_malloc was *not* scanned. Consequently, the GC had to be told explicitly about pointers to live objects contained in the memory block, e.g., *via* SMOB mark functions (see Section 6.8 [Smobs], page 241)

When *mem* is NULL, this function behaves like `scm_malloc` and allocates a new block of size *new_size*.

When not enough memory is available, signal an error. This function runs the GC to free up some memory when it deems it appropriate.

This function will call `scm_gc_register_allocation`.

void * `scm_gc_malloc` (*size_t* `size`, *const char* `*what`)	[C Function]
void * `scm_gc_malloc_pointerless` (*size_t* `size`, *const char* `*what`)	[C Function]
void * `scm_gc_realloc` (*void* `*mem`, *size_t* `old_size`, *size_t* `new_size`, *const char* `*what`);	[C Function]
void * `scm_gc_calloc` (*size_t* `size`, *const char* `*what`)	[C Function]

Allocate *size* bytes of automatically-managed memory. The memory is automatically freed when no longer referenced from any live memory block.

Memory allocated with `scm_gc_malloc` or `scm_gc_calloc` is scanned for pointers. Memory allocated by `scm_gc_malloc_pointerless` is not scanned.

The `scm_gc_realloc` call preserves the "pointerlessness" of the memory area pointed to by *mem*. Note that you need to pass the old size of a reallocated memory block as well. See below for a motivation.

void `scm_gc_free` (*void* `*mem`, *size_t* `size`, *const char* `*what`)　　　[C Function]

Explicitly free the memory block pointed to by *mem*, which was previously allocated by one of the above `scm_gc` functions.

Note that you need to explicitly pass the *size* parameter. This is done since it should normally be easy to provide this parameter (for memory that is associated with GC controlled objects) and help keep the memory management overhead very low. However, in Guile 2.x, *size* is always ignored.

void `scm_gc_register_allocation` (*size_t* `size`)　　　　　　　　[C Function]

Informs the garbage collector that *size* bytes have been allocated, which the collector would otherwise not have known about.

In general, Scheme will decide to collect garbage only after some amount of memory has been allocated. Calling this function will make the Scheme garbage collector know about more allocation, and thus run more often (as appropriate).

It is especially important to call this function when large unmanaged allocations, like images, may be freed by small Scheme allocations, like SMOBs.

void `scm_dynwind_free` (*void* `*mem`)　　　　　　　　　　　[C Function]

Equivalent　　to　　`scm_dynwind_unwind_handler` (`free`, *mem*, SCM_F_WIND_ EXPLICITLY). That is, the memory block at *mem* will be freed (using `free` from the C library) when the current dynwind is left.

`malloc-stats`　　　　　　　　　　　　　　　　　　　[Scheme Procedure]

Return an alist ((*what* . *n*) ...) describing number of malloced objects. *what* is the second argument to `scm_gc_malloc`, *n* is the number of objects of that type currently allocated.

This function is only available if the GUILE_DEBUG_MALLOC preprocessor macro was defined when Guile was compiled.

6.18.2.1 Upgrading from scm_must_malloc et al.

Version 1.6 of Guile and earlier did not have the functions from the previous section. In their place, it had the functions scm_must_malloc, scm_must_realloc and scm_must_free. This section explains why we want you to stop using them, and how to do this.

The functions scm_must_malloc and scm_must_realloc behaved like scm_gc_malloc and scm_gc_realloc do now, respectively. They would inform the GC about the newly allocated memory via the internal equivalent of scm_gc_register_allocation. However, scm_must_free did not unregister the memory it was about to free. The usual way to unregister memory was to return its size from a smob free function.

This disconnectedness of the actual freeing of memory and reporting this to the GC proved to be bad in practice. It was easy to make mistakes and report the wrong size because allocating and freeing was not done with symmetric code, and because it is cumbersome to compute the total size of nested data structures that were freed with multiple calls to scm_must_free. Additionally, there was no equivalent to scm_malloc, and it was tempting to just use scm_must_malloc and never to tell the GC that the memory has been freed.

The effect was that the internal statistics kept by the GC drifted out of sync with reality and could even overflow in long running programs. When this happened, the result was a dramatic increase in (senseless) GC activity which would effectively stop the program dead.

The functions scm_done_malloc and scm_done_free were introduced to help restore balance to the force, but existing bugs did not magically disappear, of course.

Therefore we decided to force everybody to review their code by deprecating the existing functions and introducing new ones in their place that are hopefully easier to use correctly.

For every use of scm_must_malloc you need to decide whether to use scm_malloc or scm_gc_malloc in its place. When the memory block is not part of a smob or some other Scheme object whose lifetime is ultimately managed by the garbage collector, use scm_malloc and free. When it is part of a smob, use scm_gc_malloc and change the smob free function to use scm_gc_free instead of scm_must_free or free and make it return zero.

The important thing is to always pair scm_malloc with free; and to always pair scm_gc_malloc with scm_gc_free.

The same reasoning applies to scm_must_realloc and scm_realloc versus scm_gc_realloc.

6.18.3 Weak References

[FIXME: This chapter is based on Mikael Djurfeldt's answer to a question by Michael Livshin. Any mistakes are not theirs, of course.]

Weak references let you attach bookkeeping information to data so that the additional information automatically disappears when the original data is no longer in use and gets garbage collected. In a weak key hash, the hash entry for that key disappears as soon as the key is no longer referenced from anywhere else. For weak value hashes, the same happens as soon as the value is no longer in use. Entries in a doubly weak hash disappear when either the key or the value are not used anywhere else anymore.

Object properties offer the same kind of functionality as weak key hashes in many situations. (see Section 6.11.2 [Object Properties], page 278)

Here's an example (a little bit strained perhaps, but one of the examples is actually used in Guile):

Assume that you're implementing a debugging system where you want to associate information about filename and position of source code expressions with the expressions themselves.

Hashtables can be used for that, but if you use ordinary hash tables it will be impossible for the scheme interpreter to "forget" old source when, for example, a file is reloaded.

To implement the mapping from source code expressions to positional information it is necessary to use weak-key tables since we don't want the expressions to be remembered just because they are in our table.

To implement a mapping from source file line numbers to source code expressions you would use a weak-value table.

To implement a mapping from source code expressions to the procedures they constitute a doubly-weak table has to be used.

6.18.3.1 Weak hash tables

`make-weak-key-hash-table` [*size*]	[Scheme Procedure]
`make-weak-value-hash-table` [*size*]	[Scheme Procedure]
`make-doubly-weak-hash-table` [*size*]	[Scheme Procedure]
`scm_make_weak_key_hash_table` (*size*)	[C Function]
`scm_make_weak_value_hash_table` (*size*)	[C Function]
`scm_make_doubly_weak_hash_table` (*size*)	[C Function]

> Return a weak hash table with *size* buckets. As with any hash table, choosing a good size for the table requires some caution.
>
> You can modify weak hash tables in exactly the same way you would modify regular hash tables. (see Section 6.7.14 [Hash Tables], page 236)

`weak-key-hash-table?` *obj*	[Scheme Procedure]
`weak-value-hash-table?` *obj*	[Scheme Procedure]
`doubly-weak-hash-table?` *obj*	[Scheme Procedure]
`scm_weak_key_hash_table_p` (*obj*)	[C Function]
`scm_weak_value_hash_table_p` (*obj*)	[C Function]
`scm_doubly_weak_hash_table_p` (*obj*)	[C Function]

> Return #t if *obj* is the specified weak hash table. Note that a doubly weak hash table is neither a weak key nor a weak value hash table.

6.18.3.2 Weak vectors

`make-weak-vector` *size* [*fill*]	[Scheme Procedure]
`scm_make_weak_vector` (*size, fill*)	[C Function]

> Return a weak vector with *size* elements. If the optional argument *fill* is given, all entries in the vector will be set to *fill*. The default value for *fill* is the empty list.

`weak-vector` *elem* ...	[Scheme Procedure]
`list->weak-vector` *l*	[Scheme Procedure]

`scm_weak_vector` (*l*)   [C Function]
> Construct a weak vector from a list: `weak-vector` uses the list of its arguments while `list->weak-vector` uses its only argument *l* (a list) to construct a weak vector the same way `list->vector` would.

`weak-vector?` *obj*   [Scheme Procedure]
`scm_weak_vector_p` (*obj*)   [C Function]
> Return #t if *obj* is a weak vector.

`weak-vector-ref` *wvect k*   [Scheme Procedure]
`scm_weak_vector_ref` (*wvect, k*)   [C Function]
> Return the *k*th element of the weak vector *wvect*, or #f if that element has been collected.

`weak-vector-set!` *wvect k elt*   [Scheme Procedure]
`scm_weak_vector_set_x` (*wvect, k, elt*)   [C Function]
> Set the *k*th element of the weak vector *wvect* to *elt*.

6.18.4 Guardians

Guardians provide a way to be notified about objects that would otherwise be collected as garbage. Guarding them prevents the objects from being collected and cleanup actions can be performed on them, for example.

See R. Kent Dybvig, Carl Bruggeman, and David Eby (1993) "Guardians in a Generation-Based Garbage Collector". ACM SIGPLAN Conference on Programming Language Design and Implementation, June 1993.

`make-guardian`   [Scheme Procedure]
`scm_make_guardian` ()   [C Function]
> Create a new guardian. A guardian protects a set of objects from garbage collection, allowing a program to apply cleanup or other actions.
>
> `make-guardian` returns a procedure representing the guardian. Calling the guardian procedure with an argument adds the argument to the guardian's set of protected objects. Calling the guardian procedure without an argument returns one of the protected objects which are ready for garbage collection, or #f if no such object is available. Objects which are returned in this way are removed from the guardian.
>
> You can put a single object into a guardian more than once and you can put a single object into more than one guardian. The object will then be returned multiple times by the guardian procedures.
>
> An object is eligible to be returned from a guardian when it is no longer referenced from outside any guardian.
>
> There is no guarantee about the order in which objects are returned from a guardian. If you want to impose an order on finalization actions, for example, you can do that by keeping objects alive in some global data structure until they are no longer needed for finalizing other objects.
>
> Being an element in a weak vector, a key in a hash table with weak keys, or a value in a hash table with weak values does not prevent an object from being returned by a guardian. But as long as an object can be returned from a guardian it will not be

removed from such a weak vector or hash table. In other words, a weak link does not prevent an object from being considered collectable, but being inside a guardian prevents a weak link from being broken.

A key in a weak key hash table can be thought of as having a strong reference to its associated value as long as the key is accessible. Consequently, when the key is only accessible from within a guardian, the reference from the key to the value is also considered to be coming from within a guardian. Thus, if there is no other reference to the value, it is eligible to be returned from a guardian.

6.19 Modules

When programs become large, naming conflicts can occur when a function or global variable defined in one file has the same name as a function or global variable in another file. Even just a *similarity* between function names can cause hard-to-find bugs, since a programmer might type the wrong function name.

The approach used to tackle this problem is called *information encapsulation*, which consists of packaging functional units into a given name space that is clearly separated from other name spaces.

The language features that allow this are usually called *the module system* because programs are broken up into modules that are compiled separately (or loaded separately in an interpreter).

Older languages, like C, have limited support for name space manipulation and protection. In C a variable or function is public by default, and can be made local to a module with the `static` keyword. But you cannot reference public variables and functions from another module with different names.

More advanced module systems have become a common feature in recently designed languages: ML, Python, Perl, and Modula 3 all allow the *renaming* of objects from a foreign module, so they will not clutter the global name space.

In addition, Guile offers variables as first-class objects. They can be used for interacting with the module system.

6.19.1 General Information about Modules

A Guile module can be thought of as a collection of named procedures, variables and macros. More precisely, it is a set of *bindings* of symbols (names) to Scheme objects.

Within a module, all bindings are visible. Certain bindings can be declared *public*, in which case they are added to the module's so-called *export list*; this set of public bindings is called the module's *public interface* (see Section 6.19.3 [Creating Guile Modules], page 383).

A client module *uses* a providing module's bindings by either accessing the providing module's public interface, or by building a custom interface (and then accessing that). In a custom interface, the client module can *select* which bindings to access and can also algorithmically *rename* bindings. In contrast, when using the providing module's public interface, the entire export list is available without renaming (see Section 6.19.2 [Using Guile Modules], page 382).

All Guile modules have a unique *module name*, for example `(ice-9 popen)` or `(srfi srfi-11)`. Module names are lists of one or more symbols.

When Guile goes to use an interface from a module, for example (ice-9 popen), Guile first looks to see if it has loaded (ice-9 popen) for any reason. If the module has not been loaded yet, Guile searches a *load path* for a file that might define it, and loads that file.

The following subsections go into more detail on using, creating, installing, and otherwise manipulating modules and the module system.

6.19.2 Using Guile Modules

To use a Guile module is to access either its public interface or a custom interface (see Section 6.19.1 [General Information about Modules], page 381). Both types of access are handled by the syntactic form use-modules, which accepts one or more interface specifications and, upon evaluation, arranges for those interfaces to be available to the current module. This process may include locating and loading code for a given module if that code has not yet been loaded, following %load-path (see Section 6.19.4 [Modules and the File System], page 386).

An *interface specification* has one of two forms. The first variation is simply to name the module, in which case its public interface is the one accessed. For example:

```
(use-modules (ice-9 popen))
```

Here, the interface specification is (ice-9 popen), and the result is that the current module now has access to open-pipe, close-pipe, open-input-pipe, and so on (see Section 7.2.10 [Pipes], page 500).

Note in the previous example that if the current module had already defined open-pipe, that definition would be overwritten by the definition in (ice-9 popen). For this reason (and others), there is a second variation of interface specification that not only names a module to be accessed, but also selects bindings from it and renames them to suit the current module's needs. For example:

```
(use-modules ((ice-9 popen)
              #:select ((open-pipe . pipe-open) close-pipe)
              #:renamer (symbol-prefix-proc 'unixy:)))
```

Here, the interface specification is more complex than before, and the result is that a custom interface with only two bindings is created and subsequently accessed by the current module. The mapping of old to new names is as follows:

```
(ice-9 popen) sees:          current module sees:
open-pipe                    unixy:pipe-open
close-pipe                   unixy:close-pipe
```

This example also shows how to use the convenience procedure symbol-prefix-proc.

You can also directly refer to bindings in a module by using the @ syntax. For example, instead of using the use-modules statement from above and writing unixy:pipe-open to refer to the pipe-open from the (ice-9 popen), you could also write (@ (ice-9 popen) open-pipe). Thus an alternative to the complete use-modules statement would be

```
(define unixy:pipe-open (@ (ice-9 popen) open-pipe))
(define unixy:close-pipe (@ (ice-9 popen) close-pipe))
```

There is also @@, which can be used like @, but does not check whether the variable that is being accessed is actually exported. Thus, @@ can be thought of as the impolite version of @ and should only be used as a last resort or for debugging, for example.

Note that just as with a `use-modules` statement, any module that has not yet been loaded yet will be loaded when referenced by a @ or @@ form.

You can also use the @ and @@ syntaxes as the target of a `set!` when the binding refers to a variable.

`symbol-prefix-proc` *prefix-sym*   [Scheme Procedure]
    Return a procedure that prefixes its arg (a symbol) with *prefix-sym*.

`use-modules` *spec . . .*   [syntax]
    Resolve each interface specification *spec* into an interface and arrange for these to be accessible by the current module. The return value is unspecified.

    spec can be a list of symbols, in which case it names a module whose public interface is found and used.

    spec can also be of the form:

        `(MODULE-NAME [#:select SELECTION] [#:renamer RENAMER])`

    in which case a custom interface is newly created and used. *module-name* is a list of symbols, as above; *selection* is a list of selection-specs; and *renamer* is a procedure that takes a symbol and returns its new name. A selection-spec is either a symbol or a pair of symbols `(ORIG . SEEN)`, where *orig* is the name in the used module and *seen* is the name in the using module. Note that *seen* is also passed through *renamer*.

    The `#:select` and `#:renamer` clauses are optional. If both are omitted, the returned interface has no bindings. If the `#:select` clause is omitted, *renamer* operates on the used module's public interface.

    In addition to the above, *spec* can also include a `#:version` clause, of the form:

        `#:version VERSION-SPEC`

    where *version-spec* is an R6RS-compatible version reference. An error will be signaled in the case in which a module with the same name has already been loaded, if that module specifies a version and that version is not compatible with *version-spec*. See Section 6.19.5 [R6RS Version References], page 387, for more on version references.

    If the module name is not resolvable, `use-modules` will signal an error.

@ *module-name binding-name*   [syntax]
    Refer to the binding named *binding-name* in module *module-name*. The binding must have been exported by the module.

@@ *module-name binding-name*   [syntax]
    Refer to the binding named *binding-name* in module *module-name*. The binding must not have been exported by the module. This syntax is only intended for debugging purposes or as a last resort.

6.19.3 Creating Guile Modules

When you want to create your own modules, you have to take the following steps:

- Create a Scheme source file and add all variables and procedures you wish to export, or which are required by the exported procedures.

- Add a `define-module` form at the beginning.

- Export all bindings which should be in the public interface, either by using define-public or export (both documented below).

define-module *module-name option ...*   [syntax]

    module-name is a list of one or more symbols.

        `(define-module (ice-9 popen))`

define-module makes this module available to Guile programs under the given *module-name*.

option ... are keyword/value pairs which specify more about the defined module. The recognized options and their meaning are shown in the following table.

#:use-module *interface-specification*

    Equivalent to a (use-modules *interface-specification*) (see Section 6.19.2 [Using Guile Modules], page 382).

#:autoload *module symbol-list*

    Load *module* when any of *symbol-list* are accessed. For example,

```
(define-module (my mod)
  #:autoload (srfi srfi-1) (partition delete-duplicates))
...
(if something
    (set! foo (delete-duplicates ...)))
```

    When a module is autoloaded, all its bindings become available. *symbol-list* is just those that will first trigger the load.

    An autoload is a good way to put off loading a big module until it's really needed, for instance for faster startup or if it will only be needed in certain circumstances.

    @ can do a similar thing (see Section 6.19.2 [Using Guile Modules], page 382), but in that case an @ form must be written every time a binding from the module is used.

#:export *list*

    Export all identifiers in *list* which must be a list of symbols or pairs of symbols. This is equivalent to (export *list*) in the module body.

#:re-export *list*

    Re-export all identifiers in *list* which must be a list of symbols or pairs of symbols. The symbols in *list* must be imported by the current module from other modules. This is equivalent to re-export below.

#:replace *list*

    Export all identifiers in *list* (a list of symbols or pairs of symbols) and mark them as *replacing bindings*. In the module user's name space, this will have the effect of replacing any binding with the same name that is not also "replacing". Normally a replacement results in an "override" warning message, #:replace avoids that.

    In general, a module that exports a binding for which the (guile) module already has a definition should use #:replace instead of #:export.

`#:replace`, in a sense, lets Guile know that the module *purposefully* replaces a core binding. It is important to note, however, that this binding replacement is confined to the name space of the module user. In other words, the value of the core binding in question remains unchanged for other modules.

Note that although it is often a good idea for the replaced binding to remain compatible with a binding in `(guile)`, to avoid surprising the user, sometimes the bindings will be incompatible. For example, SRFI-19 exports its own version of `current-time` (see Section 7.5.16.2 [SRFI-19 Time], page 584) which is not compatible with the core `current-time` function (see Section 7.2.5 [Time], page 485). Guile assumes that a user importing a module knows what she is doing, and uses `#:replace` for this binding rather than `#:export`.

A `#:replace` clause is equivalent to `(export! list)` in the module body.

The `#:duplicates` (see below) provides fine-grain control about duplicate binding handling on the module-user side.

`#:version` *list*

Specify a version for the module in the form of *list*, a list of zero or more exact, nonnegative integers. The corresponding `#:version` option in the `use-modules` form allows callers to restrict the value of this option in various ways.

`#:duplicates` *list*

Tell Guile to handle duplicate bindings for the bindings imported by the current module according to the policy defined by *list*, a list of symbols. *list* must contain symbols representing a duplicate binding handling policy chosen among the following:

check   Raises an error when a binding is imported from more than one place.

warn   Issue a warning when a binding is imported from more than one place and leave the responsibility of actually handling the duplication to the next duplicate binding handler.

replace   When a new binding is imported that has the same name as a previously imported binding, then do the following:

1. If the old binding was said to be *replacing* (via the `#:replace` option above) and the new binding is not replacing, the keep the old binding.

2. If the old binding was not said to be replacing and the new binding is replacing, then replace the old binding with the new one.

3. If neither the old nor the new binding is replacing, then keep the old one.

warn-override-core

Issue a warning when a core binding is being overwritten and actually override the core binding with the new one.

first   In case of duplicate bindings, the firstly imported binding is
               always the one which is kept.

last   In case of duplicate bindings, the lastly imported binding is
               always the one which is kept.

noop   In case of duplicate bindings, leave the responsibility to the
               next duplicate handler.

If *list* contains more than one symbol, then the duplicate binding handlers
which appear first will be used first when resolving a duplicate binding
situation. As mentioned above, some resolution policies may explicitly
leave the responsibility of handling the duplication to the next handler
in *list*.

If GOOPS has been loaded before the `#:duplicates` clause is processed,
there are additional strategies available for dealing with generic functions.
See Section 8.6.3 [Merging Generics], page 728, for more information.

The default duplicate binding resolution policy is given by the `default-
duplicate-binding-handler` procedure, and is

```
(replace warn-override-core warn last)
```

`#:pure`   Create a *pure* module, that is a module which does not contain any of the
               standard procedure bindings except for the syntax forms. This is useful
               if you want to create *safe* modules, that is modules which do not know
               anything about dangerous procedures.

export *variable* . . .   [syntax]
    Add all *variable*s (which must be symbols or pairs of symbols) to the list of exported
    bindings of the current module. If *variable* is a pair, its `car` gives the name of the
    variable as seen by the current module and its `cdr` specifies a name for the binding
    in the current module's public interface.

define-public . . .   [syntax]
    Equivalent to `(begin (define foo ...) (export foo))`.

re-export *variable* . . .   [syntax]
    Add all *variable*s (which must be symbols or pairs of symbols) to the list of re-exported
    bindings of the current module. Pairs of symbols are handled as in `export`. Re-
    exported bindings must be imported by the current module from some other module.

export! *variable* . . .   [syntax]
    Like `export`, but marking the exported variables as replacing. Using a module with
    replacing bindings will cause any existing bindings to be replaced without issuing any
    warnings. See the discussion of `#:replace` above.

6.19.4 Modules and the File System

Typical programs only use a small subset of modules installed on a Guile system. In order to
keep startup time down, Guile only loads modules when a program uses them, on demand.

When a program evaluates `(use-modules (ice-9 popen))`, and the module is not
loaded, Guile searches for a conventionally-named file from in the *load path*.

In this case, loading (ice-9 popen) will eventually cause Guile to run (primitive-load-path "ice-9/popen"). primitive-load-path will search for a file ice-9/popen in the %load-path (see Section 6.17.7 [Load Paths], page 368). For each directory in %load-path, Guile will try to find the file name, concatenated with the extensions from %load-extensions. By default, this will cause Guile to stat ice-9/popen.scm, and then ice-9/popen. See Section 6.17.7 [Load Paths], page 368, for more on primitive-load-path.

If a corresponding compiled .go file is found in the %load-compiled-path or in the fallback path, and is as fresh as the source file, it will be loaded instead of the source file. If no compiled file is found, Guile may try to compile the source file and cache away the resulting .go file. See Section 6.17.5 [Compilation], page 364, for more on compilation.

Once Guile finds a suitable source or compiled file is found, the file will be loaded. If, after loading the file, the module under consideration is still not defined, Guile will signal an error.

For more information on where and how to install Scheme modules, See Section 4.7 [Installing Site Packages], page 55.

6.19.5 R6RS Version References

Guile's module system includes support for locating modules based on a declared version specifier of the same form as the one described in R6RS (see Section "Library form" in *The Revised^6 Report on the Algorithmic Language Scheme*). By using the #:version keyword in a define-module form, a module may specify a version as a list of zero or more exact, nonnegative integers.

This version can then be used to locate the module during the module search process. Client modules and callers of the use-modules function may specify constraints on the versions of target modules by providing a *version reference*, which has one of the following forms:

```
(sub-version-reference ...)
(and version-reference ...)
(or version-reference ...)
(not version-reference)
```

in which *sub-version-reference* is in turn one of:

```
(sub-version)
(>= sub-version)
(<= sub-version)
(and sub-version-reference ...)
(or sub-version-reference ...)
(not sub-version-reference)
```

in which *sub-version* is an exact, nonnegative integer as above. A version reference matches a declared module version if each element of the version reference matches a corresponding element of the module version, according to the following rules:

- The **and** sub-form matches a version or version element if every element in the tail of the sub-form matches the specified version or version element.

- The **or** sub-form matches a version or version element if any element in the tail of the sub-form matches the specified version or version element.

- The **not** sub-form matches a version or version element if the tail of the sub-form does not match the version or version element.

- The **>=** sub-form matches a version element if the element is greater than or equal to the *sub-version* in the tail of the sub-form.

- The **<=** sub-form matches a version element if the version is less than or equal to the *sub-version* in the tail of the sub-form.

- A *sub-version* matches a version element if one is *eqv?* to the other.

For example, a module declared as:

```
(define-module (mylib mymodule) #:version (1 2 0))
```

would be successfully loaded by any of the following **use-modules** expressions:

```
(use-modules ((mylib mymodule) #:version (1 2 (>= 0))))
(use-modules ((mylib mymodule) #:version (or (1 2 0) (1 2 1))))
(use-modules ((mylib mymodule) #:version ((and (>= 1) (not 2)) 2 0)))
```

6.19.6 R6RS Libraries

In addition to the API described in the previous sections, you also have the option to create modules using the portable **library** form described in R6RS (see Section "Library form" in *The Revised^6 Report on the Algorithmic Language Scheme*), and to import libraries created in this format by other programmers. Guile's R6RS library implementation takes advantage of the flexibility built into the module system by expanding the R6RS library form into a corresponding Guile **define-module** form that specifies equivalent import and export requirements and includes the same body expressions. The library expression:

```
(library (mylib (1 2))
  (import (otherlib (3)))
  (export mybinding))
```

is equivalent to the module definition:

```
(define-module (mylib)
  #:version (1 2)
  #:use-module ((otherlib) #:version (3))
  #:export (mybinding))
```

Central to the mechanics of R6RS libraries is the concept of import and export *levels*, which control the visibility of bindings at various phases of a library's lifecycle — macros necessary to expand forms in the library's body need to be available at expand time; variables used in the body of a procedure exported by the library must be available at runtime. R6RS specifies the optional **for** sub-form of an *import set* specification (see below) as a mechanism by which a library author can indicate that a particular library import should take place at a particular phase with respect to the lifecycle of the importing library.

Guile's library implementation uses a technique called *implicit phasing* (first described by Abdulaziz Ghuloum and R. Kent Dybvig), which allows the expander and compiler to automatically determine the necessary visibility of a binding imported from another library. As such, the **for** sub-form described below is ignored by Guile (but may be required by Schemes in which phasing is explicit).

`library` *name* (`export` *export-spec* ...) (`import` *import-spec* ...) *body*   [Scheme Syntax]
       ...

Defines a new library with the specified name, exports, and imports, and evaluates the specified body expressions in this library's environment.

The library *name* is a non-empty list of identifiers, optionally ending with a version specification of the form described above (see Section 6.19.3 [Creating Guile Modules], page 383).

Each *export-spec* is the name of a variable defined or imported by the library, or must take the form (`rename` (`internal-name external-name`) ...), where the identifier *internal-name* names a variable defined or imported by the library and *external-name* is the name by which the variable is seen by importing libraries.

Each *import-spec* must be either an *import set* (see below) or must be of the form (`for import-set import-level` ...), where each *import-level* is one of:

```
run
expand
(meta level)
```

where *level* is an integer. Note that since Guile does not require explicit phase specification, any *import-sets* found inside of `for` sub-forms will be "unwrapped" during expansion and processed as if they had been specified directly.

Import sets in turn take one of the following forms:

```
library-reference
(library library-reference)
(only import-set identifier ...)
(except import-set identifier ...)
(prefix import-set identifier)
(rename import-set (internal-identifier external-identifier) ...)
```

where *library-reference* is a non-empty list of identifiers ending with an optional version reference (see Section 6.19.5 [R6RS Version References], page 387), and the other sub-forms have the following semantics, defined recursively on nested *import-sets*:

- The `library` sub-form is used to specify libraries for import whose names begin with the identifier "library."

- The `only` sub-form imports only the specified *identifiers* from the given *import-set*.

- The `except` sub-form imports all of the bindings exported by *import-set* except for those that appear in the specified list of *identifiers*.

- The `prefix` sub-form imports all of the bindings exported by *import-set*, first prefixing them with the specified *identifier*.

- The `rename` sub-form imports all of the identifiers exported by *import-set*. The binding for each *internal-identifier* among these identifiers is made visible to the importing library as the corresponding *external-identifier*; all other bindings are imported using the names provided by *import-set*.

Note that because Guile translates R6RS libraries into module definitions, an import specification may be used to declare a dependency on a native Guile module — although doing so may make your libraries less portable to other Schemes.

import *import-spec ...*   [Scheme Syntax]

   Import into the current environment the libraries specified by the given import specifications, where each *import-spec* takes the same form as in the **library** form described
   above.

6.19.7 Variables

Each module has its own hash table, sometimes known as an *obarray*, that maps the names
defined in that module to their corresponding variable objects.

   A variable is a box-like object that can hold any Scheme value. It is said to be *undefined*
if its box holds a special Scheme value that denotes undefined-ness (which is different from
all other Scheme values, including for example **#f**); otherwise the variable is *defined*.

   On its own, a variable object is anonymous. A variable is said to be *bound* when it is
associated with a name in some way, usually a symbol in a module obarray. When this
happens, the name is said to be bound to the variable, in that module.

   (That's the theory, anyway. In practice, defined-ness and bound-ness sometimes get
confused, because Lisp and Scheme implementations have often conflated — or deliberately
drawn no distinction between — a name that is unbound and a name that is bound to a
variable whose value is undefined. We will try to be clear about the difference and explain
any confusion where it is unavoidable.)

   Variables do not have a read syntax. Most commonly they are created and bound
implicitly by **define** expressions: a top-level **define** expression of the form

        (define name value)

creates a variable with initial value *value* and binds it to the name *name* in the current module. But they can also be created dynamically by calling one of the constructor procedures
make-variable and **make-undefined-variable**.

make-undefined-variable   [Scheme Procedure]
scm_make_undefined_variable ()   [C Function]
   Return a variable that is initially unbound.

make-variable *init*   [Scheme Procedure]
scm_make_variable (*init*)   [C Function]
   Return a variable initialized to value *init*.

variable-bound? *var*   [Scheme Procedure]
scm_variable_bound_p (*var*)   [C Function]
   Return **#t** if *var* is bound to a value, or **#f** otherwise. Throws an error if *var* is not
   a variable object.

variable-ref *var*   [Scheme Procedure]
scm_variable_ref (*var*)   [C Function]
   Dereference *var* and return its value. *var* must be a variable object; see **make-
   variable** and **make-undefined-variable**.

variable-set! *var val*   [Scheme Procedure]
scm_variable_set_x (*var, val*)   [C Function]
   Set the value of the variable *var* to *val*. *var* must be a variable object, *val* can be any
   value. Return an unspecified value.

variable-unset! *var*   [Scheme Procedure]
scm_variable_unset_x (*var*)   [C Function]
>   Unset the value of the variable *var*, leaving *var* unbound.

variable? *obj*   [Scheme Procedure]
scm_variable_p (*obj*)   [C Function]
>   Return #t if *obj* is a variable object, else return #f.

6.19.8 Module System Reflection

The previous sections have described a declarative view of the module system. You can also work with it programmatically by accessing and modifying various parts of the Scheme objects that Guile uses to implement the module system.

At any time, there is a *current module*. This module is the one where a top-level define and similar syntax will add new bindings. You can find other module objects with resolve-module, for example.

These module objects can be used as the second argument to eval.

current-module   [Scheme Procedure]
scm_current_module ()   [C Function]
>   Return the current module object.

set-current-module *module*   [Scheme Procedure]
scm_set_current_module (*module*)   [C Function]
>   Set the current module to *module* and return the previous current module.

save-module-excursion *thunk*   [Scheme Procedure]
>   Call *thunk* within a dynamic-wind such that the module that is current at invocation time is restored when *thunk*'s dynamic extent is left (see Section 6.13.10 [Dynamic Wind], page 309).
>
>   More precisely, if *thunk* escapes non-locally, the current module (at the time of escape) is saved, and the original current module (at the time *thunk*'s dynamic extent was last entered) is restored. If *thunk*'s dynamic extent is re-entered, then the current module is saved, and the previously saved inner module is set current again.

resolve-module *name* [*autoload=#t*] [*version=#f*]   [Scheme Procedure]
>   [*#:ensure=#t*]
scm_resolve_module (*name*)   [C Function]
>   Find the module named *name* and return it. When it has not already been defined and *autoload* is true, try to auto-load it. When it can't be found that way either, create an empty module if *ensure* is true, otherwise return #f. If *version* is true, ensure that the resulting module is compatible with the given version reference (see Section 6.19.5 [R6RS Version References], page 387). The name is a list of symbols.

resolve-interface *name* [*#:select=#f*] [*#:hide='()*]   [Scheme Procedure]
>   [*#:prefix=#f*] [*#:renamer=#f*] [*#:version=#f*]
>   Find the module named *name* as with resolve-module and return its interface. The interface of a module is also a module object, but it contains only the exported bindings.

module-uses *module*   [Scheme Procedure]
    Return a list of the interfaces used by *module*.

module-use! *module interface*   [Scheme Procedure]
    Add *interface* to the front of the use-list of *module*. Both arguments should be module
    objects, and *interface* should very likely be a module returned by `resolve-interface`.

reload-module *module*   [Scheme Procedure]
    Revisit the source file that corresponds to *module*. Raises an error if no source file is
    associated with the given module.

As mentioned in the previous section, modules contain a mapping between identifiers
(as symbols) and storage locations (as variables). Guile defines a number of procedures
to allow access to this mapping. If you are programming in C, Section 6.19.9 [Accessing
Modules from C], page 392.

module-variable *module name*   [Scheme Procedure]
    Return the variable bound to *name* (a symbol) in *module*, or `#f` if *name* is unbound.

module-add! *module name var*   [Scheme Procedure]
    Define a new binding between *name* (a symbol) and *var* (a variable) in *module*.

module-ref *module name*   [Scheme Procedure]
    Look up the value bound to *name* in *module*. Like `module-variable`, but also does
    a `variable-ref` on the resulting variable, raising an error if *name* is unbound.

module-define! *module name value*   [Scheme Procedure]
    Locally bind *name* to *value* in *module*. If *name* was already locally bound in *module*,
    i.e., defined locally and not by an imported module, the value stored in the existing
    variable will be updated. Otherwise, a new variable will be added to the module, via
    `module-add!`.

module-set! *module name value*   [Scheme Procedure]
    Update the binding of *name* in *module* to *value*, raising an error if *name* is not already
    bound in *module*.

There are many other reflective procedures available in the default environment. If you
find yourself using one of them, please contact the Guile developers so that we can commit
to stability for that interface.

6.19.9 Accessing Modules from C

The last sections have described how modules are used in Scheme code, which is the recommended way of creating and accessing modules. You can also work with modules from
C, but it is more cumbersome.

    The following procedures are available.

SCM **scm_c_call_with_current_module** (*SCM module, SCM*   [C Function]
        (*`*func`*)(*void *), void *`data`*)
    Call *func* and make *module* the current module during the call. The argument *data* is
    passed to *func*. The return value of `scm_c_call_with_current_module` is the return
    value of *func*.

SCM **scm_public_variable** (*SCM module_name*, *SCM name*)   [C Function]
SCM **scm_c_public_variable** (*const char *module_name*, *const char*   [C Function]
    *name)

Find a the variable bound to the symbol *name* in the public interface of the module
named *module_name*.

module_name should be a list of symbols, when represented as a Scheme object, or a
space-separated string, in the `const char *` case. See `scm_c_define_module` below,
for more examples.

Signals an error if no module was found with the given name. If *name* is not bound
in the module, just returns `#f`.

SCM **scm_private_variable** (*SCM module_name*, *SCM name*)   [C Function]
SCM **scm_c_private_variable** (*const char *module_name*, *const*   [C Function]
    char *name)

Like `scm_public_variable`, but looks in the internals of the module named *module_name* instead of the public interface. Logically, these procedures should only be
called on modules you write.

SCM **scm_public_lookup** (*SCM module_name*, *SCM name*)   [C Function]
SCM **scm_c_public_lookup** (*const char *module_name*, *const char*   [C Function]
    *name)
SCM **scm_private_lookup** (*SCM module_name*, *SCM name*)   [C Function]
SCM **scm_c_private_lookup** (*const char *module_name*, *const char*   [C Function]
    *name)

Like `scm_public_variable` or `scm_private_variable`, but if the *name* is not bound
in the module, signals an error. Returns a variable, always.

```
static SCM eval_string_var;

/* NOTE: It is important that the call to 'my_init'
   happens-before all calls to 'my_eval_string'. */
void my_init (void)
{
  eval_string_var = scm_c_public_lookup ("ice-9 eval-string",
                                         "eval-string");
}

SCM my_eval_string (SCM str)
{
  return scm_call_1 (scm_variable_ref (eval_string_var), str);
}
```

SCM **scm_public_ref** (*SCM module_name*, *SCM name*)   [C Function]
SCM **scm_c_public_ref** (*const char *module_name*, *const char *name*)   [C Function]
SCM **scm_private_ref** (*SCM module_name*, *SCM name*)   [C Function]

SCM **scm_c_private_ref** (*const char *module_name, const char*   [C Function]
    *name)
> Like `scm_public_lookup` or `scm_private_lookup`, but additionally dereferences the
> variable. If the variable object is unbound, signals an error. Returns the value bound
> to *name* in *module_name*.

In addition, there are a number of other lookup-related procedures. We suggest that
you use the `scm_public_` and `scm_private_` family of procedures instead, if possible.

SCM **scm_c_lookup** (*const char *name*)   [C Function]
> Return the variable bound to the symbol indicated by *name* in the current module.
> If there is no such binding or the symbol is not bound to a variable, signal an error.

SCM **scm_lookup** (*SCM name*)   [C Function]
> Like `scm_c_lookup`, but the symbol is specified directly.

SCM **scm_c_module_lookup** (*SCM module, const char *name*)   [C Function]
SCM **scm_module_lookup** (*SCM module, SCM name*)   [C Function]
> Like `scm_c_lookup` and `scm_lookup`, but the specified module is used instead of the
> current one.

SCM **scm_module_variable** (*SCM module, SCM name*)   [C Function]
> Like `scm_module_lookup`, but if the binding does not exist, just returns `#f` instead
> of raising an error.

To define a value, use `scm_define`:

SCM **scm_c_define** (*const char *name, SCM val*)   [C Function]
> Bind the symbol indicated by *name* to a variable in the current module and set that
> variable to *val*. When *name* is already bound to a variable, use that. Else create a
> new variable.

SCM **scm_define** (*SCM name, SCM val*)   [C Function]
> Like `scm_c_define`, but the symbol is specified directly.

SCM **scm_c_module_define** (*SCM module, const char *name, SCM*   [C Function]
    val)
SCM **scm_module_define** (*SCM module, SCM name, SCM val*)   [C Function]
> Like `scm_c_define` and `scm_define`, but the specified module is used instead of the
> current one.

In some rare cases, you may need to access the variable that `scm_module_define` would
have accessed, without changing the binding of the existing variable, if one is present. In
that case, use `scm_module_ensure_local_variable`:

SCM **scm_module_ensure_local_variable** (*SCM module, SCM*   [C Function]
    sym)
> Like `scm_module_define`, but if the *sym* is already locally bound in that module, the
> variable's existing binding is not reset. Returns a variable.

SCM `scm_module_reverse_lookup` (*SCM module, SCM variable*)   [C Function]
> Find the symbol that is bound to *variable* in *module*. When no such binding is found, return `#f`.

SCM `scm_c_define_module` (*const char *name, void (*init)(void *)*,   [C Function]
> *void *data*)
> Define a new module named *name* and make it current while *init* is called, passing it *data*. Return the module.
>
> The parameter *name* is a string with the symbols that make up the module name, separated by spaces. For example, '`"foo bar"`' names the module '`(foo bar)`'.
>
> When there already exists a module named *name*, it is used unchanged, otherwise, an empty module is created.

SCM `scm_c_resolve_module` (*const char *name*)   [C Function]
> Find the module name *name* and return it. When it has not already been defined, try to auto-load it. When it can't be found that way either, create an empty module. The name is interpreted as for `scm_c_define_module`.

SCM `scm_c_use_module` (*const char *name*)   [C Function]
> Add the module named *name* to the uses list of the current module, as with (`use-modules name`). The name is interpreted as for `scm_c_define_module`.

SCM `scm_c_export` (*const char *name, ...*)   [C Function]
> Add the bindings designated by *name*, ... to the public interface of the current module. The list of names is terminated by `NULL`.

6.19.10 provide and require

Aubrey Jaffer, mostly to support his portable Scheme library SLIB, implemented a provide/require mechanism for many Scheme implementations. Library files in SLIB *provide* a feature, and when user programs *require* that feature, the library file is loaded in.

For example, the file `random.scm` in the SLIB package contains the line

    (provide 'random)

so to use its procedures, a user would type

    (require 'random)

and they would magically become available, *but still have the same names!* So this method is nice, but not as good as a full-featured module system.

When SLIB is used with Guile, provide and require can be used to access its facilities.

6.19.11 Environments

Scheme, as defined in R5RS, does *not* have a full module system. However it does define the concept of a top-level *environment*. Such an environment maps identifiers (symbols) to Scheme objects such as procedures and lists: Section 3.4 [About Closure], page 26. In other words, it implements a set of *bindings*.

Environments in R5RS can be passed as the second argument to `eval` (see Section 6.17.4 [Fly Evaluation], page 362). Three procedures are defined to return environments:

`scheme-report-environment`, `null-environment` and `interaction-environment` (see Section 6.17.4 [Fly Evaluation], page 362).

In addition, in Guile any module can be used as an R5RS environment, i.e., passed as the second argument to `eval`.

Note: the following two procedures are available only when the (`ice-9 r5rs`) module is loaded:

```
(use-modules (ice-9 r5rs))
```

`scheme-report-environment` *version*   [Scheme Procedure]
`null-environment` *version*   [Scheme Procedure]
> *version* must be the exact integer '5', corresponding to revision 5 of the Scheme report (the Revised^5 Report on Scheme). `scheme-report-environment` returns a specifier for an environment that is empty except for all bindings defined in the report that are either required or both optional and supported by the implementation. `null-environment` returns a specifier for an environment that is empty except for the (syntactic) bindings for all syntactic keywords defined in the report that are either required or both optional and supported by the implementation.
>
> Currently Guile does not support values of *version* for other revisions of the report.
>
> The effect of assigning (through the use of `eval`) a variable bound in a `scheme-report-environment` (for example `car`) is unspecified. Currently the environments specified by `scheme-report-environment` are not immutable in Guile.

6.20 Foreign Function Interface

The more one hacks in Scheme, the more one realizes that there are actually two computational worlds: one which is warm and alive, that land of parentheses, and one cold and dead, the land of C and its ilk.

But yet we as programmers live in both worlds, and Guile itself is half implemented in C. So it is that Guile's living half pays respect to its dead counterpart, via a spectrum of interfaces to C ranging from dynamic loading of Scheme primitives to dynamic binding of stock C library procedures.

6.20.1 Foreign Libraries

Most modern Unices have something called *shared libraries*. This ordinarily means that they have the capability to share the executable image of a library between several running programs to save memory and disk space. But generally, shared libraries give a lot of additional flexibility compared to the traditional static libraries. In fact, calling them 'dynamic' libraries is as correct as calling them 'shared'.

Shared libraries really give you a lot of flexibility in addition to the memory and disk space savings. When you link a program against a shared library, that library is not closely incorporated into the final executable. Instead, the executable of your program only contains enough information to find the needed shared libraries when the program is actually run. Only then, when the program is starting, is the final step of the linking process performed. This means that you need not recompile all programs when you install a new, only slightly modified version of a shared library. The programs will pick up the changes automatically the next time they are run.

Now, when all the necessary machinery is there to perform part of the linking at run-time, why not take the next step and allow the programmer to explicitly take advantage of it from within his program? Of course, many operating systems that support shared libraries do just that, and chances are that Guile will allow you to access this feature from within your Scheme programs. As you might have guessed already, this feature is called *dynamic linking*.[14]

We titled this section "foreign libraries" because although the name "foreign" doesn't leak into the API, the world of C really is foreign to Scheme – and that estrangement extends to components of foreign libraries as well, as we see in future sections.

`dynamic-link` [*library*]   [Scheme Procedure]
`scm_dynamic_link` (*library*)   [C Function]

> Find the shared library denoted by *library* (a string) and link it into the running Guile application. When everything works out, return a Scheme object suitable for representing the linked object file. Otherwise an error is thrown. How object files are searched is system dependent.
>
> Normally, *library* is just the name of some shared library file that will be searched for in the places where shared libraries usually reside, such as in `/usr/lib` and `/usr/local/lib`.
>
> *library* should not contain an extension such as `.so`. The correct file name extension for the host operating system is provided automatically, according to libltdl's rules (see Section "lt_dlopenext" in *Shared Library Support for GNU*).
>
> When *library* is omitted, a *global symbol handle* is returned. This handle provides access to the symbols available to the program at run-time, including those exported by the program itself and the shared libraries already loaded.

`dynamic-object?` *obj*   [Scheme Procedure]
`scm_dynamic_object_p` (*obj*)   [C Function]

> Return `#t` if *obj* is a dynamic library handle, or `#f` otherwise.

`dynamic-unlink` *dobj*   [Scheme Procedure]
`scm_dynamic_unlink` (*dobj*)   [C Function]

> Unlink the indicated object file from the application. The argument *dobj* must have been obtained by a call to `dynamic-link`. After `dynamic-unlink` has been called on *dobj*, its content is no longer accessible.
>
> ```
> (define libgl-obj (dynamic-link "libGL"))
> libgl-obj
> ⇒ #<dynamic-object "libGL">
> (dynamic-unlink libGL-obj)
> libGL-obj
> ⇒ #<dynamic-object "libGL" (unlinked)>
> ```

As you can see, after calling `dynamic-unlink` on a dynamically linked library, it is marked as '`(unlinked)`' and you are no longer able to use it with `dynamic-call`, etc.

---

[14] Some people also refer to the final linking stage at program startup as 'dynamic linking', so if you want to make yourself perfectly clear, it is probably best to use the more technical term *dlopening*, as suggested by Gordon Matzigkeit in his libtool documentation.

Whether the library is really removed from you program is system-dependent and will generally not happen when some other parts of your program still use it.

When dynamic linking is disabled or not supported on your system, the above functions throw errors, but they are still available.

6.20.2 Foreign Functions

The most natural thing to do with a dynamic library is to grovel around in it for a function pointer: a *foreign function*. `dynamic-func` exists for that purpose.

dynamic-func *name dobj*   [Scheme Procedure]
scm_dynamic_func (*name, dobj*)   [C Function]
> Return a "handle" for the func *name* in the shared object referred to by *dobj*. The handle can be passed to `dynamic-call` to actually call the function.

> Regardless whether your C compiler prepends an underscore '_' to the global names in a program, you should **not** include this underscore in *name* since it will be added automatically when necessary.

Guile has static support for calling functions with no arguments, `dynamic-call`.

dynamic-call *func dobj*   [Scheme Procedure]
scm_dynamic_call (*func, dobj*)   [C Function]
> Call the C function indicated by *func* and *dobj*. The function is passed no arguments and its return value is ignored. When *function* is something returned by `dynamic-func`, call that function and ignore *dobj*. When *func* is a string , look it up in *dynobj*; this is equivalent to

> ```
> (dynamic-call (dynamic-func func dobj) #f)
> ```

`dynamic-call` is not very powerful. It is mostly intended to be used for calling specially written initialization functions that will then add new primitives to Guile. For example, we do not expect that you will dynamically link `libX11` with `dynamic-link` and then construct a beautiful graphical user interface just by using `dynamic-call`. Instead, the usual way would be to write a special Guile-to-X11 glue library that has intimate knowledge about both Guile and X11 and does whatever is necessary to make them inter-operate smoothly. This glue library could then be dynamically linked into a vanilla Guile interpreter and activated by calling its initialization function. That function would add all the new types and primitives to the Guile interpreter that it has to offer.

(There is actually another, better option: simply to create a `libX11` wrapper in Scheme via the dynamic FFI. See Section 6.20.6 [Dynamic FFI], page 407, for more information.)

Given some set of C extensions to Guile, the next logical step is to integrate these glue libraries into the module system of Guile so that you can load new primitives into a running system just as you can load new Scheme code.

load-extension *lib init*   [Scheme Procedure]
scm_load_extension (*lib, init*)   [C Function]
> Load and initialize the extension designated by LIB and INIT. When there is no pre-registered function for LIB/INIT, this is equivalent to

```
(dynamic-call INIT (dynamic-link LIB))
```

When there is a pre-registered function, that function is called instead.

Normally, there is no pre-registered function. This option exists only for situations where dynamic linking is unavailable or unwanted. In that case, you would statically link your program with the desired library, and register its init function right after Guile has been initialized.

As for `dynamic-link`, *lib* should not contain any suffix such as `.so` (see Section 6.20.1 [Foreign Libraries], page 396). It should also not contain any directory components. Libraries that implement Guile Extensions should be put into the normal locations for shared libraries. We recommend to use the naming convention `libguile-bla-blum` for a extension related to a module (`bla blum`).

The normal way for a extension to be used is to write a small Scheme file that defines a module, and to load the extension into this module. When the module is auto-loaded, the extension is loaded as well. For example,

```
(define-module (bla blum))
```

```
(load-extension "libguile-bla-blum" "bla_init_blum")
```

6.20.3 C Extensions

The most interesting application of dynamically linked libraries is probably to use them for providing *compiled code modules* to Scheme programs. As much fun as programming in Scheme is, every now and then comes the need to write some low-level C stuff to make Scheme even more fun.

Not only can you put these new primitives into their own module (see the previous section), you can even put them into a shared library that is only then linked to your running Guile image when it is actually needed.

An example will hopefully make everything clear. Suppose we want to make the Bessel functions of the C library available to Scheme in the module '(`math bessel`)'. First we need to write the appropriate glue code to convert the arguments and return values of the functions from Scheme to C and back. Additionally, we need a function that will add them to the set of Guile primitives. Because this is just an example, we will only implement this for the j0 function.

```
#include <math.h>
#include <libguile.h>

SCM
j0_wrapper (SCM x)
{
  return scm_from_double (j0 (scm_to_double (x, "j0")));
}

void
init_math_bessel ()
{
  scm_c_define_gsubr ("j0", 1, 0, 0, j0_wrapper);
}
```

We can already try to bring this into action by manually calling the low level functions for performing dynamic linking. The C source file needs to be compiled into a shared library.

Here is how to do it on GNU/Linux, please refer to the `libtool` documentation for how to create dynamically linkable libraries portably.

```
gcc -shared -o libbessel.so -fPIC bessel.c
```

Now fire up Guile:

```
(define bessel-lib (dynamic-link "./libbessel.so"))
(dynamic-call "init_math_bessel" bessel-lib)
(j0 2)
⇒ 0.223890779141236
```

The filename `./libbessel.so` should be pointing to the shared library produced with the `gcc` command above, of course. The second line of the Guile interaction will call the `init_math_bessel` function which in turn will register the C function `j0_wrapper` with the Guile interpreter under the name `j0`. This function becomes immediately available and we can call it from Scheme.

Fun, isn't it? But we are only half way there. This is what `apropos` has to say about `j0`:

```
(apropos "j0")
⊣ (guile-user): j0      #<primitive-procedure j0>
```

As you can see, `j0` is contained in the root module, where all the other Guile primitives like `display`, etc live. In general, a primitive is put into whatever module is the *current module* at the time `scm_c_define_gsubr` is called.

A compiled module should have a specially named *module init function*. Guile knows about this special name and will call that function automatically after having linked in the shared library. For our example, we replace `init_math_bessel` with the following code in `bessel.c`:

```
void
init_math_bessel (void *unused)
{
  scm_c_define_gsubr ("j0", 1, 0, 0, j0_wrapper);
  scm_c_export ("j0", NULL);
}

void
scm_init_math_bessel_module ()
{
  scm_c_define_module ("math bessel", init_math_bessel, NULL);
}
```

The general pattern for the name of a module init function is: 'scm_init_', followed by the name of the module where the individual hierarchical components are concatenated with underscores, followed by '_module'.

After `libbessel.so` has been rebuilt, we need to place the shared library into the right place.

Once the module has been correctly installed, it should be possible to use it like this:

```
guile> (load-extension "./libbessel.so" "scm_init_math_bessel_module")
guile> (use-modules (math bessel))
guile> (j0 2)
0.223890779141236
guile> (apropos "j0")
⊣ (math bessel): j0      #<primitive-procedure j0>
```

That's it!

6.20.4 Modules and Extensions

The new primitives that you add to Guile with `scm_c_define_gsubr` (see Section 6.9.2 [Primitive Procedures], page 245) or with any of the other mechanisms are placed into the module that is current when the `scm_c_define_gsubr` is executed. Extensions loaded from the REPL, for example, will be placed into the `(guile-user)` module, if the REPL module was not changed.

To define C primitives within a specific module, the simplest way is:

```
(define-module (foo bar))
(load-extension "foobar-c-code" "foo_bar_init")
```

When loaded with `(use-modules (foo bar))`, the `load-extension` call looks for the `foobar-c-code.so` (etc) object file in Guile's `extensiondir`, which is usually a subdirectory of the `libdir`. For example, if your libdir is `/usr/lib`, the `extensiondir` for the Guile 2.0.x series will be `/usr/lib/guile/2.0/`.

The extension path includes the major and minor version of Guile (the "effective version"), because Guile guarantees compatibility within a given effective version. This allows you to install different versions of the same extension for different versions of Guile.

If the extension is not found in the `extensiondir`, Guile will also search the standard system locations, such as `/usr/lib` or `/usr/local/lib`. It is preferable, however, to keep your extension out of the system library path, to prevent unintended interference with other dynamically-linked C libraries.

If someone installs your module to a non-standard location then the object file won't be found. You can address this by inserting the install location in the `foo/bar.scm` file. This is convenient for the user and also guarantees the intended object is read, even if stray older or newer versions are in the loader's path.

The usual way to specify an install location is with a `prefix` at the configure stage, for instance '`./configure prefix=/opt`' results in library files as say `/opt/lib/foobar-c-code.so`. When using Autoconf (see Section "Introduction" in *The GNU Autoconf Manual*), the library location is in a `libdir` variable. Its value is intended to be expanded by `make`, and can by substituted into a source file like `foo.scm.in`

```
(define-module (foo bar))
(load-extension "XXextensiondirXX/foobar-c-code" "foo_bar_init")
```

with the following in a `Makefile`, using `sed` (see Section "Introduction" in *SED*),

```
foo.scm: foo.scm.in
        sed 's|XXextensiondirXX|$(libdir)/guile/2.0|' <foo.scm.in >foo.scm
```

The actual pattern `XXextensiondirXX` is arbitrary, it's only something which doesn't otherwise occur. If several modules need the value, it can be easier to create one `foo/config.scm` with a define of the `extensiondir` location, and use that as required.

```
(define-module (foo config))
(define-public foo-config-extensiondir "XXextensiondirXX"")
```

Such a file might have other locations too, for instance a data directory for auxiliary files, or `localedir` if the module has its own `gettext` message catalogue (see Section 6.24 [Internationalization], page 436).

It will be noted all of the above requires that the Scheme code to be found in `%load-path` (see Section 6.17.7 [Load Paths], page 368). Presently it's left up to the system administrator or each user to augment that path when installing Guile modules in non-default locations. But having reached the Scheme code, that code should take care of hitting any of its own private files etc.

6.20.5 Foreign Pointers

The previous sections have shown how Guile can be extended at runtime by loading compiled C extensions. This approach is all well and good, but wouldn't it be nice if we didn't have to write any C at all? This section takes up the problem of accessing C values from Scheme, and the next discusses C functions.

6.20.5.1 Foreign Types

The first impedance mismatch that one sees between C and Scheme is that in C, the storage locations (variables) are typed, but in Scheme types are associated with values, not variables. See Section 3.1.2 [Values and Variables], page 15.

So when describing a C function or a C structure so that it can be accessed from Scheme, the data types of the parameters or fields must be passed explicitly.

These "C type values" may be constructed using the constants and procedures from the (system foreign) module, which may be loaded like this:

```
(use-modules (system foreign))
```

(system foreign) exports a number of values expressing the basic C types:

int8	[Scheme Variable]
uint8	[Scheme Variable]
uint16	[Scheme Variable]
int16	[Scheme Variable]
uint32	[Scheme Variable]
int32	[Scheme Variable]
uint64	[Scheme Variable]
int64	[Scheme Variable]
float	[Scheme Variable]
double	[Scheme Variable]

These values represent the C numeric types of the specified sizes and signednesses.

In addition there are some convenience bindings for indicating types of platform-dependent size:

int	[Scheme Variable]
unsigned-int	[Scheme Variable]
long	[Scheme Variable]
unsigned-long	[Scheme Variable]
size_t	[Scheme Variable]
ssize_t	[Scheme Variable]
ptrdiff_t	[Scheme Variable]

Values exported by the (system foreign) module, representing C numeric types. For example, long may be equal? to int64 on a 64-bit platform.

void   [Scheme Variable]
    The `void` type. It can be used as the first argument to `pointer->procedure` to wrap
    a C function that returns nothing.

In addition, the symbol `*` is used by convention to denote pointer types. Procedures
detailed in the following sections, such as `pointer->procedure`, accept it as a type descriptor.

6.20.5.2 Foreign Variables

Pointers to variables in the current address space may be looked up dynamically using
`dynamic-pointer`.

dynamic-pointer *name* *dobj*   [Scheme Procedure]
scm_dynamic_pointer (*name*, *dobj*)   [C Function]
    Return a "wrapped pointer" for the symbol *name* in the shared object referred to by
    dobj. The returned pointer points to a C object.

    Regardless whether your C compiler prepends an underscore '`_`' to the global names
    in a program, you should **not** include this underscore in *name* since it will be added
    automatically when necessary.

For example, currently Guile has a variable, `scm_numptob`, as part of its API. It is
declared as a C `long`. So, to create a handle pointing to that foreign value, we do:

```
(use-modules (system foreign))
(define numptob (dynamic-pointer "scm_numptob" (dynamic-link)))
numptob
⇒ #<pointer 0x7fb35b1b4688>
```

(The next section discusses ways to dereference pointers.)

A value returned by `dynamic-pointer` is a Scheme wrapper for a C pointer.

pointer-address *pointer*   [Scheme Procedure]
scm_pointer_address (*pointer*)   [C Function]
    Return the numerical value of *pointer*.

```
(pointer-address numptob)
⇒ 139984413364296 ; YMMV
```

make-pointer *address* [*finalizer*]   [Scheme Procedure]
    Return a foreign pointer object pointing to *address*. If *finalizer* is passed, it should
    be a pointer to a one-argument C function that will be called when the pointer object
    becomes unreachable.

pointer? *obj*   [Scheme Procedure]
    Return `#t` if *obj* is a pointer object, `#f` otherwise.

%null-pointer   [Scheme Variable]
    A foreign pointer whose value is 0.

null-pointer? *pointer*   [Scheme Procedure]
    Return `#t` if *pointer* is the null pointer, `#f` otherwise.

For the purpose of passing SCM values directly to foreign functions, and allowing them to return SCM values, Guile also supports some unsafe casting operators.

scm->pointer *scm*   [Scheme Procedure]
    Return a foreign pointer object with the **object-address** of *scm*.

pointer->scm *pointer*   [Scheme Procedure]
    Unsafely cast *pointer* to a Scheme object. Cross your fingers!

Sometimes you want to give C extensions access to the dynamic FFI. At that point, the names get confusing, because "pointer" can refer to a SCM object that wraps a pointer, or to a **void*** value. We will try to use "pointer object" to refer to Scheme objects, and "pointer value" to refer to **void *** values.

SCM scm_from_pointer (*void *ptr, void (*finalizer) (void*)*)   [C Function]
    Create a pointer object from a pointer value.

    If *finalizer* is non-null, Guile arranges to call it on the pointer value at some point after the pointer object becomes collectable.

void* scm_to_pointer (*SCM obj*)   [C Function]
    Unpack the pointer value from a pointer object.

6.20.5.3 Void Pointers and Byte Access

Wrapped pointers are untyped, so they are essentially equivalent to C **void** pointers. As in C, the memory region pointed to by a pointer can be accessed at the byte level. This is achieved using *bytevectors* (see Section 6.6.6 [Bytevectors], page 163). The (**rnrs bytevectors**) module contains procedures that can be used to convert byte sequences to Scheme objects such as strings, floating point numbers, or integers.

pointer->bytevector *pointer len* [*offset* [*uvec_type*]]   [Scheme Procedure]
scm_pointer_to_bytevector (*pointer, len, offset, uvec_type*)   [C Function]
    Return a bytevector aliasing the *len* bytes pointed to by *pointer*.

    The user may specify an alternate default interpretation for the memory by passing the *uvec_type* argument, to indicate that the memory is an array of elements of that type. *uvec_type* should be something that **array-type** would return, like **f32** or **s16**.

    When *offset* is passed, it specifies the offset in bytes relative to *pointer* of the memory region aliased by the returned bytevector.

    Mutating the returned bytevector mutates the memory pointed to by *pointer*, so buckle your seatbelts.

bytevector->pointer *bv* [*offset*]   [Scheme Procedure]
scm_bytevector_to_pointer (*bv, offset*)   [C Function]
    Return a pointer pointer aliasing the memory pointed to by *bv* or *offset* bytes after *bv* when *offset* is passed.

In addition to these primitives, convenience procedures are available:

dereference-pointer *pointer*   [Scheme Procedure]
    Assuming *pointer* points to a memory region that holds a pointer, return this pointer.

string->pointer *string* [*encoding*]   [Scheme Procedure]

> Return a foreign pointer to a nul-terminated copy of *string* in the given *encoding*, defaulting to the current locale encoding. The C string is freed when the returned foreign pointer becomes unreachable.
>
> This is the Scheme equivalent of `scm_to_stringn`.

pointer->string *pointer* [*length*] [*encoding*]   [Scheme Procedure]

> Return the string representing the C string pointed to by *pointer*. If *length* is omitted or `-1`, the string is assumed to be nul-terminated. Otherwise *length* is the number of bytes in memory pointed to by *pointer*. The C string is assumed to be in the given *encoding*, defaulting to the current locale encoding.
>
> This is the Scheme equivalent of `scm_from_stringn`.

Most object-oriented C libraries use pointers to specific data structures to identify objects. It is useful in such cases to reify the different pointer types as disjoint Scheme types. The `define-wrapped-pointer-type` macro simplifies this.

define-wrapped-pointer-type *type-name pred wrap unwrap*   [Scheme Syntax]
      print

> Define helper procedures to wrap pointer objects into Scheme objects with a disjoint type. Specifically, this macro defines:
>
> - *pred*, a predicate for the new Scheme type;
> - *wrap*, a procedure that takes a pointer object and returns an object that satisfies *pred*;
> - *unwrap*, which does the reverse.
>
> *wrap* preserves pointer identity, for two pointer objects *p1* and *p2* that are `equal?`, `(eq? (wrap p1) (wrap p2))` ⇒ `#t`.
>
> Finally, *print* should name a user-defined procedure to print such objects. The procedure is passed the wrapped object and a port to write to.
>
> For example, assume we are wrapping a C library that defines a type, `bottle_t`, and functions that can be passed `bottle_t *` pointers to manipulate them. We could write:
>
> ```
> (define-wrapped-pointer-type bottle
>   bottle?
>   wrap-bottle unwrap-bottle
>   (lambda (b p)
>     (format p "#<bottle of ~a ~x>"
>             (bottle-contents b)
>             (pointer-address (unwrap-bottle b)))))
>
> (define grab-bottle
>   ;; Wrapper for 'bottle_t *grab (void)'.
>   (let ((grab (pointer->procedure '*
>                                   (dynamic-func "grab_bottle" libbottle)
>                                   '())))
>     (lambda ()
> ```

```
                   "Return a new bottle."
                   (wrap-bottle (grab)))))

          (define bottle-contents
            ;; Wrapper for 'const char *bottle_contents (bottle_t *)'.
            (let ((contents (pointer->procedure '*
                                                 (dynamic-func "bottle_contents"
                                                               libbottle)
                                                 '(*))))
              (lambda (b)
                "Return the contents of B."
                (pointer->string (contents (unwrap-bottle b))))))

          (write (grab-bottle))
          ⇒ #<bottle of Château Haut-Brion 803d36>
```

In this example, `grab-bottle` is guaranteed to return a genuine `bottle` object satisfying `bottle?`. Likewise, `bottle-contents` errors out when its argument is not a genuine `bottle` object.

Going back to the `scm_numptob` example above, here is how we can read its value as a C `long` integer:

```
          (use-modules (rnrs bytevectors))

          (bytevector-uint-ref (pointer->bytevector numptob (sizeof long))
                               0 (native-endianness)
                               (sizeof long))
          ⇒ 8
```

If we wanted to corrupt Guile's internal state, we could set `scm_numptob` to another value; but we shouldn't, because that variable is not meant to be set. Indeed this point applies more widely: the C API is a dangerous place to be. Not only might setting a value crash your program, simply accessing the data pointed to by a dangling pointer or similar can prove equally disastrous.

6.20.5.4 Foreign Structs

Finally, one last note on foreign values before moving on to actually calling foreign functions. Sometimes you need to deal with C structs, which requires interpreting each element of the struct according to the its type, offset, and alignment. Guile has some primitives to support this.

`sizeof` *type*   [Scheme Procedure]
`scm_sizeof` (*type*)   [C Function]
> Return the size of *type*, in bytes.
>
> *type* should be a valid C type, like `int`. Alternately *type* may be the symbol `*`, in which case the size of a pointer is returned. *type* may also be a list of types, in which case the size of a `struct` with ABI-conventional packing is returned.

`alignof` *type*   [Scheme Procedure]

`scm_alignof` (*type*)   [C Function]

    Return the alignment of *type*, in bytes.

    type should be a valid C type, like `int`. Alternately *type* may be the symbol `*`, in which case the alignment of a pointer is returned. *type* may also be a list of types, in which case the alignment of a `struct` with ABI-conventional packing is returned.

Guile also provides some convenience methods to pack and unpack foreign pointers wrapping C structs.

`make-c-struct` *types vals*   [Scheme Procedure]

    Create a foreign pointer to a C struct containing *vals* with types `types`.

    vals and `types` should be lists of the same length.

`parse-c-struct` *foreign types*   [Scheme Procedure]

    Parse a foreign pointer to a C struct, returning a list of values.

    `types` should be a list of C types.

For example, to create and parse the equivalent of a `struct { int64_t a; uint8_t b; };`:

```
(parse-c-struct (make-c-struct (list int64 uint8)
                               (list 300 43))
                (list int64 uint8))
```
  ⇒ (300 43)

As yet, Guile only has convenience routines to support conventionally-packed structs. But given the `bytevector->pointer` and `pointer->bytevector` routines, one can create and parse tightly packed structs and unions by hand. See the code for (`system foreign`) for details.

6.20.6 Dynamic FFI

Of course, the land of C is not all nouns and no verbs: there are functions too, and Guile allows you to call them.

`pointer->procedure` *return_type func_ptr arg_types*   [Scheme Procedure]

`scm_pointer_to_procedure` (*return_type, func_ptr, arg_types*)   [C Procedure]

    Make a foreign function.

    Given the foreign void pointer *func_ptr*, its argument and return types *arg_types* and *return_type*, return a procedure that will pass arguments to the foreign function and return appropriate values.

    arg_types should be a list of foreign types. `return_type` should be a foreign type. See Section 6.20.5.1 [Foreign Types], page 402, for more information on foreign types.

Here is a better definition of (`math bessel`):

```
(define-module (math bessel)
  #:use-module (system foreign)
  #:export (j0))
```

```
(define libm (dynamic-link "libm"))

(define j0
  (pointer->procedure double
                      (dynamic-func "j0" libm)
                      (list double)))
```

That's it! No C at all.

Numeric arguments and return values from foreign functions are represented as Scheme values. For example, j0 in the above example takes a Scheme number as its argument, and returns a Scheme number.

Pointers may be passed to and returned from foreign functions as well. In that case the type of the argument or return value should be the symbol *, indicating a pointer. For example, the following code makes memcpy available to Scheme:

```
(define memcpy
  (let ((this (dynamic-link)))
    (pointer->procedure '*
                        (dynamic-func "memcpy" this)
                        (list '* '* size_t))))
```

To invoke memcpy, one must pass it foreign pointers:

```
(use-modules (rnrs bytevectors))

(define src-bits
  (u8-list->bytevector '(0 1 2 3 4 5 6 7)))
(define src
  (bytevector->pointer src-bits))
(define dest
  (bytevector->pointer (make-bytevector 16 0)))

(memcpy dest src (bytevector-length src-bits))

(bytevector->u8-list (pointer->bytevector dest 16))
⇒ (0 1 2 3 4 5 6 7 0 0 0 0 0 0 0 0)
```

One may also pass structs as values, passing structs as foreign pointers. See Section 6.20.5.4 [Foreign Structs], page 406, for more information on how to express struct types and struct values.

"Out" arguments are passed as foreign pointers. The memory pointed to by the foreign pointer is mutated in place.

```
;; struct timeval {
;;      time_t      tv_sec;     /* seconds */
;;      suseconds_t tv_usec;    /* microseconds */
;; };
;; assuming fields are of type "long"

(define gettimeofday
  (let ((f (pointer->procedure
```

```
                  int
                  (dynamic-func "gettimeofday" (dynamic-link))
                  (list '* '*)))
              (tv-type (list long long)))
          (lambda ()
            (let* ((timeval (make-c-struct tv-type (list 0 0)))
                   (ret (f timeval %null-pointer)))
              (if (zero? ret)
                  (apply values (parse-c-struct timeval tv-type))
                  (error "gettimeofday returned an error" ret))))))

      (gettimeofday)
      ⇒ 1270587589
      ⇒ 499553
```

As you can see, this interface to foreign functions is at a very low, somewhat dangerous level[15].

The FFI can also work in the opposite direction: making Scheme procedures callable from C. This makes it possible to use Scheme procedures as "callbacks" expected by C function.

procedure->pointer *return-type proc arg-types*   [Scheme Procedure]
scm_procedure_to_pointer (*return_type, proc, arg_types*)   [C Function]
    Return a pointer to a C function of type *return-type* taking arguments of types *arg-types* (a list) and behaving as a proxy to procedure *proc*. Thus *proc*'s arity, supported argument types, and return type should match *return-type* and *arg-types*.

As an example, here's how the C library's `qsort` array sorting function can be made accessible to Scheme (see Section "Array Sort Function" in *The GNU C Library Reference Manual*):

```
(define qsort!
  (let ((qsort (pointer->procedure void
                                   (dynamic-func "qsort"
                                                 (dynamic-link))
                                   (list '* size_t size_t '*))))
    (lambda (bv compare)
      ;; Sort bytevector BV in-place according to comparison
      ;; procedure COMPARE.
      (let ((ptr (procedure->pointer int
                                     (lambda (x y)
                                       ;; X and Y are pointers so,
                                       ;; for convenience, dereference
                                       ;; them before calling COMPARE.
                                       (compare (dereference-uint8* x)
                                                (dereference-uint8* y)))
                                     (list '* '*))))
```

---

[15] A contribution to Guile in the form of a high-level FFI would be most welcome.

```
          (qsort (bytevector->pointer bv)
                 (bytevector-length bv) 1 ;; we're sorting bytes
                 ptr)))))

(define (dereference-uint8* ptr)
  ;; Helper function: dereference the byte pointed to by PTR.
  (let ((b (pointer->bytevector ptr 1)))
    (bytevector-u8-ref b 0)))

(define bv
  ;; An unsorted array of bytes.
  (u8-list->bytevector '(7 1 127 3 5 4 77 2 9 0)))

;; Sort BV.
(qsort! bv (lambda (x y) (- x y)))

;; Let's see what the sorted array looks like:
(bytevector->u8-list bv)
⇒ (0 1 2 3 4 5 7 9 77 127)
```

And voilà!

Note that `procedure->pointer` is not supported (and not defined) on a few exotic architectures. Thus, user code may need to check `(defined? 'procedure->pointer)`. Nevertheless, it is available on many architectures, including (as of libffi 3.0.9) x86, ia64, SPARC, PowerPC, ARM, and MIPS, to name a few.

6.21 Threads, Mutexes, Asyncs and Dynamic Roots

6.21.1 Arbiters

Arbiters are synchronization objects, they can be used by threads to control access to a shared resource. An arbiter can be locked to indicate a resource is in use, and unlocked when done.

An arbiter is like a light-weight mutex (see Section 6.21.4 [Mutexes and Condition Variables], page 415). It uses less memory and may be faster, but there's no way for a thread to block waiting on an arbiter, it can only test and get the status returned.

make-arbiter *name*   [Scheme Procedure]
scm_make_arbiter (*name*)   [C Function]
    Return an object of type arbiter and name *name*. Its state is initially unlocked. Arbiters are a way to achieve process synchronization.

try-arbiter *arb*   [Scheme Procedure]
scm_try_arbiter (*arb*)   [C Function]
    If *arb* is unlocked, then lock it and return #t. If *arb* is already locked, then do nothing and return #f.

release-arbiter *arb*   [Scheme Procedure]
scm_release_arbiter (*arb*)   [C Function]
> If *arb* is locked, then unlock it and return #t. If *arb* is already unlocked, then do
> nothing and return #f.
>
> Typical usage is for the thread which locked an arbiter to later release it, but that's
> not required, any thread can release it.

6.21.2 Asyncs

Asyncs are a means of deferring the execution of Scheme code until it is safe to do so.

Guile provides two kinds of asyncs that share the basic concept but are otherwise quite
different: system asyncs and user asyncs. System asyncs are integrated into the core of
Guile and are executed automatically when the system is in a state to allow the execution
of Scheme code. For example, it is not possible to execute Scheme code in a POSIX signal
handler, but such a signal handler can queue a system async to be executed in the near
future, when it is safe to do so.

System asyncs can also be queued for threads other than the current one. This way, you
can cause threads to asynchronously execute arbitrary code.

User asyncs offer a convenient means of queuing procedures for future execution and
triggering this execution. They will not be executed automatically.

6.21.2.1 System asyncs

To cause the future asynchronous execution of a procedure in a given thread, use system-
async-mark.

Automatic invocation of system asyncs can be temporarily disabled by calling call-
with-blocked-asyncs. This function works by temporarily increasing the *async blocking
level* of the current thread while a given procedure is running. The blocking level starts out
at zero, and whenever a safe point is reached, a blocking level greater than zero will prevent
the execution of queued asyncs.

Analogously, the procedure call-with-unblocked-asyncs will temporarily decrease the
blocking level of the current thread. You can use it when you want to disable asyncs by
default and only allow them temporarily.

In addition to the C versions of call-with-blocked-asyncs and call-with-
unblocked-asyncs, C code can use scm_dynwind_block_asyncs and scm_dynwind_
unblock_asyncs inside a *dynamic context* (see Section 6.13.10 [Dynamic Wind], page 309)
to block or unblock system asyncs temporarily.

system-async-mark *proc* [*thread*]   [Scheme Procedure]
scm_system_async_mark (*proc*)   [C Function]
scm_system_async_mark_for_thread (*proc, thread*)   [C Function]
> Mark *proc* (a procedure with zero arguments) for future execution in *thread*. When
> *proc* has already been marked for *thread* but has not been executed yet, this call
> has no effect. When *thread* is omitted, the thread that called system-async-mark is
> used.
>
> This procedure is not safe to be called from signal handlers. Use scm_sigaction or
> scm_sigaction_for_thread to install signal handlers.

`call-with-blocked-asyncs` *proc*   [Scheme Procedure]
`scm_call_with_blocked_asyncs` (*proc*)   [C Function]
> Call *proc* and block the execution of system asyncs by one level for the current thread
> while it is running. Return the value returned by *proc*. For the first two variants, call
> *proc* with no arguments; for the third, call it with *data*.

`void * scm_c_call_with_blocked_asyncs` (*void * (*proc*) (*void*   [C Function]
> **data*), *void *data*)
> The same but with a C function *proc* instead of a Scheme thunk.

`call-with-unblocked-asyncs` *proc*   [Scheme Procedure]
`scm_call_with_unblocked_asyncs` (*proc*)   [C Function]
> Call *proc* and unblock the execution of system asyncs by one level for the current
> thread while it is running. Return the value returned by *proc*. For the first two
> variants, call *proc* with no arguments; for the third, call it with *data*.

`void * scm_c_call_with_unblocked_asyncs` (*void *(*proc*) (*void*   [C Function]
> **data*), *void *data*)
> The same but with a C function *proc* instead of a Scheme thunk.

`void scm_dynwind_block_asyncs` ()   [C Function]
> During the current dynwind context, increase the blocking of asyncs by one level.
> This function must be used inside a pair of calls to `scm_dynwind_begin` and `scm_dynwind_end` (see Section 6.13.10 [Dynamic Wind], page 309).

`void scm_dynwind_unblock_asyncs` ()   [C Function]
> During the current dynwind context, decrease the blocking of asyncs by one level.
> This function must be used inside a pair of calls to `scm_dynwind_begin` and `scm_dynwind_end` (see Section 6.13.10 [Dynamic Wind], page 309).

6.21.2.2 User asyncs

A user async is a pair of a thunk (a parameterless procedure) and a mark. Setting the
mark on a user async will cause the thunk to be executed when the user async is passed to
`run-asyncs`. Setting the mark more than once is satisfied by one execution of the thunk.

User asyncs are created with `async`. They are marked with `async-mark`.

`async` *thunk*   [Scheme Procedure]
`scm_async` (*thunk*)   [C Function]
> Create a new user async for the procedure *thunk*.

`async-mark` *a*   [Scheme Procedure]
`scm_async_mark` (*a*)   [C Function]
> Mark the user async *a* for future execution.

`run-asyncs` *list_of_a*   [Scheme Procedure]
`scm_run_asyncs` (*list_of_a*)   [C Function]
> Execute all thunks from the marked asyncs of the list *list_of_a*.

6.21.3 Threads

Guile supports POSIX threads, unless it was configured with `--without-threads` or the host lacks POSIX thread support. When thread support is available, the `threads` feature is provided (see Section 6.22.2.1 [Feature Manipulation], page 429).

The procedures below manipulate Guile threads, which are wrappers around the system's POSIX threads. For application-level parallelism, using higher-level constructs, such as futures, is recommended (see Section 6.21.9 [Futures], page 424).

`all-threads`   [Scheme Procedure]
`scm_all_threads ()`   [C Function]
>   Return a list of all threads.

`current-thread`   [Scheme Procedure]
`scm_current_thread ()`   [C Function]
>   Return the thread that called this function.

`call-with-new-thread` *thunk* [*handler*]   [Scheme Procedure]
>   Call `thunk` in a new thread and with a new dynamic state, returning the new thread. The procedure *thunk* is called via `with-continuation-barrier`.
>
>   When *handler* is specified, then *thunk* is called from within a `catch` with tag `#t` that has *handler* as its handler. This catch is established inside the continuation barrier.
>
>   Once *thunk* or *handler* returns, the return value is made the *exit value* of the thread and the thread is terminated.

`SCM scm_spawn_thread` (*scm_t_catch_body body, void *body_data,*   [C Function]
>   *scm_t_catch_handler handler, void *handler_data*)
>   Call *body* in a new thread, passing it *body_data*, returning the new thread. The function *body* is called via `scm_c_with_continuation_barrier`.
>
>   When *handler* is non-`NULL`, *body* is called via `scm_internal_catch` with tag `SCM_BOOL_T` that has *handler* and *handler_data* as the handler and its data. This catch is established inside the continuation barrier.
>
>   Once *body* or *handler* returns, the return value is made the *exit value* of the thread and the thread is terminated.

`thread?` *obj*   [Scheme Procedure]
`scm_thread_p` (*obj*)   [C Function]
>   Return `#t` ff *obj* is a thread; otherwise, return `#f`.

`join-thread` *thread* [*timeout* [*timeoutval*]]   [Scheme Procedure]
`scm_join_thread` (*thread*)   [C Function]
`scm_join_thread_timed` (*thread, timeout, timeoutval*)   [C Function]
>   Wait for *thread* to terminate and return its exit value. Threads that have not been created with `call-with-new-thread` or `scm_spawn_thread` have an exit value of `#f`. When *timeout* is given, it specifies a point in time where the waiting should be aborted. It can be either an integer as returned by `current-time` or a pair as returned by `gettimeofday`. When the waiting is aborted, *timeoutval* is returned (if it is specified; `#f` is returned otherwise).

`thread-exited?` *thread*   [Scheme Procedure]
`scm_thread_exited_p` (*thread*)   [C Function]
> Return `#t` if *thread* has exited, or `#f` otherwise.

`yield`   [Scheme Procedure]
> If one or more threads are waiting to execute, calling yield forces an immediate context switch to one of them. Otherwise, yield has no effect.

`cancel-thread` *thread*   [Scheme Procedure]
`scm_cancel_thread` (*thread*)   [C Function]
> Asynchronously notify *thread* to exit. Immediately after receiving this notification, *thread* will call its cleanup handler (if one has been set) and then terminate, aborting any evaluation that is in progress.

> Because Guile threads are isomorphic with POSIX threads, *thread* will not receive its cancellation signal until it reaches a cancellation point. See your operating system's POSIX threading documentation for more information on cancellation points; note that in Guile, unlike native POSIX threads, a thread can receive a cancellation notification while attempting to lock a mutex.

`set-thread-cleanup!` *thread proc*   [Scheme Procedure]
`scm_set_thread_cleanup_x` (*thread, proc*)   [C Function]
> Set *proc* as the cleanup handler for the thread *thread*. *proc*, which must be a thunk, will be called when *thread* exits, either normally or by being canceled. Thread cleanup handlers can be used to perform useful tasks like releasing resources, such as locked mutexes, when thread exit cannot be predicted.

> The return value of *proc* will be set as the *exit value* of *thread*.

> To remove a cleanup handler, pass `#f` for *proc*.

`thread-cleanup` *thread*   [Scheme Procedure]
`scm_thread_cleanup` (*thread*)   [C Function]
> Return the cleanup handler currently installed for the thread *thread*. If no cleanup handler is currently installed, thread-cleanup returns `#f`.

Higher level thread procedures are available by loading the (`ice-9 threads`) module. These provide standardized thread creation.

`make-thread` *proc arg* ...   [macro]
> Apply *proc* to *arg* ... in a new thread formed by `call-with-new-thread` using a default error handler that display the error to the current error port. The *arg* ... expressions are evaluated in the new thread.

`begin-thread` *expr1 expr2* ...   [macro]
> Evaluate forms *expr1 expr2* ... in a new thread formed by `call-with-new-thread` using a default error handler that display the error to the current error port.

6.21.4 Mutexes and Condition Variables

A mutex is a thread synchronization object, it can be used by threads to control access to a shared resource. A mutex can be locked to indicate a resource is in use, and other threads can then block on the mutex to wait for the resource (or can just test and do something else if not available). "Mutex" is short for "mutual exclusion".

There are two types of mutexes in Guile, "standard" and "recursive". They're created by `make-mutex` and `make-recursive-mutex` respectively, the operation functions are then common to both.

Note that for both types of mutex there's no protection against a "deadly embrace". For instance if one thread has locked mutex A and is waiting on mutex B, but another thread owns B and is waiting on A, then an endless wait will occur (in the current implementation). Acquiring requisite mutexes in a fixed order (like always A before B) in all threads is one way to avoid such problems.

`make-mutex` *flag* ...   [Scheme Procedure]
`scm_make_mutex` ()   [C Function]
`scm_make_mutex_with_flags` (*SCM flags*)   [C Function]

> Return a new mutex. It is initially unlocked. If *flag* ... is specified, it must be a list of symbols specifying configuration flags for the newly-created mutex. The supported flags are:
>
> `unchecked-unlock`
>
> > Unless this flag is present, a call to 'unlock-mutex' on the returned mutex when it is already unlocked will cause an error to be signalled.
>
> `allow-external-unlock`
>
> > Allow the returned mutex to be unlocked by the calling thread even if it was originally locked by a different thread.
>
> `recursive`
>
> > The returned mutex will be recursive.

`mutex?` *obj*   [Scheme Procedure]
`scm_mutex_p` (*obj*)   [C Function]

> Return `#t` if *obj* is a mutex; otherwise, return `#f`.

`make-recursive-mutex`   [Scheme Procedure]
`scm_make_recursive_mutex` ()   [C Function]

> Create a new recursive mutex. It is initially unlocked. Calling this function is equivalent to calling 'make-mutex' and specifying the `recursive` flag.

`lock-mutex` *mutex* [*timeout* [*owner*]]   [Scheme Procedure]
`scm_lock_mutex` (*mutex*)   [C Function]
`scm_lock_mutex_timed` (*mutex, timeout, owner*)   [C Function]

> Lock *mutex*. If the mutex is already locked, then block and return only when *mutex* has been acquired.
>
> When *timeout* is given, it specifies a point in time where the waiting should be aborted. It can be either an integer as returned by `current-time` or a pair as returned by `gettimeofday`. When the waiting is aborted, `#f` is returned.

When *owner* is given, it specifies an owner for *mutex* other than the calling thread. *owner* may also be `#f`, indicating that the mutex should be locked but left unowned.

For standard mutexes (`make-mutex`), and error is signalled if the thread has itself already locked *mutex*.

For a recursive mutex (`make-recursive-mutex`), if the thread has itself already locked *mutex*, then a further `lock-mutex` call increments the lock count. An additional `unlock-mutex` will be required to finally release.

If *mutex* was locked by a thread that exited before unlocking it, the next attempt to lock *mutex* will succeed, but `abandoned-mutex-error` will be signalled.

When a system async (see Section 6.21.2.1 [System asyncs], page 411) is activated for a thread blocked in `lock-mutex`, the wait is interrupted and the async is executed. When the async returns, the wait resumes.

void scm_dynwind_lock_mutex (*SCM mutex*)   [C Function]
Arrange for *mutex* to be locked whenever the current dynwind context is entered and to be unlocked when it is exited.

try-mutex *mx*   [Scheme Procedure]
scm_try_mutex (*mx*)   [C Function]
Try to lock *mutex* as per `lock-mutex`. If *mutex* can be acquired immediately then this is done and the return is `#t`. If *mutex* is locked by some other thread then nothing is done and the return is `#f`.

unlock-mutex *mutex* [*condvar* [*timeout*]]   [Scheme Procedure]
scm_unlock_mutex (*mutex*)   [C Function]
scm_unlock_mutex_timed (*mutex, condvar, timeout*)   [C Function]
Unlock *mutex*. An error is signalled if *mutex* is not locked and was not created with the `unchecked-unlock` flag set, or if *mutex* is locked by a thread other than the calling thread and was not created with the `allow-external-unlock` flag set.

If *condvar* is given, it specifies a condition variable upon which the calling thread will wait to be signalled before returning. (This behavior is very similar to that of `wait-condition-variable`, except that the mutex is left in an unlocked state when the function returns.)

When *timeout* is also given and not false, it specifies a point in time where the waiting should be aborted. It can be either an integer as returned by `current-time` or a pair as returned by `gettimeofday`. When the waiting is aborted, `#f` is returned. Otherwise the function returns `#t`.

mutex-owner *mutex*   [Scheme Procedure]
scm_mutex_owner (*mutex*)   [C Function]
Return the current owner of *mutex*, in the form of a thread or `#f` (indicating no owner). Note that a mutex may be unowned but still locked.

mutex-level *mutex*   [Scheme Procedure]
scm_mutex_level (*mutex*)   [C Function]
Return the current lock level of *mutex*. If *mutex* is currently unlocked, this value will be 0; otherwise, it will be the number of times *mutex* has been recursively locked by its current owner.

`mutex-locked?` *mutex*   [Scheme Procedure]
`scm_mutex_locked_p` (*mutex*)   [C Function]
> Return `#t` if *mutex* is locked, regardless of ownership; otherwise, return `#f`.

`make-condition-variable`   [Scheme Procedure]
`scm_make_condition_variable` ()   [C Function]
> Return a new condition variable.

`condition-variable?` *obj*   [Scheme Procedure]
`scm_condition_variable_p` (*obj*)   [C Function]
> Return `#t` if *obj* is a condition variable; otherwise, return `#f`.

`wait-condition-variable` *condvar mutex* [*time*]   [Scheme Procedure]
`scm_wait_condition_variable` (*condvar, mutex, time*)   [C Function]
> Wait until *condvar* has been signalled. While waiting, *mutex* is atomically unlocked
> (as with `unlock-mutex`) and is locked again when this function returns. When *time*
> is given, it specifies a point in time where the waiting should be aborted. It can be
> either a integer as returned by `current-time` or a pair as returned by `gettimeofday`.
> When the waiting is aborted, `#f` is returned. When the condition variable has in
> fact been signalled, `#t` is returned. The mutex is re-locked in any case before `wait-`
> `condition-variable` returns.
>
> When a system async is activated for a thread that is blocked in a call to `wait-`
> `condition-variable`, the waiting is interrupted, the mutex is locked, and the async
> is executed. When the async returns, the mutex is unlocked again and the waiting is
> resumed. When the thread block while re-acquiring the mutex, execution of asyncs
> is blocked.

`signal-condition-variable` *condvar*   [Scheme Procedure]
`scm_signal_condition_variable` (*condvar*)   [C Function]
> Wake up one thread that is waiting for *condvar*.

`broadcast-condition-variable` *condvar*   [Scheme Procedure]
`scm_broadcast_condition_variable` (*condvar*)   [C Function]
> Wake up all threads that are waiting for *condvar*.

The following are higher level operations on mutexes. These are available from

`(use-modules (ice-9 threads))`

`with-mutex` *mutex body1 body2* ...   [macro]
> Lock *mutex*, evaluate the body *body1 body2* ..., then unlock *mutex*. The return
> value is that returned by the last body form.
>
> The lock, body and unlock form the branches of a `dynamic-wind` (see Section 6.13.10
> [Dynamic Wind], page 309), so *mutex* is automatically unlocked if an error or new
> continuation exits the body, and is re-locked if the body is re-entered by a captured
> continuation.

monitor *body1 body2 ...*   [macro]
>   Evaluate the body form *body1 body2 ...* with a mutex locked so only one thread
>   can execute that code at any one time. The return value is the return from the last
>   body form.
>
>   Each `monitor` form has its own private mutex and the locking and evaluation is as
>   per `with-mutex` above. A standard mutex (`make-mutex`) is used, which means the
>   body must not recursively re-enter the `monitor` form.
>
>   The term "monitor" comes from operating system theory, where it means a particular
>   bit of code managing access to some resource and which only ever executes on behalf
>   of one process at any one time.

6.21.5 Blocking in Guile Mode

Up to Guile version 1.8, a thread blocked in guile mode would prevent the garbage collector
from running. Thus threads had to explicitly leave guile mode with `scm_without_guile`
() before making a potentially blocking call such as a mutex lock, a `select` () system call,
etc. The following functions could be used to temporarily leave guile mode or to perform
some common blocking operations in a supported way.

Starting from Guile 2.0, blocked threads no longer hinder garbage collection. Thus, the
functions below are not needed anymore. They can still be used to inform the GC that a
thread is about to block, giving it a (small) optimization opportunity for "stop the world"
garbage collections, should they occur while the thread is blocked.

void * scm_without_guile (*void *(*func) (void *), void *data*)   [C Function]
>   Leave guile mode, call *func* on *data*, enter guile mode and return the result of calling
>   *func*.
>
>   While a thread has left guile mode, it must not call any libguile functions except
>   `scm_with_guile` or `scm_without_guile` and must not use any libguile macros. Also,
>   local variables of type SCM that are allocated while not in guile mode are not protected
>   from the garbage collector.
>
>   When used from non-guile mode, calling `scm_without_guile` is still allowed: it simply
>   calls *func*. In that way, you can leave guile mode without having to know whether
>   the current thread is in guile mode or not.

int scm_pthread_mutex_lock (*pthread_mutex_t *mutex*)   [C Function]
>   Like `pthread_mutex_lock`, but leaves guile mode while waiting for the mutex.

int scm_pthread_cond_wait (*pthread_cond_t *cond,*   [C Function]
>   *pthread_mutex_t *mutex*)
int scm_pthread_cond_timedwait (*pthread_cond_t *cond,*   [C Function]
>   *pthread_mutex_t *mutex, struct timespec *abstime*)
>   Like `pthread_cond_wait` and `pthread_cond_timedwait`, but leaves guile mode while
>   waiting for the condition variable.

int scm_std_select (*int nfds, fd_set *readfds, fd_set *writefds, fd_set*   [C Function]
>   **exceptfds, struct timeval *timeout*)
>   Like `select` but leaves guile mode while waiting. Also, the delivery of a system async
>   causes this function to be interrupted with error code EINTR.

unsigned int scm_std_sleep (*unsigned int seconds*)   [C Function]
Like **sleep**, but leaves guile mode while sleeping. Also, the delivery of a system async causes this function to be interrupted.

unsigned long scm_std_usleep (*unsigned long usecs*)   [C Function]
Like **usleep**, but leaves guile mode while sleeping. Also, the delivery of a system async causes this function to be interrupted.

6.21.6 Critical Sections

SCM_CRITICAL_SECTION_START   [C Macro]
SCM_CRITICAL_SECTION_END   [C Macro]
These two macros can be used to delimit a critical section. Syntactically, they are both statements and need to be followed immediately by a semicolon.

Executing **SCM_CRITICAL_SECTION_START** will lock a recursive mutex and block the executing of system asyncs. Executing **SCM_CRITICAL_SECTION_END** will unblock the execution of system asyncs and unlock the mutex. Thus, the code that executes between these two macros can only be executed in one thread at any one time and no system asyncs will run. However, because the mutex is a recursive one, the code might still be reentered by the same thread. You must either allow for this or avoid it, both by careful coding.

On the other hand, critical sections delimited with these macros can be nested since the mutex is recursive.

You must make sure that for each **SCM_CRITICAL_SECTION_START**, the corresponding **SCM_CRITICAL_SECTION_END** is always executed. This means that no non-local exit (such as a signalled error) might happen, for example.

void scm_dynwind_critical_section (*SCM mutex*)   [C Function]
Call **scm_dynwind_lock_mutex** on *mutex* and call **scm_dynwind_block_asyncs**. When *mutex* is false, a recursive mutex provided by Guile is used instead.

The effect of a call to **scm_dynwind_critical_section** is that the current dynwind context (see Section 6.13.10 [Dynamic Wind], page 309) turns into a critical section. Because of the locked mutex, no second thread can enter it concurrently and because of the blocked asyncs, no system async can reenter it from the current thread.

When the current thread reenters the critical section anyway, the kind of *mutex* determines what happens: When *mutex* is recursive, the reentry is allowed. When it is a normal mutex, an error is signalled.

6.21.7 Fluids and Dynamic States

A *fluid* is an object that can store one value per *dynamic state*. Each thread has a current dynamic state, and when accessing a fluid, this current dynamic state is used to provide the actual value. In this way, fluids can be used for thread local storage, but they are in fact more flexible: dynamic states are objects of their own and can be made current for more than one thread at the same time, or only be made current temporarily, for example.

Fluids can also be used to simulate the desirable effects of dynamically scoped variables. Dynamically scoped variables are useful when you want to set a variable to a value during some dynamic extent in the execution of your program and have them revert to their original value when the control flow is outside of this dynamic extent. See the description of with-fluids below for details.

New fluids are created with make-fluid and fluid? is used for testing whether an object is actually a fluid. The values stored in a fluid can be accessed with fluid-ref and fluid-set!.

make-fluid [*dflt*]   [Scheme Procedure]
scm_make_fluid ()   [C Function]
scm_make_fluid_with_default (*dflt*)   [C Function]
> Return a newly created fluid, whose initial value is *dflt*, or #f if *dflt* is not given. Fluids are objects that can hold one value per dynamic state. That is, modifications to this value are only visible to code that executes with the same dynamic state as the modifying code. When a new dynamic state is constructed, it inherits the values from its parent. Because each thread normally executes with its own dynamic state, you can use fluids for thread local storage.

make-unbound-fluid   [Scheme Procedure]
scm_make_unbound_fluid ()   [C Function]
> Return a new fluid that is initially unbound (instead of being implicitly bound to some definite value).

fluid? *obj*   [Scheme Procedure]
scm_fluid_p (*obj*)   [C Function]
> Return #t if *obj* is a fluid; otherwise, return #f.

fluid-ref *fluid*   [Scheme Procedure]
scm_fluid_ref (*fluid*)   [C Function]
> Return the value associated with *fluid* in the current dynamic root. If *fluid* has not been set, then return its default value. Calling fluid-ref on an unbound fluid produces a runtime error.

fluid-set! *fluid value*   [Scheme Procedure]
scm_fluid_set_x (*fluid, value*)   [C Function]
> Set the value associated with *fluid* in the current dynamic root.

fluid-unset! *fluid*   [Scheme Procedure]
scm_fluid_unset_x (*fluid*)   [C Function]
> Disassociate the given fluid from any value, making it unbound.

fluid-bound? *fluid*   [Scheme Procedure]
scm_fluid_bound_p (*fluid*)   [C Function]
> Returns #t if the given fluid is bound to a value, otherwise #f.

with-fluids* temporarily changes the values of one or more fluids, so that the given procedure and each procedure called by it access the given values. After the procedure returns, the old values are restored.

`with-fluid*` *fluid value thunk*   [Scheme Procedure]
`scm_with_fluid` (*fluid, value, thunk*)   [C Function]
> Set *fluid* to *value* temporarily, and call *thunk*. *thunk* must be a procedure with no
> argument.

`with-fluids*` *fluids values thunk*   [Scheme Procedure]
`scm_with_fluids` (*fluids, values, thunk*)   [C Function]
> Set *fluids* to *values* temporary, and call *thunk*. *fluids* must be a list of fluids and
> *values* must be the same number of their values to be applied. Each substitution is
> done in the order given. *thunk* must be a procedure with no argument. It is called
> inside a `dynamic-wind` and the fluids are set/restored when control enter or leaves
> the established dynamic extent.

`with-fluids` ((*fluid value*) ...) *body1 body2* ...   [Scheme Macro]
> Execute body *body1 body2* ... while each *fluid* is set to the corresponding *value*.
> Both *fluid* and *value* are evaluated and *fluid* must yield a fluid. The body is executed
> inside a `dynamic-wind` and the fluids are set/restored when control enter or leaves
> the established dynamic extent.

SCM `scm_c_with_fluids` (*SCM fluids, SCM vals, SCM* (**cproc*)(*void*   [C Function]
>   **), void *data*)
SCM `scm_c_with_fluid` (*SCM fluid, SCM val, SCM* (**cproc*)(*void **),   [C Function]
>   *void *data*)
> The function `scm_c_with_fluids` is like `scm_with_fluids` except that it takes a C
> function to call instead of a Scheme thunk.
>
> The function `scm_c_with_fluid` is similar but only allows one fluid to be set instead
> of a list.

void `scm_dynwind_fluid` (*SCM fluid, SCM val*)   [C Function]
> This function must be used inside a pair of calls to `scm_dynwind_begin` and `scm_`
> `dynwind_end` (see Section 6.13.10 [Dynamic Wind], page 309). During the dynwind
> context, the fluid *fluid* is set to *val*.
>
> More precisely, the value of the fluid is swapped with a 'backup' value whenever
> the dynwind context is entered or left. The backup value is initialized with the *val*
> argument.

`make-dynamic-state` [*parent*]   [Scheme Procedure]
`scm_make_dynamic_state` (*parent*)   [C Function]
> Return a copy of the dynamic state object *parent* or of the current dynamic state
> when *parent* is omitted.

`dynamic-state?` *obj*   [Scheme Procedure]
`scm_dynamic_state_p` (*obj*)   [C Function]
> Return #t if *obj* is a dynamic state object; return #f otherwise.

int `scm_is_dynamic_state` (*SCM obj*)   [C Procedure]
> Return non-zero if *obj* is a dynamic state object; return zero otherwise.

`current-dynamic-state`   [Scheme Procedure]
`scm_current_dynamic_state ()`   [C Function]
> Return the current dynamic state object.

`set-current-dynamic-state` *state*   [Scheme Procedure]
`scm_set_current_dynamic_state (`*state*`)`   [C Function]
> Set the current dynamic state object to *state* and return the previous current dynamic state object.

`with-dynamic-state` *state proc*   [Scheme Procedure]
`scm_with_dynamic_state (`*state, proc*`)`   [C Function]
> Call *proc* while *state* is the current dynamic state object.

`void scm_dynwind_current_dynamic_state (`*SCM state*`)`   [C Procedure]
> Set the current dynamic state to *state* for the current dynwind context.

`void * scm_c_with_dynamic_state (`*SCM state, void*   [C Procedure]
> `*(*func)(`*void ***`), void *data*`)`
> Like `scm_with_dynamic_state`, but call *func* with *data*.

6.21.8 Parameters

A parameter object is a procedure. Calling it with no arguments returns its value. Calling it with one argument sets the value.

```
(define my-param (make-parameter 123))
(my-param)  ⇒ 123
(my-param 456)
(my-param)  ⇒ 456
```

The `parameterize` special form establishes new locations for parameters, those new locations having effect within the dynamic scope of the `parameterize` body. Leaving restores the previous locations. Re-entering (through a saved continuation) will again use the new locations.

```
(parameterize ((my-param 789))
  (my-param))  ⇒ 789
(my-param)  ⇒ 456
```

Parameters are like dynamically bound variables in other Lisp dialects. They allow an application to establish parameter settings (as the name suggests) just for the execution of a particular bit of code, restoring when done. Examples of such parameters might be case-sensitivity for a search, or a prompt for user input.

Global variables are not as good as parameter objects for this sort of thing. Changes to them are visible to all threads, but in Guile parameter object locations are per-thread, thereby truly limiting the effect of `parameterize` to just its dynamic execution.

Passing arguments to functions is thread-safe, but that soon becomes tedious when there's more than a few or when they need to pass down through several layers of calls before reaching the point they should affect. And introducing a new setting to existing code is often easier with a parameter object than adding arguments.

make-parameter *init* [*converter*]   [Scheme Procedure]
>   Return a new parameter object, with initial value *init*.
>
>   If a *converter* is given, then a call (`converter` val) is made for each value set, its
>   return is the value stored. Such a call is made for the *init* initial value too.
>
>   A *converter* allows values to be validated, or put into a canonical form. For example,
>
> ```
> (define my-param (make-parameter 123
>                   (lambda (val)
>                     (if (not (number? val))
>                         (error "must be a number"))
>                     (inexact->exact val))))
>
> (my-param 0.75)
> (my-param) ⇒ 3/4
> ```

parameterize ((*param value*) ...) *body1 body2* ...   [library syntax]
>   Establish a new dynamic scope with the given *param*s bound to new locations and set
>   to the given *value*s. *body1 body2* ... is evaluated in that environment. The value
>   returned is that of last body form.
>
>   Each *param* is an expression which is evaluated to get the parameter object. Often
>   this will just be the name of a variable holding the object, but it can be anything
>   that evaluates to a parameter.
>
>   The *param* expressions and *value* expressions are all evaluated before establishing the
>   new dynamic bindings, and they're evaluated in an unspecified order.
>
>   For example,
>
> ```
> (define prompt (make-parameter "Type something: "))
> (define (get-input)
>   (display (prompt))
>   ...)
>
> (parameterize ((prompt "Type a number: "))
>   (get-input)
>   ...)
> ```

Parameter objects are implemented using fluids (see Section 6.21.7 [Fluids and Dynamic
States], page 419), so each dynamic state has its own parameter locations. That includes
the separate locations when outside any **parameterize** form. When a parameter is created
it gets a separate initial location in each dynamic state, all initialized to the given *init* value.

New code should probably just use parameters instead of fluids, because the interface is
better. But for migrating old code or otherwise providing interoperability, Guile provides
the **fluid->parameter** procedure:

fluid->parameter *fluid* [*conv*]   [Scheme Procedure]
>   Make a parameter that wraps a fluid.
>
>   The value of the parameter will be the same as the value of the fluid. If the parameter
>   is rebound in some dynamic extent, perhaps via **parameterize**, the new value will be
>   run through the optional *conv* procedure, as with any parameter. Note that unlike
>   **make-parameter**, *conv* is not applied to the initial value.

As alluded to above, because each thread usually has a separate dynamic state, each thread has its own locations behind parameter objects, and changes in one thread are not visible to any other. When a new dynamic state or thread is created, the values of parameters in the originating context are copied, into new locations.

Guile's parameters conform to SRFI-39 (see Section 7.5.26 [SRFI-39], page 599).

6.21.9 Futures

The (ice-9 futures) module provides *futures*, a construct for fine-grain parallelism. A future is a wrapper around an expression whose computation may occur in parallel with the code of the calling thread, and possibly in parallel with other futures. Like promises, futures are essentially proxies that can be queried to obtain the value of the enclosed expression:

```
(touch (future (+ 2 3)))
⇒ 5
```

However, unlike promises, the expression associated with a future may be evaluated on another CPU core, should one be available. This supports *fine-grain parallelism*, because even relatively small computations can be embedded in futures. Consider this sequential code:

```
(define (find-prime lst1 lst2)
  (or (find prime? lst1)
      (find prime? lst2)))
```

The two arms of or are potentially computation-intensive. They are independent of one another, yet, they are evaluated sequentially when the first one returns #f. Using futures, one could rewrite it like this:

```
(define (find-prime lst1 lst2)
  (let ((f (future (find prime? lst2))))
    (or (find prime? lst1)
        (touch f))))
```

This preserves the semantics of **find-prime**. On a multi-core machine, though, the computation of (find prime? lst2) may be done in parallel with that of the other **find** call, which can reduce the execution time of **find-prime**.

Futures may be nested: a future can itself spawn and then **touch** other futures, leading to a directed acyclic graph of futures. Using this facility, a parallel **map** procedure can be defined along these lines:

```
(use-modules (ice-9 futures) (ice-9 match))

(define (par-map proc lst)
  (match lst
    (()
     '())
    ((head tail ...)
     (let ((tail (future (par-map proc tail)))
           (head (proc head)))
       (cons head (touch tail))))))
```

Note that futures are intended for the evaluation of purely functional expressions. Expressions that have side-effects or rely on I/O may require additional care, such as explicit synchronization (see Section 6.21.4 [Mutexes and Condition Variables], page 415).

Guile's futures are implemented on top of POSIX threads (see Section 6.21.3 [Threads], page 413). Internally, a fixed-size pool of threads is used to evaluate futures, such that offloading the evaluation of an expression to another thread doesn't incur thread creation costs. By default, the pool contains one thread per available CPU core, minus one, to account for the main thread. The number of available CPU cores is determined using `current-processor-count` (see Section 7.2.7 [Processes], page 490).

When a thread touches a future that has not completed yet, it processes any pending future while waiting for it to complete, or just waits if there are no pending futures. When `touch` is called from within a future, the execution of the calling future is suspended, allowing its host thread to process other futures, and resumed when the touched future has completed. This suspend/resume is achieved by capturing the calling future's continuation, and later reinstating it (see Section 6.13.5 [Prompts], page 296).

Note that `par-map` above is not tail-recursive. This could lead to stack overflows when *lst* is large compared to (`current-processor-count`). To address that, `touch` uses the suspend mechanism described above to limit the number of nested futures executing on the same stack. Thus, the above code should never run into stack overflows.

`future` *exp*   [Scheme Syntax]

> Return a future for expression *exp*. This is equivalent to:
>
>   (make-future (lambda () exp))

`make-future` *thunk*   [Scheme Procedure]

> Return a future for *thunk*, a zero-argument procedure.
>
> This procedure returns immediately. Execution of *thunk* may begin in parallel with the calling thread's computations, if idle CPU cores are available, or it may start when `touch` is invoked on the returned future.
>
> If the execution of *thunk* throws an exception, that exception will be re-thrown when `touch` is invoked on the returned future.

`future?` *obj*   [Scheme Procedure]

> Return #t if *obj* is a future.

`touch` *f*   [Scheme Procedure]

> Return the result of the expression embedded in future *f*.
>
> If the result was already computed in parallel, `touch` returns instantaneously. Otherwise, it waits for the computation to complete, if it already started, or initiates it. In the former case, the calling thread may process other futures in the meantime.

6.21.10 Parallel forms

The functions described in this section are available from

    (use-modules (ice-9 threads))

They provide high-level parallel constructs. The following functions are implemented in terms of futures (see Section 6.21.9 [Futures], page 424). Thus they are relatively cheap as they re-use existing threads, and portable, since they automatically use one thread per available CPU core.

parallel *expr* ...   [syntax]

> Evaluate each *expr* expression in parallel, each in its own thread. Return the results of *n* expressions as a set of *n* multiple values (see Section 6.13.7 [Multiple Values], page 301).

letpar ((*var expr*) ...) *body1 body2* ...   [syntax]

> Evaluate each *expr* in parallel, each in its own thread, then bind the results to the corresponding *var* variables, and then evaluate *body1 body2* ...
>
> **letpar** is like **let** (see Section 6.12.2 [Local Bindings], page 287), but all the expressions for the bindings are evaluated in parallel.

par-map *proc lst1 lst2* ...   [Scheme Procedure]
par-for-each *proc lst1 lst2* ...   [Scheme Procedure]

> Call *proc* on the elements of the given lists. **par-map** returns a list comprising the return values from *proc*. **par-for-each** returns an unspecified value, but waits for all calls to complete.
>
> The *proc* calls are (*proc elem1 elem2* ...), where each *elem* is from the corresponding *lst* . Each *lst* must be the same length. The calls are potentially made in parallel, depending on the number of CPU cores available.
>
> These functions are like **map** and **for-each** (see Section 6.7.2.8 [List Mapping], page 193), but make their *proc* calls in parallel.

Unlike those above, the functions described below take a number of threads as an argument. This makes them inherently non-portable since the specified number of threads may differ from the number of available CPU cores as returned by **current-processor-count** (see Section 7.2.7 [Processes], page 490). In addition, these functions create the specified number of threads when they are called and terminate them upon completion, which makes them quite expensive.

Therefore, they should be avoided.

n-par-map *n proc lst1 lst2* ...   [Scheme Procedure]
n-par-for-each *n proc lst1 lst2* ...   [Scheme Procedure]

> Call *proc* on the elements of the given lists, in the same way as **par-map** and **par-for-each** above, but use no more than *n* threads at any one time. The order in which calls are initiated within that threads limit is unspecified.
>
> These functions are good for controlling resource consumption if *proc* calls might be costly, or if there are many to be made. On a dual-CPU system for instance *n* = 4 might be enough to keep the CPUs utilized, and not consume too much memory.

n-for-each-par-map *n sproc pproc lst1 lst2* ...   [Scheme Procedure]

> Apply *pproc* to the elements of the given lists, and apply *sproc* to each result returned by *pproc*. The final return value is unspecified, but all calls will have been completed before returning.
>
> The calls made are (*sproc* (*pproc elem1* ... *elemN*)), where each *elem* is from the corresponding *lst*. Each *lst* must have the same number of elements.

The *pproc* calls are made in parallel, in separate threads. No more than *n* threads are used at any one time. The order in which *pproc* calls are initiated within that limit is unspecified.

The *sproc* calls are made serially, in list element order, one at a time. *pproc* calls on later elements may execute in parallel with the *sproc* calls. Exactly which thread makes each *sproc* call is unspecified.

This function is designed for individual calculations that can be done in parallel, but with results needing to be handled serially, for instance to write them to a file. The *n* limit on threads controls system resource usage when there are many calculations or when they might be costly.

It will be seen that `n-for-each-par-map` is like a combination of `n-par-map` and `for-each`,

```
(for-each sproc (n-par-map n pproc lst1 ... lstN))
```

But the actual implementation is more efficient since each *sproc* call, in turn, can be initiated once the relevant *pproc* call has completed, it doesn't need to wait for all to finish.

6.22 Configuration, Features and Runtime Options

Why is my Guile different from your Guile? There are three kinds of possible variation:

- build differences — different versions of the Guile source code, installation directories, configuration flags that control pieces of functionality being included or left out, etc.

- differences in dynamically loaded code — behaviour and features provided by modules that can be dynamically loaded into a running Guile

- different runtime options — some of the options that are provided for controlling Guile's behaviour may be set differently.

Guile provides "introspective" variables and procedures to query all of these possible variations at runtime. For runtime options, it also provides procedures to change the settings of options and to obtain documentation on what the options mean.

6.22.1 Configuration, Build and Installation

The following procedures and variables provide information about how Guile was configured, built and installed on your system.

`version`	[Scheme Procedure]
`effective-version`	[Scheme Procedure]
`major-version`	[Scheme Procedure]
`minor-version`	[Scheme Procedure]
`micro-version`	[Scheme Procedure]
`scm_version ()`	[C Function]
`scm_effective_version ()`	[C Function]
`scm_major_version ()`	[C Function]
`scm_minor_version ()`	[C Function]
`scm_micro_version ()`	[C Function]

Return a string describing Guile's full version number, effective version number, major, minor or micro version number, respectively. The `effective-version` function returns the version name that should remain unchanged during a stable series. Currently that means that it omits the micro version. The effective version should be used for items like the versioned share directory name i.e. `/usr/share/guile/2.0/`

```
(version) ⇒ "2.0.4"
(effective-version) ⇒ "2.0"
(major-version) ⇒ "2"
(minor-version) ⇒ "0"
(micro-version) ⇒ "4"
```

%package-data-dir   [Scheme Procedure]
scm_sys_package_data_dir ()   [C Function]
> Return the name of the directory under which Guile Scheme files in general are stored. On Unix-like systems, this is usually `/usr/local/share/guile` or `/usr/share/guile`.

%library-dir   [Scheme Procedure]
scm_sys_library_dir ()   [C Function]
> Return the name of the directory where the Guile Scheme files that belong to the core Guile installation (as opposed to files from a 3rd party package) are installed. On Unix-like systems this is usually `/usr/local/share/guile/`*GUILE_EFFECTIVE_VERSION* or `/usr/share/guile/`*GUILE_EFFECTIVE_VERSION*;
>
> for example `/usr/local/share/guile/2.0`.

%site-dir   [Scheme Procedure]
scm_sys_site_dir ()   [C Function]
> Return the name of the directory where Guile Scheme files specific to your site should be installed. On Unix-like systems, this is usually `/usr/local/share/guile/site` or `/usr/share/guile/site`.

%site-ccache-dir   [Scheme Procedure]
scm_sys_site_ccache_dir ()   [C Function]
> Return the directory where users should install compiled `.go` files for use with this version of Guile. Might look something like `/usr/lib/guile/2.0/site-ccache`.

%guile-build-info   [Variable]
> Alist of information collected during the building of a particular Guile. Entries can be grouped into one of several categories: directories, env vars, and versioning info.
>
> Briefly, here are the keys in **%guile-build-info**, by group:
>
> directories srcdir, top_srcdir, prefix, exec_prefix, bindir, sbindir, libexecdir, datadir, sysconfdir, sharedstatedir, localstatedir, libdir, infodir, mandir, includedir, pkgdatadir, pkglibdir, pkgincludedir
>
> env vars   LIBS
>
> versioning info
>   guileversion, libguileinterface, buildstamp
>
> Values are all strings. The value for **LIBS** is typically found also as a part of `pkg-config --libs guile-2.0` output. The value for **guileversion** has form X.Y.Z, and

should be the same as returned by (version). The value for libguileinterface is libtool compatible and has form CURRENT:REVISION:AGE (see Section "Library interface versions" in *GNU Libtool*). The value for buildstamp is the output of the command 'date -u +'%Y-%m-%d %T'' (UTC).

In the source, %guile-build-info is initialized from libguile/libpath.h, which is completely generated, so deleting this file before a build guarantees up-to-date values for that build.

%host-type   [Variable]
        The canonical host type (GNU triplet) of the host Guile was configured for, e.g.,
        "x86_64-unknown-linux-gnu" (see Section "Canonicalizing" in *The GNU Autoconf Manual*).

6.22.2 Feature Tracking

Guile has a Scheme level variable *features* that keeps track to some extent of the features that are available in a running Guile. *features* is a list of symbols, for example threads, each of which describes a feature of the running Guile process.

features   [Variable]
        A list of symbols describing available features of the Guile process.

You shouldn't modify the *features* variable directly using set!. Instead, see the procedures that are provided for this purpose in the following subsection.

6.22.2.1 Feature Manipulation

To check whether a particular feature is available, use the provided? procedure:

provided? *feature*   [Scheme Procedure]
feature? *feature*   [Deprecated Scheme Procedure]
        Return #t if the specified *feature* is available, otherwise #f.

To advertise a feature from your own Scheme code, you can use the provide procedure:

provide *feature*   [Scheme Procedure]
        Add *feature* to the list of available features in this Guile process.

For C code, the equivalent function takes its feature name as a char * argument for convenience:

void scm_add_feature (*const char *str*)   [C Function]
        Add a symbol with name *str* to the list of available features in this Guile process.

6.22.2.2 Common Feature Symbols

In general, a particular feature may be available for one of two reasons. Either because the Guile library was configured and compiled with that feature enabled — i.e. the feature is built into the library on your system. Or because some C or Scheme code that was dynamically loaded by Guile has added that feature to the list.

In the first category, here are the features that the current version of Guile may define (depending on how it is built), and what they mean.

array   Indicates support for arrays (see Section 6.7.5 [Arrays], page 200).

array-for-each
             Indicates availability of **array-for-each** and other array mapping procedures
             (see Section 6.7.5 [Arrays], page 200).

char-ready?
             Indicates that the **char-ready?** function is available (see Section 6.14.2 [Read-
             ing], page 318).

complex   Indicates support for complex numbers.

current-time
             Indicates availability of time-related functions: **times**, **get-internal-run-
             time** and so on (see Section 7.2.5 [Time], page 485).

debug-extensions
             Indicates that the debugging evaluator is available, together with the options
             for controlling it.

delay   Indicates support for promises (see Section 6.17.9 [Delayed Evaluation],
             page 371).

EIDs   Indicates that the **geteuid** and **getegid** really return effective user and group
             IDs (see Section 7.2.7 [Processes], page 490).

inexact   Indicates support for inexact numbers.

i/o-extensions
             Indicates availability of the following extended I/O procedures: **ftell**,
             redirect-port, **dup->fdes**, **dup2**, **fileno**, **isatty?**, **fdopen**, **primitive-
             move->fdes** and **fdes->ports** (see Section 7.2.2 [Ports and File Descriptors],
             page 469).

net-db   Indicates availability of network database functions: **scm_gethost**,
             scm_getnet, **scm_getproto**, **scm_getserv**, **scm_sethost**, **scm_setnet**,
             scm_setproto, **scm_setserv**, and their 'byXXX' variants (see Section 7.2.11.2
             [Network Databases], page 503).

posix   Indicates support for POSIX functions: **pipe**, **getgroups**, **kill**, **execl** and so
             on (see Section 7.2 [POSIX], page 468).

fork   Indicates support for the POSIX **fork** function (see Section 7.2.7 [Processes],
             page 490). This is a prerequisite for the **(ice-9 popen)** module (see
             Section 7.2.10 [Pipes], page 500).

random   Indicates availability of random number generation functions: **random**, **copy-
             random-state**, **random-uniform** and so on (see Section 6.6.2.14 [Random],
             page 127).

reckless   Indicates that Guile was built with important checks omitted — you should
             never see this!

regex   Indicates support for POSIX regular expressions using **make-regexp**, **regexp-
             exec** and friends (see Section 6.15.1 [Regexp Functions], page 350).

socket   Indicates availability of socket-related functions: `socket`, `bind`, `connect` and so on (see Section 7.2.11.4 [Network Sockets and Communication], page 511).

sort   Indicates availability of sorting and merging functions (see Section 6.11.3 [Sorting], page 279).

system   Indicates that the `system` function is available (see Section 7.2.7 [Processes], page 490).

threads   Indicates support for multithreading (see Section 6.21.3 [Threads], page 413).

values   Indicates support for multiple return values using `values` and `call-with-values` (see Section 6.13.7 [Multiple Values], page 301).

Available features in the second category depend, by definition, on what additional code your Guile process has loaded in. The following table lists features that you might encounter for this reason.

defmacro   Indicates that the `defmacro` macro is available (see Section 6.10 [Macros], page 257).

describe   Indicates that the `(oop goops describe)` module has been loaded, which provides a procedure for describing the contents of GOOPS instances.

readline   Indicates that Guile has loaded in Readline support, for command line editing (see Section 7.8 [Readline Support], page 660).

record   Indicates support for record definition using `make-record-type` and friends (see Section 6.7.9 [Records], page 219).

Although these tables may seem exhaustive, it is probably unwise in practice to rely on them, as the correspondences between feature symbols and available procedures/behaviour are not strictly defined. If you are writing code that needs to check for the existence of some procedure, it is probably safer to do so directly using the `defined?` procedure than to test for the corresponding feature using `provided?`.

6.22.3 Runtime Options

There are a number of runtime options available for paramaterizing built-in procedures, like `read`, and built-in behavior, like what happens on an uncaught error.

For more information on reader options, See Section 6.17.2 [Scheme Read], page 360.

For more information on print options, See Section 6.17.3 [Scheme Write], page 361.

Finally, for more information on debugger options, See Section 6.25.3.4 [Debug Options], page 454.

6.22.3.1 Examples of option use

Here is an example of a session in which some read and debug option handling procedures are used. In this example, the user

1. Notices that the symbols `abc` and `aBc` are not the same

2. Examines the `read-options`, and sees that `case-insensitive` is set to "no".

3. Enables `case-insensitive`

4. Quits the recursive prompt

5. Verifies that now aBc and abc are the same

```
scheme@(guile-user)> (define abc "hello")
scheme@(guile-user)> abc
$1 = "hello"
scheme@(guile-user)> aBc
<unknown-location>: warning: possibly unbound variable 'aBc'
ERROR: In procedure module-lookup:
ERROR: Unbound variable: aBc
Entering a new prompt.  Type ',bt' for a backtrace or ',q' to continue.
scheme@(guile-user) [1]> (read-options 'help)
copy                no    Copy source code expressions.
positions           yes   Record positions of source code expressions.
case-insensitive    no    Convert symbols to lower case.
keywords            #f    Style of keyword recognition: #f, 'prefix or 'postfix.
r6rs-hex-escapes    no    Use R6RS variable-length character and string hex escapes.
square-brackets     yes   Treat '[' and ']' as parentheses, for R6RS compatibility.
hungry-eol-escapes no     In strings, consume leading whitespace after an
                          escaped end-of-line.
curly-infix         no    Support SRFI-105 curly infix expressions.
scheme@(guile-user) [1]> (read-enable 'case-insensitive)
$2 = (square-brackets keywords #f case-insensitive positions)
scheme@(guile-user) [1]> ,q
scheme@(guile-user)> aBc
$3 = "hello"
```

6.23 Support for Other Languages

In addition to Scheme, a user may write a Guile program in an increasing number of other languages. Currently supported languages include Emacs Lisp and ECMAScript.

Guile is still fundamentally a Scheme, but it tries to support a wide variety of language building-blocks, so that other languages can be implemented on top of Guile. This allows users to write or extend applications in languages other than Scheme, too. This section describes the languages that have been implemented.

(For details on how to implement a language, See Section 9.4 [Compiling to the Virtual Machine], page 791.)

6.23.1 Using Other Languages

There are currently only two ways to access other languages from within Guile: at the REPL, and programmatically, via compile, read-and-compile, and compile-file.

The REPL is Guile's command prompt (see Section 4.4 [Using Guile Interactively], page 46). The REPL has a concept of the "current language", which defaults to Scheme. The user may change that language, via the meta-command ,language.

For example, the following meta-command enables Emacs Lisp input:

```
scheme@(guile-user)> ,language elisp
Happy hacking with Emacs Lisp!  To switch back, type ',L scheme'.
elisp@(guile-user)> (eq 1 2)
$1 = #nil
```

Each language has its short name: for example, elisp, for Elisp. The same short name may be used to compile source code programmatically, via compile:

```
elisp@(guile-user)> ,L scheme
```

```
Happy hacking with Guile Scheme!  To switch back, type ',L elisp'.
scheme@(guile-user)> (compile '(eq 1 2) #:from 'elisp)
$2 = #nil
```

Granted, as the input to `compile` is a datum, this works best for Lispy languages, which have a straightforward datum representation. Other languages that need more parsing are better dealt with as strings.

The easiest way to deal with syntax-heavy language is with files, via `compile-file` and friends. However it is possible to invoke a language's reader on a port, and then compile the resulting expression (which is a datum at that point). For more information, See Section 6.17.5 [Compilation], page 364.

For more details on introspecting aspects of different languages, See Section 9.4.1 [Compiler Tower], page 792.

6.23.2 Emacs Lisp

Emacs Lisp (Elisp) is a dynamically-scoped Lisp dialect used in the Emacs editor. See Section "Overview" in *Emacs Lisp*, for more information on Emacs Lisp.

We hope that eventually Guile's implementation of Elisp will be good enough to replace Emacs' own implementation of Elisp. For that reason, we have thought long and hard about how to support the various features of Elisp in a performant and compatible manner.

Readers familiar with Emacs Lisp might be curious about how exactly these various Elisp features are supported in Guile. The rest of this section focuses on addressing these concerns of the Elisp elect.

6.23.2.1 Nil

`nil` in ELisp is an amalgam of Scheme's `#f` and `'()`. It is false, and it is the end-of-list; thus it is a boolean, and a list as well.

Guile has chosen to support `nil` as a separate value, distinct from `#f` and `'()`. This allows existing Scheme and Elisp code to maintain their current semantics. `nil`, which in Elisp would just be written and read as `nil`, in Scheme has the external representation `#nil`.

This decision to have `nil` as a low-level distinct value facilitates interoperability between the two languages. Guile has chosen to have Scheme deal with `nil` as follows:

```
(boolean? #nil) ⇒ #t
(not #nil) ⇒ #t
(null? #nil) ⇒ #t
```

And in C, one has:

```
scm_is_bool (SCM_ELISP_NIL) ⇒ 1
scm_is_false (SCM_ELISP_NIL) ⇒ 1
scm_is_null (SCM_ELISP_NIL) ⇒ 1
```

In this way, a version of `fold` written in Scheme can correctly fold a function written in Elisp (or in fact any other language) over a nil-terminated list, as Elisp makes. The converse holds as well; a version of `fold` written in Elisp can fold over a `'()`-terminated list, as made by Scheme.

On a low level, the bit representations for #f, #t, nil, and '() are made in such a way that they differ by only one bit, and so a test for, for example, #f-or-nil may be made very efficiently. See libguile/boolean.h, for more information.

6.23.2.2 Equality

Since Scheme's equal? must be transitive, and '() is not equal? to #f, to Scheme nil is not equal? to #f or '().

```
(eq? #f '()) ⇒ #f
(eq? #nil '()) ⇒ #f
(eq? #nil #f) ⇒ #f
(eqv? #f '()) ⇒ #f
(eqv? #nil '()) ⇒ #f
(eqv? #nil #f) ⇒ #f
(equal? #f '()) ⇒ #f
(equal? #nil '()) ⇒ #f
(equal? #nil #f) ⇒ #f
```

However, in Elisp, '(), #f, and nil are all equal (though not eq).

```
(defvar f (make-scheme-false))
(defvar eol (make-scheme-null))
(eq f eol) ⇒ nil
(eq nil eol) ⇒ nil
(eq nil f) ⇒ nil
(equal f eol) ⇒ t
(equal nil eol) ⇒ t
(equal nil f) ⇒ t
```

These choices facilitate interoperability between Elisp and Scheme code, but they are not perfect. Some code that is correct standard Scheme is not correct in the presence of a second false and null value. For example:

```
(define (truthiness x)
  (if (eq? x #f)
      #f
      #t))
```

This code seems to be meant to test a value for truth, but now that there are two false values, #f and nil, it is no longer correct.

Similarly, there is the loop:

```
(define (my-length l)
  (let lp ((l l) (len 0))
    (if (eq? l '())
        len
        (lp (cdr l) (1+ len)))))
```

Here, my-length will raise an error if *l* is a nil-terminated list.

Both of these examples are correct standard Scheme, but, depending on what they really want to do, they are not correct Guile Scheme. Correctly written, they would test the *properties* of falsehood or nullity, not the individual members of that set. That is to say, they should use `not` or `null?` to test for falsehood or nullity, not `eq?` or `memv` or the like.

Fortunately, using `not` and `null?` is in good style, so all well-written standard Scheme programs are correct, in Guile Scheme.

Here are correct versions of the above examples:

```
(define (truthiness* x)
  (if (not x)
      #f
      #t))
;; or: (define (t* x) (not (not x)))
;; or: (define (t** x) x)

(define (my-length* l)
  (let lp ((l l) (len 0))
    (if (null? l)
        len
        (lp (cdr l) (1+ len)))))
```

This problem has a mirror-image case in Elisp:

```
(deffn my-falsep (x)
  (if (eq x nil)
      t
      nil))
```

Guile can warn when compiling code that has equality comparisons with `#f`, `'()`, or `nil`. See Section 6.17.5 [Compilation], page 364, for details.

6.23.2.3 Dynamic Binding

In contrast to Scheme, which uses "lexical scoping", Emacs Lisp scopes its variables dynamically. Guile supports dynamic scoping with its "fluids" facility. See Section 6.21.7 [Fluids and Dynamic States], page 419, for more information.

6.23.2.4 Other Elisp Features

Buffer-local and mode-local variables should be mentioned here, along with buckybits on characters, Emacs primitive data types, the Lisp-2-ness of Elisp, and other things. Contributions to the documentation are most welcome!

6.23.3 ECMAScript

ECMAScript was not the first non-Schemey language implemented by Guile, but it was the first implemented for Guile's bytecode compiler. The goal was to support ECMAScript version 3.1, a relatively small language, but the implementor was completely irresponsible and got distracted by other things before finishing the standard library, and even some bits of the syntax. So, ECMAScript does deserve a mention in the manual, but it doesn't deserve an endorsement until its implementation is completed, perhaps by some more responsible hacker.

In the meantime, the charitable user might investigate such invocations as `,L ecmascript` and `cat test-suite/tests/ecmascript.test`.

6.24 Support for Internationalization

Guile provides internationalization[16] support for Scheme programs in two ways. First, procedures to manipulate text and data in a way that conforms to particular cultural conventions (i.e., in a "locale-dependent" way) are provided in the (ice-9 i18n). Second, Guile allows the use of GNU `gettext` to translate program message strings.

6.24.1 Internationalization with Guile

In order to make use of the functions described thereafter, the (ice-9 i18n) module must be imported in the usual way:

```
(use-modules (ice-9 i18n))
```

The (ice-9 i18n) module provides procedures to manipulate text and other data in a way that conforms to the cultural conventions chosen by the user. Each region of the world or language has its own customs to, for instance, represent real numbers, classify characters, collate text, etc. All these aspects comprise the so-called "cultural conventions" of that region or language.

Computer systems typically refer to a set of cultural conventions as a *locale*. For each particular aspect that comprise those cultural conventions, a *locale category* is defined. For instance, the way characters are classified is defined by the `LC_CTYPE` category, while the language in which program messages are issued to the user is defined by the `LC_MESSAGES` category (see Section 7.2.13 [Locales], page 518 for details).

The procedures provided by this module allow the development of programs that adapt automatically to any locale setting. As we will see later, many of these procedures can optionally take a *locale object* argument. This additional argument defines the locale settings that must be followed by the invoked procedure. When it is omitted, then the current locale settings of the process are followed (see Section 7.2.13 [Locales], page 518).

The following procedures allow the manipulation of such locale objects.

`make-locale` *category-list locale-name* [*base-locale*]   [Scheme Procedure]
`scm_make_locale` (*category_list, locale_name, base_locale*)   [C Function]

> Return a reference to a data structure representing a set of locale datasets. *locale-name* should be a string denoting a particular locale (e.g., `"aa_DJ"`) and *category-list* should be either a list of locale categories or a single category as used with `setlocale` (see Section 7.2.13 [Locales], page 518). Optionally, if `base-locale` is passed, it should be a locale object denoting settings for categories not listed in *category-list*.
>
> The following invocation creates a locale object that combines the use of Swedish for messages and character classification with the default settings for the other categories (i.e., the settings of the default `C` locale which usually represents conventions in use in the USA):
>
> ```
> (make-locale (list LC_MESSAGES LC_CTYPE) "sv_SE")
> ```
>
> The following example combines the use of Esperanto messages and conventions with monetary conventions from Croatia:
>
> ```
> (make-locale LC_MONETARY "hr_HR"
>              (make-locale LC_ALL "eo_EO"))
> ```

---

[16] For concision and style, programmers often like to refer to internationalization as "i18n".

A `system-error` exception (see Section 6.13.11 [Handling Errors], page 313) is raised by `make-locale` when *locale-name* does not match any of the locales compiled on the system. Note that on non-GNU systems, this error may be raised later, when the locale object is actually used.

`locale?` *obj*	[Scheme Procedure]
`scm_locale_p` (*obj*)	[C Function]

Return true if *obj* is a locale object.

`%global-locale`	[Scheme Variable]
`scm_global_locale`	[C Variable]

This variable is bound to a locale object denoting the current process locale as installed using `setlocale ()` (see Section 7.2.13 [Locales], page 518). It may be used like any other locale object, including as a third argument to `make-locale`, for instance.

6.24.2 Text Collation

The following procedures provide support for text collation, i.e., locale-dependent string and character sorting.

`string-locale<?` *s1 s2* [*locale*]	[Scheme Procedure]
`scm_string_locale_lt` (*s1, s2, locale*)	[C Function]
`string-locale>?` *s1 s2* [*locale*]	[Scheme Procedure]
`scm_string_locale_gt` (*s1, s2, locale*)	[C Function]
`string-locale-ci<?` *s1 s2* [*locale*]	[Scheme Procedure]
`scm_string_locale_ci_lt` (*s1, s2, locale*)	[C Function]
`string-locale-ci>?` *s1 s2* [*locale*]	[Scheme Procedure]
`scm_string_locale_ci_gt` (*s1, s2, locale*)	[C Function]

Compare strings *s1* and *s2* in a locale-dependent way. If *locale* is provided, it should be locale object (as returned by `make-locale`) and will be used to perform the comparison; otherwise, the current system locale is used. For the `-ci` variants, the comparison is made in a case-insensitive way.

`string-locale-ci=?` *s1 s2* [*locale*]	[Scheme Procedure]
`scm_string_locale_ci_eq` (*s1, s2, locale*)	[C Function]

Compare strings *s1* and *s2* in a case-insensitive, and locale-dependent way. If *locale* is provided, it should be a locale object (as returned by `make-locale`) and will be used to perform the comparison; otherwise, the current system locale is used.

`char-locale<?` *c1 c2* [*locale*]	[Scheme Procedure]
`scm_char_locale_lt` (*c1, c2, locale*)	[C Function]
`char-locale>?` *c1 c2* [*locale*]	[Scheme Procedure]
`scm_char_locale_gt` (*c1, c2, locale*)	[C Function]
`char-locale-ci<?` *c1 c2* [*locale*]	[Scheme Procedure]
`scm_char_locale_ci_lt` (*c1, c2, locale*)	[C Function]
`char-locale-ci>?` *c1 c2* [*locale*]	[Scheme Procedure]

`scm_char_locale_ci_gt` (*c1, c2, locale*)   [C Function]
> Compare characters *c1* and *c2* according to either *locale* (a locale object as returned by `make-locale`) or the current locale. For the `-ci` variants, the comparison is made in a case-insensitive way.

`char-locale-ci=?` *c1 c2* [*locale*]   [Scheme Procedure]
`scm_char_locale_ci_eq` (*c1, c2, locale*)   [C Function]
> Return true if character *c1* is equal to *c2*, in a case insensitive way according to *locale* or to the current locale.

6.24.3 Character Case Mapping

The procedures below provide support for "character case mapping", i.e., to convert characters or strings to their upper-case or lower-case equivalent. Note that SRFI-13 provides procedures that look similar (see Section 6.6.5.9 [Alphabetic Case Mapping], page 154). However, the SRFI-13 procedures are locale-independent. Therefore, they do not take into account specificities of the customs in use in a particular language or region of the world. For instance, while most languages using the Latin alphabet map lower-case letter "i" to upper-case letter "I", Turkish maps lower-case "i" to "Latin capital letter I with dot above". The following procedures allow programmers to provide idiomatic character mapping.

`char-locale-downcase` *chr* [*locale*]   [Scheme Procedure]
`scm_char_locale_upcase` (*chr, locale*)   [C Function]
> Return the lowercase character that corresponds to *chr* according to either *locale* or the current locale.

`char-locale-upcase` *chr* [*locale*]   [Scheme Procedure]
`scm_char_locale_downcase` (*chr, locale*)   [C Function]
> Return the uppercase character that corresponds to *chr* according to either *locale* or the current locale.

`char-locale-titlecase` *chr* [*locale*]   [Scheme Procedure]
`scm_char_locale_titlecase` (*chr, locale*)   [C Function]
> Return the titlecase character that corresponds to *chr* according to either *locale* or the current locale.

`string-locale-upcase` *str* [*locale*]   [Scheme Procedure]
`scm_string_locale_upcase` (*str, locale*)   [C Function]
> Return a new string that is the uppercase version of *str* according to either *locale* or the current locale.

`string-locale-downcase` *str* [*locale*]   [Scheme Procedure]
`scm_string_locale_downcase` (*str, locale*)   [C Function]
> Return a new string that is the down-case version of *str* according to either *locale* or the current locale.

`string-locale-titlecase` *str* [*locale*]   [Scheme Procedure]
`scm_string_locale_titlecase` (*str, locale*)   [C Function]
> Return a new string that is the titlecase version of *str* according to either *locale* or the current locale.

6.24.4 Number Input and Output

The following procedures allow programs to read and write numbers written according to a particular locale. As an example, in English, "ten thousand and a half" is usually written 10,000.5 while in French it is written 10 000,5. These procedures allow such differences to be taken into account.

locale-string->integer *str* [*base* [*locale*]] [Scheme Procedure]
scm_locale_string_to_integer (*str*, *base*, *locale*) [C Function]

> Convert string *str* into an integer according to either *locale* (a locale object as returned by make-locale) or the current process locale. If *base* is specified, then it determines the base of the integer being read (e.g., 16 for an hexadecimal number, 10 for a decimal number); by default, decimal numbers are read. Return two values (see Section 6.13.7 [Multiple Values], page 301): an integer (on success) or #f, and the number of characters read from *str* (0 on failure).

> This function is based on the C library's strtol function (see Section "Parsing of Integers" in *The GNU C Library Reference Manual*).

locale-string->inexact *str* [*locale*] [Scheme Procedure]
scm_locale_string_to_inexact (*str*, *locale*) [C Function]

> Convert string *str* into an inexact number according to either *locale* (a locale object as returned by make-locale) or the current process locale. Return two values (see Section 6.13.7 [Multiple Values], page 301): an inexact number (on success) or #f, and the number of characters read from *str* (0 on failure).

> This function is based on the C library's strtod function (see Section "Parsing of Floats" in *The GNU C Library Reference Manual*).

number->locale-string *number* [*fraction-digits* [*locale*]] [Scheme Procedure]

> Convert *number* (an inexact) into a string according to the cultural conventions of either *locale* (a locale object) or the current locale. Optionally, *fraction-digits* may be bound to an integer specifying the number of fractional digits to be displayed.

monetary-amount->locale-string *amount intl?* [*locale*] [Scheme Procedure]

> Convert *amount* (an inexact denoting a monetary amount) into a string according to the cultural conventions of either *locale* (a locale object) or the current locale. If *intl?* is true, then the international monetary format for the given locale is used (see Section "Currency Symbol" in *The GNU C Library Reference Manual*).

6.24.5 Accessing Locale Information

It is sometimes useful to obtain very specific information about a locale such as the word it uses for days or months, its format for representing floating-point figures, etc. The (ice-9 i18n) module provides support for this in a way that is similar to the libc functions nl_langinfo () and localeconv () (see Section "Locale Information" in *The GNU C Library Reference Manual*). The available functions are listed below.

locale-encoding [*locale*] [Scheme Procedure]

> Return the name of the encoding (a string whose interpretation is system-dependent) of either *locale* or the current locale.

The following functions deal with dates and times.

`locale-day` *day* [*locale*]   [Scheme Procedure]
`locale-day-short` *day* [*locale*]   [Scheme Procedure]
`locale-month` *month* [*locale*]   [Scheme Procedure]
`locale-month-short` *month* [*locale*]   [Scheme Procedure]

> Return the word (a string) used in either *locale* or the current locale to name the day (or month) denoted by *day* (or *month*), an integer between 1 and 7 (or 1 and 12). The `-short` variants provide an abbreviation instead of a full name.

`locale-am-string` [*locale*]   [Scheme Procedure]
`locale-pm-string` [*locale*]   [Scheme Procedure]

> Return a (potentially empty) string that is used to denote *ante meridiem* (or *post meridiem*) hours in 12-hour format.

`locale-date+time-format` [*locale*]   [Scheme Procedure]
`locale-date-format` [*locale*]   [Scheme Procedure]
`locale-time-format` [*locale*]   [Scheme Procedure]
`locale-time+am/pm-format` [*locale*]   [Scheme Procedure]
`locale-era-date-format` [*locale*]   [Scheme Procedure]
`locale-era-date+time-format` [*locale*]   [Scheme Procedure]
`locale-era-time-format` [*locale*]   [Scheme Procedure]

> These procedures return format strings suitable to `strftime` (see Section 7.2.5 [Time], page 485) that may be used to display (part of) a date/time according to certain constraints and to the conventions of either *locale* or the current locale (see Section "The Elegant and Fast Way" in *The GNU C Library Reference Manual*).

`locale-era` [*locale*]   [Scheme Procedure]
`locale-era-year` [*locale*]   [Scheme Procedure]

> These functions return, respectively, the era and the year of the relevant era used in *locale* or the current locale. Most locales do not define this value. In this case, the empty string is returned. An example of a locale that does define this value is the Japanese one.

The following procedures give information about number representation.

`locale-decimal-point` [*locale*]   [Scheme Procedure]
`locale-thousands-separator` [*locale*]   [Scheme Procedure]

> These functions return a string denoting the representation of the decimal point or that of the thousand separator (respectively) for either *locale* or the current locale.

`locale-digit-grouping` [*locale*]   [Scheme Procedure]

> Return a (potentially circular) list of integers denoting how digits of the integer part of a number are to be grouped, starting at the decimal point and going to the left. The list contains integers indicating the size of the successive groups, from right to left. If the list is non-circular, then no grouping occurs for digits beyond the last group.
>
> For instance, if the returned list is a circular list that contains only 3 and the thousand separator is `","` (as is the case with English locales), then the number `12345678` should be printed `12,345,678`.

The following procedures deal with the representation of monetary amounts. Some of them take an additional *intl?* argument (a boolean) that tells whether the international or local monetary conventions for the given locale are to be used.

`locale-monetary-decimal-point` [*locale*]   [Scheme Procedure]
`locale-monetary-thousands-separator` [*locale*]   [Scheme Procedure]
`locale-monetary-grouping` [*locale*]   [Scheme Procedure]
> These are the monetary counterparts of the above procedures. These procedures apply to monetary amounts.

`locale-currency-symbol` *intl?* [*locale*]   [Scheme Procedure]
> Return the currency symbol (a string) of either *locale* or the current locale.
>
> The following example illustrates the difference between the local and international monetary formats:
>
> ```
> (define us (make-locale LC_MONETARY "en_US"))
> (locale-currency-symbol #f us)
> ⇒ "-$"
> (locale-currency-symbol #t us)
> ⇒ "USD "
> ```

`locale-monetary-fractional-digits` *intl?* [*locale*]   [Scheme Procedure]
> Return the number of fractional digits to be used when printing monetary amounts according to either *locale* or the current locale. If the locale does not specify it, then `#f` is returned.

`locale-currency-symbol-precedes-positive?` *intl?*   [Scheme Procedure]
> [*locale*]
`locale-currency-symbol-precedes-negative?` *intl?*   [Scheme Procedure]
> [*locale*]
`locale-positive-separated-by-space?` *intl?* [*locale*]   [Scheme Procedure]
`locale-negative-separated-by-space?` *intl?* [*locale*]   [Scheme Procedure]
> These procedures return a boolean indicating whether the currency symbol should precede a positive/negative number, and whether a whitespace should be inserted between the currency symbol and a positive/negative amount.

`locale-monetary-positive-sign` [*locale*]   [Scheme Procedure]
`locale-monetary-negative-sign` [*locale*]   [Scheme Procedure]
> Return a string denoting the positive (respectively negative) sign that should be used when printing a monetary amount.

`locale-positive-sign-position`   [Scheme Procedure]
`locale-negative-sign-position`   [Scheme Procedure]
> These functions return a symbol telling where a sign of a positive/negative monetary amount is to appear when printing it. The possible values are:
>
> `parenthesize`
>> The currency symbol and quantity should be surrounded by parentheses.
>
> `sign-before`
>> Print the sign string before the quantity and currency symbol.

sign-after
> Print the sign string after the quantity and currency symbol.

sign-before-currency-symbol
> Print the sign string right before the currency symbol.

sign-after-currency-symbol
> Print the sign string right after the currency symbol.

unspecified
> Unspecified. We recommend you print the sign after the currency symbol.

Finally, the two following procedures may be helpful when programming user interfaces:

locale-yes-regexp [*locale*]   [Scheme Procedure]
locale-no-regexp [*locale*]   [Scheme Procedure]
> Return a string that can be used as a regular expression to recognize a positive (respectively, negative) response to a yes/no question. For the C locale, the default values are typically `"^[yY]"` and `"^[nN]"`, respectively.

> Here is an example:

```
(use-modules (ice-9 rdelim))
(format #t "Does Guile rock?~%")
(let lp ((answer (read-line)))
  (cond ((string-match (locale-yes-regexp) answer)
         (format #t "High fives!~%"))
        ((string-match (locale-no-regexp) answer)
         (format #t "How about now? Does it rock yet?~%")
         (lp (read-line)))
        (else
         (format #t "What do you mean?~%")
         (lp (read-line)))))
```

> For an internationalized yes/no string output, `gettext` should be used (see Section 6.24.6 [Gettext Support], page 442).

Example uses of some of these functions are the implementation of the `number->locale-string` and `monetary-amount->locale-string` procedures (see Section 6.24.4 [Number Input and Output], page 439), as well as that the SRFI-19 date and time conversion to/from strings (see Section 7.5.16 [SRFI-19], page 583).

6.24.6 Gettext Support

Guile provides an interface to GNU `gettext` for translating message strings (see Section "Introduction" in *GNU* `gettext` *utilities*).

Messages are collected in domains, so different libraries and programs maintain different message catalogues. The *domain* parameter in the functions below is a string (it becomes part of the message catalog filename).

When `gettext` is not available, or if Guile was configured '`--without-nls`', dummy functions doing no translation are provided. When `gettext` support is available in Guile, the `i18n` feature is provided (see Section 6.22.2 [Feature Tracking], page 429).

`gettext` *msg* [*domain* [*category*]]   [Scheme Procedure]
`scm_gettext` (*msg, domain, category*)   [C Function]
　　　Return the translation of *msg* in *domain*. *domain* is optional and defaults to the
　　　domain set through `textdomain` below. *category* is optional and defaults to `LC_`
　　　`MESSAGES` (see Section 7.2.13 [Locales], page 518).

　　　Normal usage is for *msg* to be a literal string. `xgettext` can extract those from the
　　　source to form a message catalogue ready for translators (see Section "Invoking the
　　　xgettext Program" in *GNU* gettext *utilities*).

```
(display (gettext "You are in a maze of twisty passages."))
```

　　　_ is a commonly used shorthand, an application can make that an alias for `gettext`.
　　　Or a library can make a definition that uses its specific *domain* (so an application can
　　　change the default without affecting the library).

```
(define (_ msg) (gettext msg "mylibrary"))
(display (_ "File not found."))
```

　　　_ is also a good place to perhaps strip disambiguating extra text from the message
　　　string, as for instance in Section "How to use gettext in GUI programs" in *GNU*
　　　gettext *utilities*.

`ngettext` *msg msgplural n* [*domain* [*category*]]   [Scheme Procedure]
`scm_ngettext` (*msg, msgplural, n, domain, category*)   [C Function]
　　　Return the translation of *msg*/*msgplural* in *domain*, with a plural form chosen ap-
　　　propriately for the number *n*. *domain* is optional and defaults to the domain set
　　　through `textdomain` below. *category* is optional and defaults to `LC_MESSAGES` (see
　　　Section 7.2.13 [Locales], page 518).

　　　msg is the singular form, and *msgplural* the plural. When no translation is available,
　　　msg is used if $n = 1$, or *msgplural* otherwise. When translated, the message catalogue
　　　can have a different rule, and can have more than two possible forms.

　　　As per `gettext` above, normal usage is for *msg* and *msgplural* to be literal strings,
　　　since `xgettext` can extract them from the source to build a message catalogue. For
　　　example,

```
(define (done n)
  (format #t (ngettext "~a file processed\n"
                       "~a files processed\n" n)
          n))

(done 1)  ⊣ 1 file processed
(done 3)  ⊣ 3 files processed
```

　　　It's important to use `ngettext` rather than plain `gettext` for plurals, since the rules
　　　for singular and plural forms in English are not the same in other languages. Only
　　　`ngettext` will allow translators to give correct forms (see Section "Additional func-
　　　tions for plural forms" in *GNU* gettext *utilities*).

`textdomain` [*domain*]   [Scheme Procedure]
`scm_textdomain` (*domain*)   [C Function]

Get or set the default gettext domain. When called with no parameter the current domain is returned. When called with a parameter, *domain* is set as the current domain, and that new value returned. For example,

```
(textdomain "myprog")
⇒ "myprog"
```

`bindtextdomain` *domain* [*directory*]   [Scheme Procedure]
`scm_bindtextdomain` (*domain, directory*)   [C Function]

Get or set the directory under which to find message files for *domain*. When called without a *directory* the current setting is returned. When called with a *directory*, *directory* is set for *domain* and that new setting returned. For example,

```
(bindtextdomain "myprog" "/my/tree/share/locale")
⇒ "/my/tree/share/locale"
```

When using Autoconf/Automake, an application should arrange for the configured `localedir` to get into the program (by substituting, or by generating a config file) and set that for its domain. This ensures the catalogue can be found even when installed in a non-standard location.

`bind-textdomain-codeset` *domain* [*encoding*]   [Scheme Procedure]
`scm_bind_textdomain_codeset` (*domain, encoding*)   [C Function]

Get or set the text encoding to be used by `gettext` for messages from *domain*. *encoding* is a string, the name of a coding system, for instance `"8859_1"`. (On a Unix/POSIX system the `iconv` program can list all available encodings.)

When called without an *encoding* the current setting is returned, or `#f` if none yet set. When called with an *encoding*, it is set for *domain* and that new setting returned. For example,

```
(bind-textdomain-codeset "myprog")
⇒ #f
(bind-textdomain-codeset "myprog" "latin-9")
⇒ "latin-9"
```

The encoding requested can be different from the translated data file, messages will be recoded as necessary. But note that when there is no translation, `gettext` returns its *msg* unchanged, ie. without any recoding. For that reason source message strings are best as plain ASCII.

Currently Guile has no understanding of multi-byte characters, and string functions won't recognise character boundaries in multi-byte strings. An application will at least be able to pass such strings through to some output though. Perhaps this will change in the future.

6.25 Debugging Infrastructure

In order to understand Guile's debugging facilities, you first need to understand a little about how Guile represent the Scheme control stack. With that in place we explain the low level trap calls that the virtual machine can be configured to make, and the trap and breakpoint infrastructure that builds on top of those calls.

6.25.1 Evaluation and the Scheme Stack

The idea of the Scheme stack is central to a lot of debugging. The Scheme stack is a reified representation of the pending function returns in an expression's continuation. As Guile implements function calls using a stack, this reification takes the form of a number of nested stack frames, each of which corresponds to the application of a procedure to a set of arguments.

A Scheme stack always exists implicitly, and can be summoned into concrete existence as a first-class Scheme value by the `make-stack` call, so that an introspective Scheme program – such as a debugger – can present it in some way and allow the user to query its details. The first thing to understand, therefore, is how Guile's function call convention creates the stack.

Broadly speaking, Guile represents all control flow on a stack. Calling a function involves pushing an empty frame on the stack, then evaluating the procedure and its arguments, then fixing up the new frame so that it points to the old one. Frames on the stack are thus linked together. A tail call is the same, except it reuses the existing frame instead of pushing on a new one.

In this way, the only frames that are on the stack are "active" frames, frames which need to do some work before the computation is complete. On the other hand, a function that has tail-called another function will not be on the stack, as it has no work left to do.

Therefore, when an error occurs in a running program, or the program hits a breakpoint, or in fact at any point that the programmer chooses, its state at that point can be represented by a *stack* of all the procedure applications that are logically in progress at that time, each of which is known as a *frame*. The programmer can learn more about the program's state at that point by inspecting the stack and its frames.

6.25.1.1 Stack Capture

A Scheme program can use the `make-stack` primitive anywhere in its code, with first arg `#t`, to construct a Scheme value that describes the Scheme stack at that point.

```
(make-stack #t)
⇒
#<stack 25205a0>
```

Use `start-stack` to limit the stack extent captured by future `make-stack` calls.

`make-stack` *obj* arg . . .   [Scheme Procedure]
`scm_make_stack` (*obj*, *args*)   [C Function]

> Create a new stack. If *obj* is `#t`, the current evaluation stack is used for creating the stack frames, otherwise the frames are taken from *obj* (which must be a continuation or a frame object).
>
> *arg* . . . can be any combination of integer, procedure, prompt tag and `#t` values.
>
> These values specify various ways of cutting away uninteresting stack frames from the top and bottom of the stack that `make-stack` returns. They come in pairs like this: (*inner_cut_1 outer_cut_1 inner_cut_2 outer_cut_2* . . .).
>
> Each *inner_cut_i* can be `#t`, an integer, a prompt tag, or a procedure. `#t` means to cut away all frames up to but excluding the first user module frame. An integer means to cut away exactly that number of frames. A prompt tag means to cut away

all frames that are inside a prompt with the given tag. A procedure means to cut away all frames up to but excluding the application frame whose procedure matches the specified one.

Each *outer_cut_i* can be an integer, a prompt tag, or a procedure. An integer means to cut away that number of frames. A prompt tag means to cut away all frames that are outside a prompt with the given tag. A procedure means to cut away frames down to but excluding the application frame whose procedure matches the specified one.

If the *outer_cut_i* of the last pair is missing, it is taken as 0.

start-stack *id exp*   [Scheme Syntax]

Evaluate *exp* on a new calling stack with identity *id*. If *exp* is interrupted during evaluation, backtraces will not display frames farther back than *exp*'s top-level form. This macro is a way of artificially limiting backtraces and stack procedures, largely as a convenience to the user.

6.25.1.2 Stacks

stack? *obj*   [Scheme Procedure]
scm_stack_p (*obj*)   [C Function]

Return #t if *obj* is a calling stack.

stack-id *stack*   [Scheme Procedure]
scm_stack_id (*stack*)   [C Function]

Return the identifier given to *stack* by **start-stack**.

stack-length *stack*   [Scheme Procedure]
scm_stack_length (*stack*)   [C Function]

Return the length of *stack*.

stack-ref *stack index*   [Scheme Procedure]
scm_stack_ref (*stack, index*)   [C Function]

Return the *index*'th frame from *stack*.

display-backtrace *stack port* [*first* [*depth* [*highlights*]]]   [Scheme Procedure]
scm_display_backtrace_with_highlights (*stack, port, first,*   [C Function]
    depth, highlights)
scm_display_backtrace (*stack, port, first, depth*)   [C Function]

Display a backtrace to the output port *port*. *stack* is the stack to take the backtrace from, *first* specifies where in the stack to start and *depth* how many frames to display. *first* and *depth* can be #f, which means that default values will be used. If *highlights* is given it should be a list; the elements of this list will be highlighted wherever they appear in the backtrace.

6.25.1.3 Frames

frame? *obj*   [Scheme Procedure]
scm_frame_p (*obj*)   [C Function]

Return #t if *obj* is a stack frame.

`frame-previous` *frame*   [Scheme Procedure]

`scm_frame_previous` (*frame*)   [C Function]

> Return the previous frame of *frame*, or `#f` if *frame* is the first frame in its stack.

`frame-procedure` *frame*   [Scheme Procedure]

`scm_frame_procedure` (*frame*)   [C Function]

> Return the procedure for *frame*, or `#f` if no procedure is associated with *frame*.

`frame-arguments` *frame*   [Scheme Procedure]

`scm_frame_arguments` (*frame*)   [C Function]

> Return the arguments of *frame*.

`frame-address` *frame*   [Scheme Procedure]

`frame-instruction-pointer` *frame*   [Scheme Procedure]

`frame-stack-pointer` *frame*   [Scheme Procedure]

> Accessors for the three VM registers associated with this frame: the frame pointer
> (fp), instruction pointer (ip), and stack pointer (sp), respectively. See Section 9.3.2
> [VM Concepts], page 773, for more information.

`frame-dynamic-link` *frame*   [Scheme Procedure]

`frame-return-address` *frame*   [Scheme Procedure]

`frame-mv-return-address` *frame*   [Scheme Procedure]

> Accessors for the three saved VM registers in a frame: the previous frame pointer, the
> single-value return address, and the multiple-value return address. See Section 9.3.3
> [Stack Layout], page 774, for more information.

`frame-num-locals` *frame*   [Scheme Procedure]

`frame-local-ref` *frame i*   [Scheme Procedure]

`frame-local-set!` *frame i val*   [Scheme Procedure]

> Accessors for the temporary values corresponding to *frame*'s procedure application.
> The first local is the first argument given to the procedure. After the arguments,
> there are the local variables, and after that temporary values. See Section 9.3.3
> [Stack Layout], page 774, for more information.

`display-application` *frame* [*port* [*indent*]]   [Scheme Procedure]

`scm_display_application` (*frame, port, indent*)   [C Function]

> Display a procedure application *frame* to the output port *port*. *indent* specifies the
> indentation of the output.

Additionally, the `(system vm frame)` module defines a number of higher-level introspective procedures, for example to retrieve the names of local variables, and the source location
to correspond to a frame. See its source code for more details.

6.25.2 Source Properties

As Guile reads in Scheme code from file or from standard input, it remembers the file name,
line number and column number where each expression begins. These pieces of information
are known as the *source properties* of the expression. Syntax expanders and the compiler
propagate these source properties to compiled procedures, so that, if an error occurs when

evaluating the transformed expression, Guile's debugger can point back to the file and location where the expression originated.

The way that source properties are stored means that Guile cannot associate source properties with individual symbols, keywords, characters, booleans, or small integers. This can be seen by typing (xxx) and xxx at the Guile prompt (where the variable xxx has not been defined):

```
scheme@(guile-user)> (xxx)
<unnamed port>:4:1: In procedure module-lookup:
<unnamed port>:4:1: Unbound variable: xxx

scheme@(guile-user)> xxx
ERROR: In procedure module-lookup:
ERROR: Unbound variable: xxx
```

In the latter case, no source properties were stored, so the error doesn't have any source information.

supports-source-properties? *obj*   [Scheme Procedure]
scm_supports_source_properties_p (*obj*)   [C Function]
    Return #t if source properties can be associated with *obj*, otherwise return #f.

The recording of source properties is controlled by the read option named "positions" (see Section 6.17.2 [Scheme Read], page 360). This option is switched *on* by default.

The following procedures can be used to access and set the source properties of read expressions.

set-source-properties! *obj alist*   [Scheme Procedure]
scm_set_source_properties_x (*obj, alist*)   [C Function]
    Install the association list *alist* as the source property list for *obj*.

set-source-property! *obj key datum*   [Scheme Procedure]
scm_set_source_property_x (*obj, key, datum*)   [C Function]
    Set the source property of object *obj*, which is specified by *key* to *datum*. Normally, the key will be a symbol.

source-properties *obj*   [Scheme Procedure]
scm_source_properties (*obj*)   [C Function]
    Return the source property association list of *obj*.

source-property *obj key*   [Scheme Procedure]
scm_source_property (*obj, key*)   [C Function]
    Return the property specified by *key* from *obj*'s source properties.

If the **positions** reader option is enabled, supported expressions will have values set for the **filename**, **line** and **column** properties.

Source properties are also associated with syntax objects. Procedural macros can get at the source location of their input using the **syntax-source** accessor. See Section 6.10.4 [Syntax Transformer Helpers], page 268, for more.

Guile also defines a couple of convenience macros built on **syntax-source**:

current-source-location   [Scheme Syntax]
> Expands to the source properties corresponding to the location of the (current-source-location) form.

current-filename   [Scheme Syntax]
> Expands to the current filename: the filename that the (current-filename) form appears in. Expands to #f if this information is unavailable.

If you're stuck with defmacros (see Section 6.10.5 [Defmacros], page 270), and want to preserve source information, the following helper function might be useful to you:

cons-source *xorig x y*   [Scheme Procedure]
scm_cons_source (*xorig, x, y*)   [C Function]
> Create and return a new pair whose car and cdr are *x* and *y*. Any source properties associated with *xorig* are also associated with the new pair.

6.25.3 Programmatic Error Handling

For better or for worse, all programs have bugs, and dealing with bugs is part of programming. This section deals with that class of bugs that causes an exception to be raised – from your own code, from within a library, or from Guile itself.

6.25.3.1 Catching Exceptions

A common requirement is to be able to show as much useful context as possible when a Scheme program hits an error. The most immediate information about an error is the kind of error that it is – such as "division by zero" – and any parameters that the code which signalled the error chose explicitly to provide. This information originates with the error or throw call (or their C code equivalents, if the error is detected by C code) that signals the error, and is passed automatically to the handler procedure of the innermost applicable catch or with-throw-handler expression.

Therefore, to catch errors that occur within a chunk of Scheme code, and to intercept basic information about those errors, you need to execute that code inside the dynamic context of a catch or with-throw-handler expression, or the equivalent in C. In Scheme, this means you need something like this:

```
(catch #t
       (lambda ()
         ;; Execute the code in which
         ;; you want to catch errors here.
         ...)
       (lambda (key . parameters)
         ;; Put the code which you want
         ;; to handle an error here.
         ...))
```

The catch here can also be with-throw-handler; see Section 6.13.8.3 [Throw Handlers], page 306 for information on the when you might want to use with-throw-handler instead of catch.

For example, to print out a message and return #f when an error occurs, you might use:

```
(define (catch-all thunk)
  (catch #t
    thunk
    (lambda (key . parameters)
      (format (current-error-port)
              "Uncaught throw to '~a: ~a\n" key parameters)
        #f)))

(catch-all
 (lambda () (error "Not a vegetable: tomato")))
⊣ Uncaught throw to 'misc-error: (#f ~A (Not a vegetable: tomato) #f)
⇒ #f
```

The #t means that the catch is applicable to all kinds of error. If you want to restrict your catch to just one kind of error, you can put the symbol for that kind of error instead of #t. The equivalent to this in C would be something like this:

```
SCM my_body_proc (void *body_data)
{
  /* Execute the code in which
     you want to catch errors here. */
  ...
}


SCM my_handler_proc (void *handler_data,
                     SCM key,
                     SCM parameters)
{
  /* Put the code which you want
     to handle an error here. */
  ...
}


{
  ...
  scm_c_catch (SCM_BOOL_T,
               my_body_proc, body_data,
               my_handler_proc, handler_data,
               NULL, NULL);
  ...
}
```

Again, as with the Scheme version, scm_c_catch could be replaced by scm_c_with_throw_handler, and SCM_BOOL_T could instead be the symbol for a particular kind of error.

6.25.3.2 Capturing the full error stack

The other interesting information about an error is the full Scheme stack at the point where the error occurred; in other words what innermost expression was being evaluated, what was the expression that called that one, and so on. If you want to write your code so that it captures and can display this information as well, there are a couple important things to understand.

Firstly, the stack at the point of the error needs to be explicitly captured by a `make-stack` call (or the C equivalent `scm_make_stack`). The Guile library does not do this "automatically" for you, so you will need to write code with a `make-stack` or `scm_make_stack` call yourself. (We emphasise this point because some people are misled by the fact that the Guile interactive REPL code *does* capture and display the stack automatically. But the Guile interactive REPL is itself a Scheme program[17] running on top of the Guile library, and which uses `catch` and `make-stack` in the way we are about to describe to capture the stack when an error occurs.)

And secondly, in order to capture the stack effectively at the point where the error occurred, the `make-stack` call must be made before Guile unwinds the stack back to the location of the prevailing catch expression. This means that the `make-stack` call must be made within the handler of a `with-throw-handler` expression, or the optional "pre-unwind" handler of a `catch`. (For the full story of how these alternatives differ from each other, see Section 6.13.8 [Exceptions], page 303. The main difference is that `catch` terminates the error, whereas `with-throw-handler` only intercepts it temporarily and then allow it to continue propagating up to the next innermost handler.)

So, here are some examples of how to do all this in Scheme and in C. For the purpose of these examples we assume that the captured stack should be stored in a variable, so that it can be displayed or arbitrarily processed later on. In Scheme:

```scheme
(let ((captured-stack #f))
  (catch #t
         (lambda ()
           ;; Execute the code in which
           ;; you want to catch errors here.
           ...)
         (lambda (key . parameters)
           ;; Put the code which you want
           ;; to handle an error after the
           ;; stack has been unwound here.
           ...)
         (lambda (key . parameters)
           ;; Capture the stack here:
           (set! captured-stack (make-stack #t))))
  ...
  (if captured-stack
      (begin
        ;; Display or process the captured stack.
        ...))
  ...)
```

And in C:

```c
SCM my_body_proc (void *body_data)
{
  /* Execute the code in which
```

---

[17] In effect, it is the default program which is run when no commands or script file are specified on the Guile command line.

```
      you want to catch errors here. */
  ...
}

SCM my_handler_proc (void *handler_data,
                     SCM key,
                     SCM parameters)
{
  /* Put the code which you want
     to handle an error after the
     stack has been unwound here. */
  ...
}

SCM my_preunwind_proc (void *handler_data,
                       SCM key,
                       SCM parameters)
{
  /* Capture the stack here: */
  *(SCM *)handler_data = scm_make_stack (SCM_BOOL_T, SCM_EOL);
}

{
  SCM captured_stack = SCM_BOOL_F;
  ...
  scm_c_catch (SCM_BOOL_T,
               my_body_proc, body_data,
               my_handler_proc, handler_data,
               my_preunwind_proc, &captured_stack);
  ...
  if (captured_stack != SCM_BOOL_F)
  {
    /* Display or process the captured stack. */
    ...
  }
  ...
}
```

Once you have a captured stack, you can interrogate and display its details in any way that you want, using the stack-... and frame-... API described in Section 6.25.1.2 [Stacks], page 446 and Section 6.25.1.3 [Frames], page 446.

If you want to print out a backtrace in the same format that the Guile REPL does, you can use the display-backtrace procedure to do so. You can also use display-application to display an individual frame in the Guile REPL format.

6.25.3.3 Pre-Unwind Debugging

Instead of saving a stack away and waiting for the `catch` to return, you can handle errors directly, from within the pre-unwind handler.

For example, to show a backtrace when an error is thrown, you might want to use a procedure like this:

```
(define (with-backtrace thunk)
  (with-throw-handler #t
                      thunk
                      (lambda args (backtrace))))
(with-backtrace (lambda () (error "Not a vegetable: tomato")))
```

Since we used `with-throw-handler` here, we didn't actually catch the error. See Section 6.13.8.3 [Throw Handlers], page 306, for more information. However, we did print out a context at the time of the error, using the built-in procedure, `backtrace`.

`backtrace` [*highlights*]   [Scheme Procedure]
`scm_backtrace_with_highlights` (*highlights*)   [C Function]
`scm_backtrace` ()   [C Function]

> Display a backtrace of the current stack to the current output port. If *highlights* is given it should be a list; the elements of this list will be highlighted wherever they appear in the backtrace.

The Guile REPL code (in `system/repl/repl.scm` and related files) uses a `catch` with a pre-unwind handler to capture the stack when an error occurs in an expression that was typed into the REPL, and debug that stack interactively in the context of the error.

These procedures are available for use by user programs, in the (`system repl error-handling`) module.

```
(use-modules (system repl error-handling))
```

`call-with-error-handling` *thunk* [*#:on-error*   [Scheme Procedure]
> *on-error='debug*] [*#:post-error post-error='catch*] [*#:pass-keys*
> *pass-keys='(quit)*] [*#:trap-handler trap-handler='debug*]
> Call a thunk in a context in which errors are handled.

> There are four keyword arguments:

> *on-error*   Specifies what to do before the stack is unwound.

> > Valid options are `debug` (the default), which will enter a debugger; `pass`, in which case nothing is done, and the exception is rethrown; or a procedure, which will be the pre-unwind handler.

> *post-error* Specifies what to do after the stack is unwound.

> > Valid options are `catch` (the default), which will silently catch errors, returning the unspecified value; `report`, which prints out a description of the error (via `display-error`), and then returns the unspecified value; or a procedure, which will be the catch handler.

> *trap-handler*

> > Specifies a trap handler: what to do when a breakpoint is hit.

Valid options are `debug`, which will enter the debugger; `pass`, which does
nothing; or `disabled`, which disables traps entirely. See Section 6.25.4
[Traps], page 455, for more information.

pass-keys   A set of keys to ignore, as a list.

6.25.3.4 Debug options

The behavior of the `backtrace` procedure and of the default error handler can be parame-
terized via the debug options.

`debug-options` [*setting*]   [Scheme Procedure]
> Display the current settings of the debug options. If *setting* is omitted, only a short
> form of the current read options is printed. Otherwise if *setting* is the symbol `help`,
> a complete options description is displayed.

The set of available options, and their default values, may be had by invoking `debug-`
`options` at the prompt.

```
scheme@(guile-user)>
backwards       no       Display backtrace in anti-chronological order.
width           79       Maximal width of backtrace.
depth           20       Maximal length of printed backtrace.
backtrace       yes      Show backtrace on error.
stack           1048576  Stack size limit (measured in words;
                         0 = no check).
show-file-name  #t       Show file names and line numbers in backtraces
                         when not '#f'.  A value of 'base' displays only
                         base names, while '#t' displays full names.
warn-deprecated no       Warn when deprecated features are used.
```

The boolean options may be toggled with `debug-enable` and `debug-disable`. The
non-boolean `keywords` option must be set using `debug-set!`.

`debug-enable` *option-name*   [Scheme Procedure]
`debug-disable` *option-name*   [Scheme Procedure]
`debug-set!` *option-name value*   [Scheme Syntax]
> Modify the debug options. `debug-enable` should be used with boolean options and
> switches them on, `debug-disable` switches them off.
>
> `debug-set!` can be used to set an option to a specific value. Due to historical oddities,
> it is a macro that expects an unquoted option name.

Stack overflow

Stack overflow errors are caused by a computation trying to use more stack space than has
been enabled by the `stack` option. There are actually two kinds of stack that can overflow,
the C stack and the Scheme stack.

Scheme stack overflows can occur if Scheme procedures recurse too far deeply. An
example would be the following recursive loop:

```
scheme@(guile-user)> (let lp () (+ 1 (lp)))
<unnamed port>:8:17: In procedure vm-run:
<unnamed port>:8:17: VM: Stack overflow
```

The default stack size should allow for about 10000 frames or so, so one usually doesn't
hit this level of recursion. Unfortunately there is no way currently to make a VM with a

bigger stack. If you are in this unfortunate situation, please file a bug, and in the meantime, rewrite your code to be tail-recursive (see Section 3.3.2 [Tail Calls], page 24).

The other limit you might hit would be C stack overflows. If you call a primitive procedure which then calls a Scheme procedure in a loop, you will consume C stack space. Guile tries to detect excessive consumption of C stack space, throwing an error when you have hit 80% of the process' available stack (as allocated by the operating system), or 160 kilowords in the absence of a strict limit.

For example, looping through `call-with-vm`, a primitive that calls a thunk, gives us the following:

```
scheme@(guile-user)> (use-modules (system vm vm))
scheme@(guile-user)> (debug-set! stack 10000)
scheme@(guile-user)> (let lp () (call-with-vm (the-vm) lp))
ERROR: In procedure call-with-vm:
ERROR: Stack overflow
```

If you get an error like this, you can either try rewriting your code to use less stack space, or increase the maximum stack size. To increase the maximum stack size, use `debug-set!`, for example:

```
(debug-set! stack 200000)
```

But of course it's better to have your code operate without so much resource consumption, avoiding loops through C trampolines.

6.25.4 Traps

Guile's virtual machine can be configured to call out at key points to arbitrary user-specified procedures.

In principle, these *hooks* allow Scheme code to implement any model it chooses for examining the evaluation stack as program execution proceeds, and for suspending execution to be resumed later.

VM hooks are very low-level, though, and so Guile also has a library of higher-level *traps* on top of the VM hooks. A trap is an execution condition that, when fulfilled, will fire a handler. For example, Guile defines a trap that fires when control reaches a certain source location.

Finally, Guile also defines a third level of abstractions: per-thread *trap states*. A trap state exists to give names to traps, and to hold on to the set of traps so that they can be enabled, disabled, or removed. The trap state infrastructure defines the most useful abstractions for most cases. For example, Guile's REPL uses trap state functions to set breakpoints and tracepoints.

The following subsections describe all this in detail, for both the user wanting to use traps, and the developer interested in understanding how the interface hangs together.

6.25.4.1 VM Hooks

Everything that runs in Guile runs on its virtual machine, a C program that defines a number of operations that Scheme programs can perform.

Note that there are multiple VM "engines" for Guile. Only some of them have support for hooks compiled in. Normally the deal is that you get hooks if you are running interactively, and otherwise they are disabled, as they do have some overhead (about 10 or 20 percent).

To ensure that you are running with hooks, pass `--debug` to Guile when running your program, or otherwise use the `call-with-vm` and `set-vm-engine!` procedures to ensure that you are running in a VM with the `debug` engine.

To digress, Guile's VM has 6 different hooks (see Section 6.11.6 [Hooks], page 281) that can be fired at different times, which may be accessed with the following procedures.

All hooks are called with one argument, the frame in question. See Section 6.25.1.3 [Frames], page 446. Since these hooks may be fired very frequently, Guile does a terrible thing: it allocates the frames on the C stack instead of the garbage-collected heap.

The upshot here is that the frames are only valid within the dynamic extent of the call to the hook. If a hook procedure keeps a reference to the frame outside the extent of the hook, bad things will happen.

The interface to hooks is provided by the `(system vm vm)` module:

```
(use-modules (system vm vm))
```

The result of calling `the-vm` is usually passed as the *vm* argument to all of these procedures.

`vm-next-hook` *vm*   [Scheme Procedure]
  The hook that will be fired before an instruction is retired (and executed).

`vm-push-continuation-hook` *vm*   [Scheme Procedure]
  The hook that will be fired after preparing a new frame. Fires just before applying a procedure in a non-tail context, just before the corresponding apply-hook.

`vm-pop-continuation-hook` *vm*   [Scheme Procedure]
  The hook that will be fired before returning from a frame.

  This hook is a bit trickier than the rest, in that there is a particular interpretation of the values on the stack. Specifically, the top value on the stack is the number of values being returned, and the next *n* values are the actual values being returned, with the last value highest on the stack.

`vm-apply-hook` *vm*   [Scheme Procedure]
  The hook that will be fired before a procedure is applied. The frame's procedure will have already been set to the new procedure.

  Note that procedure application is somewhat orthogonal to continuation pushes and pops. A non-tail call to a procedure will result first in a firing of the push-continuation hook, then this application hook, whereas a tail call will run without having fired a push-continuation hook.

`vm-abort-continuation-hook` *vm*   [Scheme Procedure]
  The hook that will be called after aborting to a prompt. See Section 6.13.5 [Prompts], page 296. The stack will be in the same state as for `vm-pop-continuation-hook`.

`vm-restore-continuation-hook` *vm*   [Scheme Procedure]
  The hook that will be called after restoring an undelimited continuation. Unfortunately it's not currently possible to introspect on the values that were given to the continuation.

These hooks do impose a performance penalty, if they are on. Obviously, the `vm-next-hook` has quite an impact, performance-wise. Therefore Guile exposes a single, heavy-handed knob to turn hooks on or off, the *VM trace level*. If the trace level is positive, hooks run; otherwise they don't.

For convenience, when the VM fires a hook, it does so with the trap level temporarily set to 0. That way the hooks don't fire while you're handling a hook. The trace level is restored to whatever it was once the hook procedure finishes.

`vm-trace-level` *vm*   [Scheme Procedure]
> Retrieve the "trace level" of the VM. If positive, the trace hooks associated with *vm* will be run. The initial trace level is 0.

`set-vm-trace-level!` *vm level*   [Scheme Procedure]
> Set the "trace level" of the VM.

See Section 9.3 [A Virtual Machine for Guile], page 772, for more information on Guile's virtual machine.

6.25.4.2 Trap Interface

The capabilities provided by hooks are great, but hooks alone rarely correspond to what users want to do.

For example, if a user wants to break when and if control reaches a certain source location, how do you do it? If you install a "next" hook, you get unacceptable overhead for the execution of the entire program. It would be possible to install an "apply" hook, then if the procedure encompasses those source locations, install a "next" hook, but already you're talking about one concept that might be implemented by a varying number of lower-level concepts.

It's best to be clear about things and define one abstraction for all such conditions: the *trap*.

Considering the myriad capabilities offered by the hooks though, there is only a minimum of functionality shared by all traps. Guile's current take is to reduce this to the absolute minimum, and have the only standard interface of a trap be "turn yourself on" or "turn yourself off".

This interface sounds a bit strange, but it is useful to procedurally compose higher-level traps from lower-level building blocks. For example, Guile defines a trap that calls one handler when control enters a procedure, and another when control leaves the procedure. Given that trap, one can define a trap that adds to the next-hook only when within a given procedure. Building further, one can define a trap that fires when control reaches particular instructions within a procedure.

Or of course you can stop at any of these intermediate levels. For example, one might only be interested in calls to a given procedure. But the point is that a simple enable/disable interface is all the commonality that exists between the various kinds of traps, and further-more that such an interface serves to allow "higher-level" traps to be composed from more primitive ones.

Specifically, a trap, in Guile, is a procedure. When a trap is created, by convention the trap is enabled; therefore, the procedure that is the trap will, when called, disable the trap, and return a procedure that will enable the trap, and so on.

Trap procedures take one optional argument: the current frame. (A trap may want to add to different sets of hooks depending on the frame that is current at enable-time.)

If this all sounds very complicated, it's because it is. Some of it is essential, but probably most of it is not. The advantage of using this minimal interface is that composability is more lexically apparent than when, for example, using a stateful interface based on GOOPS. But perhaps this reflects the cognitive limitations of the programmer who made the current interface more than anything else.

6.25.4.3 Low-Level Traps

To summarize the last sections, traps are enabled or disabled, and when they are enabled, they add to various VM hooks.

Note, however, that *traps do not increase the VM trace level*. So if you create a trap, it will be enabled, but unless something else increases the VM's trace level (see Section 6.25.4.1 [VM Hooks], page 455), the trap will not fire. It turns out that getting the VM trace level right is tricky without a global view of what traps are enabled. See Section 6.25.4.5 [Trap States], page 461, for Guile's answer to this problem.

Traps are created by calling procedures. Most of these procedures share a set of common keyword arguments, so rather than document them separately, we discuss them all together here:

`#:vm`   The VM to instrument. Defaults to the current thread's VM.

`#:closure?`

> For traps that depend on the current frame's procedure, this argument specifies whether to trap on the only the specific procedure given, or on any closure that has the given procedure's code. Defaults to `#f`.

`#:current-frame`

> For traps that enable more hooks depending on their dynamic context, this argument gives the current frame that the trap is running in. Defaults to `#f`.

To have access to these procedures, you'll need to have imported the (`system vm traps`) module:

```
(use-modules (system vm traps))
```

`trap-at-procedure-call` *proc handler* [*#:vm*] [*#:closure?*]   [Scheme Procedure]
> A trap that calls *handler* when *proc* is applied.

`trap-in-procedure` *proc enter-handler exit-handler*   [Scheme Procedure]
> [*#:current-frame*] [*#:vm*] [*#:closure?*]
> A trap that calls *enter-handler* when control enters *proc*, and *exit-handler* when control leaves *proc*.

> Control can enter a procedure via:

- A procedure call.
- A return to a procedure's frame on the stack.
- A continuation returning directly to an application of this procedure.

> Control can leave a procedure via:

- A normal return from the procedure.

- An application of another procedure.

- An invocation of a continuation.

- An abort.

`trap-instructions-in-procedure` *proc next-handler*   [Scheme Procedure]
      exit-handler [*#:current-frame*] [*#:vm*] [*#:closure?*]
> A trap that calls *next-handler* for every instruction executed in *proc*, and *exit-handler*
> when execution leaves *proc*.

`trap-at-procedure-ip-in-range` *proc range handler*   [Scheme Procedure]
      [*#:current-frame*] [*#:vm*] [*#:closure?*]
> A trap that calls *handler* when execution enters a range of instructions in *proc*. *range*
> is a simple of pairs, ((`start` . `end`) ...). The *start* addresses are inclusive, and *end*
> addresses are exclusive.

`trap-at-source-location` *file user-line handler*   [Scheme Procedure]
      [*#:current-frame*] [*#:vm*]
> A trap that fires when control reaches a given source location. The *user-line* parameter
> is one-indexed, as a user counts lines, instead of zero-indexed, as Guile counts lines.

`trap-frame-finish` *frame return-handler abort-handler* [*#:vm*]   [Scheme Procedure]
> A trap that fires when control leaves the given frame. *frame* should be a live frame
> in the current continuation. *return-handler* will be called on a normal return, and
> *abort-handler* on a nonlocal exit.

`trap-in-dynamic-extent` *proc enter-handler return-handler*   [Scheme Procedure]
      abort-handler [*#:vm*] [*#:closure?*]
> A more traditional dynamic-wind trap, which fires *enter-handler* when control enters
> *proc*, *return-handler* on a normal return, and *abort-handler* on a nonlocal exit.
>
> Note that rewinds are not handled, so there is no rewind handler.

`trap-calls-in-dynamic-extent` *proc apply-handler*   [Scheme Procedure]
      return-handler [*#:current-frame*] [*#:vm*] [*#:closure?*]
> A trap that calls *apply-handler* every time a procedure is applied, and *return-handler*
> for returns, but only during the dynamic extent of an application of *proc*.

`trap-instructions-in-dynamic-extent` *proc next-handler*   [Scheme Procedure]
      [*#:current-frame*] [*#:vm*] [*#:closure?*]
> A trap that calls *next-handler* for all retired instructions within the dynamic extent
> of a call to *proc*.

`trap-calls-to-procedure` *proc apply-handler return-handler*   [Scheme Procedure]
      [*#:vm*]
> A trap that calls *apply-handler* whenever *proc* is applied, and *return-handler* when
> it returns, but with an additional argument, the call depth.
>
> That is to say, the handlers will get two arguments: the frame in question, and the
> call depth (a non-negative integer).

`trap-matching-instructions` *frame-pred handler* [*#:vm*]   [Scheme Procedure]
    A trap that calls *frame-pred* at every instruction, and if *frame-pred* returns a true value, calls *handler* on the frame.

6.25.4.4 Tracing Traps

The (`system vm trace`) module defines a number of traps for tracing of procedure applications. When a procedure is *traced*, it means that every call to that procedure is reported to the user during a program run. The idea is that you can mark a collection of procedures for tracing, and Guile will subsequently print out a line of the form

```
|  |  (procedure args ...)
```

whenever a marked procedure is about to be applied to its arguments. This can help a programmer determine whether a function is being called at the wrong time or with the wrong set of arguments.

In addition, the indentation of the output is useful for demonstrating how the traced applications are or are not tail recursive with respect to each other. Thus, a trace of a non-tail recursive factorial implementation looks like this:

```
scheme@(guile-user)> (define (fact1 n)
                       (if (zero? n) 1
                           (* n (fact1 (1- n))))))
scheme@(guile-user)> ,trace (fact1 4)
trace: (fact1 4)
trace: |  (fact1 3)
trace: |  |  (fact1 2)
trace: |  |  |  (fact1 1)
trace: |  |  |  |  (fact1 0)
trace: |  |  |  |  1
trace: |  |  |  1
trace: |  |  2
trace: |  6
trace: 24
```

While a typical tail recursive implementation would look more like this:

```
scheme@(guile-user)> (define (facti acc n)
                       (if (zero? n) acc
                           (facti (* n acc) (1- n))))
scheme@(guile-user)> (define (fact2 n) (facti 1 n))
scheme@(guile-user)> ,trace (fact2 4)
trace: (fact2 4)
trace: (facti 1 4)
trace: (facti 4 3)
trace: (facti 12 2)
trace: (facti 24 1)
trace: (facti 24 0)
trace: 24
```

The low-level traps below (see Section 6.25.4.3 [Low-Level Traps], page 458) share some common options:

#:width   The maximum width of trace output. Trace printouts will try not to exceed this
           column, but for highly nested procedure calls, it may be unavoidable. Defaults
           to 80.

#:vm   The VM on which to add the traps. Defaults to the current thread's VM.

#:prefix   A string to print out before each trace line. As seen above in the examples,
           defaults to "trace: ".

To have access to these procedures, you'll need to have imported the (system vm trace)
module:

```
(use-modules (system vm trace))
```

trace-calls-to-procedure *proc* [*#:width*] [*#:vm*] [*#:prefix*]   [Scheme Procedure]
      Print a trace at applications of and returns from *proc*.

trace-calls-in-procedure *proc* [*#:width*] [*#:vm*] [*#:prefix*]   [Scheme Procedure]
      Print a trace at all applications and returns within the dynamic extent of calls to
      proc.

trace-instructions-in-procedure *proc* [*#:width*] [*#:vm*]   [Scheme Procedure]
      Print a trace at all instructions executed in the dynamic extent of calls to *proc*.

In addition, Guile defines a procedure to call a thunk, tracing all procedure calls and
returns within the thunk.

call-with-trace *thunk* [*#:calls?=#t*] [*#:instructions?=#f*]   [Scheme Procedure]
      [*#:width=80*] [*#:vm=(the-vm)*]
      Call *thunk*, tracing all execution within its dynamic extent.

      If *calls?* is true, Guile will print a brief report at each procedure call and return, as
      given above.

      If *instructions?* is true, Guile will also print a message each time an instruction is
      executed. This is a lot of output, but it is sometimes useful when doing low-level
      optimization.

      Note that because this procedure manipulates the VM trace level directly, it doesn't
      compose well with traps at the REPL.

See Section 4.4.4.5 [Profile Commands], page 49, for more information on tracing at the
REPL.

6.25.4.5 Trap States

When multiple traps are present in a system, we begin to have a bookkeeping problem.
How are they named? How does one disable, enable, or delete them?

Guile's answer to this is to keep an implicit per-thread *trap state*. The trap state object
is not exposed to the user; rather, API that works on trap states fetches the current trap
state from the dynamic environment.

Traps are identified by integers. A trap can be enabled, disabled, or removed, and can
have an associated user-visible name.

These procedures have their own module:

```
(use-modules (system vm trap-state))
```

add-trap! *trap name*   [Scheme Procedure]
> Add a trap to the current trap state, associating the given *name* with it. Returns a
> fresh trap identifier (an integer).
>
> Note that usually the more specific functions detailed in Section 6.25.4.6 [High-Level
> Traps], page 462 are used in preference to this one.

list-traps   [Scheme Procedure]
> List the current set of traps, both enabled and disabled. Returns a list of integers.

trap-name *idx*   [Scheme Procedure]
> Returns the name associated with trap *idx*, or #f if there is no such trap.

trap-enabled? *idx*   [Scheme Procedure]
> Returns #t if trap *idx* is present and enabled, or #f otherwise.

enable-trap! *idx*   [Scheme Procedure]
> Enables trap *idx*.

disable-trap! *idx*   [Scheme Procedure]
> Disables trap *idx*.

delete-trap! *idx*   [Scheme Procedure]
> Removes trap *idx*, disabling it first, if necessary.

6.25.4.6 High-Level Traps

The low-level trap API allows one to make traps that call procedures, and the trap state
API allows one to keep track of what traps are there. But neither of these APIs directly
helps you when you want to set a breakpoint, because it's unclear what to do when the trap
fires. Do you enter a debugger, or mail a summary of the situation to your great-aunt, or
what?

So for the common case in which you just want to install breakpoints, and then have them
all result in calls to one parameterizable procedure, we have the high-level trap interface.

Perhaps we should have started this section with this interface, as it's clearly the one
most people should use. But as its capabilities and limitations proceed from the lower
layers, we felt that the character-building exercise of building a mental model might be
helpful.

These procedures share a module with trap states:

```
(use-modules (system vm trap-state))
```

with-default-trap-handler *handler thunk*   [Scheme Procedure]
> Call *thunk* in a dynamic context in which *handler* is the current trap handler.
>
> Additionally, during the execution of *thunk*, the VM trace level (see Section 6.25.4.1
> [VM Hooks], page 455) is set to the number of enabled traps. This ensures that traps
> will in fact fire.
>
> *handler* may be #f, in which case VM hooks are not enabled as they otherwise would
> be, as there is nothing to handle the traps.

The trace-level-setting behavior of `with-default-trap-handler` is one of its more useful aspects, but if you are willing to forgo that, and just want to install a global trap handler, there's a function for that too:

`install-trap-handler!` *handler*   [Scheme Procedure]
    Set the current thread's trap handler to *handler*.

Trap handlers are called when traps installed by procedures from this module fire. The current "consumer" of this API is Guile's REPL, but one might easily imagine other trap handlers being used to integrate with other debugging tools.

`add-trap-at-procedure-call!` *proc*   [Scheme Procedure]
    Install a trap that will fire when *proc* is called.

    This is a breakpoint.

`add-trace-at-procedure-call!` *proc*   [Scheme Procedure]
    Install a trap that will print a tracing message when *proc* is called. See Section 6.25.4.4 [Tracing Traps], page 460, for more information.

    This is a tracepoint.

`add-trap-at-source-location!` *file user-line*   [Scheme Procedure]
    Install a trap that will fire when control reaches the given source location. *user-line* is one-indexed, as users count lines, instead of zero-indexed, as Guile counts lines.

    This is a source breakpoint.

`add-ephemeral-trap-at-frame-finish!` *frame handler*   [Scheme Procedure]
    Install a trap that will call *handler* when *frame* finishes executing. The trap will be removed from the trap state after firing, or on nonlocal exit.

    This is a finish trap, used to implement the "finish" REPL command.

`add-ephemeral-stepping-trap!` *frame handler* [#:into?]   [Scheme Procedure]
        [#:instruction?]
    Install a trap that will call *handler* after stepping to a different source line or instruction. The trap will be removed from the trap state after firing, or on nonlocal exit.

    If *instruction?* is false (the default), the trap will fire when control reaches a new source line. Otherwise it will fire when control reaches a new instruction.

    Additionally, if *into?* is false (not the default), the trap will only fire for frames at or prior to the given frame. If *into?* is true (the default), the trap may step into nested procedure invocations.

    This is a stepping trap, used to implement the "step", "next", "step-instruction", and "next-instruction" REPL commands.

6.25.5 GDB Support

Sometimes, you may find it necessary to debug Guile applications at the C level. Doing so can be tedious, in particular because the debugger is oblivious to Guile's `SCM` type, and thus unable to display `SCM` values in any meaningful way:

```
(gdb) frame
#0  scm_display (obj=0xf04310, port=0x6f9f30) at print.c:1437
```

To address that, Guile comes with an extension of the GNU Debugger (GDB) that contains a "pretty-printer" for SCM values. With this GDB extension, the C frame in the example above shows up like this:

```
(gdb) frame
#0  scm_display (obj=("hello" GDB!), port=#<port file 6f9f30>) at print.c:1437
```

Here GDB was able to decode the list pointed to by *obj*, and to print it using Scheme's read syntax.

That extension is a `.scm` file installed alongside the `libguile` shared library. When GDB 7.8 or later is installed and compiled with support for extensions written in Guile, the extension is automatically loaded when debugging a program linked against `libguile` (see Section "Auto-loading" in *Debugging with GDB*). Note that the directory where `libguile` is installed must be among GDB's auto-loading "safe directories" (see Section "Auto-loading safe path" in *Debugging with GDB*).

6.26 Code Coverage Reports

When writing a test suite for a program or library, it is desirable to know what part of the code is *covered* by the test suite. The (`system vm coverage`) module provides tools to gather code coverage data and to present them, as detailed below.

with-code-coverage *vm thunk*   [Scheme Procedure]
> Run *thunk*, a zero-argument procedure, using *vm*; instrument *vm* to collect code coverage data. Return code coverage data and the values returned by *thunk*.

coverage-data? *obj*   [Scheme Procedure]
> Return #t if *obj* is a *coverage data* object as returned by `with-code-coverage`.

coverage-data->lcov *data port #:key modules*   [Scheme Procedure]
> Traverse code coverage information *data*, as obtained with `with-code-coverage`, and write coverage information to port in the `.info` format used by LCOV. The report will include all of *modules* (or, by default, all the currently loaded modules) even if their code was not executed.

> The generated data can be fed to LCOV's `genhtml` command to produce an HTML report, which aids coverage data visualization.

Here's an example use:

```
(use-modules (system vm coverage)
             (system vm vm))

(call-with-values (lambda ()
                    (with-code-coverage (the-vm)
                      (lambda ()
                        (do-something-tricky))))
   (lambda (data result)
     (let ((port (open-output-file "lcov.info")))
```

```
(coverage-data->lcov data port)
(close file))))
```

In addition, the module provides low-level procedures that would make it possible to write other user interfaces to the coverage data.

instrumented-source-files *data*   [Scheme Procedures]
> Return the list of "instrumented" source files, i.e., source files whose code was loaded at the time *data* was collected.

line-execution-counts *data file*   [Scheme Procedures]
> Return a list of line number/execution count pairs for *file*, or **#f** if *file* is not among the files covered by *data*. This includes lines with zero count.

instrumented/executed-lines *data file*   [Scheme Procedures]
> Return the number of instrumented and the number of executed source lines in *file* according to *data*.

procedure-execution-count *data proc*   [Scheme Procedures]
> Return the number of times *proc*'s code was executed, according to *data*, or **#f** if *proc* was not executed. When *proc* is a closure, the number of times its code was executed is returned, not the number of times this code associated with this particular closure was executed.

Appendix A GNU Free Documentation License

Version 1.3, 3 November 2008

Copyright © 2000, 2001, 2002, 2007, 2008 Free Software Foundation, Inc.
`http://fsf.org/`

Everyone is permitted to copy and distribute verbatim copies
of this license document, but changing it is not allowed.

0. PREAMBLE

The purpose of this License is to make a manual, textbook, or other functional and useful document *free* in the sense of freedom: to assure everyone the effective freedom to copy and redistribute it, with or without modifying it, either commercially or non-commercially. Secondarily, this License preserves for the author and publisher a way to get credit for their work, while not being considered responsible for modifications made by others.

This License is a kind of "copyleft", which means that derivative works of the document must themselves be free in the same sense. It complements the GNU General Public License, which is a copyleft license designed for free software.

We have designed this License in order to use it for manuals for free software, because free software needs free documentation: a free program should come with manuals providing the same freedoms that the software does. But this License is not limited to software manuals; it can be used for any textual work, regardless of subject matter or whether it is published as a printed book. We recommend this License principally for works whose purpose is instruction or reference.

1. APPLICABILITY AND DEFINITIONS

This License applies to any manual or other work, in any medium, that contains a notice placed by the copyright holder saying it can be distributed under the terms of this License. Such a notice grants a world-wide, royalty-free license, unlimited in duration, to use that work under the conditions stated herein. The "Document", below, refers to any such manual or work. Any member of the public is a licensee, and is addressed as "you". You accept the license if you copy, modify or distribute the work in a way requiring permission under copyright law.

A "Modified Version" of the Document means any work containing the Document or a portion of it, either copied verbatim, or with modifications and/or translated into another language.

A "Secondary Section" is a named appendix or a front-matter section of the Document that deals exclusively with the relationship of the publishers or authors of the Document to the Document's overall subject (or to related matters) and contains nothing that could fall directly within that overall subject. (Thus, if the Document is in part a textbook of mathematics, a Secondary Section may not explain any mathematics.) The relationship could be a matter of historical connection with the subject or with related matters, or of legal, commercial, philosophical, ethical or political position regarding them.

The "Invariant Sections" are certain Secondary Sections whose titles are designated, as being those of Invariant Sections, in the notice that says that the Document is released under this License. If a section does not fit the above definition of Secondary then it is not allowed to be designated as Invariant. The Document may contain zero Invariant Sections. If the Document does not identify any Invariant Sections then there are none.

The "Cover Texts" are certain short passages of text that are listed, as Front-Cover Texts or Back-Cover Texts, in the notice that says that the Document is released under this License. A Front-Cover Text may be at most 5 words, and a Back-Cover Text may be at most 25 words.

A "Transparent" copy of the Document means a machine-readable copy, represented in a format whose specification is available to the general public, that is suitable for revising the document straightforwardly with generic text editors or (for images composed of pixels) generic paint programs or (for drawings) some widely available drawing editor, and that is suitable for input to text formatters or for automatic translation to a variety of formats suitable for input to text formatters. A copy made in an otherwise Transparent file format whose markup, or absence of markup, has been arranged to thwart or discourage subsequent modification by readers is not Transparent. An image format is not Transparent if used for any substantial amount of text. A copy that is not "Transparent" is called "Opaque".

Examples of suitable formats for Transparent copies include plain ASCII without markup, Texinfo input format, LaTeX input format, SGML or XML using a publicly available DTD, and standard-conforming simple HTML, PostScript or PDF designed for human modification. Examples of transparent image formats include PNG, XCF and JPG. Opaque formats include proprietary formats that can be read and edited only by proprietary word processors, SGML or XML for which the DTD and/or processing tools are not generally available, and the machine-generated HTML, PostScript or PDF produced by some word processors for output purposes only.

The "Title Page" means, for a printed book, the title page itself, plus such following pages as are needed to hold, legibly, the material this License requires to appear in the title page. For works in formats which do not have any title page as such, "Title Page" means the text near the most prominent appearance of the work's title, preceding the beginning of the body of the text.

The "publisher" means any person or entity that distributes copies of the Document to the public.

A section "Entitled XYZ" means a named subunit of the Document whose title either is precisely XYZ or contains XYZ in parentheses following text that translates XYZ in another language. (Here XYZ stands for a specific section name mentioned below, such as "Acknowledgements", "Dedications", "Endorsements", or "History".) To "Preserve the Title" of such a section when you modify the Document means that it remains a section "Entitled XYZ" according to this definition.

The Document may include Warranty Disclaimers next to the notice which states that this License applies to the Document. These Warranty Disclaimers are considered to be included by reference in this License, but only as regards disclaiming warranties: any other implication that these Warranty Disclaimers may have is void and has no effect on the meaning of this License.

2. VERBATIM COPYING

You may copy and distribute the Document in any medium, either commercially or noncommercially, provided that this License, the copyright notices, and the license notice saying this License applies to the Document are reproduced in all copies, and that you add no other conditions whatsoever to those of this License. You may not use technical measures to obstruct or control the reading or further copying of the copies you make or distribute. However, you may accept compensation in exchange for copies. If you distribute a large enough number of copies you must also follow the conditions in section 3.

You may also lend copies, under the same conditions stated above, and you may publicly display copies.

3. COPYING IN QUANTITY

If you publish printed copies (or copies in media that commonly have printed covers) of the Document, numbering more than 100, and the Document's license notice requires Cover Texts, you must enclose the copies in covers that carry, clearly and legibly, all these Cover Texts: Front-Cover Texts on the front cover, and Back-Cover Texts on the back cover. Both covers must also clearly and legibly identify you as the publisher of these copies. The front cover must present the full title with all words of the title equally prominent and visible. You may add other material on the covers in addition. Copying with changes limited to the covers, as long as they preserve the title of the Document and satisfy these conditions, can be treated as verbatim copying in other respects.

If the required texts for either cover are too voluminous to fit legibly, you should put the first ones listed (as many as fit reasonably) on the actual cover, and continue the rest onto adjacent pages.

If you publish or distribute Opaque copies of the Document numbering more than 100, you must either include a machine-readable Transparent copy along with each Opaque copy, or state in or with each Opaque copy a computer-network location from which the general network-using public has access to download using public-standard network protocols a complete Transparent copy of the Document, free of added material. If you use the latter option, you must take reasonably prudent steps, when you begin distribution of Opaque copies in quantity, to ensure that this Transparent copy will remain thus accessible at the stated location until at least one year after the last time you distribute an Opaque copy (directly or through your agents or retailers) of that edition to the public.

It is requested, but not required, that you contact the authors of the Document well before redistributing any large number of copies, to give them a chance to provide you with an updated version of the Document.

4. MODIFICATIONS

You may copy and distribute a Modified Version of the Document under the conditions of sections 2 and 3 above, provided that you release the Modified Version under precisely this License, with the Modified Version filling the role of the Document, thus licensing distribution and modification of the Modified Version to whoever possesses a copy of it. In addition, you must do these things in the Modified Version:

A. Use in the Title Page (and on the covers, if any) a title distinct from that of the Document, and from those of previous versions (which should, if there were any, be listed in the History section of the Document). You may use the same title as a previous version if the original publisher of that version gives permission.

B. List on the Title Page, as authors, one or more persons or entities responsible for authorship of the modifications in the Modified Version, together with at least five of the principal authors of the Document (all of its principal authors, if it has fewer than five), unless they release you from this requirement.

C. State on the Title page the name of the publisher of the Modified Version, as the publisher.

D. Preserve all the copyright notices of the Document.

E. Add an appropriate copyright notice for your modifications adjacent to the other copyright notices.

F. Include, immediately after the copyright notices, a license notice giving the public permission to use the Modified Version under the terms of this License, in the form shown in the Addendum below.

G. Preserve in that license notice the full lists of Invariant Sections and required Cover Texts given in the Document's license notice.

H. Include an unaltered copy of this License.

I. Preserve the section Entitled "History", Preserve its Title, and add to it an item stating at least the title, year, new authors, and publisher of the Modified Version as given on the Title Page. If there is no section Entitled "History" in the Document, create one stating the title, year, authors, and publisher of the Document as given on its Title Page, then add an item describing the Modified Version as stated in the previous sentence.

J. Preserve the network location, if any, given in the Document for public access to a Transparent copy of the Document, and likewise the network locations given in the Document for previous versions it was based on. These may be placed in the "History" section. You may omit a network location for a work that was published at least four years before the Document itself, or if the original publisher of the version it refers to gives permission.

K. For any section Entitled "Acknowledgements" or "Dedications", Preserve the Title of the section, and preserve in the section all the substance and tone of each of the contributor acknowledgements and/or dedications given therein.

L. Preserve all the Invariant Sections of the Document, unaltered in their text and in their titles. Section numbers or the equivalent are not considered part of the section titles.

M. Delete any section Entitled "Endorsements". Such a section may not be included in the Modified Version.

N. Do not retitle any existing section to be Entitled "Endorsements" or to conflict in title with any Invariant Section.

O. Preserve any Warranty Disclaimers.

If the Modified Version includes new front-matter sections or appendices that qualify as Secondary Sections and contain no material copied from the Document, you may at your option designate some or all of these sections as invariant. To do this, add their titles to the list of Invariant Sections in the Modified Version's license notice. These titles must be distinct from any other section titles.

You may add a section Entitled "Endorsements", provided it contains nothing but endorsements of your Modified Version by various parties—for example, statements of peer review or that the text has been approved by an organization as the authoritative definition of a standard.

You may add a passage of up to five words as a Front-Cover Text, and a passage of up to 25 words as a Back-Cover Text, to the end of the list of Cover Texts in the Modified Version. Only one passage of Front-Cover Text and one of Back-Cover Text may be added by (or through arrangements made by) any one entity. If the Document already includes a cover text for the same cover, previously added by you or by arrangement made by the same entity you are acting on behalf of, you may not add another; but you may replace the old one, on explicit permission from the previous publisher that added the old one.

The author(s) and publisher(s) of the Document do not by this License give permission to use their names for publicity for or to assert or imply endorsement of any Modified Version.

5. COMBINING DOCUMENTS

You may combine the Document with other documents released under this License, under the terms defined in section 4 above for modified versions, provided that you include in the combination all of the Invariant Sections of all of the original documents, unmodified, and list them all as Invariant Sections of your combined work in its license notice, and that you preserve all their Warranty Disclaimers.

The combined work need only contain one copy of this License, and multiple identical Invariant Sections may be replaced with a single copy. If there are multiple Invariant Sections with the same name but different contents, make the title of each such section unique by adding at the end of it, in parentheses, the name of the original author or publisher of that section if known, or else a unique number. Make the same adjustment to the section titles in the list of Invariant Sections in the license notice of the combined work.

In the combination, you must combine any sections Entitled "History" in the various original documents, forming one section Entitled "History"; likewise combine any sections Entitled "Acknowledgements", and any sections Entitled "Dedications". You must delete all sections Entitled "Endorsements."

6. COLLECTIONS OF DOCUMENTS

You may make a collection consisting of the Document and other documents released under this License, and replace the individual copies of this License in the various documents with a single copy that is included in the collection, provided that you follow the rules of this License for verbatim copying of each of the documents in all other respects.

You may extract a single document from such a collection, and distribute it individually under this License, provided you insert a copy of this License into the extracted document, and follow this License in all other respects regarding verbatim copying of that document.

7. AGGREGATION WITH INDEPENDENT WORKS

A compilation of the Document or its derivatives with other separate and independent documents or works, in or on a volume of a storage or distribution medium, is called an "aggregate" if the copyright resulting from the compilation is not used to limit the legal rights of the compilation's users beyond what the individual works permit. When the Document is included in an aggregate, this License does not apply to the other works in the aggregate which are not themselves derivative works of the Document.

If the Cover Text requirement of section 3 is applicable to these copies of the Document, then if the Document is less than one half of the entire aggregate, the Document's Cover Texts may be placed on covers that bracket the Document within the aggregate, or the electronic equivalent of covers if the Document is in electronic form. Otherwise they must appear on printed covers that bracket the whole aggregate.

8. TRANSLATION

Translation is considered a kind of modification, so you may distribute translations of the Document under the terms of section 4. Replacing Invariant Sections with translations requires special permission from their copyright holders, but you may include translations of some or all Invariant Sections in addition to the original versions of these Invariant Sections. You may include a translation of this License, and all the license notices in the Document, and any Warranty Disclaimers, provided that you also include the original English version of this License and the original versions of those notices and disclaimers. In case of a disagreement between the translation and the original version of this License or a notice or disclaimer, the original version will prevail.

If a section in the Document is Entitled "Acknowledgements", "Dedications", or "History", the requirement (section 4) to Preserve its Title (section 1) will typically require changing the actual title.

9. TERMINATION

You may not copy, modify, sublicense, or distribute the Document except as expressly provided under this License. Any attempt otherwise to copy, modify, sublicense, or distribute it is void, and will automatically terminate your rights under this License.

However, if you cease all violation of this License, then your license from a particular copyright holder is reinstated (a) provisionally, unless and until the copyright holder explicitly and finally terminates your license, and (b) permanently, if the copyright holder fails to notify you of the violation by some reasonable means prior to 60 days after the cessation.

Moreover, your license from a particular copyright holder is reinstated permanently if the copyright holder notifies you of the violation by some reasonable means, this is the first time you have received notice of violation of this License (for any work) from that copyright holder, and you cure the violation prior to 30 days after your receipt of the notice.

Termination of your rights under this section does not terminate the licenses of parties who have received copies or rights from you under this License. If your rights have been terminated and not permanently reinstated, receipt of a copy of some or all of the same material does not give you any rights to use it.

10. FUTURE REVISIONS OF THIS LICENSE

The Free Software Foundation may publish new, revised versions of the GNU Free Documentation License from time to time. Such new versions will be similar in spirit to the present version, but may differ in detail to address new problems or concerns. See http://www.gnu.org/copyleft/.

Each version of the License is given a distinguishing version number. If the Document specifies that a particular numbered version of this License "or any later version" applies to it, you have the option of following the terms and conditions either of that specified version or of any later version that has been published (not as a draft) by the Free Software Foundation. If the Document does not specify a version number of this License, you may choose any version ever published (not as a draft) by the Free Software Foundation. If the Document specifies that a proxy can decide which future versions of this License can be used, that proxy's public statement of acceptance of a version permanently authorizes you to choose that version for the Document.

11. RELICENSING

"Massive Multiauthor Collaboration Site" (or "MMC Site") means any World Wide Web server that publishes copyrightable works and also provides prominent facilities for anybody to edit those works. A public wiki that anybody can edit is an example of such a server. A "Massive Multiauthor Collaboration" (or "MMC") contained in the site means any set of copyrightable works thus published on the MMC site.

"CC-BY-SA" means the Creative Commons Attribution-Share Alike 3.0 license published by Creative Commons Corporation, a not-for-profit corporation with a principal place of business in San Francisco, California, as well as future copyleft versions of that license published by that same organization.

"Incorporate" means to publish or republish a Document, in whole or in part, as part of another Document.

An MMC is "eligible for relicensing" if it is licensed under this License, and if all works that were first published under this License somewhere other than this MMC, and subsequently incorporated in whole or in part into the MMC, (1) had no cover texts or invariant sections, and (2) were thus incorporated prior to November 1, 2008.

The operator of an MMC Site may republish an MMC contained in the site under CC-BY-SA on the same site at any time before August 1, 2009, provided the MMC is eligible for relicensing.

ADDENDUM: How to use this License for your documents

To use this License in a document you have written, include a copy of the License in the document and put the following copyright and license notices just after the title page:

```
Copyright (C)  year  your name.
Permission is granted to copy, distribute and/or modify this document
under the terms of the GNU Free Documentation License, Version 1.3
or any later version published by the Free Software Foundation;
with no Invariant Sections, no Front-Cover Texts, and no Back-Cover
Texts.  A copy of the license is included in the section entitled ''GNU
Free Documentation License''.
```

If you have Invariant Sections, Front-Cover Texts and Back-Cover Texts, replace the "with...Texts." line with this:

```
with the Invariant Sections being list their titles, with
the Front-Cover Texts being list, and with the Back-Cover Texts
being list.
```

If you have Invariant Sections without Cover Texts, or some other combination of the three, merge those two alternatives to suit the situation.

If your document contains nontrivial examples of program code, we recommend releasing these examples in parallel under your choice of free software license, such as the GNU General Public License, to permit their use in free software.

Concept Index

This index contains concepts, keywords and non-Schemey names for several features, to make it easier to locate the desired sections.

Procedure Index

This is an alphabetical list of all the procedures and macros in Guile. It also includes Guile's Autoconf macros.

When looking for a particular procedure, please look under its Scheme name as well as under its C name. The C name can be constructed from the Scheme names by a simple transformation described in the section See Section 6.1 [API Overview], page 99.

B

C

G

H

M

O

P

Q

S

T

U

V

W

X

Y

Z

Variable Index

This is an alphabetical list of all the important variables and constants in Guile.

When looking for a particular variable or constant, please look under its Scheme name as well as under its C name. The C name can be constructed from the Scheme names by a simple transformation described in the section See Section 6.1 [API Overview], page 99.

Type Index

This is an alphabetical list of all the important data types defined in the Guile Programmers Manual.

R5RS Index